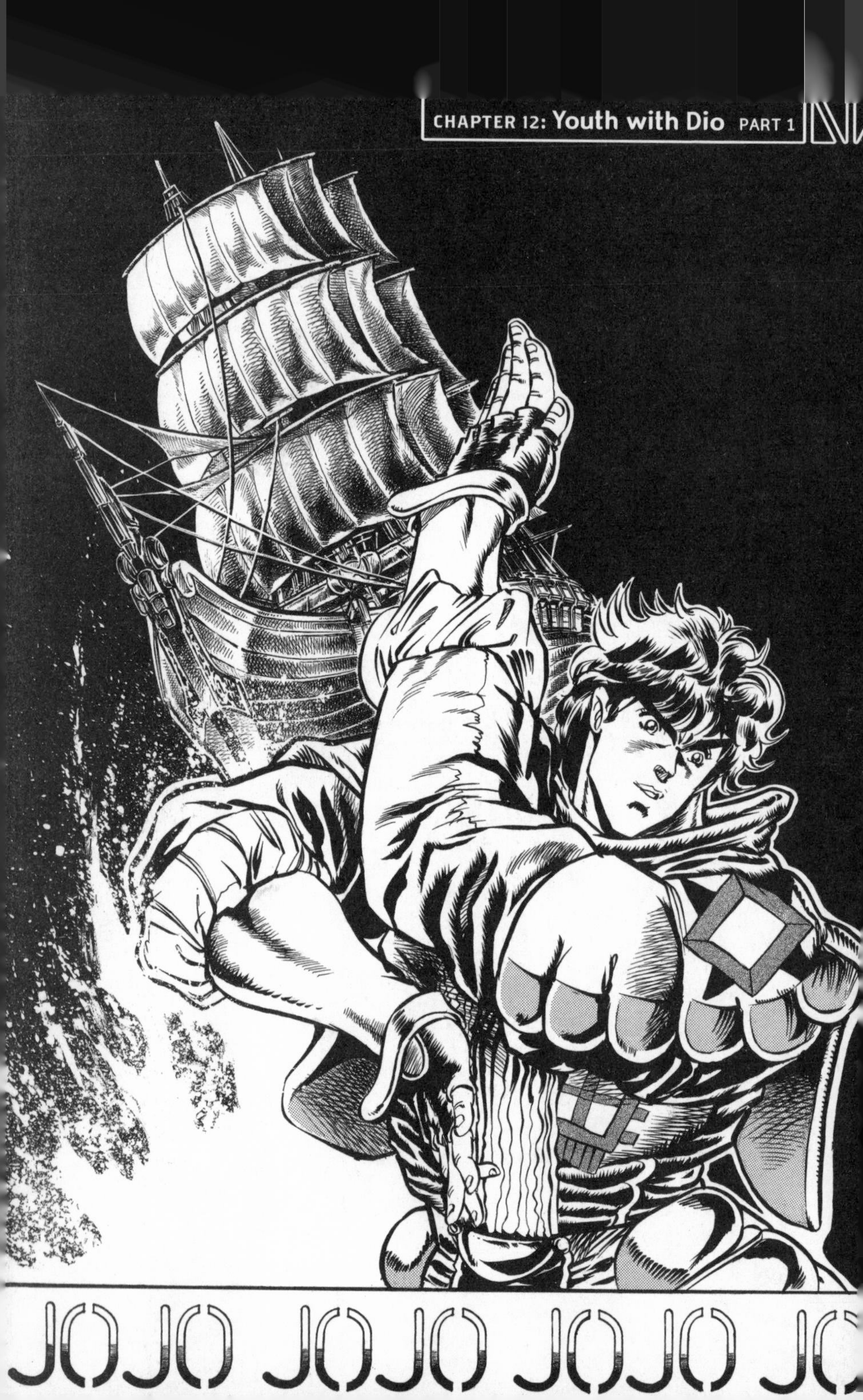
CHAPTER 12: Youth with Dio PART 1
JOJO JOJO JOJO JO

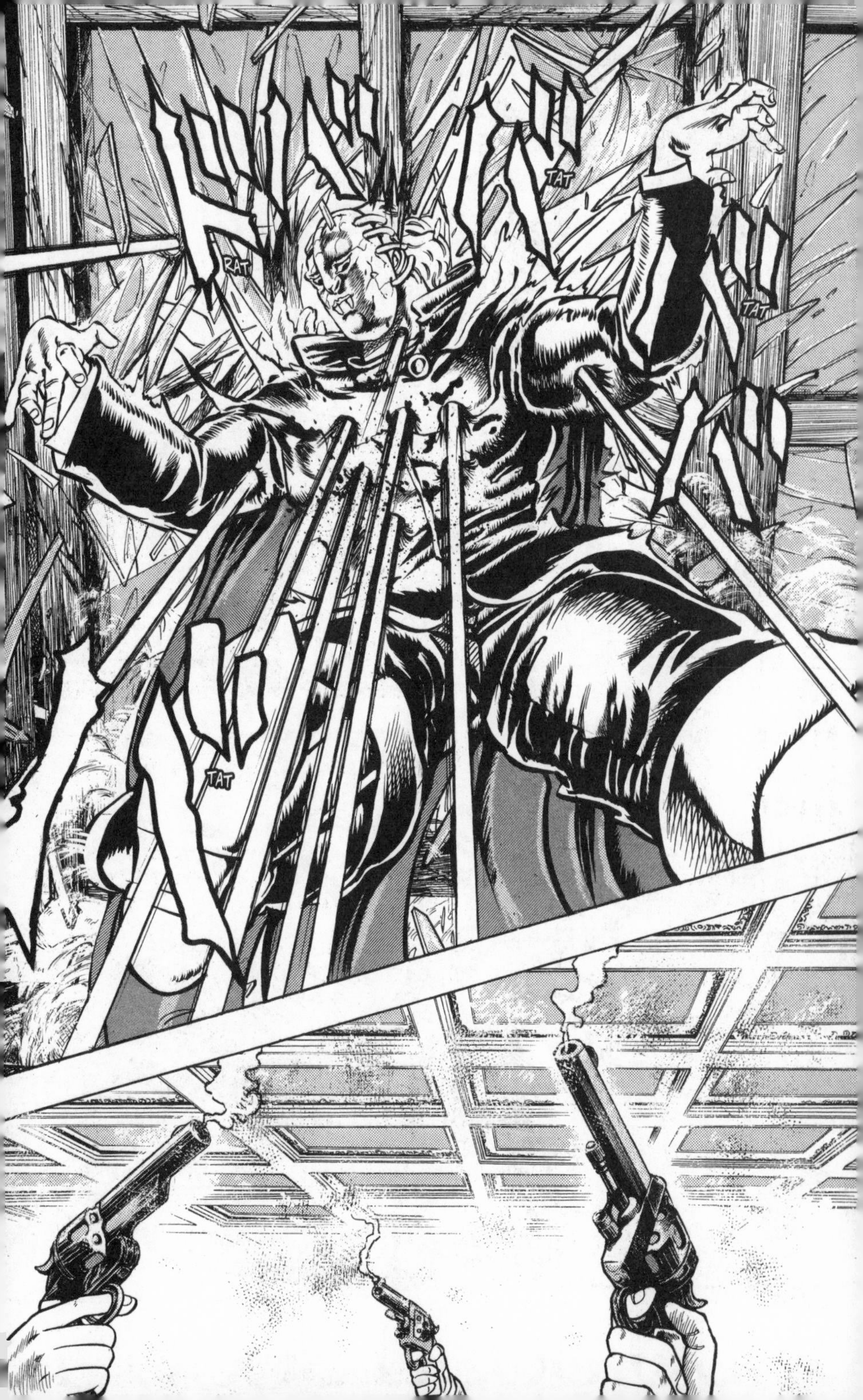
TAT
TAT
RAT
TAT

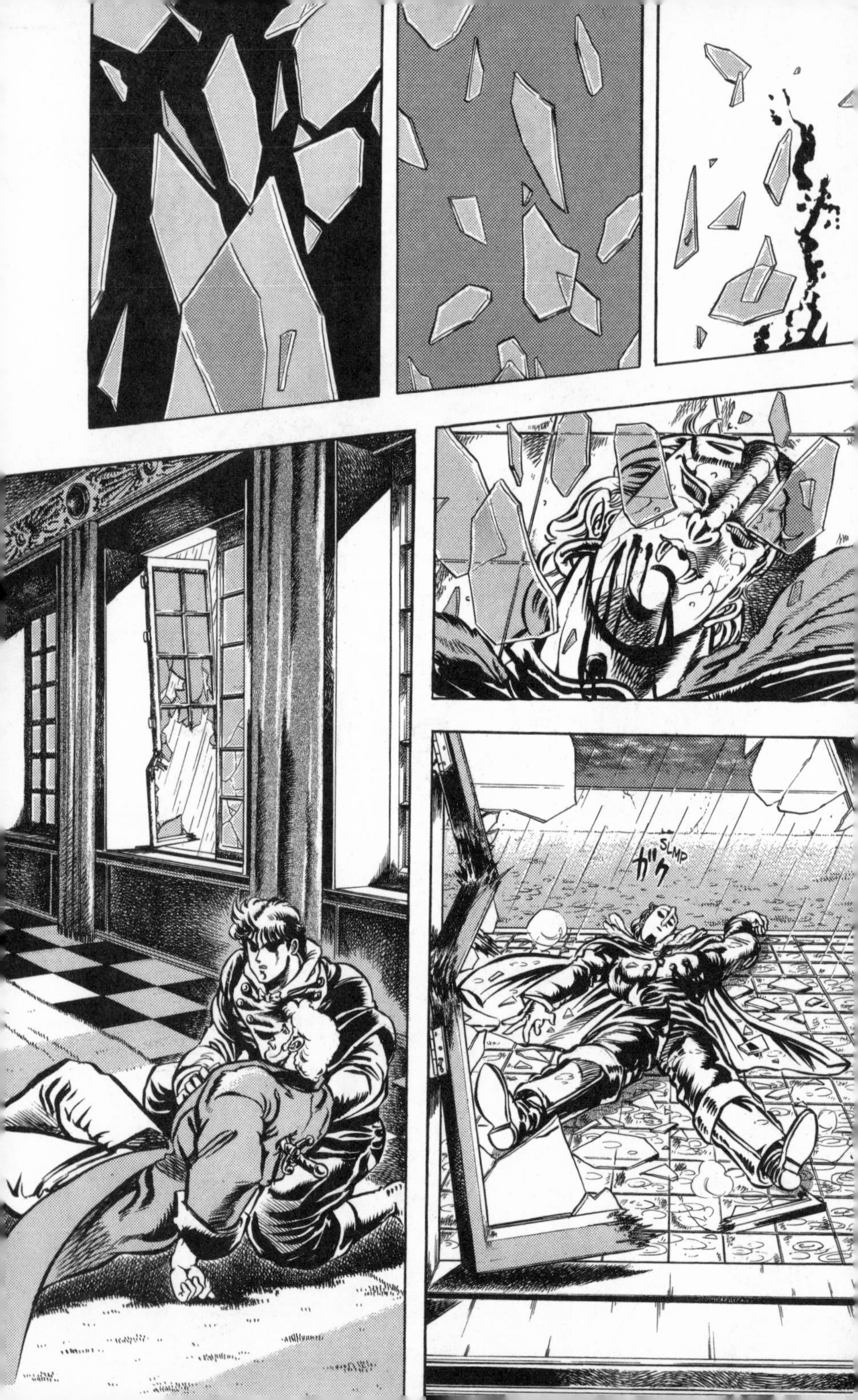
ガク
SLMP

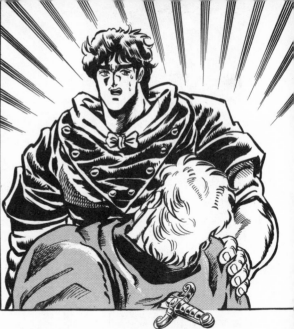
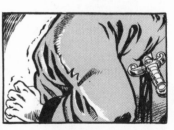
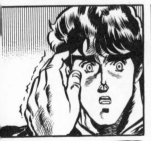
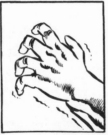
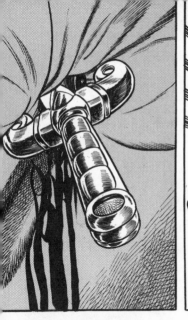

F-
FATHER...

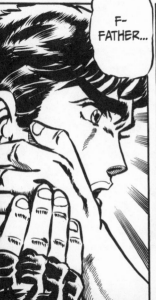
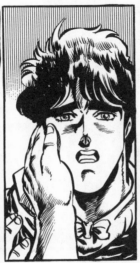
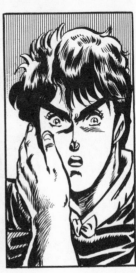

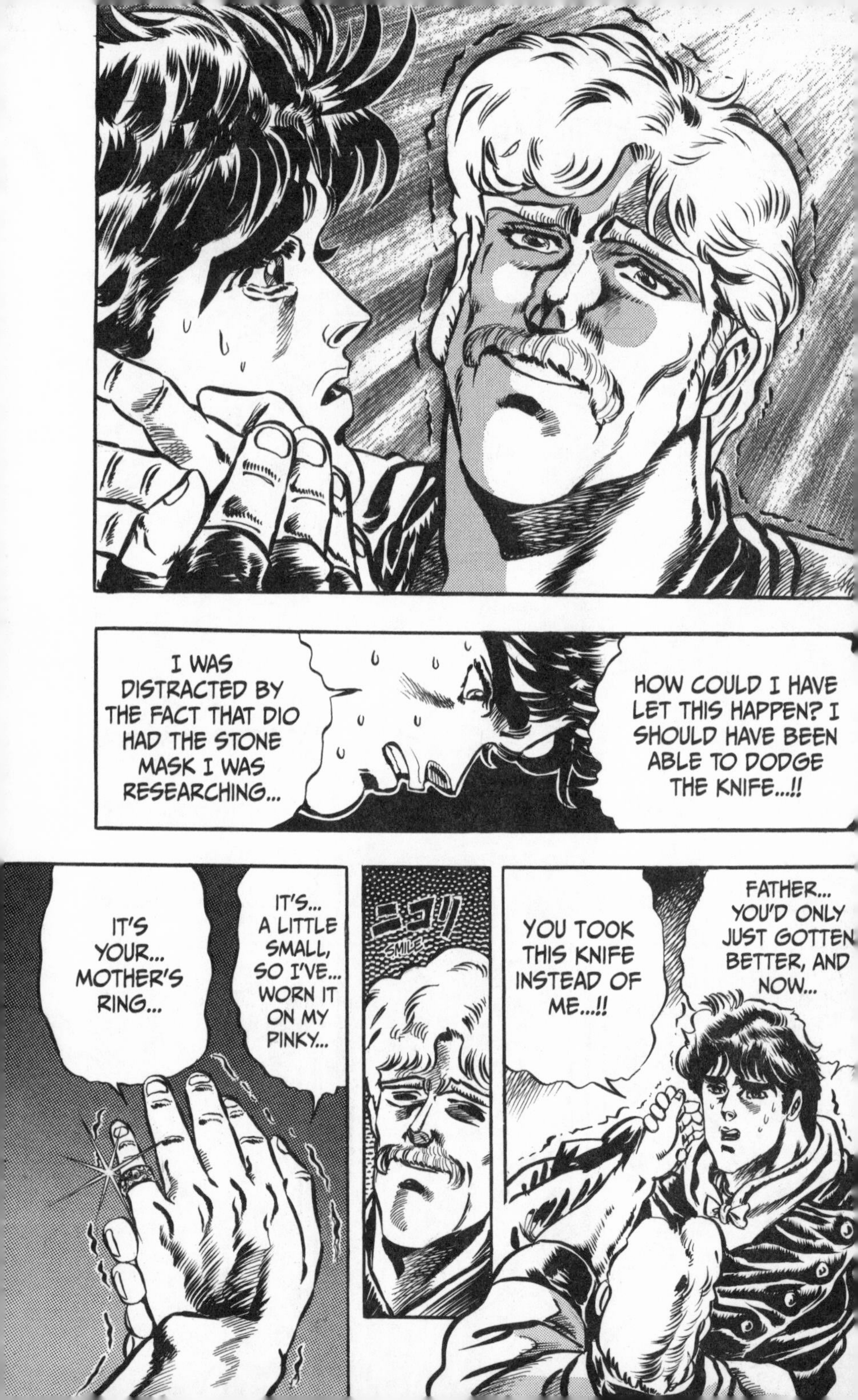
HOW COULD I HAVE LET THIS HAPPEN? I SHOULD HAVE BEEN ABLE TO DODGE THE KNIFE...!!
I WAS DISTRACTED BY THE FACT THAT DIO HAD THE STONE MASK I WAS RESEARCHING...
FATHER... YOU'D ONLY JUST GOTTEN BETTER, AND NOW...
YOU TOOK THIS KNIFE INSTEAD OF ME...!!
ニコリ
SMILE
IT'S... A LITTLE SMALL, SO I'VE... WORN IT ON MY PINKY...
IT'S YOUR... MOTHER'S RING...

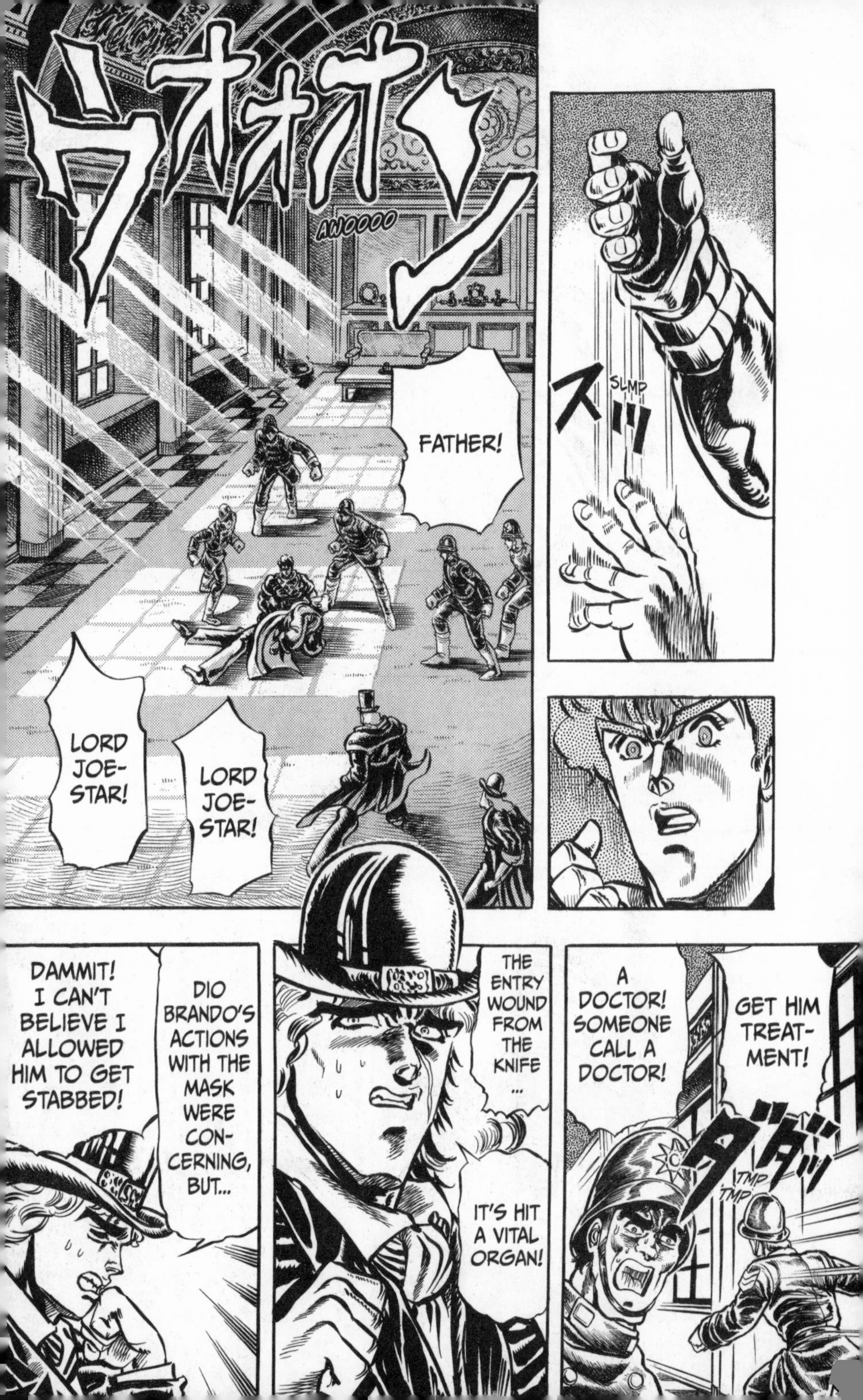
スッ
SLMP
ウオオオ〜ン
AWOOOO
FATHER!
LORD JOE-STAR!
LORD JOE-STAR!
GET HIM TREAT-MENT!
A DOCTOR! SOMEONE CALL A DOCTOR!
ダダッ
TMP TMP
THE ENTRY WOUND FROM THE KNIFE ...
IT'S HIT A VITAL ORGAN!
DIO BRANDO'S ACTIONS WITH THE MASK WERE CON-CERNING, BUT...
DAMMIT! I CAN'T BELIEVE I ALLOWED HIM TO GET STABBED!

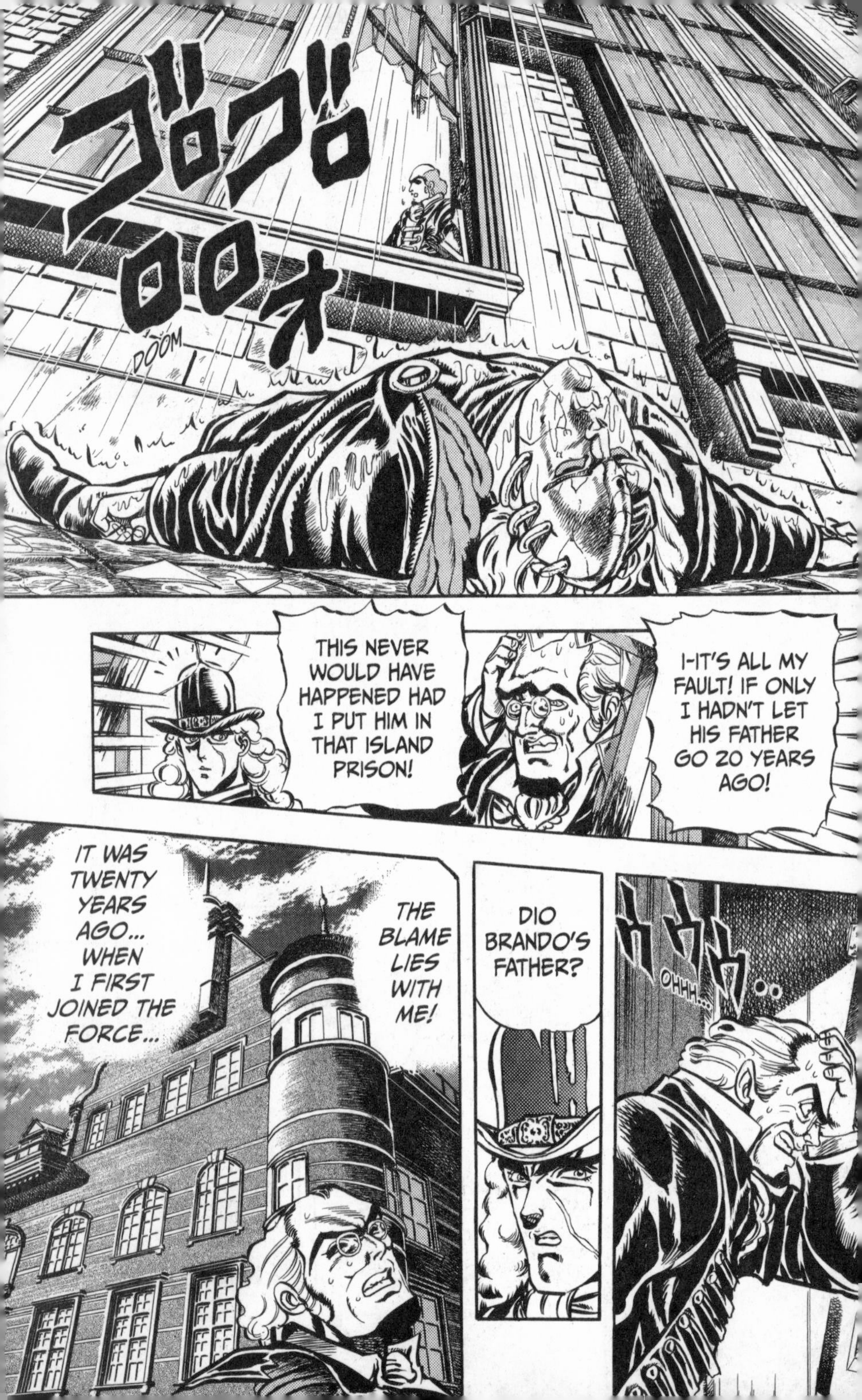
DOOM
I-IT'S ALL MY FAULT! IF ONLY I HADN'T LET HIS FATHER GO 20 YEARS AGO!
THIS NEVER WOULD HAVE HAPPENED HAD I PUT HIM IN THAT ISLAND PRISON!
OHHH...
DIO BRANDO'S FATHER?
THE BLAME LIES WITH ME!
IT WAS TWENTY YEARS AGO... WHEN I FIRST JOINED THE FORCE...

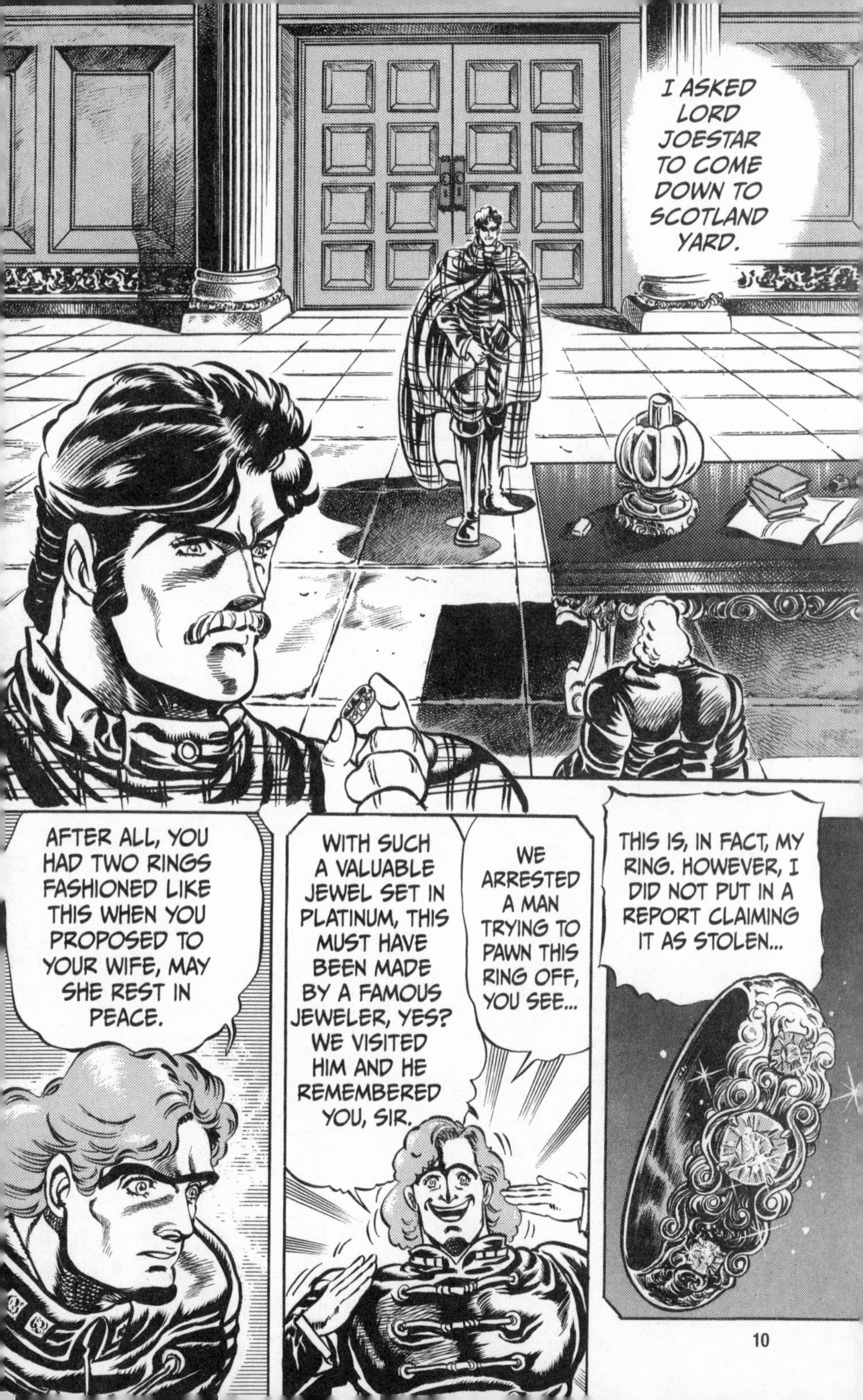
I ASKED LORD JOESTAR TO COME DOWN TO SCOTLAND YARD.
THIS IS, IN FACT, MY RING. HOWEVER, I DID NOT PUT IN A REPORT CLAIMING IT AS STOLEN...
WE ARRESTED A MAN TRYING TO PAWN THIS RING OFF, YOU SEE...
WITH SUCH A VALUABLE JEWEL SET IN PLATINUM, THIS MUST HAVE BEEN MADE BY A FAMOUS JEWELER, YES? WE VISITED HIM AND HE REMEMBERED YOU, SIR.
AFTER ALL, YOU HAD TWO RINGS FASHIONED LIKE THIS WHEN YOU PROPOSED TO YOUR WIFE, MAY SHE REST IN PEACE.

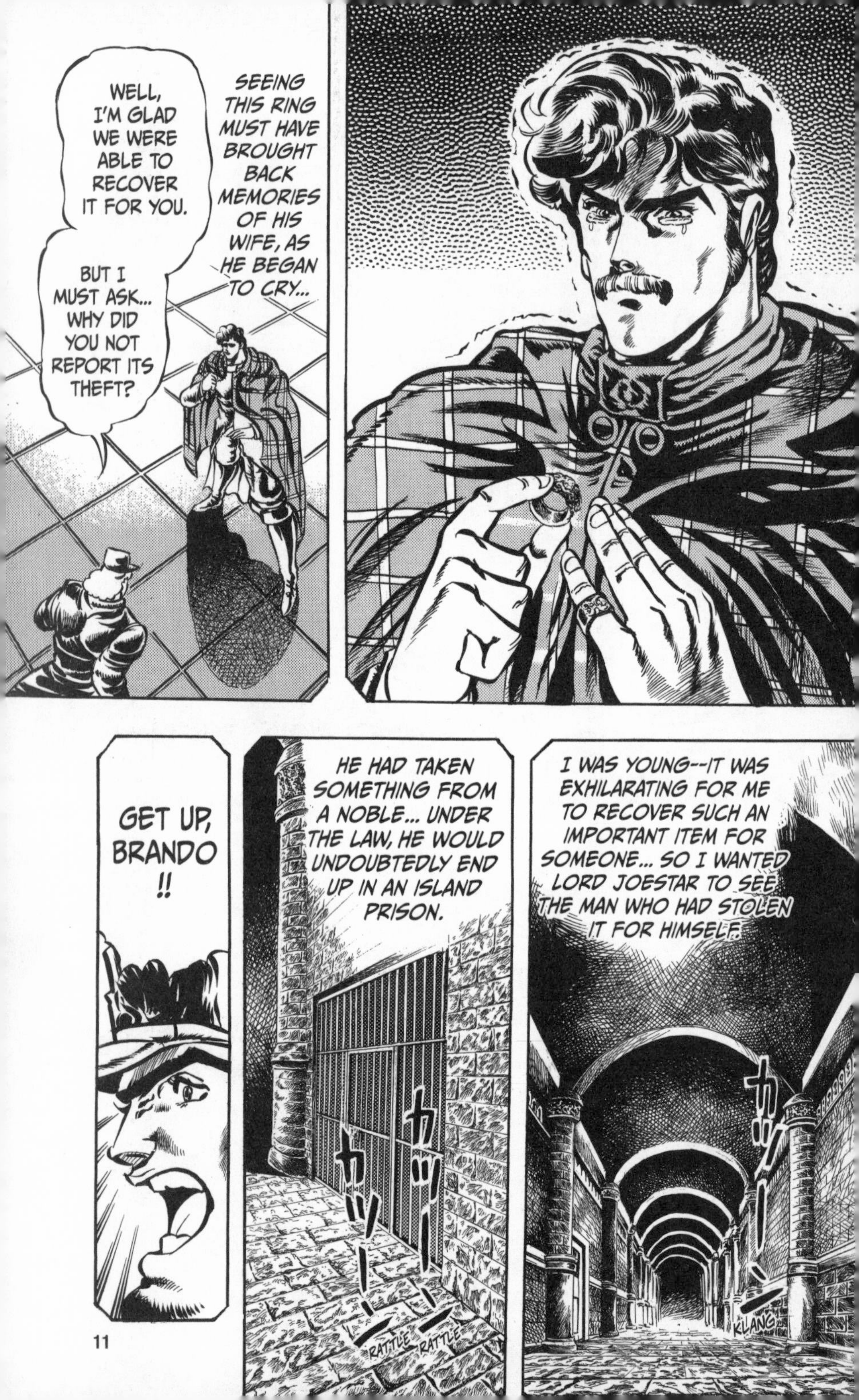
SEEING THIS RING MUST HAVE BROUGHT BACK MEMORIES OF HIS WIFE, AS HE BEGAN TO CRY...
WELL, I'M GLAD WE WERE ABLE TO RECOVER IT FOR YOU.
BUT I MUST ASK... WHY DID YOU NOT REPORT ITS THEFT?
I WAS YOUNG--IT WAS EXHILARATING FOR ME TO RECOVER SUCH AN IMPORTANT ITEM FOR SOMEONE... SO I WANTED LORD JOESTAR TO SEE THE MAN WHO HAD STOLEN IT FOR HIMSELF.
KLANG
HE HAD TAKEN SOMETHING FROM A NOBLE... UNDER THE LAW, HE WOULD UNDOUBTEDLY END UP IN AN ISLAND PRISON.
RATTLE RATTLE
GET UP, BRANDO !!

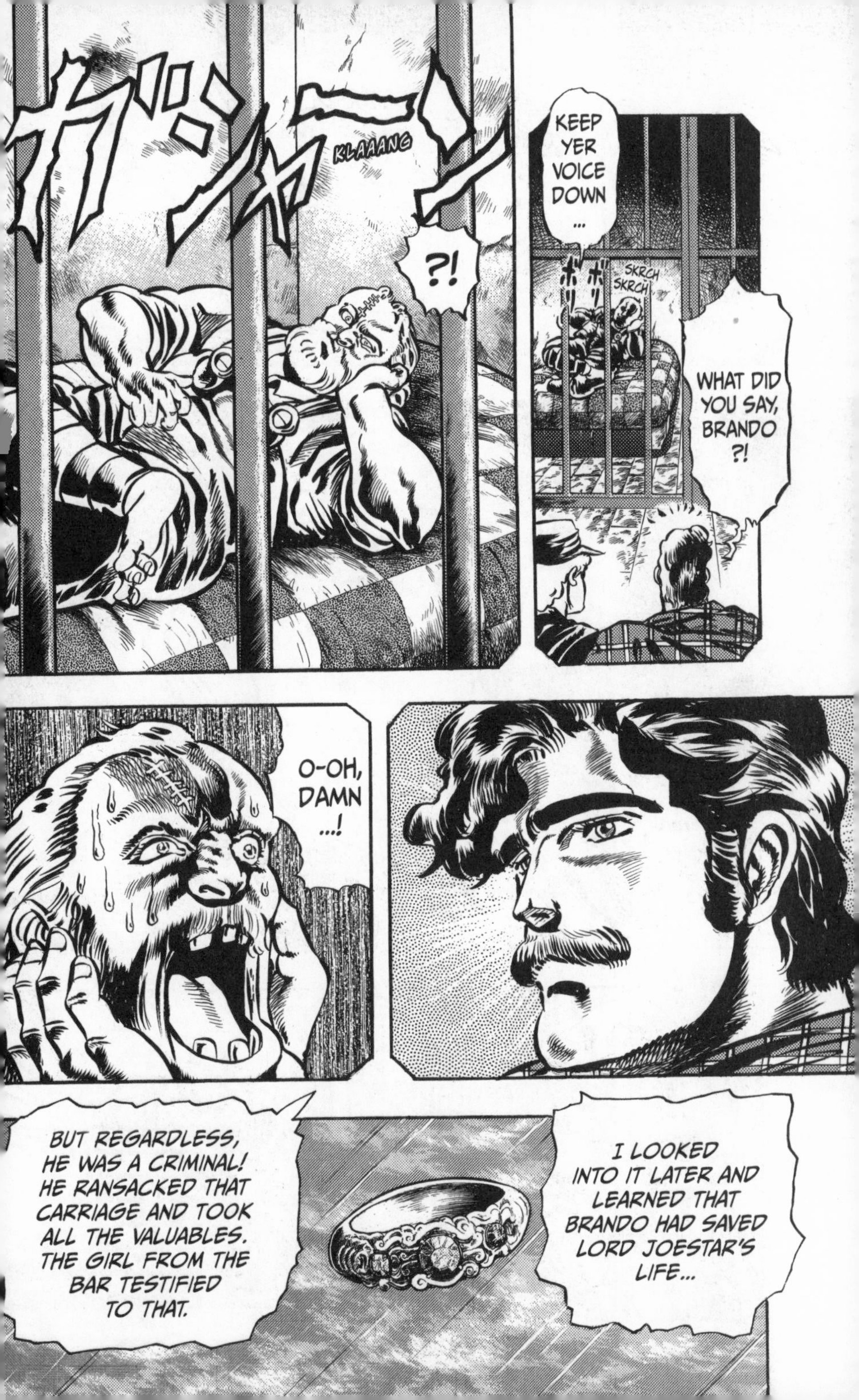
KEEP YER VOICE DOWN ...
ボリボリ
SKRCH SKRCH
WHAT DID YOU SAY, BRANDO ?!
ガシャーン
KLAAANG
?!
O-OH, DAMN ...!
I LOOKED INTO IT LATER AND LEARNED THAT BRANDO HAD SAVED LORD JOESTAR'S LIFE...
BUT REGARDLESS, HE WAS A CRIMINAL! HE RANSACKED THAT CARRIAGE AND TOOK ALL THE VALUABLES. THE GIRL FROM THE BAR TESTIFIED TO THAT.

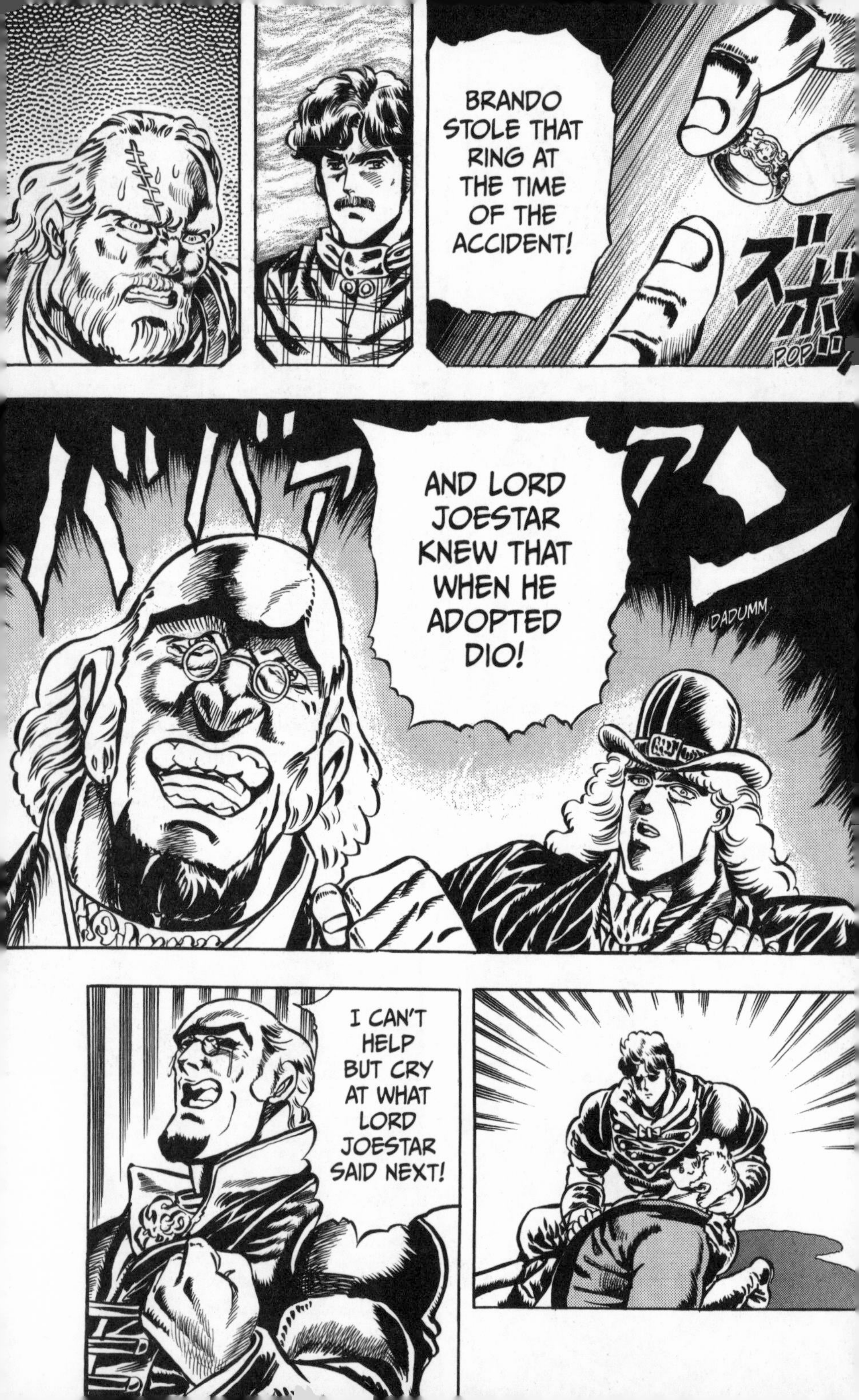
BRANDO STOLE THAT RING AT THE TIME OF THE ACCIDENT!
ズボ
POP
AND LORD JOESTAR KNEW THAT WHEN HE ADOPTED DIO!
DADUMM
I CAN'T HELP BUT CRY AT WHAT LORD JOESTAR SAID NEXT!

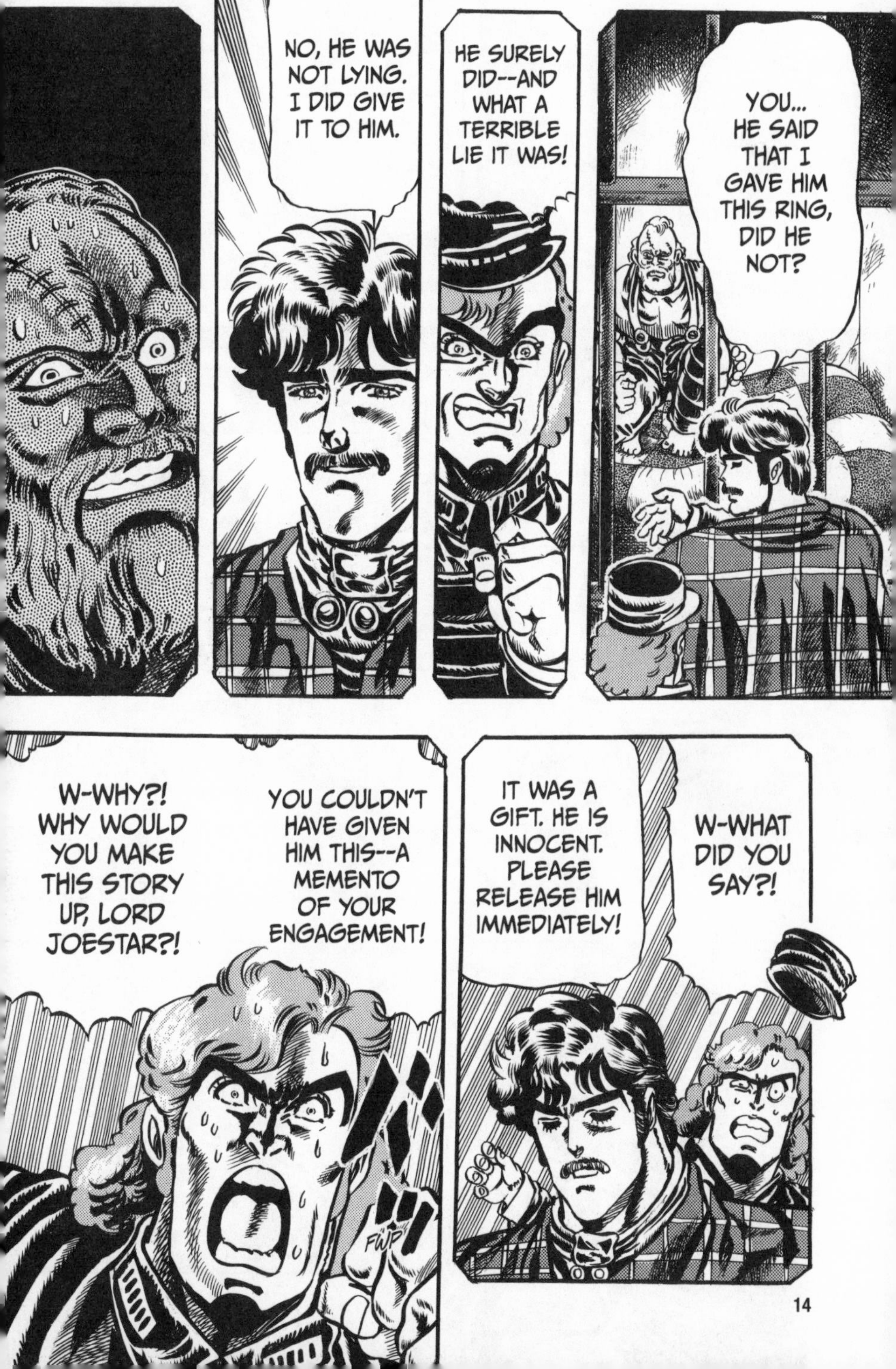
YOU... HE SAID THAT I GAVE HIM THIS RING, DID HE NOT?
HE SURELY DID--AND WHAT A TERRIBLE LIE IT WAS!
NO, HE WAS NOT LYING. I DID GIVE IT TO HIM.
IT WAS A GIFT. HE IS INNOCENT. PLEASE RELEASE HIM IMMEDIATELY!
W-WHAT DID YOU SAY?!
YOU COULDN'T HAVE GIVEN HIM THIS--A MEMENTO OF YOUR ENGAGEMENT!
W-WHY?! WHY WOULD YOU MAKE THIS STORY UP, LORD JOESTAR?!
FWP

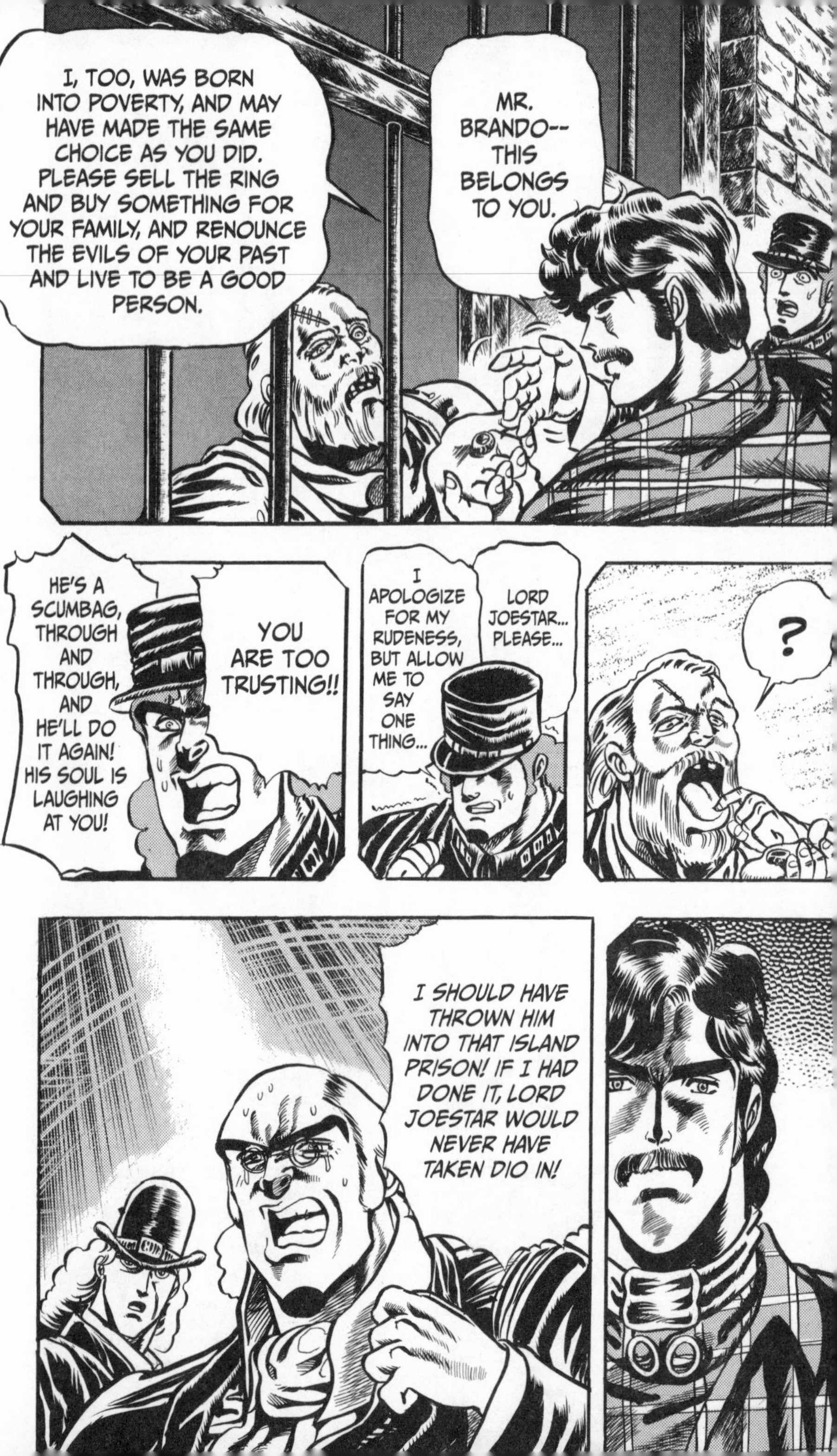
MR. BRANDO-- THIS BELONGS TO YOU.
I, TOO, WAS BORN INTO POVERTY, AND MAY HAVE MADE THE SAME CHOICE AS YOU DID. PLEASE SELL THE RING AND BUY SOMETHING FOR YOUR FAMILY, AND RENOUNCE THE EVILS OF YOUR PAST AND LIVE TO BE A GOOD PERSON.
?
LORD JOESTAR... PLEASE...
I APOLOGIZE FOR MY RUDENESS, BUT ALLOW ME TO SAY ONE THING...
YOU ARE TOO TRUSTING!!
HE'S A SCUMBAG, THROUGH AND THROUGH, AND HE'LL DO IT AGAIN! HIS SOUL IS LAUGHING AT YOU!
I SHOULD HAVE THROWN HIM INTO THAT ISLAND PRISON! IF I HAD DONE IT, LORD JOESTAR WOULD NEVER HAVE TAKEN DIO IN!

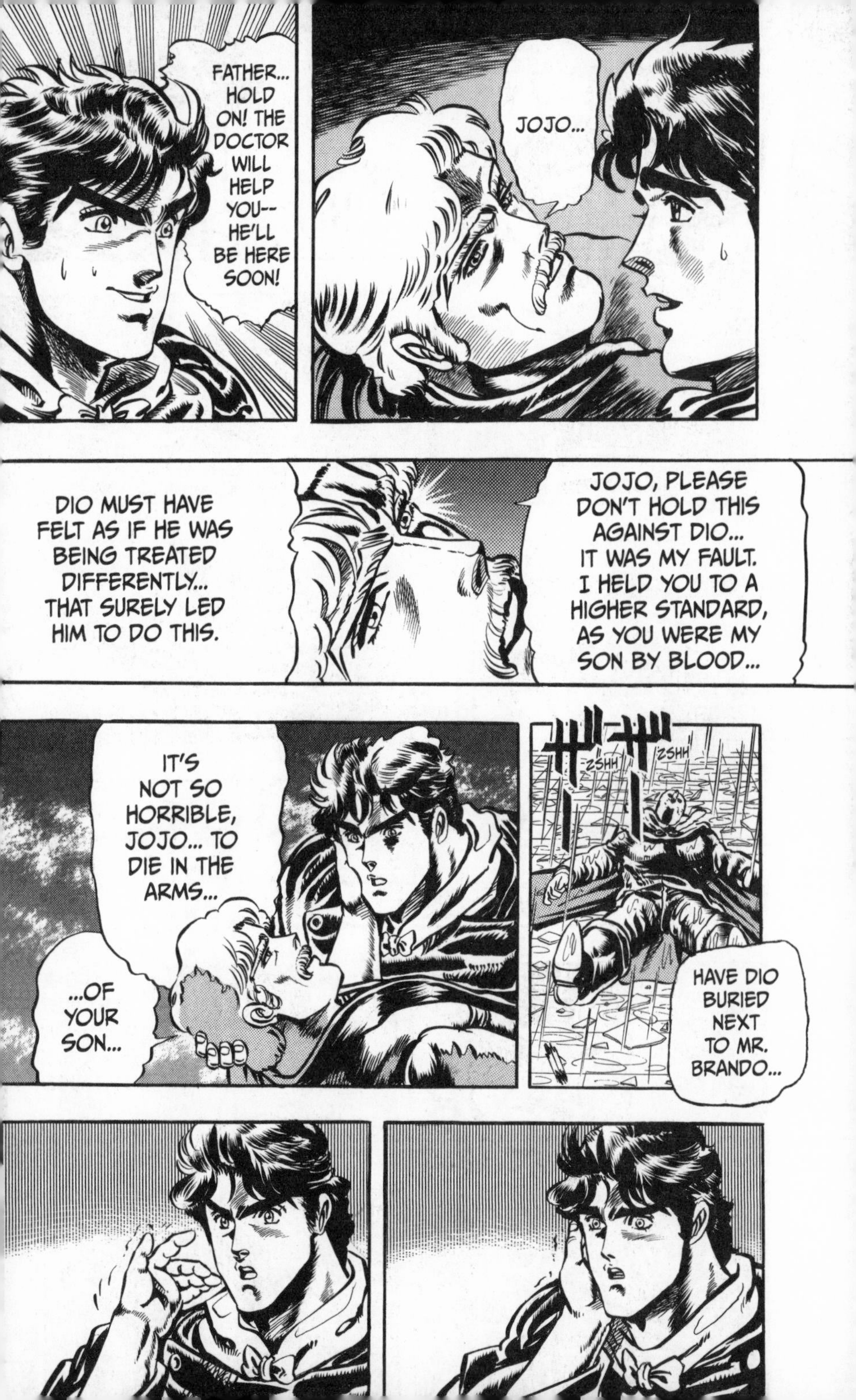
JOJO...
FATHER... HOLD ON! THE DOCTOR WILL HELP YOU-- HE'LL BE HERE SOON!
JOJO, PLEASE DON'T HOLD THIS AGAINST DIO... IT WAS MY FAULT. I HELD YOU TO A HIGHER STANDARD, AS YOU WERE MY SON BY BLOOD...
DIO MUST HAVE FELT AS IF HE WAS BEING TREATED DIFFERENTLY... THAT SURELY LED HIM TO DO THIS.
ZSHH
ZSHH
HAVE DIO BURIED NEXT TO MR. BRANDO...
IT'S NOT SO HORRIBLE, JOJO... TO DIE IN THE ARMS...
...OF YOUR SON...

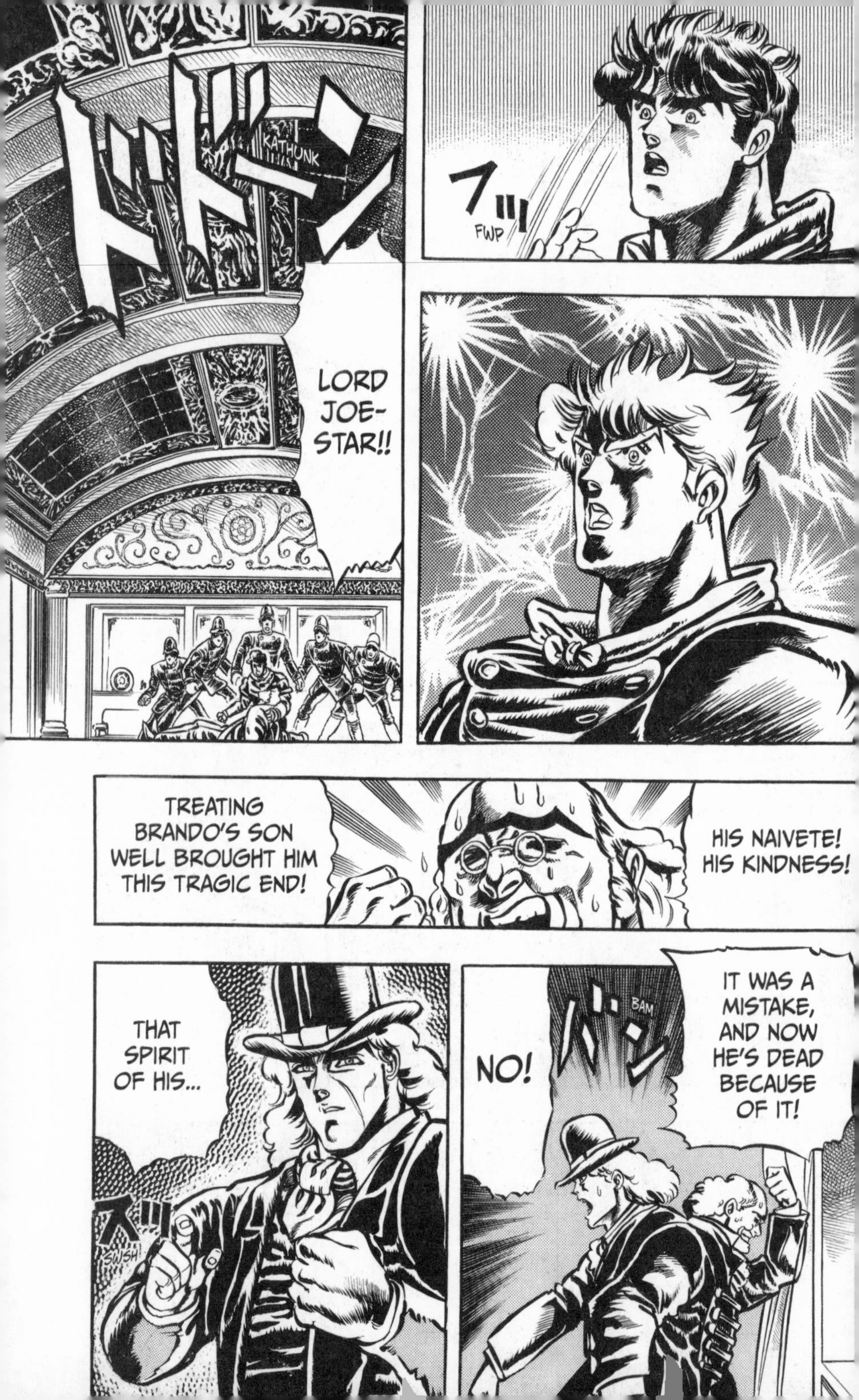
FWP
KATHUNK
LORD JOE-STAR!!
HIS NAIVETE! HIS KINDNESS!
TREATING BRANDO'S SON WELL BROUGHT HIM THIS TRAGIC END!
IT WAS A MISTAKE, AND NOW HE'S DEAD BECAUSE OF IT!
BAM
NO!
THAT SPIRIT OF HIS...
SWSH

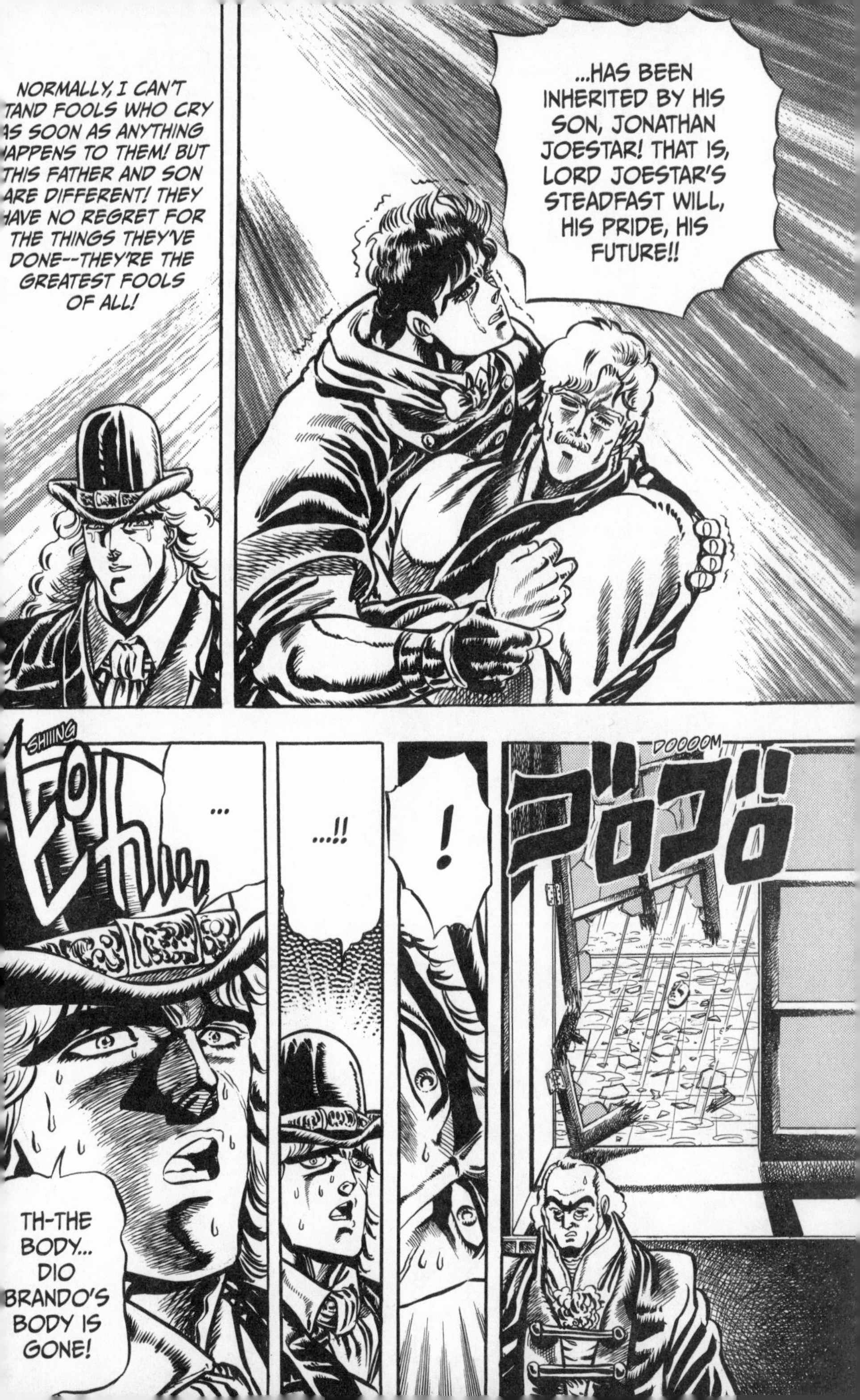
...HAS BEEN INHERITED BY HIS SON, JONATHAN JOESTAR! THAT IS, LORD JOESTAR'S STEADFAST WILL, HIS PRIDE, HIS FUTURE!!
NORMALLY, I CAN'T TAND FOOLS WHO CRY AS SOON AS ANYTHING APPENS TO THEM! BUT THIS FATHER AND SON ARE DIFFERENT! THEY HAVE NO REGRET FOR THE THINGS THEY'VE DONE--THEY'RE THE GREATEST FOOLS OF ALL!
DOOOOM
!
...!!
...
SHIIING
TH-THE BODY... DIO BRANDO'S BODY IS GONE!

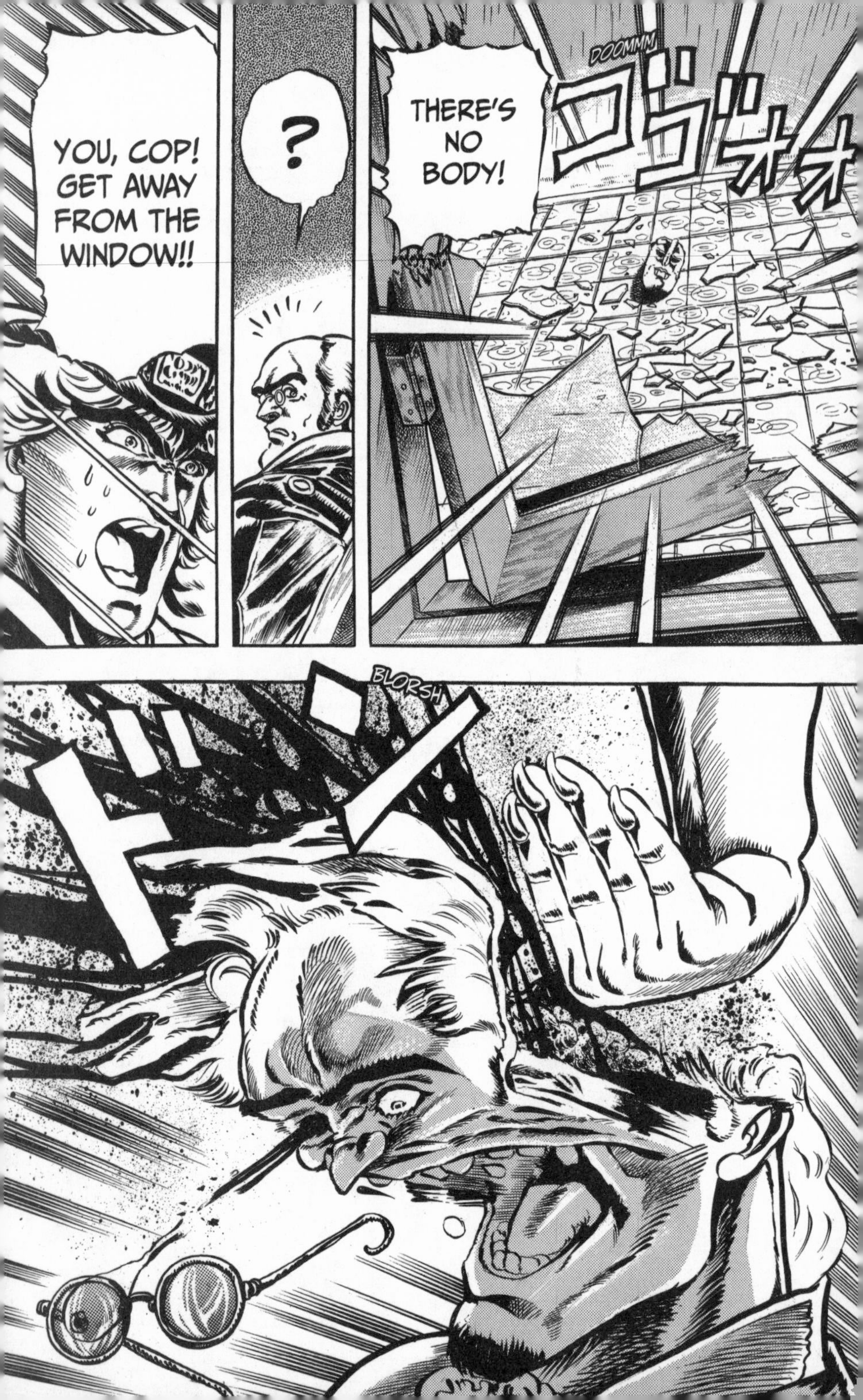
DOOMMM
ゴゴオオ
THERE'S NO BODY!
?
YOU, COP! GET AWAY FROM THE WINDOW!!
BLORSH

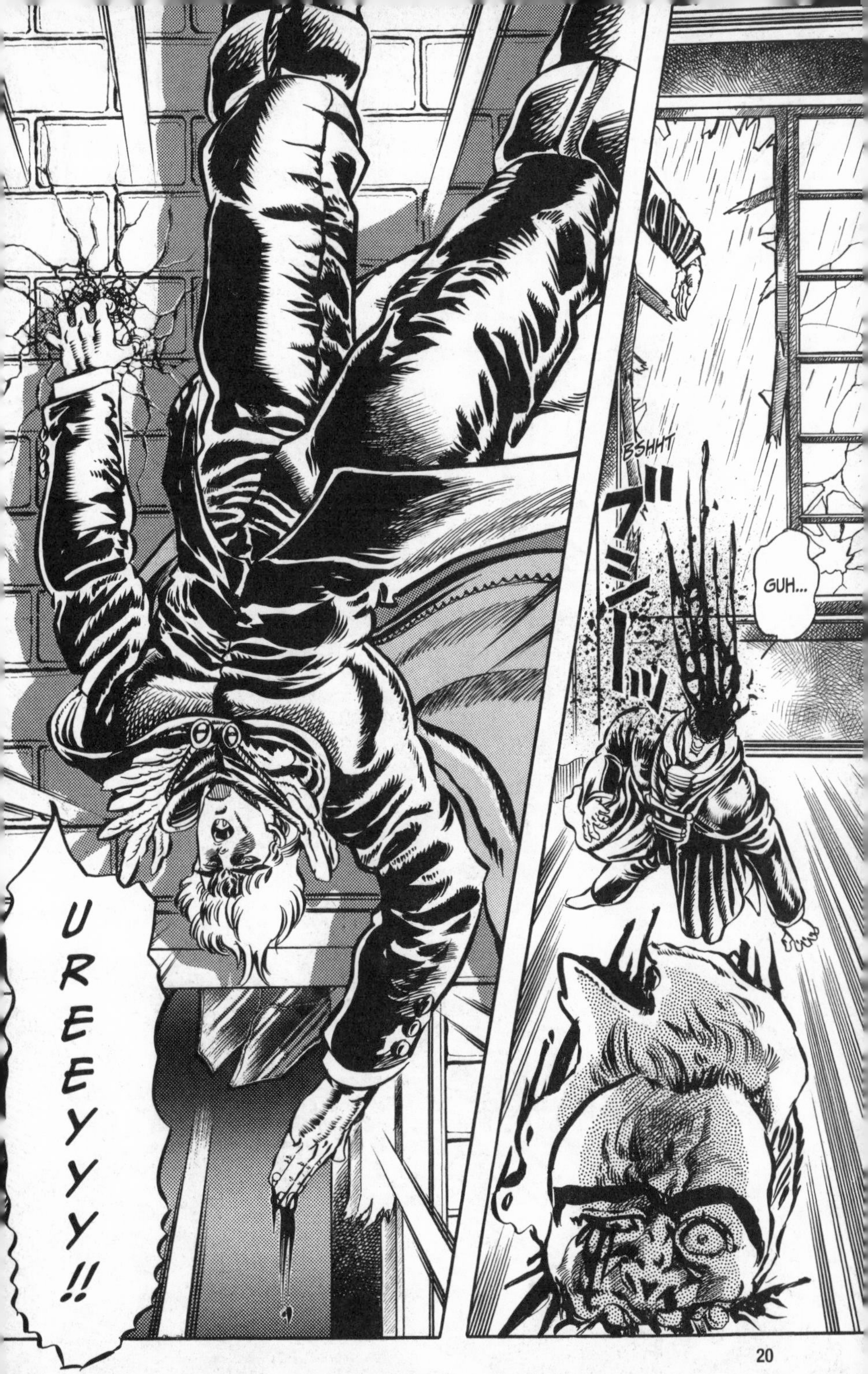
BSHHT
ブシューッ
GUH...
UREEYYY!!

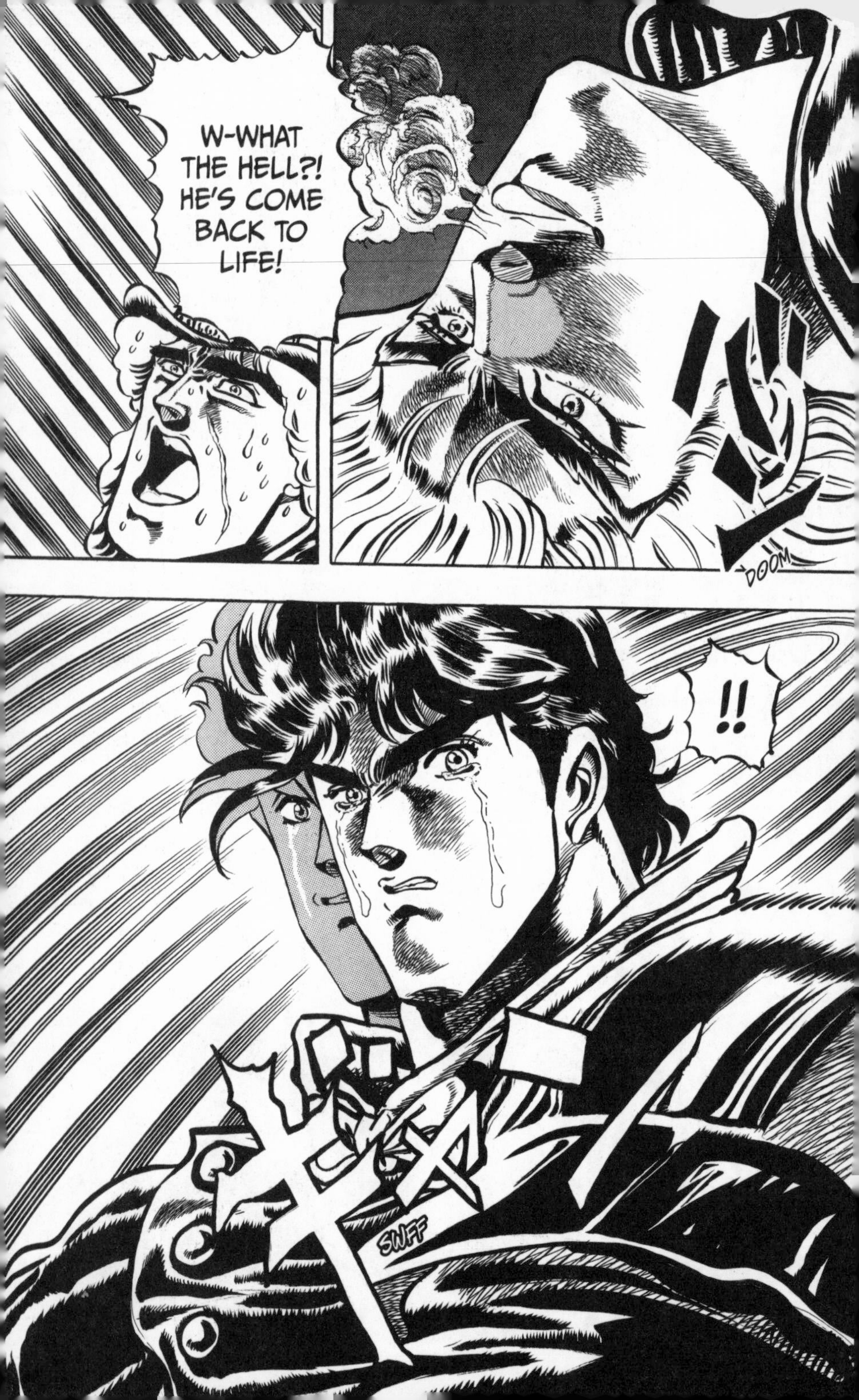
DOOM
W-WHAT THE HELL?! HE'S COME BACK TO LIFE!
!!
SNIFF

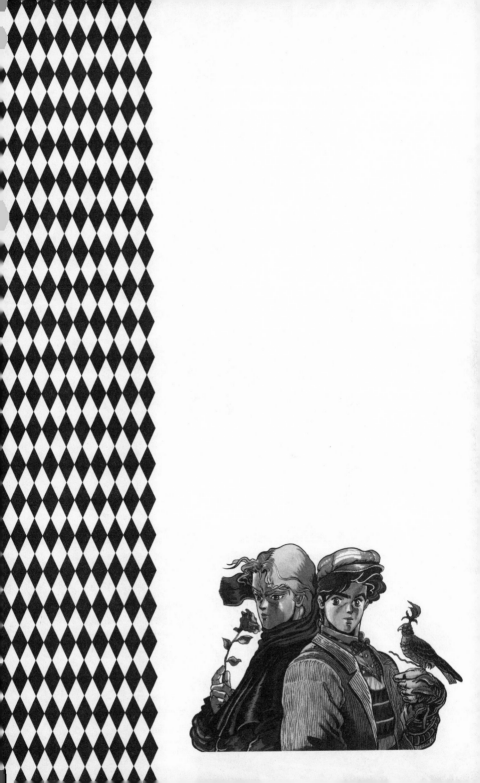

CHAPTER 13: Youth with Dio PART 2

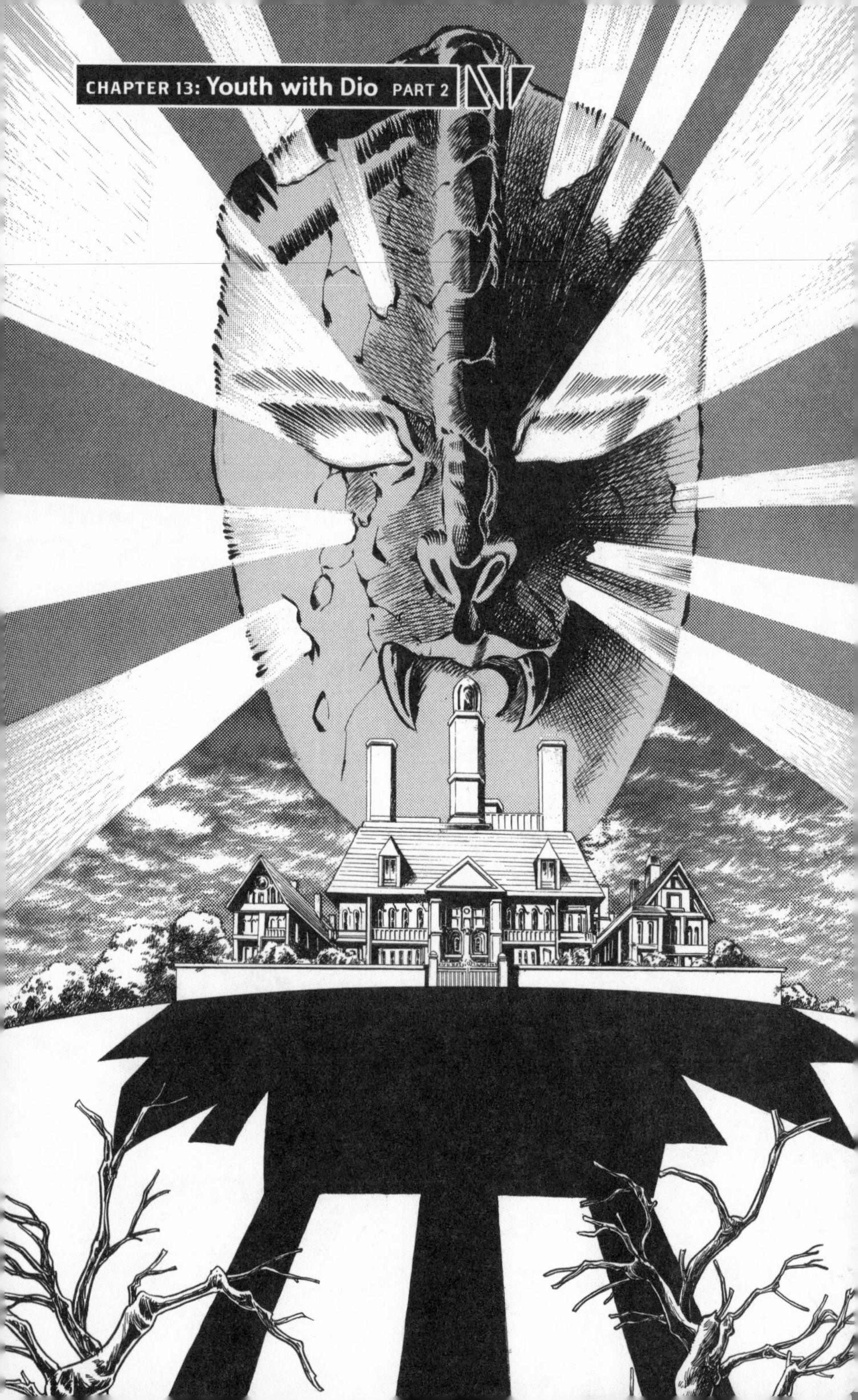

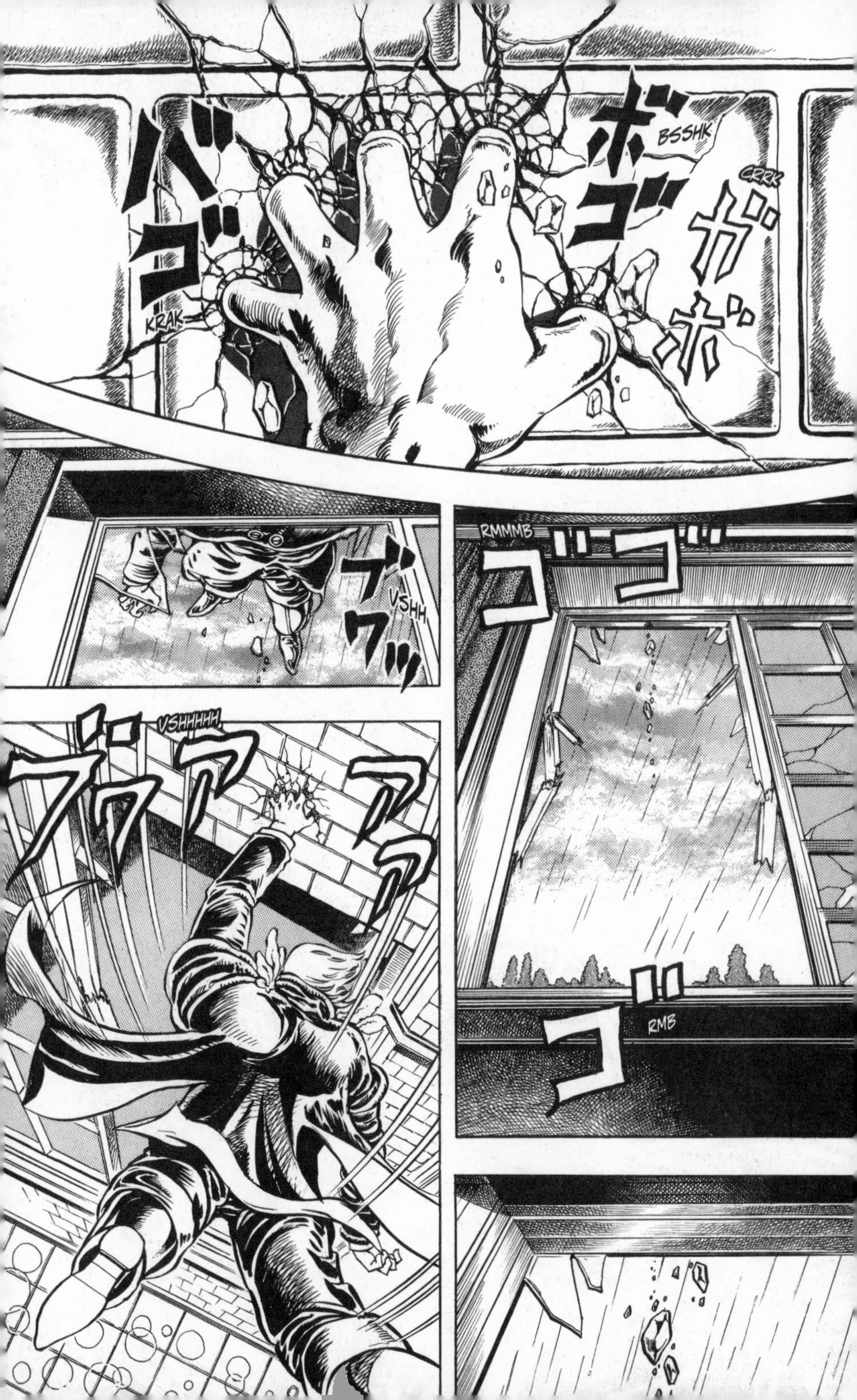
CRRK
BSSHK
KRAK
RMMMB
RMB
VSHH
VSHHHHH

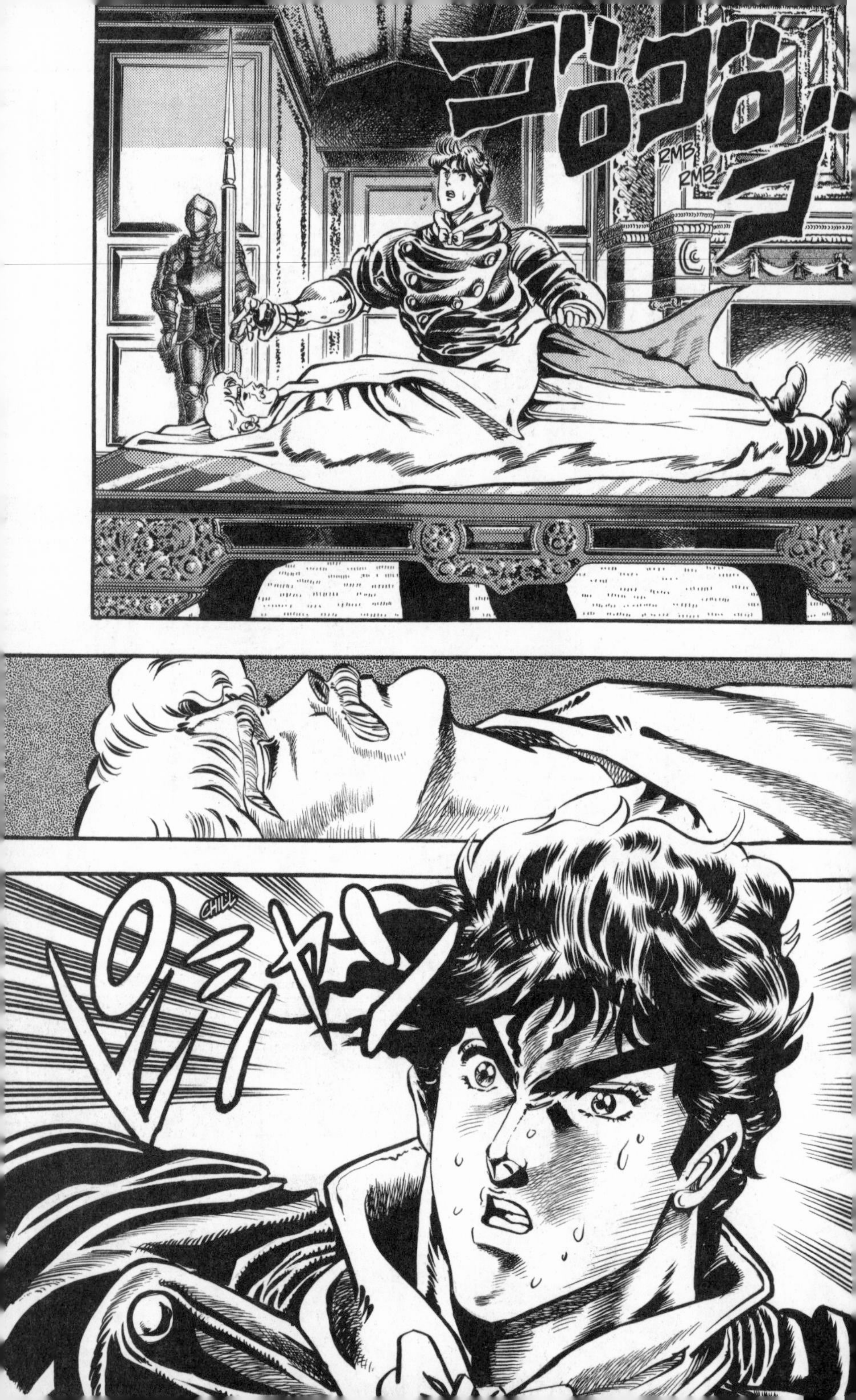
ゴゴゴゴ…
RMB
RMB
CHILL

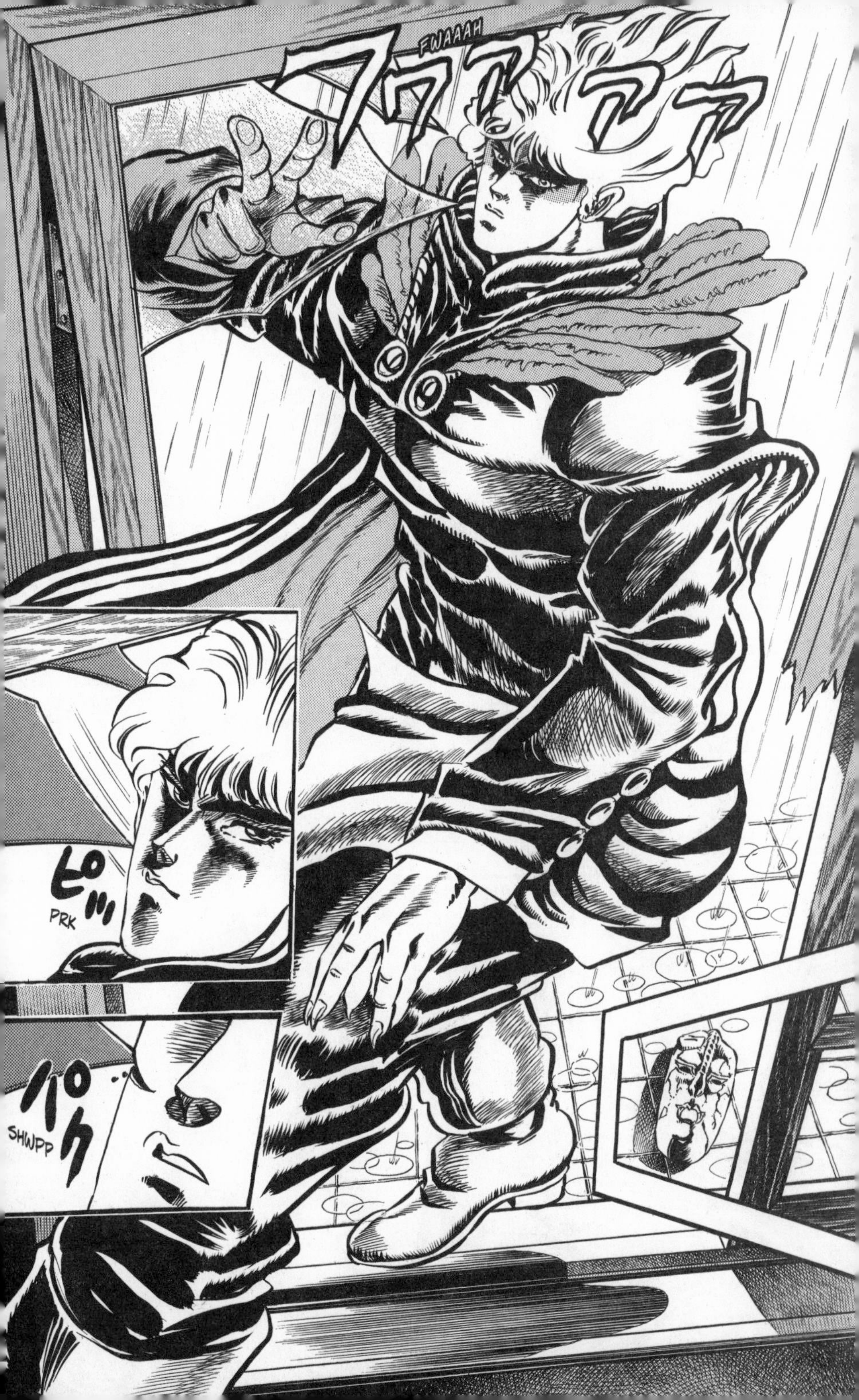
FWAAAH
ピッ
PRK
パク
SHWPP

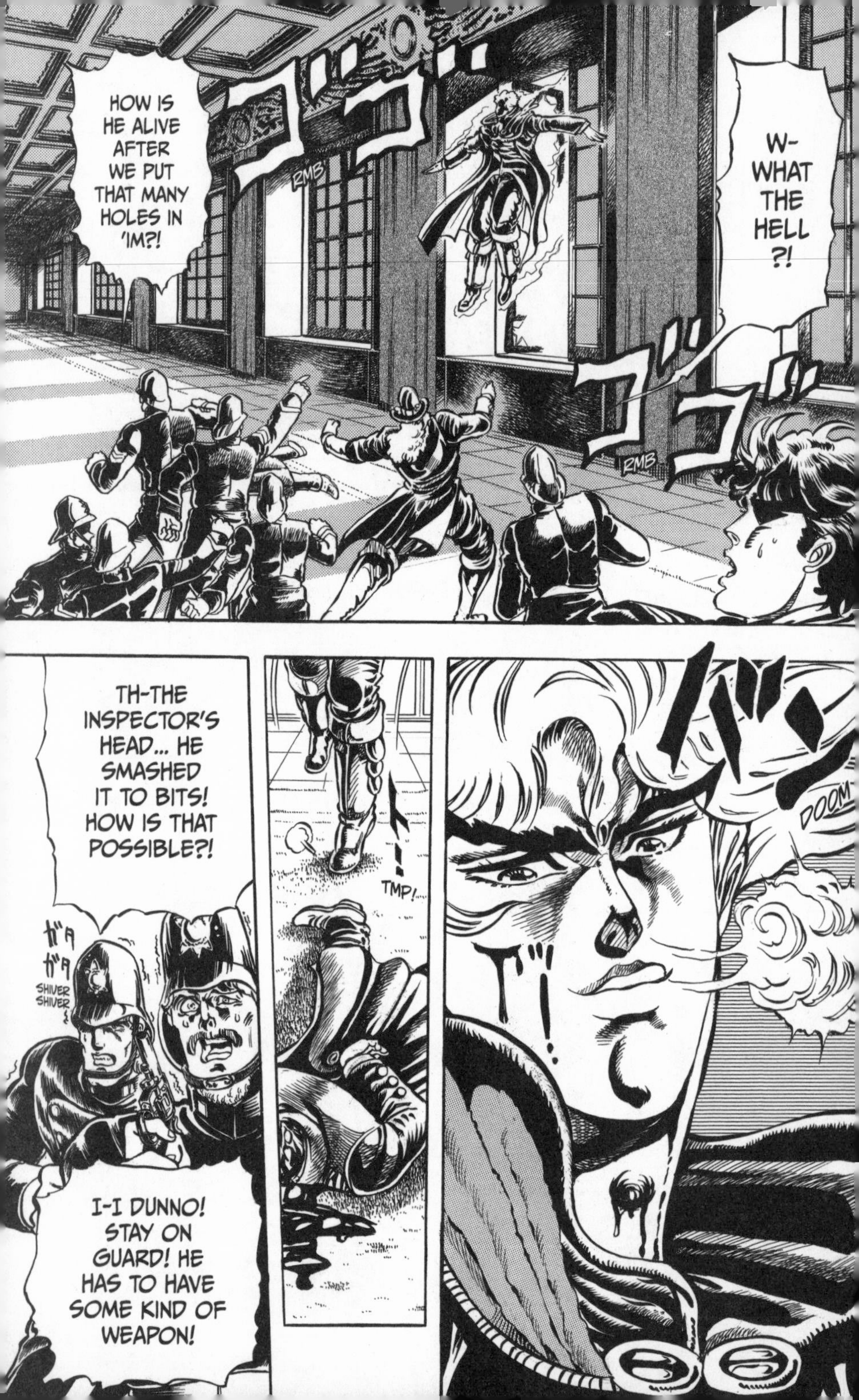
W-WHAT THE HELL?!
RMB
RMB
HOW IS HE ALIVE AFTER WE PUT THAT MANY HOLES IN 'IM?!
DOOM
TMP!
TH-THE INSPECTOR'S HEAD... HE SMASHED IT TO BITS! HOW IS THAT POSSIBLE?!
SHIVER SHIVER
I-I DUNNO! STAY ON GUARD! HE HAS TO HAVE SOME KIND OF WEAPON!

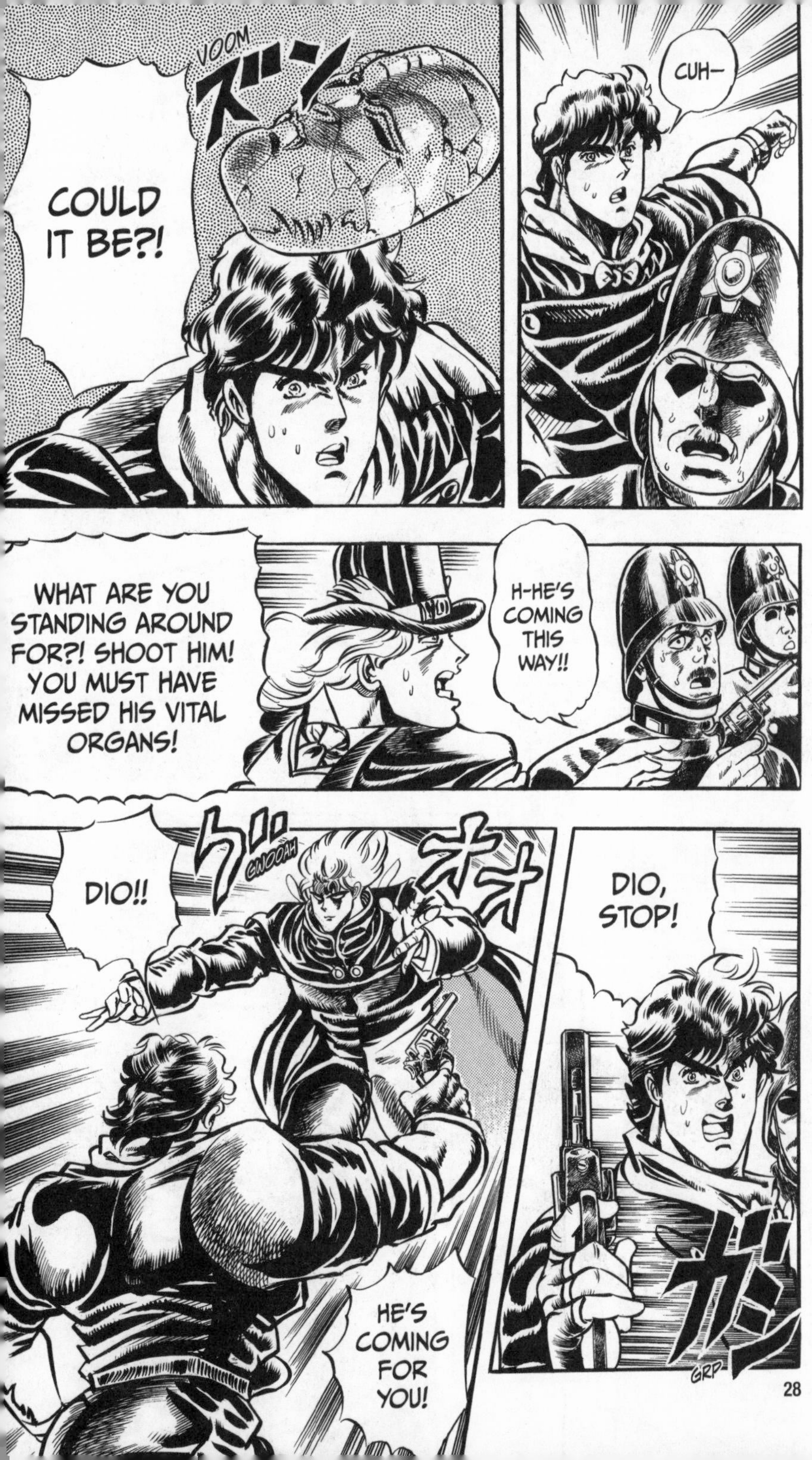
CUH—
VOOM
COULD IT BE?!
H-HE'S COMING THIS WAY!!
WHAT ARE YOU STANDING AROUND FOR?! SHOOT HIM! YOU MUST HAVE MISSED HIS VITAL ORGANS!
DIO, STOP!
GRP
CWOOAH
DIO!!
HE'S COMING FOR YOU!

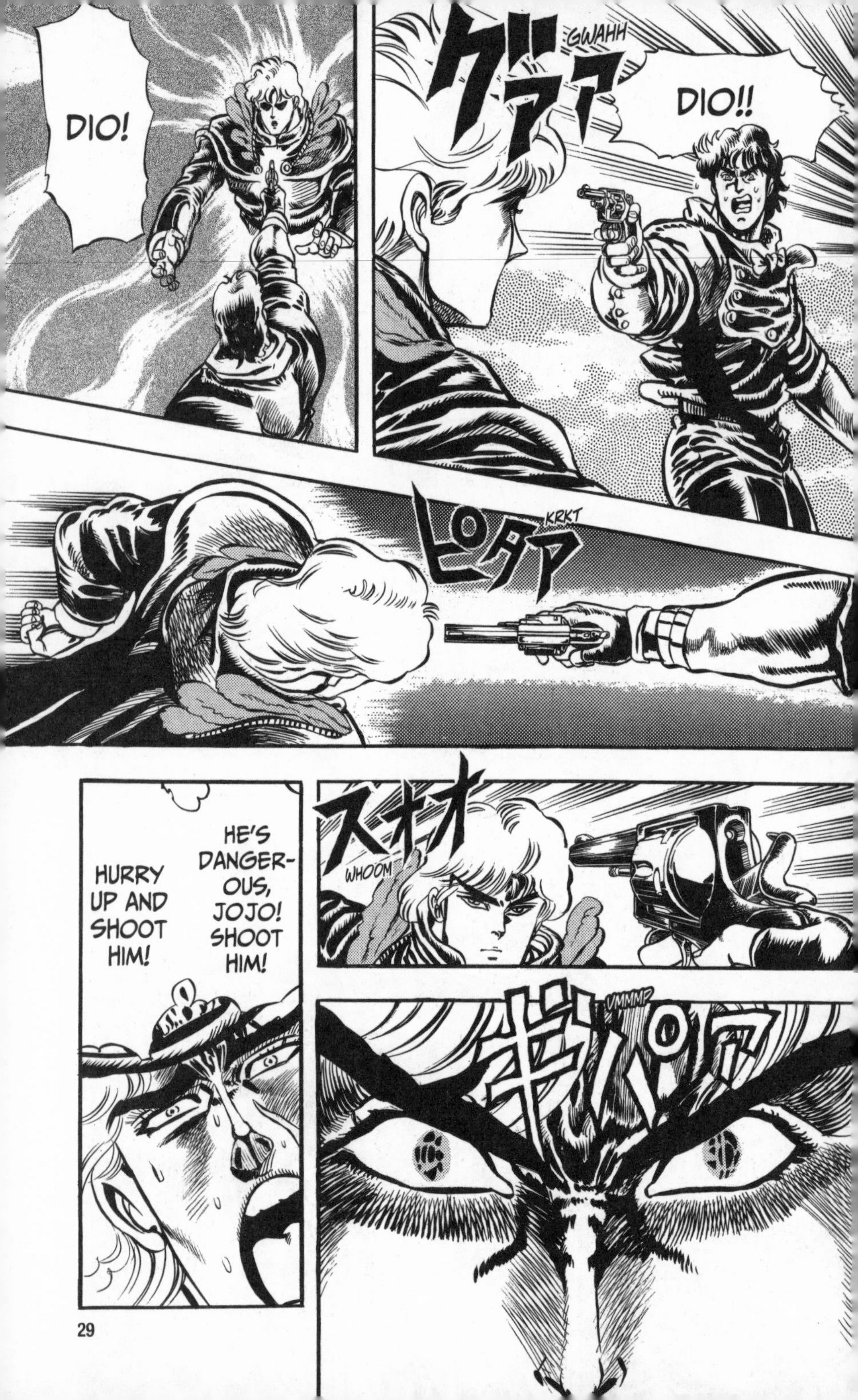
グアア
GWAHH
DIO!!
DIO!
ピタア
KRKT
スオオ
WHOOM
UMMMP
HE'S DANGEROUS, JOJO! SHOOT HIM!
HURRY UP AND SHOOT HIM!

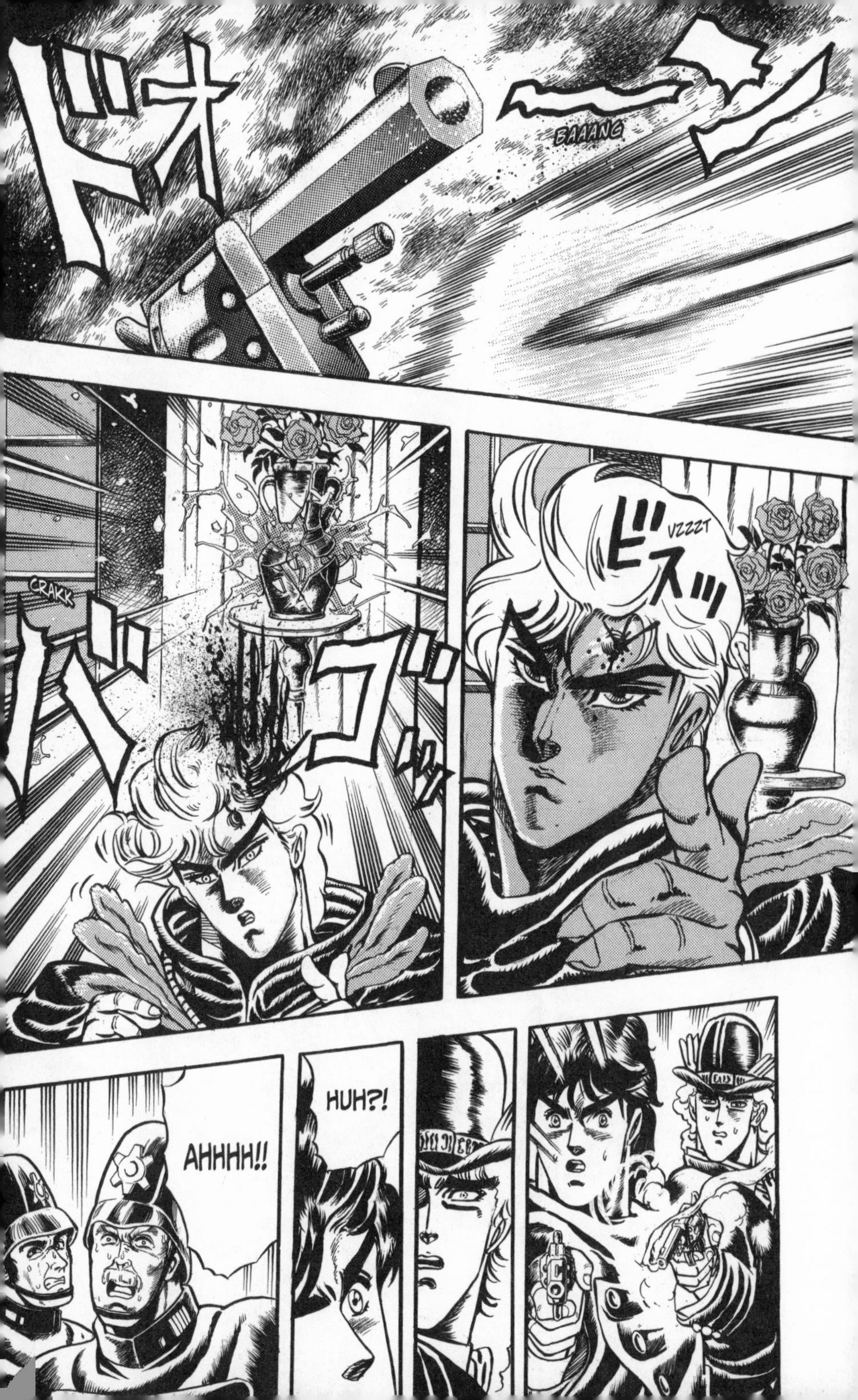
ドオーーン
BAAANG
ビスッ
VZZZT
バゴッ
CRAKK
HUH?!
AHHHH!!

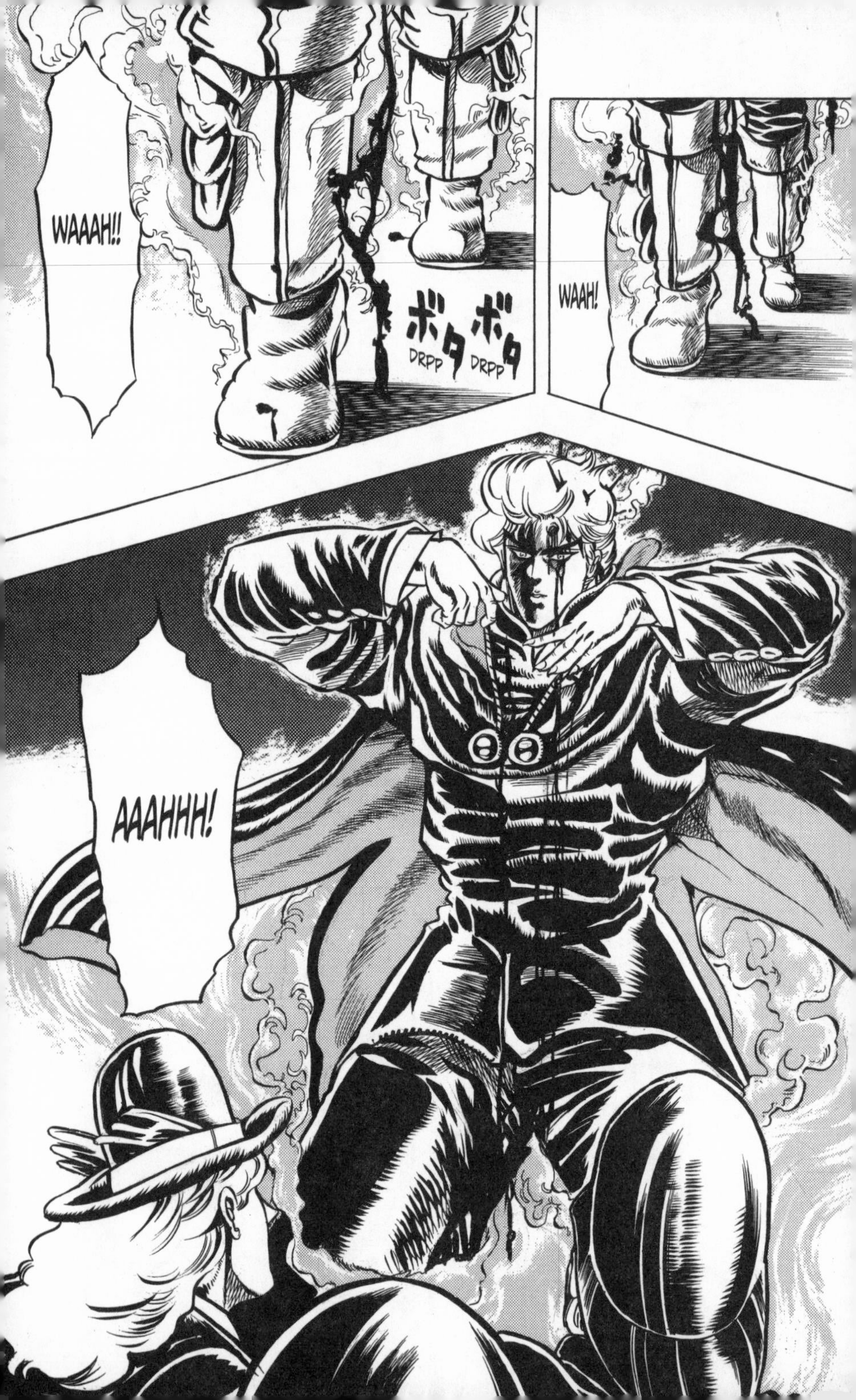
WAAH!
WAAAH!!
ボタ DRPP
ボタ DRPP
AAAHHH!

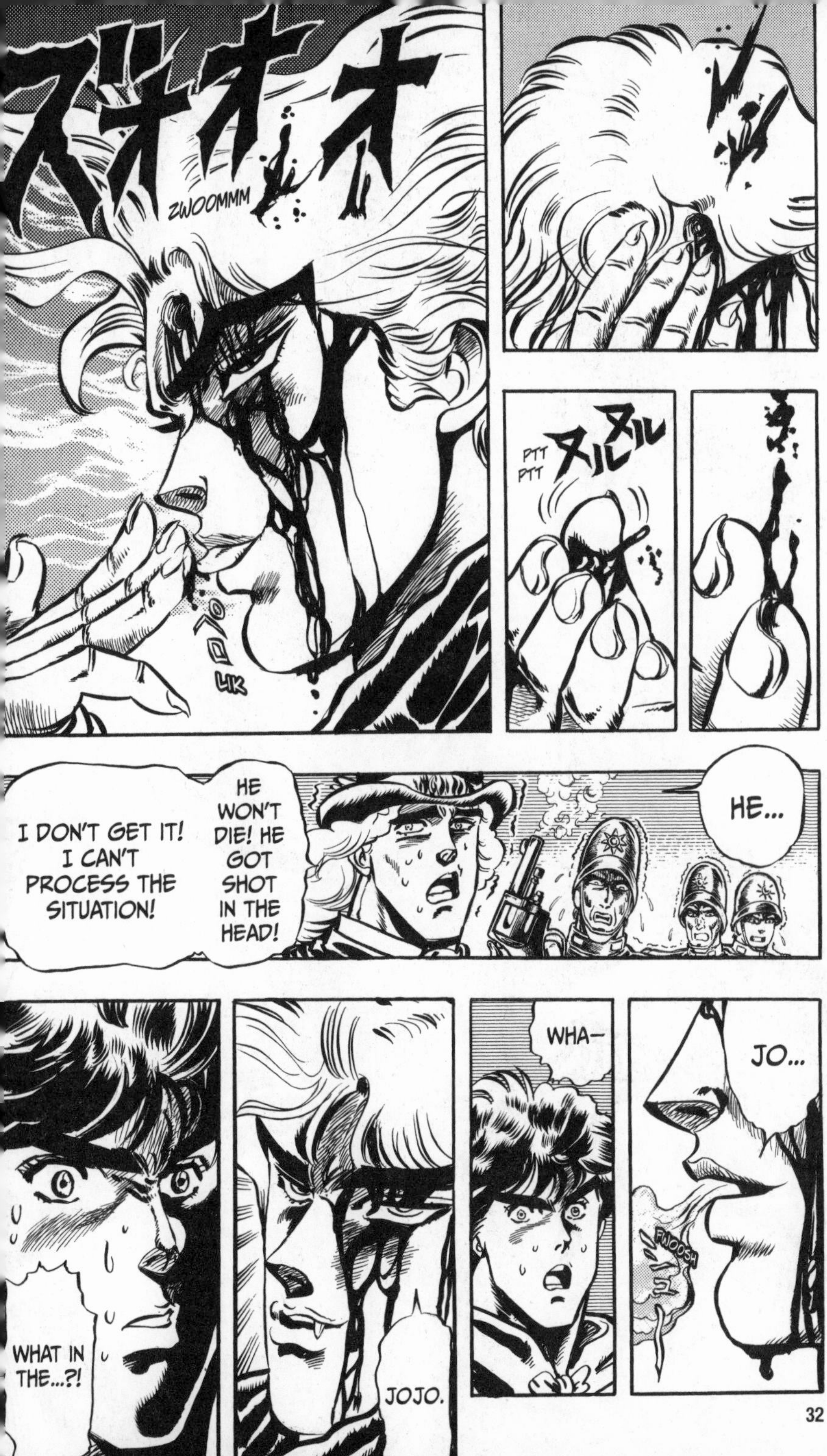
PTT
PTT
ヌルヌル
ズオオオ
ZWOOMMM
ペロ
UK
HE...
HE WON'T DIE! HE GOT SHOT IN THE HEAD!
I DON'T GET IT! I CAN'T PROCESS THE SITUATION!
JO...
FWOOSH
WHA—
JOJO.
WHAT IN THE...?!

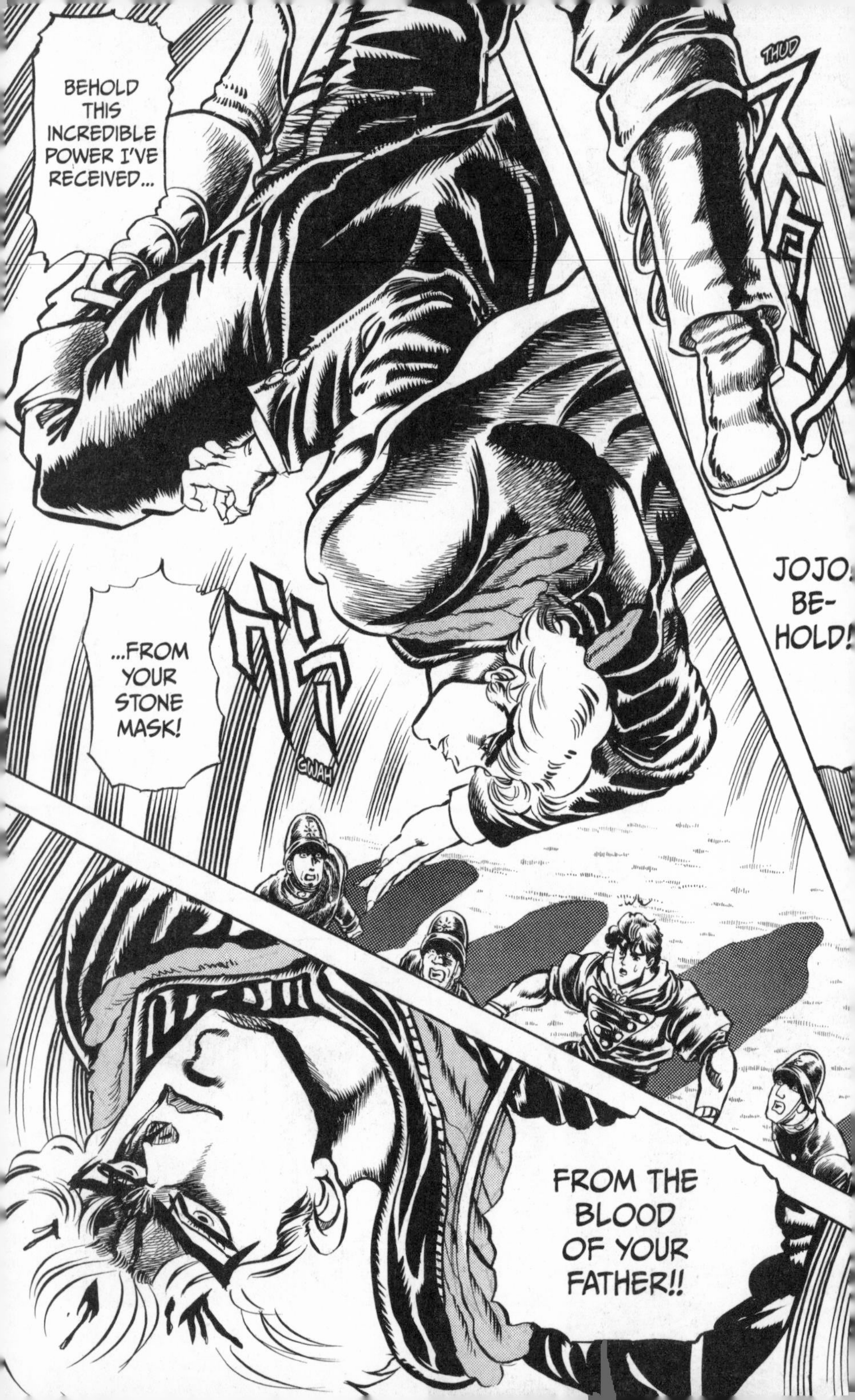
THUD
JOJO! BE-HOLD!
BEHOLD THIS INCREDIBLE POWER I'VE RECEIVED...
...FROM YOUR STONE MASK!
GNAH
FROM THE BLOOD OF YOUR FATHER!!

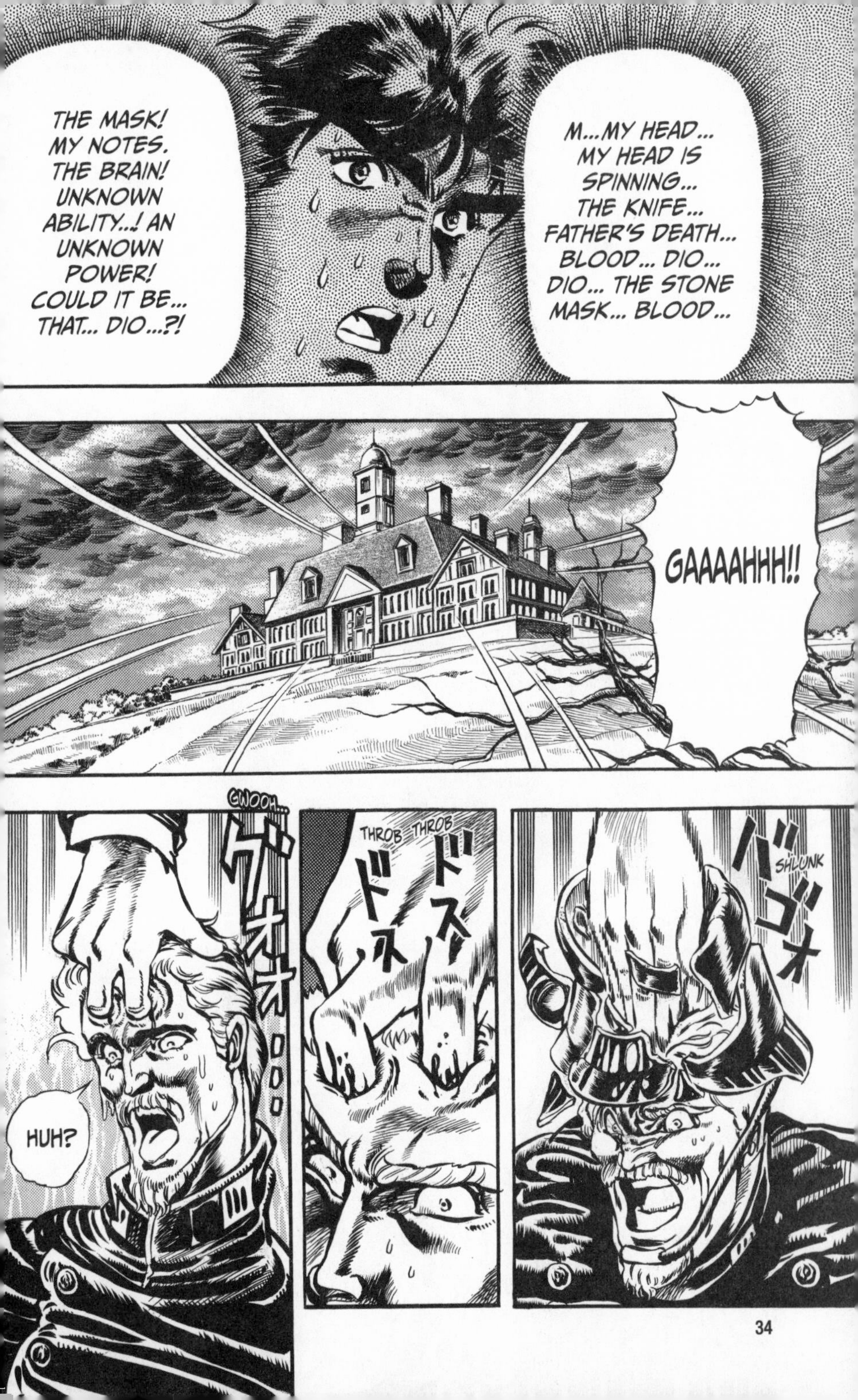
M...MY HEAD... MY HEAD IS SPINNING... THE KNIFE... FATHER'S DEATH... BLOOD... DIO... DIO... THE STONE MASK... BLOOD...
THE MASK! MY NOTES. THE BRAIN! UNKNOWN ABILITY...! AN UNKNOWN POWER! COULD IT BE... THAT... DIO...?!
GAAAAHHH!!
バゴオ
SHLUNK
THROB THROB
ドスドス
GWOOH...
HUH?

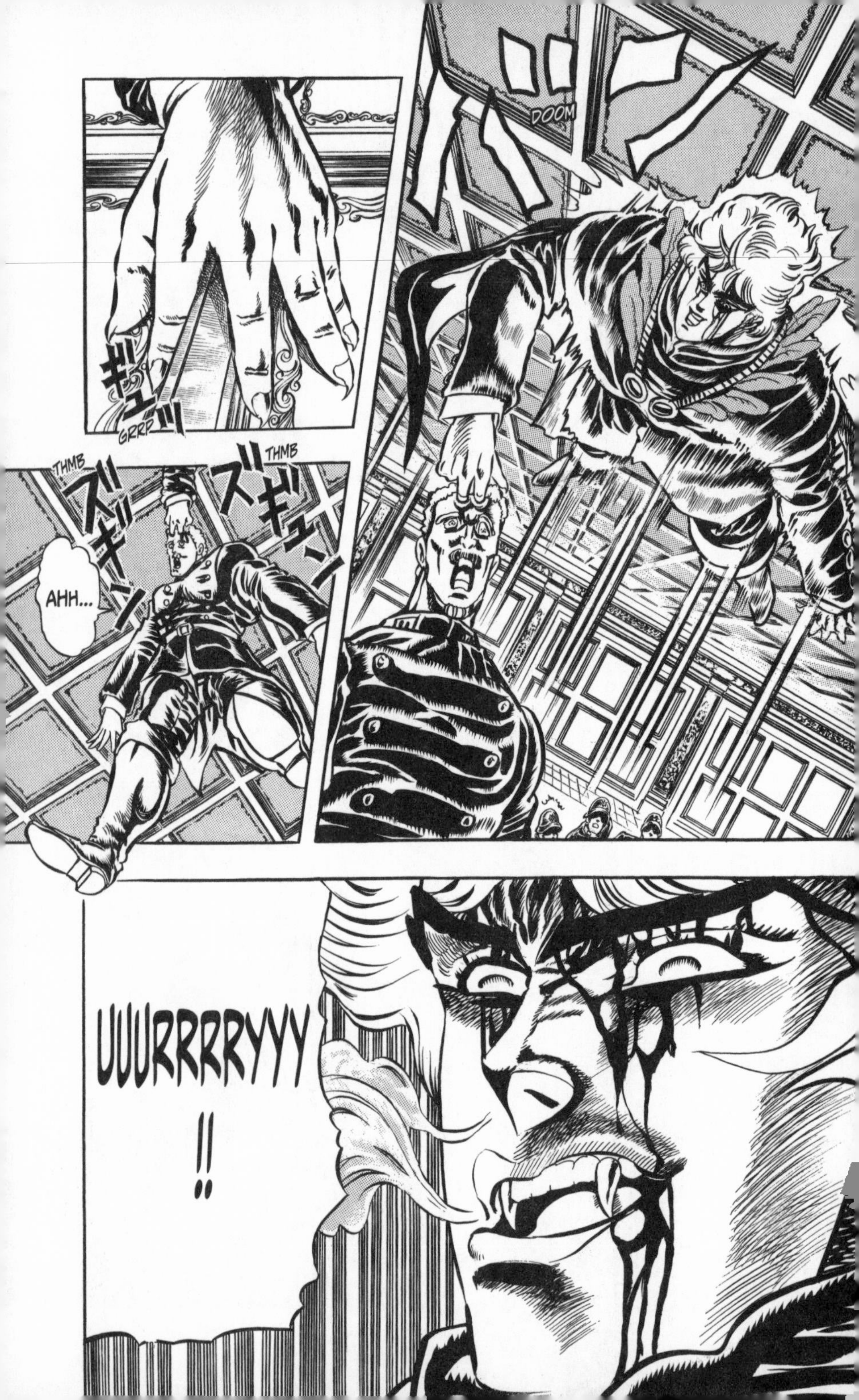
DOOM
GRRP
THMB
THMB
AHH...
UUURRRRYYY
!!

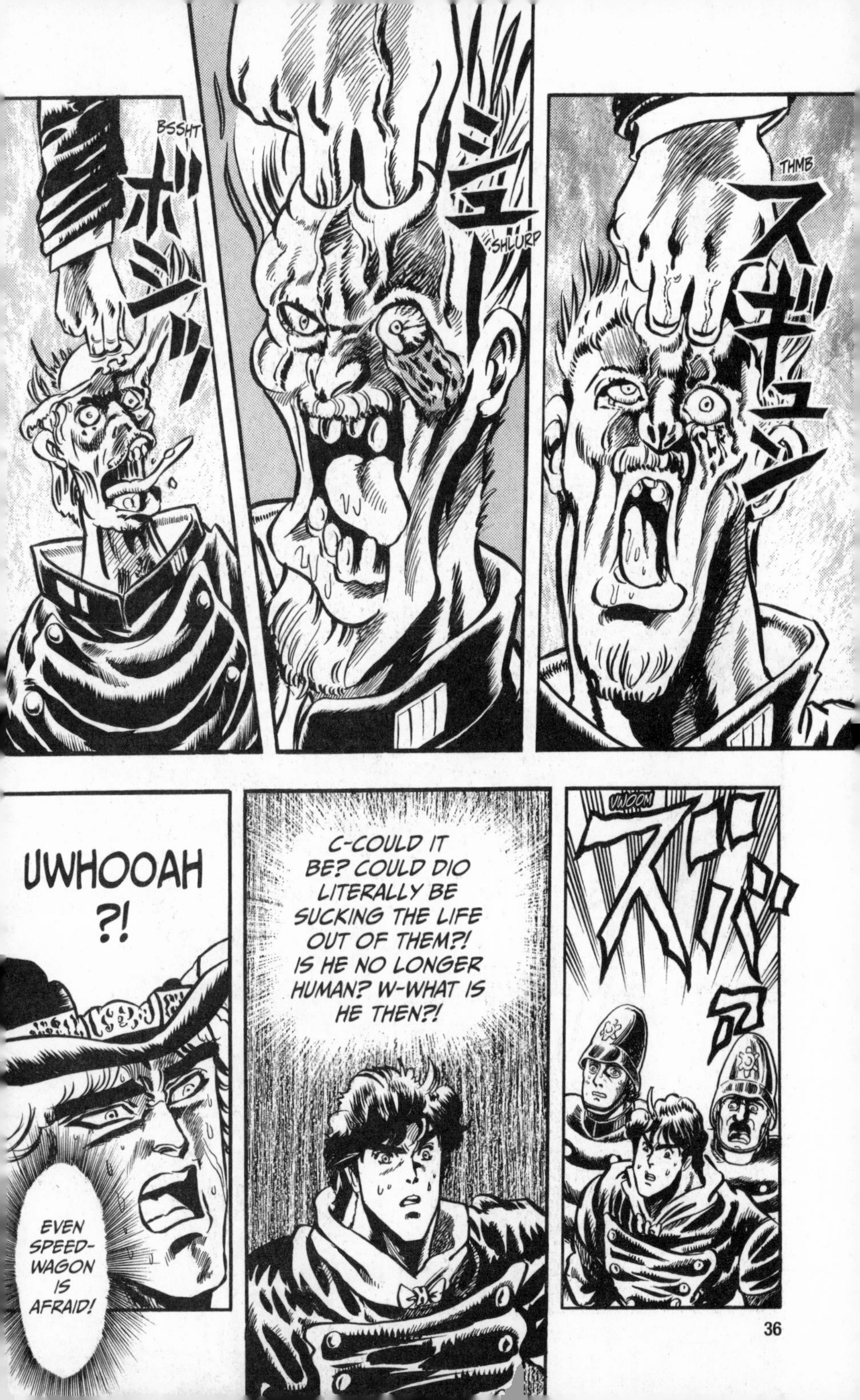
THMB
SHLURP
BSSHT
VWOOM
C-COULD IT BE? COULD DIO LITERALLY BE SUCKING THE LIFE OUT OF THEM?! IS HE NO LONGER HUMAN? W-WHAT IS HE THEN?!
UWHOOAH ?!
EVEN SPEED-WAGON IS AFRAID!

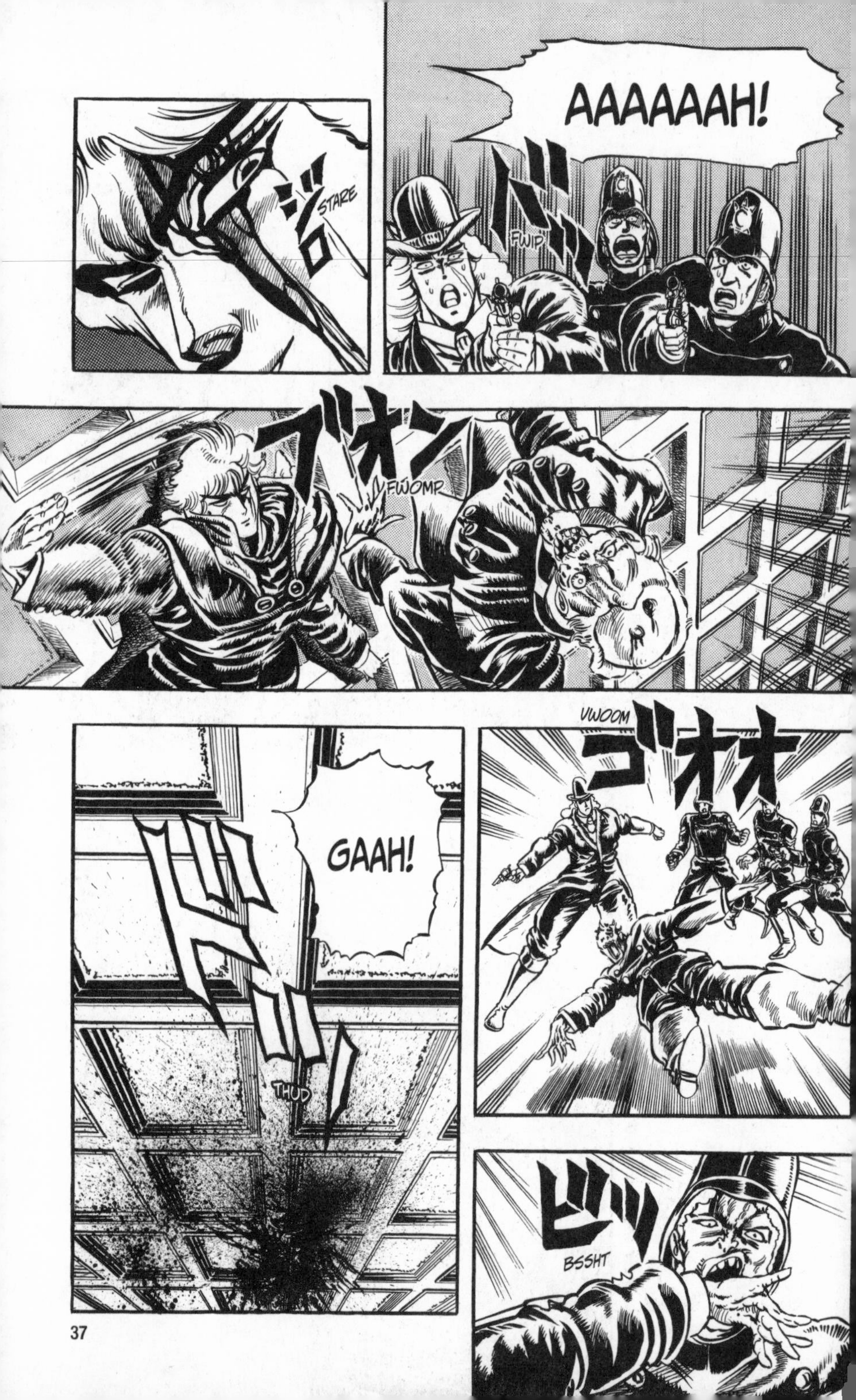
AAAAAAH!
FWIP
STARE
FWOMP
VWOOM
BSSHT
GAAH!
THUD

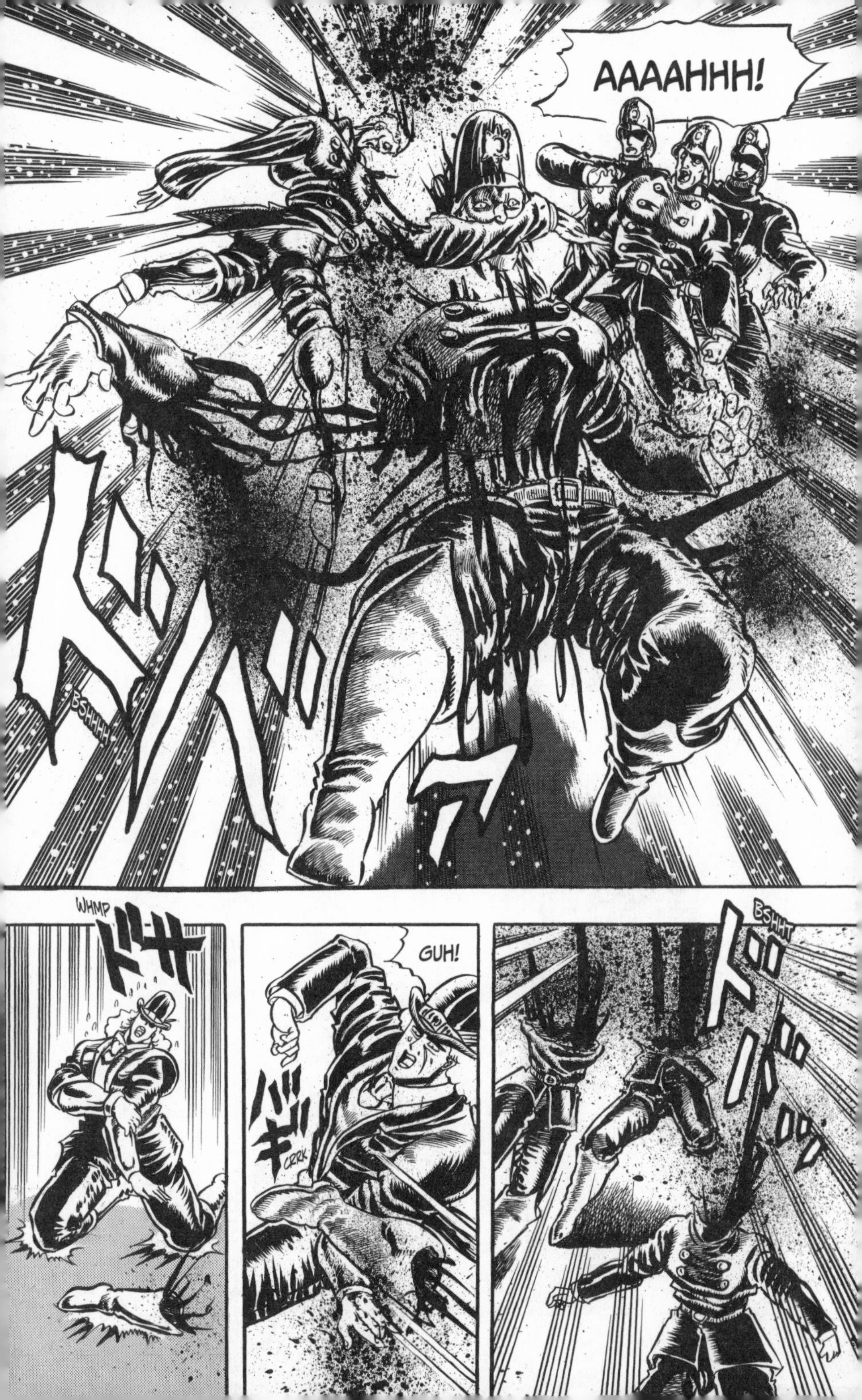
AAAAHHH!
BSHHHH
BSHHT
GUH!
CRRK
WHMP

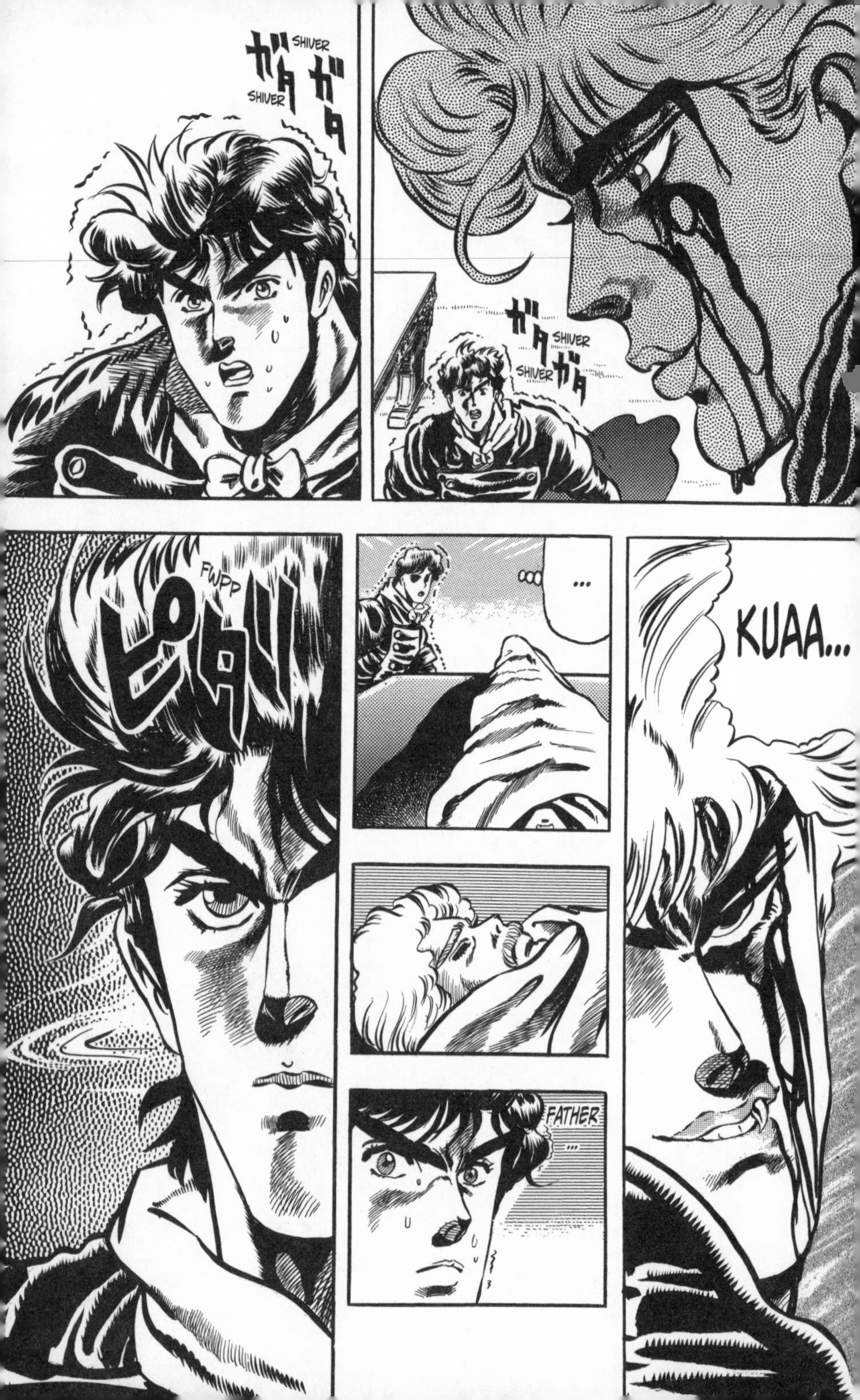
ガタ SHIVER
SHIVER ガタ
ガタ SHIVER
SHIVER ガタ
KUAA...
...
FATHER ...
FWPP
ピクリ

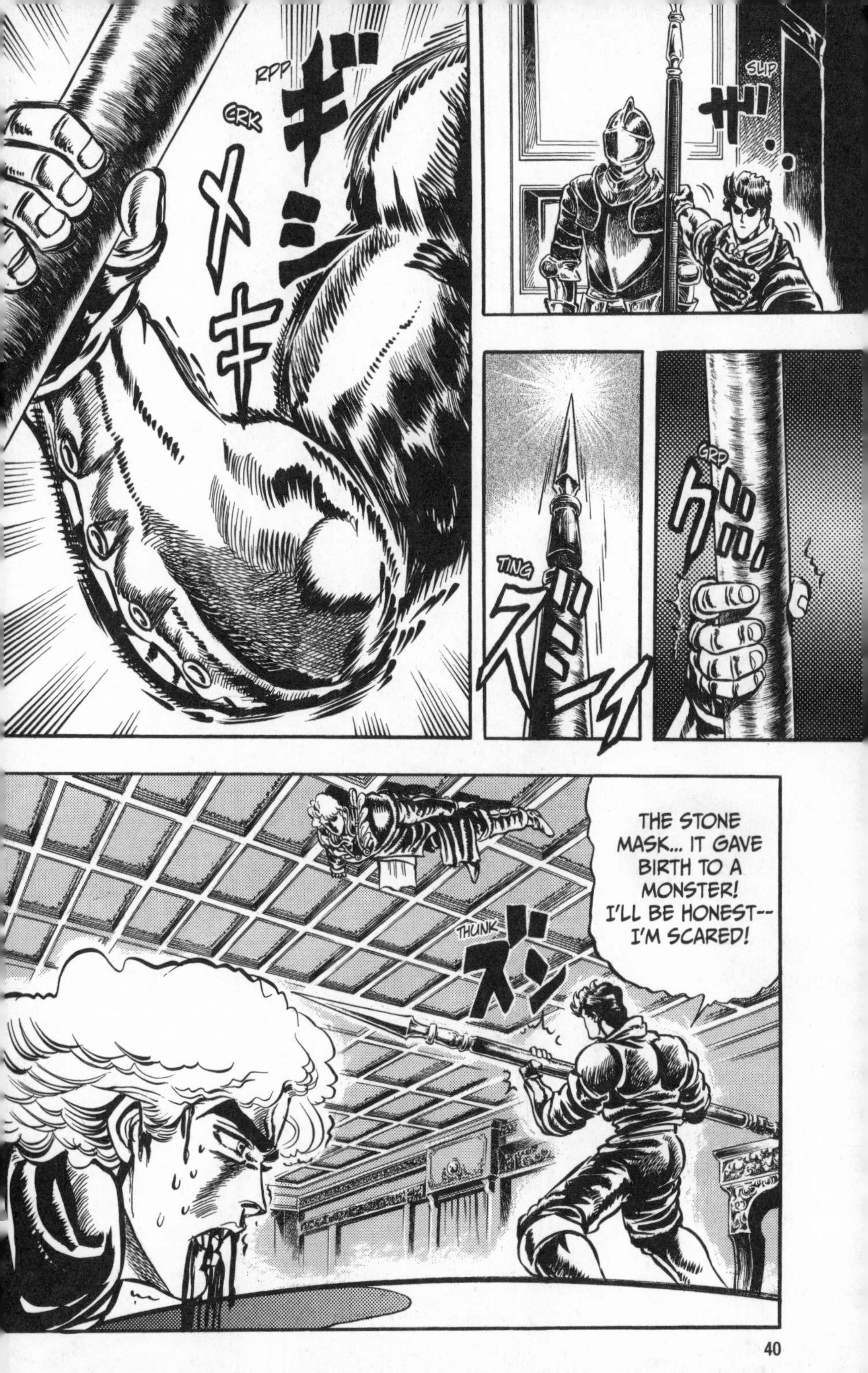
SLIP
GRP
TING
RPP
CRK
THUNK
THE STONE MASK... IT GAVE BIRTH TO A MONSTER! I'LL BE HONEST-- I'M SCARED!

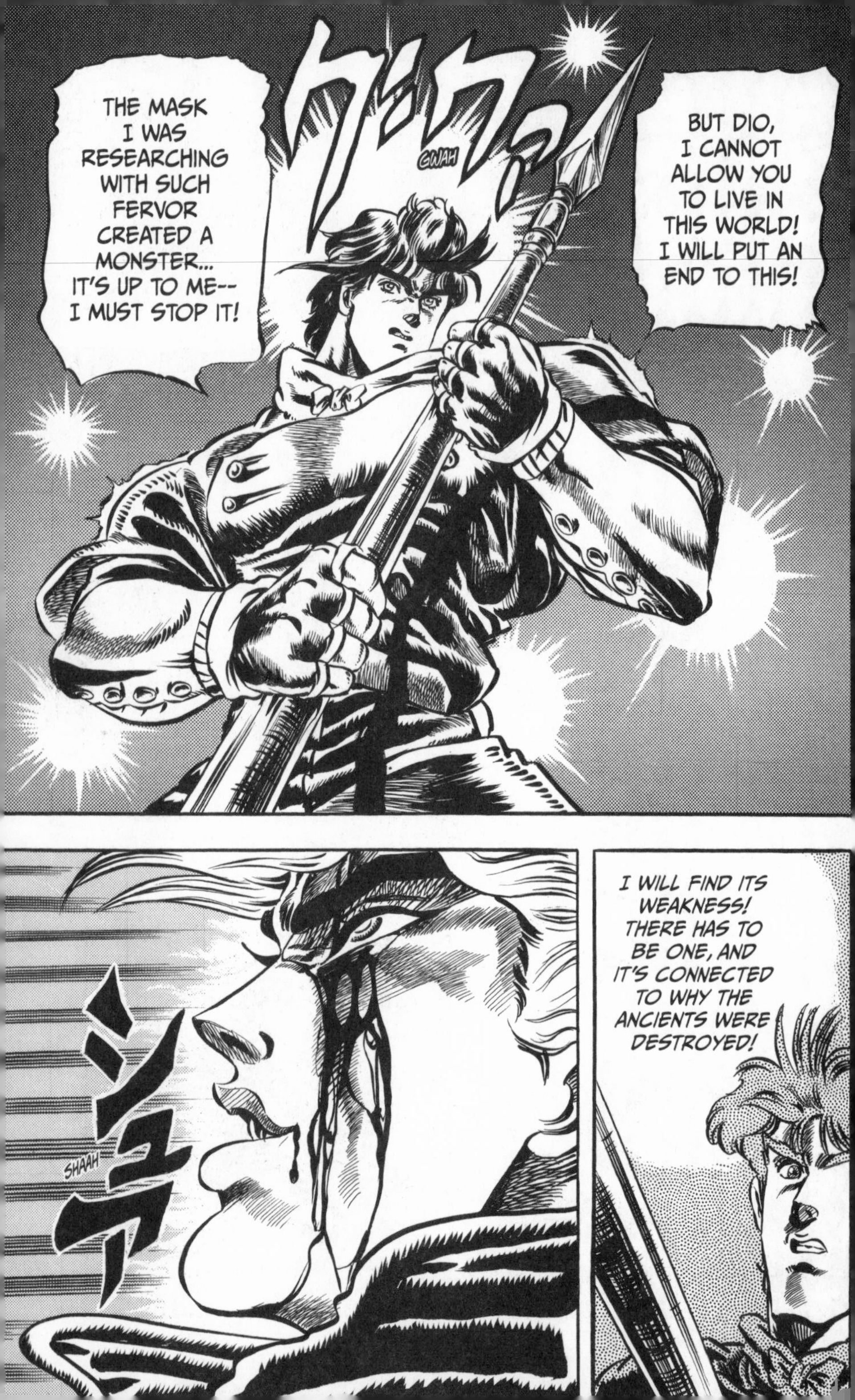
THE MASK I WAS RESEARCHING WITH SUCH FERVOR CREATED A MONSTER... IT'S UP TO ME-- I MUST STOP IT!
GWAH
BUT DIO, I CANNOT ALLOW YOU TO LIVE IN THIS WORLD! I WILL PUT AN END TO THIS!
SHAAH
I WILL FIND ITS WEAKNESS! THERE HAS TO BE ONE, AND IT'S CONNECTED TO WHY THE ANCIENTS WERE DESTROYED!

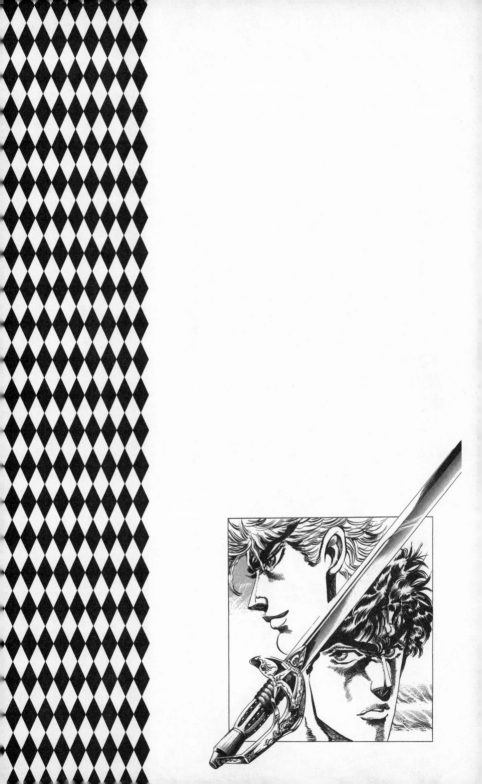

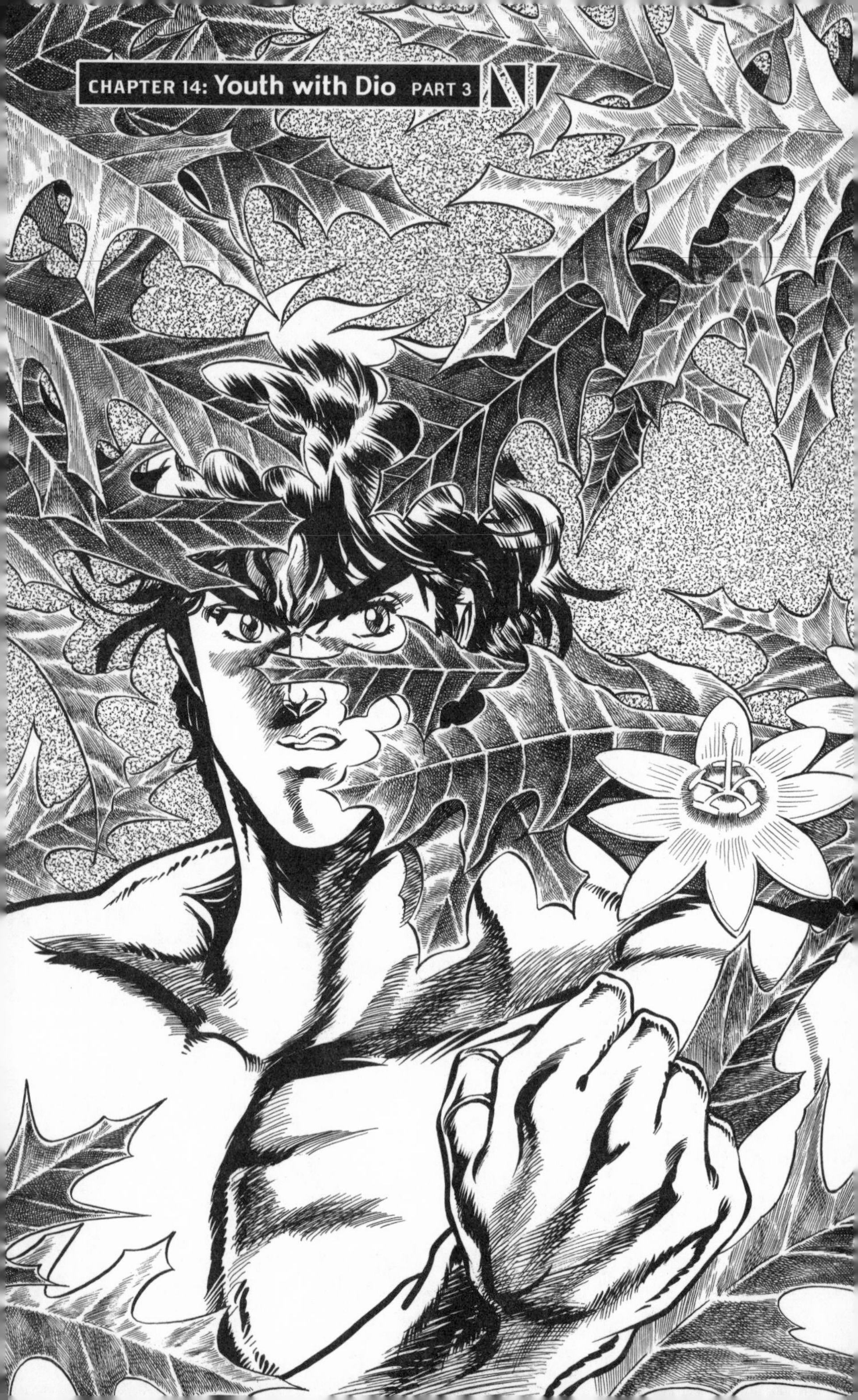
CHAPTER 14: Youth with Dio PART 3

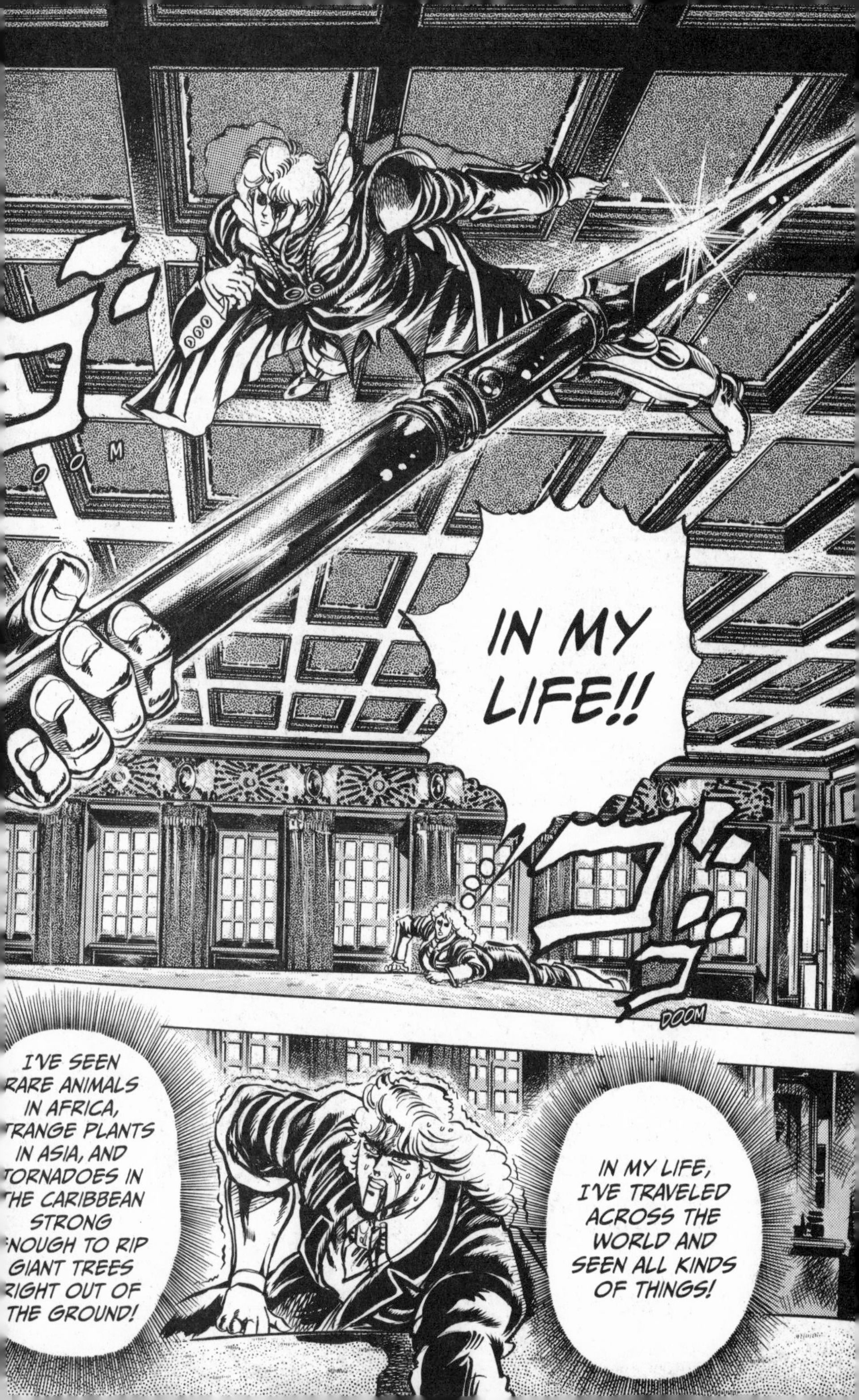
IN MY LIFE!!
M
DOOM
IN MY LIFE, I'VE TRAVELED ACROSS THE WORLD AND SEEN ALL KINDS OF THINGS!
I'VE SEEN RARE ANIMALS IN AFRICA, TRANGE PLANTS IN ASIA, AND TORNADOES IN THE CARIBBEAN STRONG NOUGH TO RIP GIANT TREES RIGHT OUT OF THE GROUND!

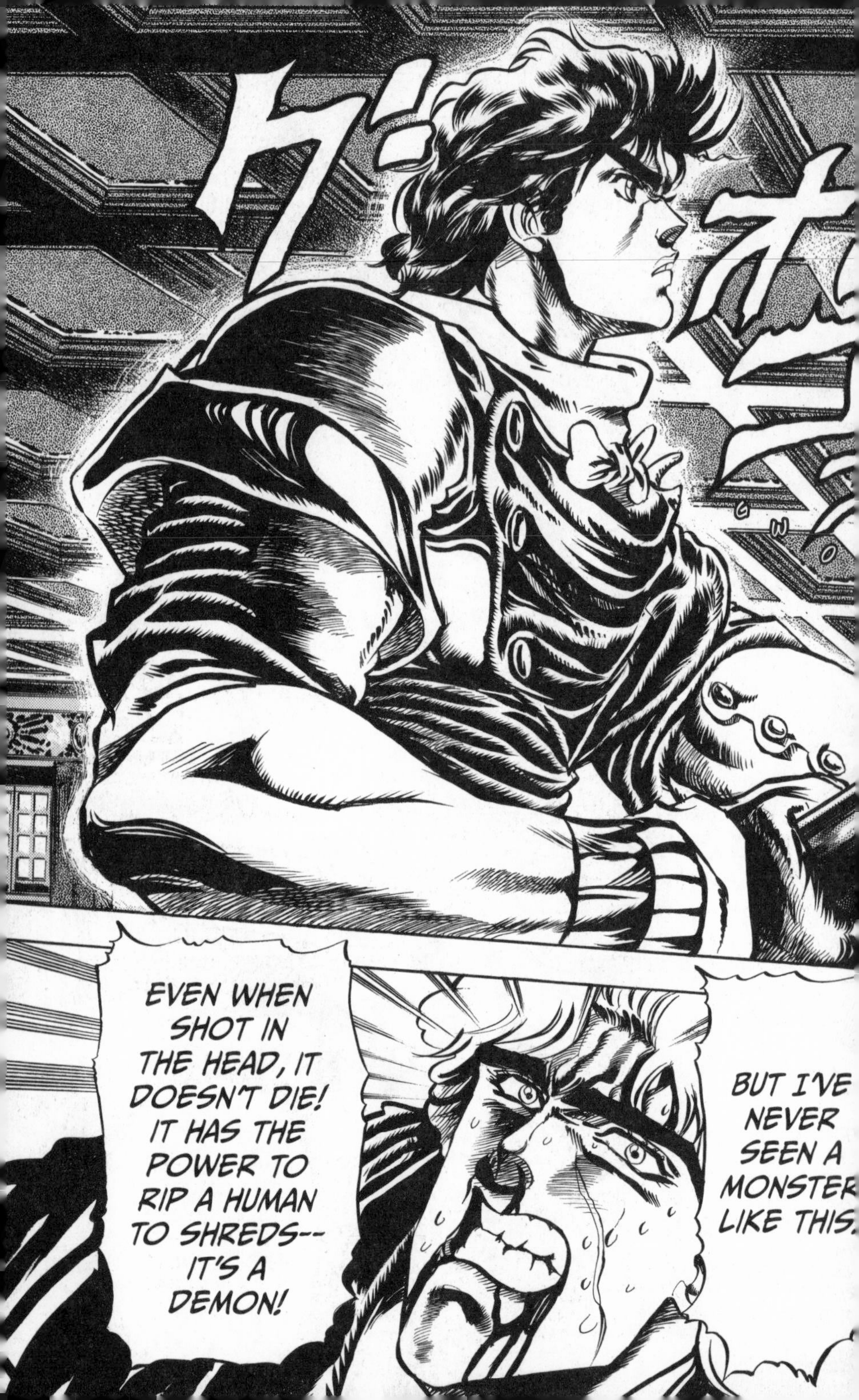
EVEN WHEN SHOT IN THE HEAD, IT DOESN'T DIE! IT HAS THE POWER TO RIP A HUMAN TO SHREDS-- IT'S A DEMON!
BUT I'VE NEVER SEEN A MONSTER LIKE THIS.

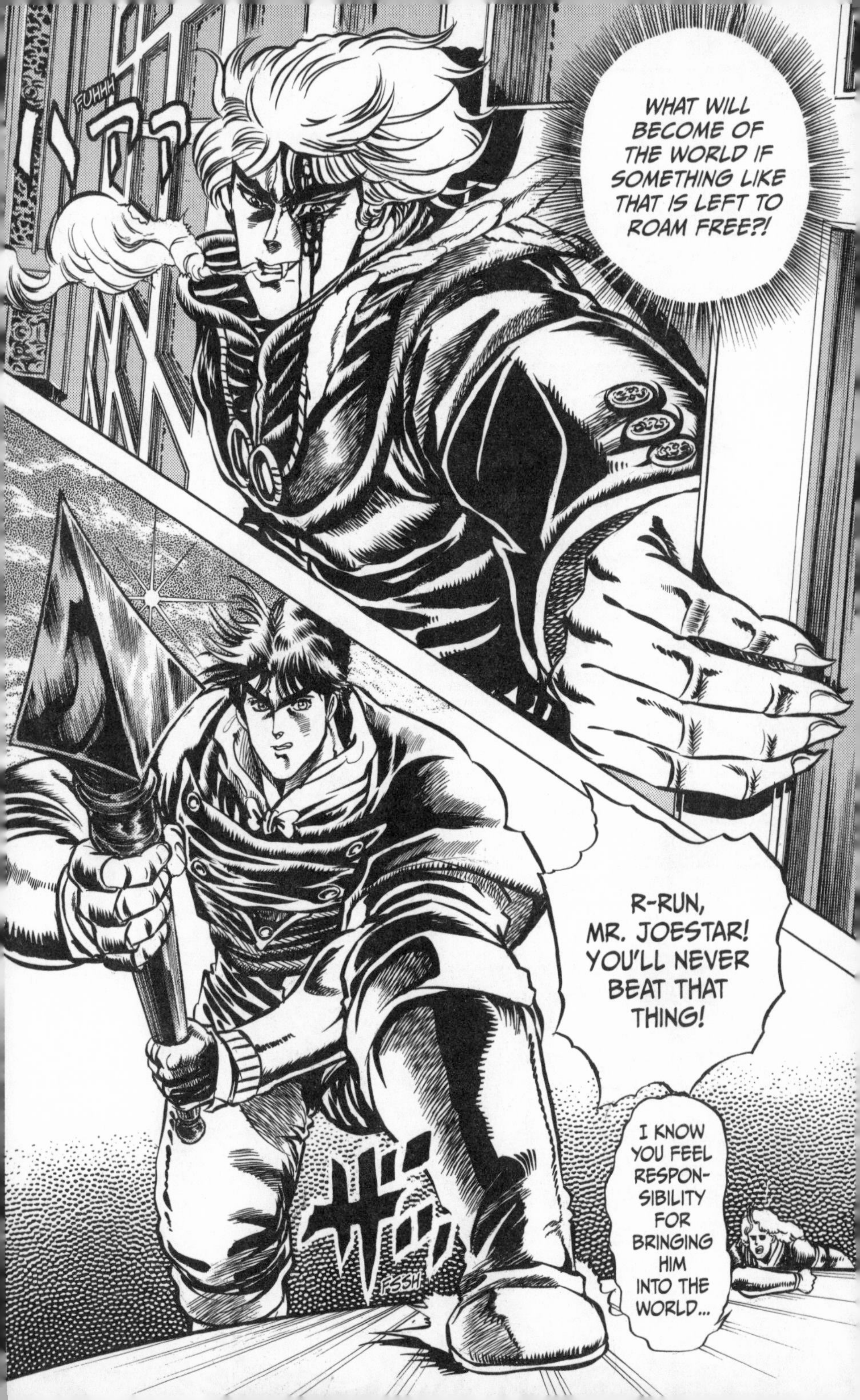
WHAT WILL BECOME OF THE WORLD IF SOMETHING LIKE THAT IS LEFT TO ROAM FREE?!
FUHHH
R-RUN, MR. JOESTAR! YOU'LL NEVER BEAT THAT THING!
I KNOW YOU FEEL RESPON-SIBILITY FOR BRINGING HIM INTO THE WORLD...
TSSH

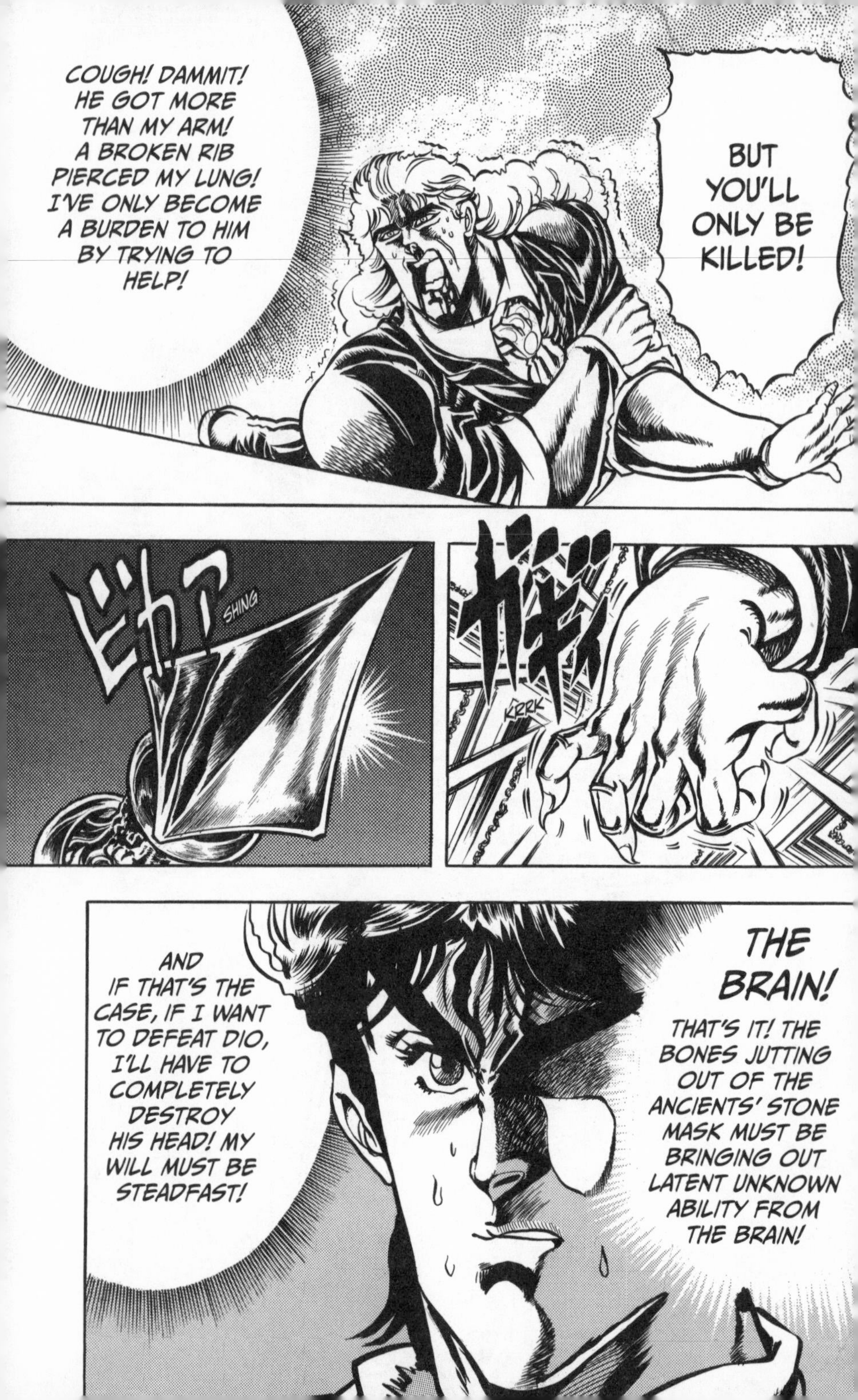
BUT YOU'LL ONLY BE KILLED!
COUGH! DAMMIT! HE GOT MORE THAN MY ARM! A BROKEN RIB PIERCED MY LUNG! I'VE ONLY BECOME A BURDEN TO HIM BY TRYING TO HELP!
KRRK
SHING
THE BRAIN!
THAT'S IT! THE BONES JUTTING OUT OF THE ANCIENTS' STONE MASK MUST BE BRINGING OUT LATENT UNKNOWN ABILITY FROM THE BRAIN!
AND IF THAT'S THE CASE, IF I WANT TO DEFEAT DIO, I'LL HAVE TO COMPLETELY DESTROY HIS HEAD! MY WILL MUST BE STEADFAST!

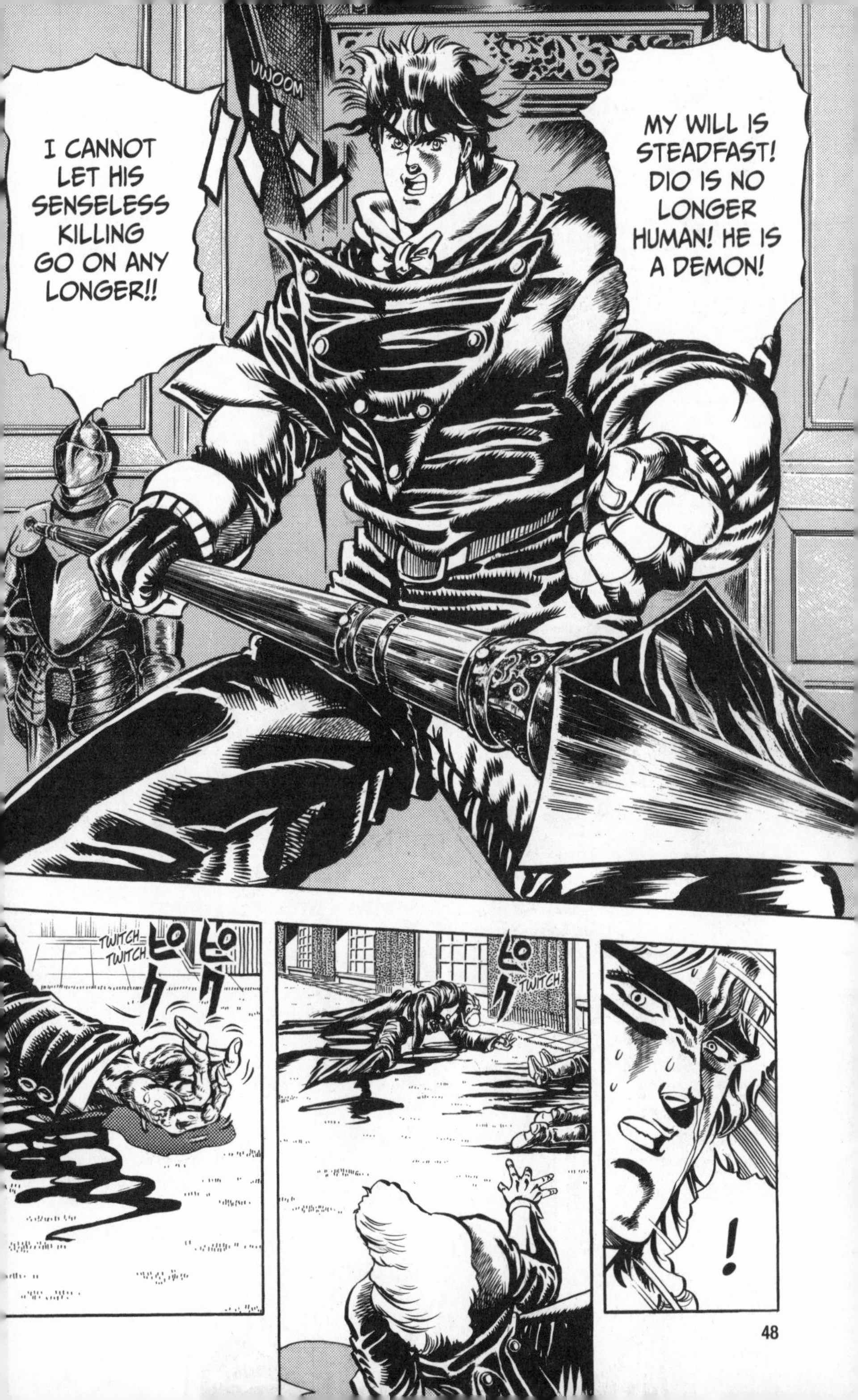

MY WILL IS STEADFAST! DIO IS NO LONGER HUMAN! HE IS A DEMON!
VWOOM
I CANNOT LET HIS SENSELESS KILLING GO ON ANY LONGER!!
!
TWITCH
TWITCH-TWITCH

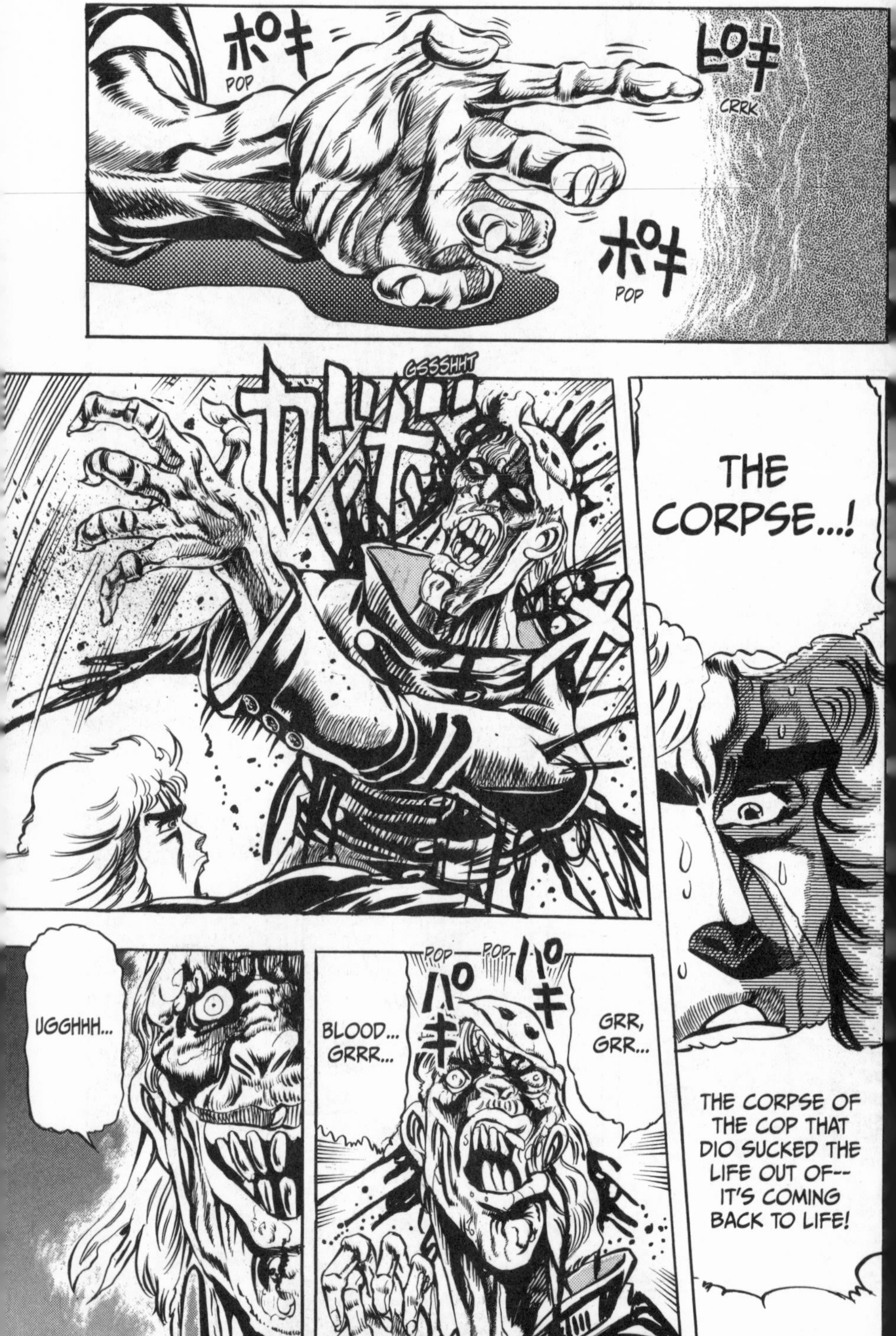
ピキ
CRRK
ポキ
POP
ポキ
POP
THE CORPSE...!
THE CORPSE OF THE COP THAT DIO SUCKED THE LIFE OUT OF-- IT'S COMING BACK TO LIFE!
GSSSHHT
POP POP
パキ パキ
GRR, GRR...
BLOOD... GRRR...
UGGHHH...

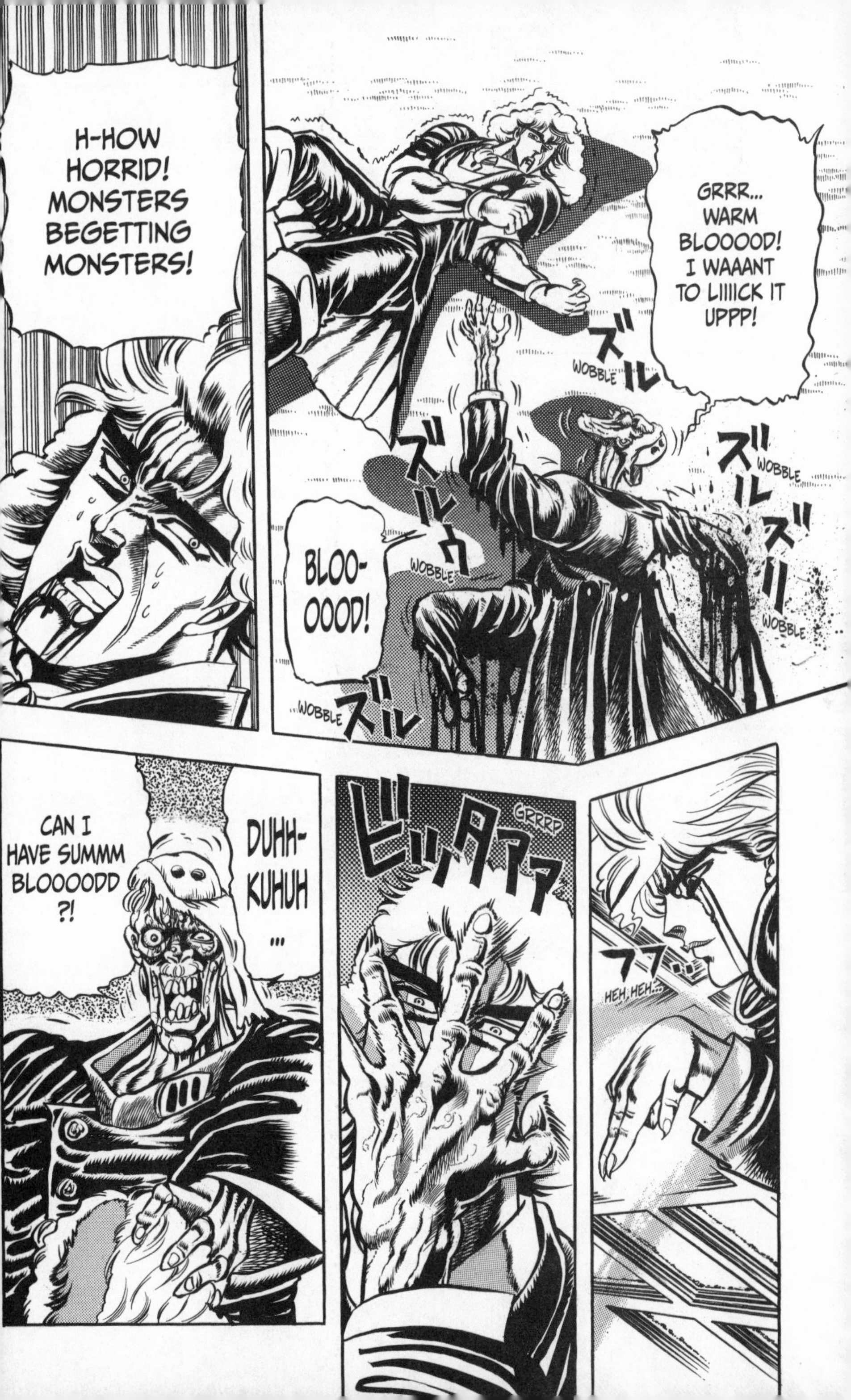

GRRR... WARM BLOOOOD! I WAAANT TO LIIIICK IT UPPP!
ズル
WOBBLE
ズル
WOBBLE
ズリ
WOBBLE
BLOO-OOOD!
WOBBLE
WOBBLE
ズル
H-HOW HORRID! MONSTERS BEGETTING MONSTERS!
HEH, HEH...
GRRRP
DUHH-KUHUH ...
CAN I HAVE SUMMM BLOOOODD ?!

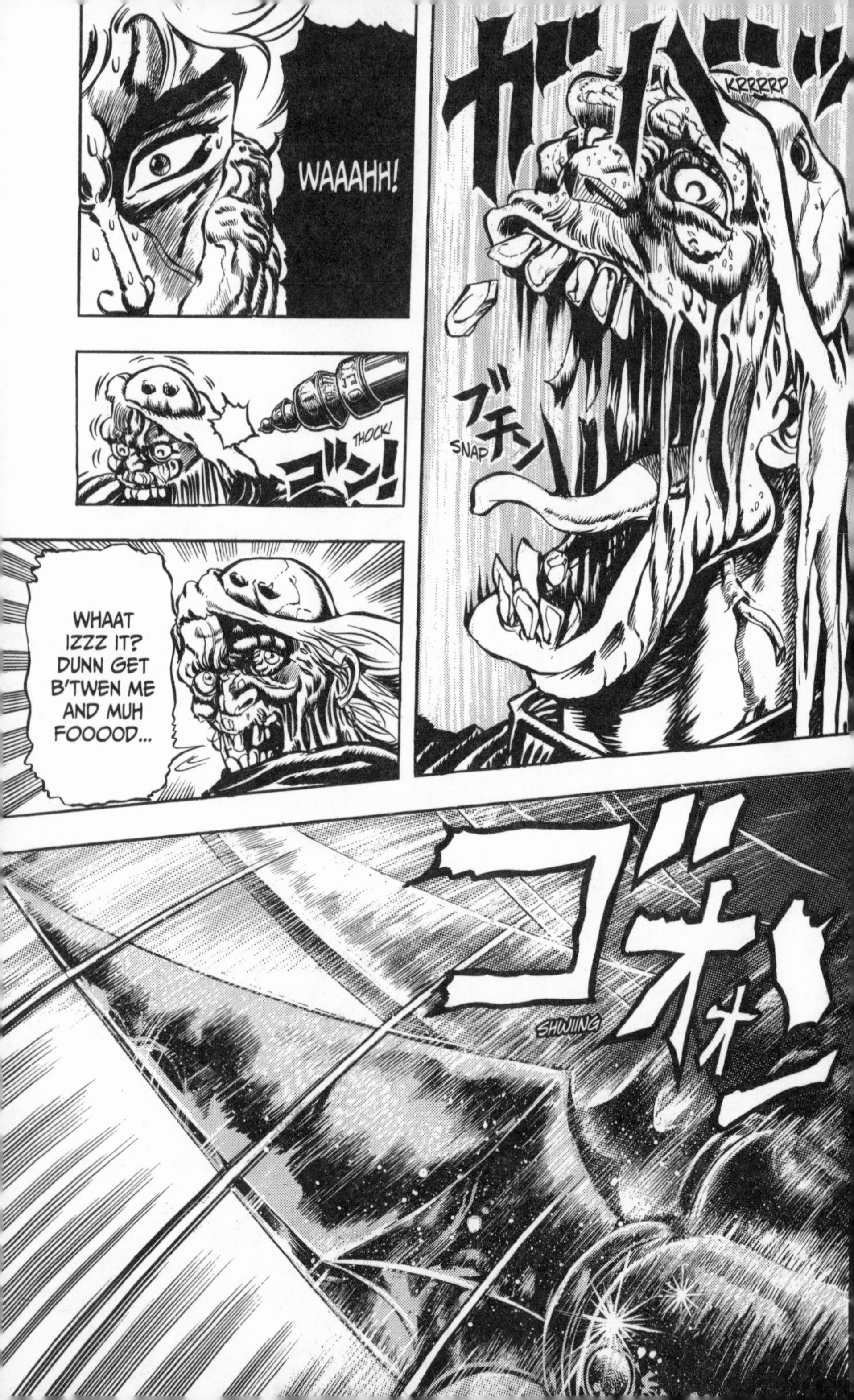
KRRRRP
SNAP
WAAAHH!
THOCK!
WHAAT IZZZ IT? DUNN GET B'TWEN ME AND MUH FOOOOD...
SHWIING

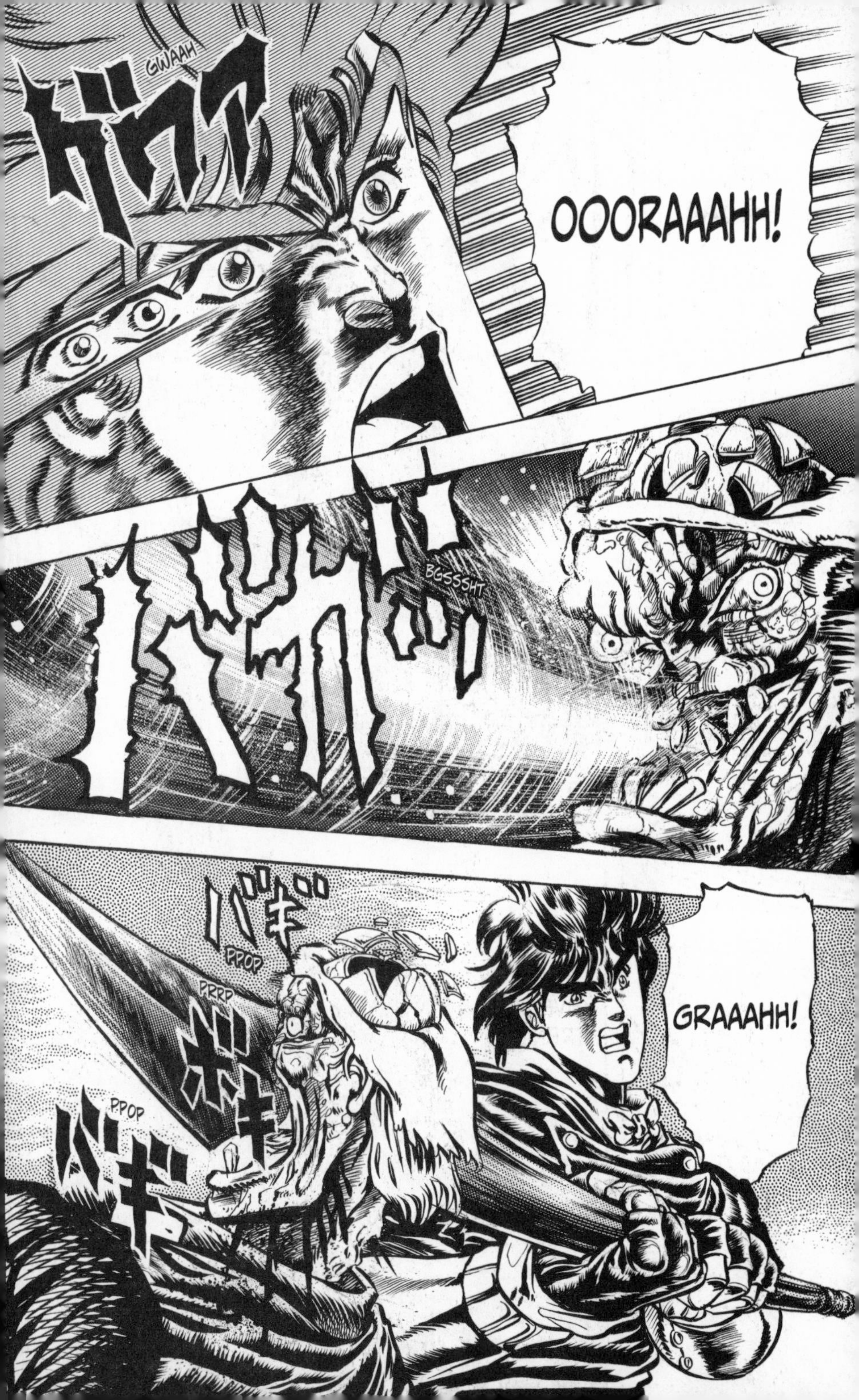
OOORAAAHH!
GWAAH
BGSSSHT
GRAAAHH!
PPOP
PRRP
PPOP

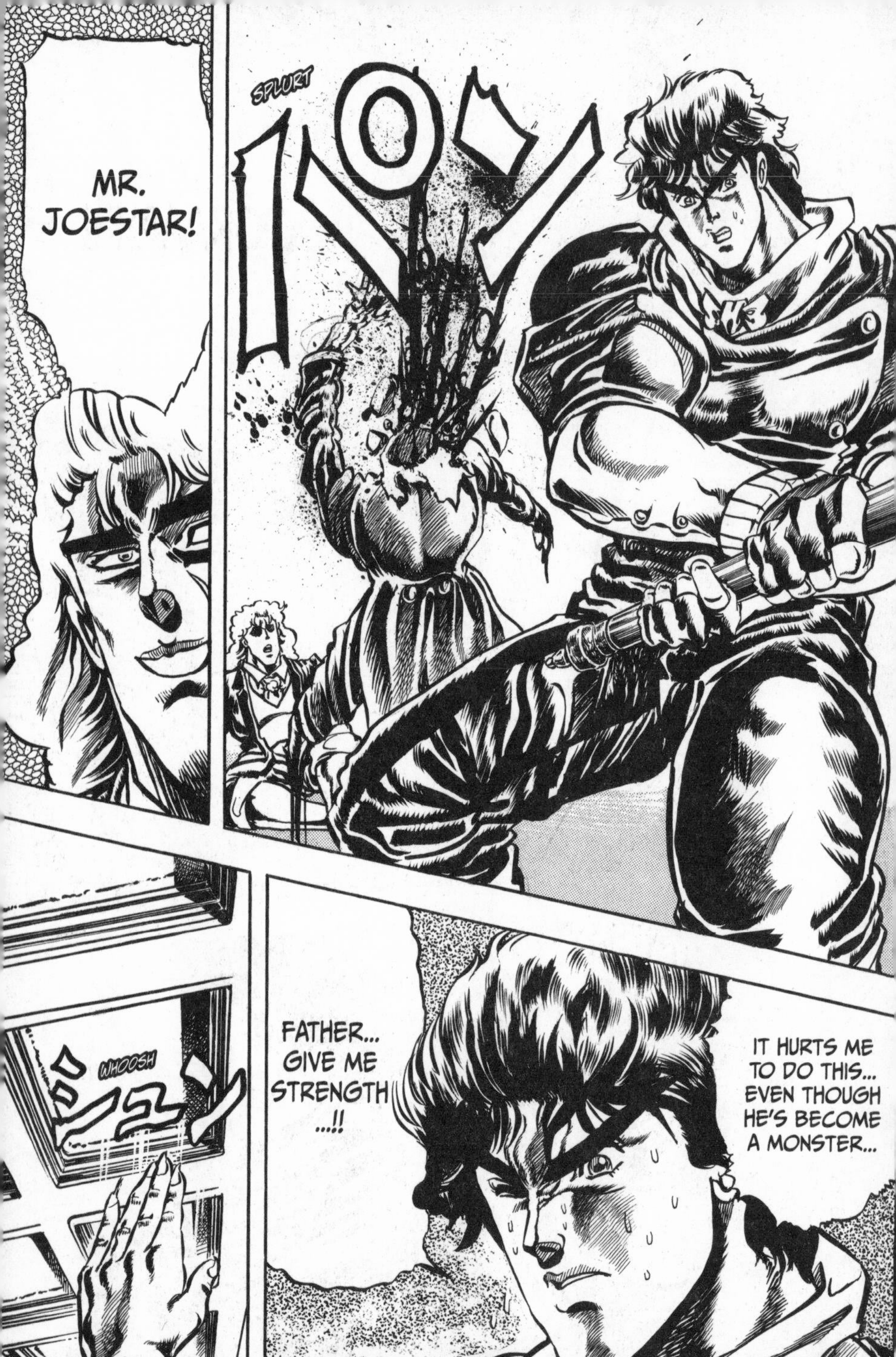
SPLURT
MR. JOESTAR!
IT HURTS ME TO DO THIS... EVEN THOUGH HE'S BECOME A MONSTER...
FATHER... GIVE ME STRENGTH ...!!
WHOOSH

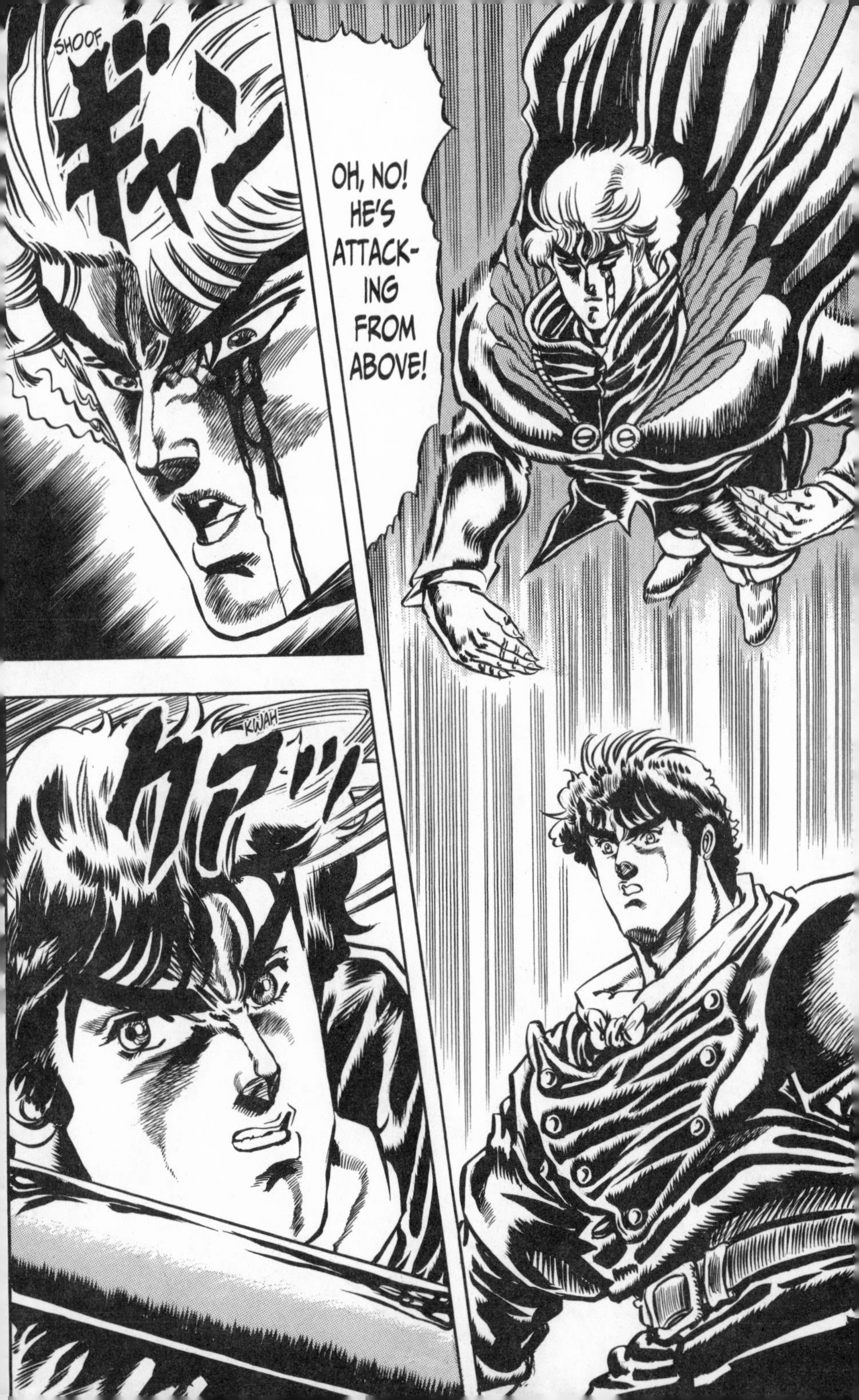
OH, NO! HE'S ATTACK-ING FROM ABOVE!
SHOOF
KWAH

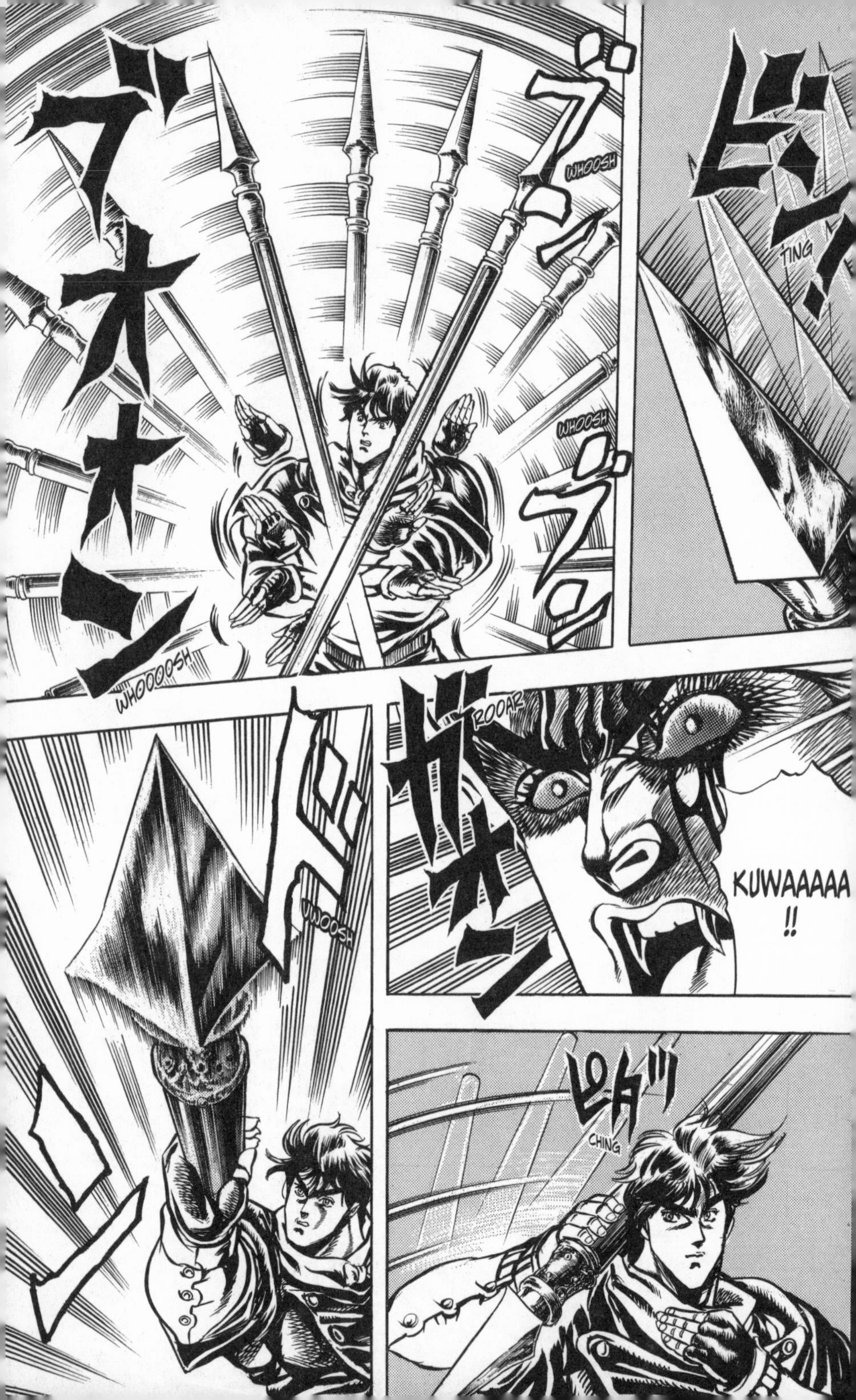
TING
WHOOSH
WHOOSH
WHOOOOSH
ROOAR
KUWAAAAA !!
CHING
VWOOSH

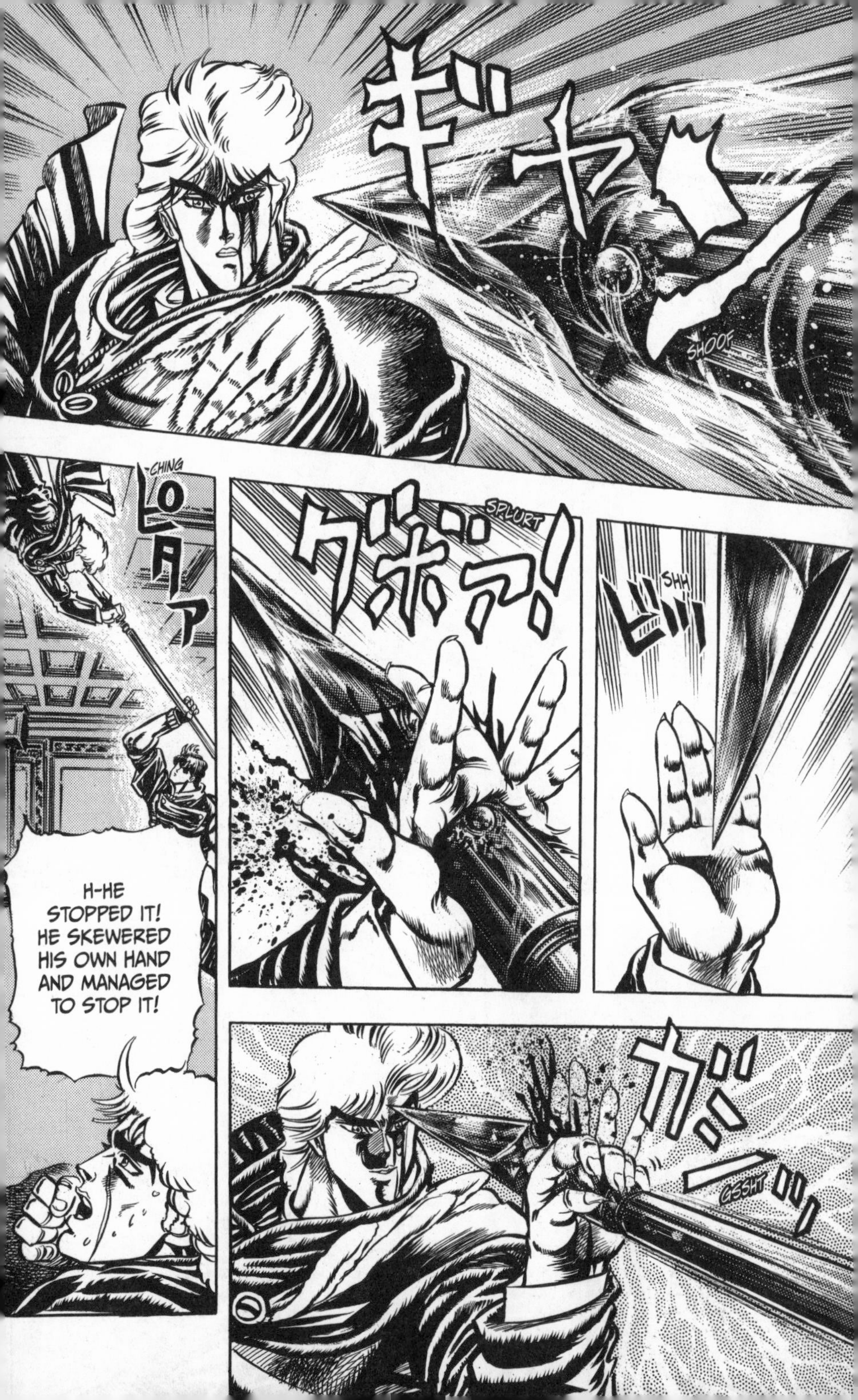
SHOOF
SHH
SPLURT
GSSHT
CHING
H-HE STOPPED IT! HE SKEWERED HIS OWN HAND AND MANAGED TO STOP IT!

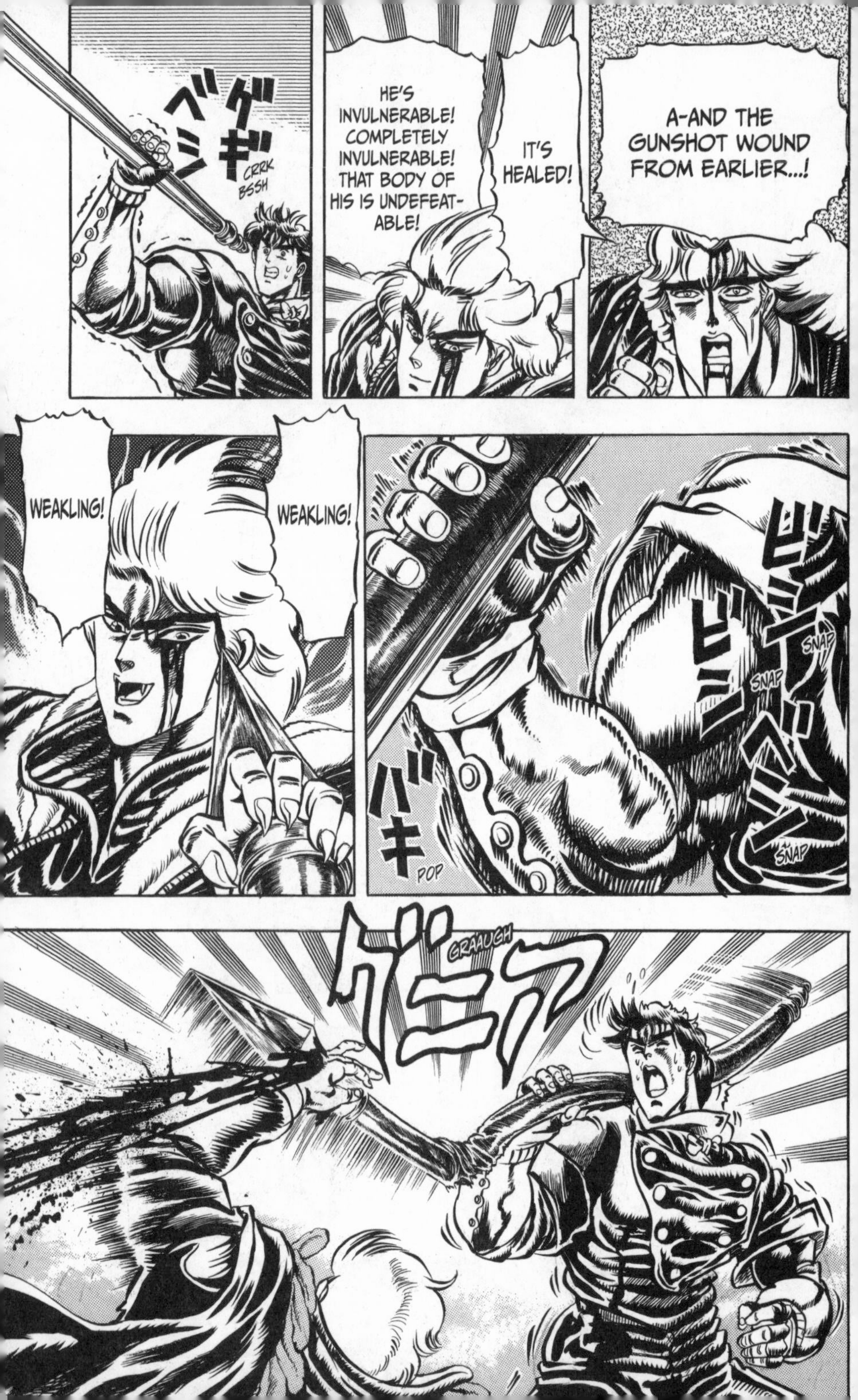
A-AND THE GUNSHOT WOUND FROM EARLIER...!
IT'S HEALED!
HE'S INVULNERABLE! COMPLETELY INVULNERABLE! THAT BODY OF HIS IS UNDEFEAT-ABLE!
CRRK
BSSH
SNAP
SNAP
SNAP
POP
WEAKLING!
WEAKLING!
GRAAUGH

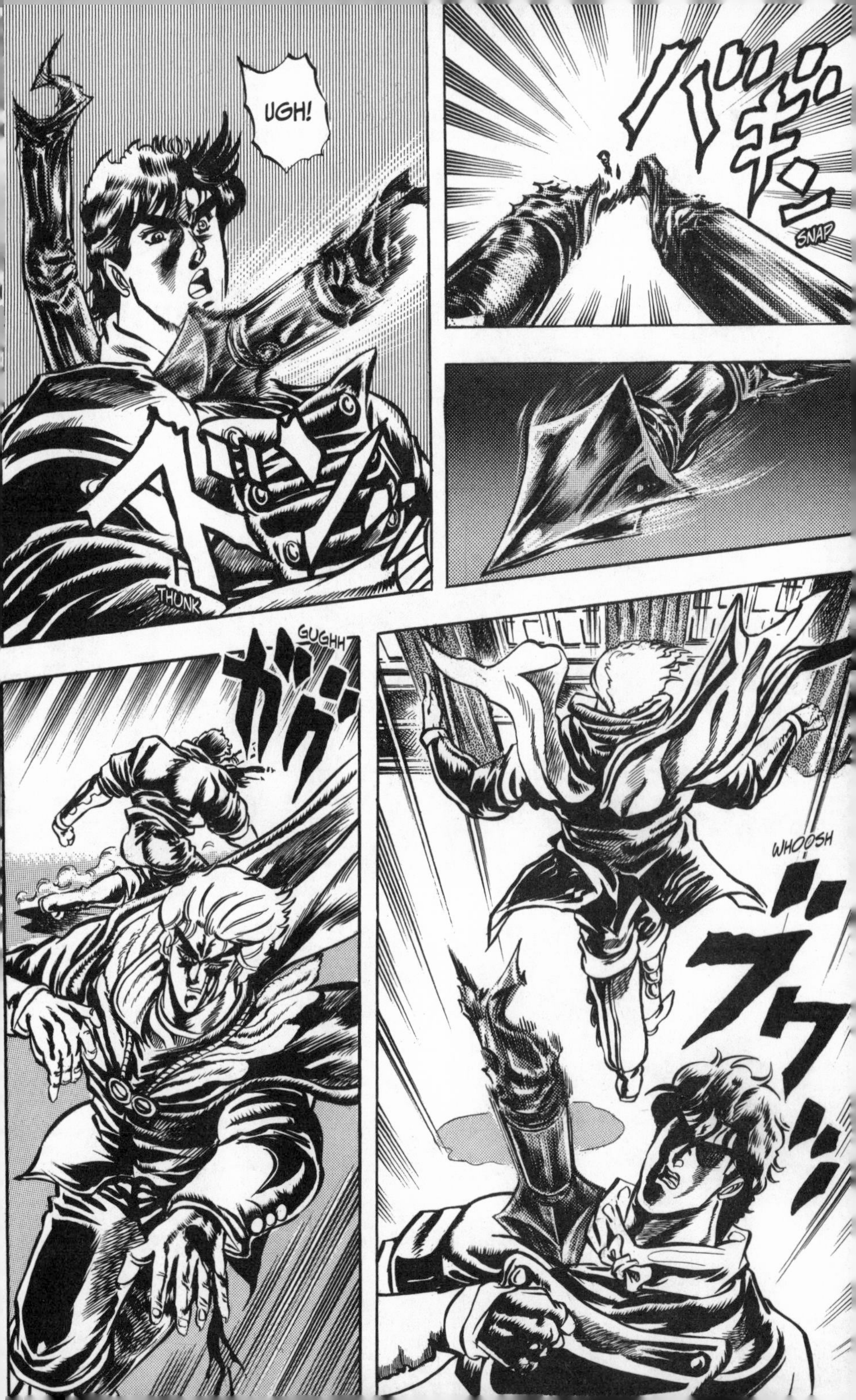
SNAP
UGH!
THUNK
WHOOSH
GUGHH

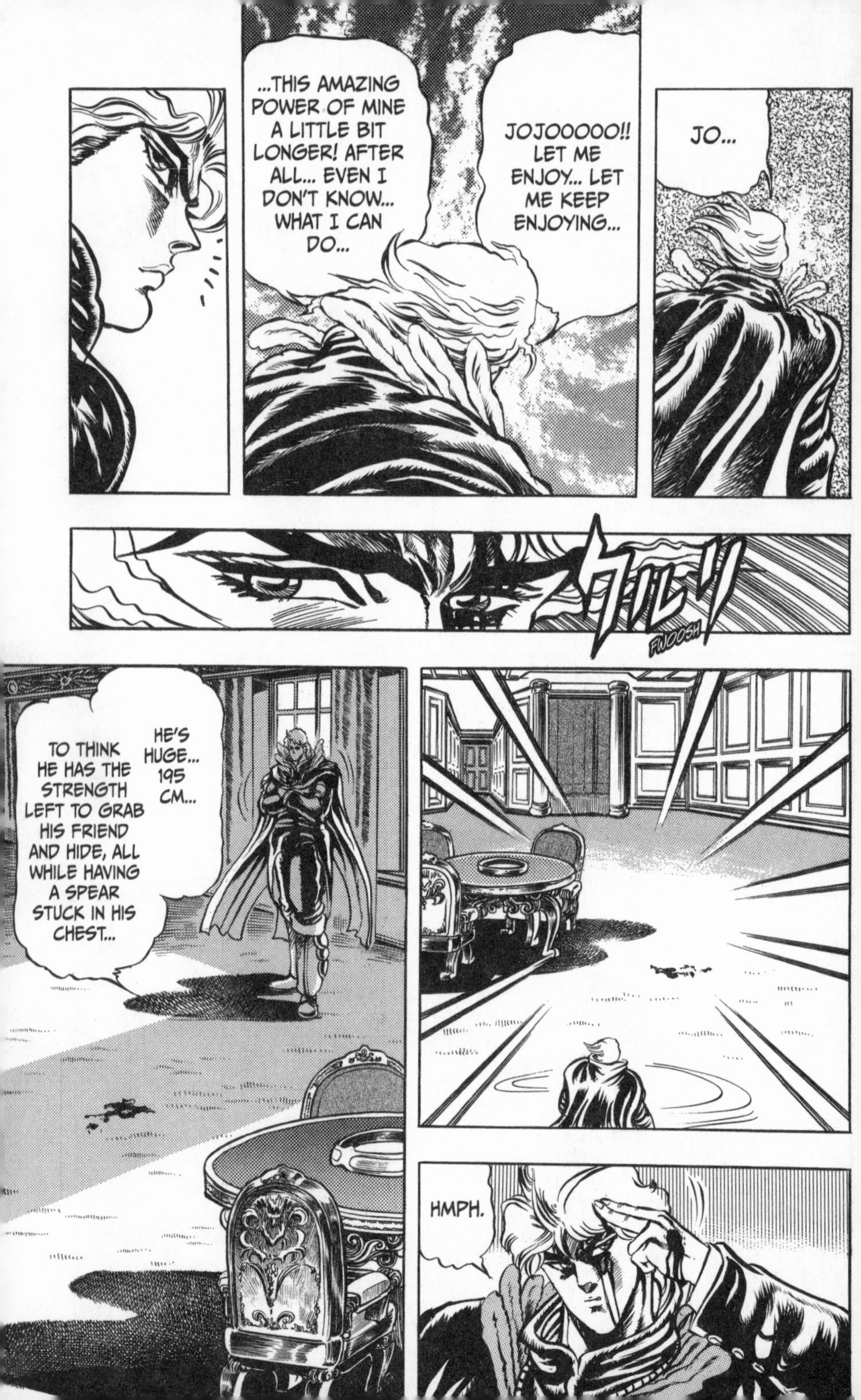
JO...
JOJOOOOO!! LET ME ENJOY... LET ME KEEP ENJOYING...
...THIS AMAZING POWER OF MINE A LITTLE BIT LONGER! AFTER ALL... EVEN I DON'T KNOW... WHAT I CAN DO...
クルリ
FWOOSH
HMPH.
HE'S HUGE... 195 CM...
TO THINK HE HAS THE STRENGTH LEFT TO GRAB HIS FRIEND AND HIDE, ALL WHILE HAVING A SPEAR STUCK IN HIS CHEST...

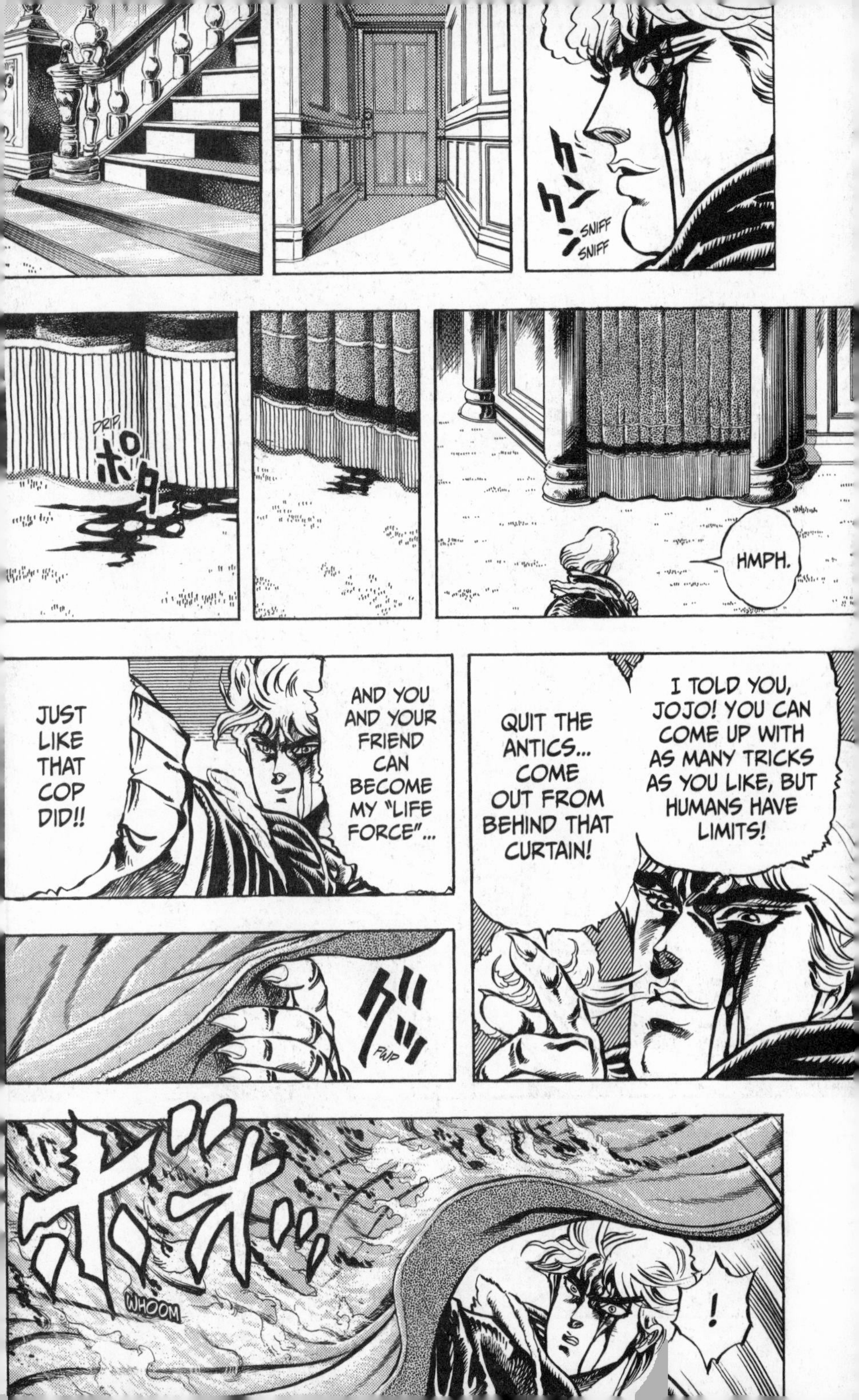
SNIFF
SNIFF
HMPH.
DRIP
I TOLD YOU, JOJO! YOU CAN COME UP WITH AS MANY TRICKS AS YOU LIKE, BUT HUMANS HAVE LIMITS!
QUIT THE ANTICS... COME OUT FROM BEHIND THAT CURTAIN!
AND YOU AND YOUR FRIEND CAN BECOME MY "LIFE FORCE"...
JUST LIKE THAT COP DID!!
FWP
!
WHOOM

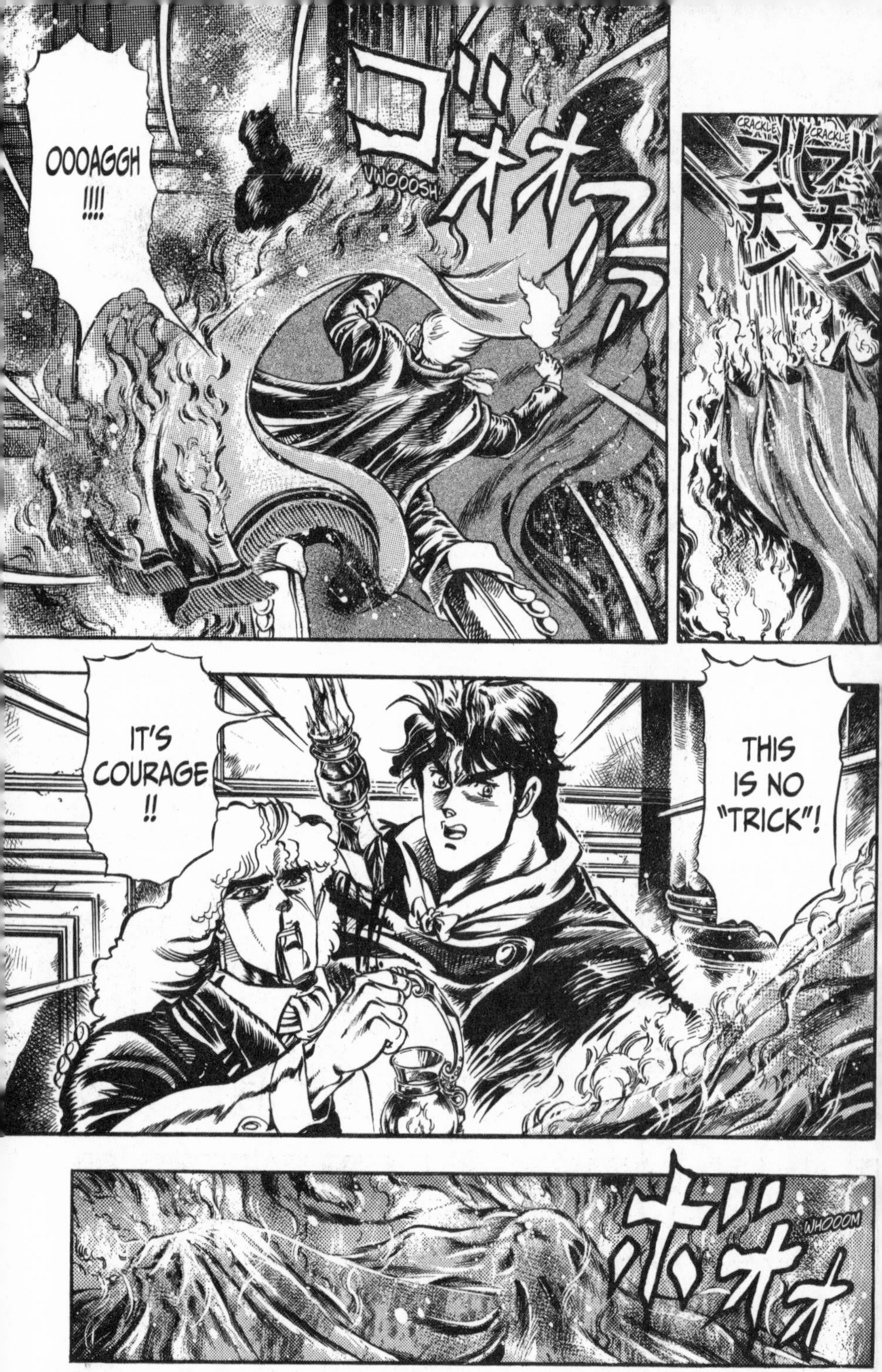
CRACKLE CRACKLE
VWOOOSH
OOOAGGH !!!!
THIS IS NO "TRICK"!
IT'S COURAGE !!
WHOOOM

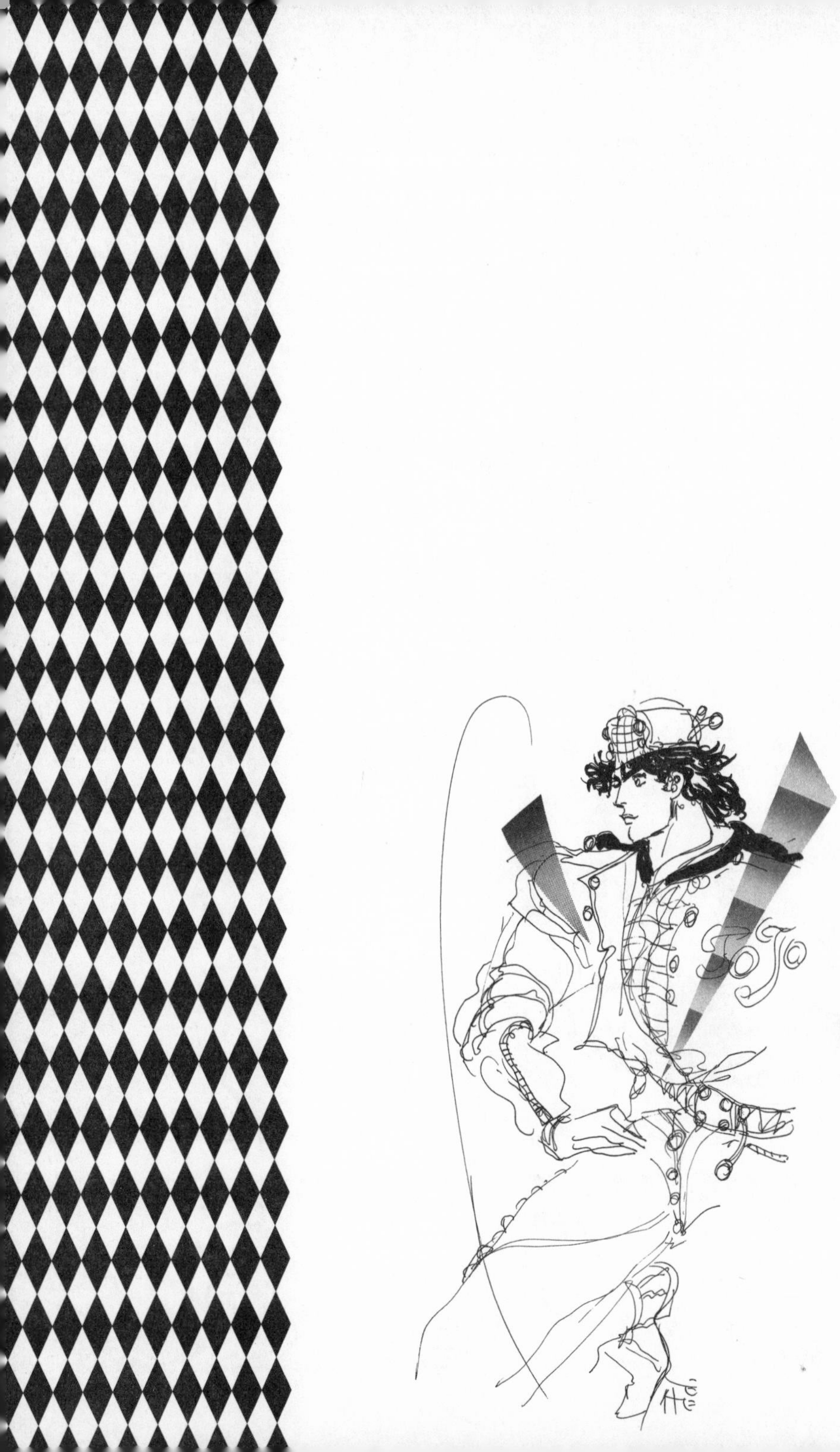
JoJo

CHAPTER 15: Youth with Dio PART 4

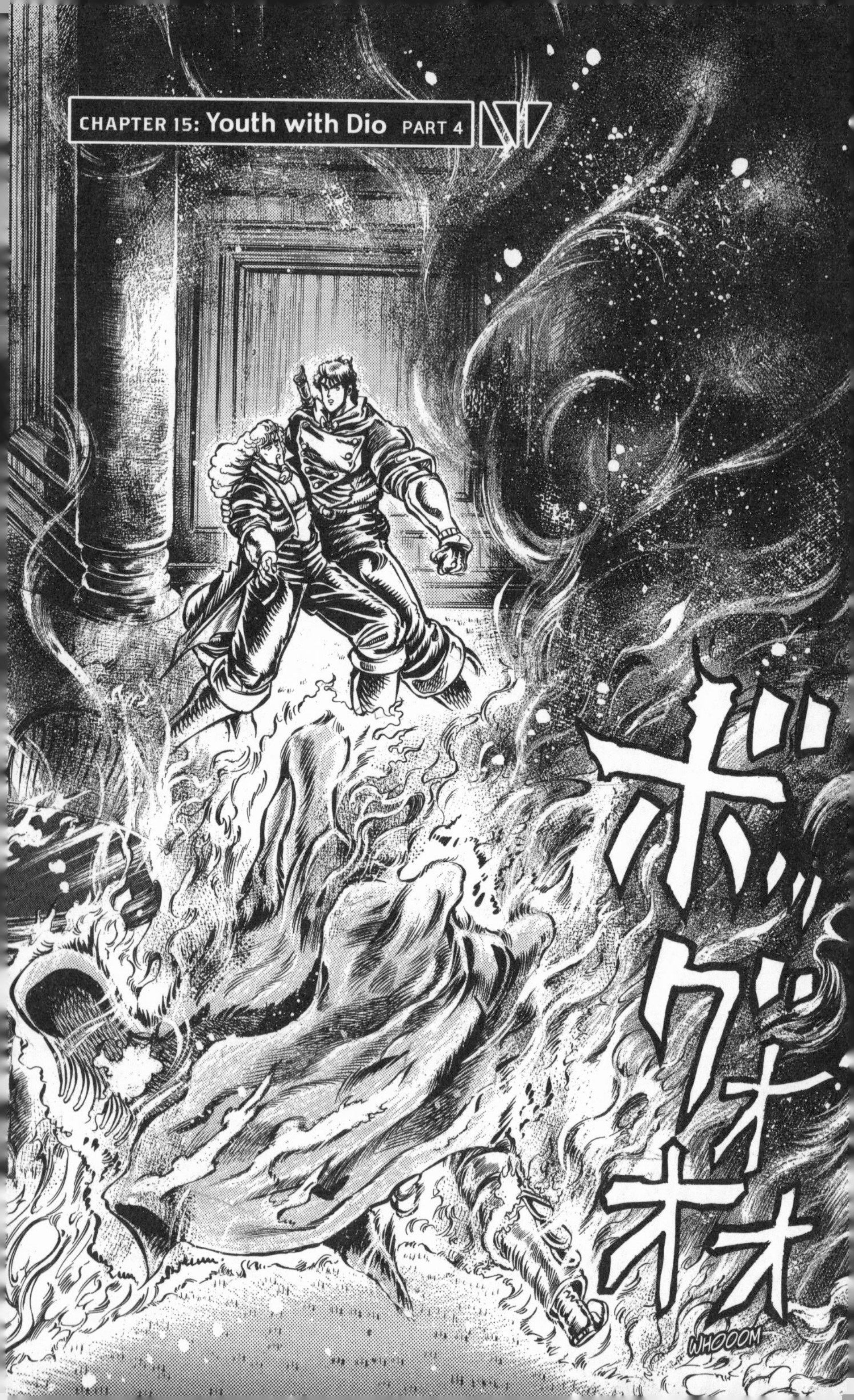
ボッグオオオ
WHOOOM

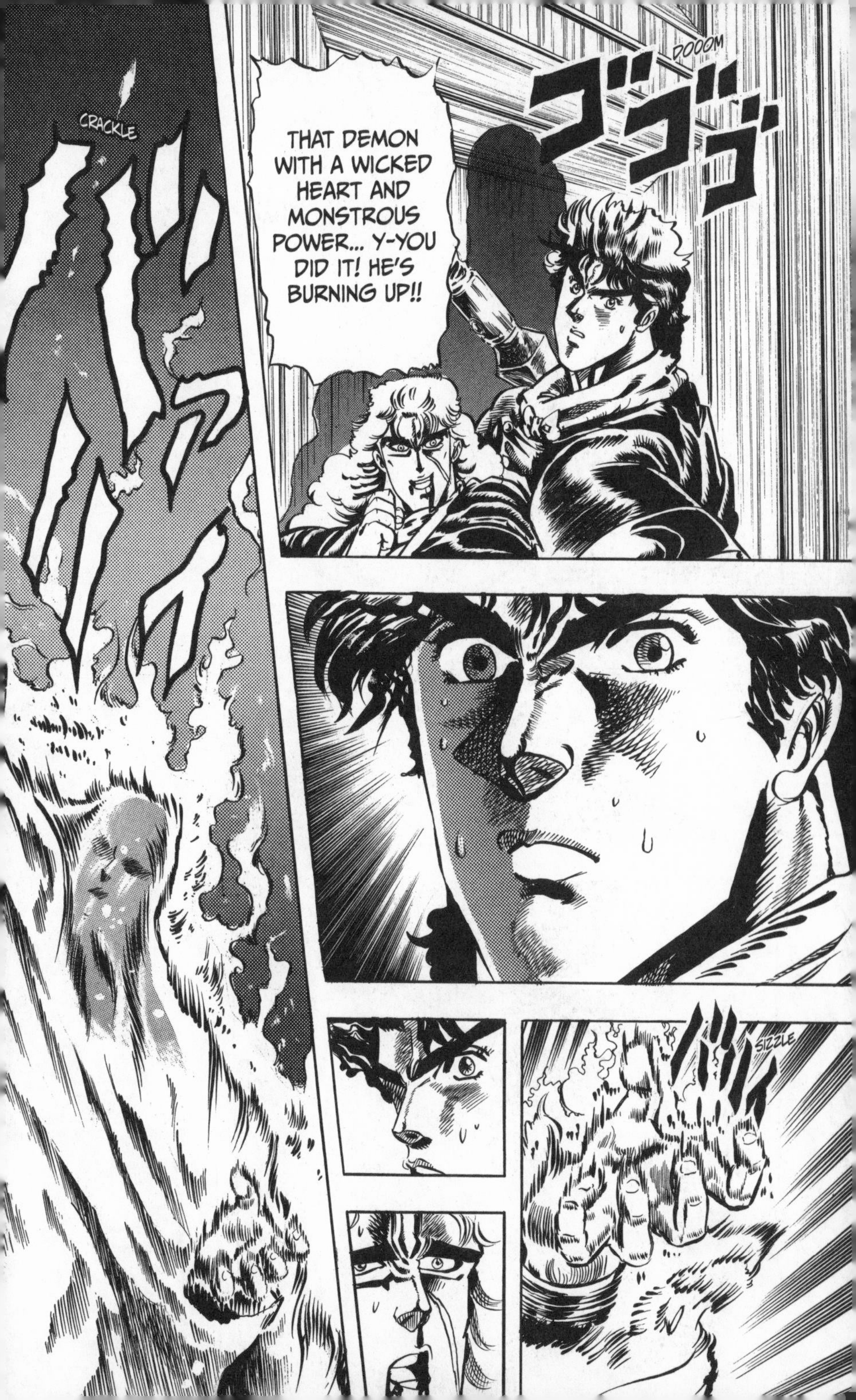
DOOOM
THAT DEMON WITH A WICKED HEART AND MONSTROUS POWER... Y-YOU DID IT! HE'S BURNING UP!!
SIZZLE
CRACKLE

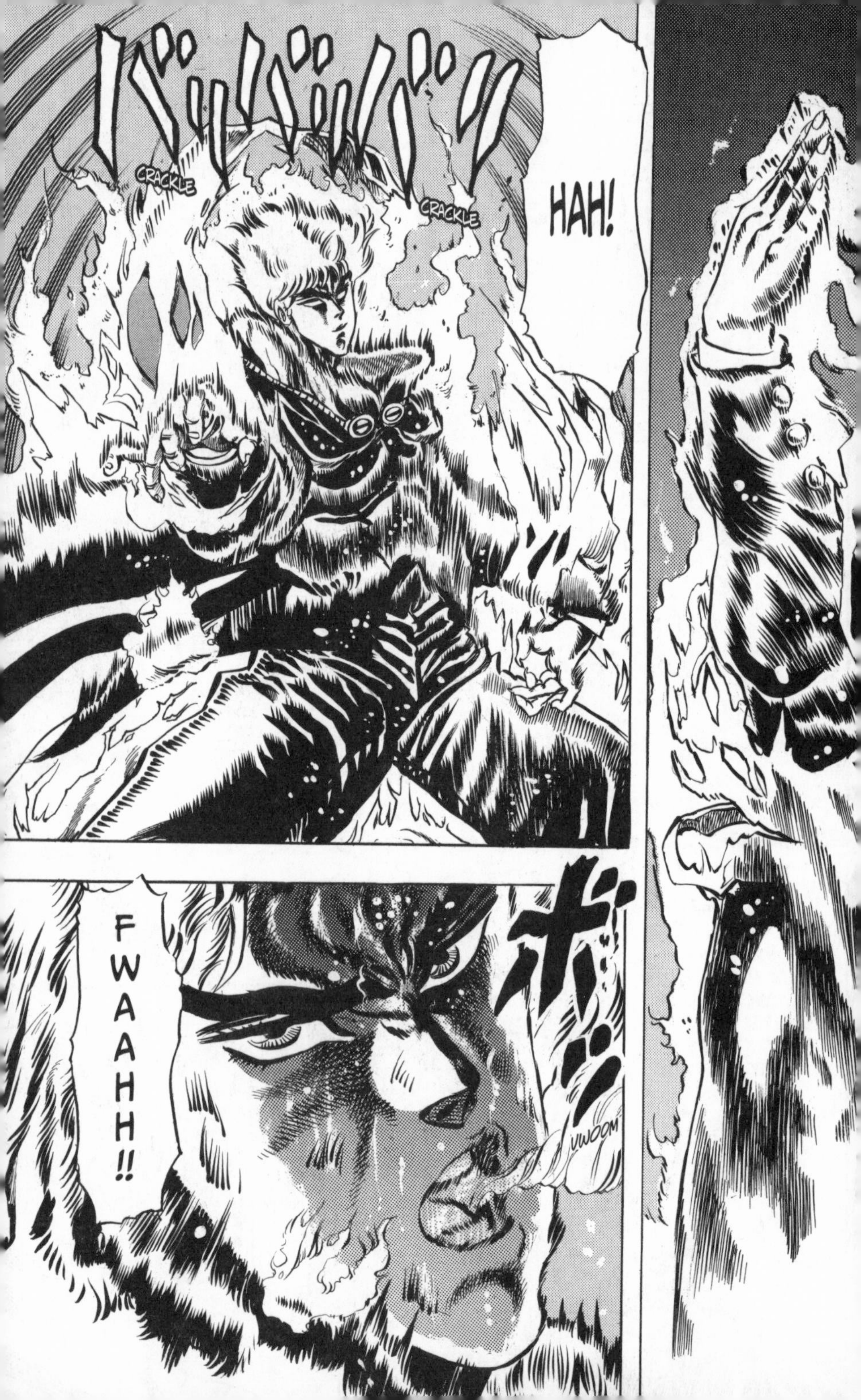
CRACKLE
CRACKLE
HAH!
FWAAAHH!!
VWOOM

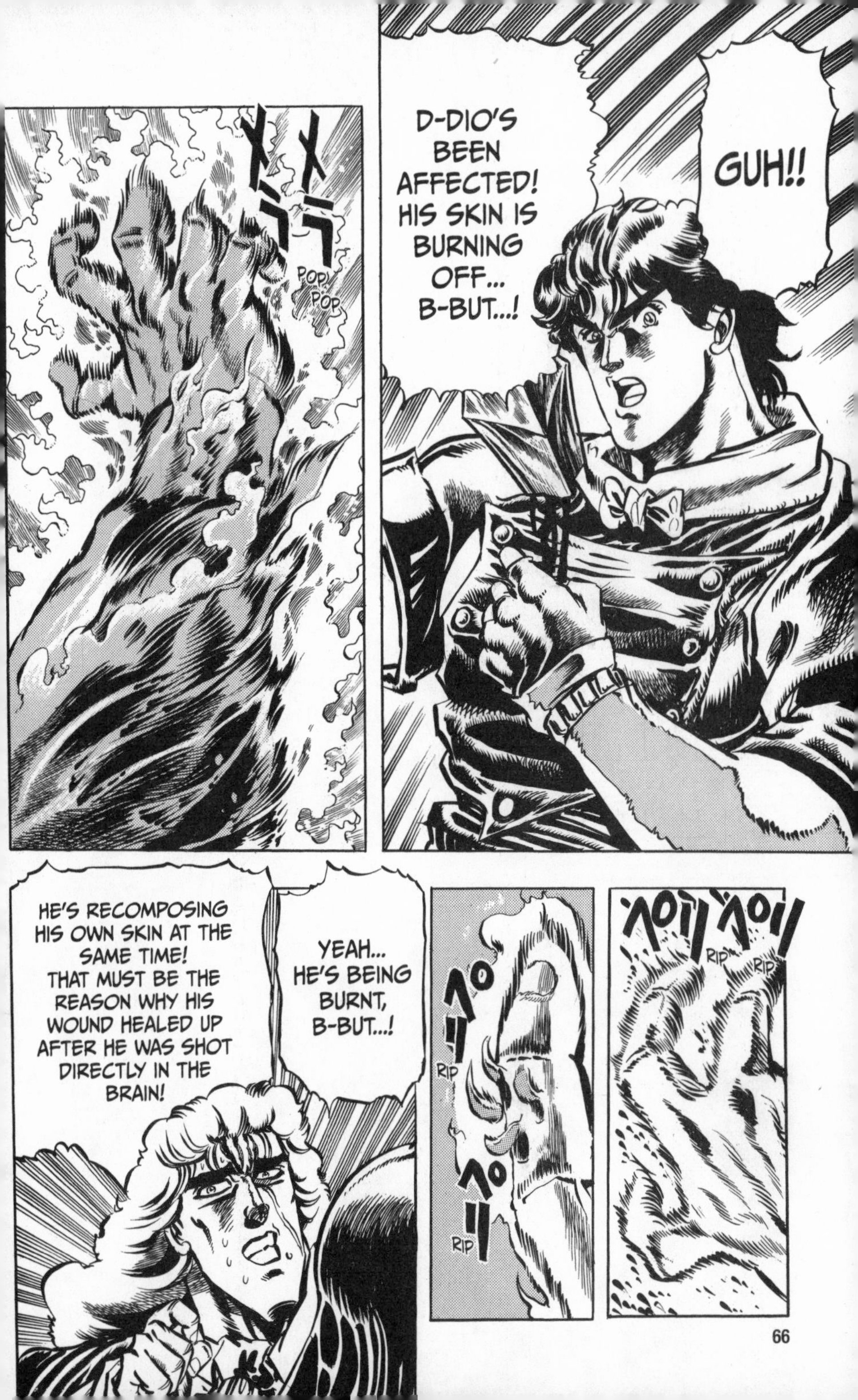
GUH!!
D-DIO'S BEEN AFFECTED! HIS SKIN IS BURNING OFF... B-BUT...!
POP POP
RIP RIP
RIP RIP
YEAH... HE'S BEING BURNT, B-BUT...!
HE'S RECOMPOSING HIS OWN SKIN AT THE SAME TIME! THAT MUST BE THE REASON WHY HIS WOUND HEALED UP AFTER HE WAS SHOT DIRECTLY IN THE BRAIN!

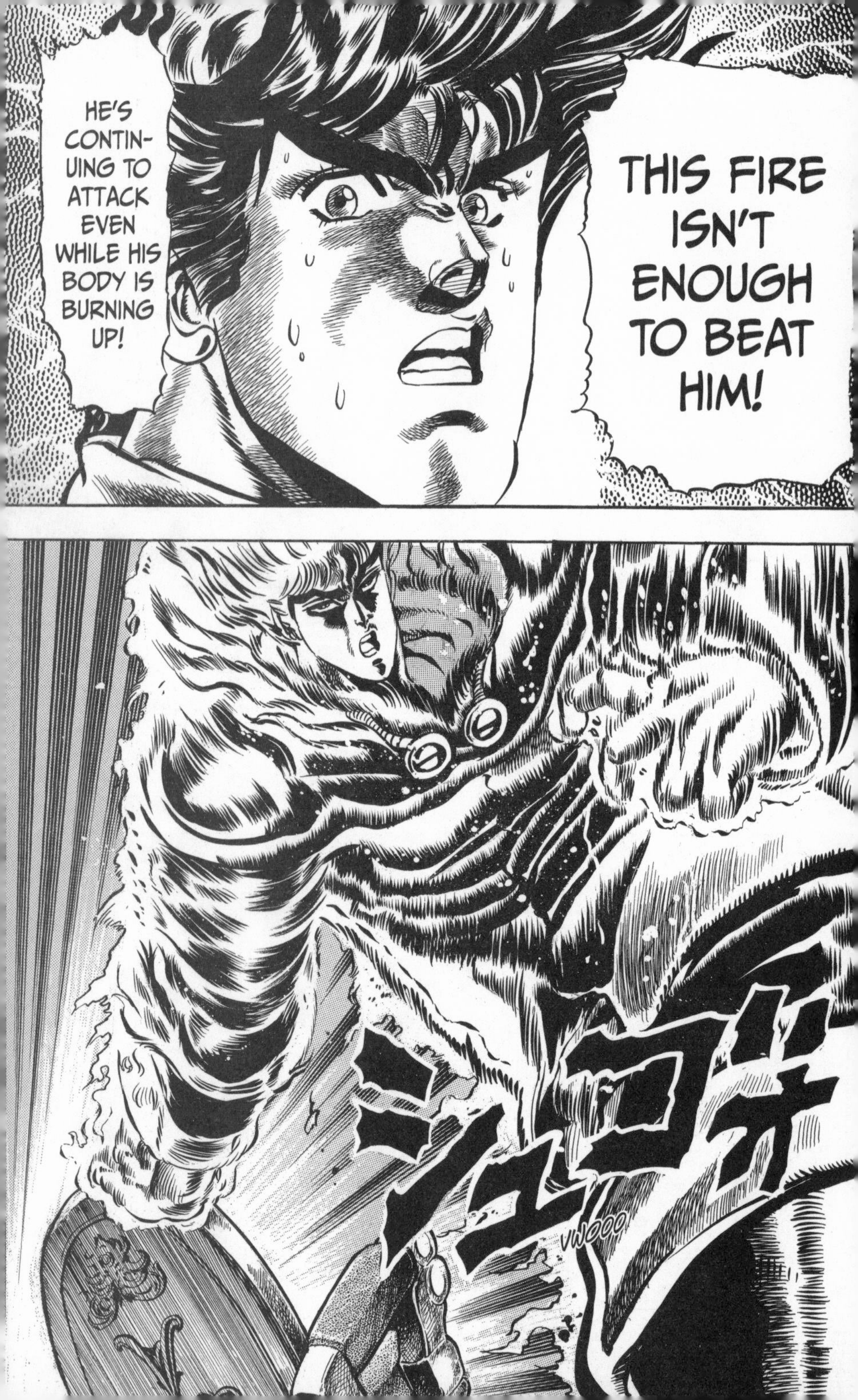
THIS FIRE ISN'T ENOUGH TO BEAT HIM!
HE'S CONTIN-UING TO ATTACK EVEN WHILE HIS BODY IS BURNING UP!
VWOOO

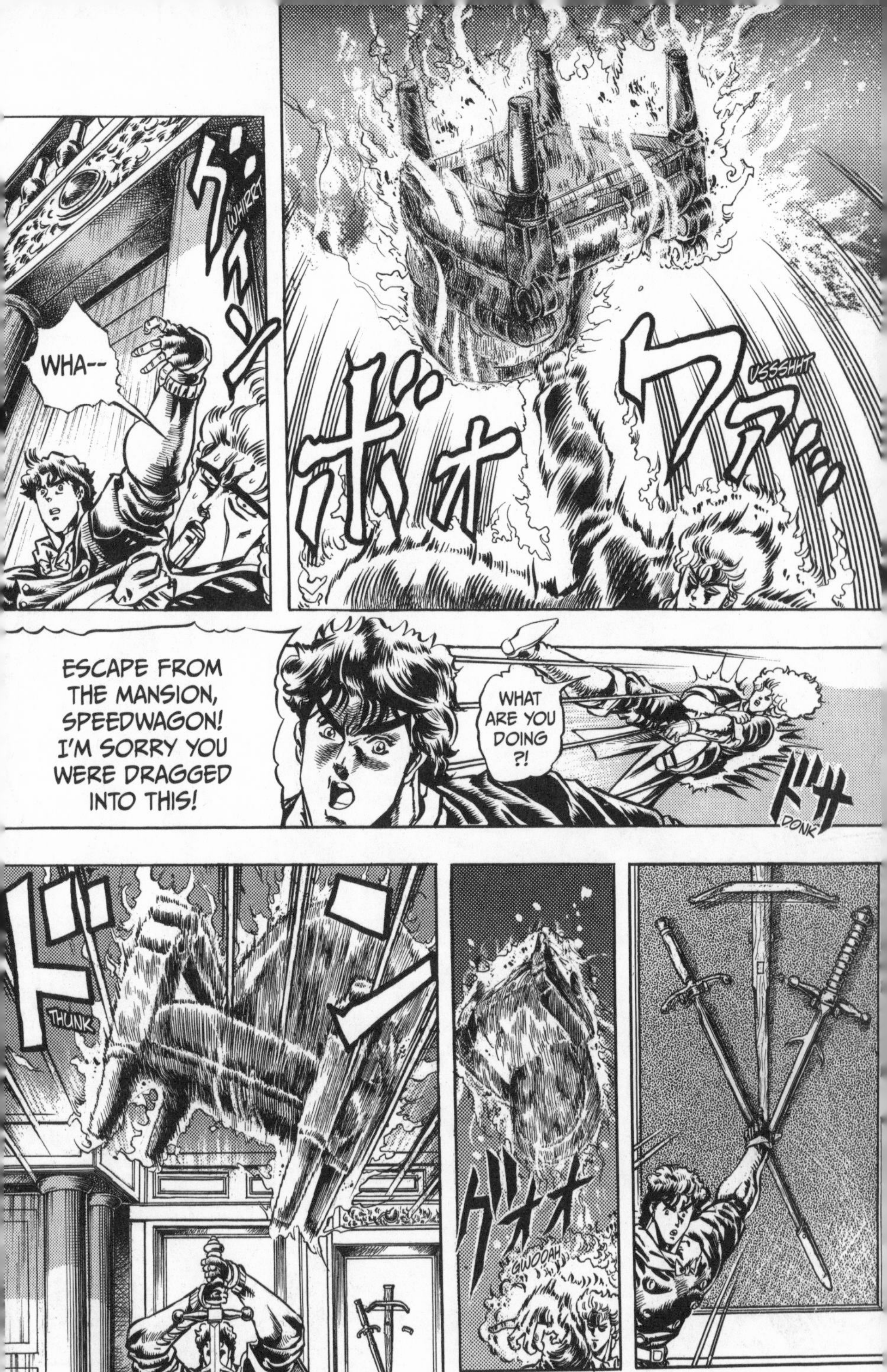
USSSHHT
WHIRRT
WHA--
WHAT ARE YOU DOING ?!
ESCAPE FROM THE MANSION, SPEEDWAGON! I'M SORRY YOU WERE DRAGGED INTO THIS!
DONK
GWOOAH
THUNK

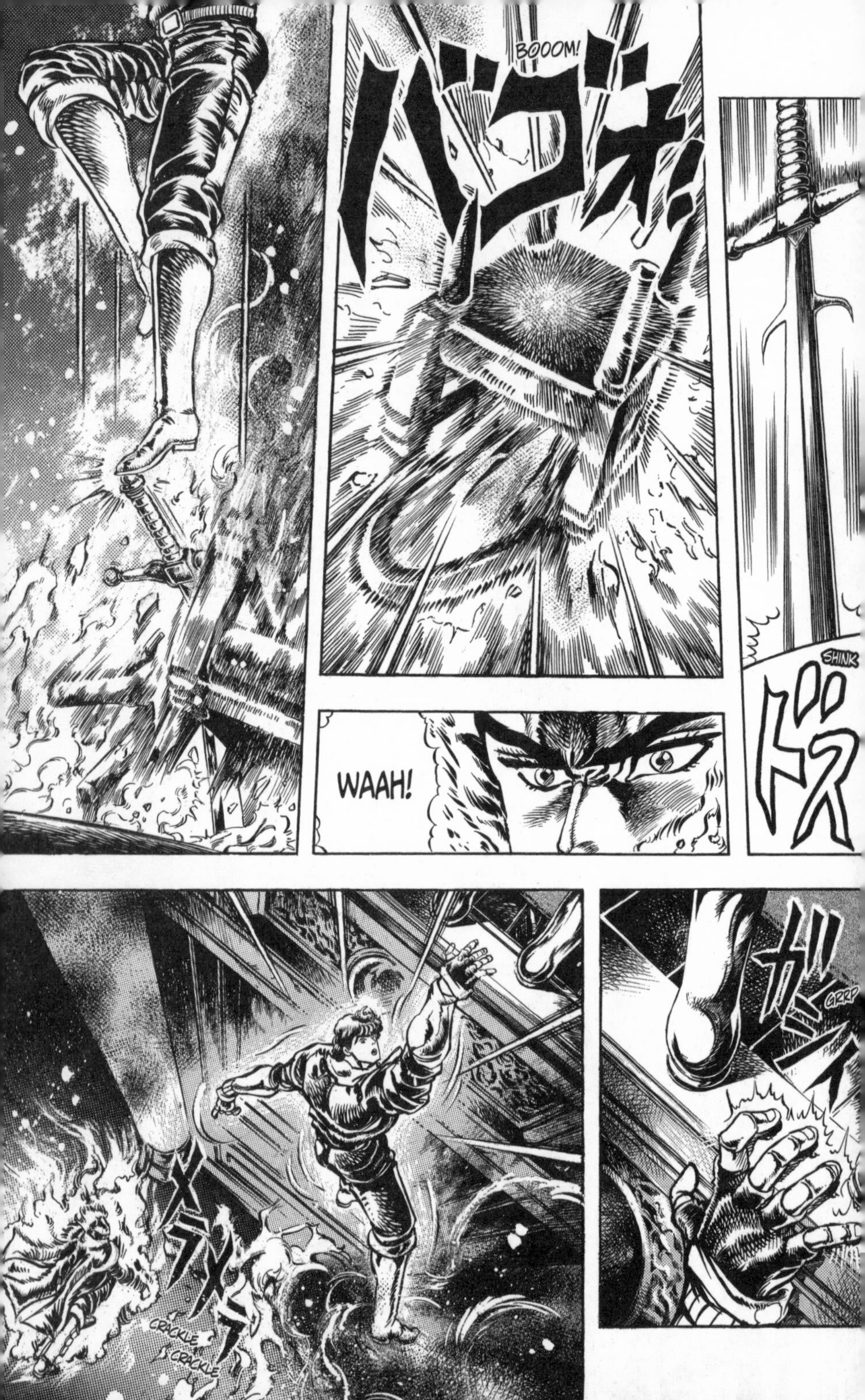
SHINK
ドス
BOOOM!
バゴォ!
WAAH!
GRRP
CRACKLE
CRACKLE

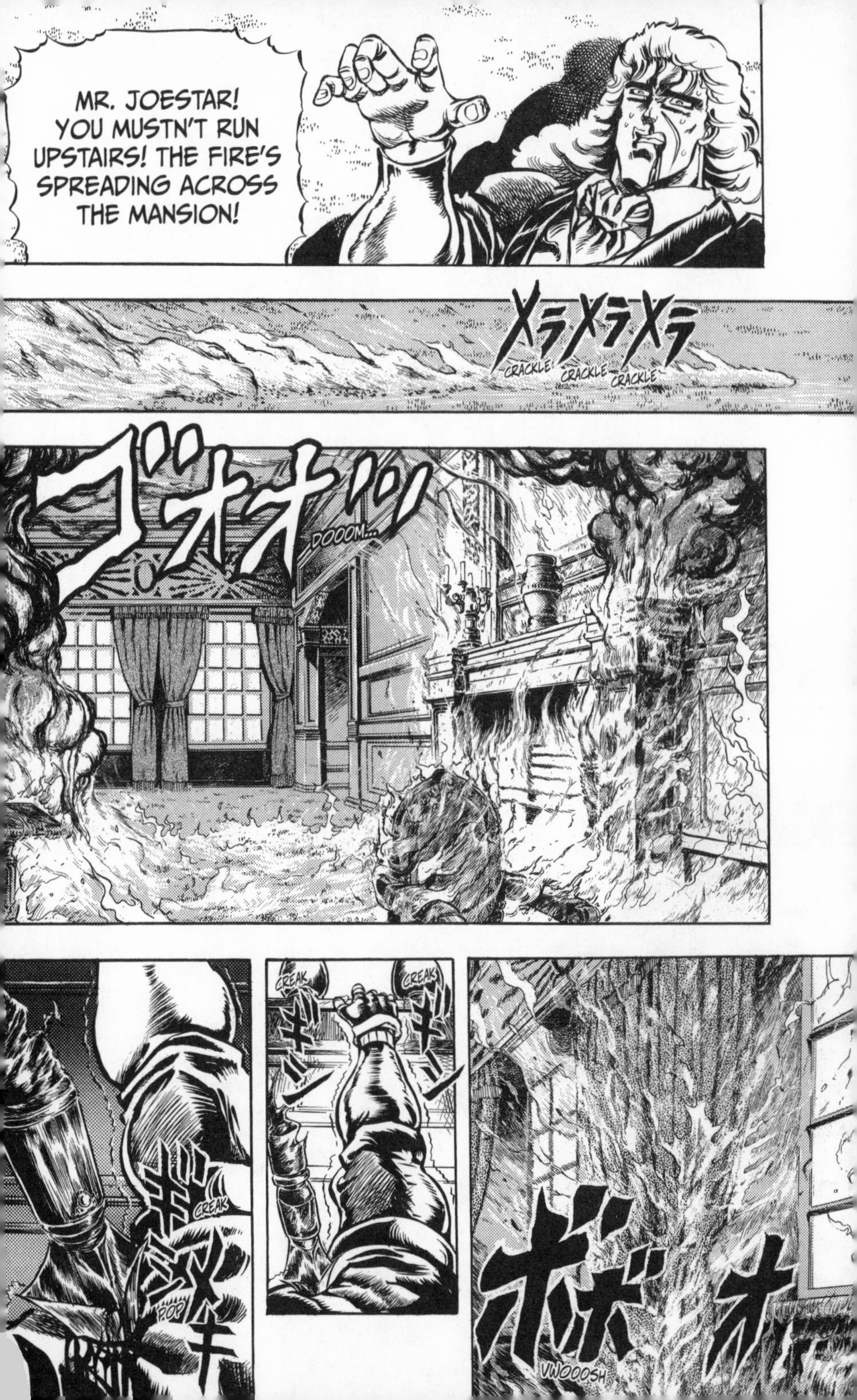
MR. JOESTAR! YOU MUSTN'T RUN UPSTAIRS! THE FIRE'S SPREADING ACROSS THE MANSION!
メラメラメラ
CRACKLE CRACKLE CRACKLE
DOOOM...
VWOOOSH
CREAK CREAK
CREAK
POP

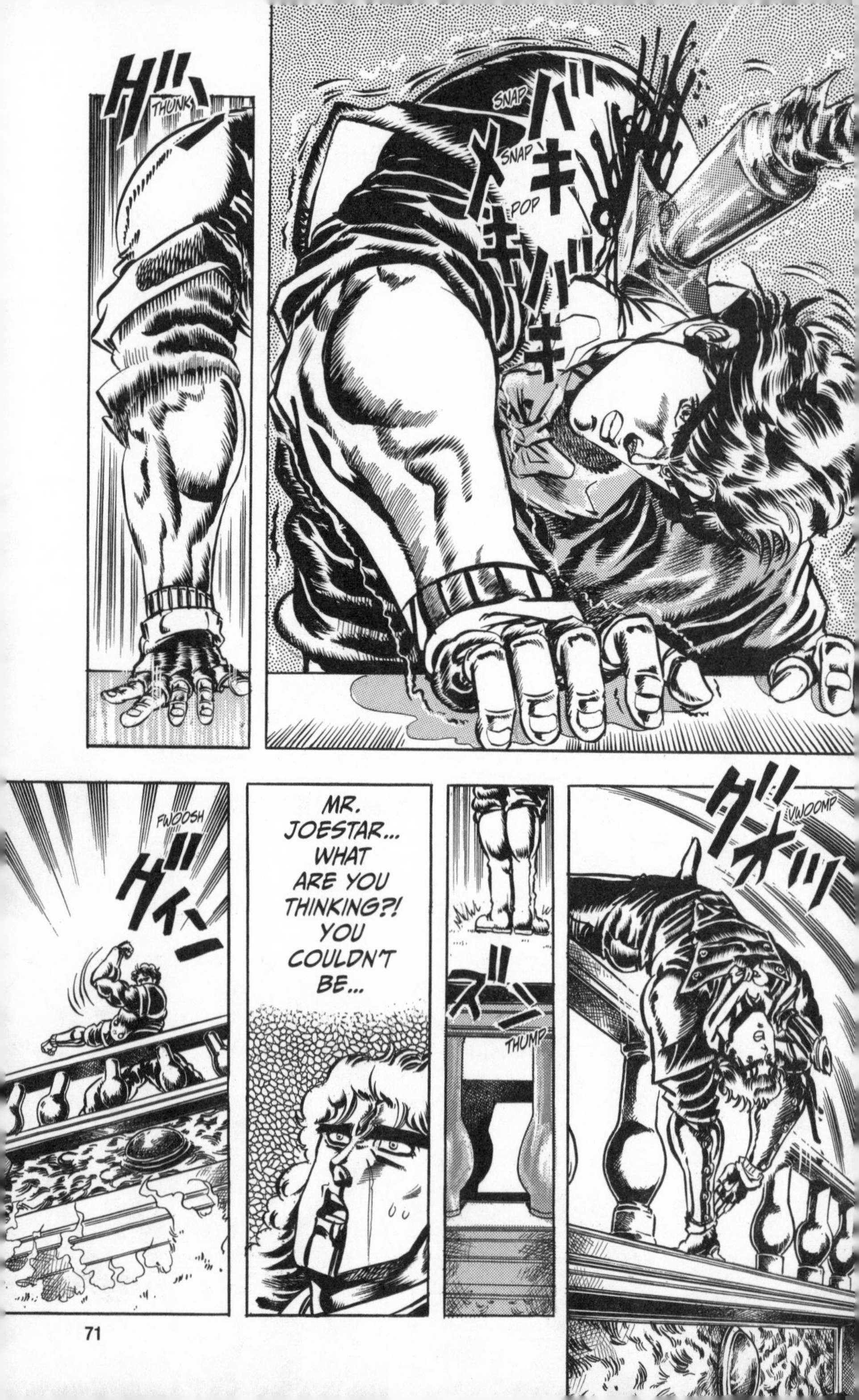
SNAP
SNAP
POP
THUNK
VWOOMP
THUMP
MR. JOESTAR... WHAT ARE YOU THINKING?! YOU COULDN'T BE...
FWOOSH

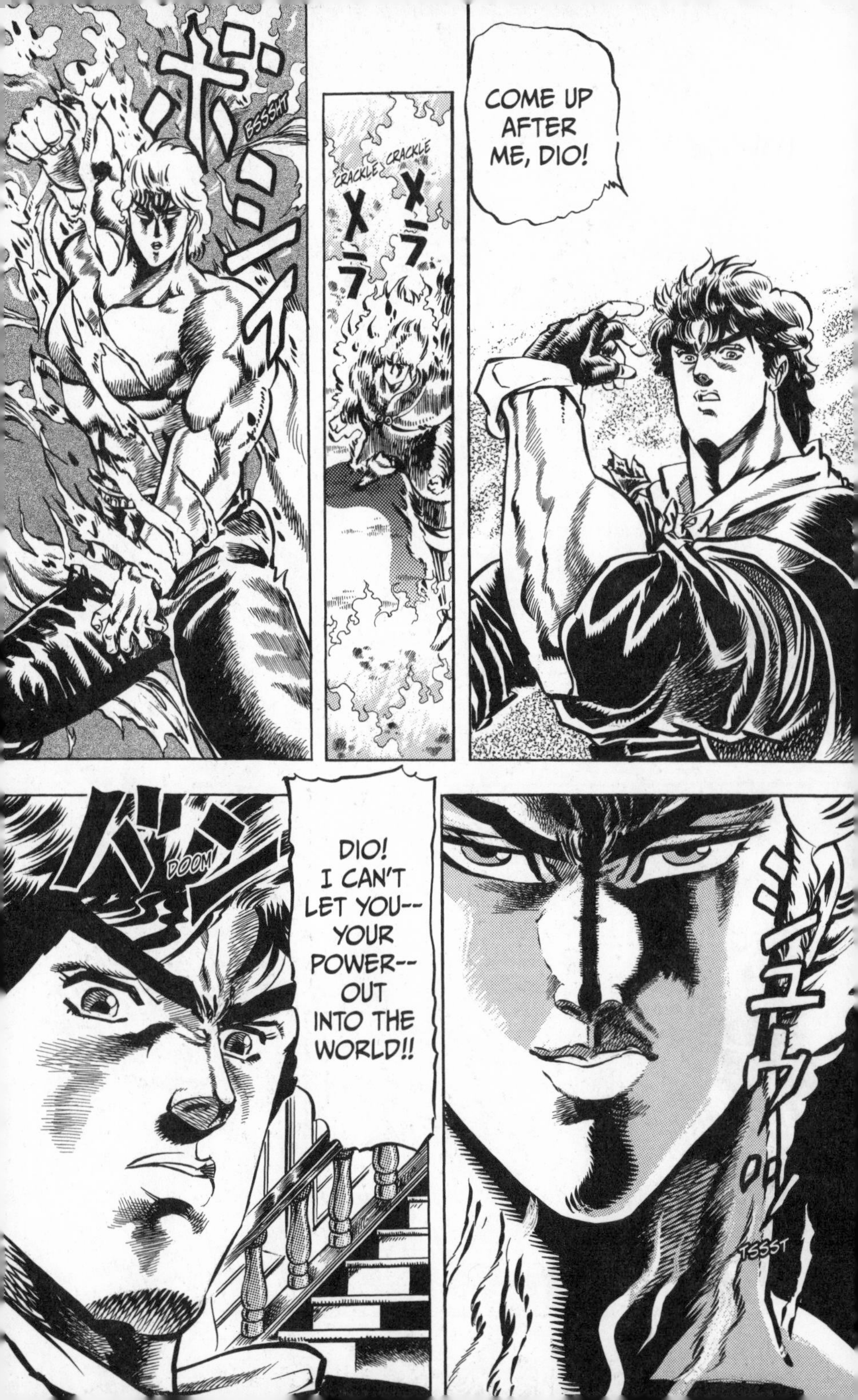
COME UP AFTER ME, DIO!
CRACKLE CRACKLE
BSSSHT
TSSST
DIO! I CAN'T LET YOU-- YOUR POWER-- OUT INTO THE WORLD!!
DOOM

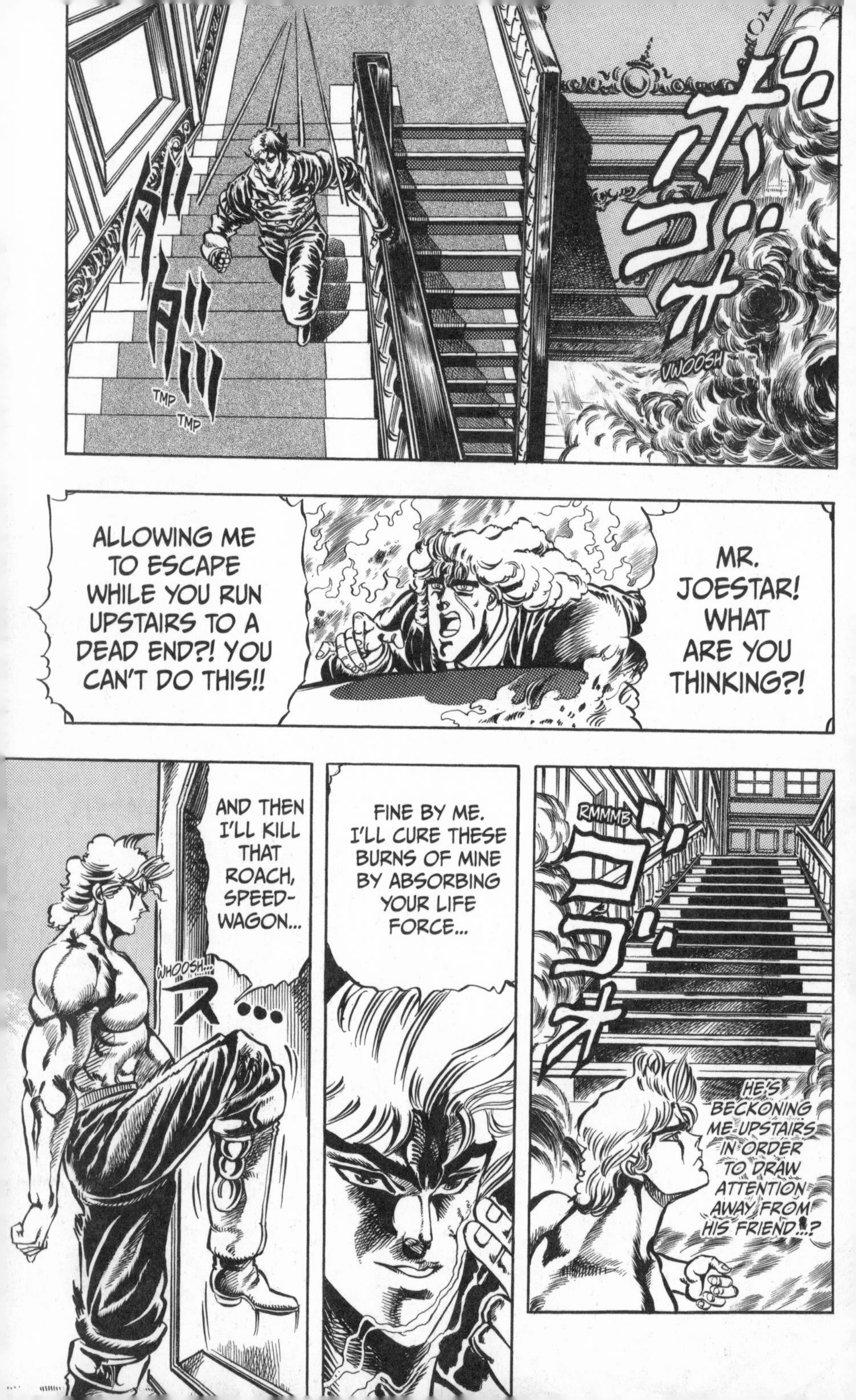
VWOOSH
TMP
TMP
MR. JOESTAR! WHAT ARE YOU THINKING?!
ALLOWING ME TO ESCAPE WHILE YOU RUN UPSTAIRS TO A DEAD END?! YOU CAN'T DO THIS!!
RMMMB
HE'S BECKONING ME UPSTAIRS IN ORDER TO DRAW ATTENTION AWAY FROM HIS FRIEND...?
FINE BY ME. I'LL CURE THESE BURNS OF MINE BY ABSORBING YOUR LIFE FORCE...
AND THEN I'LL KILL THAT ROACH, SPEED-WAGON...
WHOOSH...

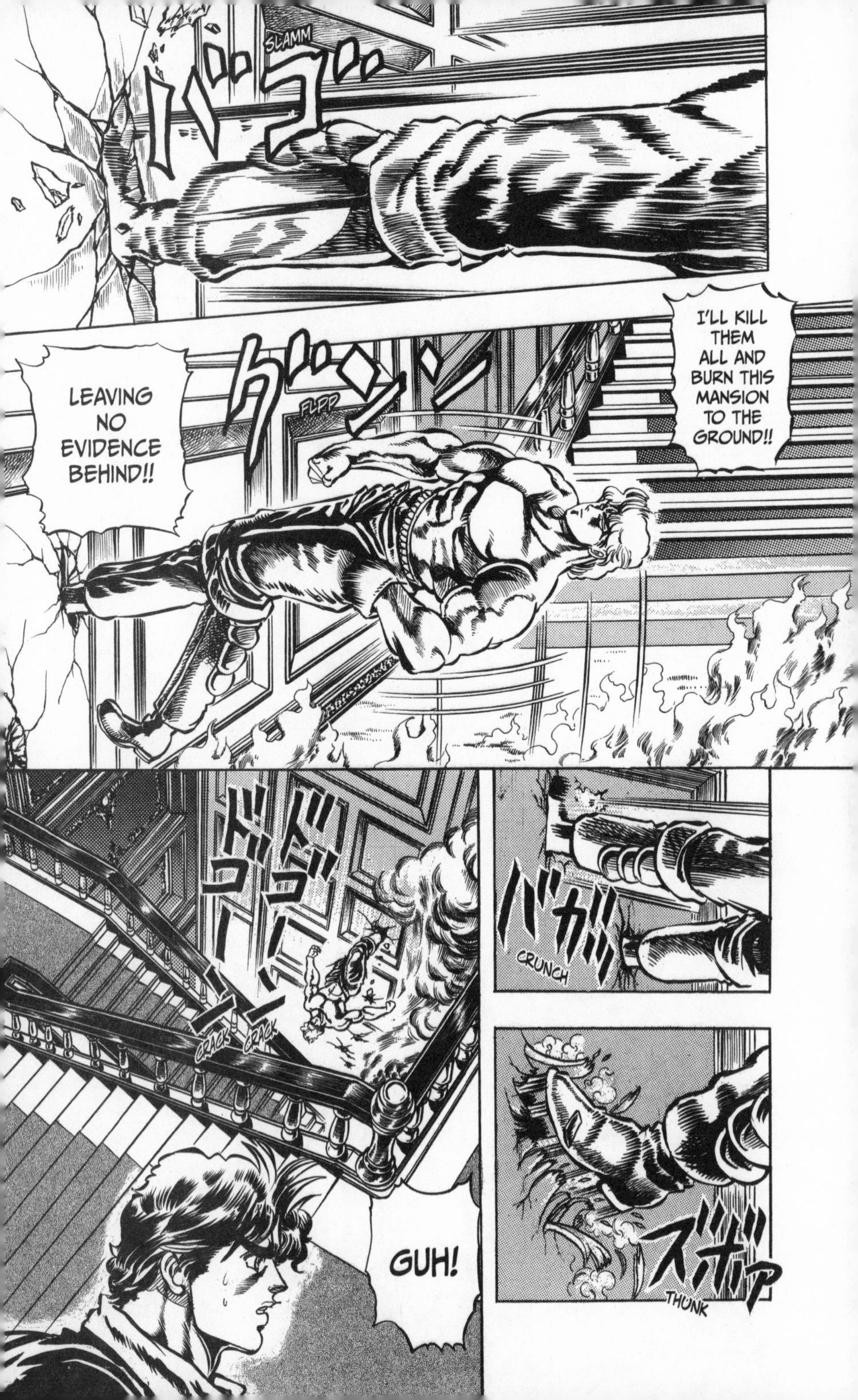
SLAMM
I'LL KILL THEM ALL AND BURN THIS MANSION TO THE GROUND!!
FLPP
LEAVING NO EVIDENCE BEHIND!!
CRUNCH
THUNK
CRACK CRACK
GUH!

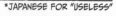

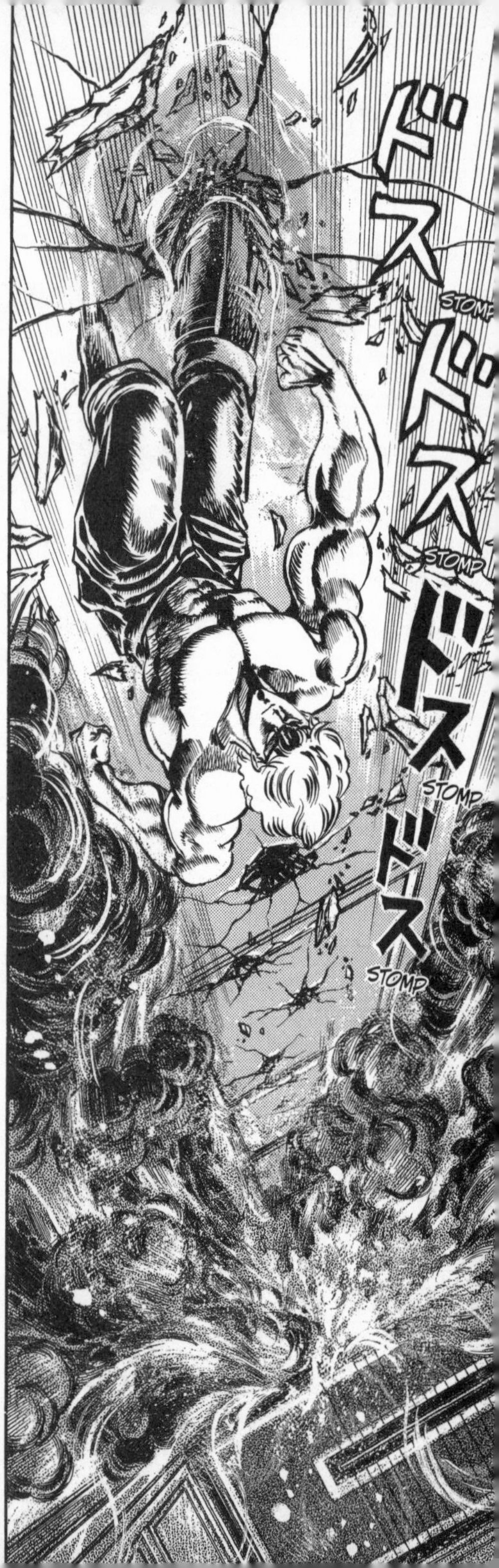
ドス
STOMP
ドス
STOMP
ドス
STOMP
ドス
STOMP

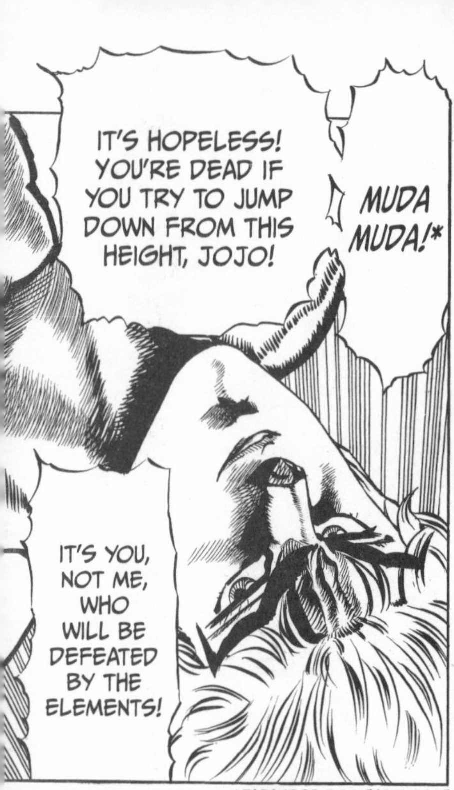
MUDA MUDA!*
IT'S HOPELESS! YOU'RE DEAD IF YOU TRY TO JUMP DOWN FROM THIS HEIGHT, JOJO!
IT'S YOU, NOT ME, WHO WILL BE DEFEATED BY THE ELEMENTS!

*JAPANESE FOR "USELESS"

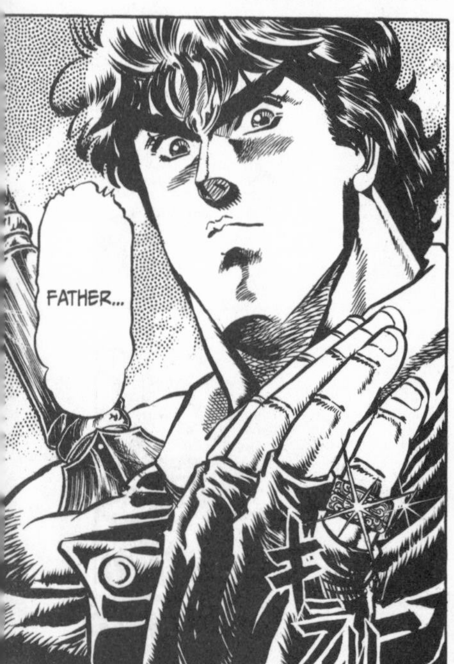
FATHER...
CHING

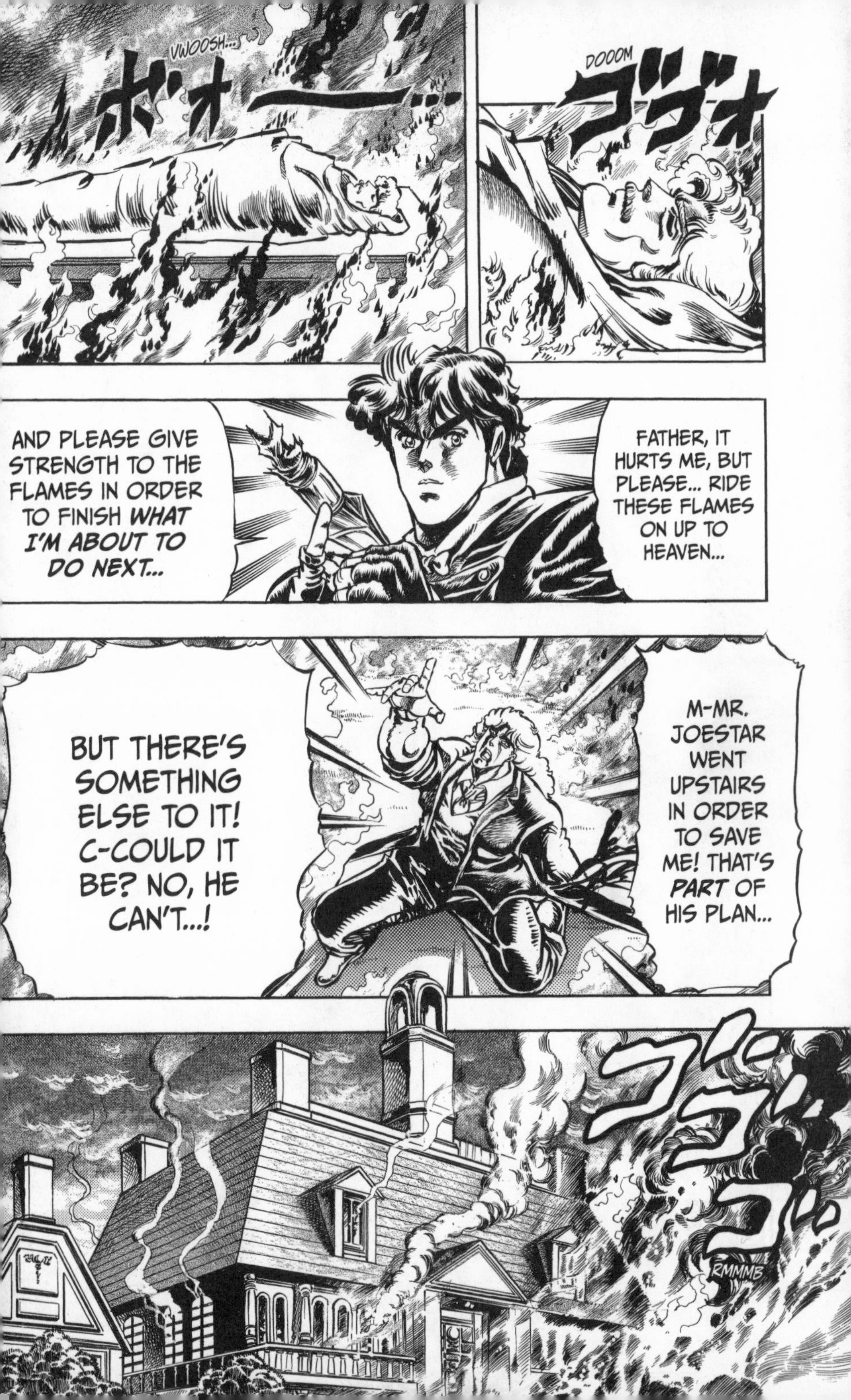
DOOOM
VWOOSH...
FATHER, IT HURTS ME, BUT PLEASE... RIDE THESE FLAMES ON UP TO HEAVEN...
AND PLEASE GIVE STRENGTH TO THE FLAMES IN ORDER TO FINISH *WHAT I'M ABOUT TO DO NEXT...*
M-MR. JOESTAR WENT UPSTAIRS IN ORDER TO SAVE ME! THAT'S *PART* OF HIS PLAN...
BUT THERE'S SOMETHING ELSE TO IT! C-COULD IT BE? NO, HE CAN'T...!
RMMMB

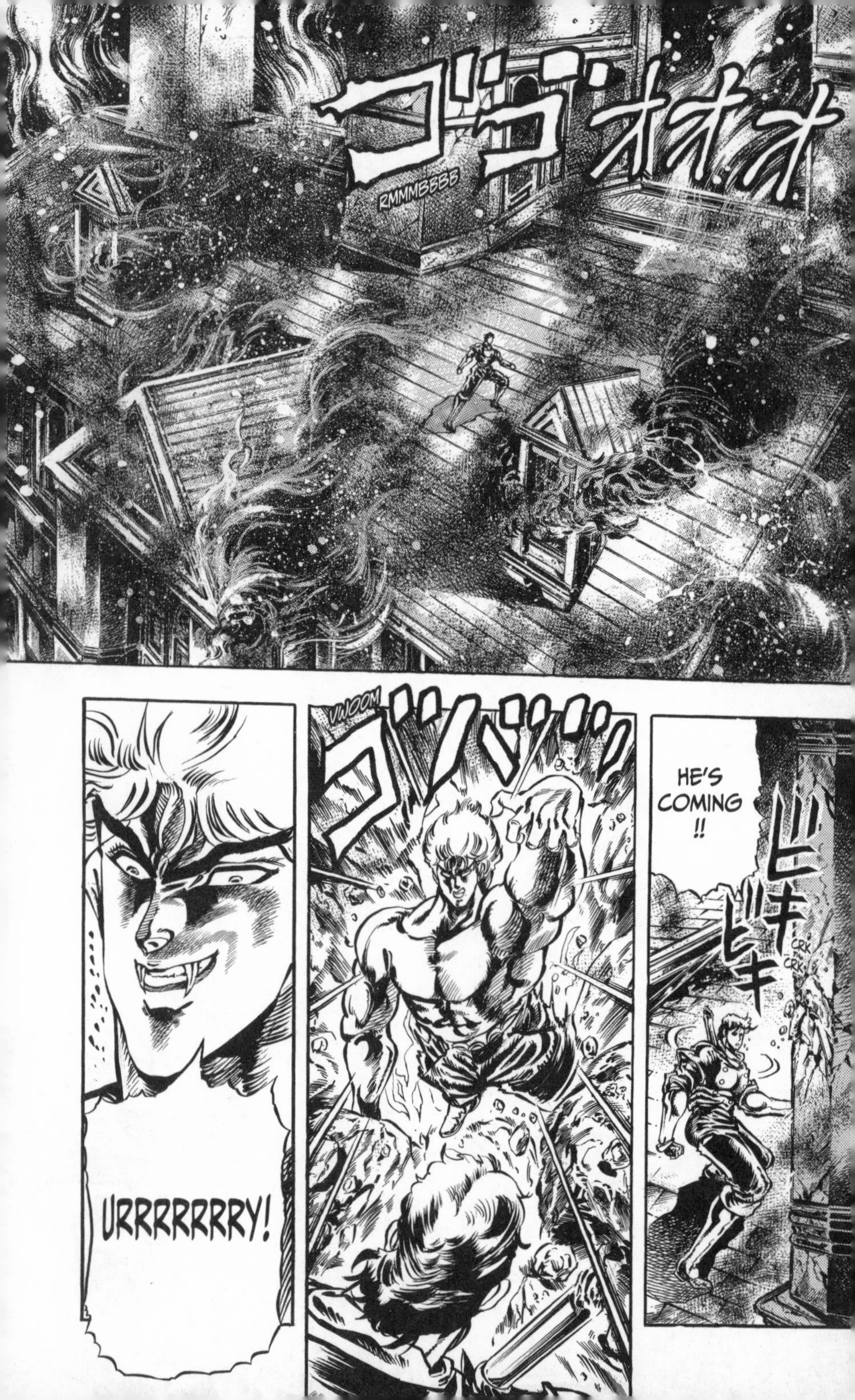

ゴゴオオオ
RMMMBBBB
HE'S COMING !!
ビキビキ
CRK CRK
VWOOM
URRRRRRRY!

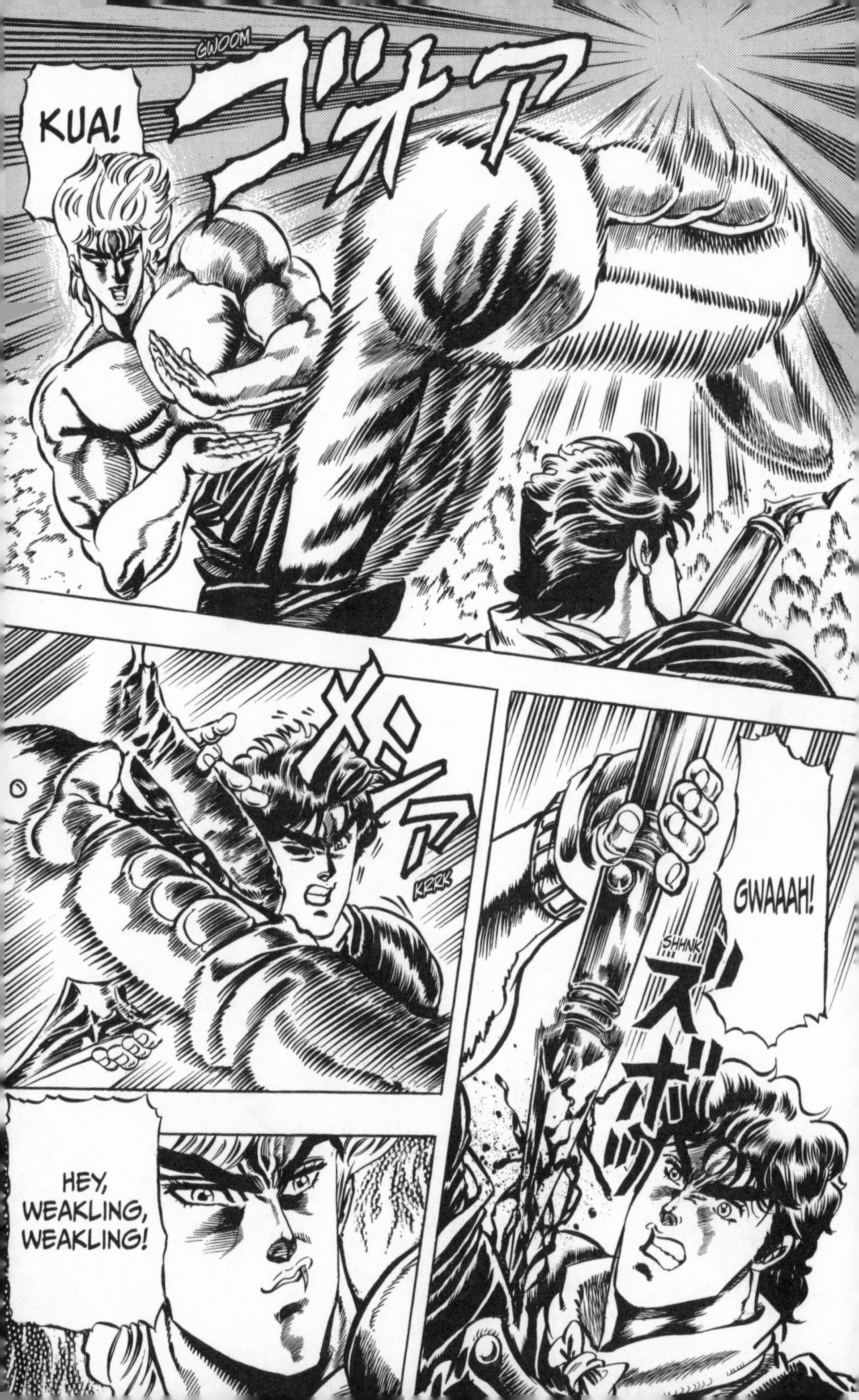
GWOOM
KUA!
GWAAAH!
SHHNK
KRRK
HEY, WEAKLING, WEAKLING!

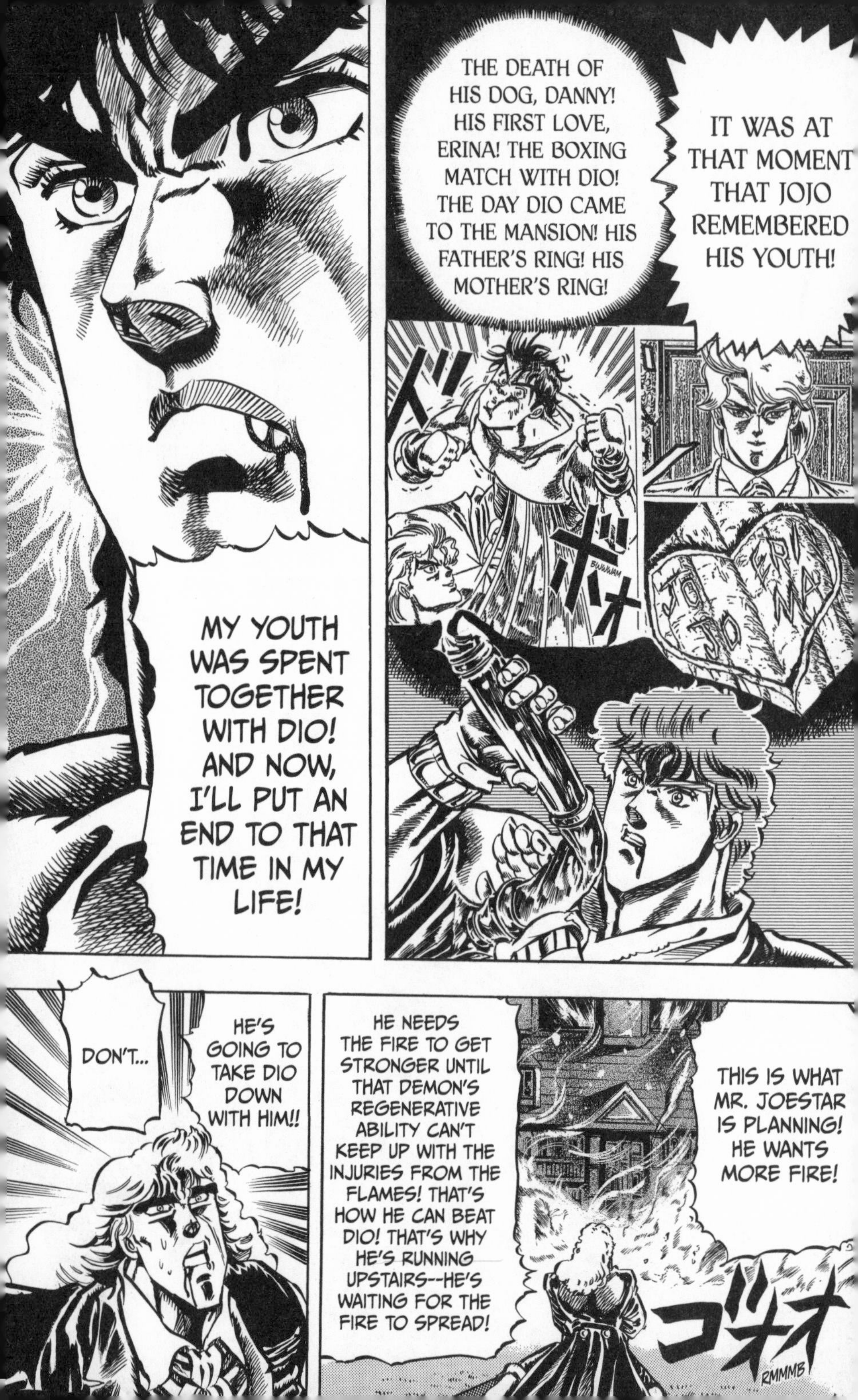
IT WAS AT THAT MOMENT THAT JOJO REMEMBERED HIS YOUTH!
THE DEATH OF HIS DOG, DANNY! HIS FIRST LOVE, ERINA! THE BOXING MATCH WITH DIO! THE DAY DIO CAME TO THE MANSION! HIS FATHER'S RING! HIS MOTHER'S RING!
MY YOUTH WAS SPENT TOGETHER WITH DIO! AND NOW, I'LL PUT AN END TO THAT TIME IN MY LIFE!
THIS IS WHAT MR. JOESTAR IS PLANNING! HE WANTS MORE FIRE!
HE NEEDS THE FIRE TO GET STRONGER UNTIL THAT DEMON'S REGENERATIVE ABILITY CAN'T KEEP UP WITH THE INJURIES FROM THE FLAMES! THAT'S HOW HE CAN BEAT DIO! THAT'S WHY HE'S RUNNING UPSTAIRS--HE'S WAITING FOR THE FIRE TO SPREAD!
RMMMB
HE'S GOING TO TAKE DIO DOWN WITH HIM!!
DON'T...

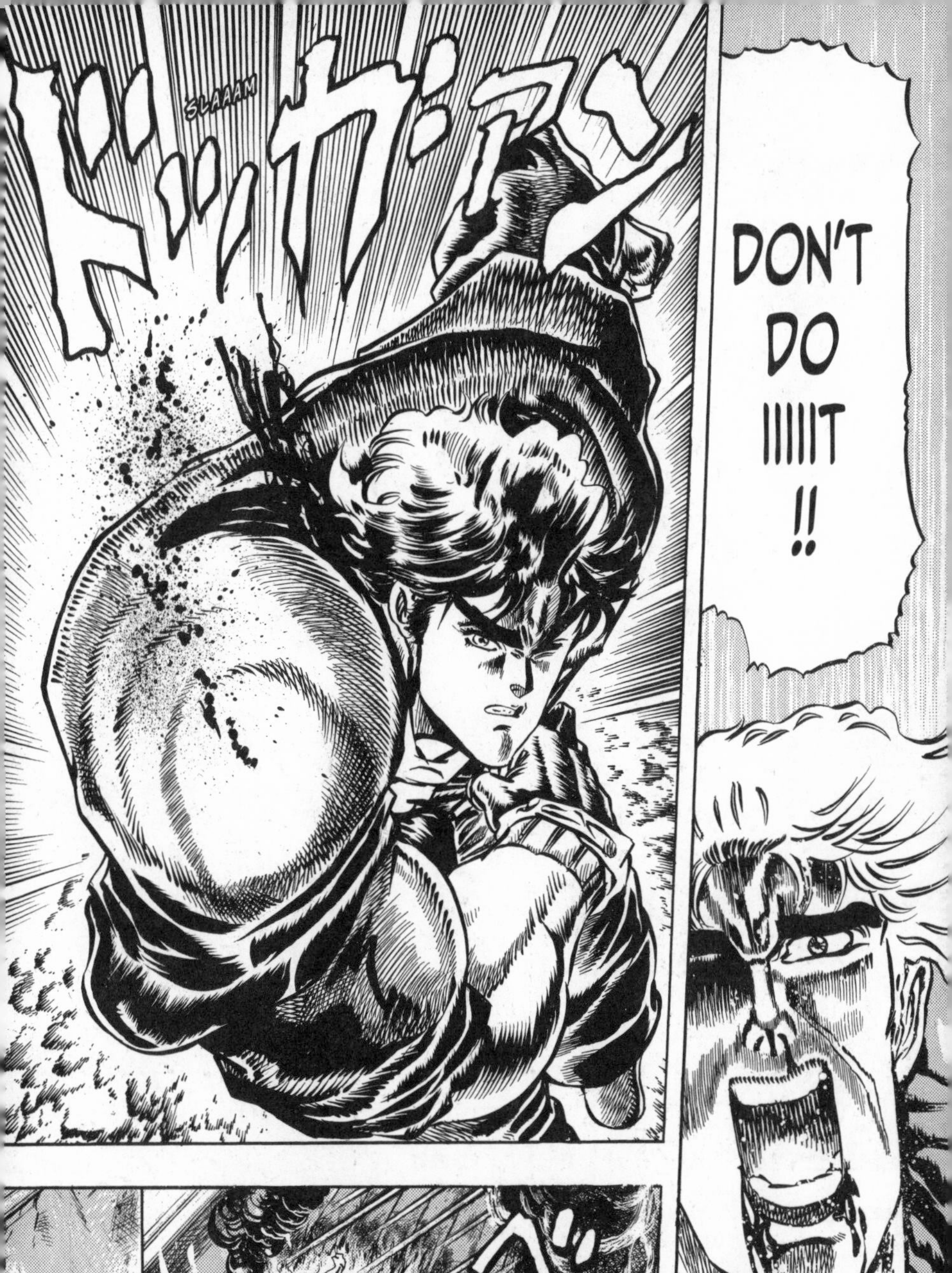
DON'T DO IIIIIT!!
SLAAAM
VGRRP

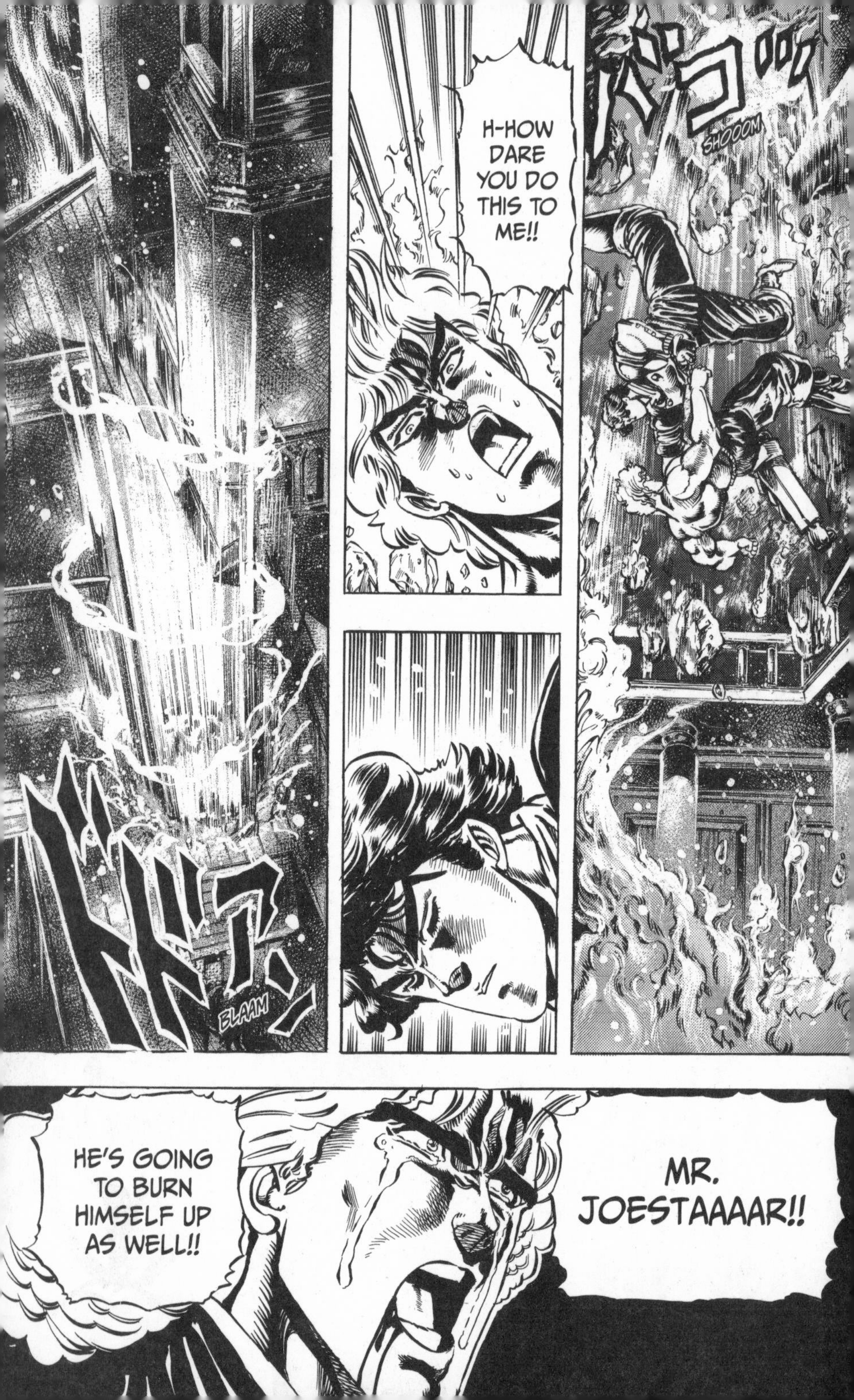
SHOOOM
H-HOW DARE YOU DO THIS TO ME!!
BLAAM
MR. JOESTAAAAR!!
HE'S GOING TO BURN HIMSELF UP AS WELL!!

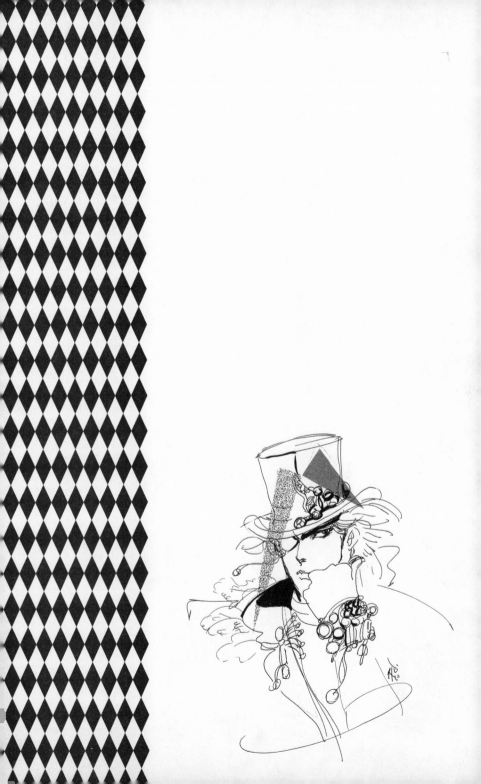

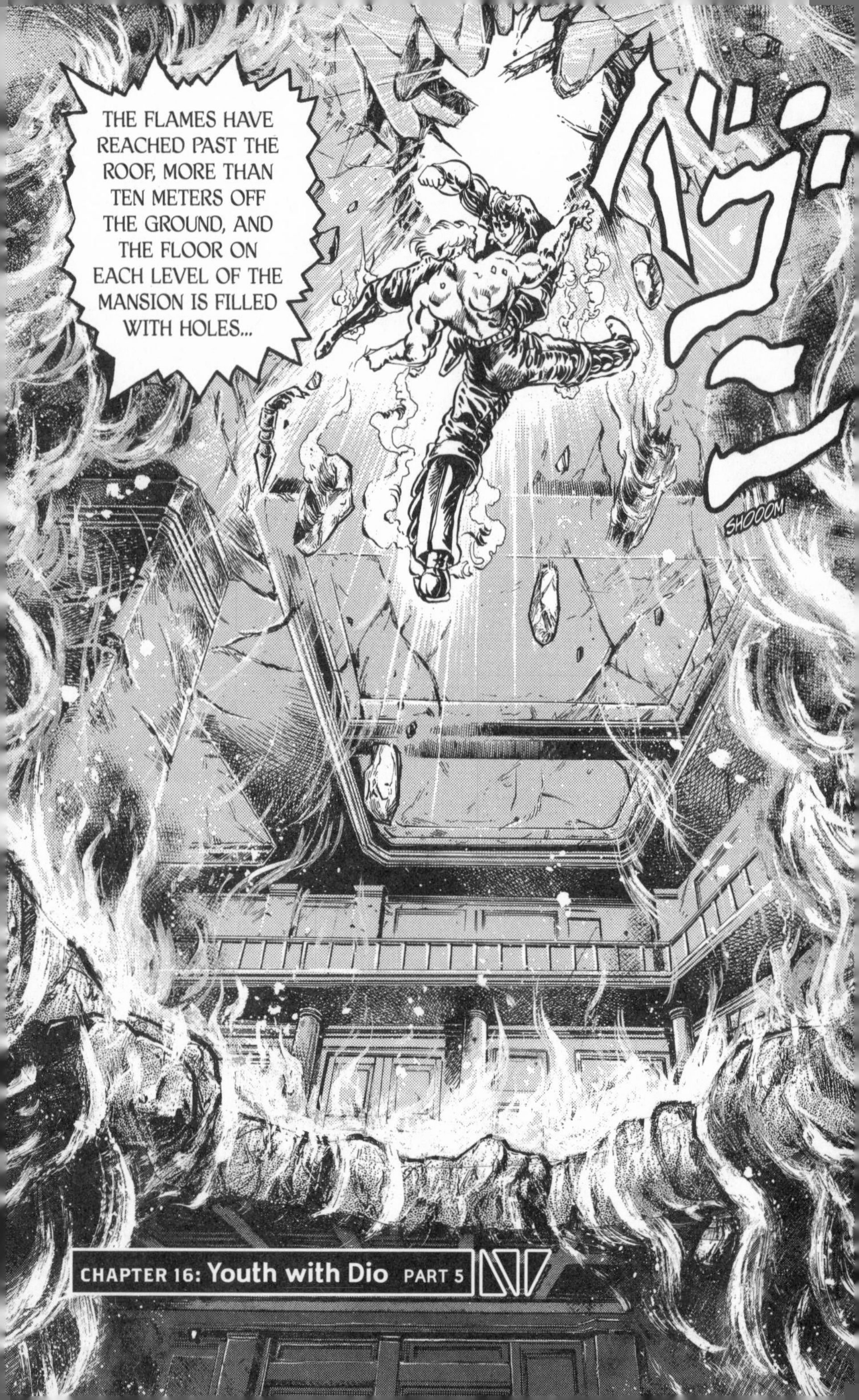
THE FLAMES HAVE REACHED PAST THE ROOF, MORE THAN TEN METERS OFF THE GROUND, AND THE FLOOR ON EACH LEVEL OF THE MANSION IS FILLED WITH HOLES...
バゴーン
SHOOOM
CHAPTER 16: Youth with Dio PART 5

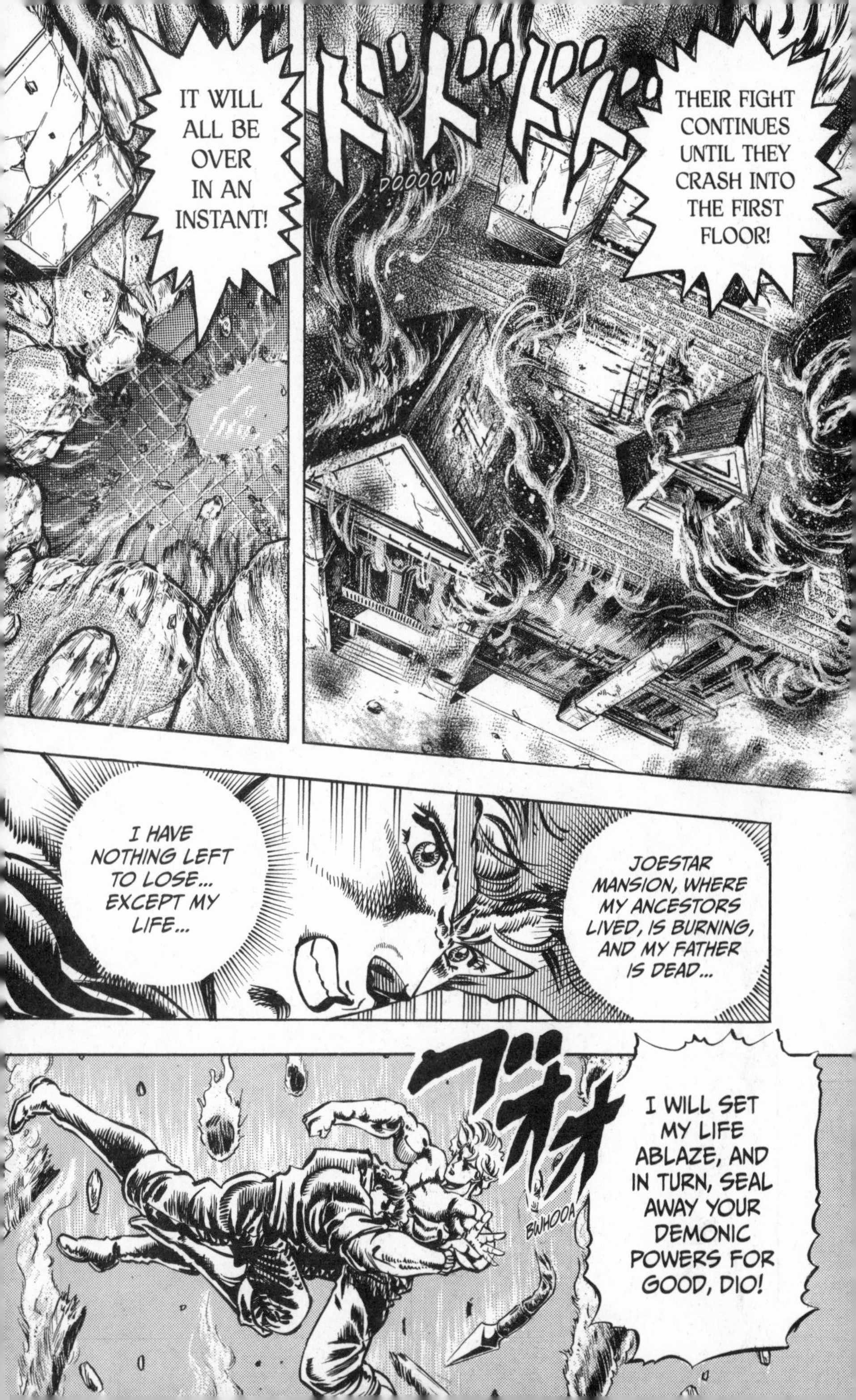
THEIR FIGHT CONTINUES UNTIL THEY CRASH INTO THE FIRST FLOOR!
DOOOOM
IT WILL ALL BE OVER IN AN INSTANT!
JOESTAR MANSION, WHERE MY ANCESTORS LIVED, IS BURNING, AND MY FATHER IS DEAD...
I HAVE NOTHING LEFT TO LOSE... EXCEPT MY LIFE...
I WILL SET MY LIFE ABLAZE, AND IN TURN, SEAL AWAY YOUR DEMONIC POWERS FOR GOOD, DIO!
BWHOOA

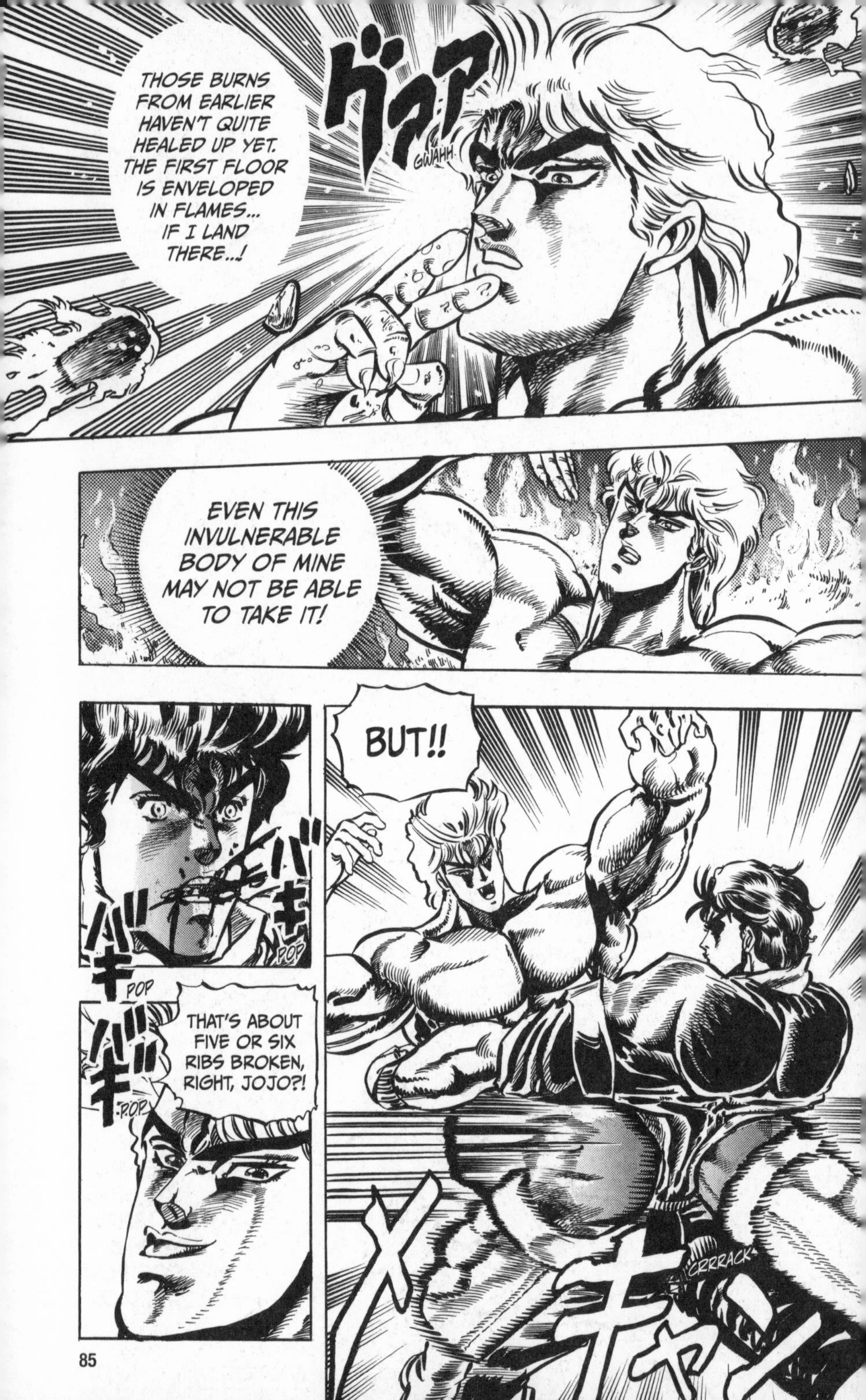
GWAHH
THOSE BURNS FROM EARLIER HAVEN'T QUITE HEALED UP YET. THE FIRST FLOOR IS ENVELOPED IN FLAMES... IF I LAND THERE...!
EVEN THIS INVULNERABLE BODY OF MINE MAY NOT BE ABLE TO TAKE IT!
BUT!!
CRRRACK
POP
POP
POP
THAT'S ABOUT FIVE OR SIX RIBS BROKEN, RIGHT, JOJO?!

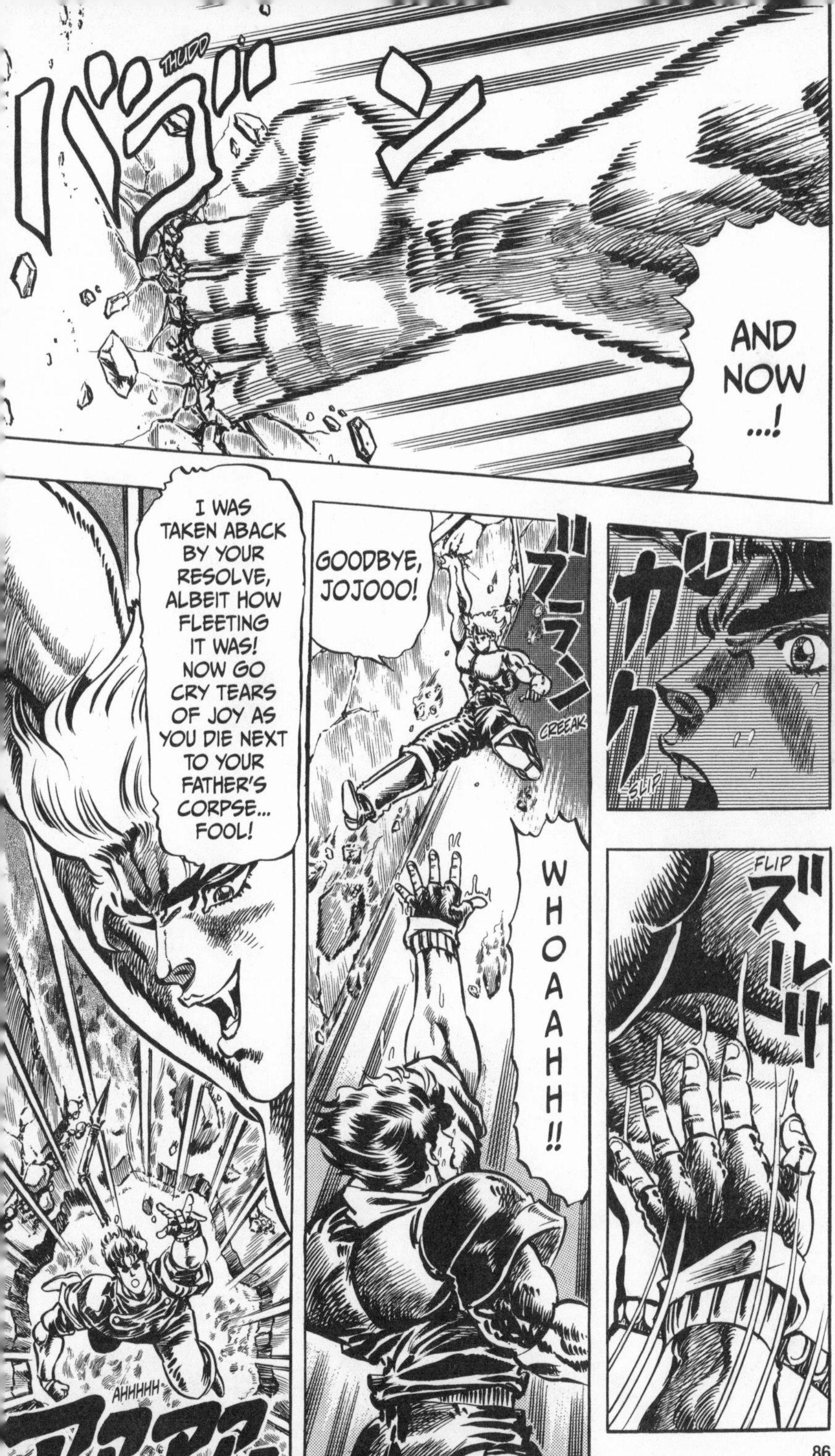
THUDD
AND NOW ...!
SLIP
FLIP
GOODBYE, JOJOOO!
CREEAK
WHOAAAHH!!
I WAS TAKEN ABACK BY YOUR RESOLVE, ALBEIT HOW FLEETING IT WAS! NOW GO CRY TEARS OF JOY AS YOU DIE NEXT TO YOUR FATHER'S CORPSE... FOOL!
AHHHHH

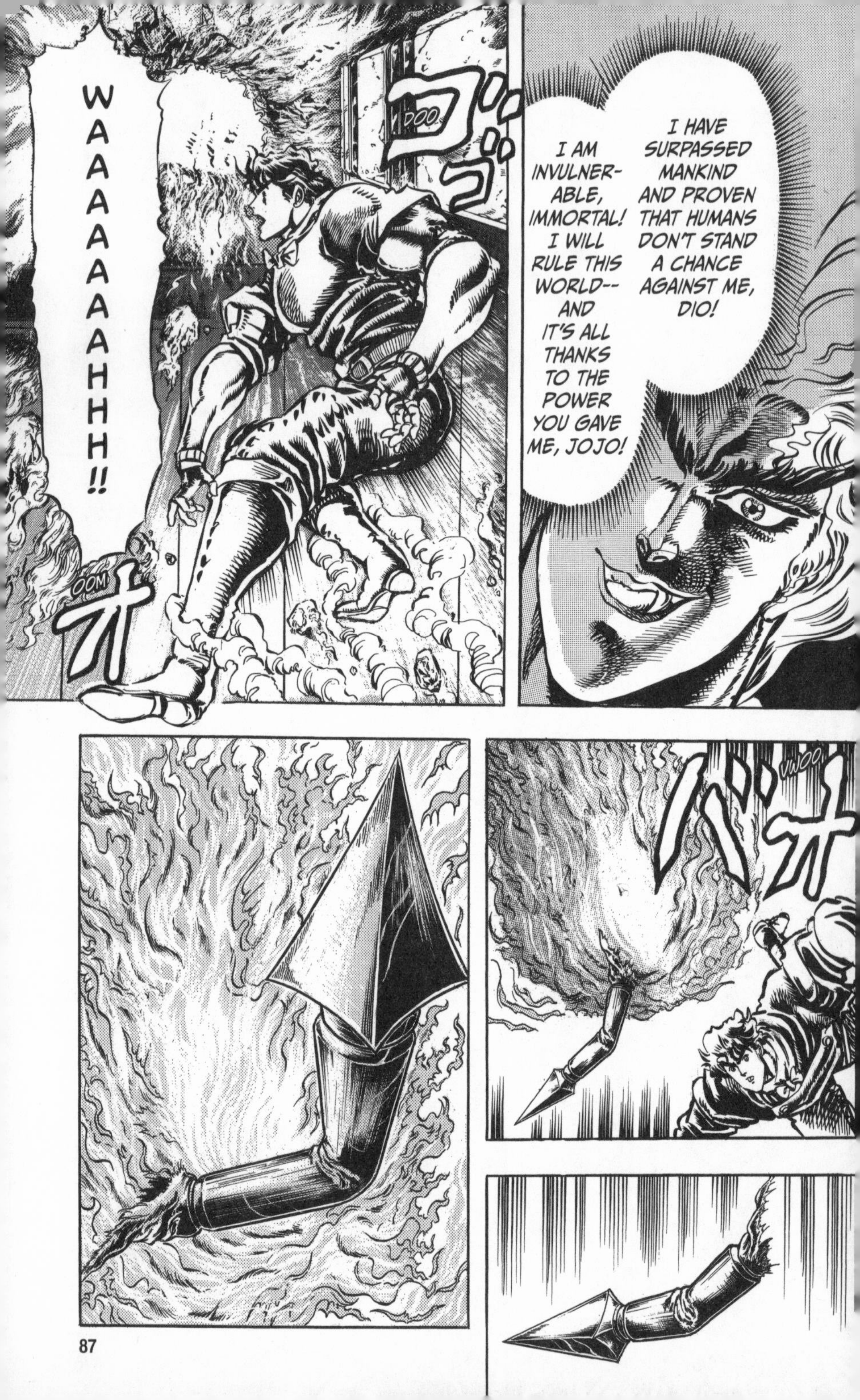
I HAVE SURPASSED MANKIND AND PROVEN THAT HUMANS DON'T STAND A CHANCE AGAINST ME, DIO!
I AM INVULNER-ABLE, IMMORTAL! I WILL RULE THIS WORLD-- AND IT'S ALL THANKS TO THE POWER YOU GAVE ME, JOJO!
DOO
WAAAAAAAAAAHHHHH!!
OOM
VWOO

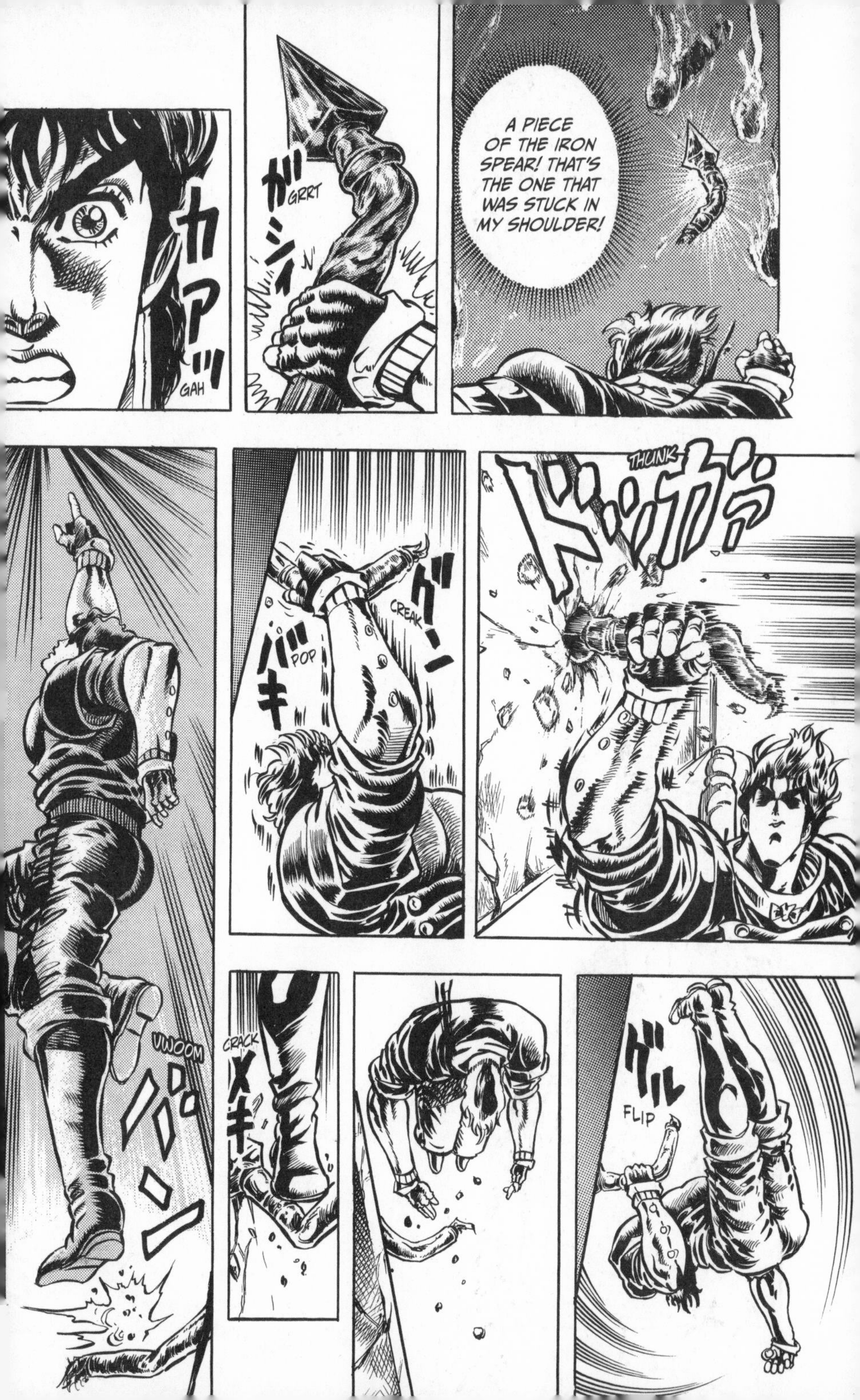
A PIECE OF THE IRON SPEAR! THAT'S THE ONE THAT WAS STUCK IN MY SHOULDER!
GRRT
カアッ
GAH
THUNK
CREAK
バキ
POP
グル
FLIP
メキ
CRACK
UWOOM

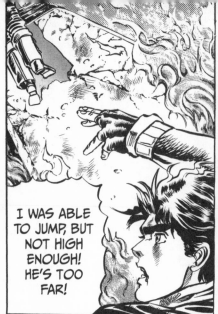

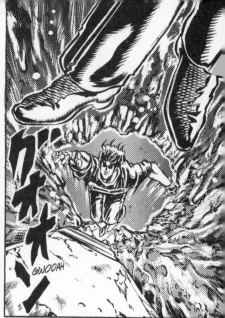

I WAS ABLE TO JUMP, BUT NOT HIGH ENOUGH! HE'S TOO FAR!

GWOOAH

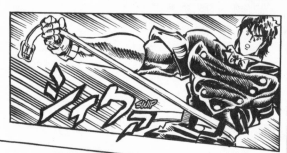

SWIP

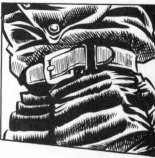

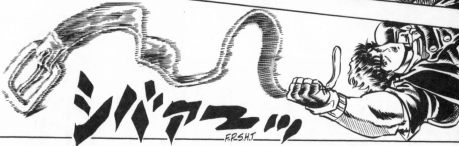

F.R.S.H.T

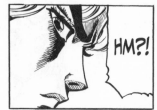

HM?!

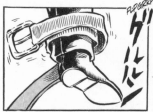

FLP.GRP

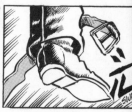

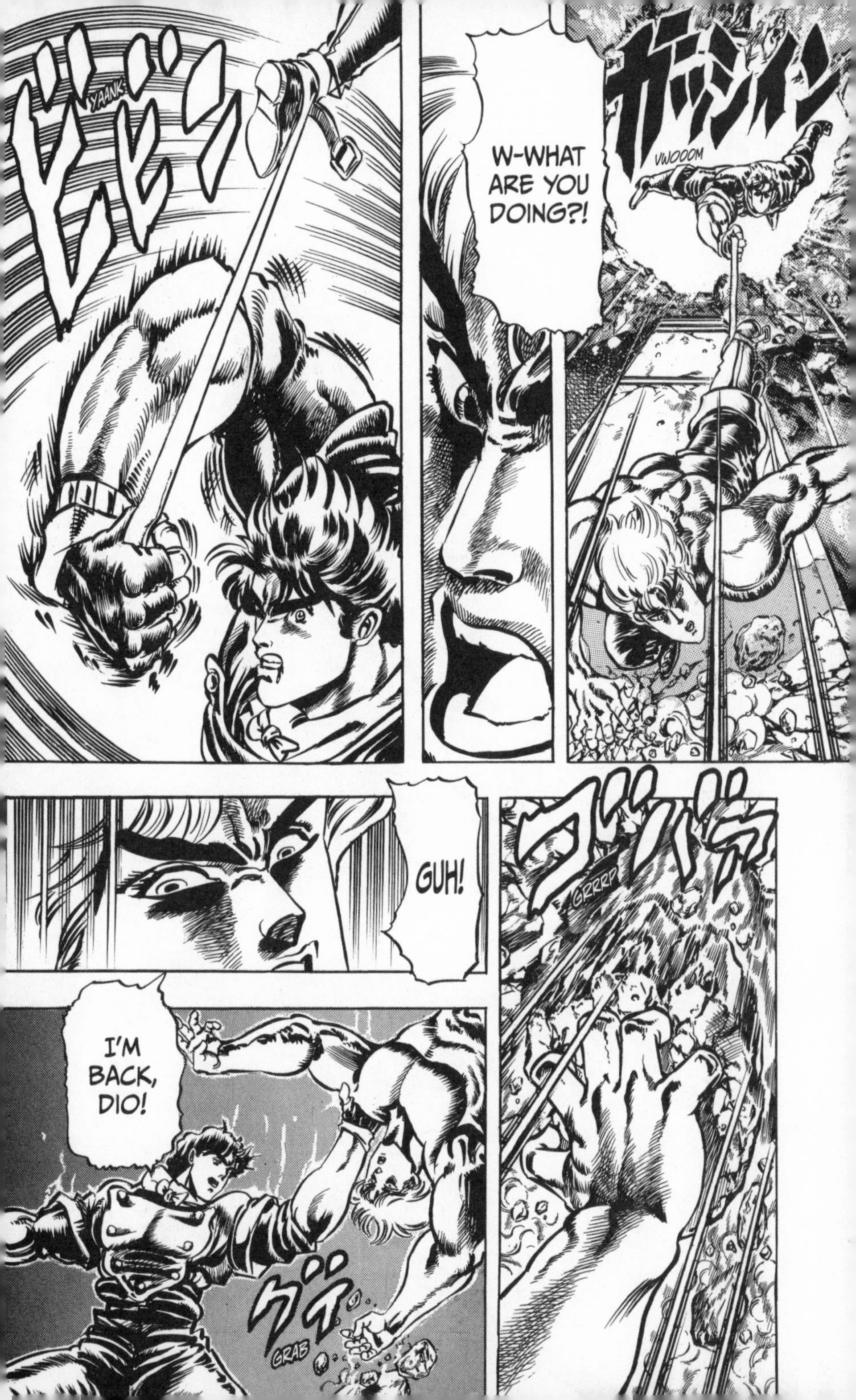
VWOOOM
W-WHAT ARE YOU DOING?!
YAANK
GRRRP
GUH!
I'M BACK, DIO!
GRAB

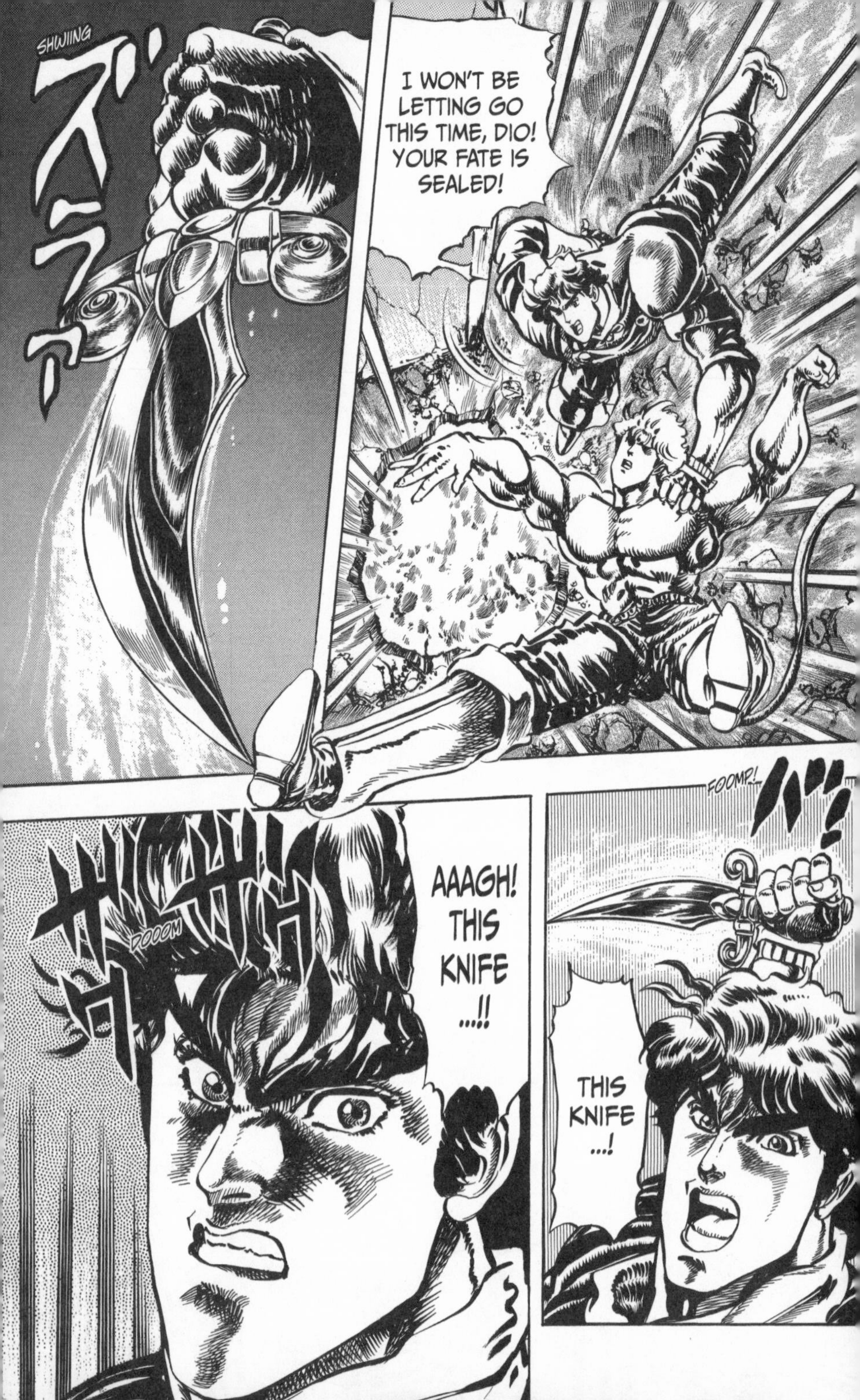
I WON'T BE LETTING GO THIS TIME, DIO! YOUR FATE IS SEALED!
SHWIING
FOOMP!
THIS KNIFE ...!
DOOOM
AAAGH! THIS KNIFE ...!!

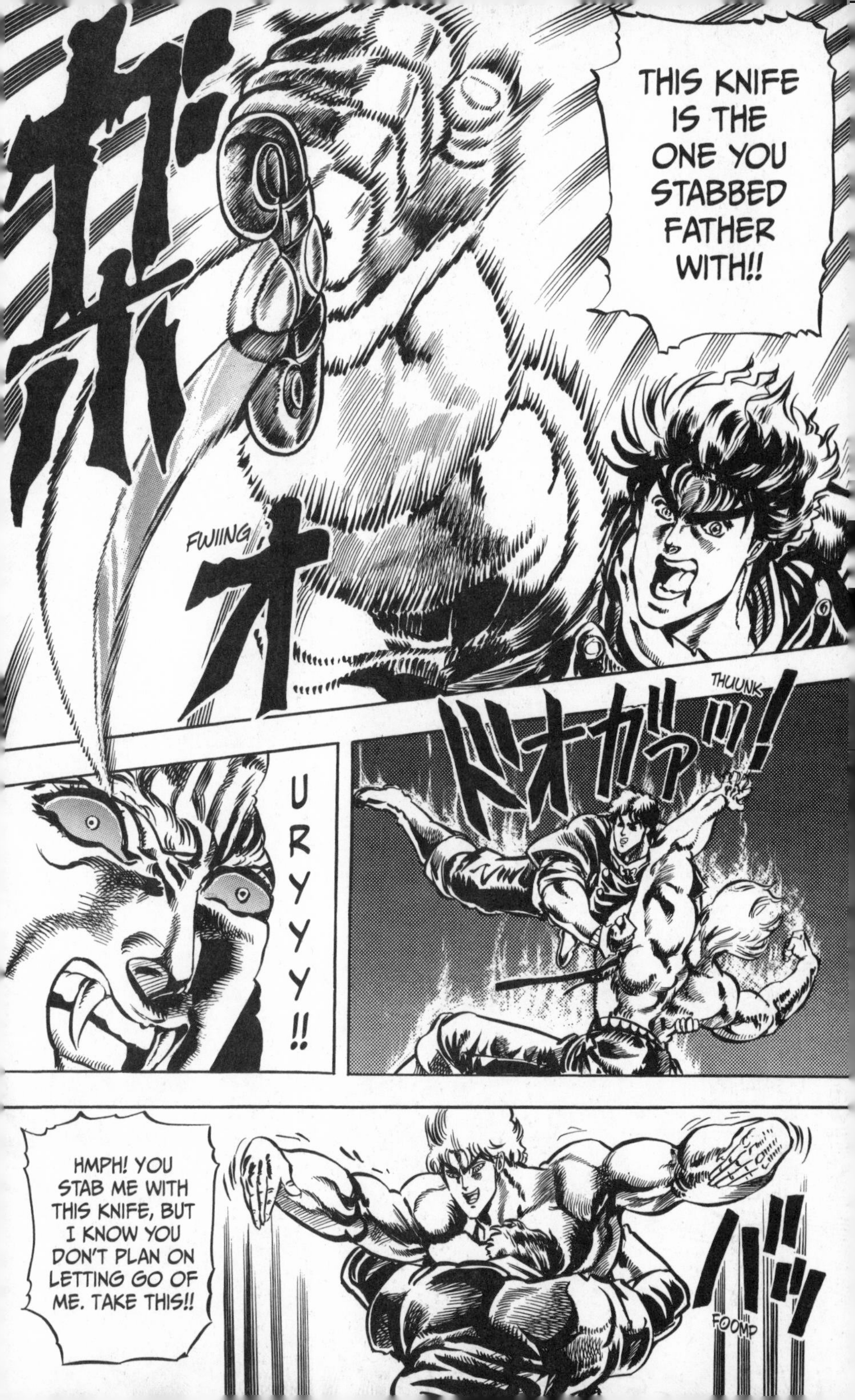
THIS KNIFE IS THE ONE YOU STABBED FATHER WITH!!
FWIING
THUUNK
URYYY!!
HMPH! YOU STAB ME WITH THIS KNIFE, BUT I KNOW YOU DON'T PLAN ON LETTING GO OF ME. TAKE THIS!!
FOOMP

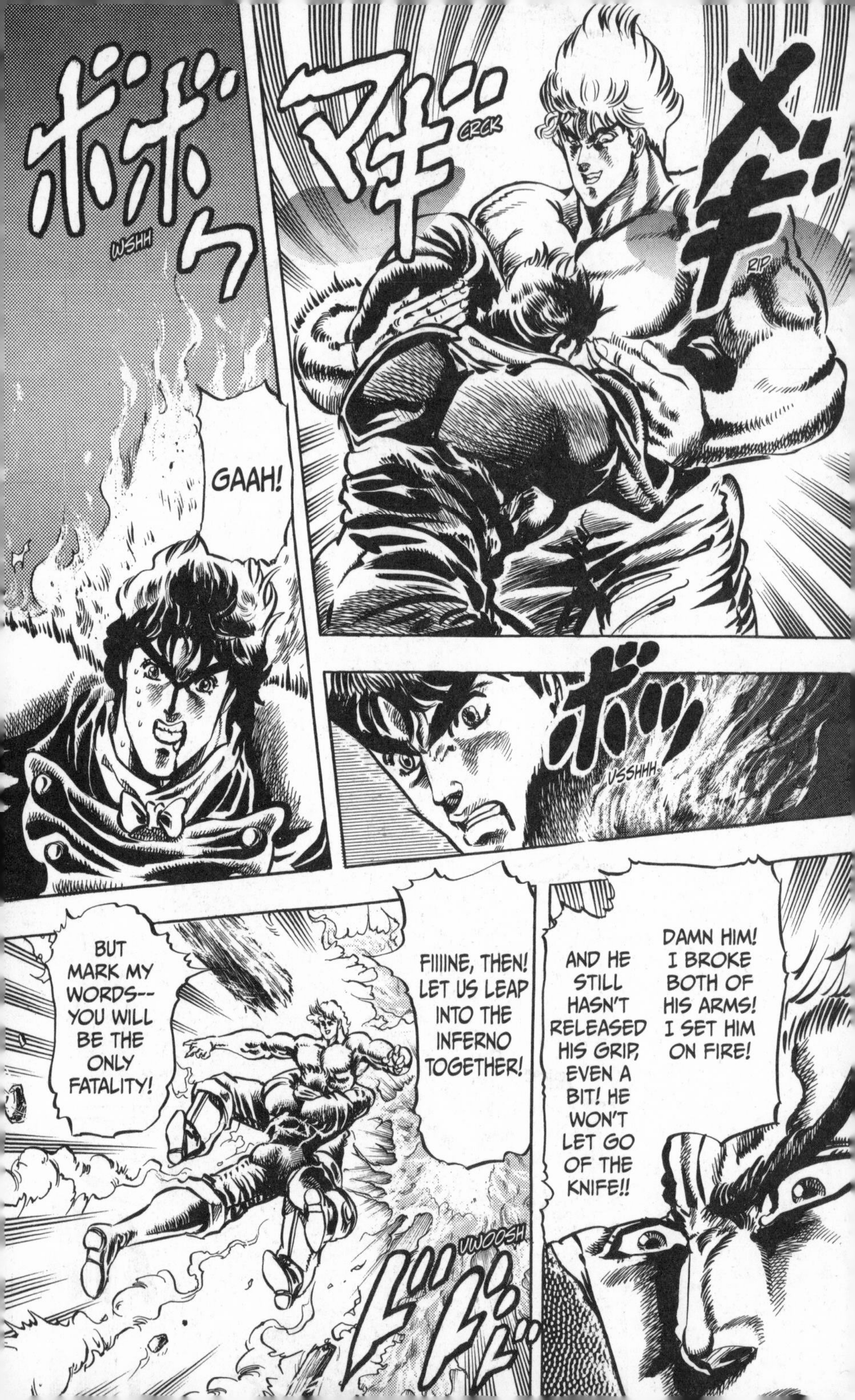
RIP
CRCK
USSHHH
WSHH
GAAH!
DAMN HIM! I BROKE BOTH OF HIS ARMS! I SET HIM ON FIRE!
AND HE STILL HASN'T RELEASED HIS GRIP, EVEN A BIT! HE WON'T LET GO OF THE KNIFE!!
FIIIINE, THEN! LET US LEAP INTO THE INFERNO TOGETHER!
VWOOSH
BUT MARK MY WORDS-- YOU WILL BE THE ONLY FATALITY!

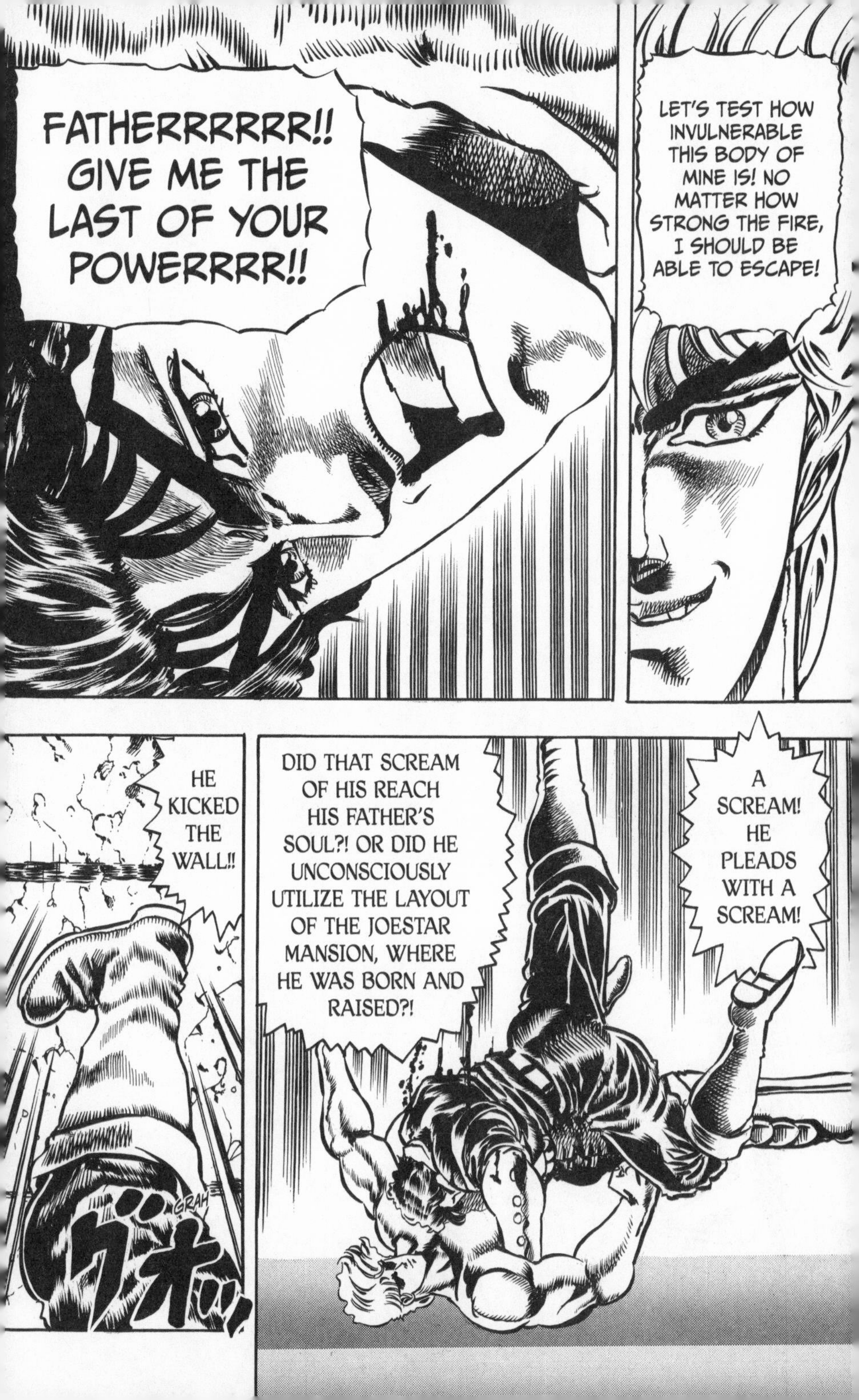
LET'S TEST HOW INVULNERABLE THIS BODY OF MINE IS! NO MATTER HOW STRONG THE FIRE, I SHOULD BE ABLE TO ESCAPE!
FATHERRRRRR!! GIVE ME THE LAST OF YOUR POWERRRR!!
A SCREAM! HE PLEADS WITH A SCREAM!
DID THAT SCREAM OF HIS REACH HIS FATHER'S SOUL?! OR DID HE UNCONSCIOUSLY UTILIZE THE LAYOUT OF THE JOESTAR MANSION, WHERE HE WAS BORN AND RAISED?!
HE KICKED THE WALL!!
ウオ…
GRAH

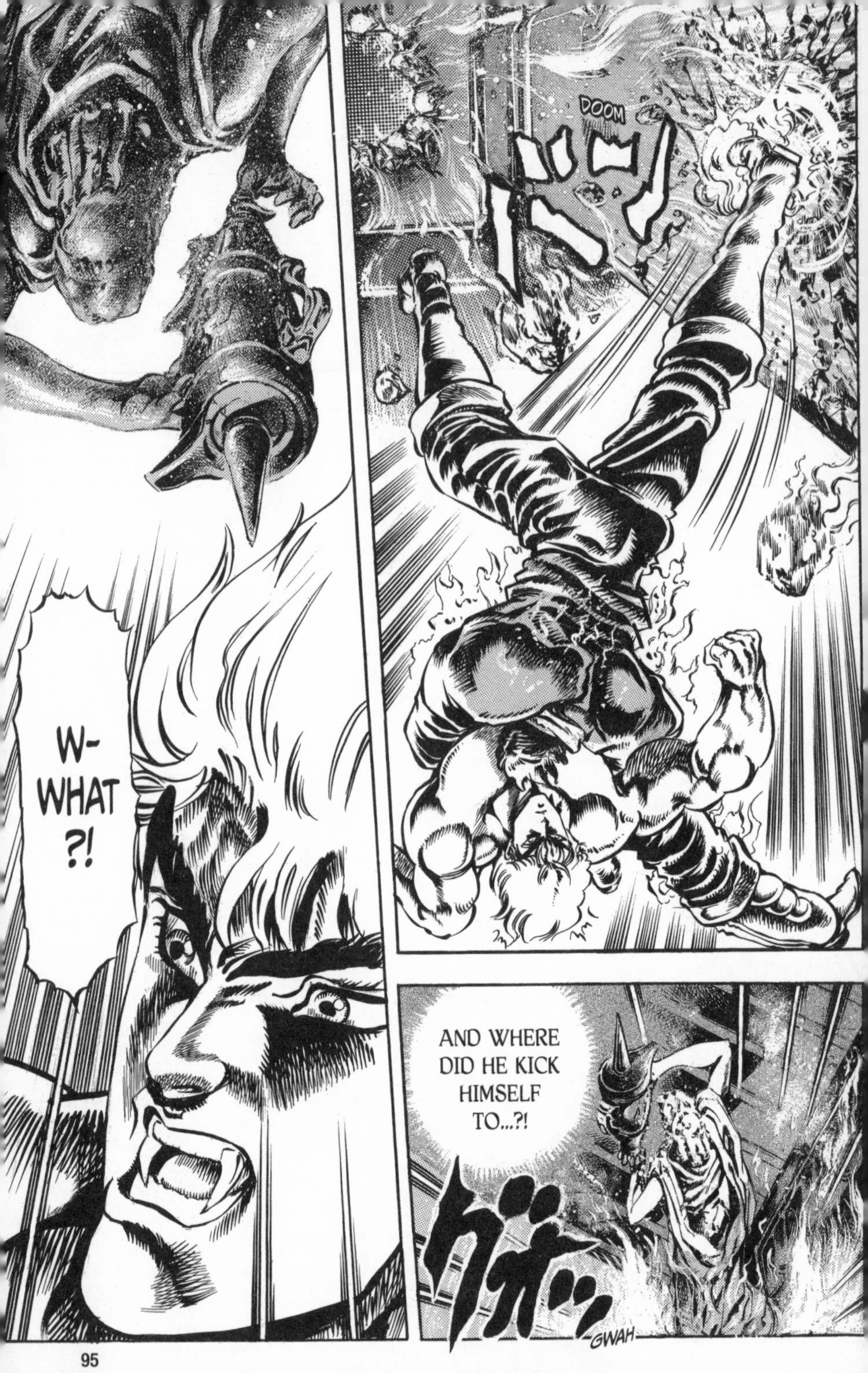
DOOM
AND WHERE DID HE KICK HIMSELF TO...?!
GWAH
W- WHAT ?!

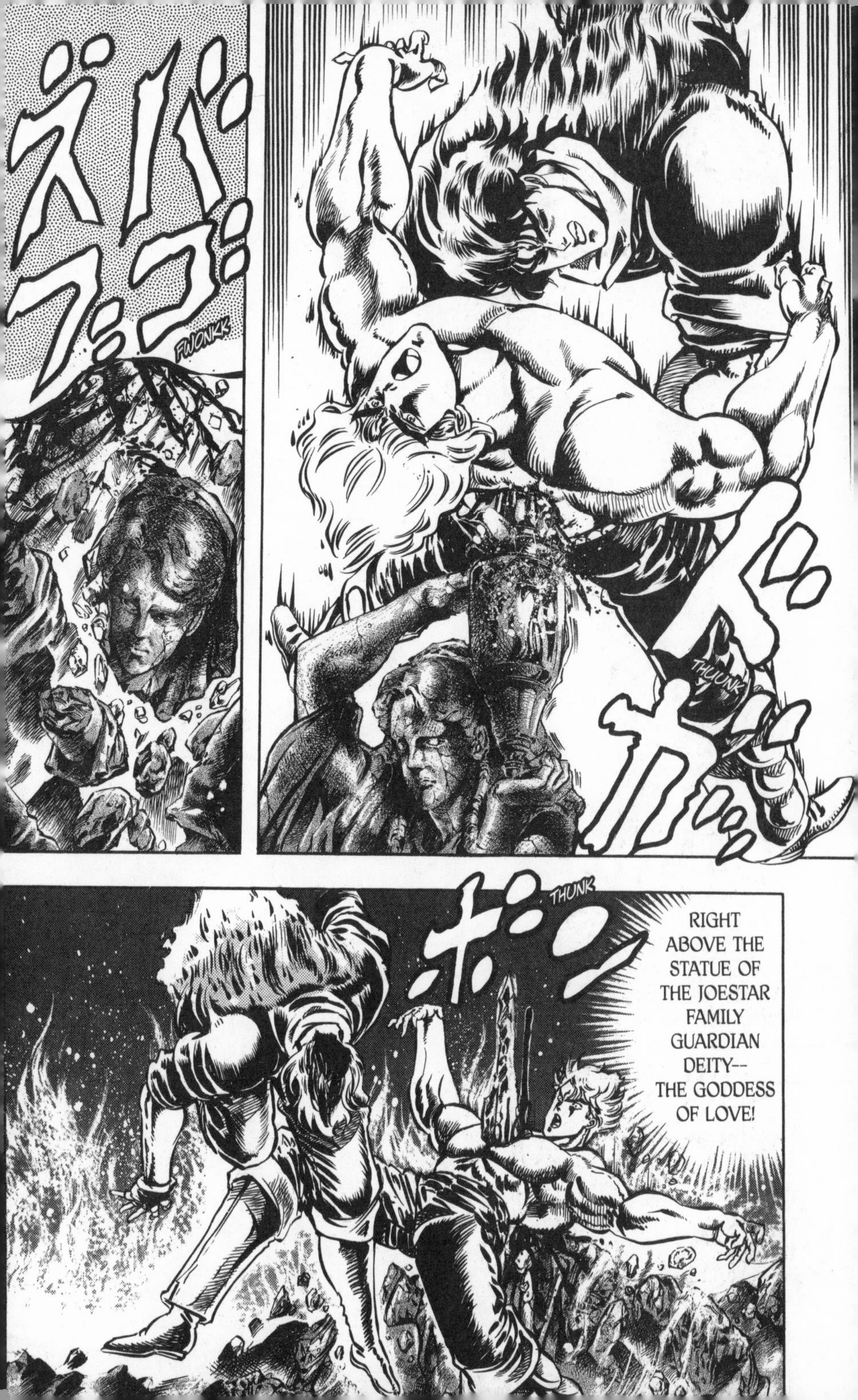
THUUNK
FWONKK
THUNK
RIGHT ABOVE THE STATUE OF THE JOESTAR FAMILY GUARDIAN DEITY-- THE GODDESS OF LOVE!

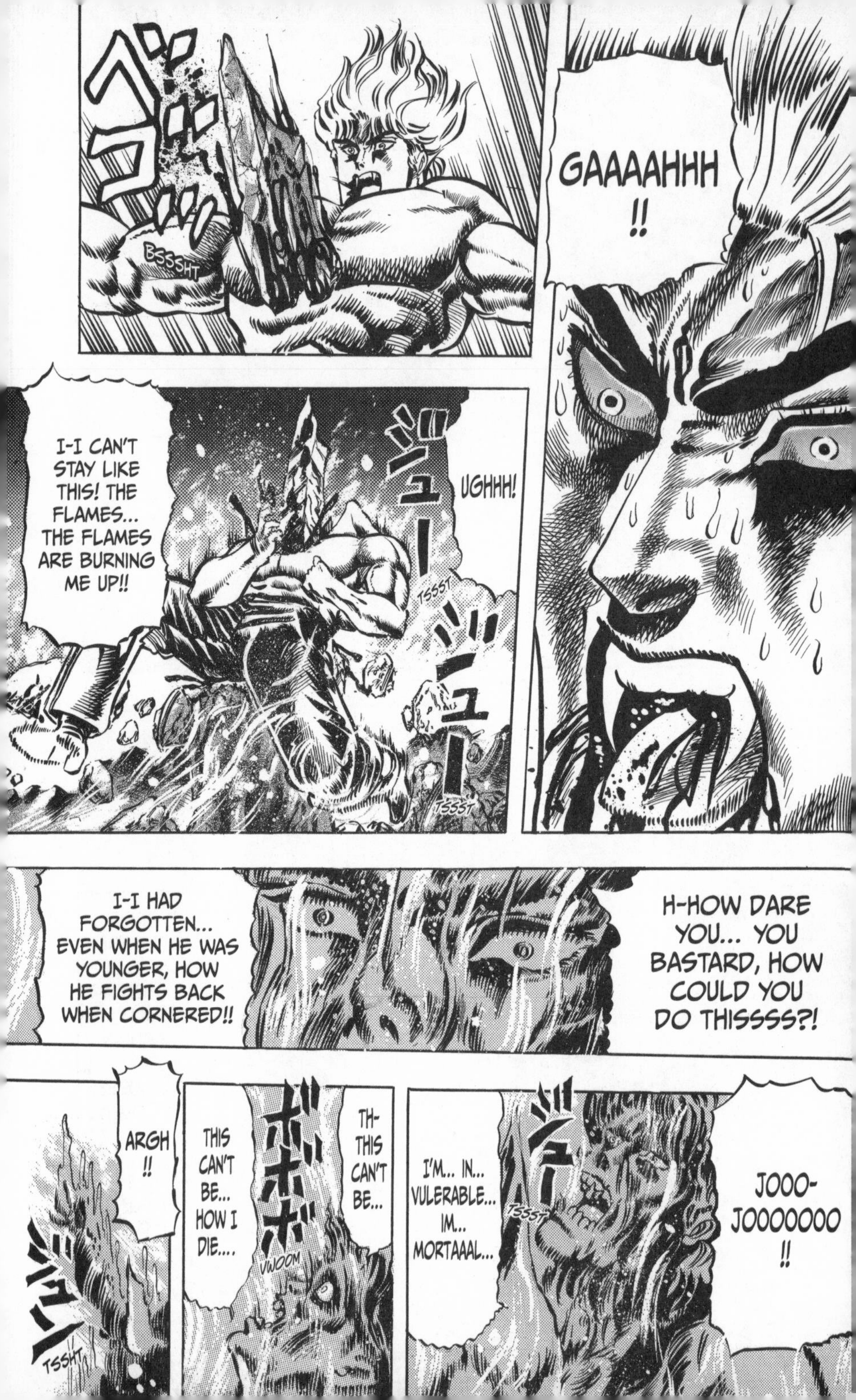
GAAAAHHH !!
BSSSHT
UGHHH!
I-I CAN'T STAY LIKE THIS! THE FLAMES... THE FLAMES ARE BURNING ME UP!!
TSSST
TSSST
H-HOW DARE YOU... YOU BASTARD, HOW COULD YOU DO THISSSS?!
I-I HAD FORGOTTEN... EVEN WHEN HE WAS YOUNGER, HOW HE FIGHTS BACK WHEN CORNERED!!
JOOO-JOOOOOOO !!
I'M... IN... VULERABLE... IM... MORTAAAL...
TSSST
TH-THIS CAN'T BE...
THIS CAN'T BE... HOW I DIE....
VWOOM
ARGH !!
TSSHT

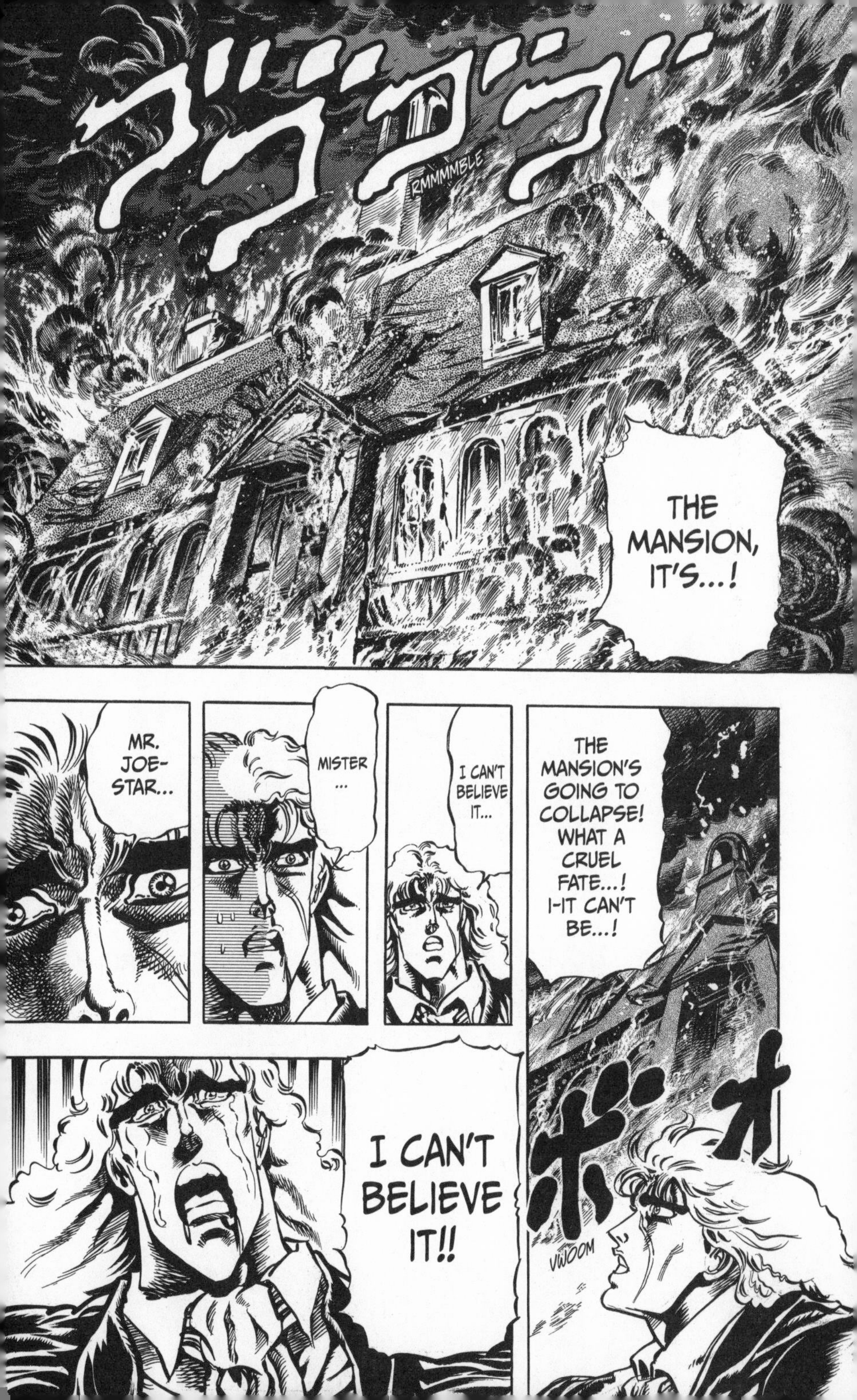
RMMMMBLE
THE MANSION, IT'S...!
THE MANSION'S GOING TO COLLAPSE! WHAT A CRUEL FATE...! I-IT CAN'T BE...!
VWOOM
I CAN'T BELIEVE IT...
MISTER ...
MR. JOE-STAR...
I CAN'T BELIEVE IT!!

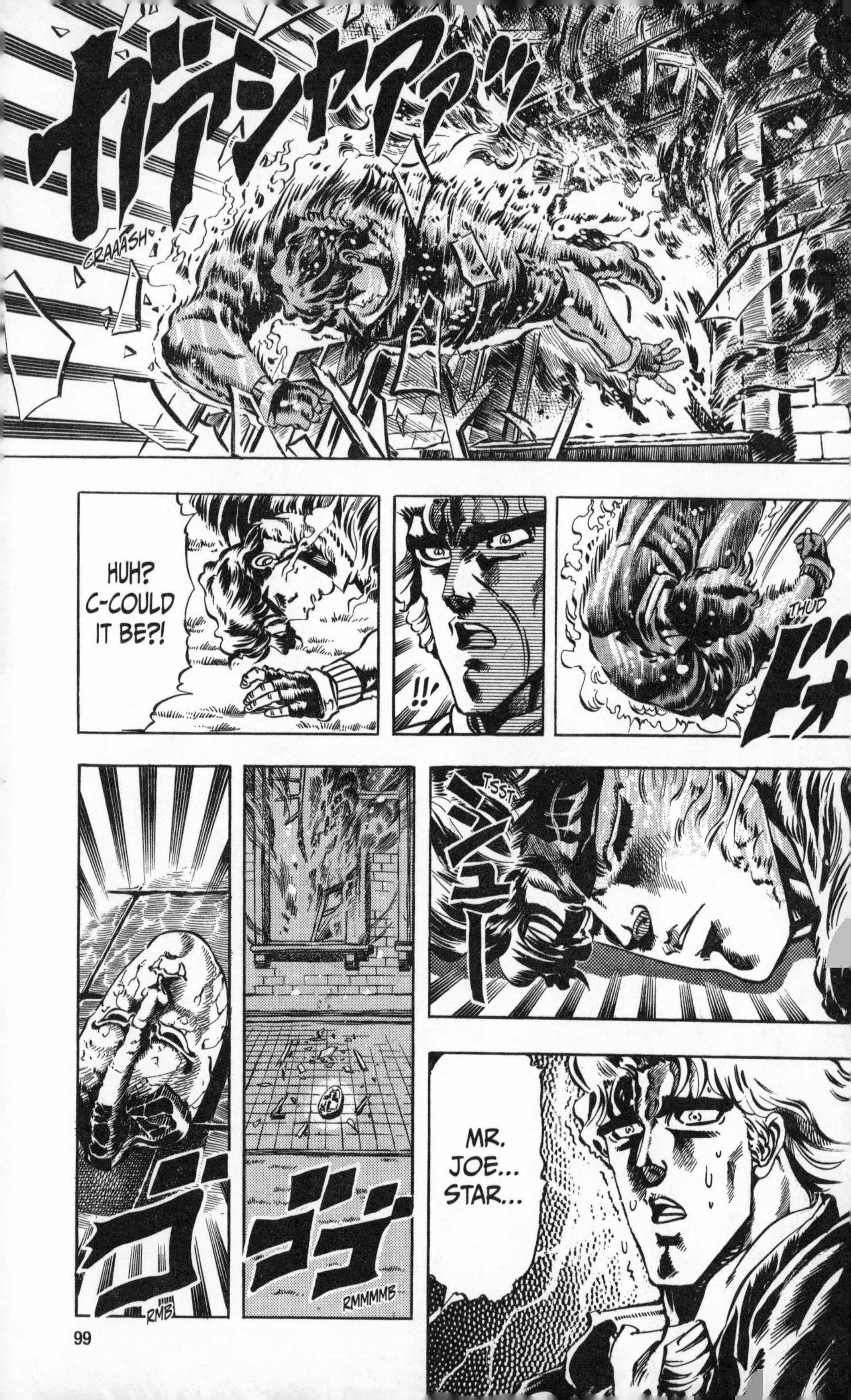
CRAAAASH
THUD
!!
HUH? C-COULD IT BE?!
TSST
MR. JOE... STAR...
RMMMMB
RMB

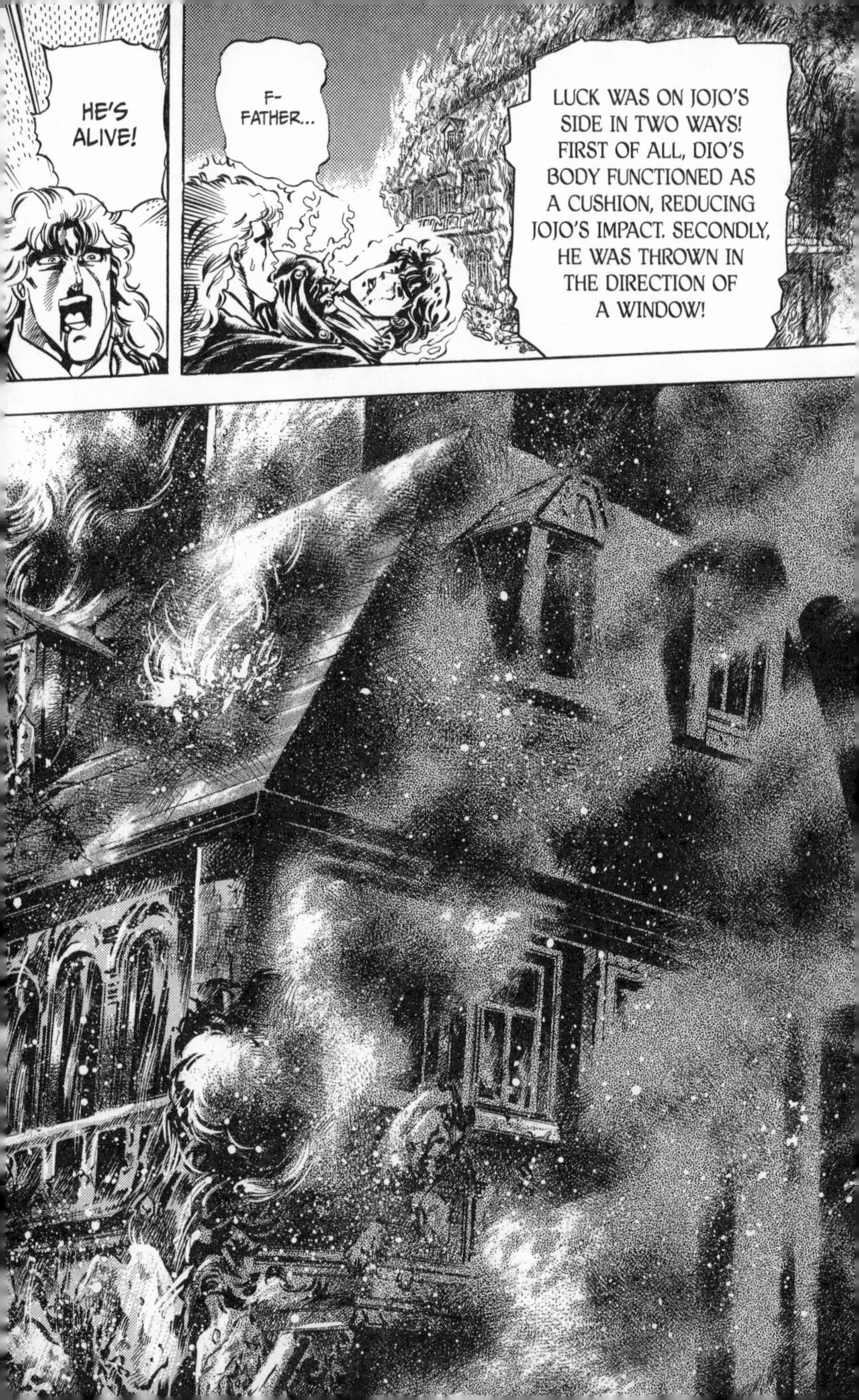
LUCK WAS ON JOJO'S SIDE IN TWO WAYS! FIRST OF ALL, DIO'S BODY FUNCTIONED AS A CUSHION, REDUCING JOJO'S IMPACT. SECONDLY, HE WAS THROWN IN THE DIRECTION OF A WINDOW!
F- FATHER...
HE'S ALIVE!

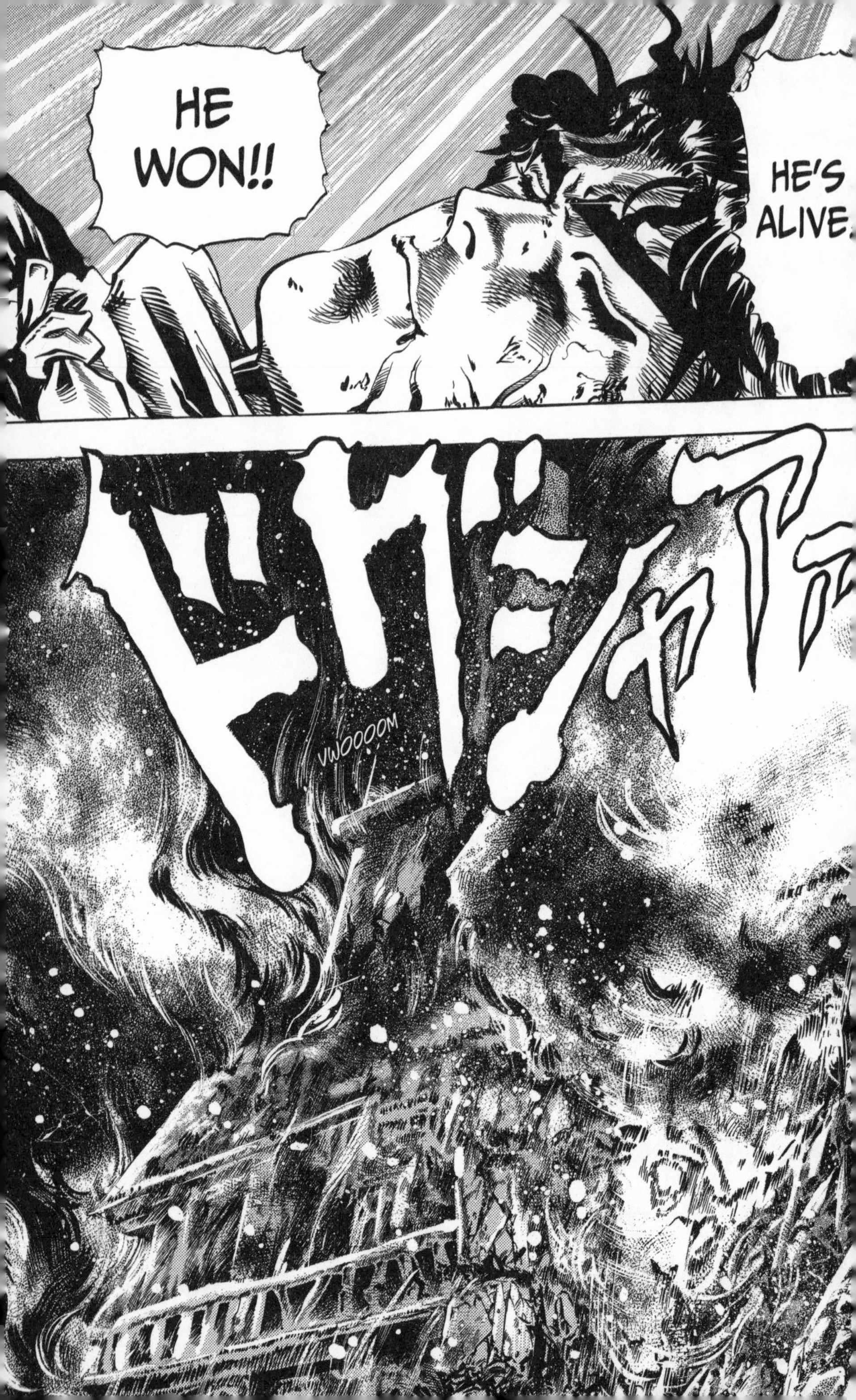
HE'S ALIVE.
HE WON!!
VWOOOOM

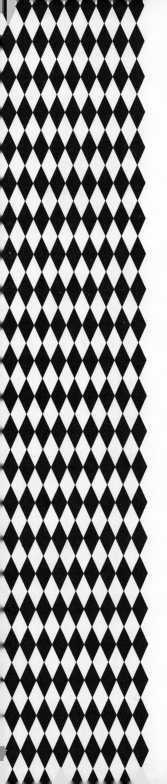

JoJo's

BIZARRE ADVENTURE

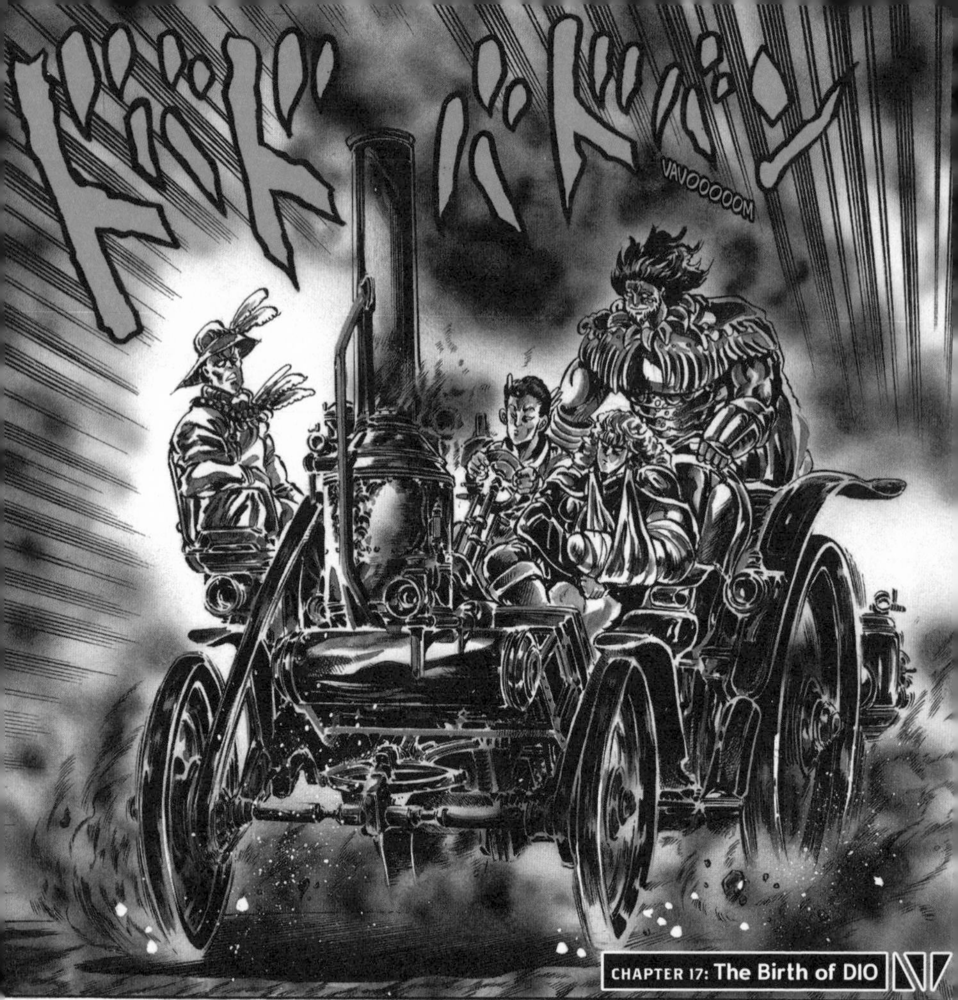
VAVOOOOOOM
CHAPTER 17: The Birth of DIO

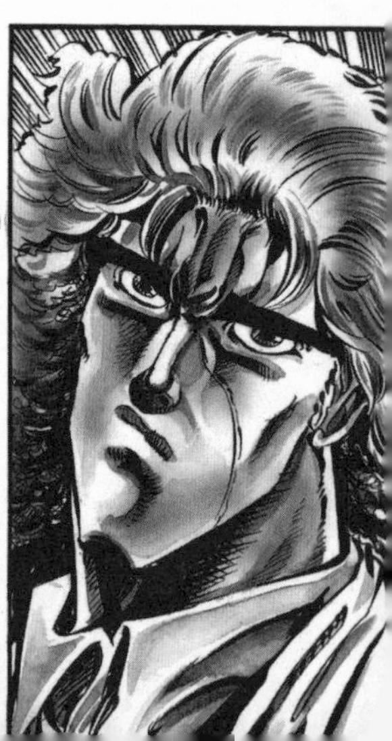

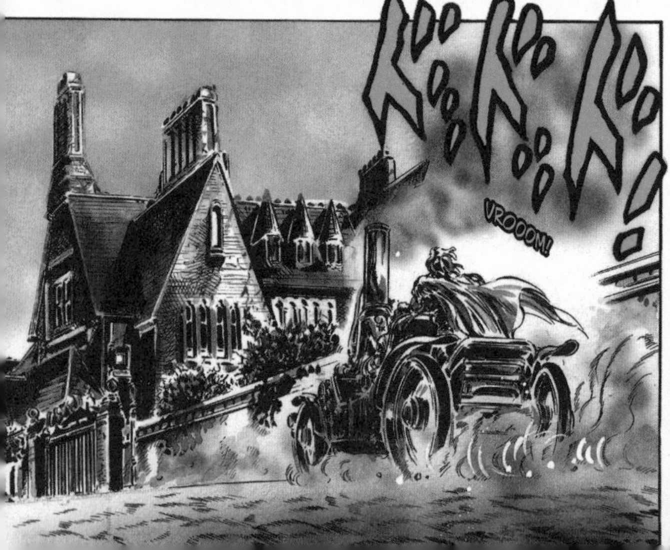
VROOOM!

CHAPTER 17: The Birth of DIO IV

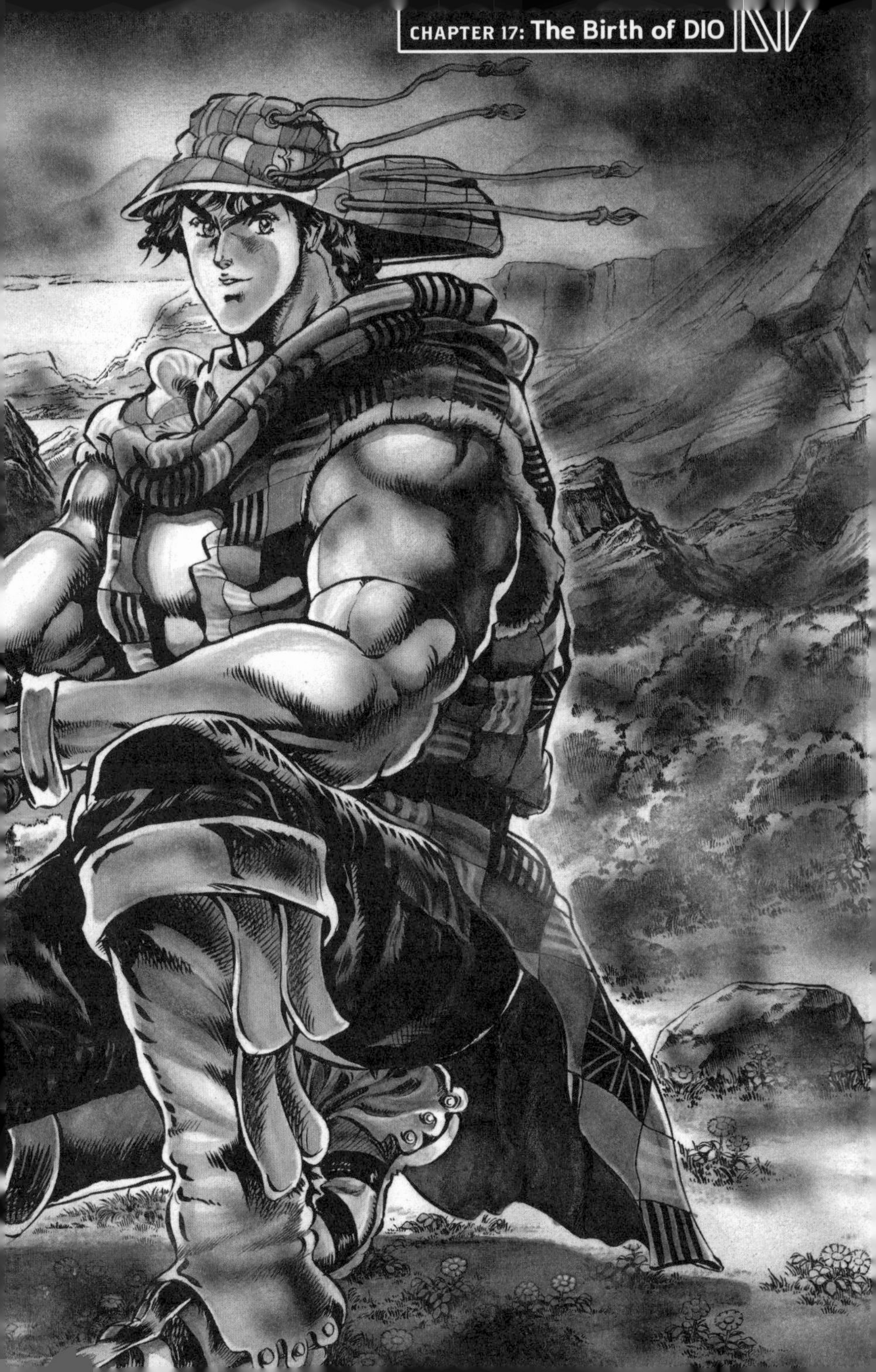

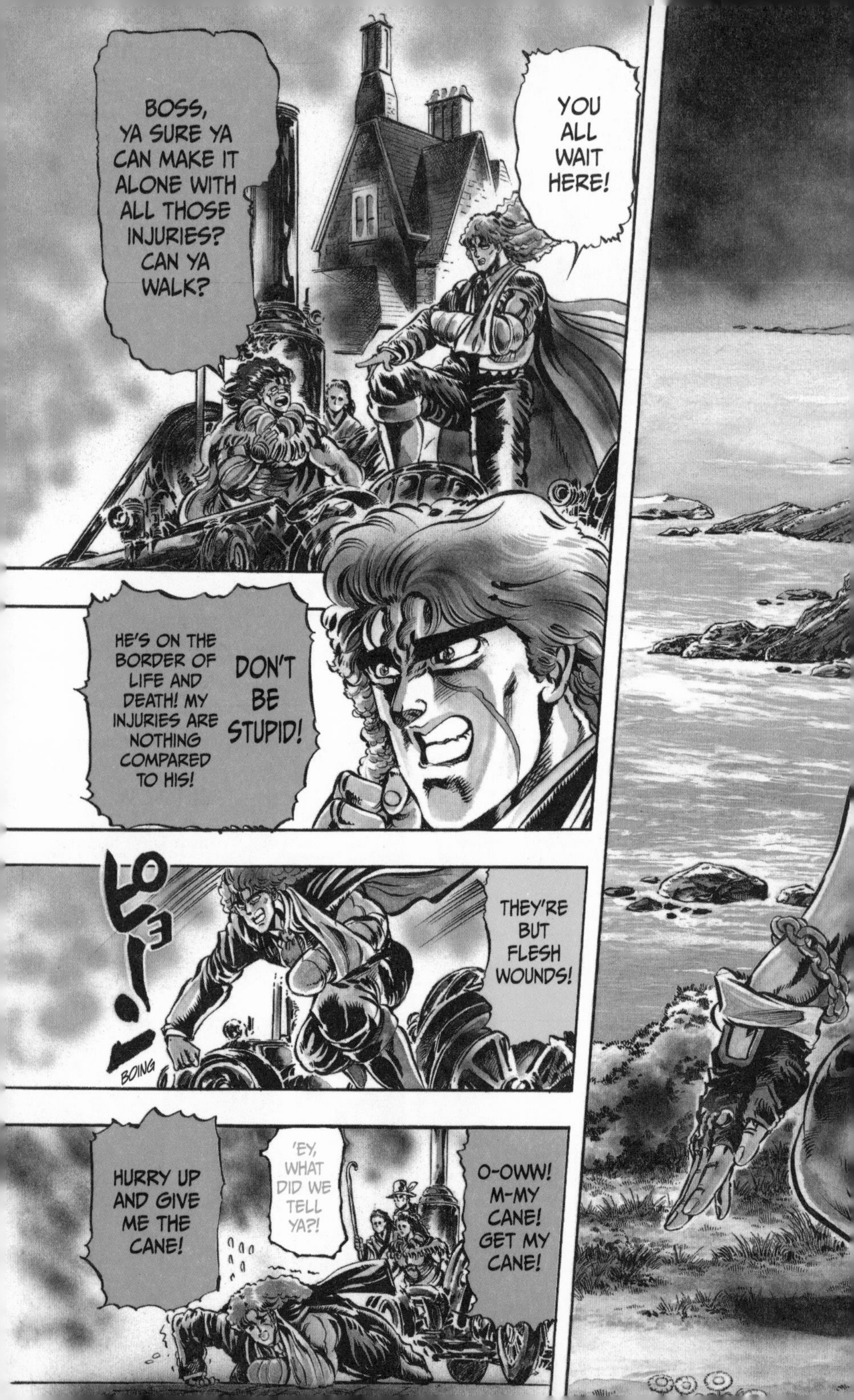
YOU ALL WAIT HERE!
BOSS, YA SURE YA CAN MAKE IT ALONE WITH ALL THOSE INJURIES? CAN YA WALK?
DON'T BE STUPID!
HE'S ON THE BORDER OF LIFE AND DEATH! MY INJURIES ARE NOTHING COMPARED TO HIS!
THEY'RE BUT FLESH WOUNDS!
BOING
O-OWW! M-MY CANE! GET MY CANE!
'EY, WHAT DID WE TELL YA?!
HURRY UP AND GIVE ME THE CANE!

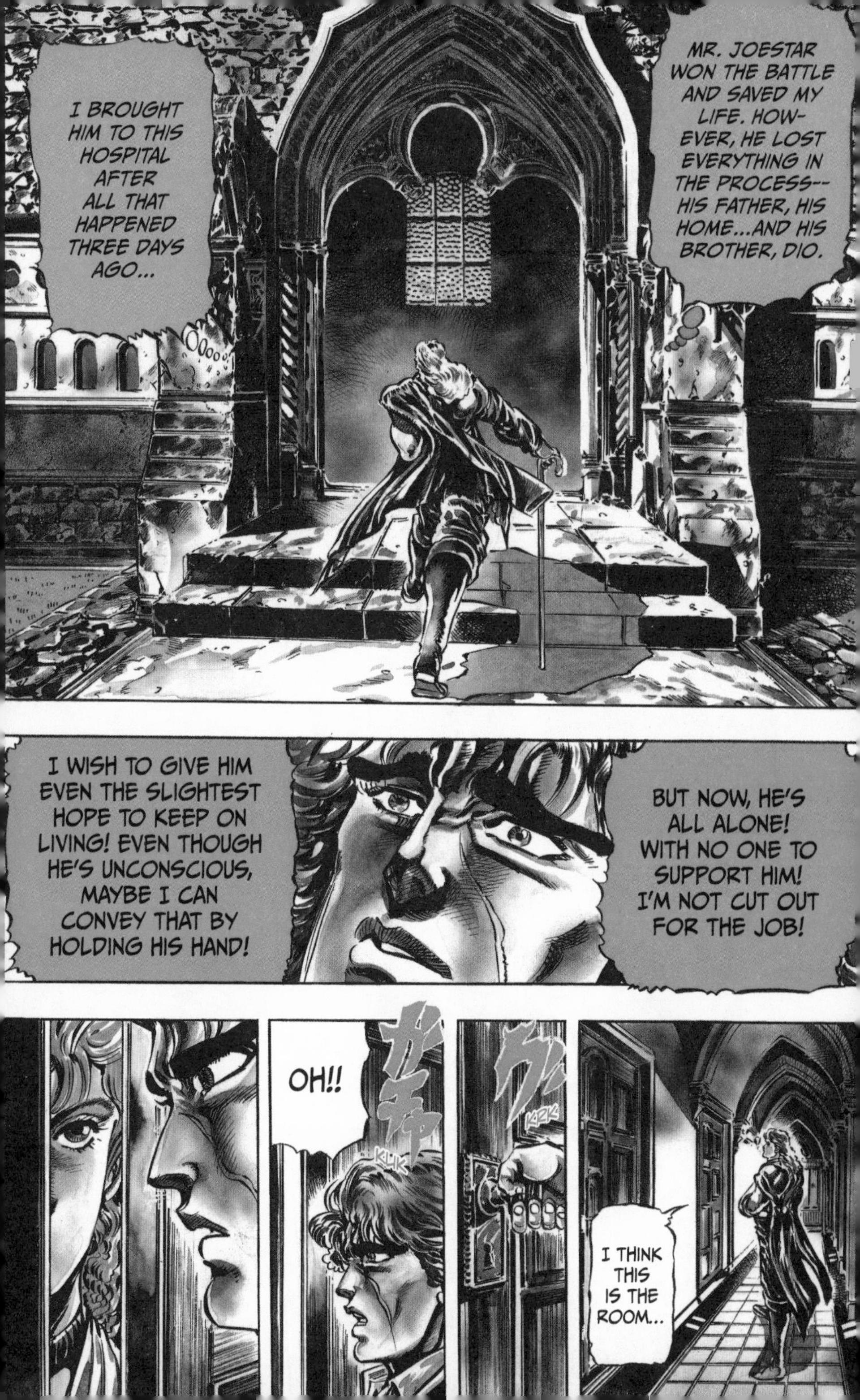
MR. JOESTAR WON THE BATTLE AND SAVED MY LIFE. HOW-EVER, HE LOST EVERYTHING IN THE PROCESS-- HIS FATHER, HIS HOME...AND HIS BROTHER, DIO.
I BROUGHT HIM TO THIS HOSPITAL AFTER ALL THAT HAPPENED THREE DAYS AGO...
BUT NOW, HE'S ALL ALONE! WITH NO ONE TO SUPPORT HIM! I'M NOT CUT OUT FOR THE JOB!
I WISH TO GIVE HIM EVEN THE SLIGHTEST HOPE TO KEEP ON LIVING! EVEN THOUGH HE'S UNCONSCIOUS, MAYBE I CAN CONVEY THAT BY HOLDING HIS HAND!
I THINK THIS IS THE ROOM...
KRK
ガチャ
KLIK
OH!!

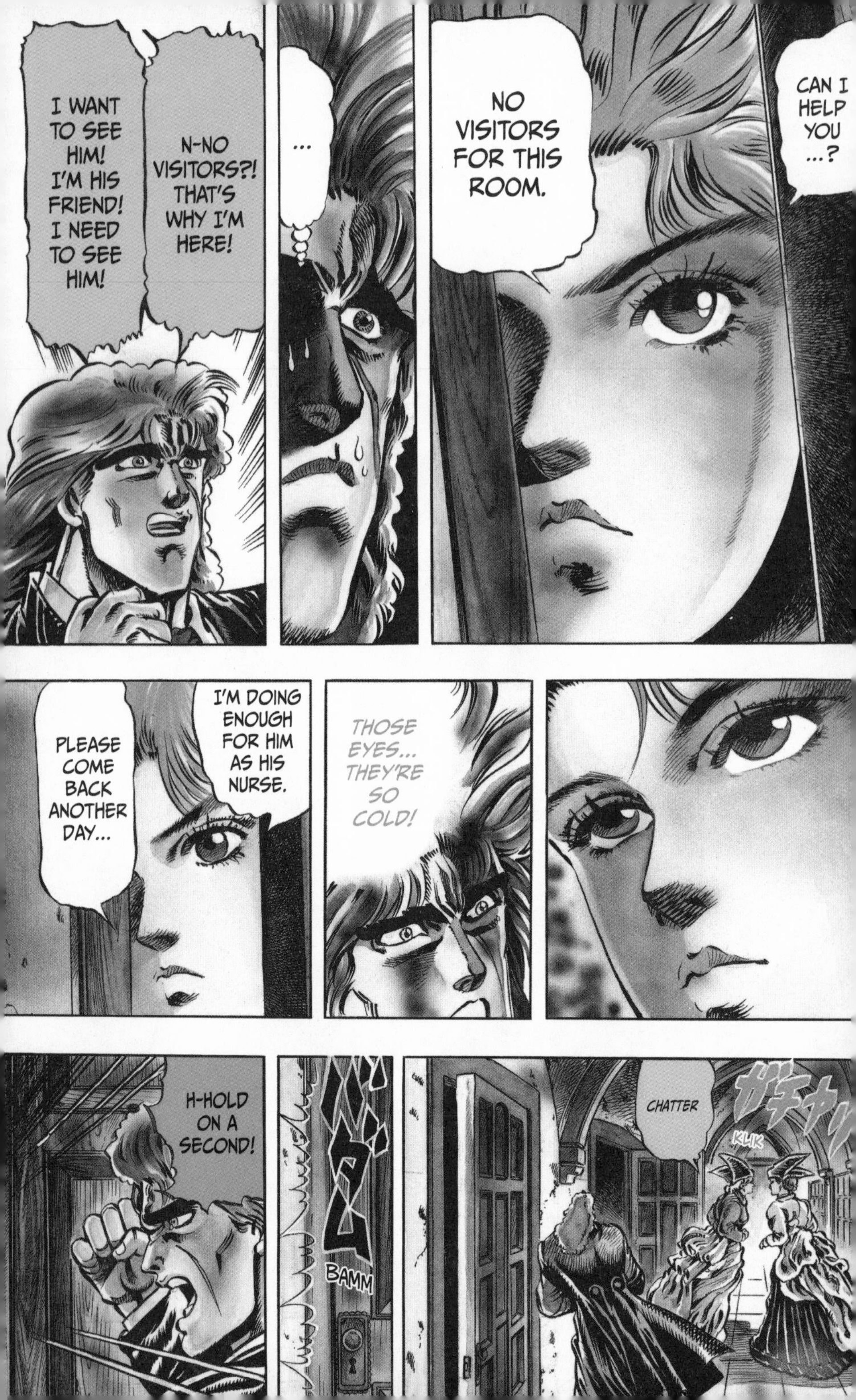
CAN I HELP YOU ...?
NO VISITORS FOR THIS ROOM.
...
N-NO VISITORS?! THAT'S WHY I'M HERE!
I WANT TO SEE HIM! I'M HIS FRIEND! I NEED TO SEE HIM!
THOSE EYES... THEY'RE SO COLD!
I'M DOING ENOUGH FOR HIM AS HIS NURSE.
PLEASE COME BACK ANOTHER DAY...
KLIK
CHATTER
BAMM
H-HOLD ON A SECOND!

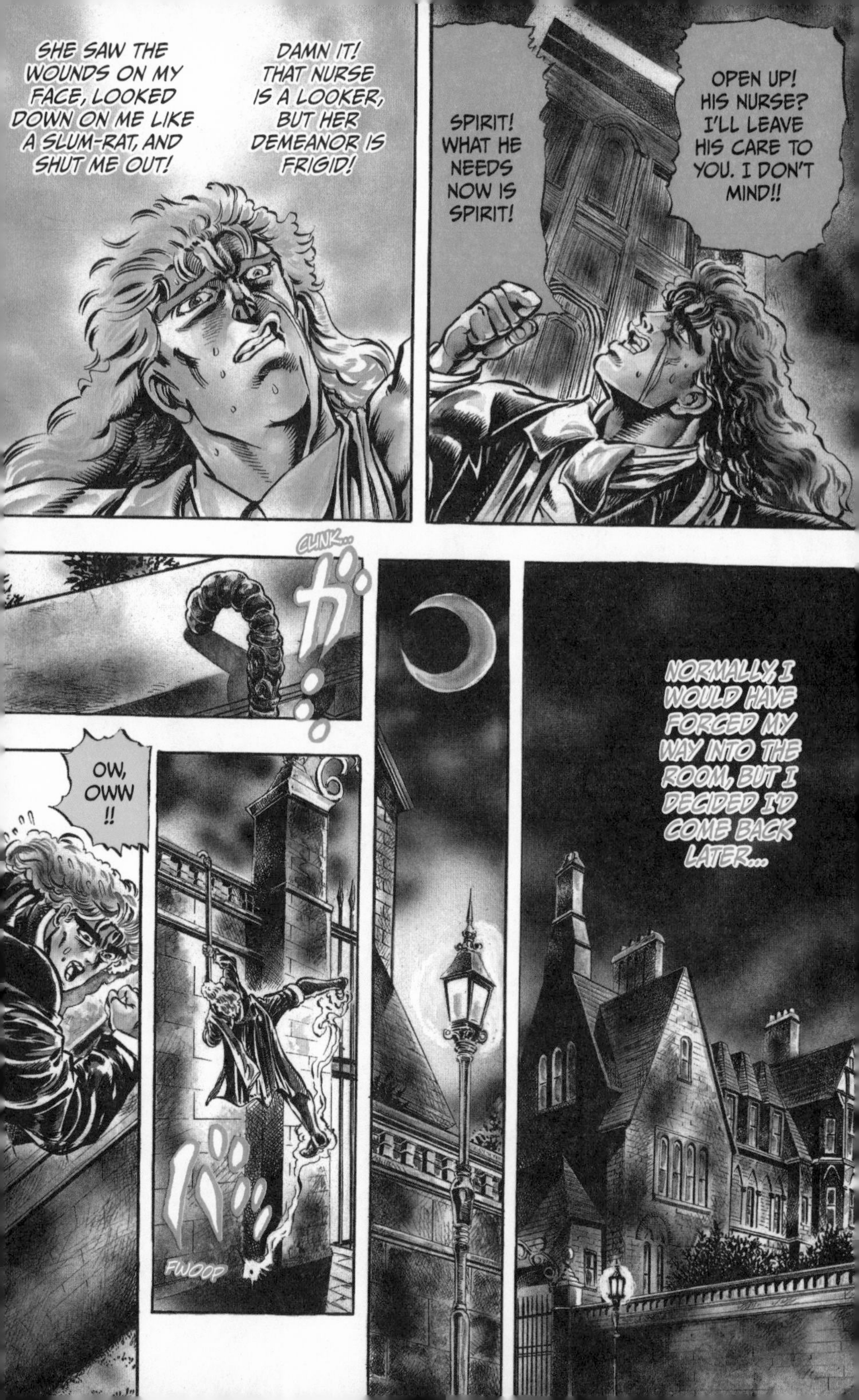
OPEN UP! HIS NURSE? I'LL LEAVE HIS CARE TO YOU. I DON'T MIND!!
SPIRIT! WHAT HE NEEDS NOW IS SPIRIT!
DAMN IT! THAT NURSE IS A LOOKER, BUT HER DEMEANOR IS FRIGID!
SHE SAW THE WOUNDS ON MY FACE, LOOKED DOWN ON ME LIKE A SLUM-RAT, AND SHUT ME OUT!
NORMALLY, I WOULD HAVE FORCED MY WAY INTO THE ROOM, BUT I DECIDED I'D COME BACK LATER...
CLUNK...
ガ
バ
FWOOP
OW, OWW !!

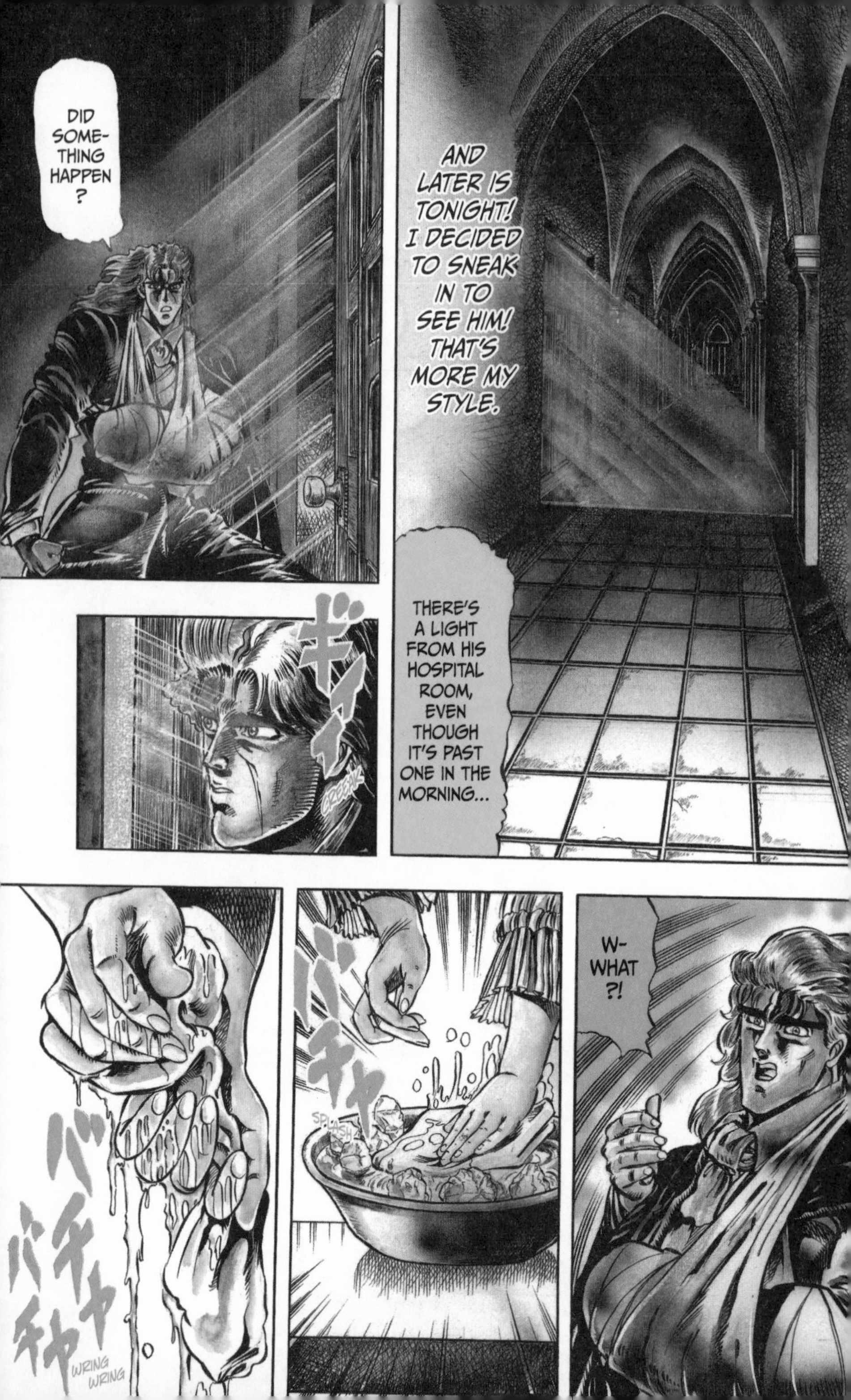
AND LATER IS TONIGHT! I DECIDED TO SNEAK IN TO SEE HIM! THAT'S MORE MY STYLE.
THERE'S A LIGHT FROM HIS HOSPITAL ROOM, EVEN THOUGH IT'S PAST ONE IN THE MORNING...
DID SOMETHING HAPPEN?
CREEAK
W-WHAT?!
SPLASH
WRING WRING

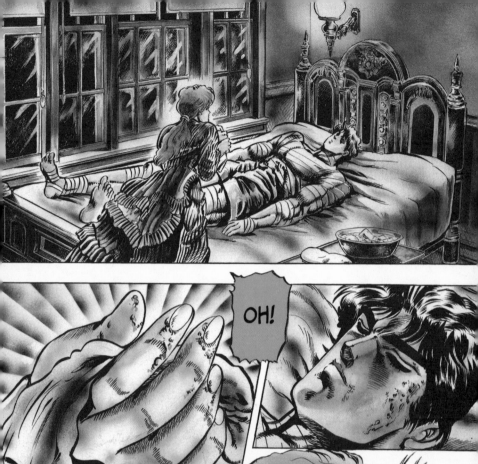

OH!

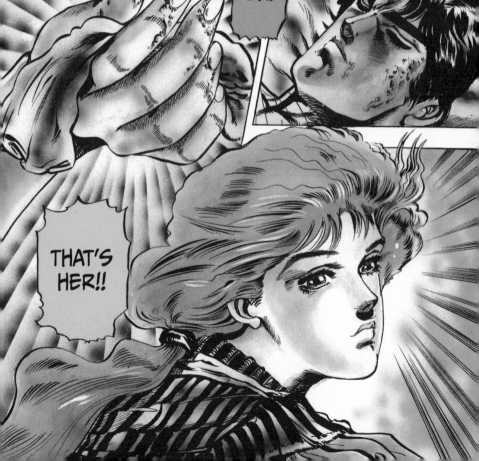

THAT'S HER!!

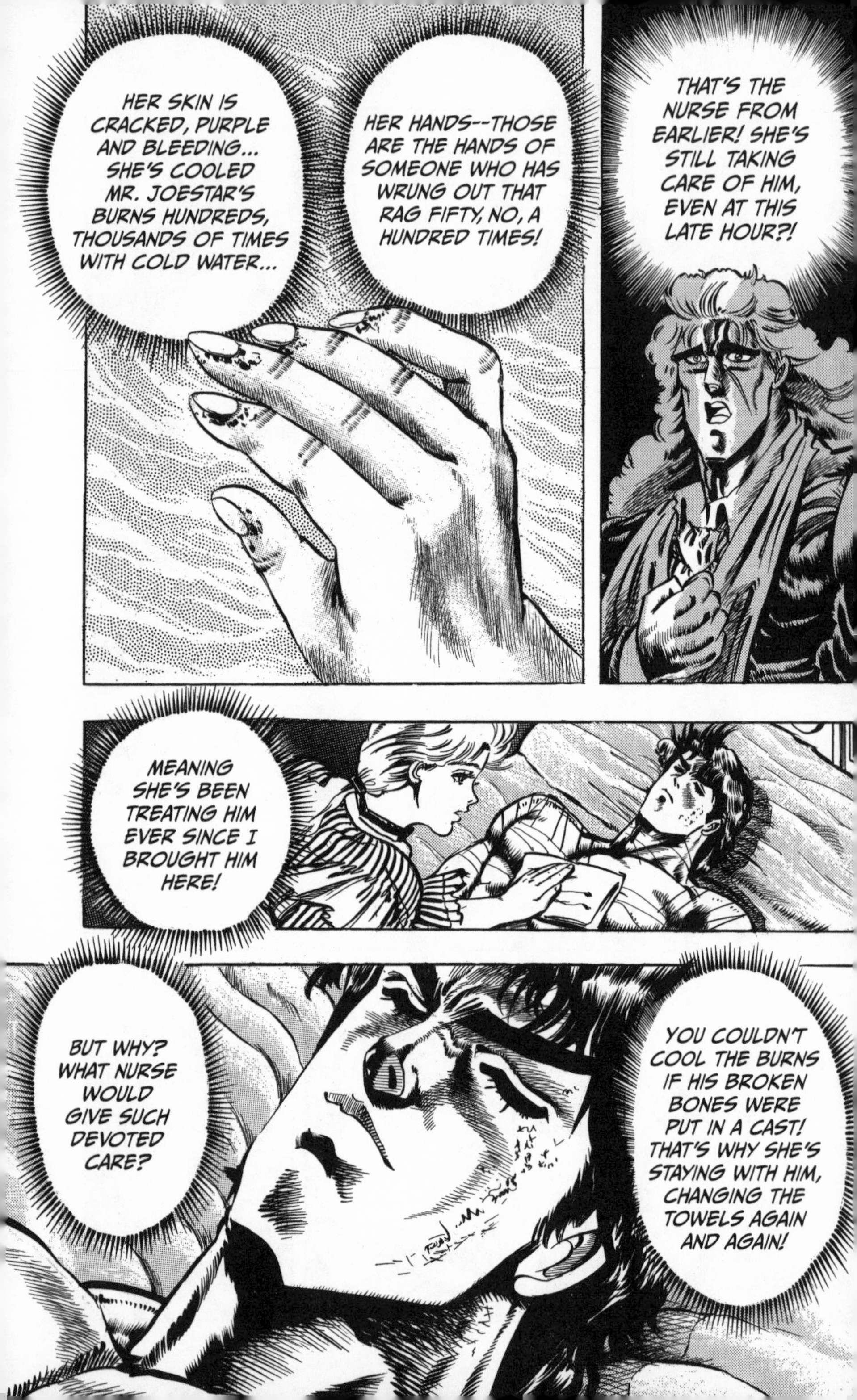
THAT'S THE NURSE FROM EARLIER! SHE'S STILL TAKING CARE OF HIM, EVEN AT THIS LATE HOUR?!
HER HANDS--THOSE ARE THE HANDS OF SOMEONE WHO HAS WRUNG OUT THAT RAG FIFTY, NO, A HUNDRED TIMES!
HER SKIN IS CRACKED, PURPLE AND BLEEDING... SHE'S COOLED MR. JOESTAR'S BURNS HUNDREDS, THOUSANDS OF TIMES WITH COLD WATER...
MEANING SHE'S BEEN TREATING HIM EVER SINCE I BROUGHT HIM HERE!
YOU COULDN'T COOL THE BURNS IF HIS BROKEN BONES WERE PUT IN A CAST! THAT'S WHY SHE'S STAYING WITH HIM, CHANGING THE TOWELS AGAIN AND AGAIN!
BUT WHY? WHAT NURSE WOULD GIVE SUCH DEVOTED CARE?

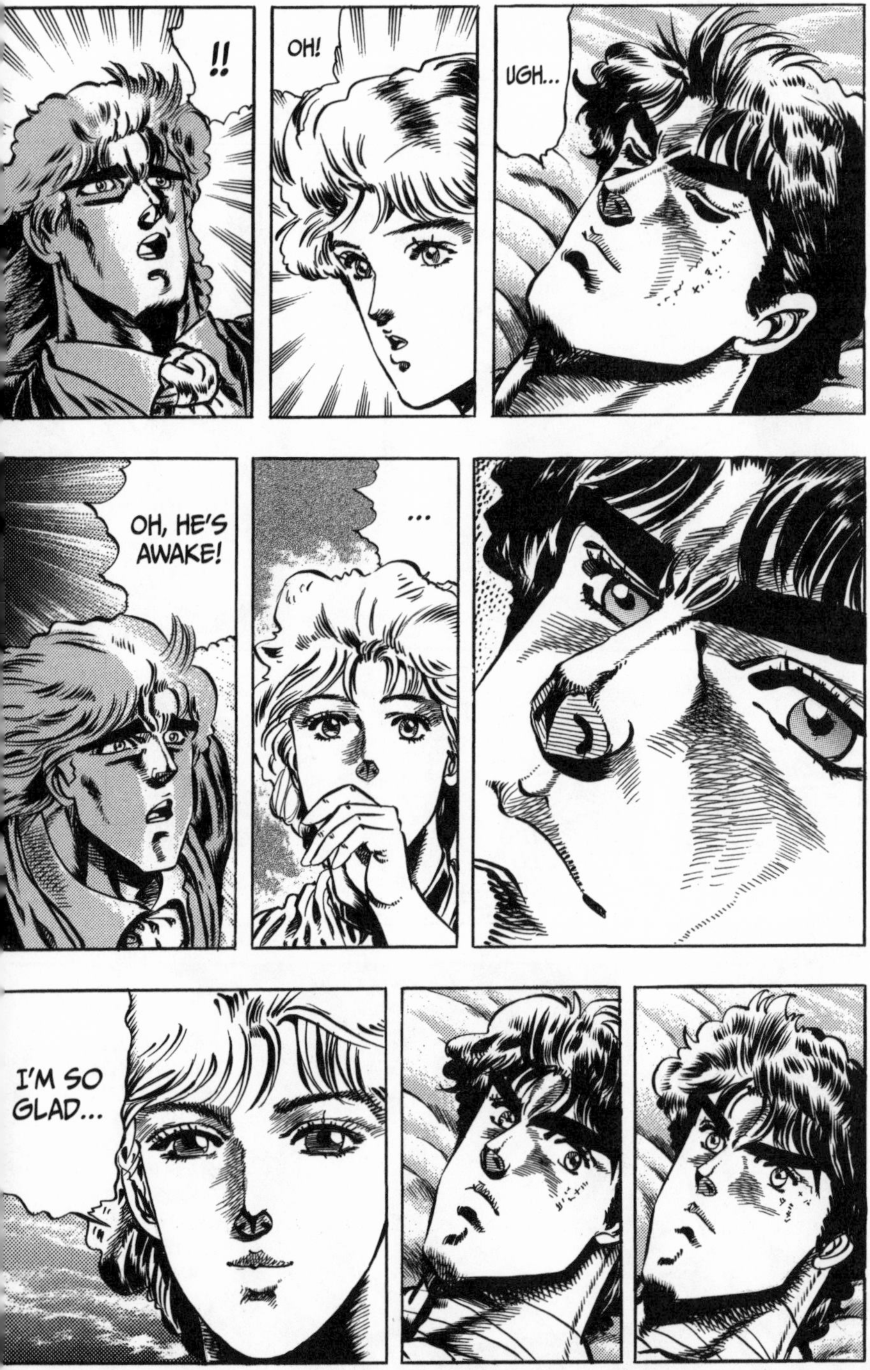
UGH...
OH!
!!
...
OH, HE'S AWAKE!
I'M SO GLAD...

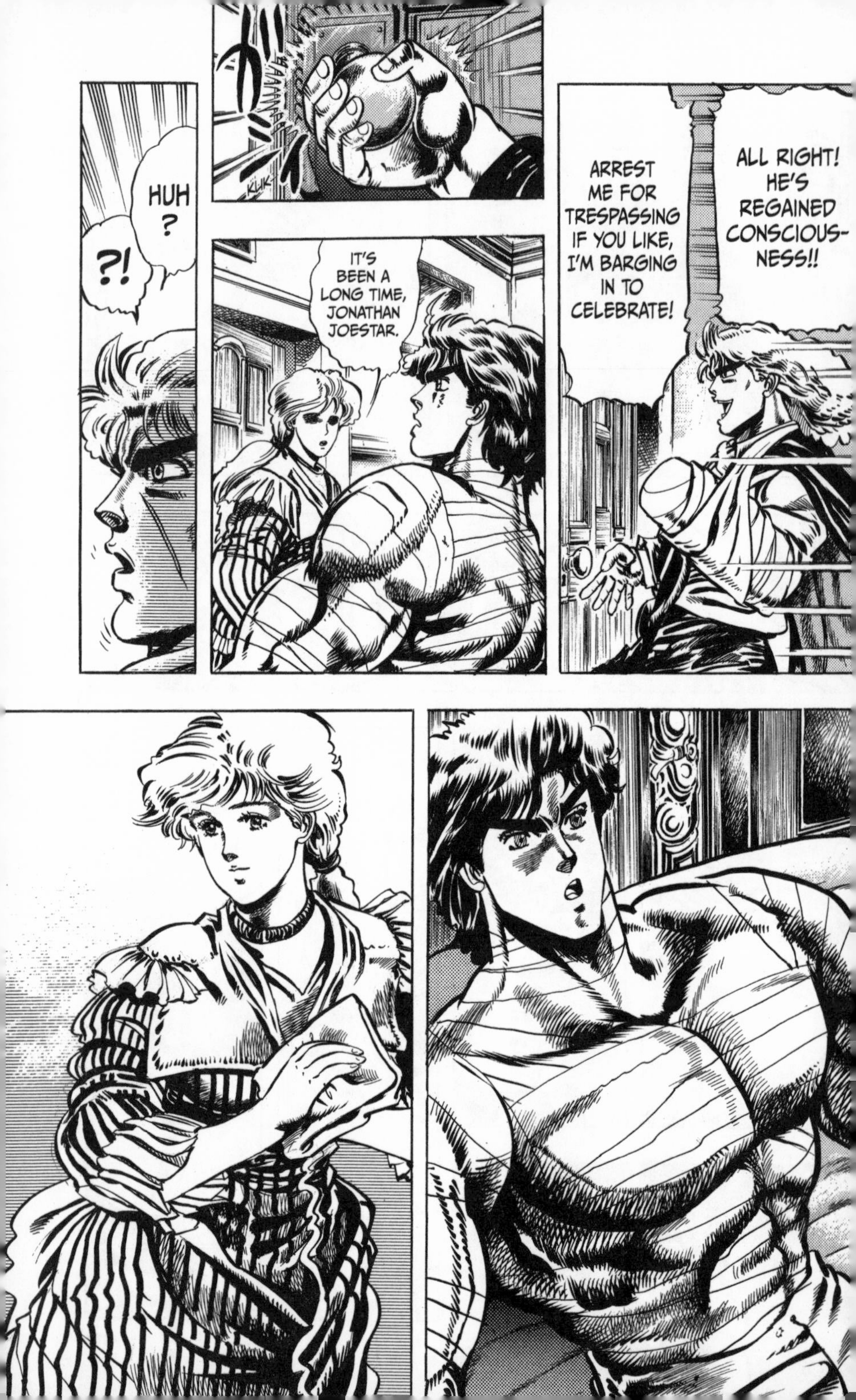

ALL RIGHT! HE'S REGAINED CONSCIOUS-NESS!!
ARREST ME FOR TRESPASSING IF YOU LIKE, I'M BARGING IN TO CELEBRATE!
KUK
IT'S BEEN A LONG TIME, JONATHAN JOESTAR.
HUH?
?!

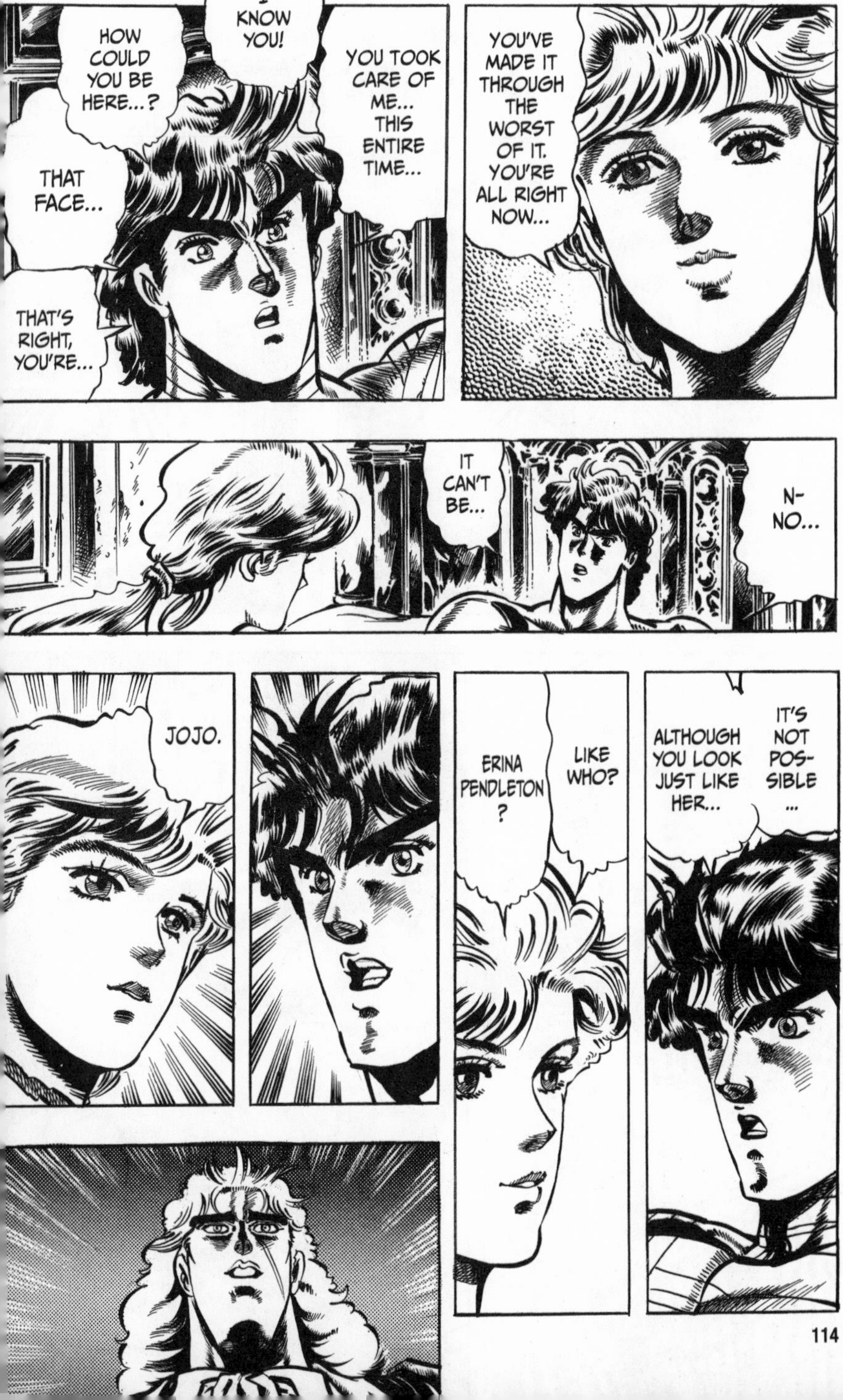
YOU'VE MADE IT THROUGH THE WORST OF IT. YOU'RE ALL RIGHT NOW...
YOU TOOK CARE OF ME... THIS ENTIRE TIME...
I KNOW YOU!
HOW COULD YOU BE HERE...?
THAT FACE...
THAT'S RIGHT, YOU'RE...
N-NO...
IT CAN'T BE...
IT'S NOT POSSIBLE...
ALTHOUGH YOU LOOK JUST LIKE HER...
LIKE WHO?
ERINA PENDLETON?
JOJO.

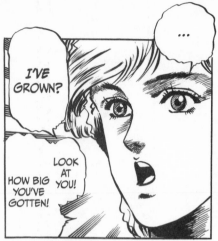

ERINA...! YOU'VE GROWN!
...
I'VE GROWN?
LOOK AT YOU!
HOW BIG YOU'VE GOTTEN!
ジワ...
SOB...
IT'S REALLY BEEN TOO LONG.
IT LOOKS AS IF THEY'RE ACQUAINTED... AND THEY'VE SHARED SOME WONDERFUL MEMORIES TOGETHER IN THE PAST.
IT SEEMS THAT IT'S BEEN YEARS SINCE THEY'VE SEEN EACH OTHER. I LEARNED THIS LATER, BUT HER FATHER RELOCATED TO INDIA SEVEN YEARS AGO FOR WORK. SHE ONLY RECENTLY RETURNED, AND IT TURNS OUT THAT THE HOSPITAL THAT I BROUGHT MR. JOESTAR TO WAS HER FATHER'S...

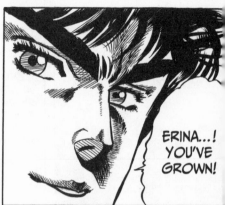

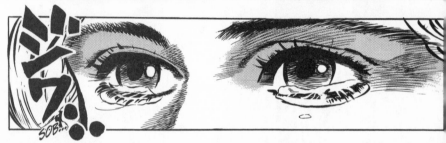

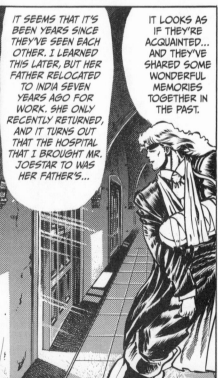

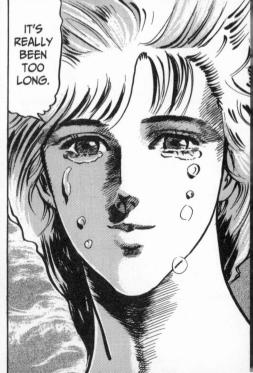

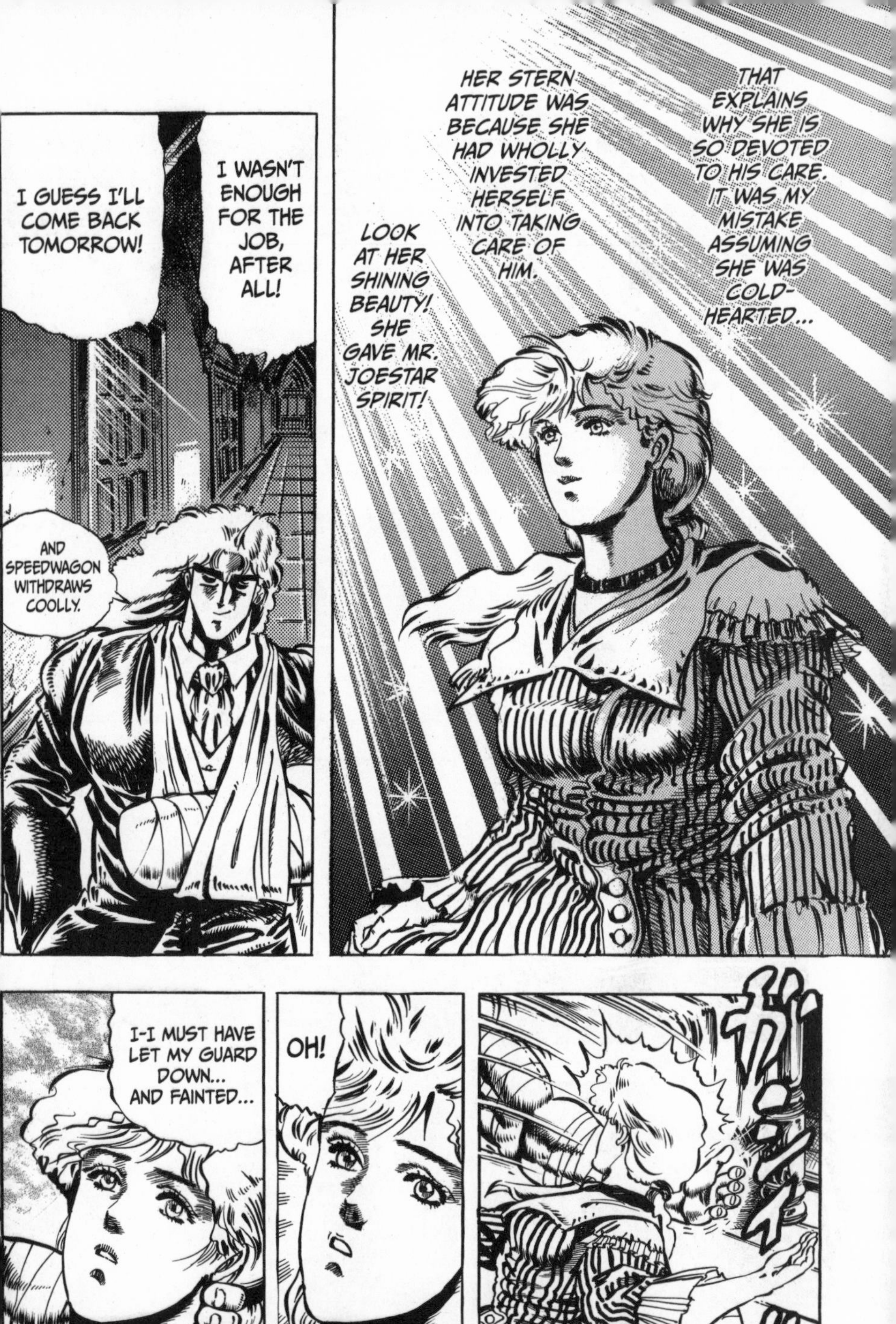
THAT EXPLAINS WHY SHE IS SO DEVOTED TO HIS CARE. IT WAS MY MISTAKE ASSUMING SHE WAS COLD-HEARTED...
HER STERN ATTITUDE WAS BECAUSE SHE HAD WHOLLY INVESTED HERSELF INTO TAKING CARE OF HIM.
LOOK AT HER SHINING BEAUTY! SHE GAVE MR. JOESTAR SPIRIT!
I WASN'T ENOUGH FOR THE JOB, AFTER ALL!
I GUESS I'LL COME BACK TOMORROW!
AND SPEEDWAGON WITHDRAWS COOLLY.
SNOOP
OH!
I-I MUST HAVE LET MY GUARD DOWN... AND FAINTED...

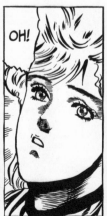

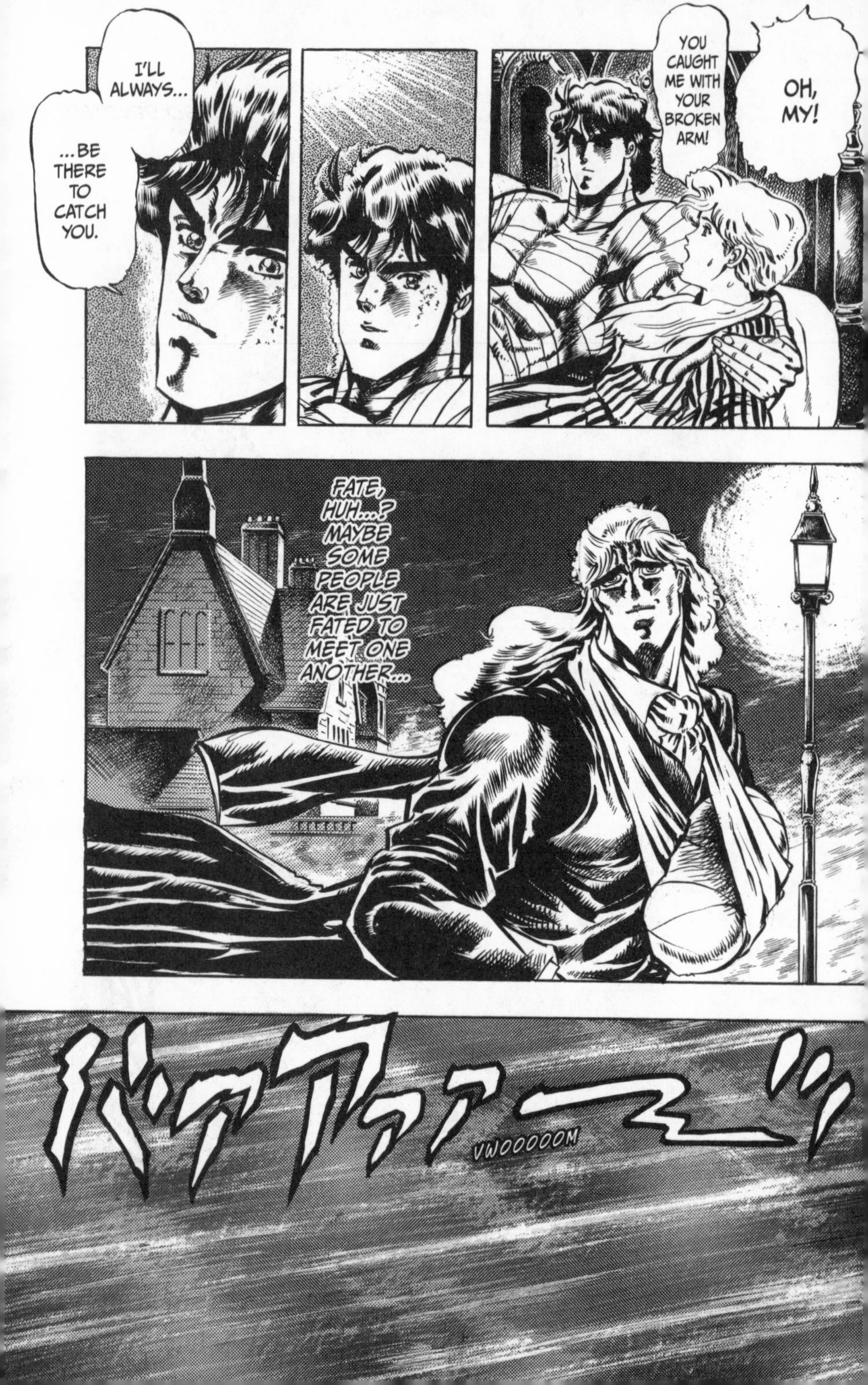
OH, MY!
YOU CAUGHT ME WITH YOUR BROKEN ARM!
I'LL ALWAYS...
...BE THERE TO CATCH YOU.
FATE, HUH...? MAYBE SOME PEOPLE ARE JUST FATED TO MEET ONE ANOTHER...
バアァァーッ
VWOOOOOM

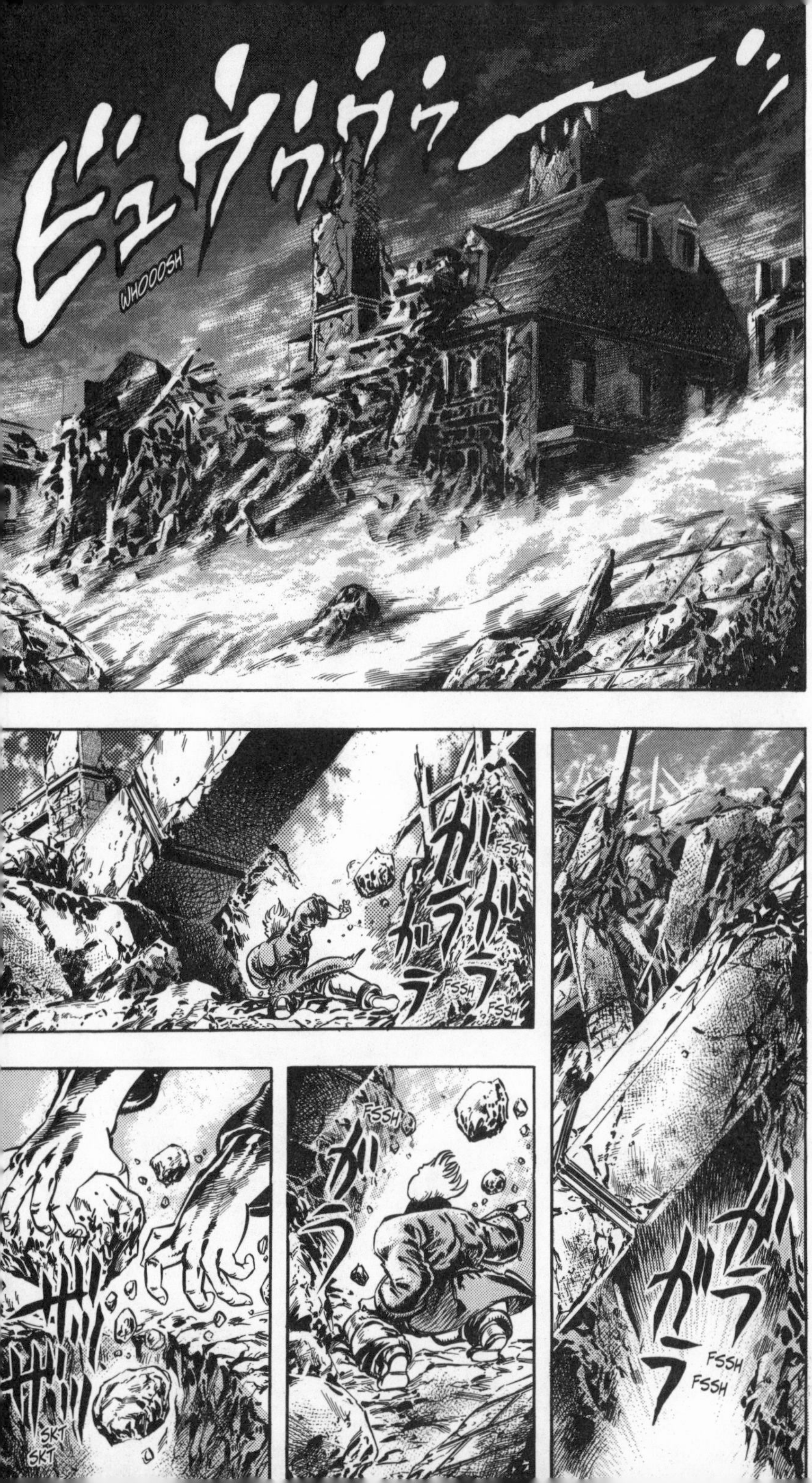

ビュウゥウゥー
WHOOOSH
ガラガラ
FSSH
FSSH
ガラガラ
FSSH
FSSH
FSSH
FSSH
ガラ
ザリ
ザリ
SKT
SKT

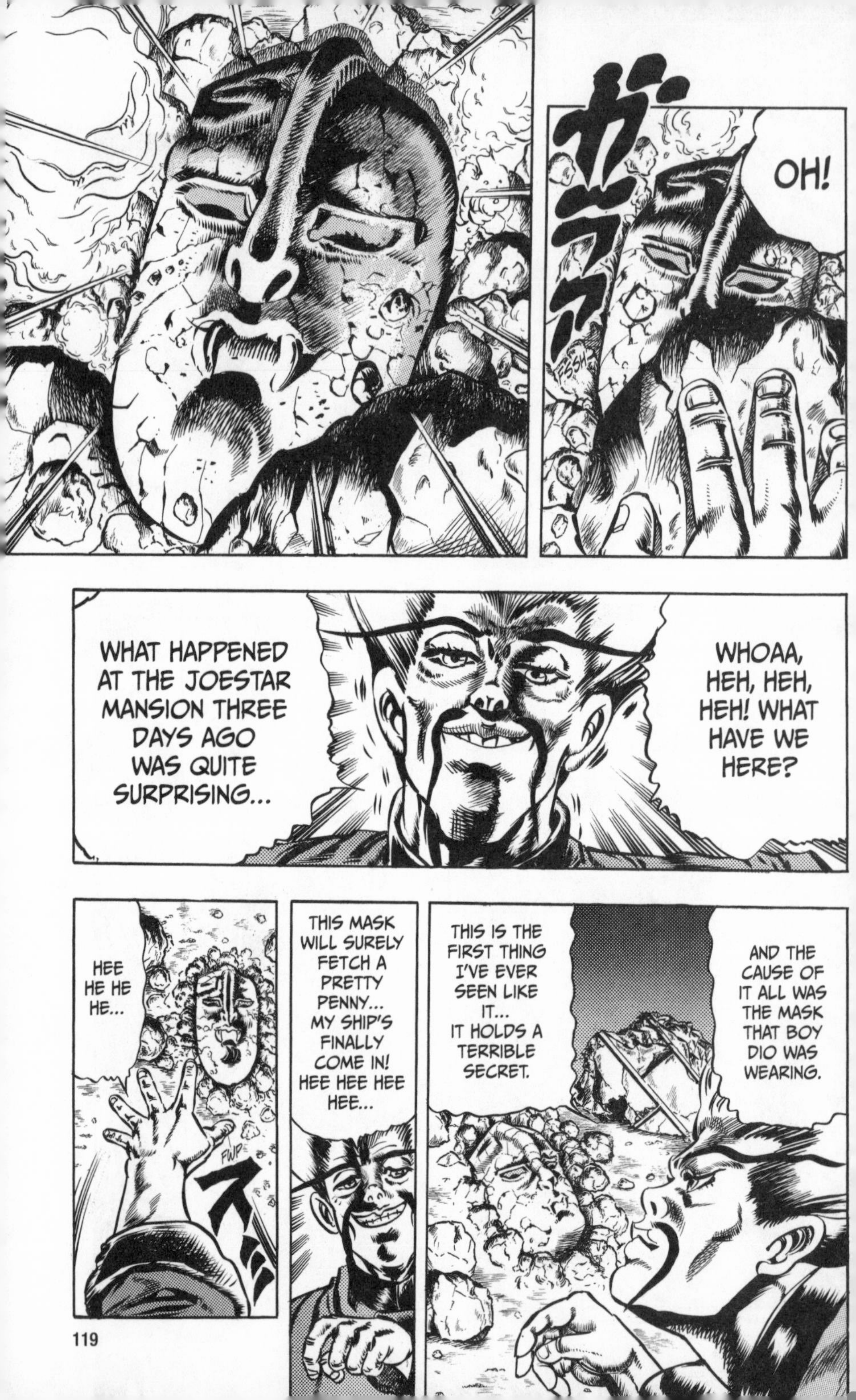
ガララ
OH!
FSSH
WHOAA, HEH, HEH, HEH! WHAT HAVE WE HERE?
WHAT HAPPENED AT THE JOESTAR MANSION THREE DAYS AGO WAS QUITE SURPRISING...
AND THE CAUSE OF IT ALL WAS THE MASK THAT BOY DIO WAS WEARING.
THIS IS THE FIRST THING I'VE EVER SEEN LIKE IT... IT HOLDS A TERRIBLE SECRET.
THIS MASK WILL SURELY FETCH A PRETTY PENNY... MY SHIP'S FINALLY COME IN! HEE HEE HEE HEE...
HEE HE HE HE...
FWP
スッ

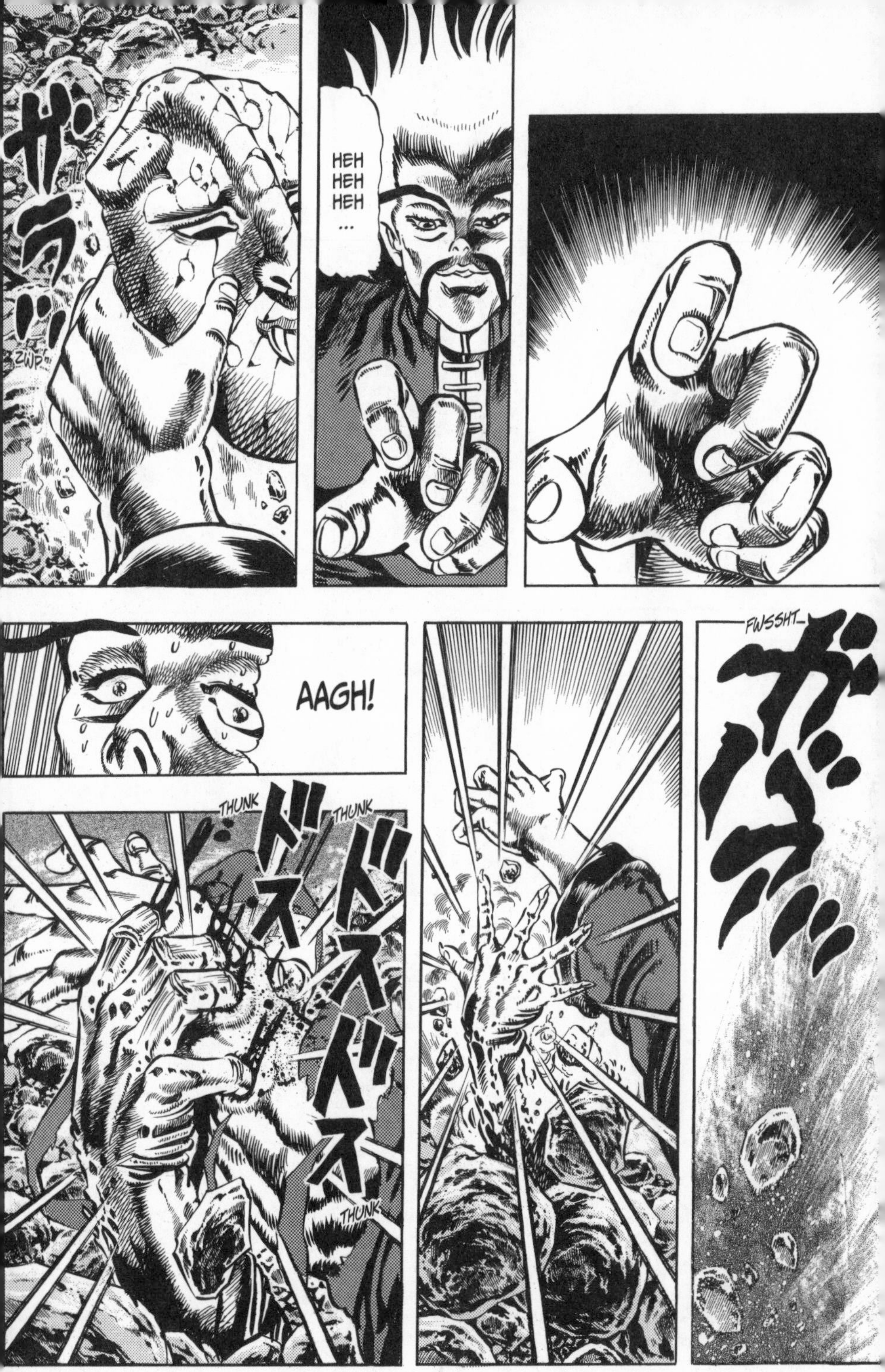
HEH
HEH
HEH
...
ZWP
FWSSHT
AAGH!
THUNK
THUNK
THUNK

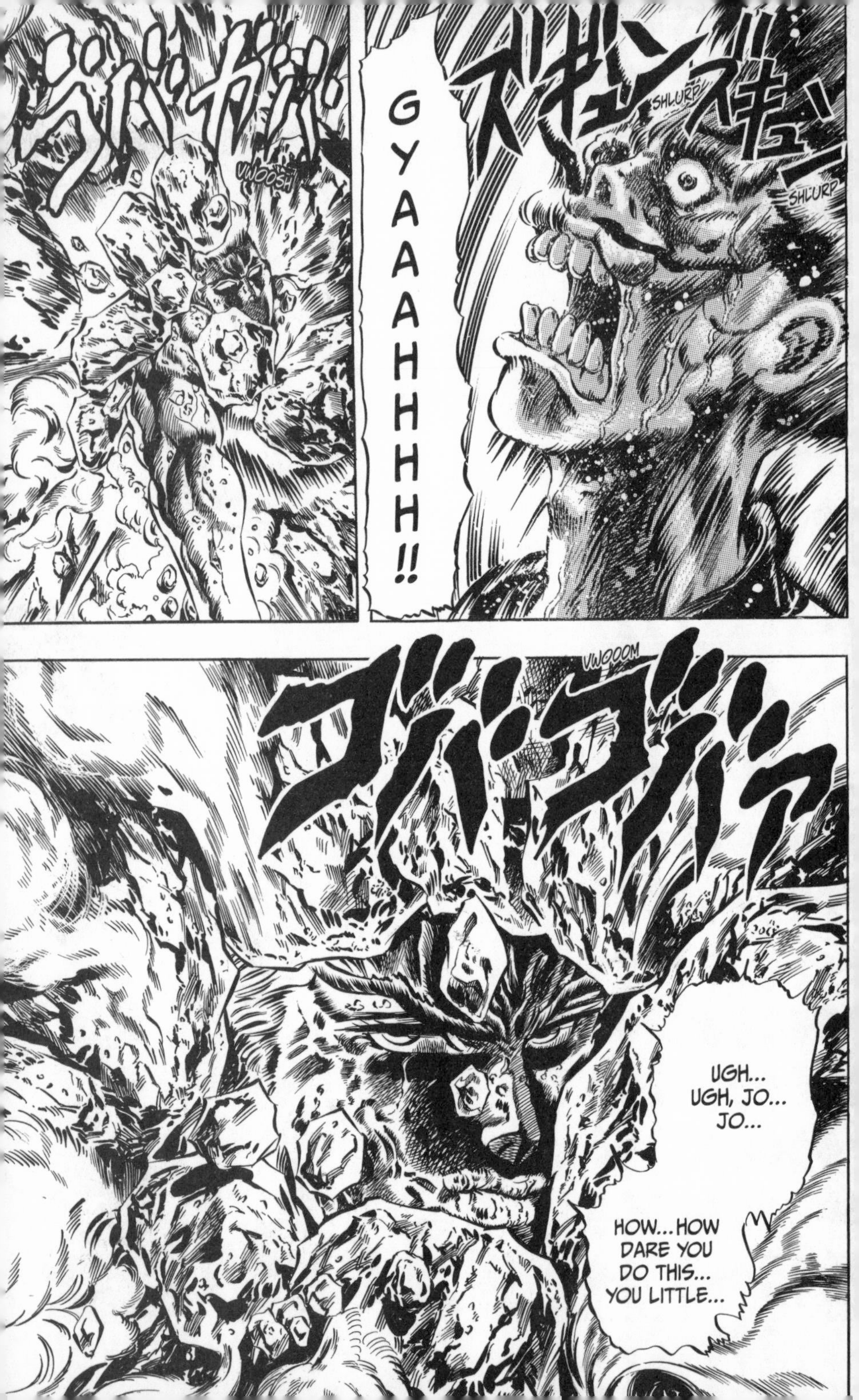
SHLURP
SHLURP
GYAAAHHHHH!!
VWOOSH
VWOOOM
UGH... UGH, JO... JO...
HOW...HOW DARE YOU DO THIS... YOU LITTLE...

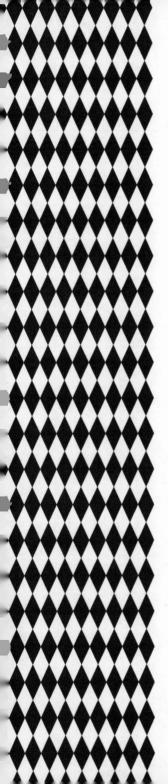

JoJo's

BIZARRE ADVENTURE

CHAPTER 18: Jack the Ripper and Zeppeli the Strange PART 1

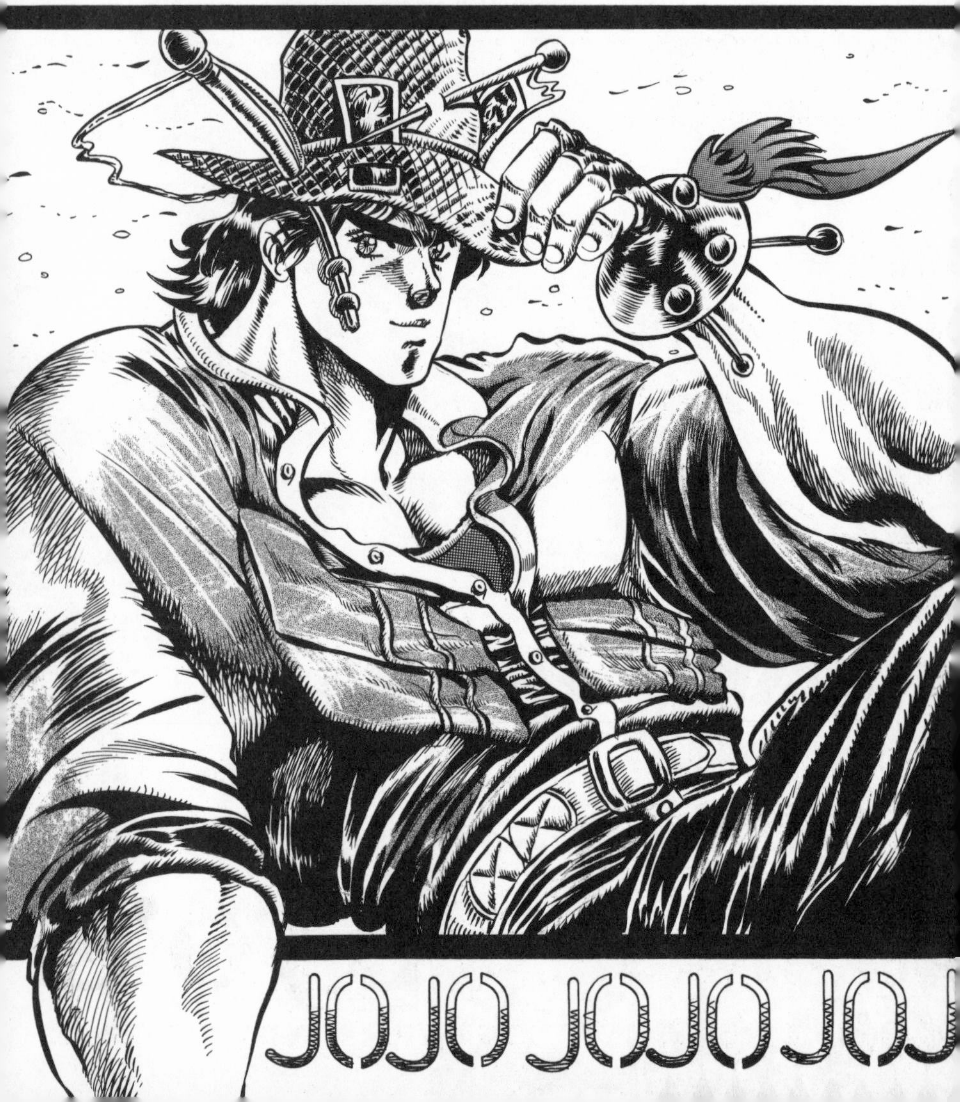
JOJO JOJO JOJ

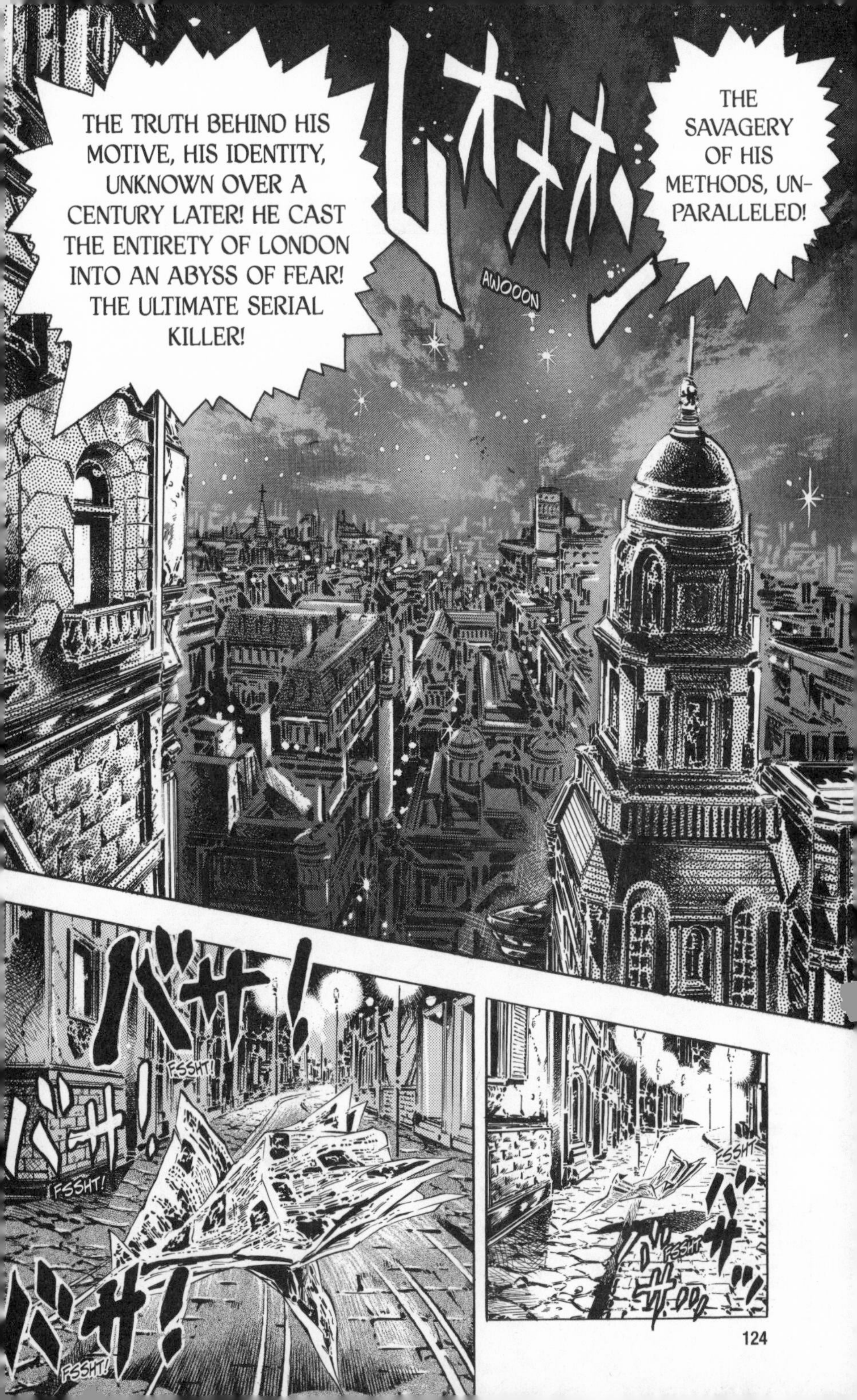
THE SAVAGERY OF HIS METHODS, UN-PARALLELED!
AWOOON
THE TRUTH BEHIND HIS MOTIVE, HIS IDENTITY, UNKNOWN OVER A CENTURY LATER! HE CAST THE ENTIRETY OF LONDON INTO AN ABYSS OF FEAR! THE ULTIMATE SERIAL KILLER!
F-SSHT
FSSHT
バサ!
FSSHT!
バサ!
FSSHT!
バサ!
FSSHT!

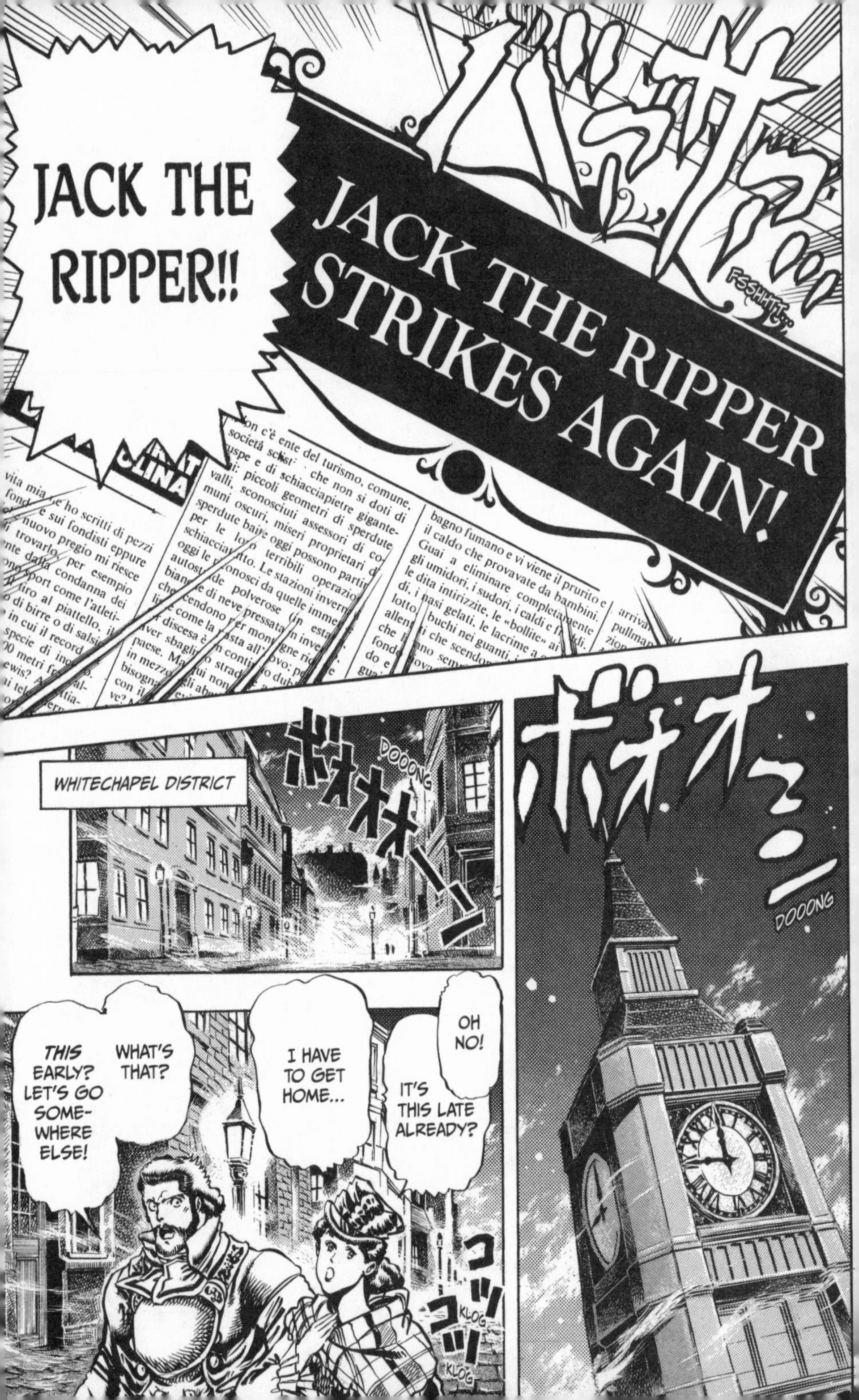
FSSHHT...
JACK THE RIPPER STRIKES AGAIN!
JACK THE RIPPER!!
DOOONG
WHITECHAPEL DISTRICT
DOOONG
OH NO!
IT'S THIS LATE ALREADY?
I HAVE TO GET HOME...
WHAT'S THAT?
THIS EARLY? LET'S GO SOMEWHERE ELSE!
KLOG
KLOG

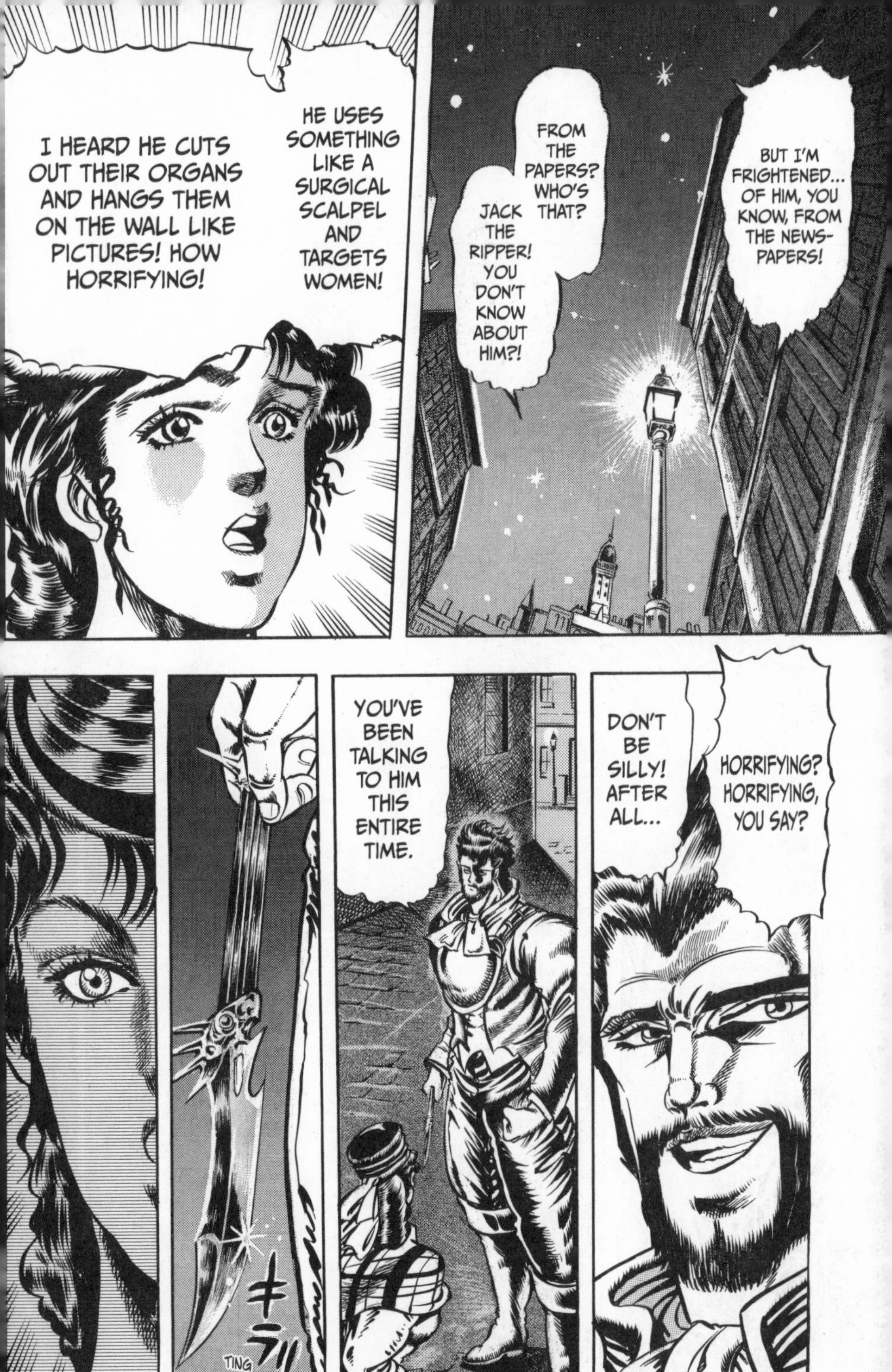
BUT I'M FRIGHTENED... OF HIM, YOU KNOW, FROM THE NEWSPAPERS!
FROM THE PAPERS? WHO'S THAT?
JACK THE RIPPER! YOU DON'T KNOW ABOUT HIM?!
HE USES SOMETHING LIKE A SURGICAL SCALPEL AND TARGETS WOMEN!
I HEARD HE CUTS OUT THEIR ORGANS AND HANGS THEM ON THE WALL LIKE PICTURES! HOW HORRIFYING!
HORRIFYING? HORRIFYING, YOU SAY?
DON'T BE SILLY! AFTER ALL...
YOU'VE BEEN TALKING TO HIM THIS ENTIRE TIME.
TING

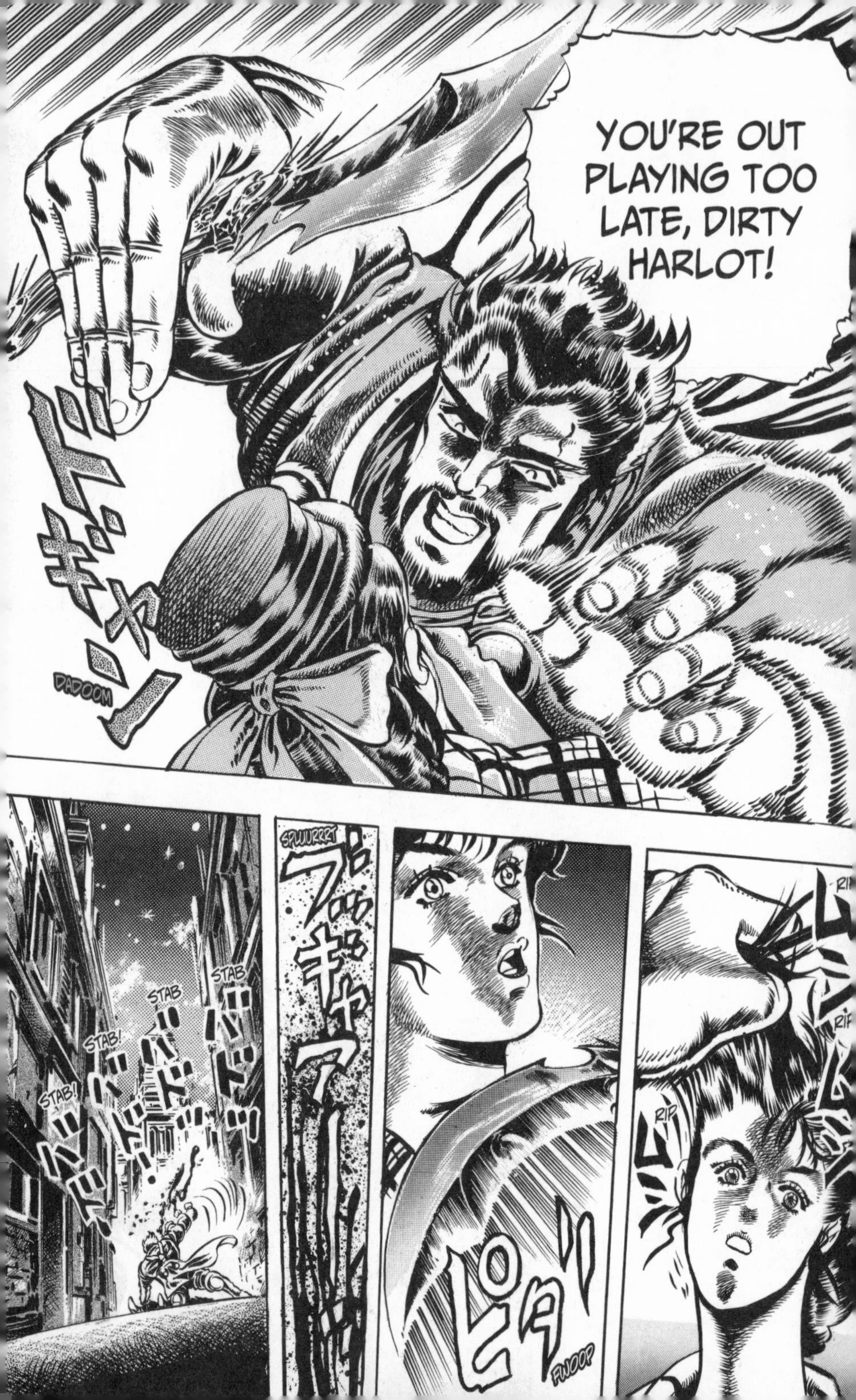
YOU'RE OUT PLAYING TOO LATE, DIRTY HARLOT!
DADOOM
RIP
RIP
RIP
FWOOP
SPLUURRRT
STAB
STAB
STAB!
STAB!

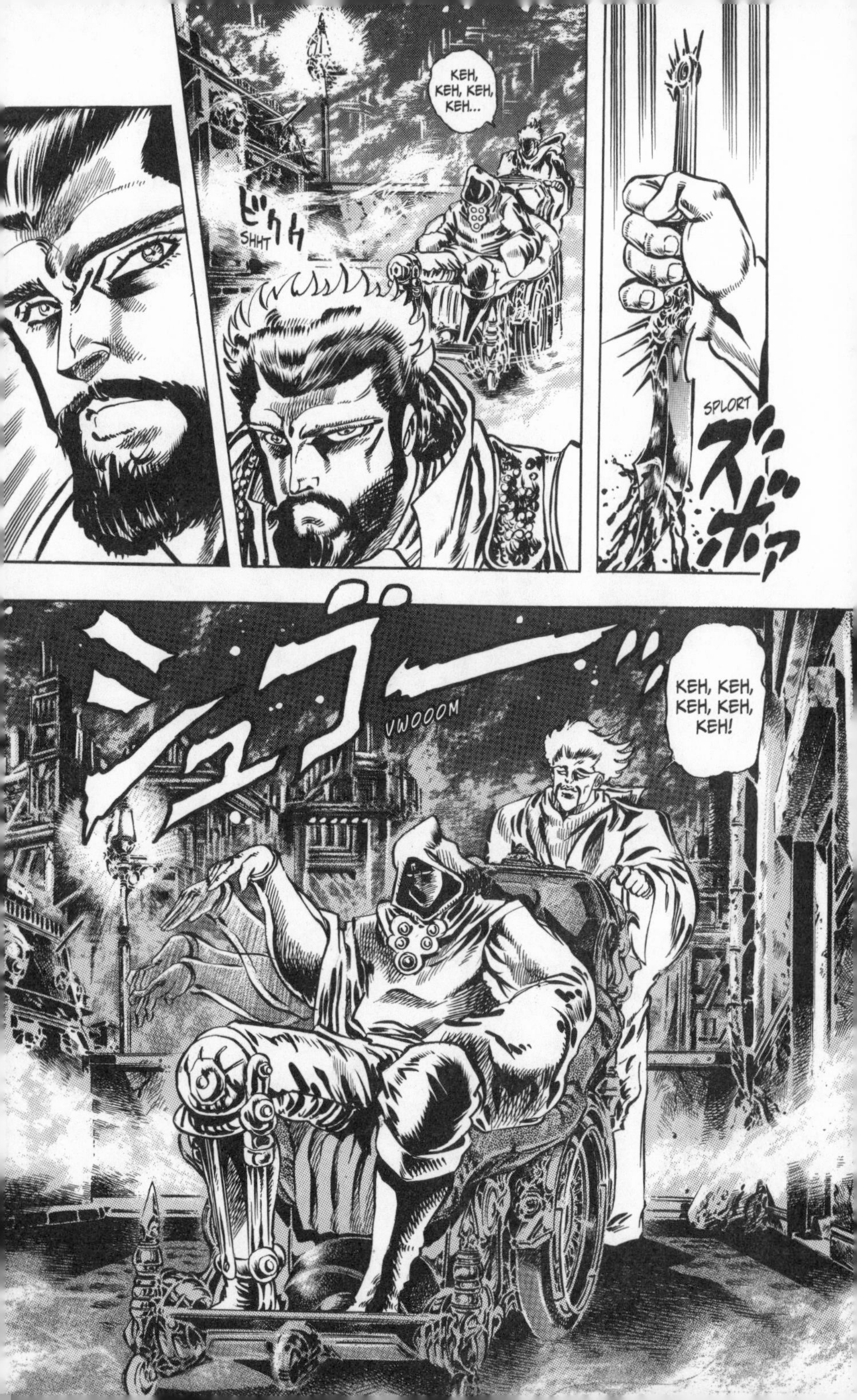
SPLORT
ズボァ
KEH, KEH, KEH, KEH...
SHHT
ジュゴー
VWOOOM
KEH, KEH, KEH, KEH, KEH!

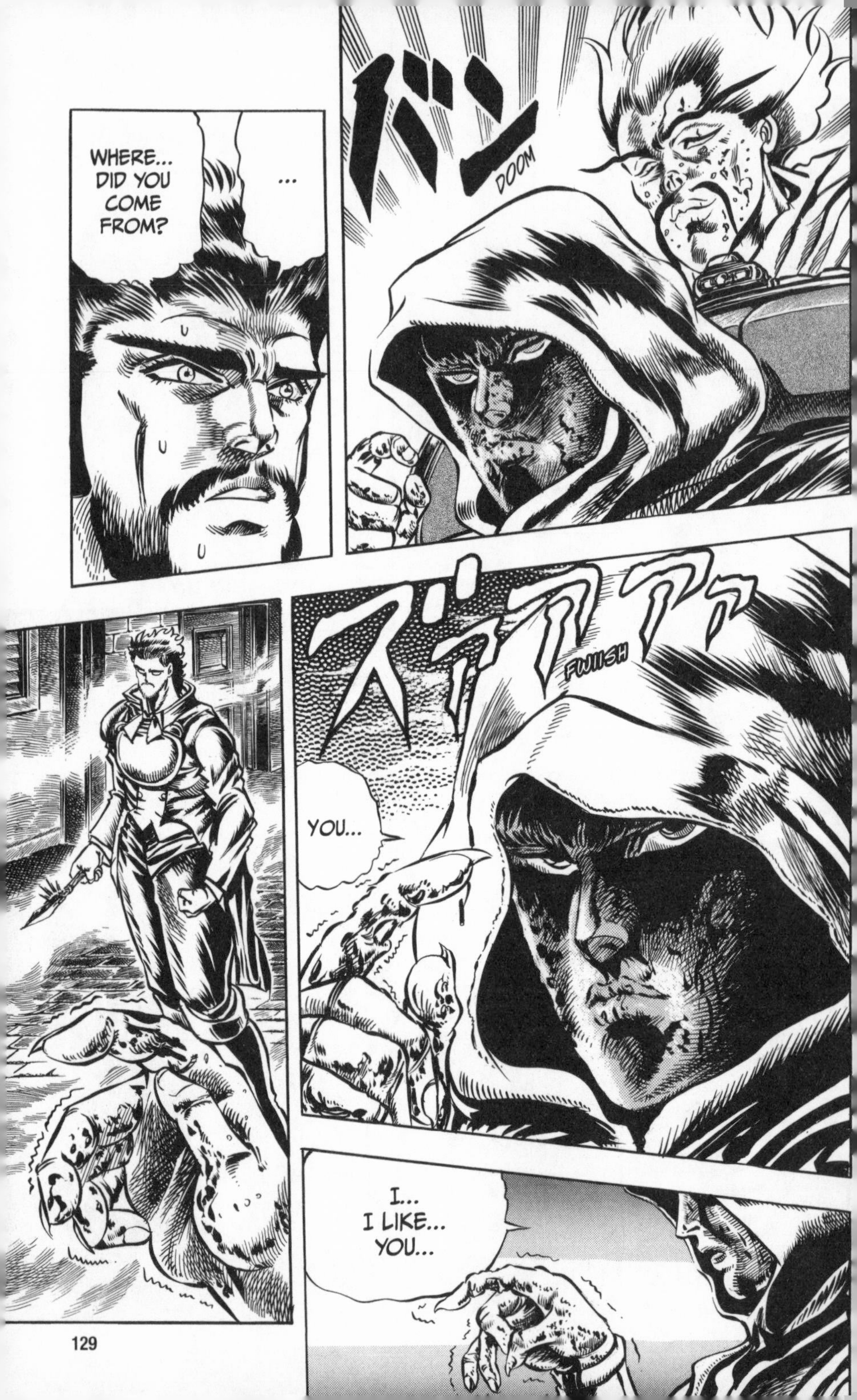

バン
DOOM
WHERE... DID YOU COME FROM?
...
ズァアアァ
FWIISH
YOU...
I... I LIKE... YOU...

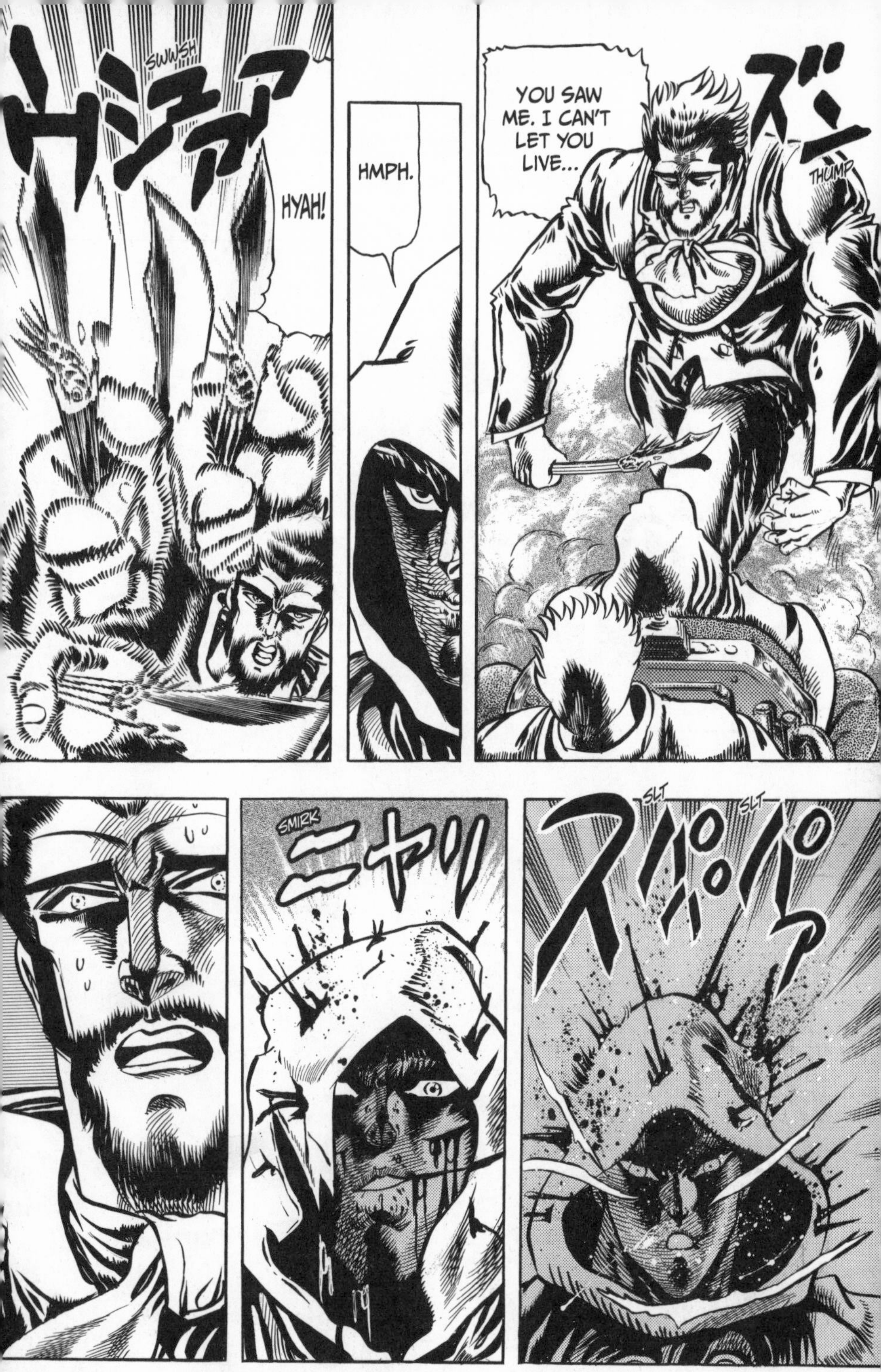
YOU SAW ME. I CAN'T LET YOU LIVE...
THUMP
HMPH.
SWWSH
HYAH!
SLT SLT
SMIRK

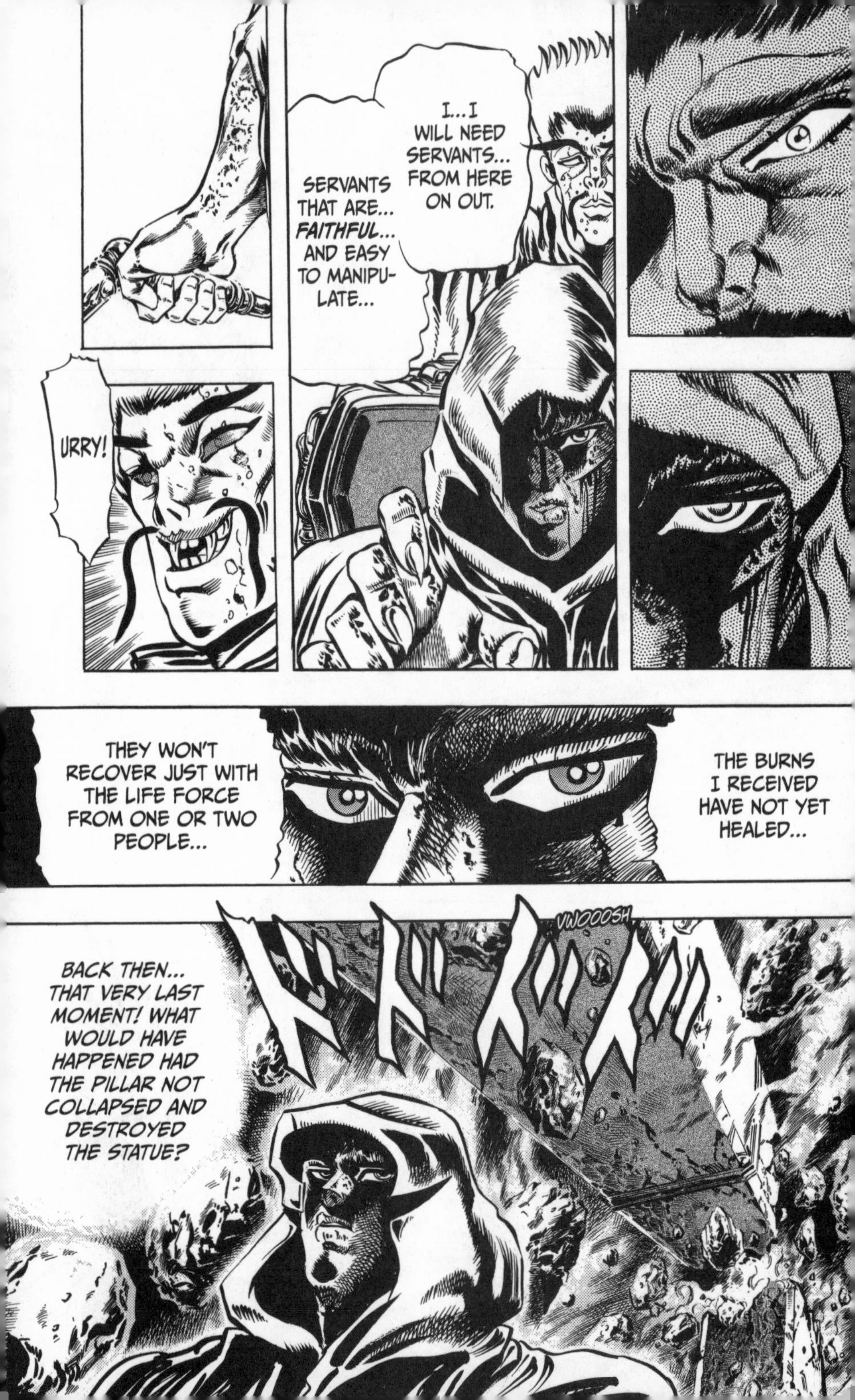
I...I WILL NEED SERVANTS... FROM HERE ON OUT.
SERVANTS THAT ARE... *FAITHFUL*... AND EASY TO MANIPULATE...
URRY!
THE BURNS I RECEIVED HAVE NOT YET HEALED...
THEY WON'T RECOVER JUST WITH THE LIFE FORCE FROM ONE OR TWO PEOPLE...
VWOOOSH
BACK THEN... THAT VERY LAST MOMENT! WHAT WOULD HAVE HAPPENED HAD THE PILLAR NOT COLLAPSED AND DESTROYED THE STATUE?

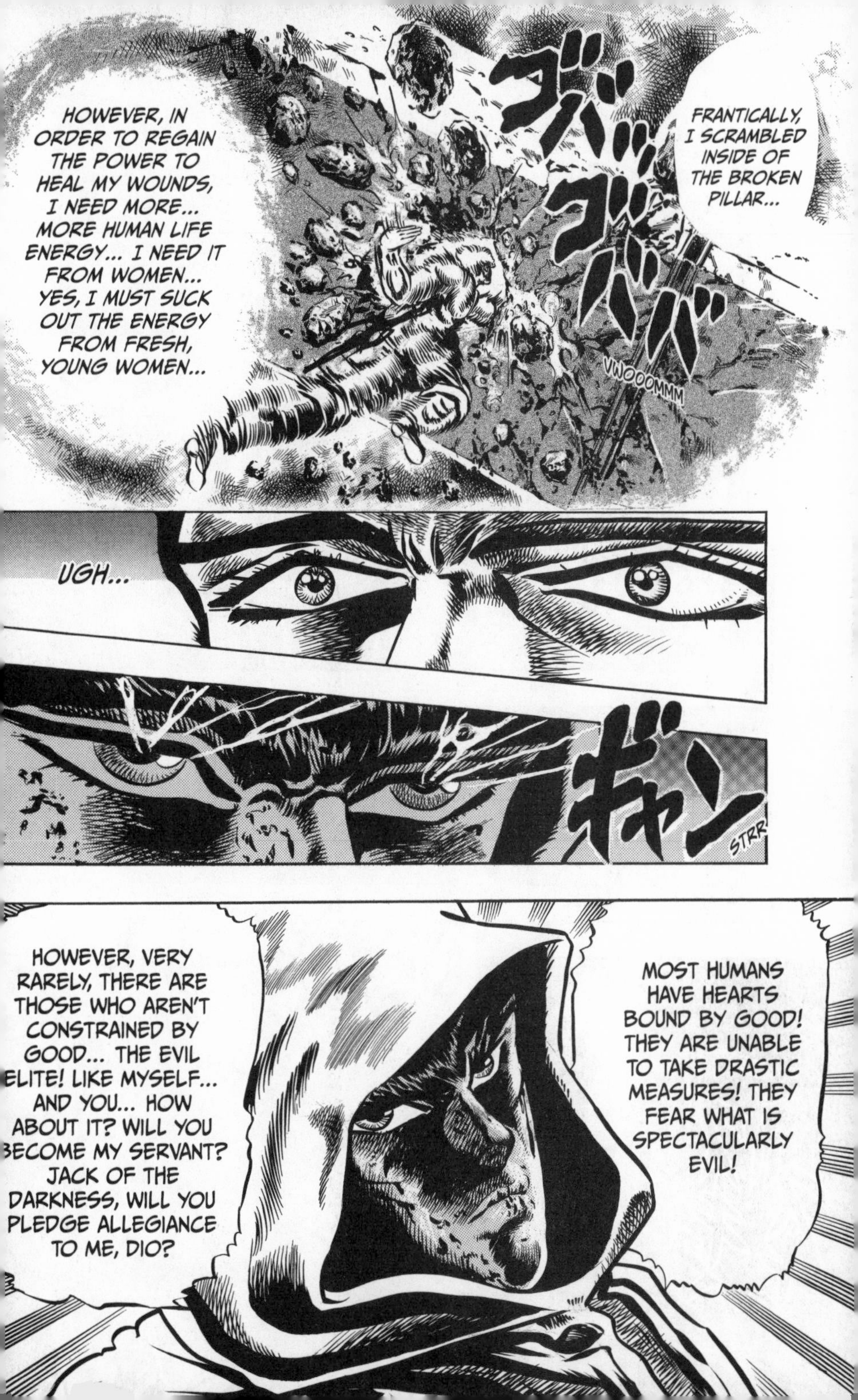
FRANTICALLY, I SCRAMBLED INSIDE OF THE BROKEN PILLAR...
ゴバッゴバババ
VWOOOMMM
HOWEVER, IN ORDER TO REGAIN THE POWER TO HEAL MY WOUNDS, I NEED MORE... MORE HUMAN LIFE ENERGY... I NEED IT FROM WOMEN... YES, I MUST SUCK OUT THE ENERGY FROM FRESH, YOUNG WOMEN...
UGH...
ギャン
STRR
MOST HUMANS HAVE HEARTS BOUND BY GOOD! THEY ARE UNABLE TO TAKE DRASTIC MEASURES! THEY FEAR WHAT IS SPECTACULARLY EVIL!
HOWEVER, VERY RARELY, THERE ARE THOSE WHO AREN'T CONSTRAINED BY GOOD... THE EVIL ELITE! LIKE MYSELF... AND YOU... HOW ABOUT IT? WILL YOU BECOME MY SERVANT? JACK OF THE DARKNESS, WILL YOU PLEDGE ALLEGIANCE TO ME, DIO?

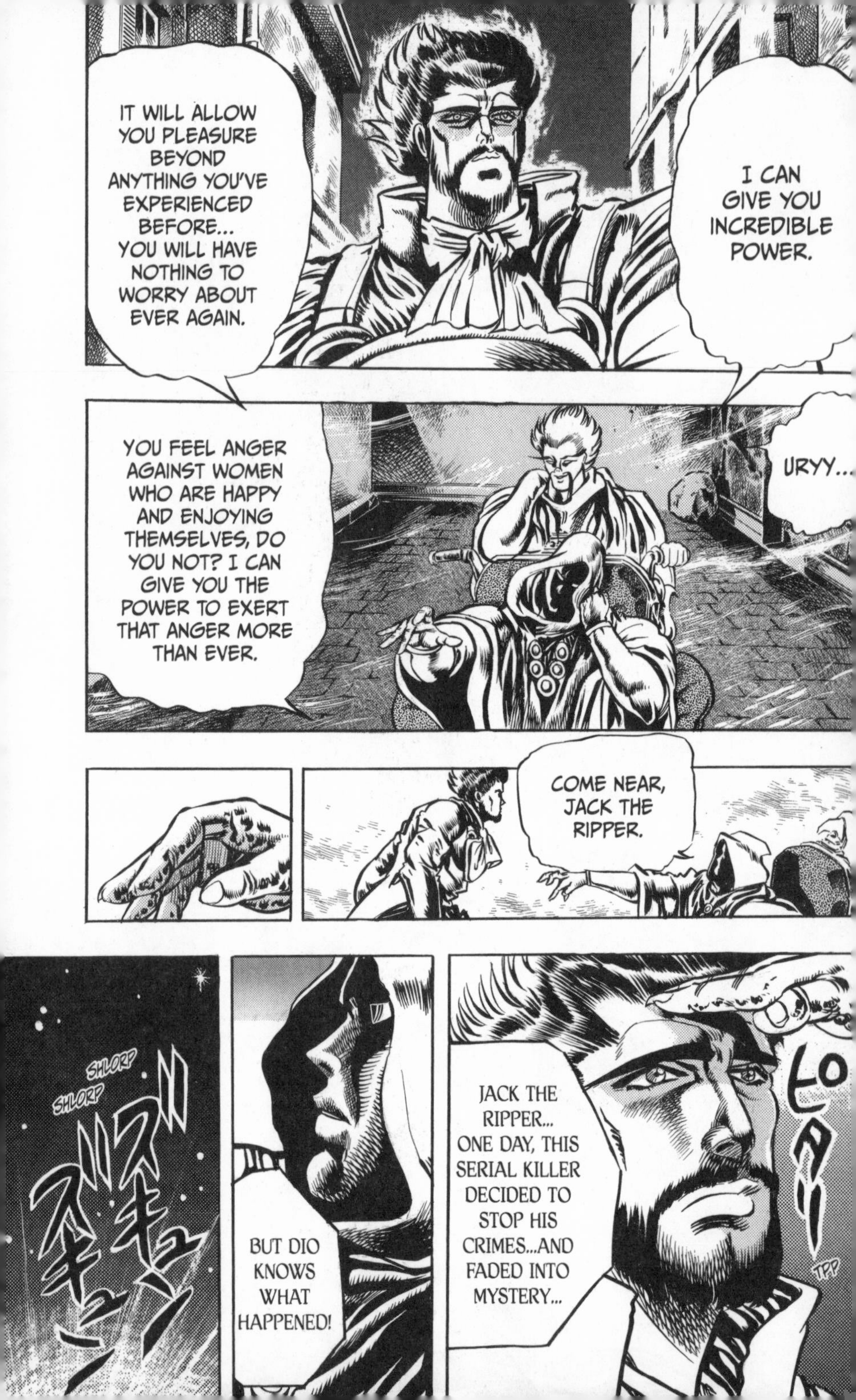
I CAN GIVE YOU INCREDIBLE POWER.
IT WILL ALLOW YOU PLEASURE BEYOND ANYTHING YOU'VE EXPERIENCED BEFORE... YOU WILL HAVE NOTHING TO WORRY ABOUT EVER AGAIN.
URYY...
YOU FEEL ANGER AGAINST WOMEN WHO ARE HAPPY AND ENJOYING THEMSELVES, DO YOU NOT? I CAN GIVE YOU THE POWER TO EXERT THAT ANGER MORE THAN EVER.
COME NEAR, JACK THE RIPPER.
TPP
JACK THE RIPPER... ONE DAY, THIS SERIAL KILLER DECIDED TO STOP HIS CRIMES...AND FADED INTO MYSTERY...
BUT DIO KNOWS WHAT HAPPENED!
SHLORP
SHLORP

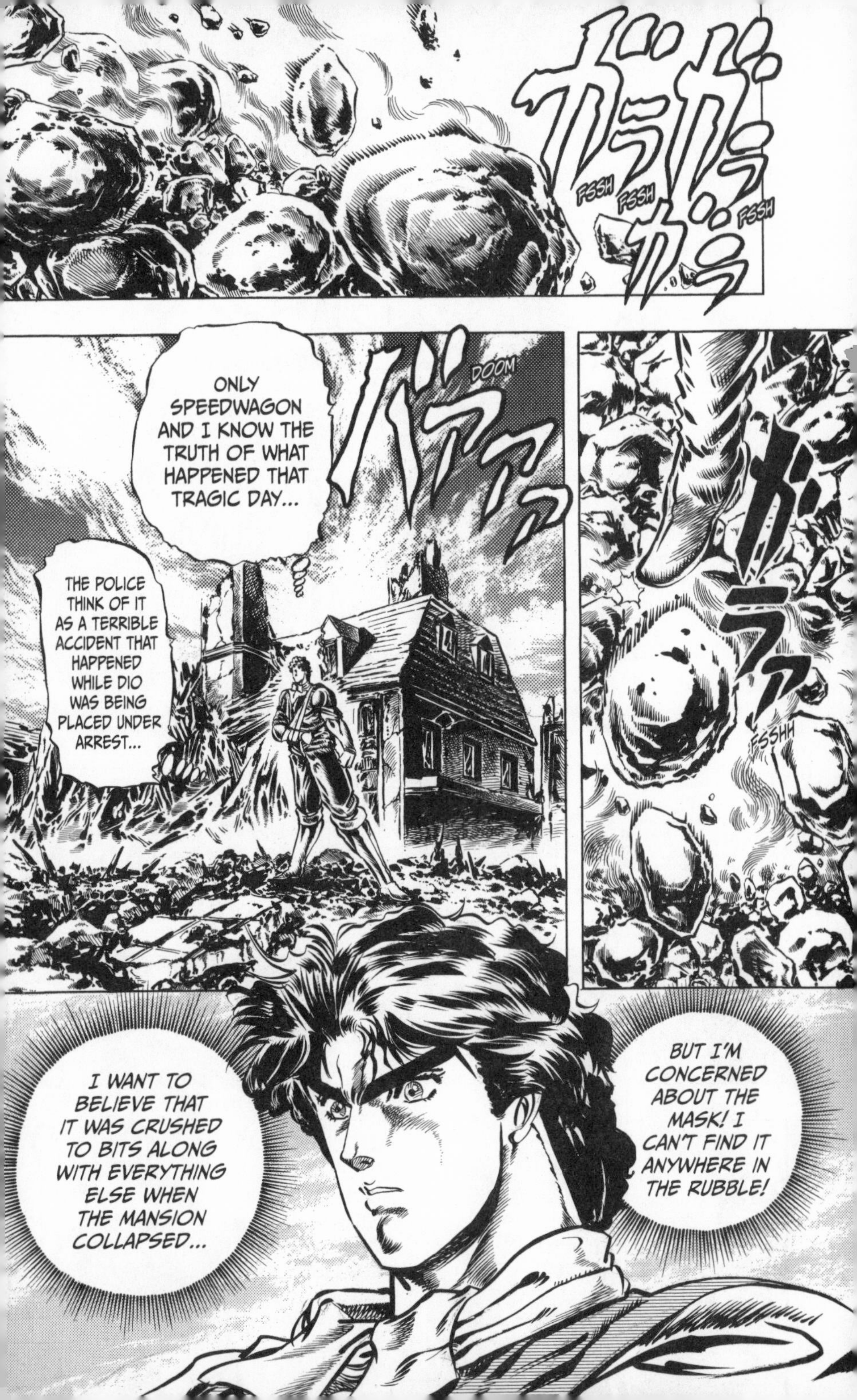
ガラガラ
FSSH FSSH
ガラ
FSSH
ガラァ
FSSHH
バァァ
DOOM
ONLY SPEEDWAGON AND I KNOW THE TRUTH OF WHAT HAPPENED THAT TRAGIC DAY...
THE POLICE THINK OF IT AS A TERRIBLE ACCIDENT THAT HAPPENED WHILE DIO WAS BEING PLACED UNDER ARREST...
BUT I'M CONCERNED ABOUT THE MASK! I CAN'T FIND IT ANYWHERE IN THE RUBBLE!
I WANT TO BELIEVE THAT IT WAS CRUSHED TO BITS ALONG WITH EVERYTHING ELSE WHEN THE MANSION COLLAPSED...

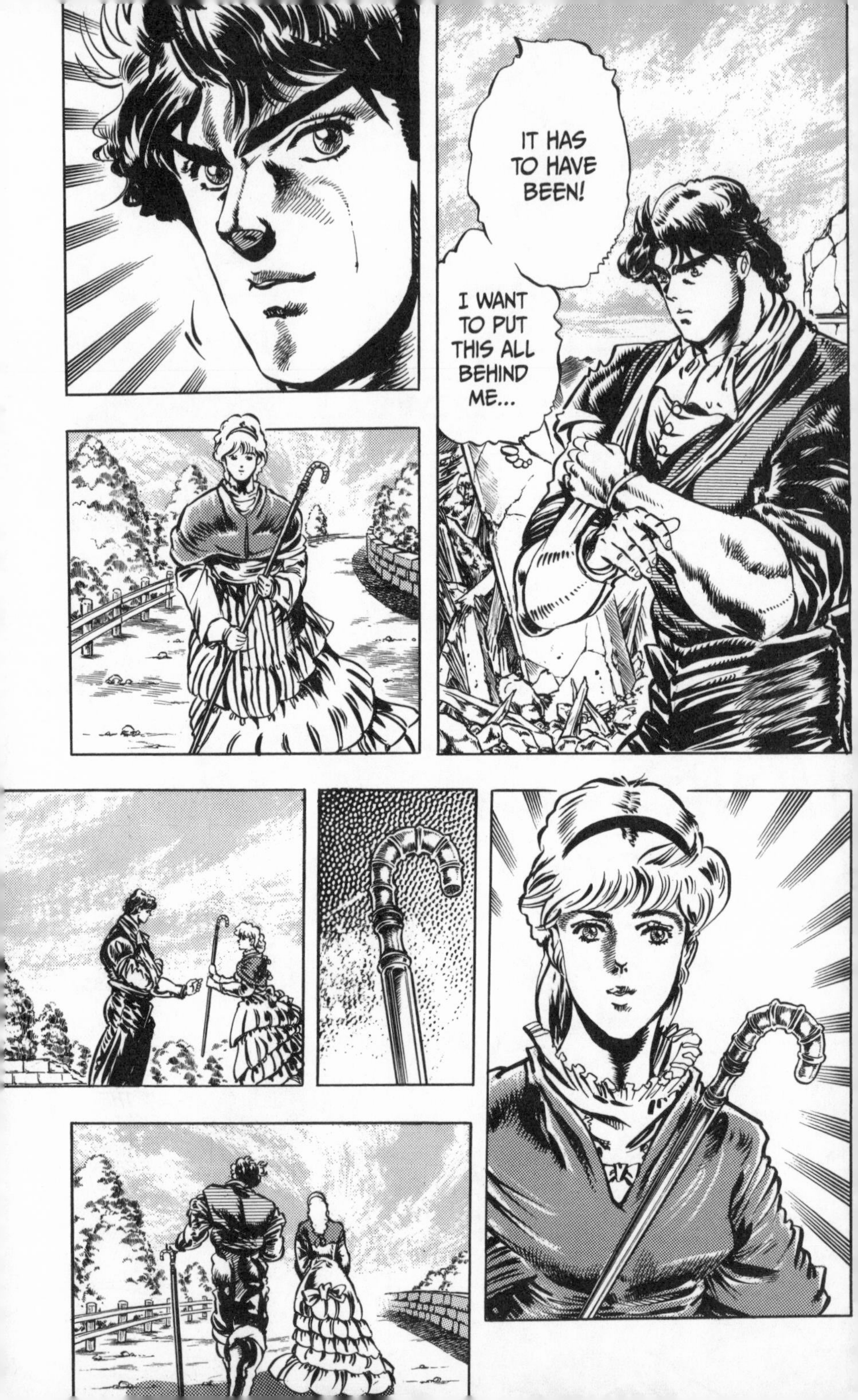
IT HAS TO HAVE BEEN!
I WANT TO PUT THIS ALL BEHIND ME...

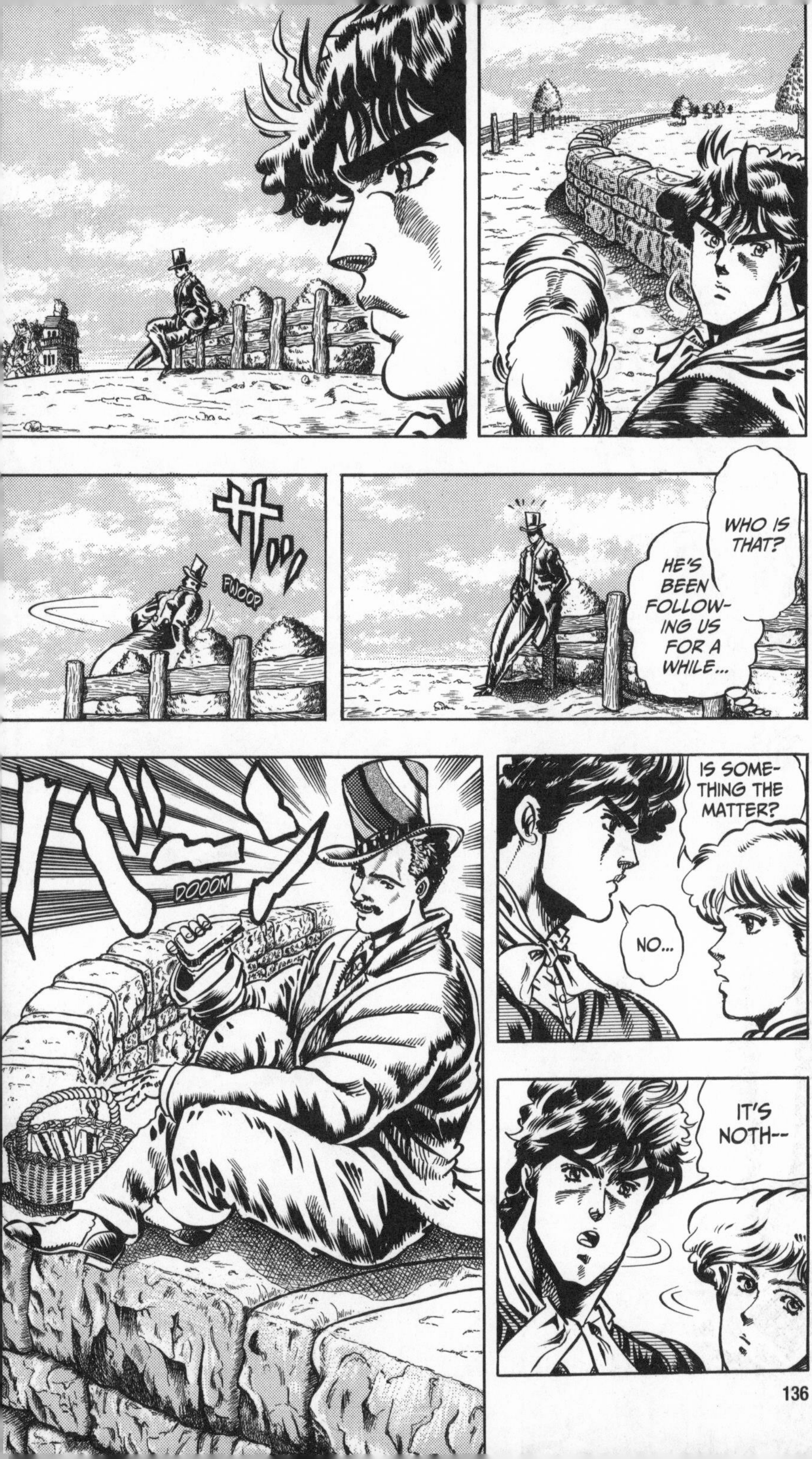
WHO IS THAT?
HE'S BEEN FOLLOWING US FOR A WHILE...
FWOOP
IS SOMETHING THE MATTER?
NO...
IT'S NOTH--
DOOOM

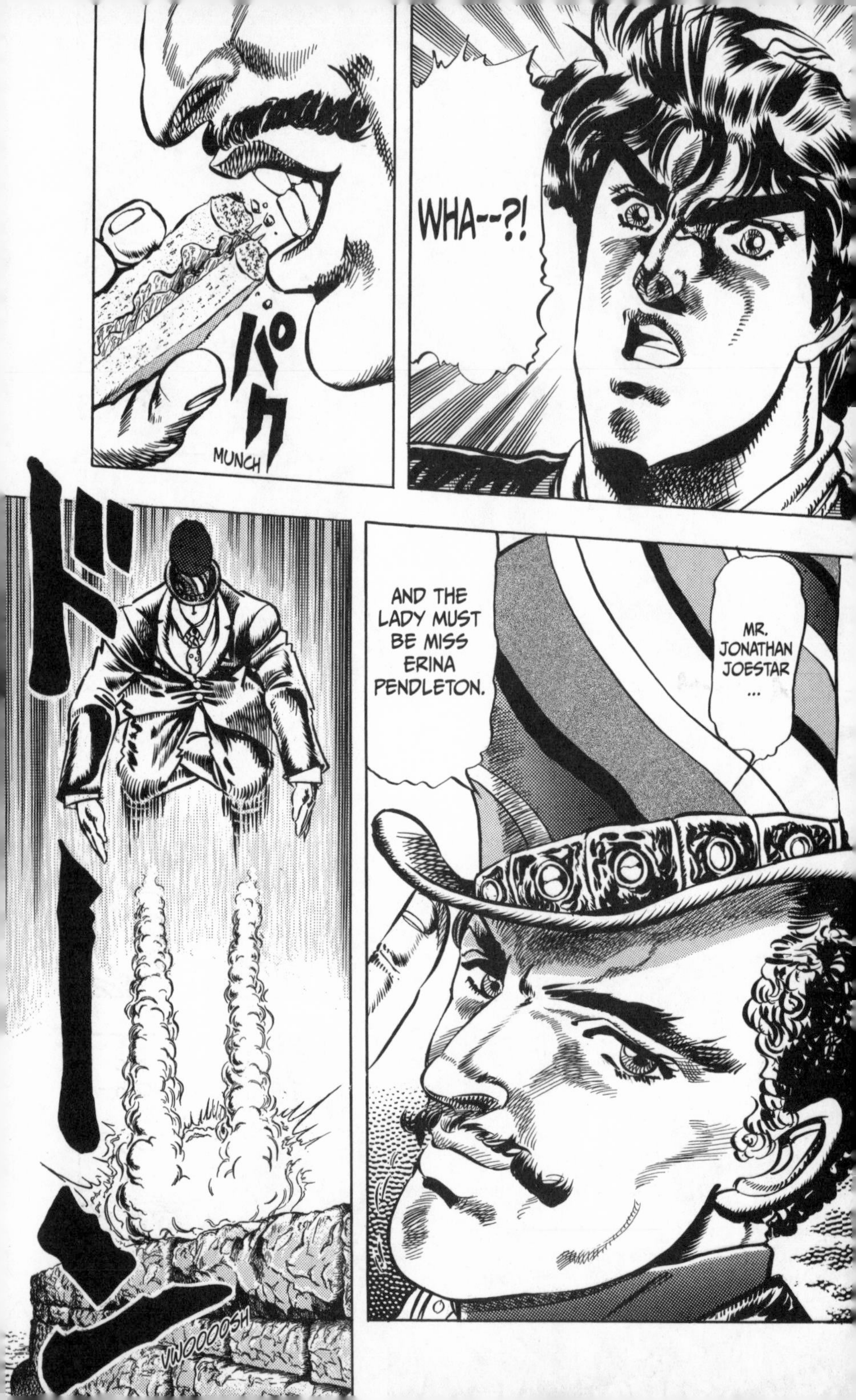
WHA--?!
パク
MUNCH
MR. JONATHAN JOESTAR ...
AND THE LADY MUST BE MISS ERINA PENDLETON.
VWOOOOSH

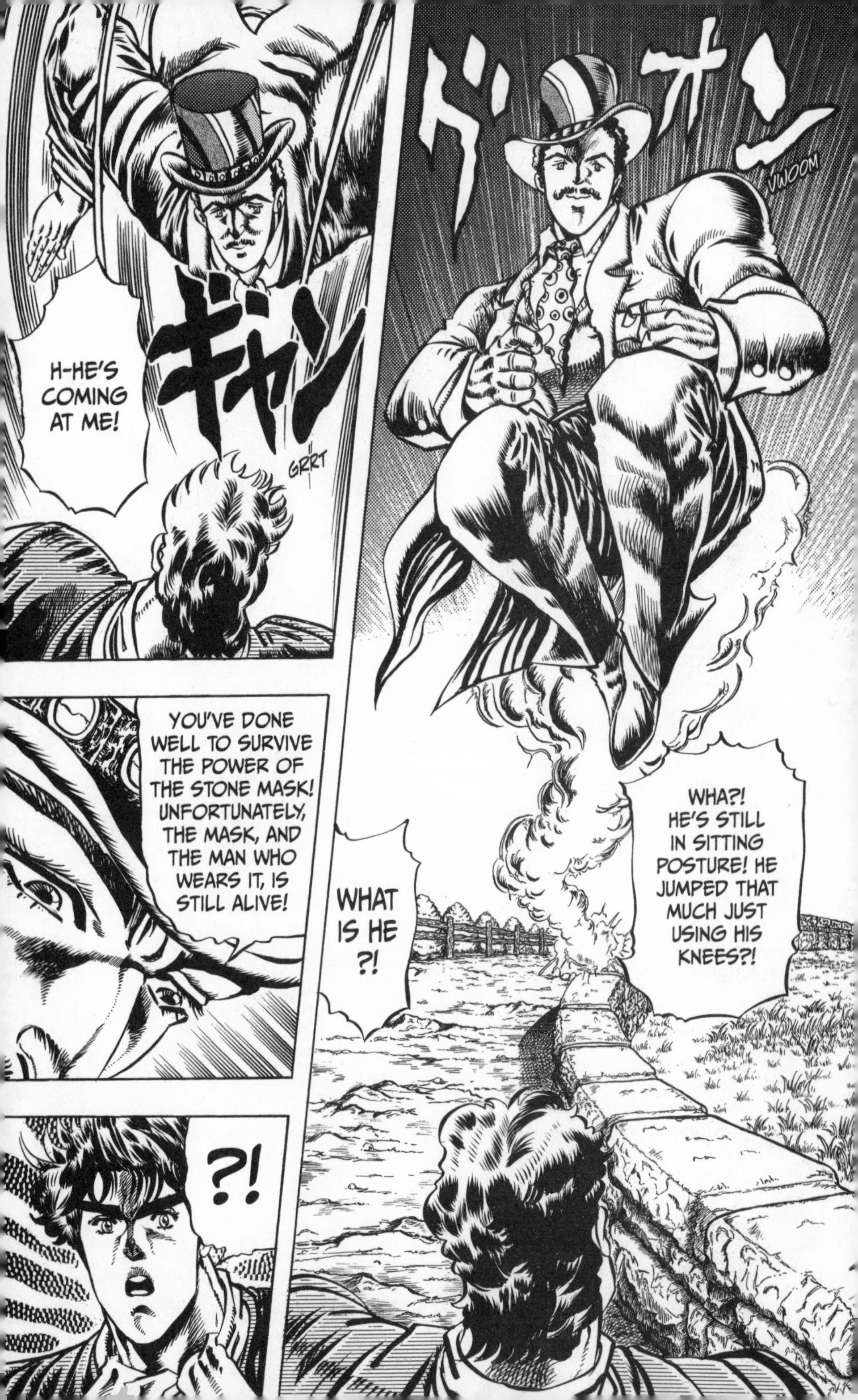

ドゥオン
VWOOM
WHA?! HE'S STILL IN SITTING POSTURE! HE JUMPED THAT MUCH JUST USING HIS KNEES?!
WHAT IS HE ?!
ギャン
GRRT
H-HE'S COMING AT ME!
YOU'VE DONE WELL TO SURVIVE THE POWER OF THE STONE MASK! UNFORTUNATELY, THE MASK, AND THE MAN WHO WEARS IT, IS STILL ALIVE!
?!

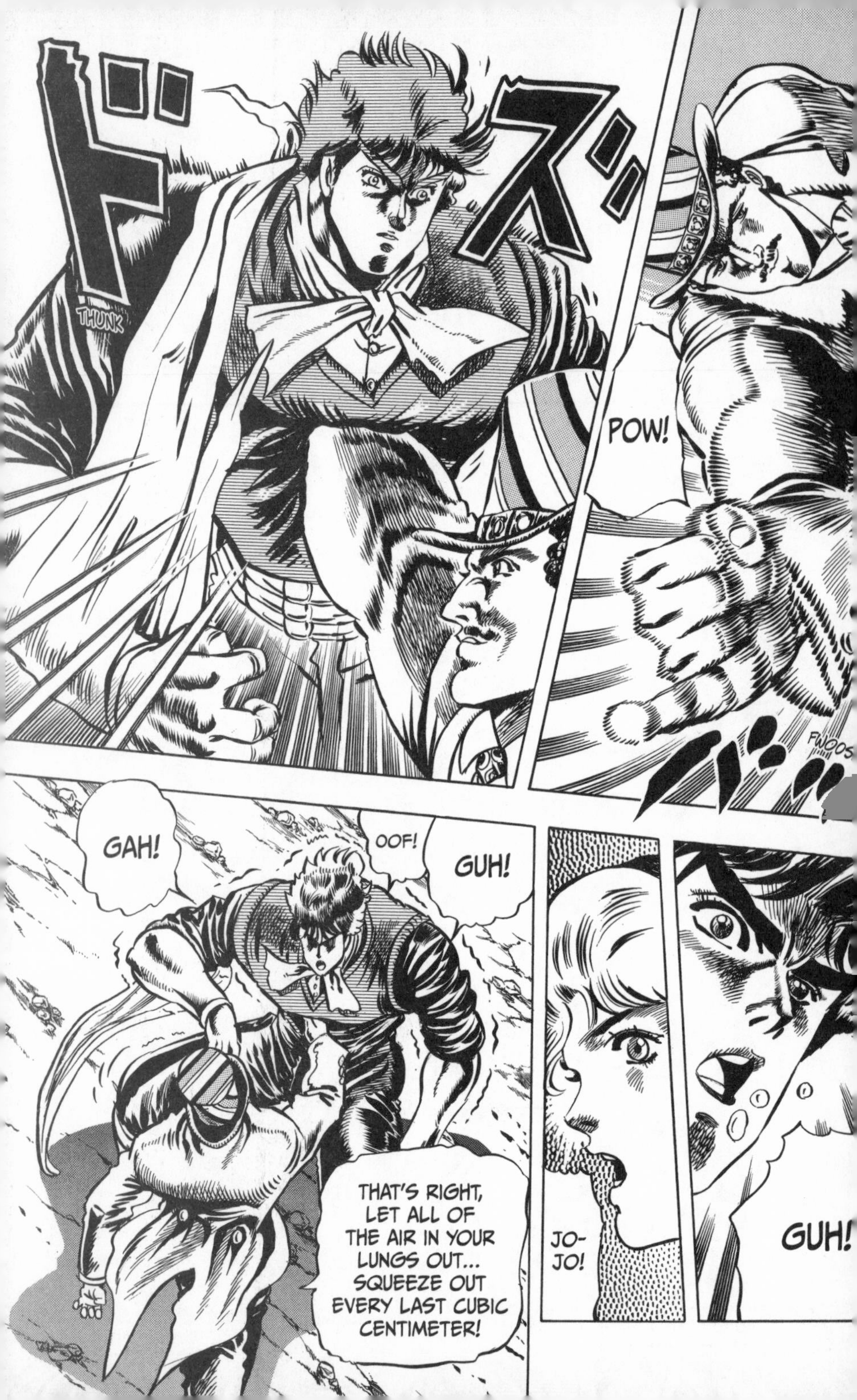
POW!
FWOOS
THUNK
GUH!
JO-JO!
GUH!
OOF!
GAH!
THAT'S RIGHT, LET ALL OF THE AIR IN YOUR LUNGS OUT... SQUEEZE OUT EVERY LAST CUBIC CENTIMETER!

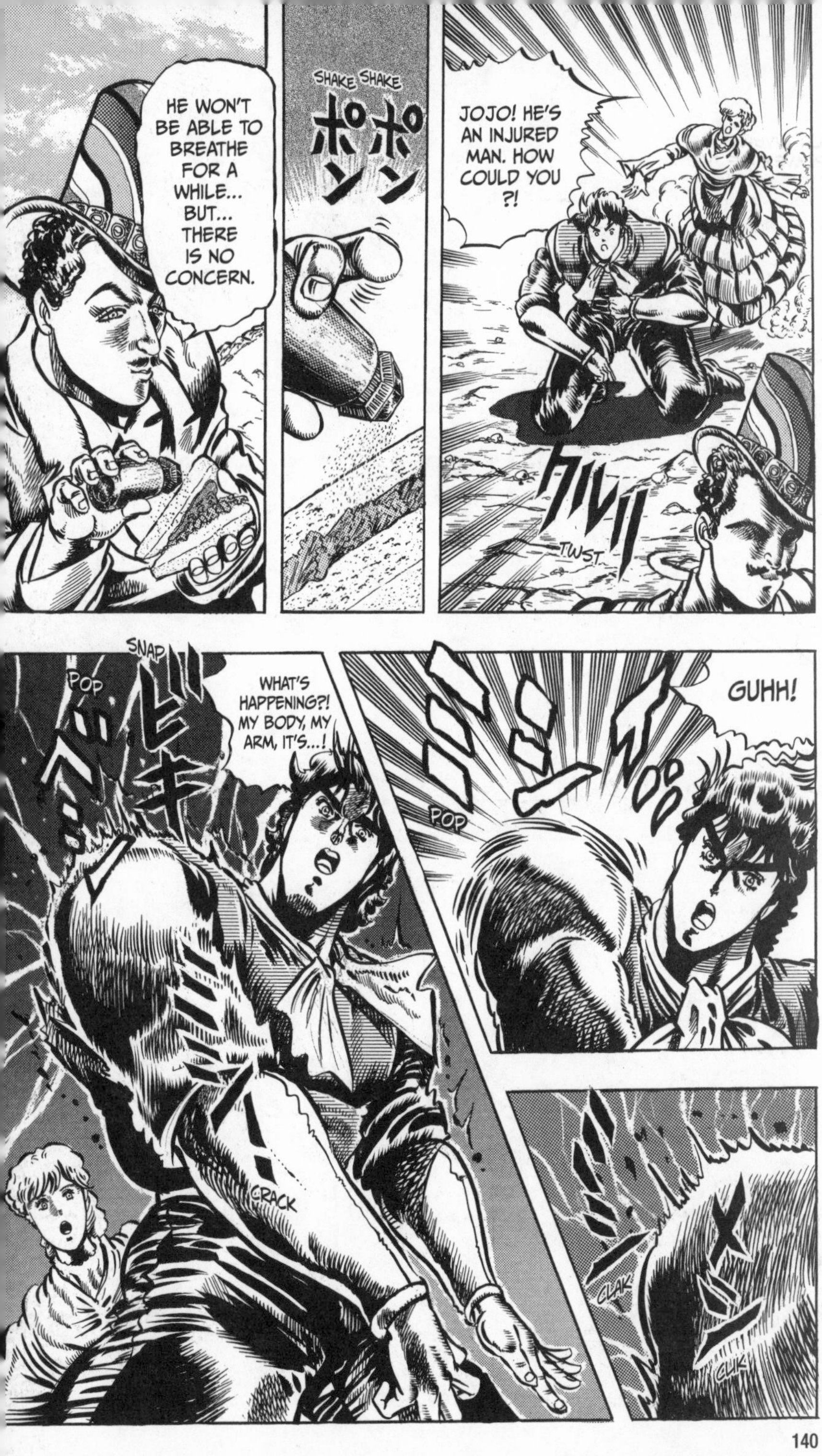
JOJO! HE'S AN INJURED MAN. HOW COULD YOU ?!
TWIST
SHAKE SHAKE
ポンポン
HE WON'T BE ABLE TO BREATHE FOR A WHILE... BUT... THERE IS NO CONCERN.
GUHH!
POP
CLAK
CLUK
SNAP
POP
WHAT'S HAPPENING?! MY BODY, MY ARM, IT'S...!
CRACK

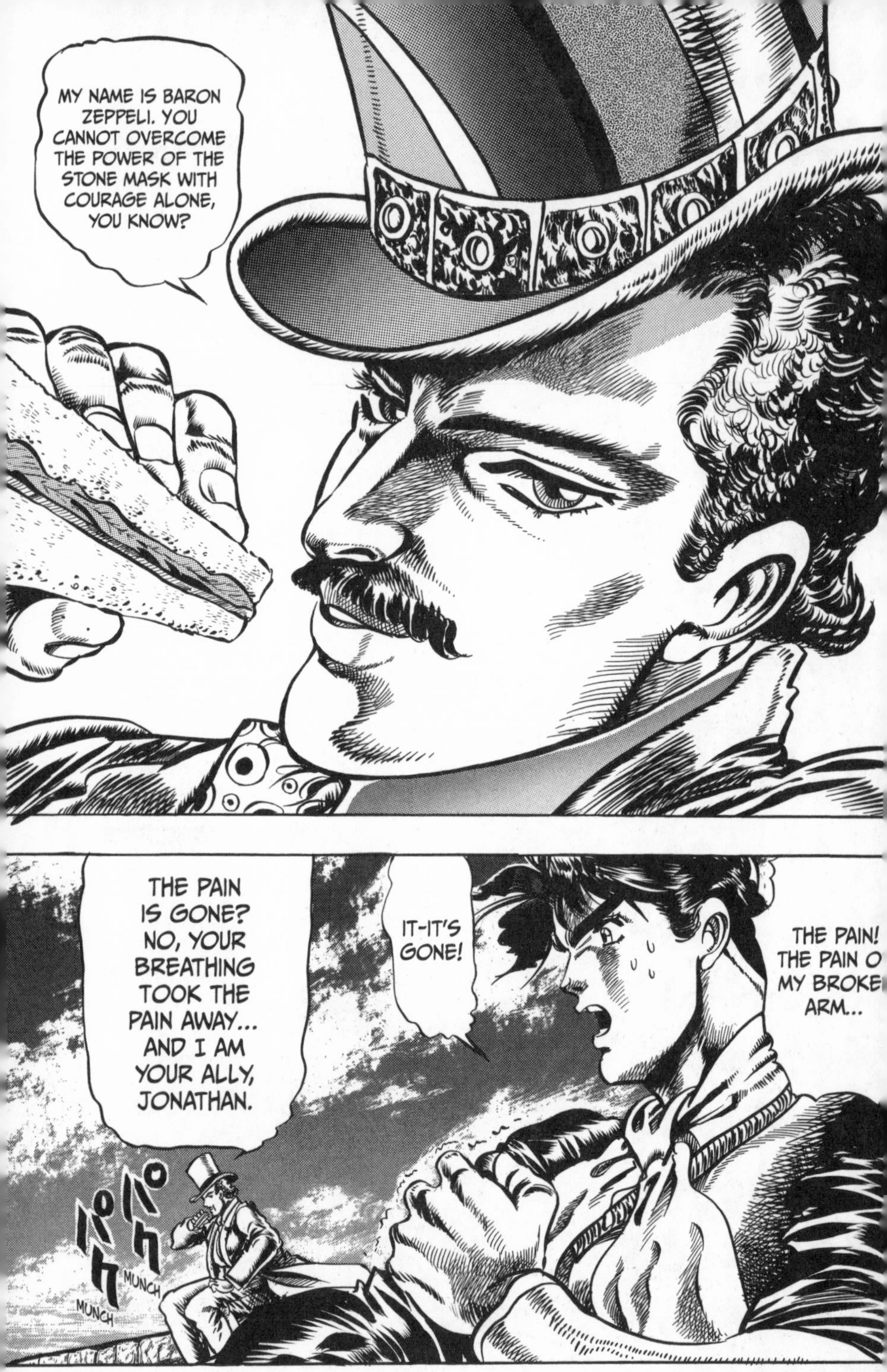
MY NAME IS BARON ZEPPELI. YOU CANNOT OVERCOME THE POWER OF THE STONE MASK WITH COURAGE ALONE, YOU KNOW?
THE PAIN! THE PAIN O MY BROKE ARM...
IT-IT'S GONE!
THE PAIN IS GONE? NO, YOUR BREATHING TOOK THE PAIN AWAY... AND I AM YOUR ALLY, JONATHAN.
MUNCH
MUNCH

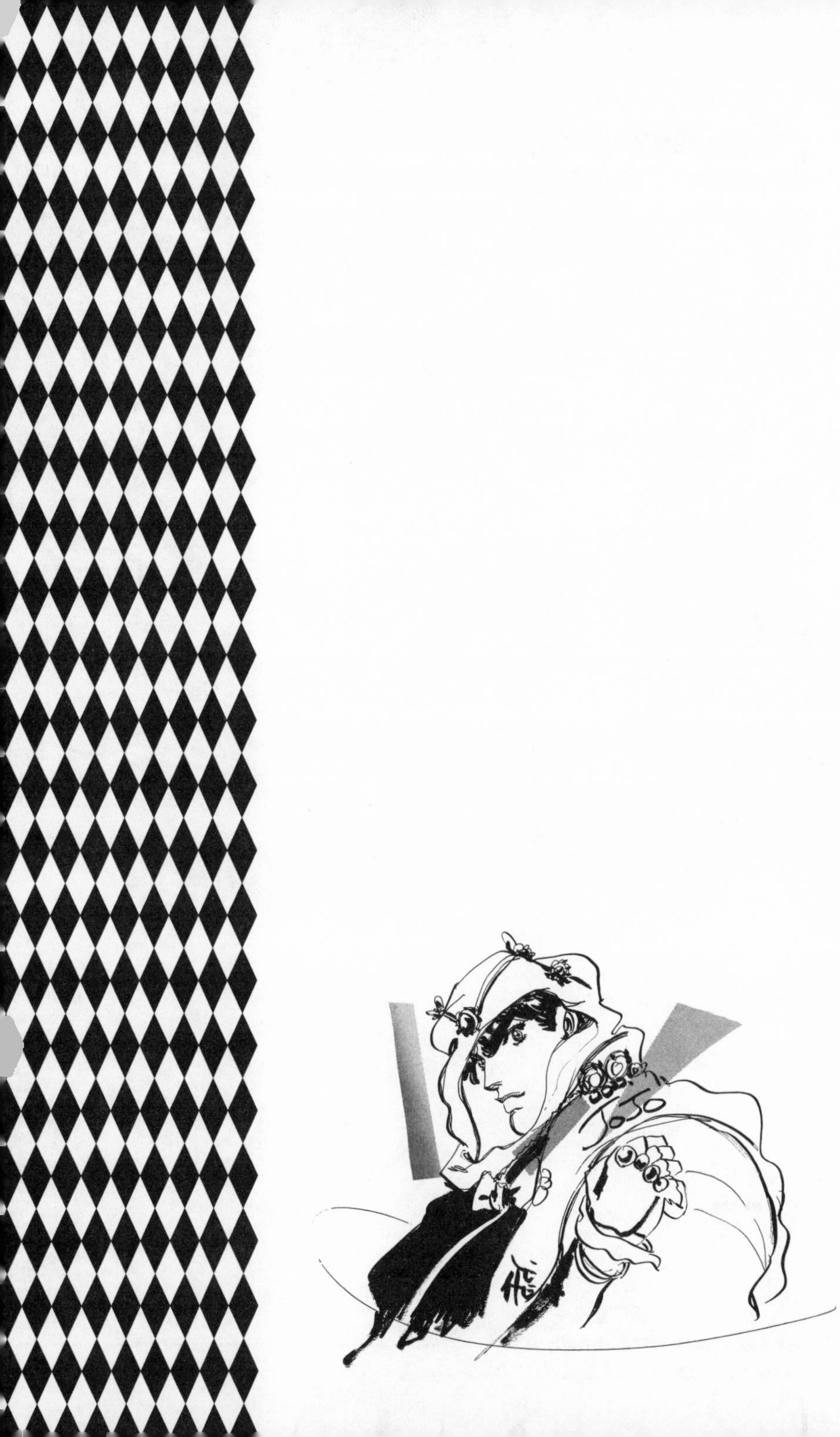
JoJo

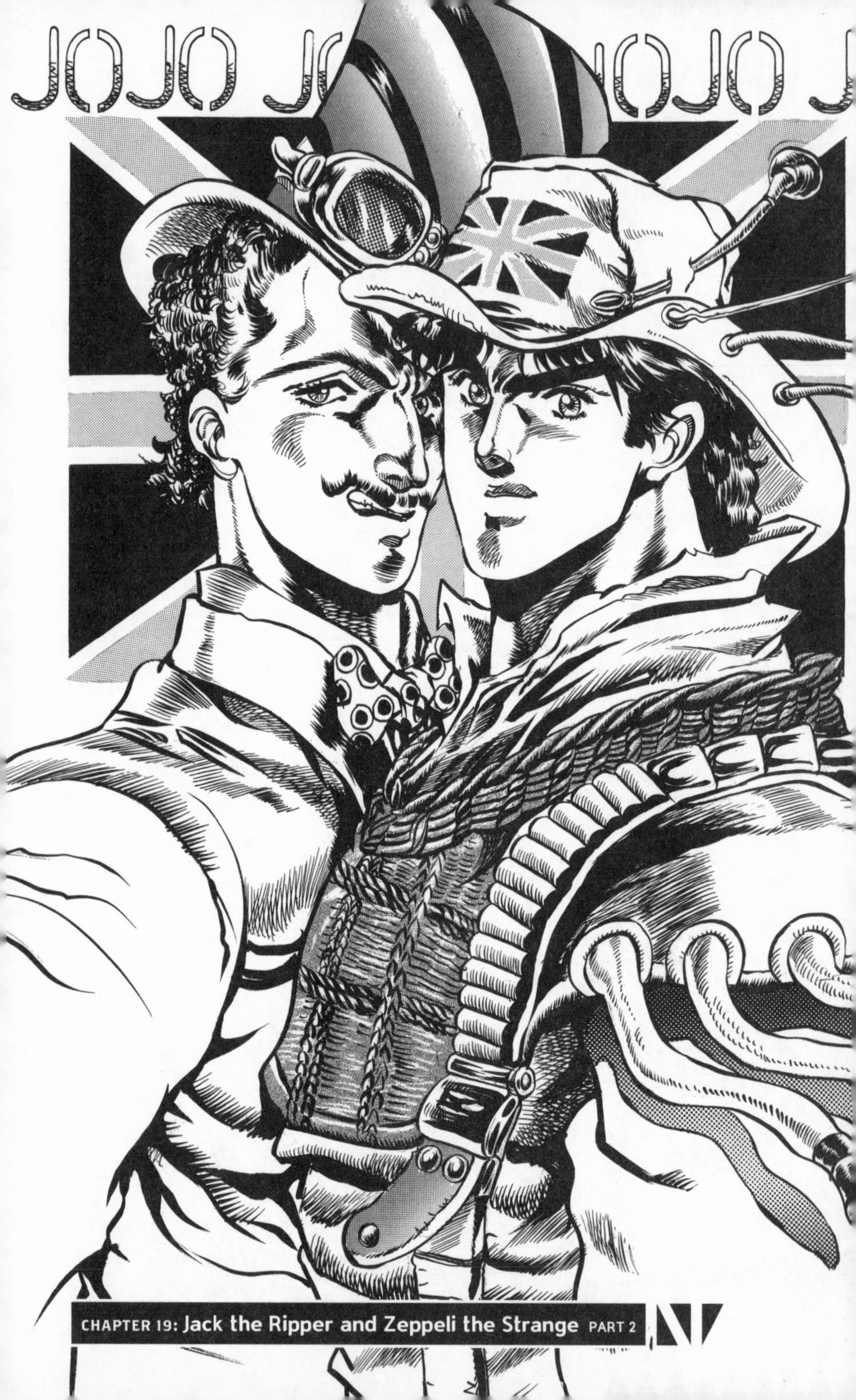
JOJO JO JOJO J

CHAPTER 19: Jack the Ripper and Zeppeli the Strange PART 2

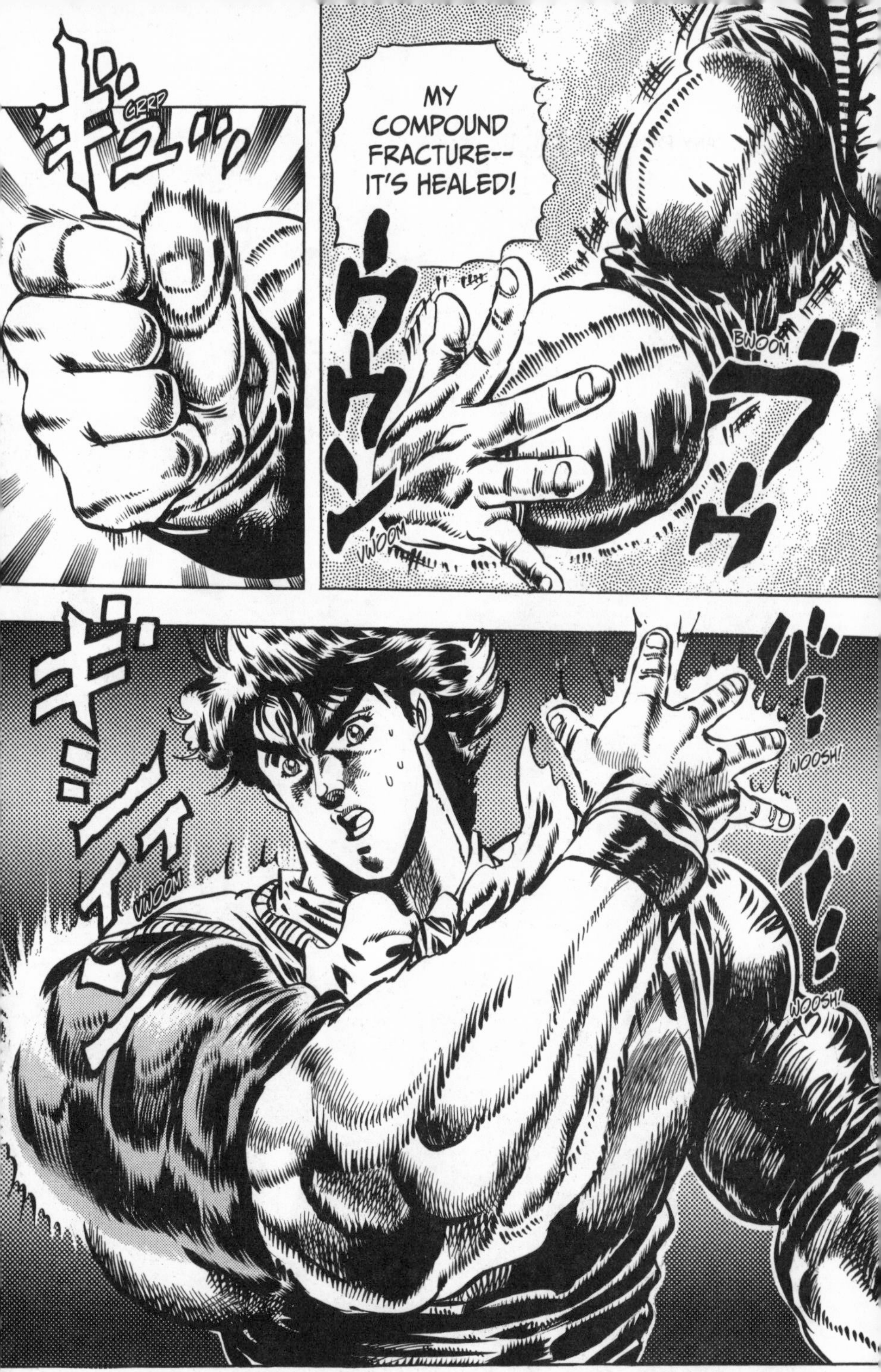
MY COMPOUND FRACTURE-- IT'S HEALED!
BWOOM
VWOOM
GRRP
WOOSH!
WOOSH!
VWOOM

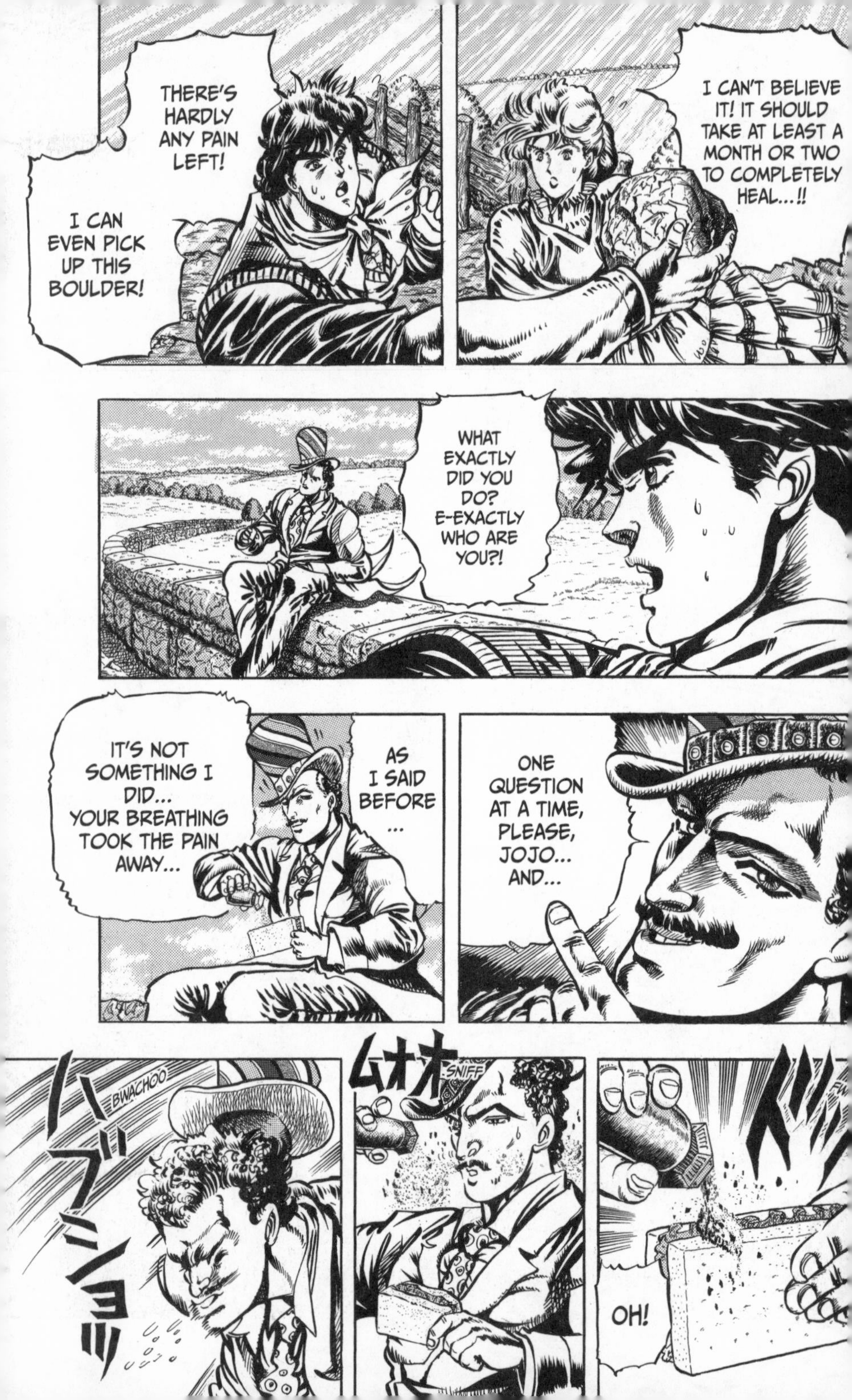
I CAN'T BELIEVE IT! IT SHOULD TAKE AT LEAST A MONTH OR TWO TO COMPLETELY HEAL...!!
THERE'S HARDLY ANY PAIN LEFT!
I CAN EVEN PICK UP THIS BOULDER!
WHAT EXACTLY DID YOU DO? E-EXACTLY WHO ARE YOU?!
ONE QUESTION AT A TIME, PLEASE, JOJO... AND...
AS I SAID BEFORE ...
IT'S NOT SOMETHING I DID... YOUR BREATHING TOOK THE PAIN AWAY...
OH!
SNIFF
BWACHOO

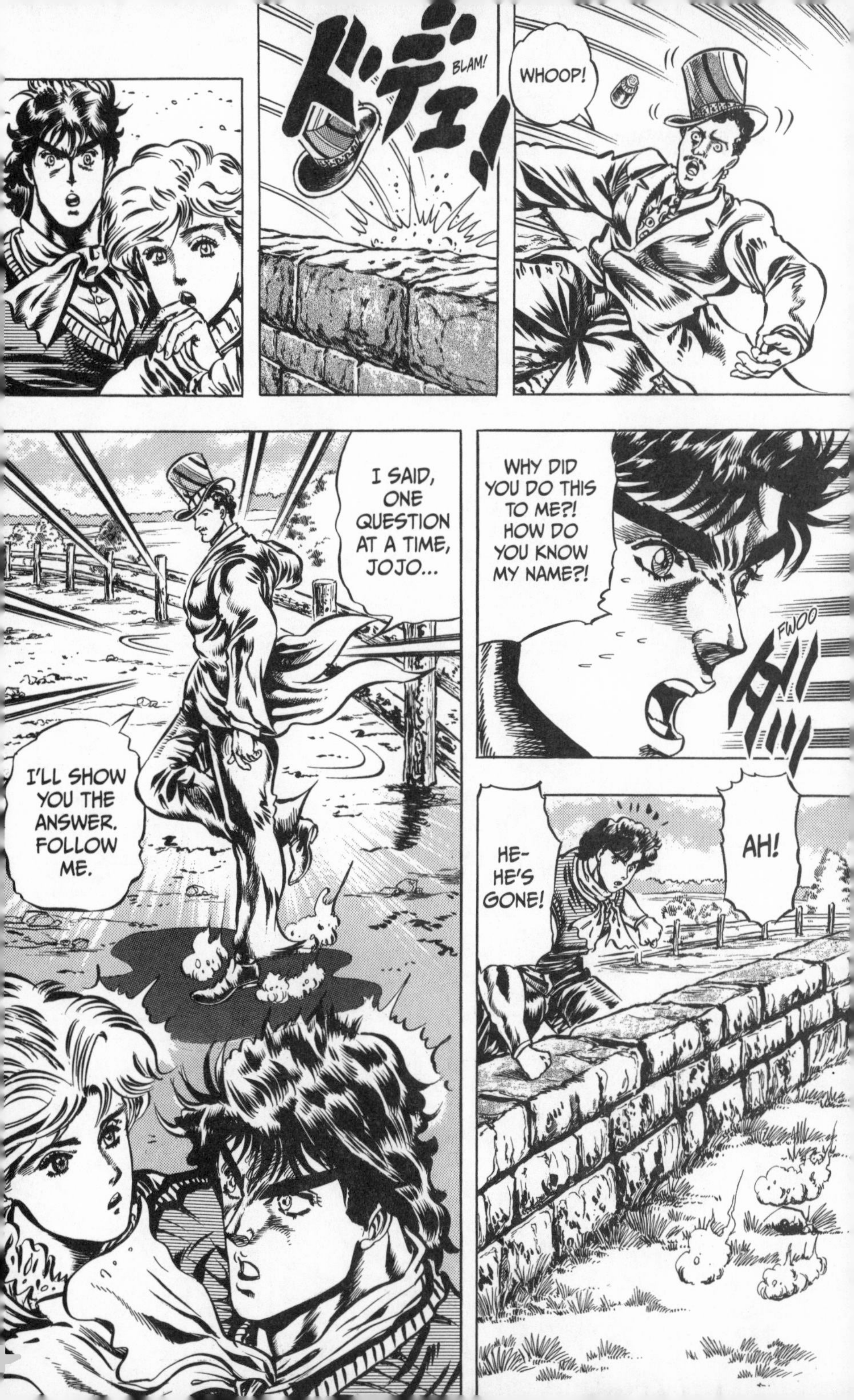
WHOOP!
ドデェ
BLAM!
WHY DID YOU DO THIS TO ME?! HOW DO YOU KNOW MY NAME?!
FWOO
AH!
HE- HE'S GONE!
I SAID, ONE QUESTION AT A TIME, JOJO...
I'LL SHOW YOU THE ANSWER. FOLLOW ME.

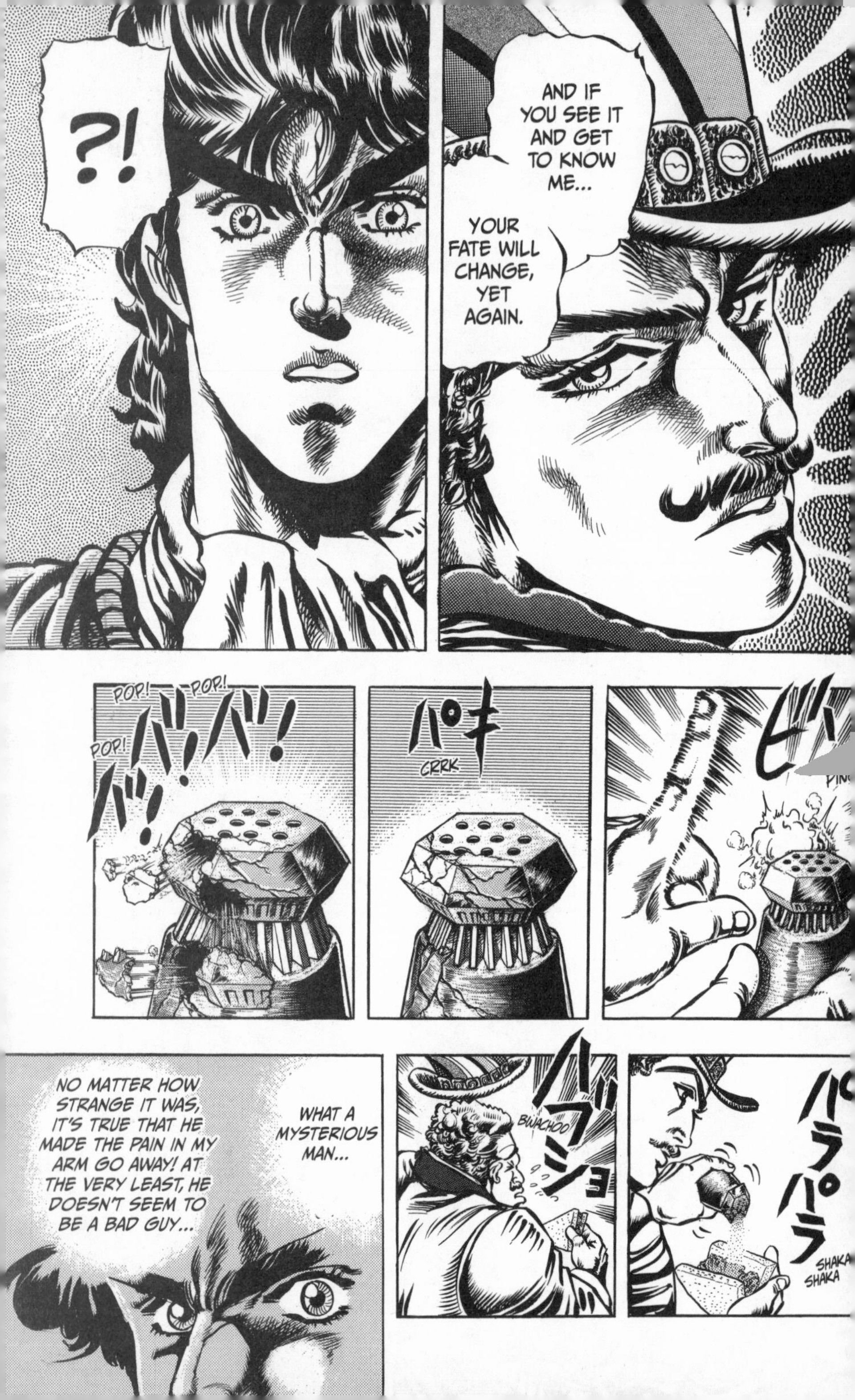
AND IF YOU SEE IT AND GET TO KNOW ME...
YOUR FATE WILL CHANGE, YET AGAIN.
?!
PING
パキ
CRRK
POP!
POP!
POP!
パラパラ
SHAKA SHAKA
BWACHOO
WHAT A MYSTERIOUS MAN...
NO MATTER HOW STRANGE IT WAS, IT'S TRUE THAT HE MADE THE PAIN IN MY ARM GO AWAY! AT THE VERY LEAST, HE DOESN'T SEEM TO BE A BAD GUY...

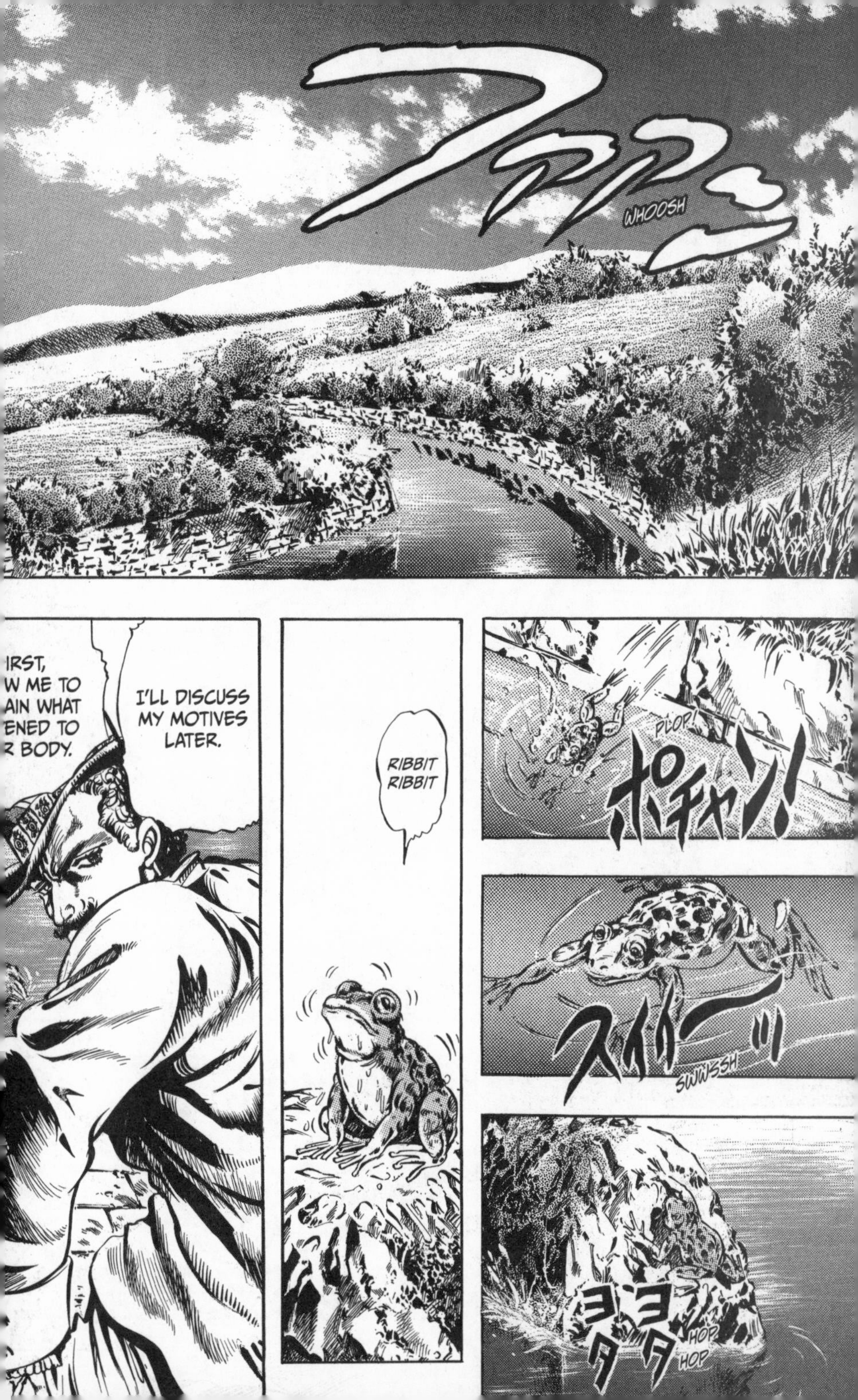
WHOOSH
PLOP!
ポチャン!
スイーッ
SWWSSH
ヨタヨタ
HOP HOP
RIBBIT RIBBIT
I'LL DISCUSS MY MOTIVES LATER.
IRST, W ME TO AIN WHAT ENED TO R BODY.

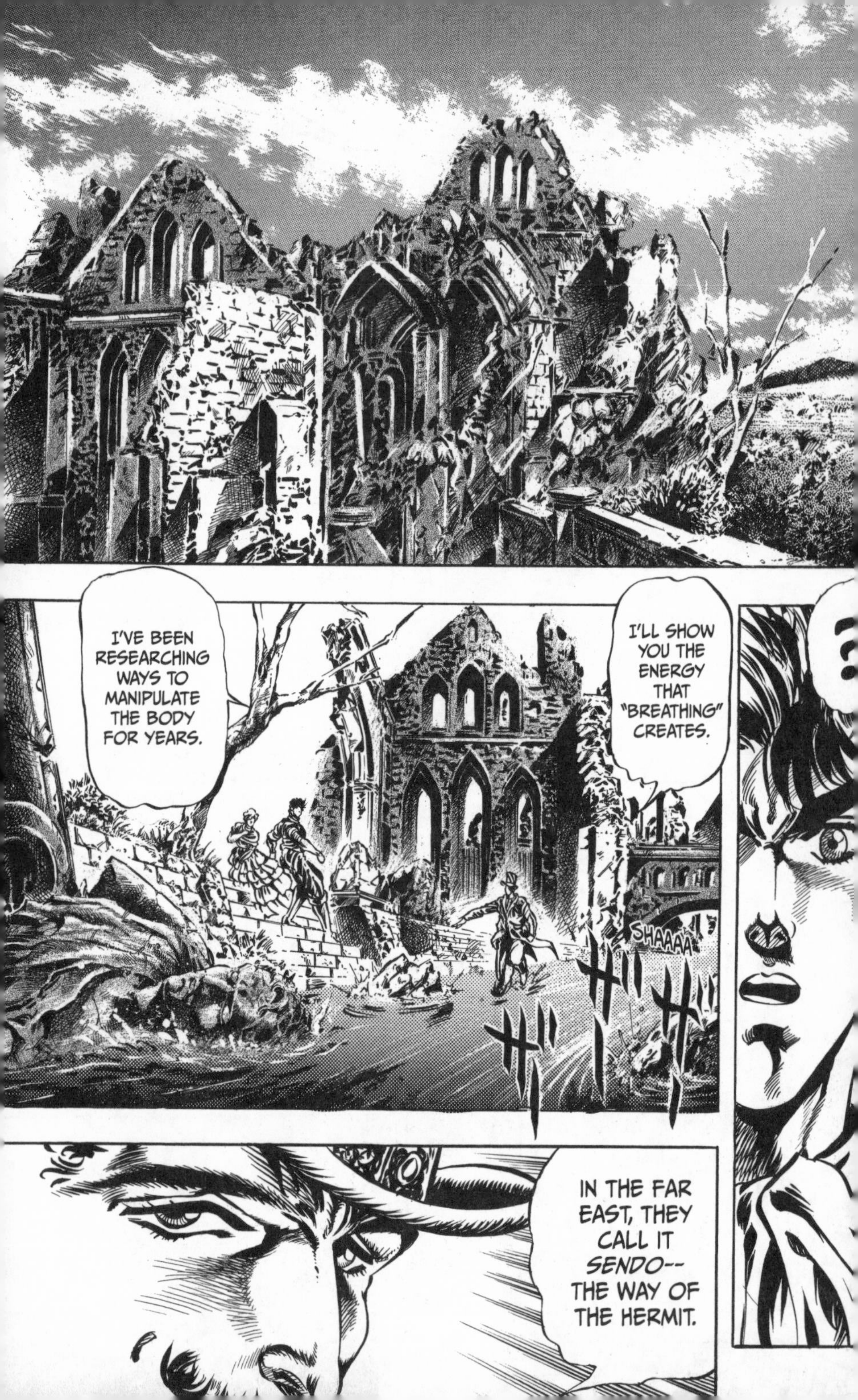
I'LL SHOW YOU THE ENERGY THAT "BREATHING" CREATES.
I'VE BEEN RESEARCHING WAYS TO MANIPULATE THE BODY FOR YEARS.
SHAAAA
IN THE FAR EAST, THEY CALL IT *SENDO*-- THE WAY OF THE HERMIT.

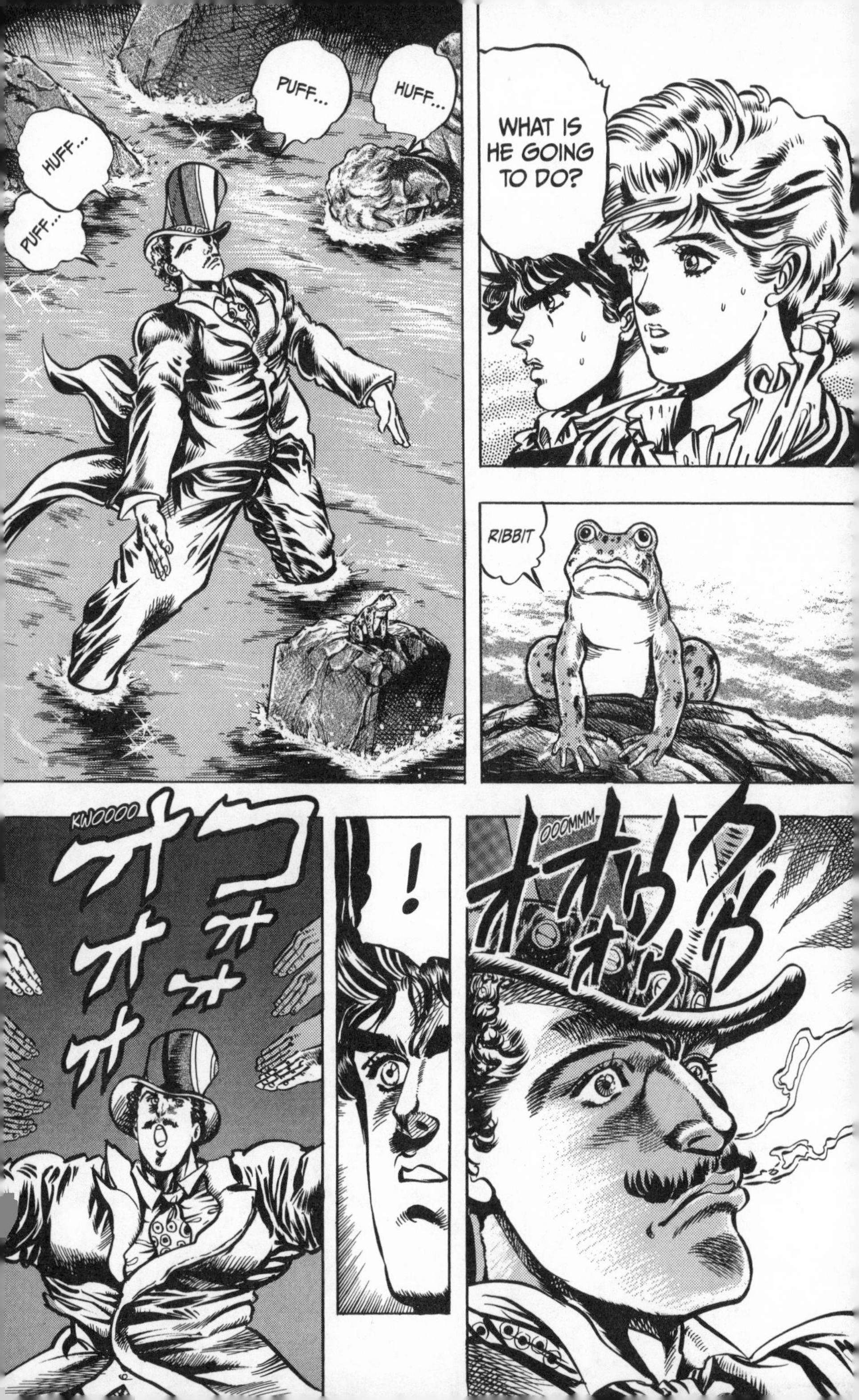

WHAT IS HE GOING TO DO?
RIBBIT
HUFF...
PUFF...
HUFF...
PUFF...
OOOMMM
!
KWOOOO

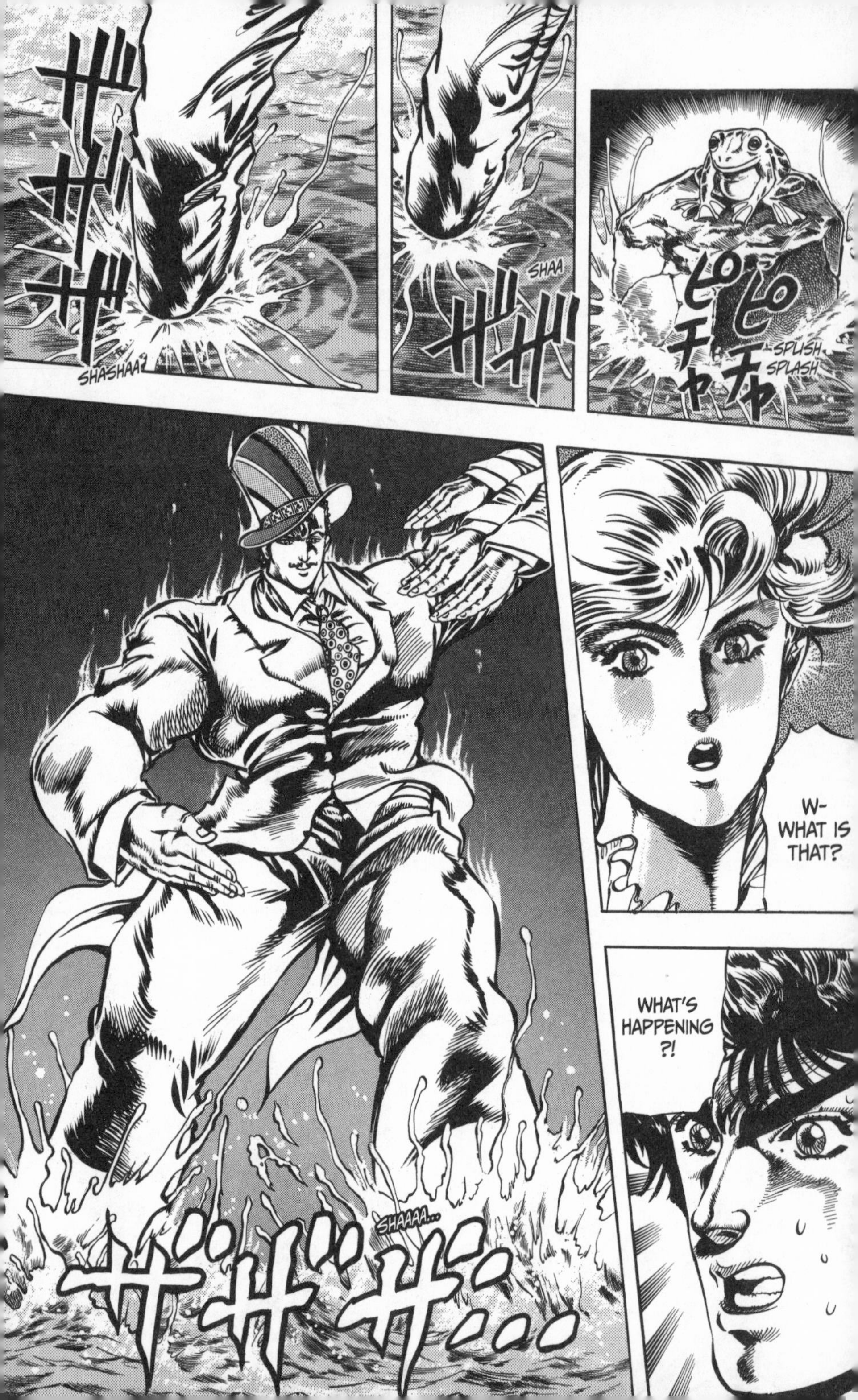
ピチャ
ピチャ
SPLISH SPLASH
SHAA
SHASHAA
W-WHAT IS THAT?
WHAT'S HAPPENING ?!
SHAAAA...

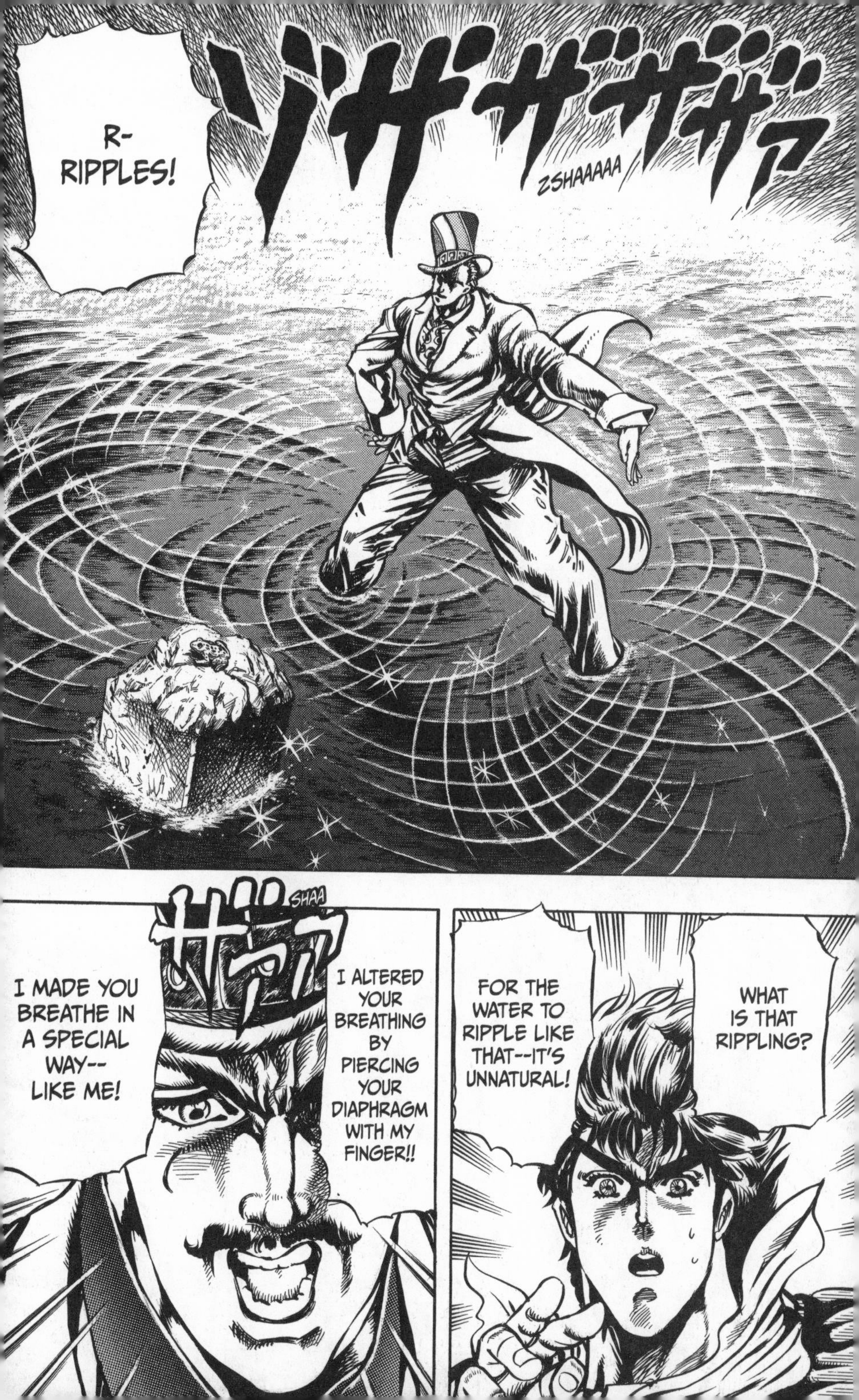
ゾザザザザァ
ZSHAAAAA
R- RIPPLES!
WHAT IS THAT RIPPLING?
FOR THE WATER TO RIPPLE LIKE THAT--IT'S UNNATURAL!
サラァ
SHAA
I ALTERED YOUR BREATHING BY PIERCING YOUR DIAPHRAGM WITH MY FINGER!!
I MADE YOU BREATHE IN A SPECIAL WAY-- LIKE ME!

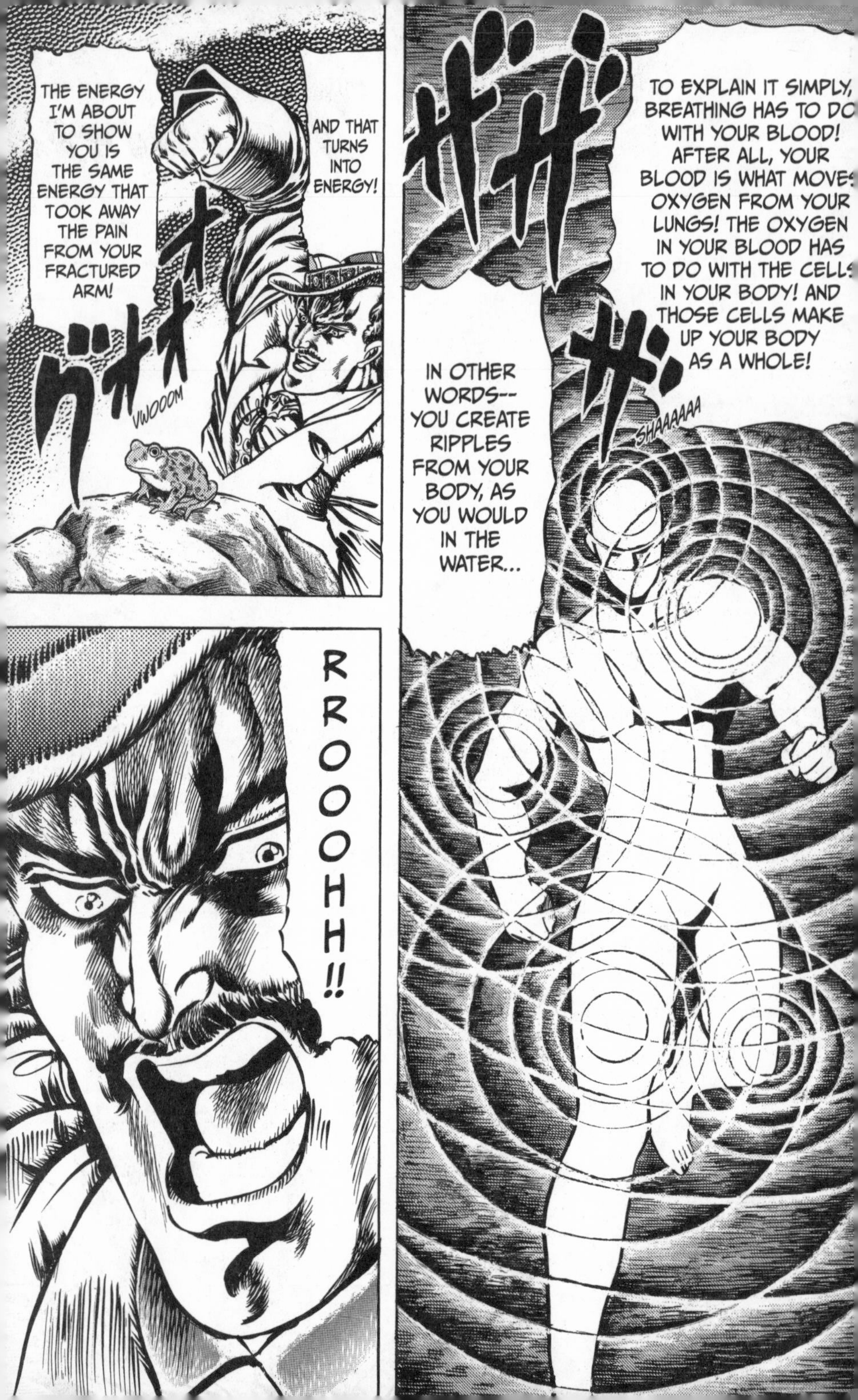
TO EXPLAIN IT SIMPLY, BREATHING HAS TO DO WITH YOUR BLOOD! AFTER ALL, YOUR BLOOD IS WHAT MOVES OXYGEN FROM YOUR LUNGS! THE OXYGEN IN YOUR BLOOD HAS TO DO WITH THE CELLS IN YOUR BODY! AND THOSE CELLS MAKE UP YOUR BODY AS A WHOLE!
IN OTHER WORDS-- YOU CREATE RIPPLES FROM YOUR BODY, AS YOU WOULD IN THE WATER...
SHAAAAAA
AND THAT TURNS INTO ENERGY!
THE ENERGY I'M ABOUT TO SHOW YOU IS THE SAME ENERGY THAT TOOK AWAY THE PAIN FROM YOUR FRACTURED ARM!
VWOOOM
RROOOOHH!!

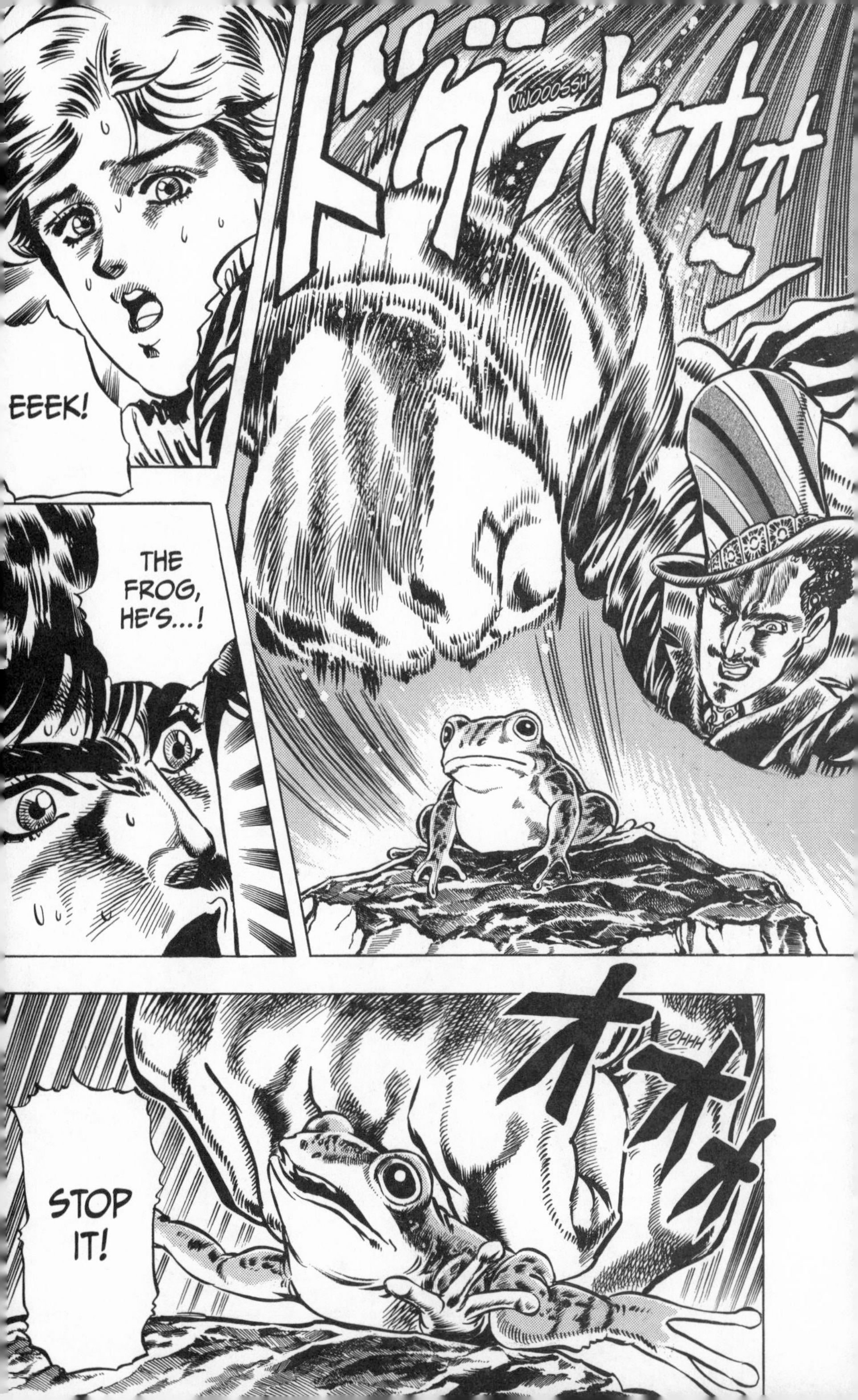
VWOOOSSH
EEEK!
THE FROG, HE'S...!
OHHH
STOP IT!

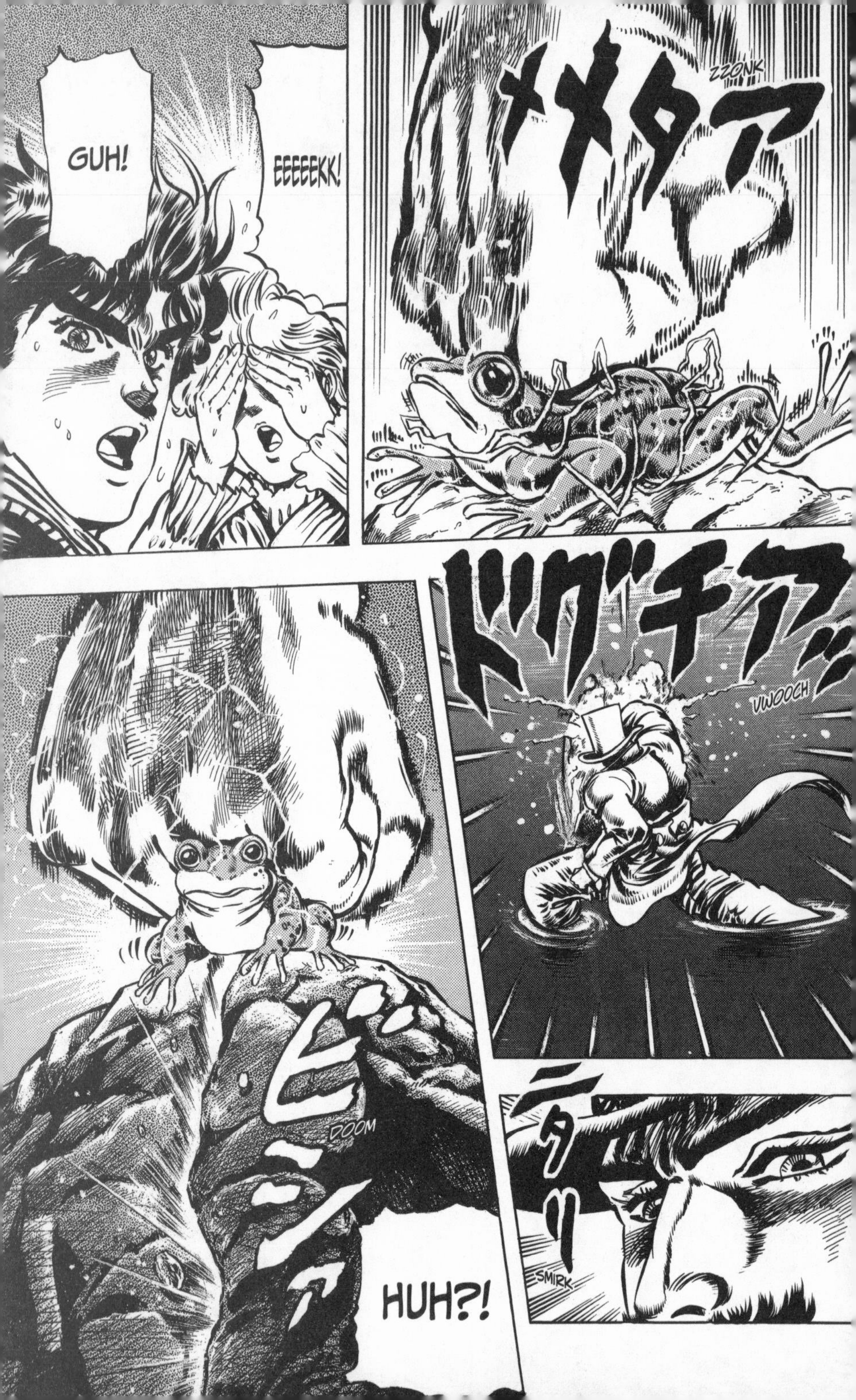

メメタァ
ZZONK
EEEEEEKK!
GUH!
ドグチアッ
UWOOCH
ニタァリ
SMIRK
DOOM
HUH?!

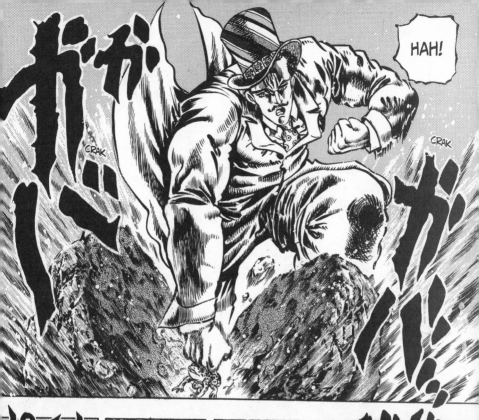

HAH!

CRAK

CRAK

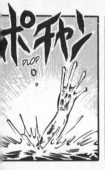

PLOP

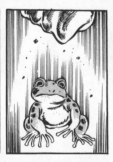

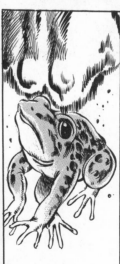

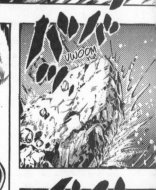

VWOOM

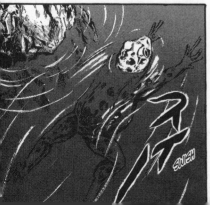

SWISH

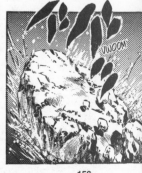

VWOOM

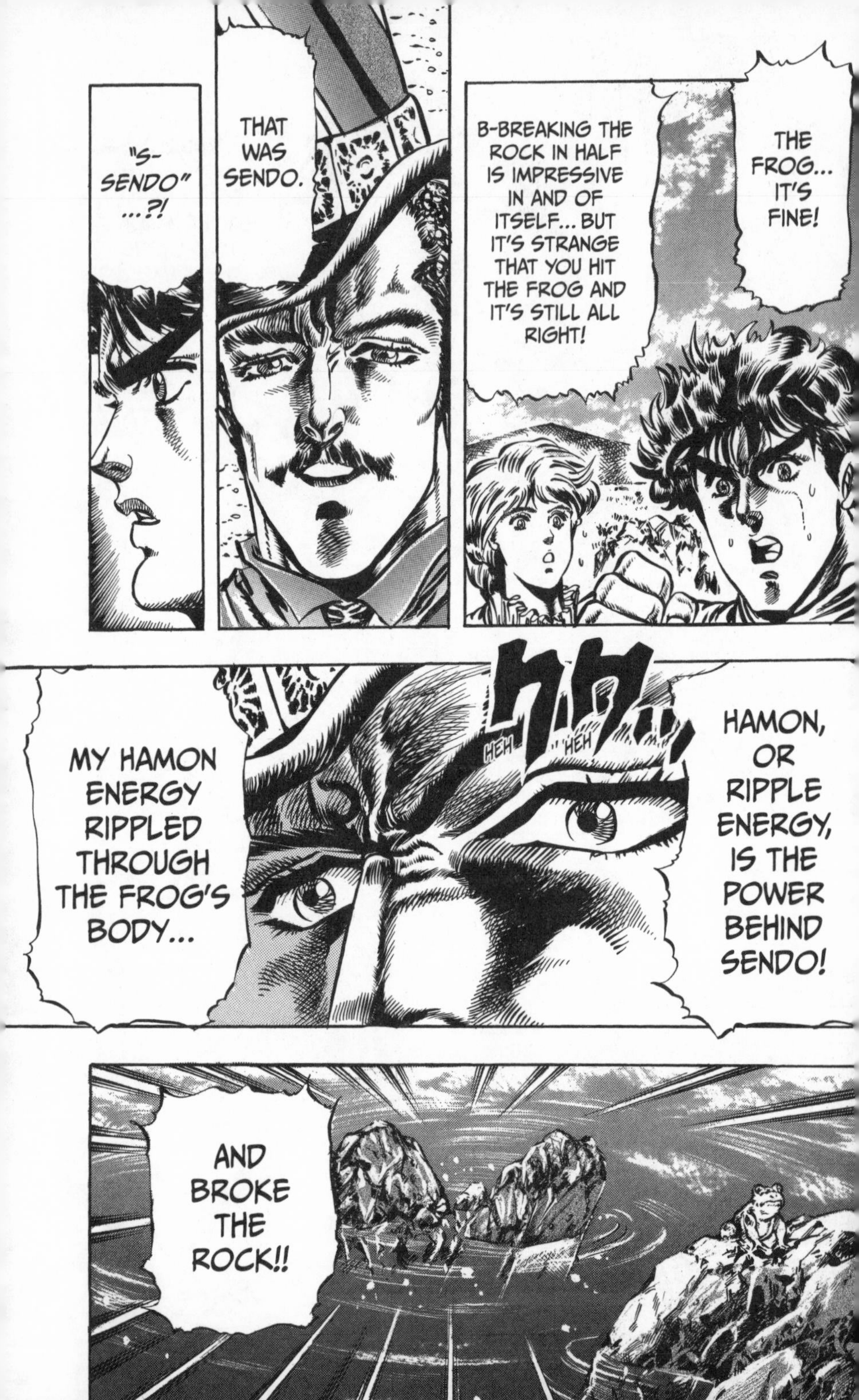
THE FROG... IT'S FINE!
B-BREAKING THE ROCK IN HALF IS IMPRESSIVE IN AND OF ITSELF... BUT IT'S STRANGE THAT YOU HIT THE FROG AND IT'S STILL ALL RIGHT!
THAT WAS SENDO.
"S-SENDO" ...?!
HAMON, OR RIPPLE ENERGY, IS THE POWER BEHIND SENDO!
HEH HEH
MY HAMON ENERGY RIPPLED THROUGH THE FROG'S BODY...
AND BROKE THE ROCK!!

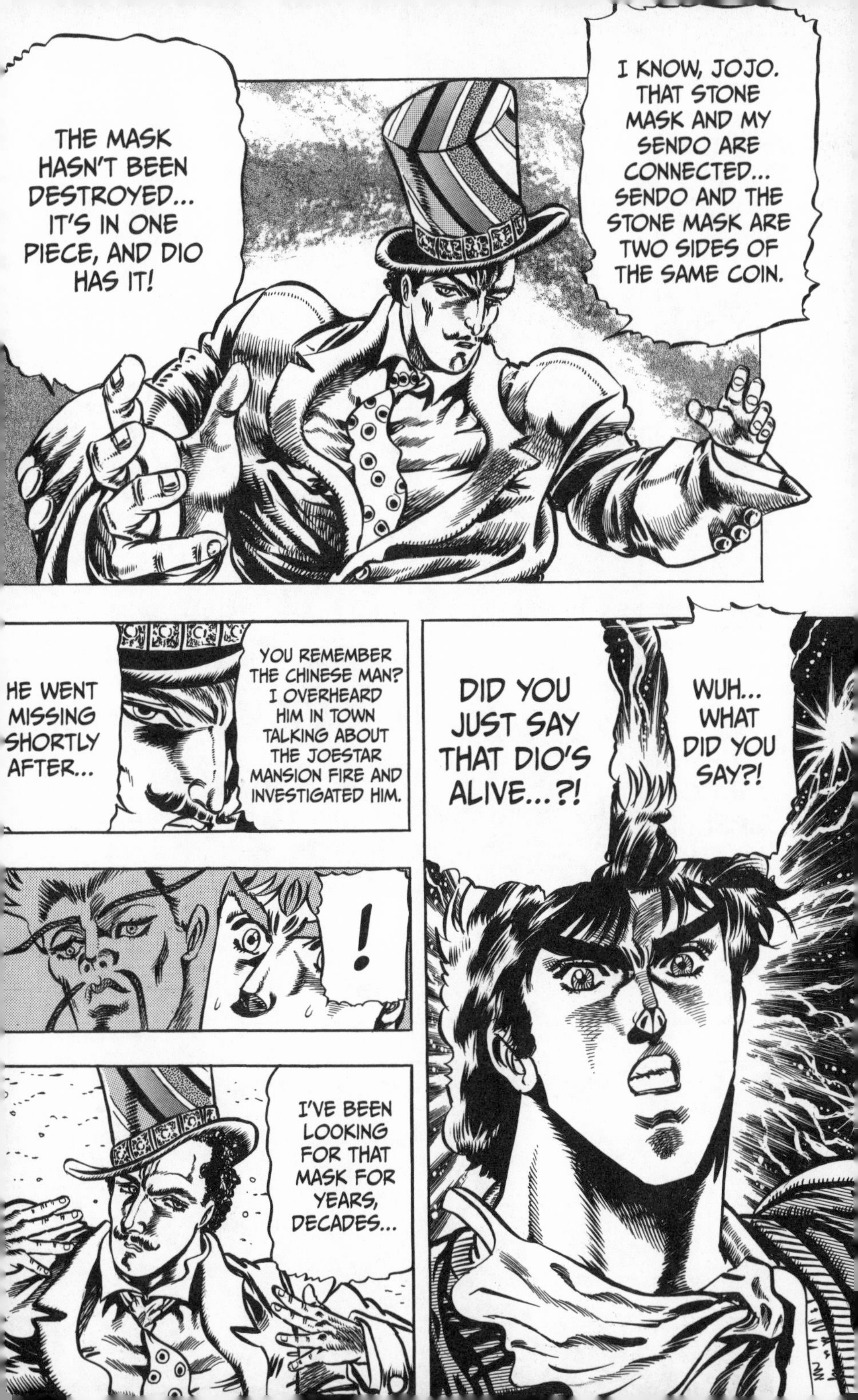
I KNOW, JOJO. THAT STONE MASK AND MY SENDO ARE CONNECTED... SENDO AND THE STONE MASK ARE TWO SIDES OF THE SAME COIN.
THE MASK HASN'T BEEN DESTROYED... IT'S IN ONE PIECE, AND DIO HAS IT!
WUH... WHAT DID YOU SAY?!
DID YOU JUST SAY THAT DIO'S ALIVE...?!
YOU REMEMBER THE CHINESE MAN? I OVERHEARD HIM IN TOWN TALKING ABOUT THE JOESTAR MANSION FIRE AND INVESTIGATED HIM.
HE WENT MISSING SHORTLY AFTER...
!
I'VE BEEN LOOKING FOR THAT MASK FOR YEARS, DECADES...

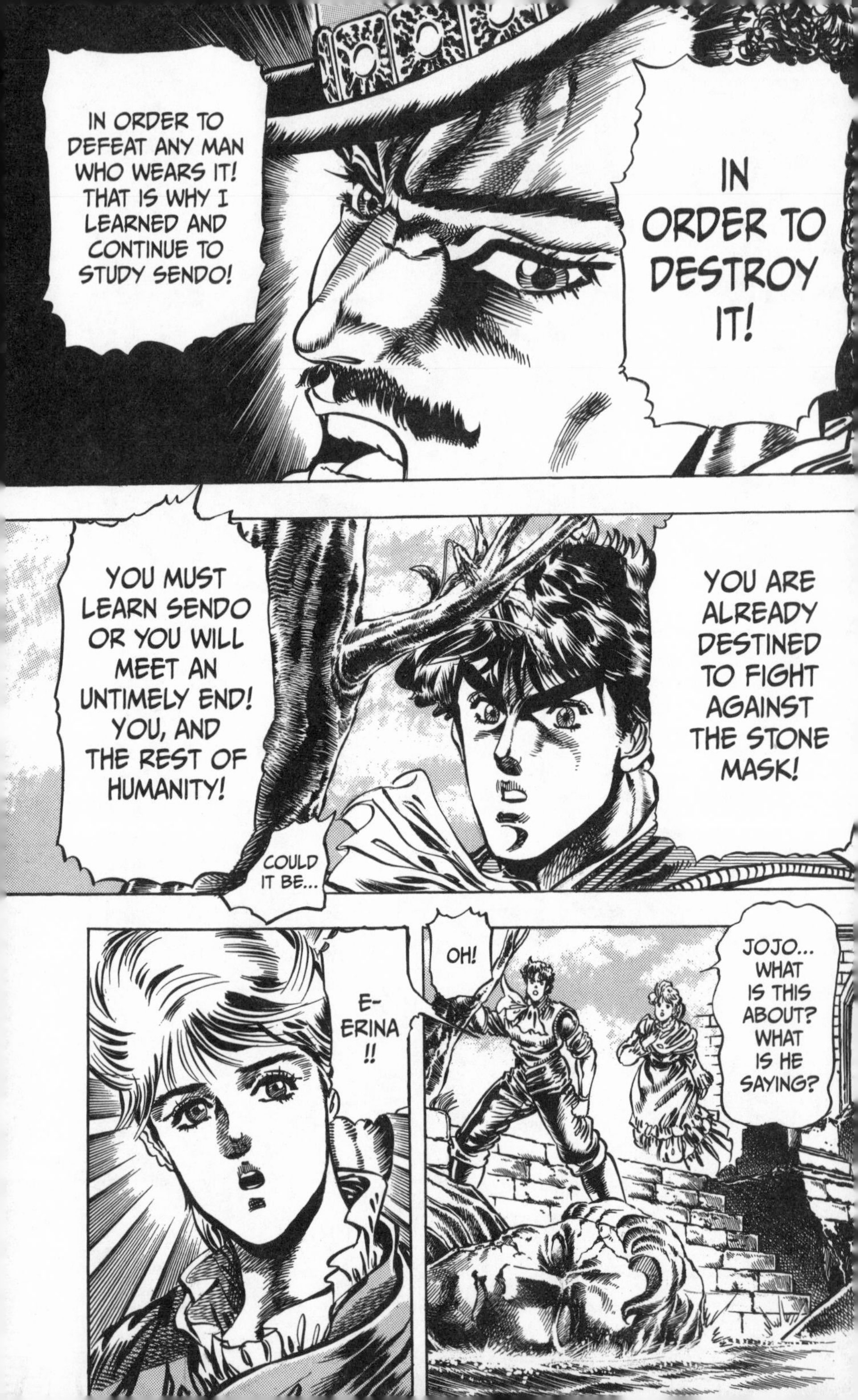
IN ORDER TO DESTROY IT!
IN ORDER TO DEFEAT ANY MAN WHO WEARS IT! THAT IS WHY I LEARNED AND CONTINUE TO STUDY SENDO!
YOU ARE ALREADY DESTINED TO FIGHT AGAINST THE STONE MASK!
YOU MUST LEARN SENDO OR YOU WILL MEET AN UNTIMELY END! YOU, AND THE REST OF HUMANITY!
COULD IT BE...
JOJO... WHAT IS THIS ABOUT? WHAT IS HE SAYING?
OH!
E-ERINA!!

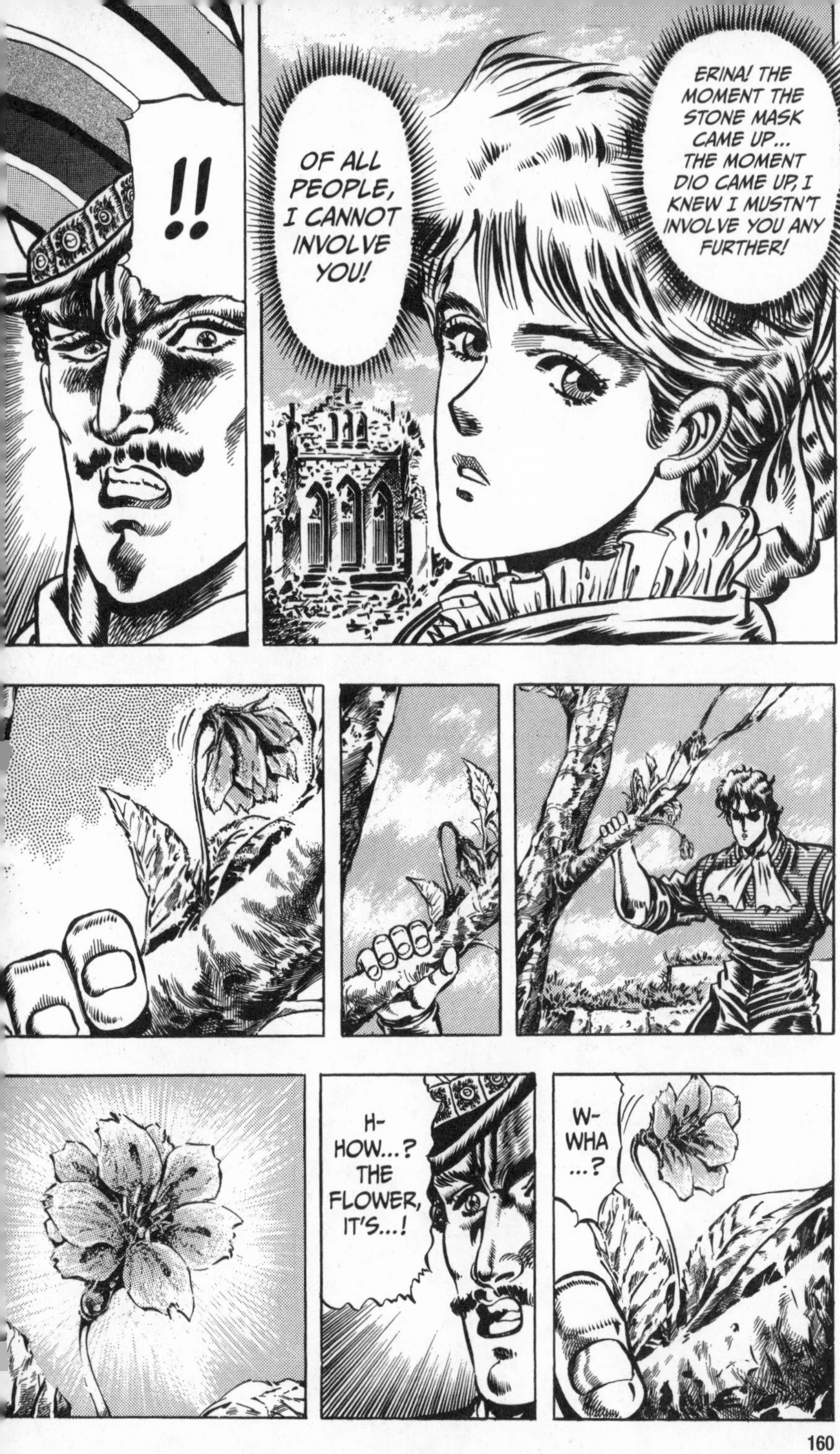
ERINA! THE MOMENT THE STONE MASK CAME UP... THE MOMENT DIO CAME UP, I KNEW I MUSTN'T INVOLVE YOU ANY FURTHER!
OF ALL PEOPLE, I CANNOT INVOLVE YOU!
!!
W-WHA...?
H-HOW...? THE FLOWER, IT'S...!

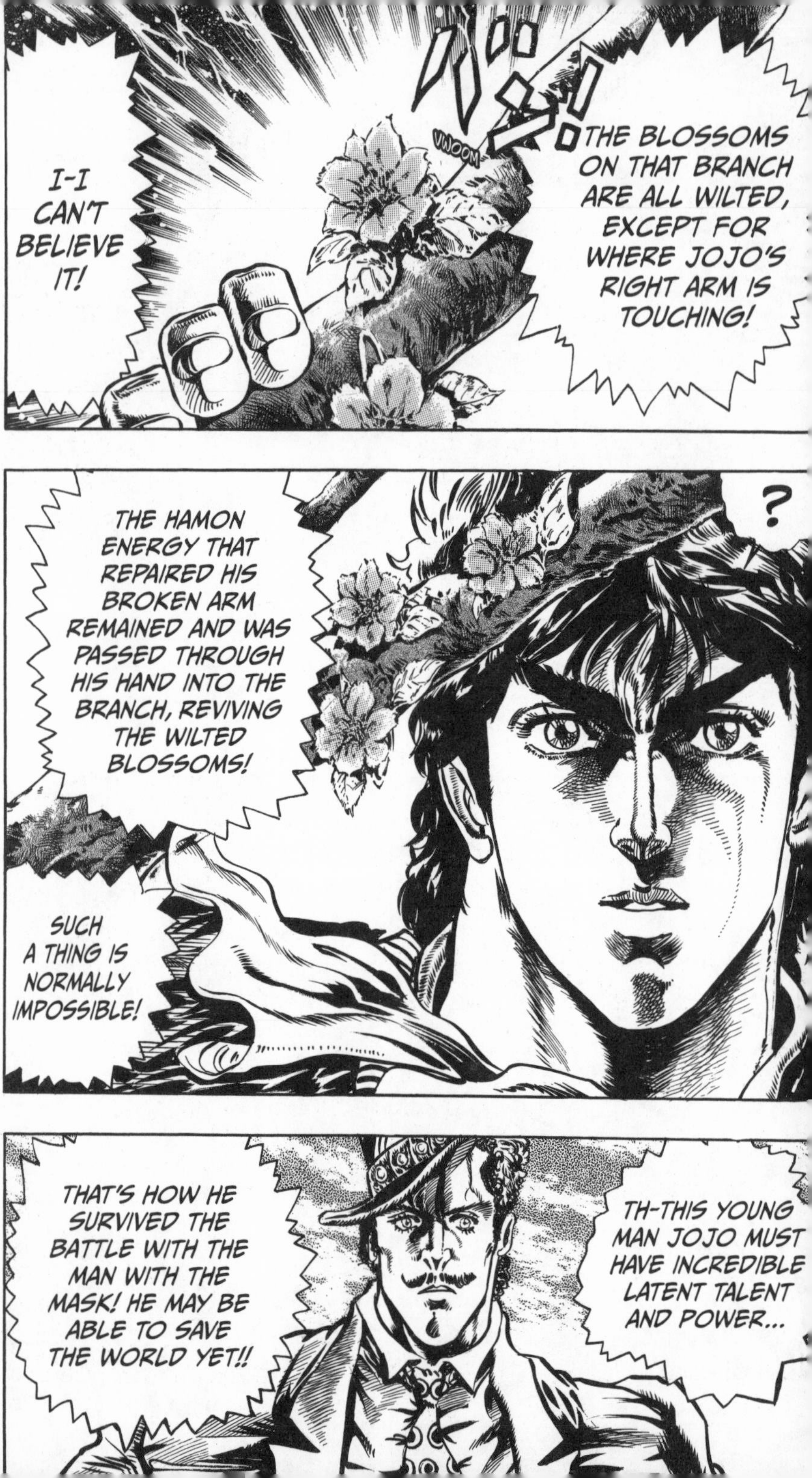
THE BLOSSOMS ON THAT BRANCH ARE ALL WILTED, EXCEPT FOR WHERE JOJO'S RIGHT ARM IS TOUCHING!
VWOOM
I-I CAN'T BELIEVE IT!
?
THE HAMON ENERGY THAT REPAIRED HIS BROKEN ARM REMAINED AND WAS PASSED THROUGH HIS HAND INTO THE BRANCH, REVIVING THE WILTED BLOSSOMS!
SUCH A THING IS NORMALLY IMPOSSIBLE!
TH-THIS YOUNG MAN JOJO MUST HAVE INCREDIBLE LATENT TALENT AND POWER...
THAT'S HOW HE SURVIVED THE BATTLE WITH THE MAN WITH THE MASK! HE MAY BE ABLE TO SAVE THE WORLD YET!!

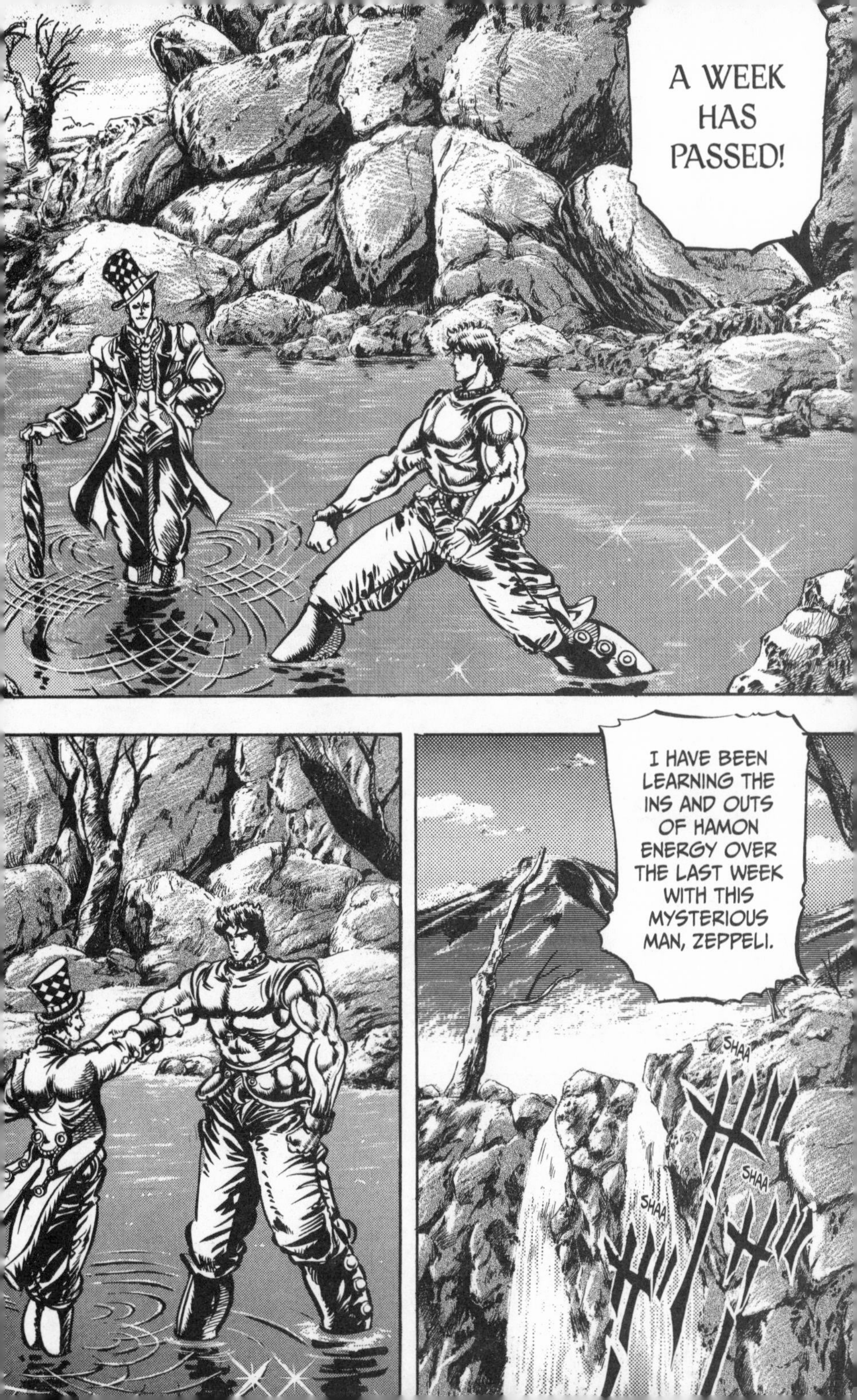
A WEEK HAS PASSED!
I HAVE BEEN LEARNING THE INS AND OUTS OF HAMON ENERGY OVER THE LAST WEEK WITH THIS MYSTERIOUS MAN, ZEPPELI.
SHAA
SHAA
SHAA

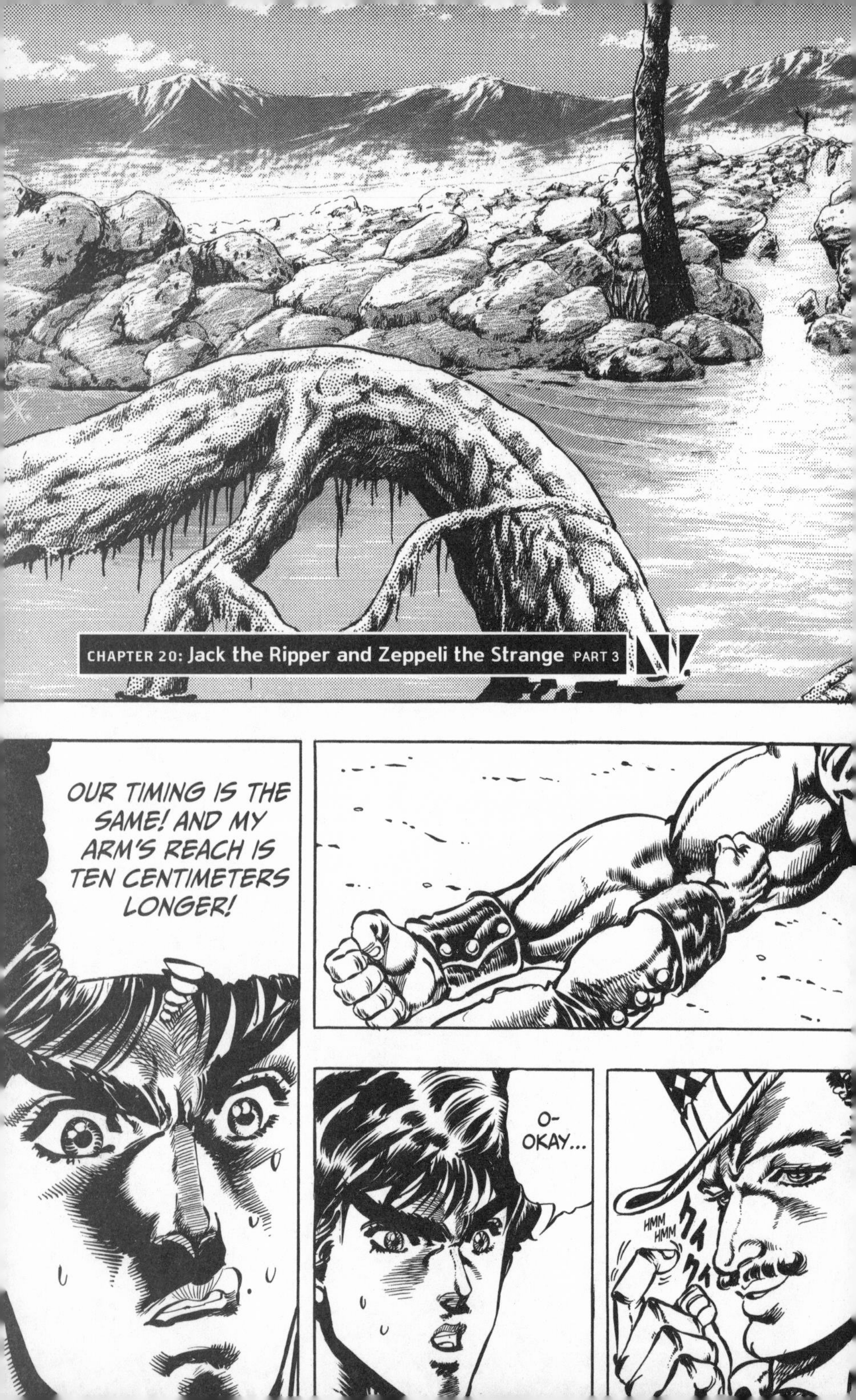
CHAPTER 20: Jack the Ripper and Zeppeli the Strange PART 3
HMM HMM
O-OKAY...
OUR TIMING IS THE SAME! AND MY ARM'S REACH IS TEN CENTIMETERS LONGER!

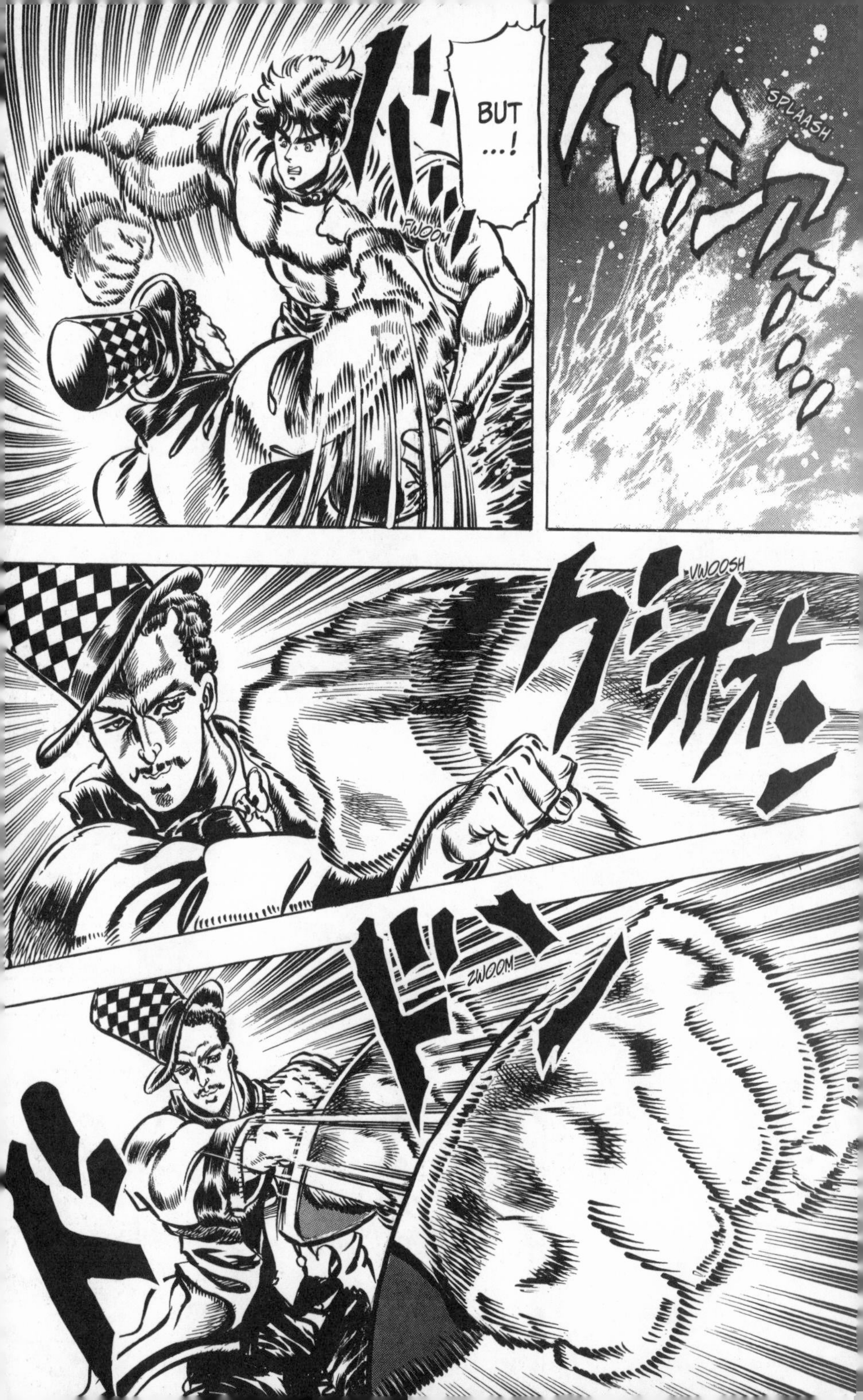
SPLAASH
BUT ...!
FWOOM
VWOOSH
ZWOOM

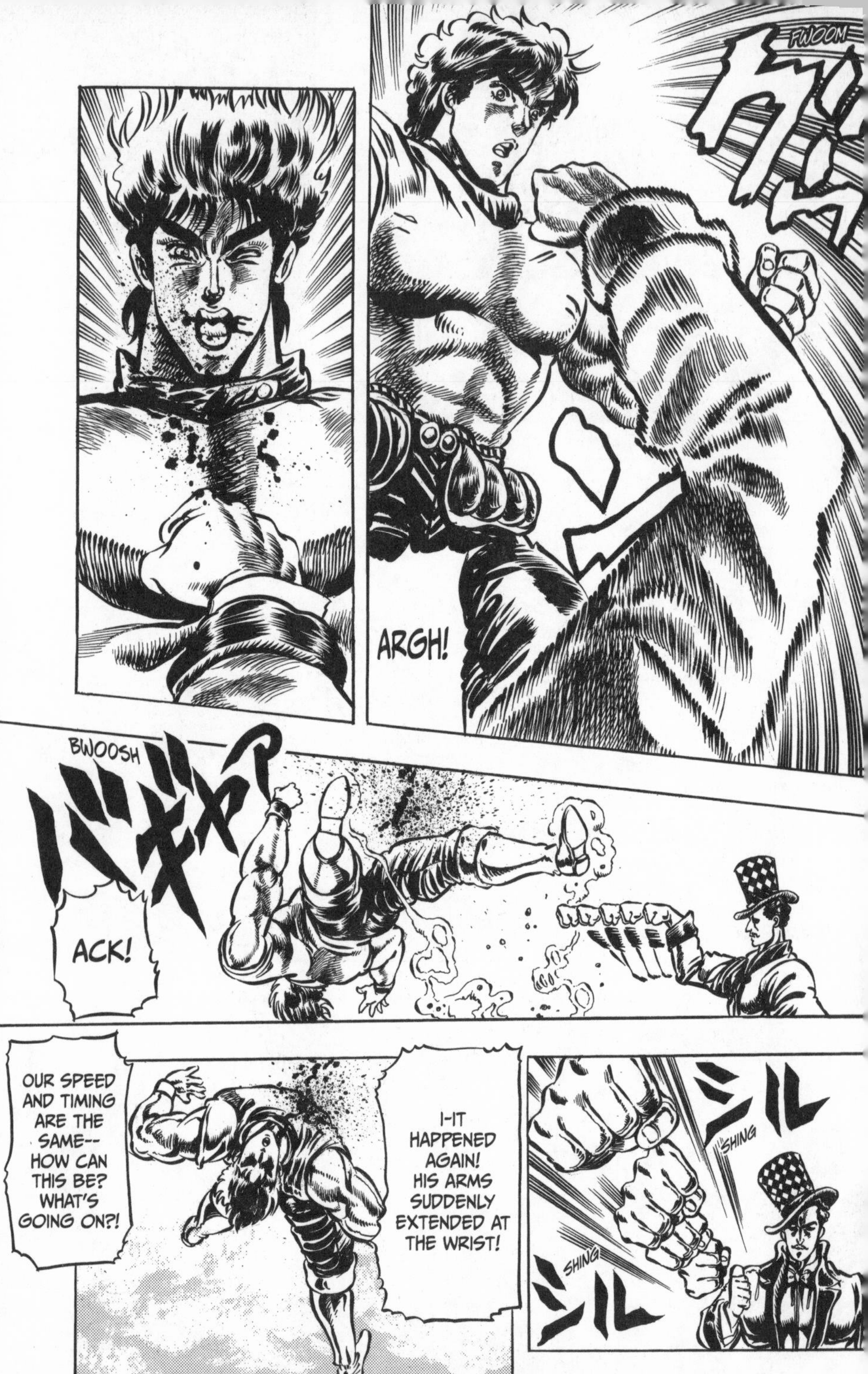
FWOON
ARGH!
BWOOSH
ACK!
SHING
SHING
I-IT HAPPENED AGAIN! HIS ARMS SUDDENLY EXTENDED AT THE WRIST!
OUR SPEED AND TIMING ARE THE SAME-- HOW CAN THIS BE? WHAT'S GOING ON?!

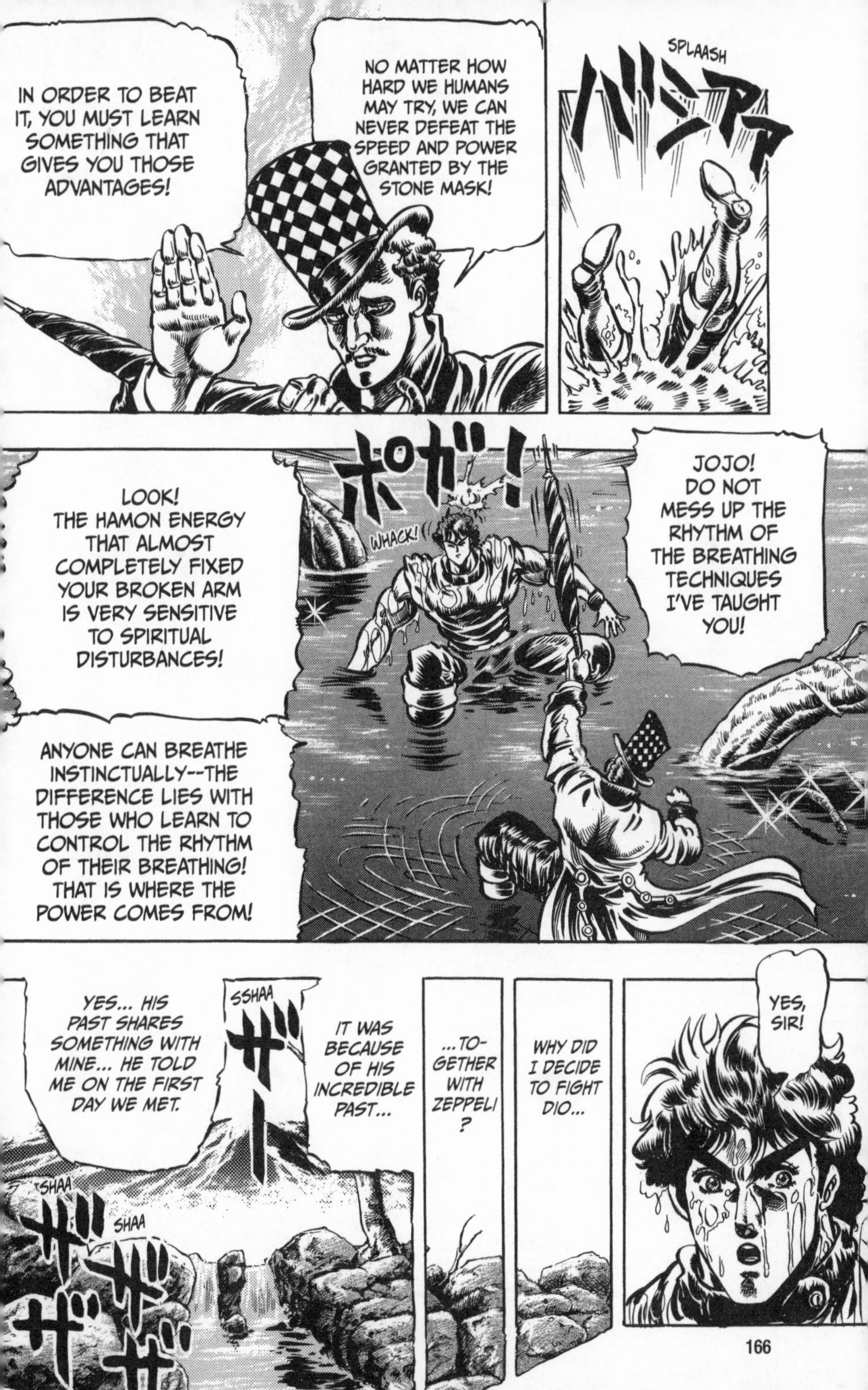
SPLAASH
NO MATTER HOW HARD WE HUMANS MAY TRY, WE CAN NEVER DEFEAT THE SPEED AND POWER GRANTED BY THE STONE MASK!
IN ORDER TO BEAT IT, YOU MUST LEARN SOMETHING THAT GIVES YOU THOSE ADVANTAGES!
JOJO! DO NOT MESS UP THE RHYTHM OF THE BREATHING TECHNIQUES I'VE TAUGHT YOU!
WHACK!
LOOK! THE HAMON ENERGY THAT ALMOST COMPLETELY FIXED YOUR BROKEN ARM IS VERY SENSITIVE TO SPIRITUAL DISTURBANCES!
ANYONE CAN BREATHE INSTINCTUALLY--THE DIFFERENCE LIES WITH THOSE WHO LEARN TO CONTROL THE RHYTHM OF THEIR BREATHING! THAT IS WHERE THE POWER COMES FROM!
YES, SIR!
WHY DID I DECIDE TO FIGHT DIO...
...TO-GETHER WITH ZEPPELI ?
IT WAS BECAUSE OF HIS INCREDIBLE PAST...
SSHAA
YES... HIS PAST SHARES SOMETHING WITH MINE... HE TOLD ME ON THE FIRST DAY WE MET.
SHAA
SHAA

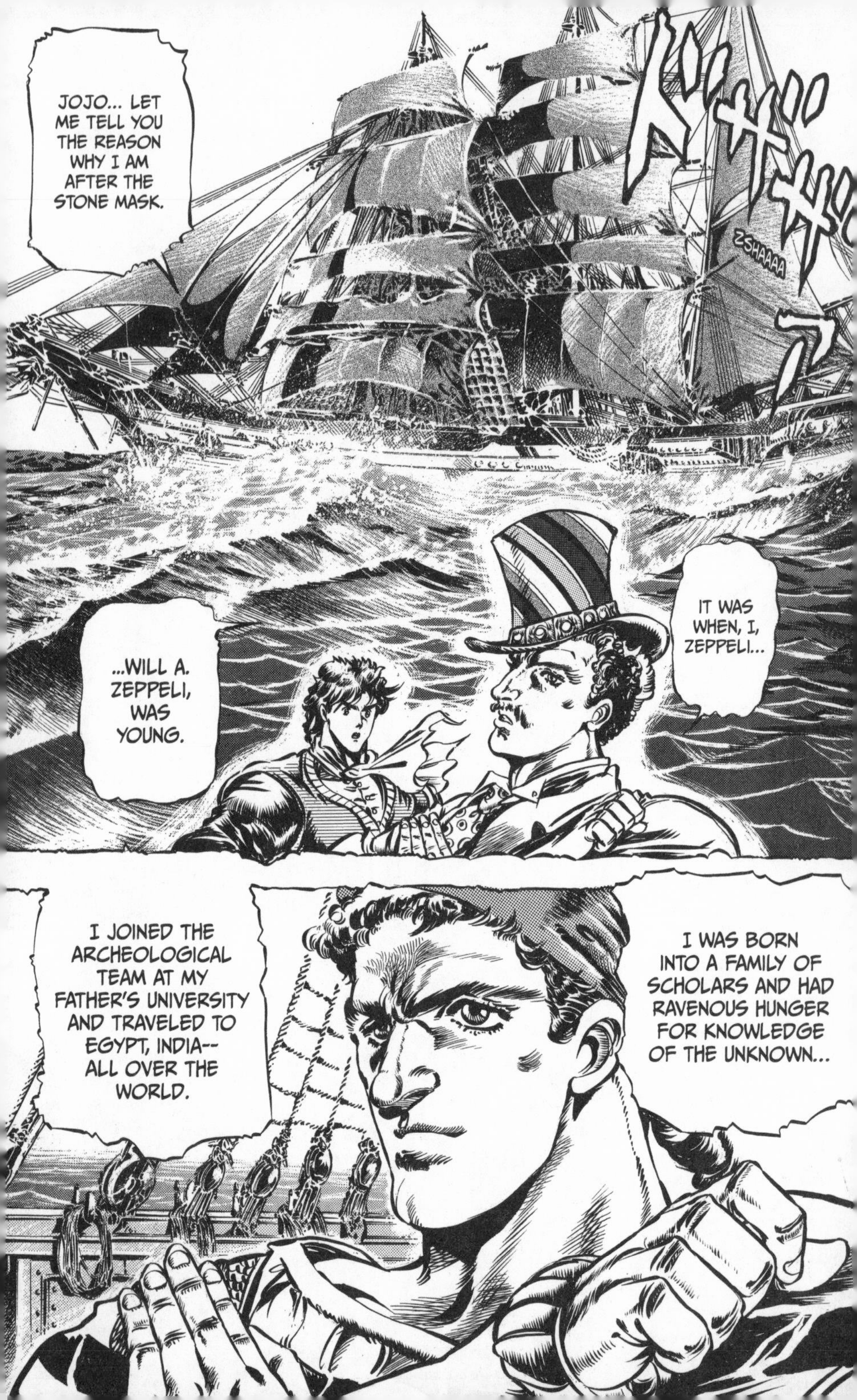
JOJO... LET ME TELL YOU THE REASON WHY I AM AFTER THE STONE MASK.
ZSHAAAA
IT WAS WHEN, I, ZEPPELI...
...WILL A. ZEPPELI, WAS YOUNG.
I WAS BORN INTO A FAMILY OF SCHOLARS AND HAD RAVENOUS HUNGER FOR KNOWLEDGE OF THE UNKNOWN...
I JOINED THE ARCHEOLOGICAL TEAM AT MY FATHER'S UNIVERSITY AND TRAVELED TO EGYPT, INDIA-- ALL OVER THE WORLD.

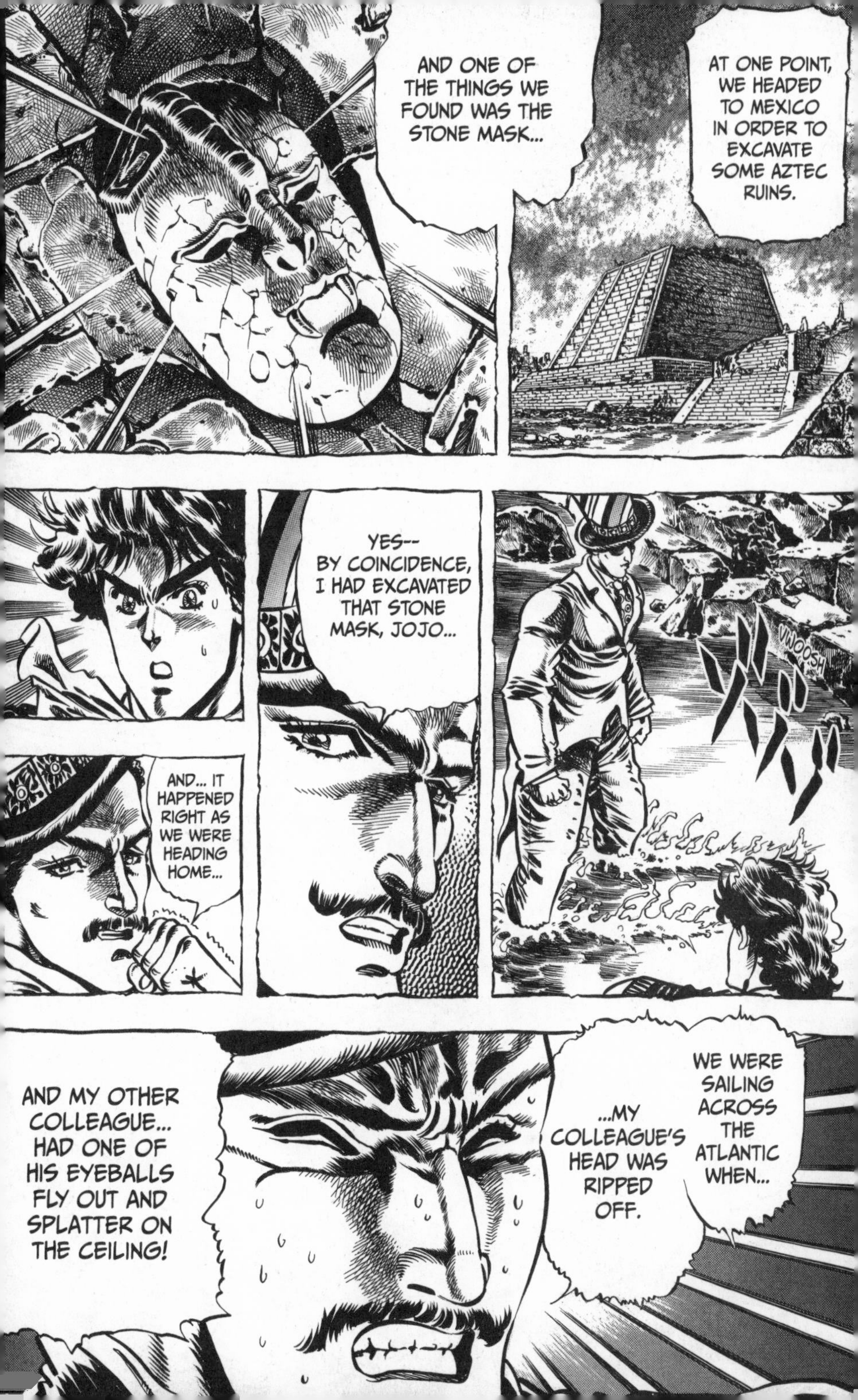
AT ONE POINT, WE HEADED TO MEXICO IN ORDER TO EXCAVATE SOME AZTEC RUINS.
AND ONE OF THE THINGS WE FOUND WAS THE STONE MASK...
VWOOSH
YES-- BY COINCIDENCE, I HAD EXCAVATED THAT STONE MASK, JOJO...
AND... IT HAPPENED RIGHT AS WE WERE HEADING HOME...
WE WERE SAILING ACROSS THE ATLANTIC WHEN...
...MY COLLEAGUE'S HEAD WAS RIPPED OFF.
AND MY OTHER COLLEAGUE... HAD ONE OF HIS EYEBALLS FLY OUT AND SPLATTER ON THE CEILING!

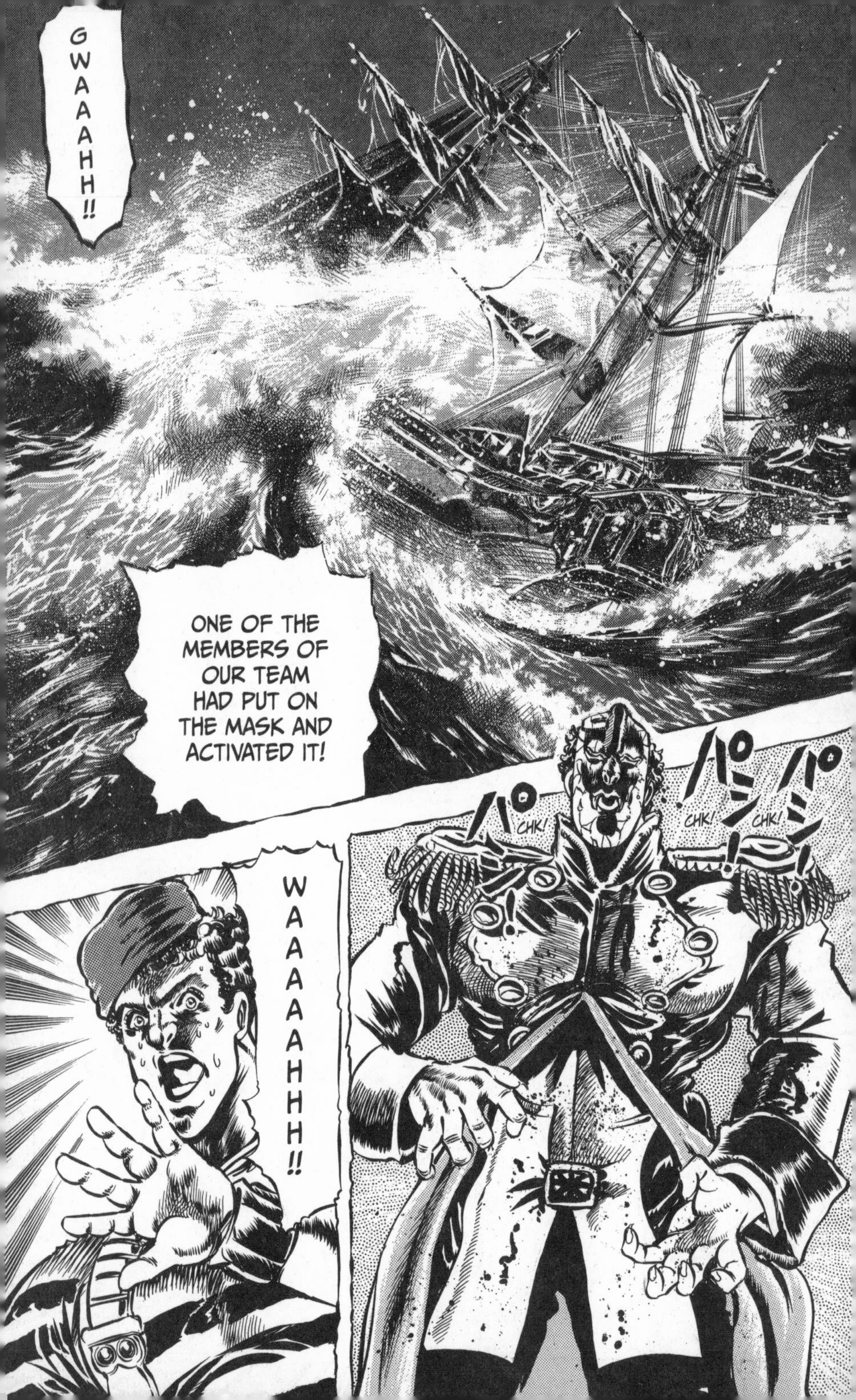
GWAAAHH!!
ONE OF THE MEMBERS OF OUR TEAM HAD PUT ON THE MASK AND ACTIVATED IT!
CHK!
CHK!
CHK!
WAAAAAHHH!!

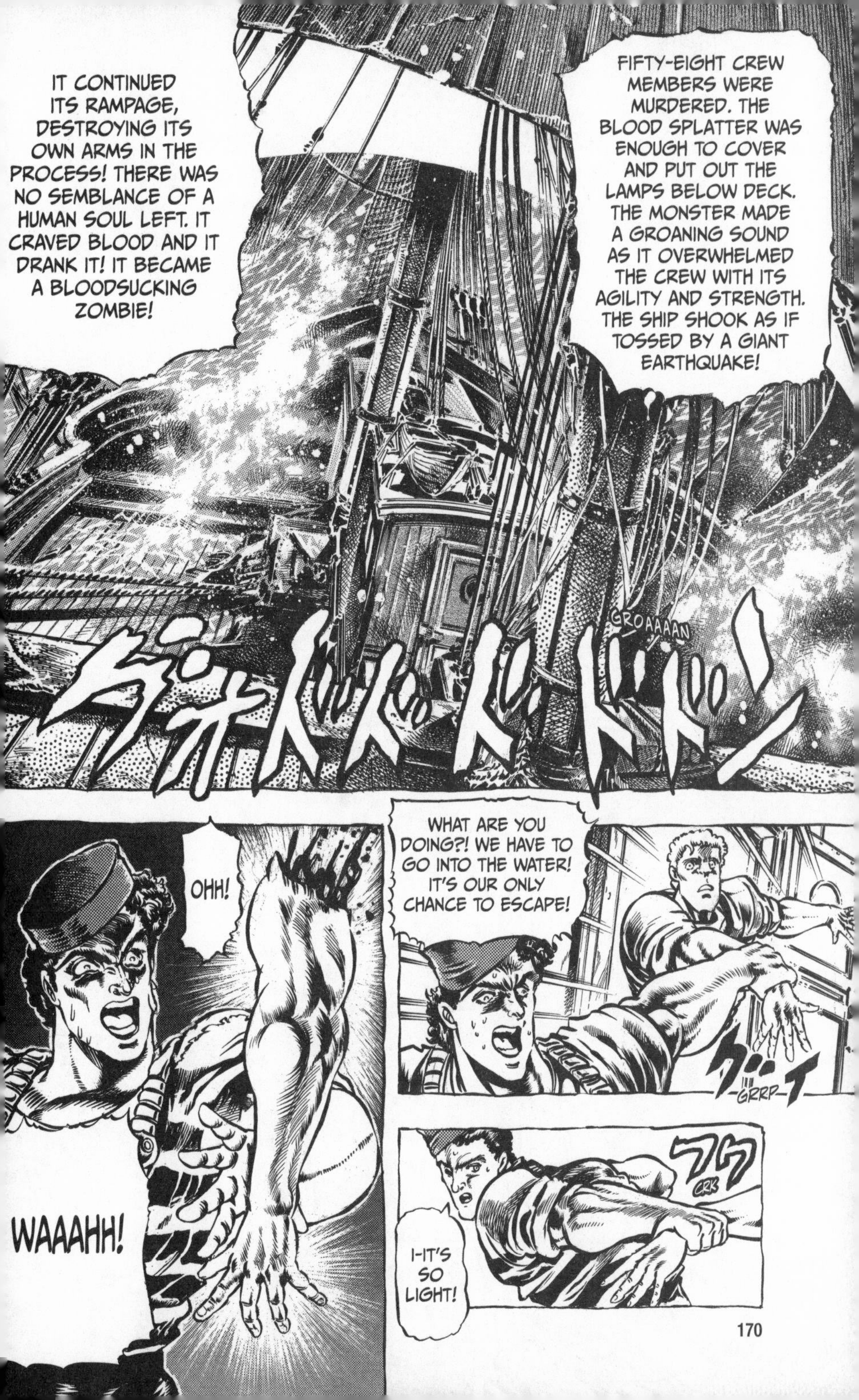
FIFTY-EIGHT CREW MEMBERS WERE MURDERED. THE BLOOD SPLATTER WAS ENOUGH TO COVER AND PUT OUT THE LAMPS BELOW DECK. THE MONSTER MADE A GROANING SOUND AS IT OVERWHELMED THE CREW WITH ITS AGILITY AND STRENGTH. THE SHIP SHOOK AS IF TOSSED BY A GIANT EARTHQUAKE!
IT CONTINUED ITS RAMPAGE, DESTROYING ITS OWN ARMS IN THE PROCESS! THERE WAS NO SEMBLANCE OF A HUMAN SOUL LEFT. IT CRAVED BLOOD AND IT DRANK IT! IT BECAME A BLOODSUCKING ZOMBIE!
GROAAAAN
WHAT ARE YOU DOING?! WE HAVE TO GO INTO THE WATER! IT'S OUR ONLY CHANCE TO ESCAPE!
GRRP
CRK
I-IT'S SO LIGHT!
OHH!
WAAAHH!

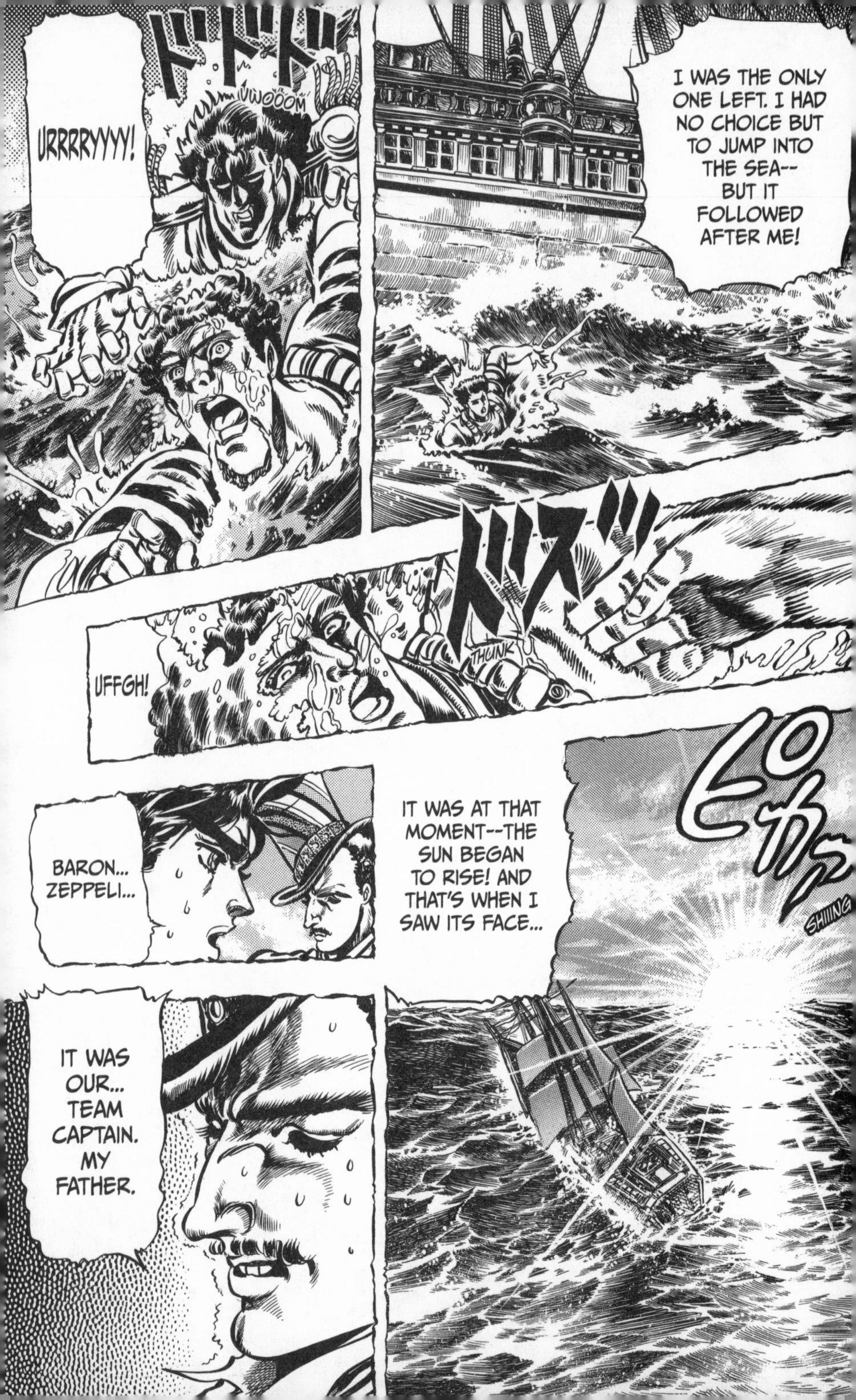
I WAS THE ONLY ONE LEFT. I HAD NO CHOICE BUT TO JUMP INTO THE SEA-- BUT IT FOLLOWED AFTER ME!
VWOOOM
URRRRYYYY!
THUNK
UFFGH!
SHIIING
IT WAS AT THAT MOMENT--THE SUN BEGAN TO RISE! AND THAT'S WHEN I SAW ITS FACE...
BARON... ZEPPELI...
IT WAS OUR... TEAM CAPTAIN. MY FATHER.

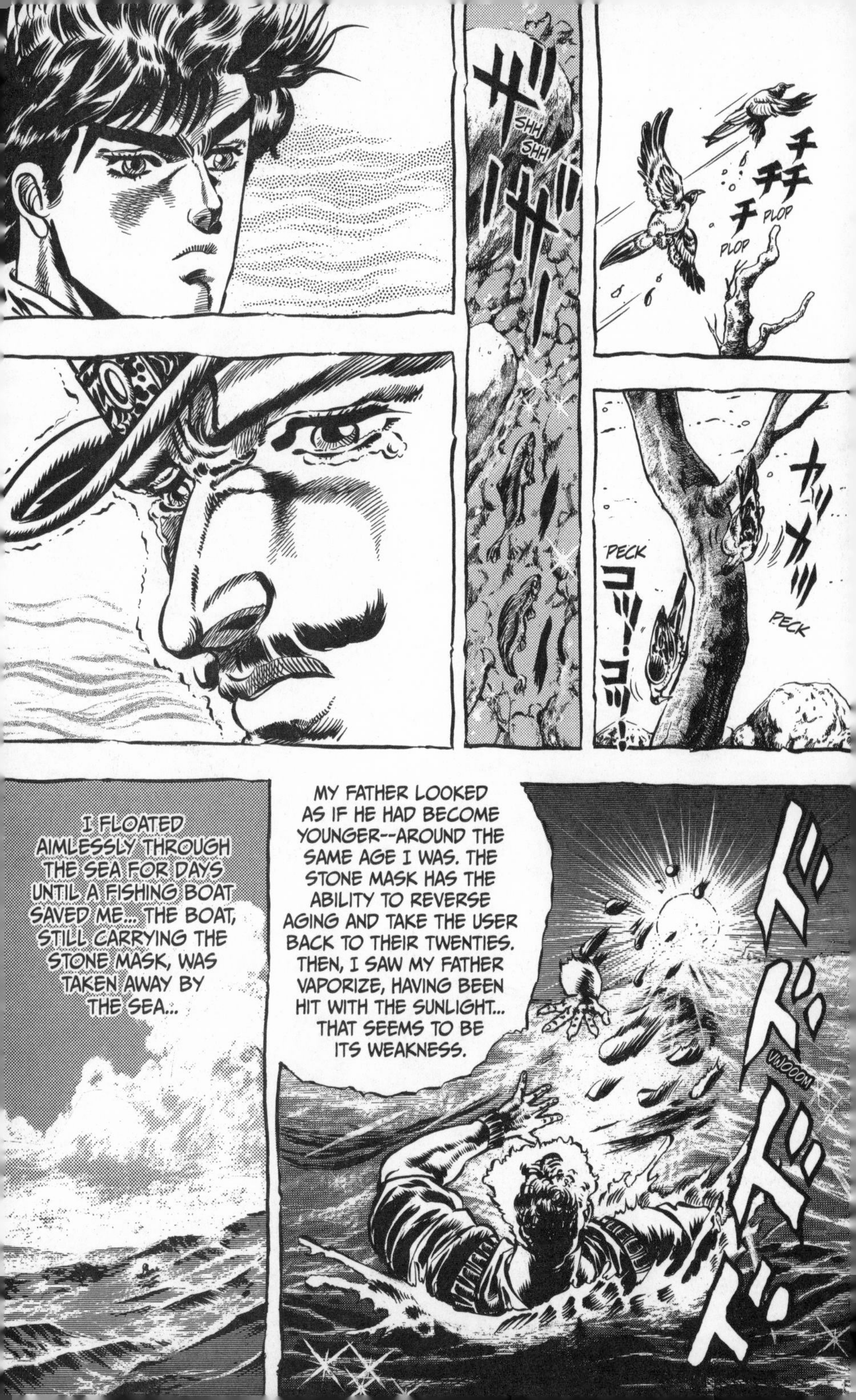

チチチ
PLOP
PLOP
カッカッ
PECK
コッコッ!
PECK
SHH
SHH
MY FATHER LOOKED AS IF HE HAD BECOME YOUNGER--AROUND THE SAME AGE I WAS. THE STONE MASK HAS THE ABILITY TO REVERSE AGING AND TAKE THE USER BACK TO THEIR TWENTIES. THEN, I SAW MY FATHER VAPORIZE, HAVING BEEN HIT WITH THE SUNLIGHT... THAT SEEMS TO BE ITS WEAKNESS.
VJOOON
I FLOATED AIMLESSLY THROUGH THE SEA FOR DAYS UNTIL A FISHING BOAT SAVED ME... THE BOAT, STILL CARRYING THE STONE MASK, WAS TAKEN AWAY BY THE SEA...

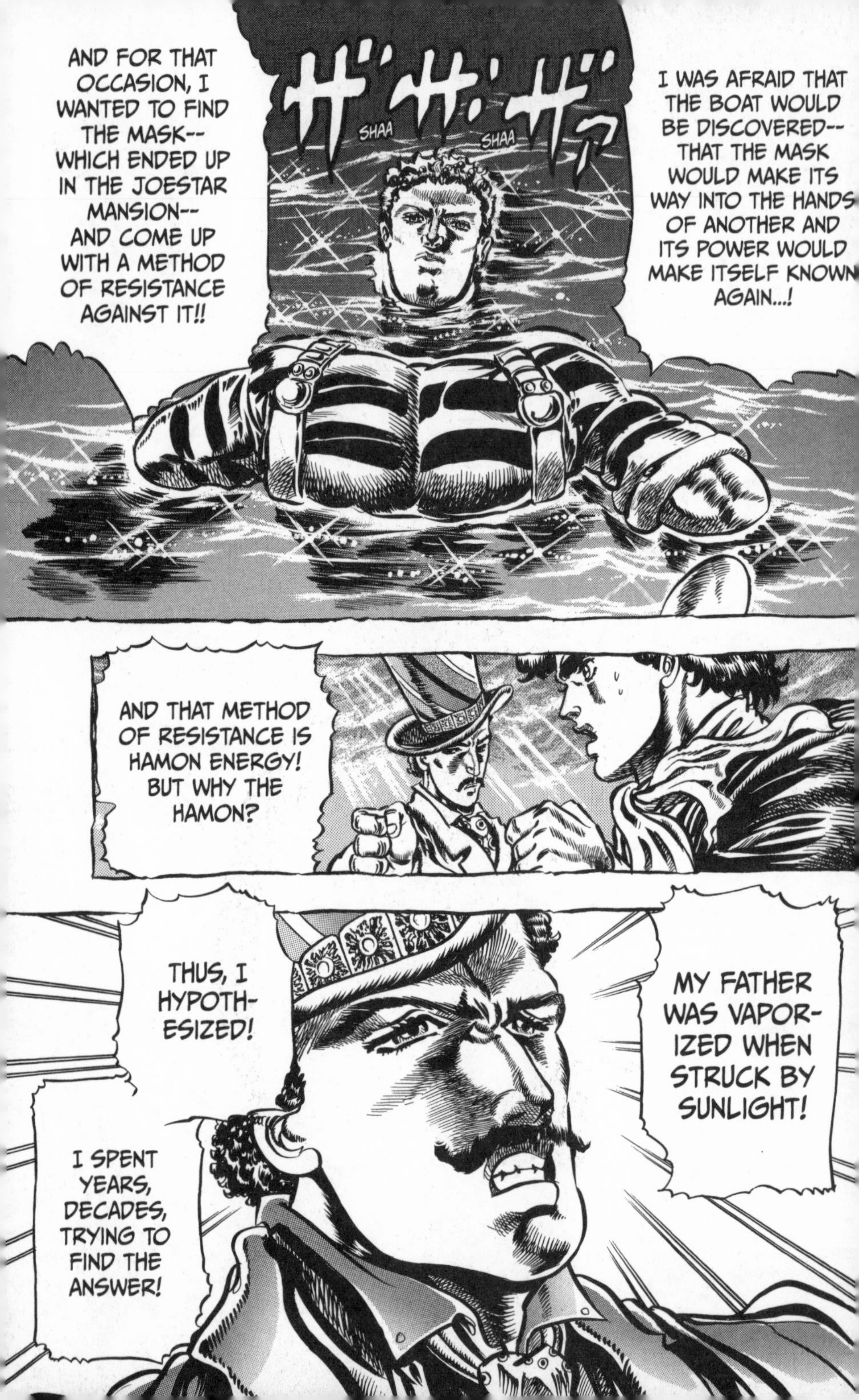
I WAS AFRAID THAT THE BOAT WOULD BE DISCOVERED-- THAT THE MASK WOULD MAKE ITS WAY INTO THE HANDS OF ANOTHER AND ITS POWER WOULD MAKE ITSELF KNOWN AGAIN...!
SHAA
SHAA
AND FOR THAT OCCASION, I WANTED TO FIND THE MASK-- WHICH ENDED UP IN THE JOESTAR MANSION-- AND COME UP WITH A METHOD OF RESISTANCE AGAINST IT!!
AND THAT METHOD OF RESISTANCE IS HAMON ENERGY! BUT WHY THE HAMON?
MY FATHER WAS VAPOR-IZED WHEN STRUCK BY SUNLIGHT!
THUS, I HYPOTH-ESIZED!
I SPENT YEARS, DECADES, TRYING TO FIND THE ANSWER!

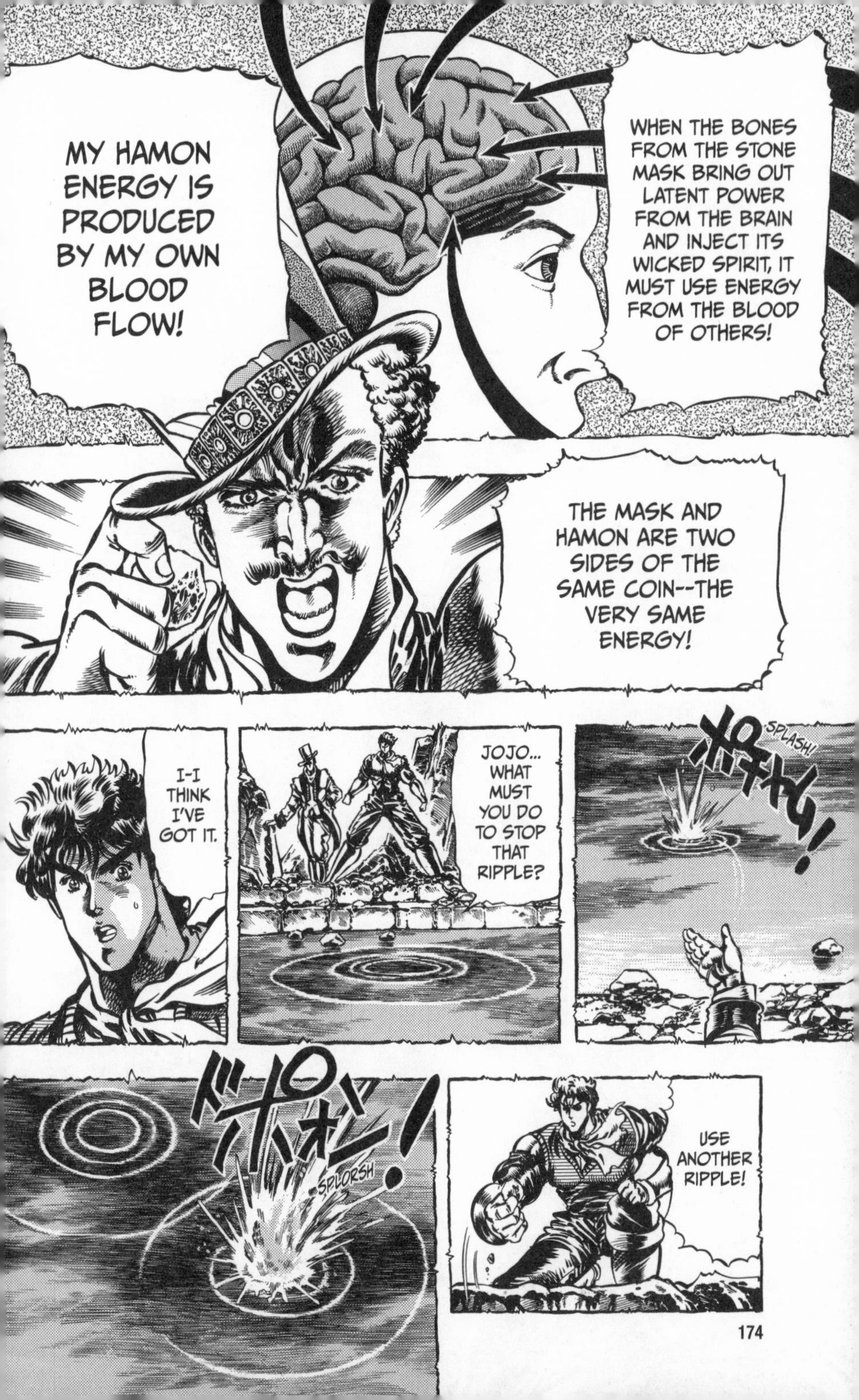
WHEN THE BONES FROM THE STONE MASK BRING OUT LATENT POWER FROM THE BRAIN AND INJECT ITS WICKED SPIRIT, IT MUST USE ENERGY FROM THE BLOOD OF OTHERS!
MY HAMON ENERGY IS PRODUCED BY MY OWN BLOOD FLOW!
THE MASK AND HAMON ARE TWO SIDES OF THE SAME COIN--THE VERY SAME ENERGY!
SPLASH!
JOJO... WHAT MUST YOU DO TO STOP THAT RIPPLE?
I-I THINK I'VE GOT IT.
USE ANOTHER RIPPLE!
SPLORSH

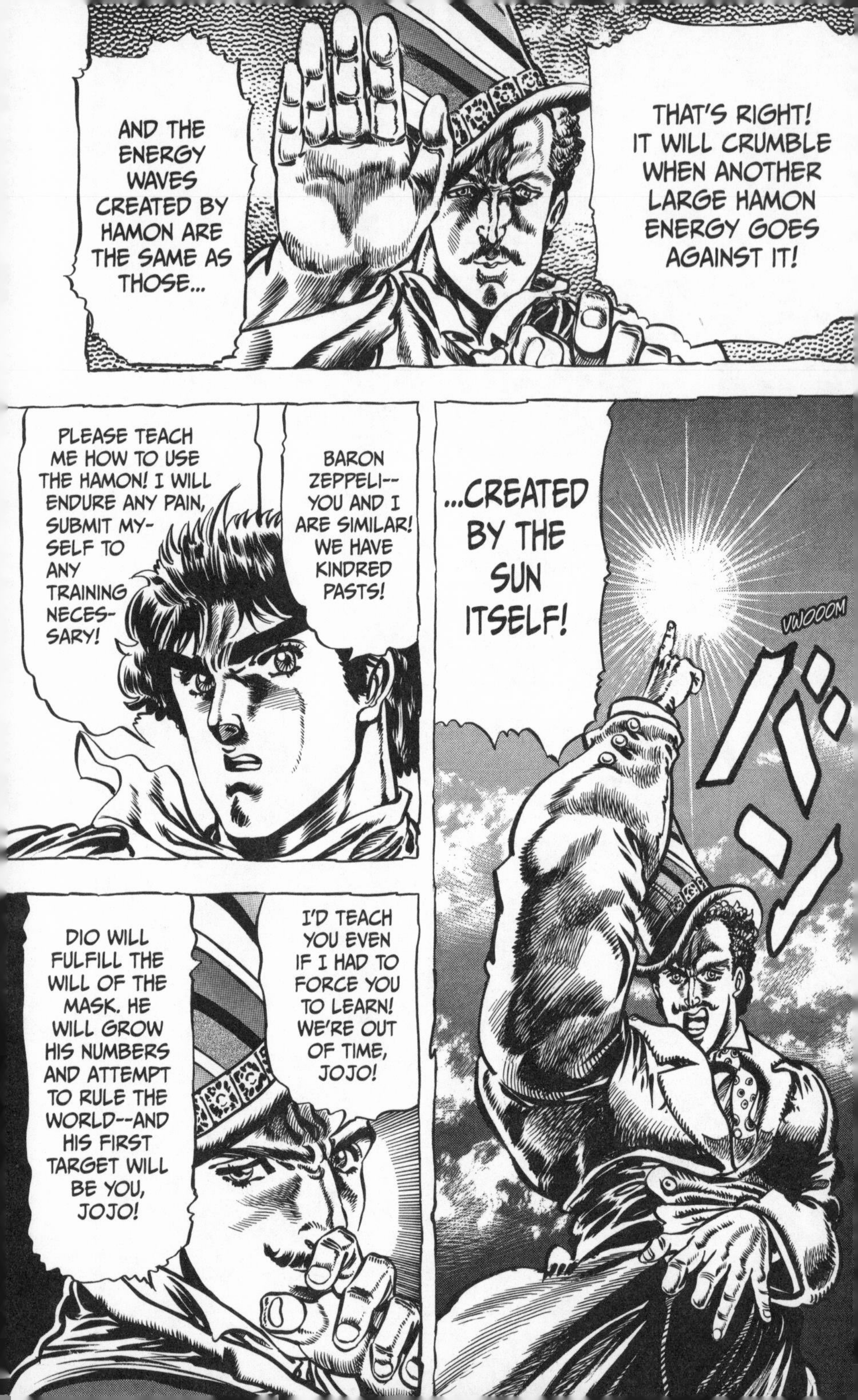
THAT'S RIGHT! IT WILL CRUMBLE WHEN ANOTHER LARGE HAMON ENERGY GOES AGAINST IT!
AND THE ENERGY WAVES CREATED BY HAMON ARE THE SAME AS THOSE...
...CREATED BY THE SUN ITSELF!
VWOOOM
BARON ZEPPELI-- YOU AND I ARE SIMILAR! WE HAVE KINDRED PASTS!
PLEASE TEACH ME HOW TO USE THE HAMON! I WILL ENDURE ANY PAIN, SUBMIT MY-SELF TO ANY TRAINING NECES-SARY!
I'D TEACH YOU EVEN IF I HAD TO FORCE YOU TO LEARN! WE'RE OUT OF TIME, JOJO!
DIO WILL FULFILL THE WILL OF THE MASK. HE WILL GROW HIS NUMBERS AND ATTEMPT TO RULE THE WORLD--AND HIS FIRST TARGET WILL BE YOU, JOJO!

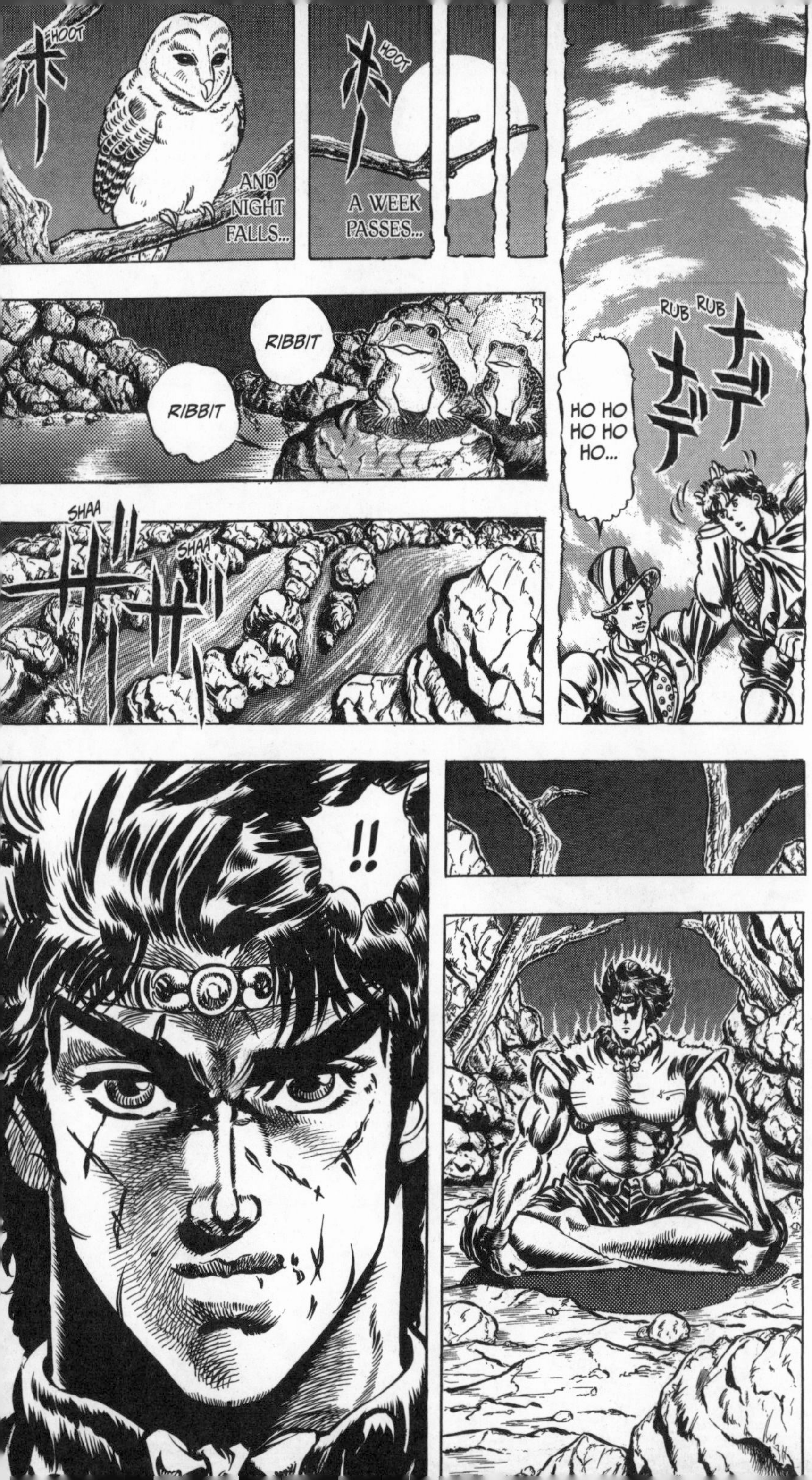
RUB RUB
HO HO HO HO HO...
HOOT
A WEEK PASSES...
HOOT
AND NIGHT FALLS...
RIBBIT
RIBBIT
SHAA
SHAA
!!

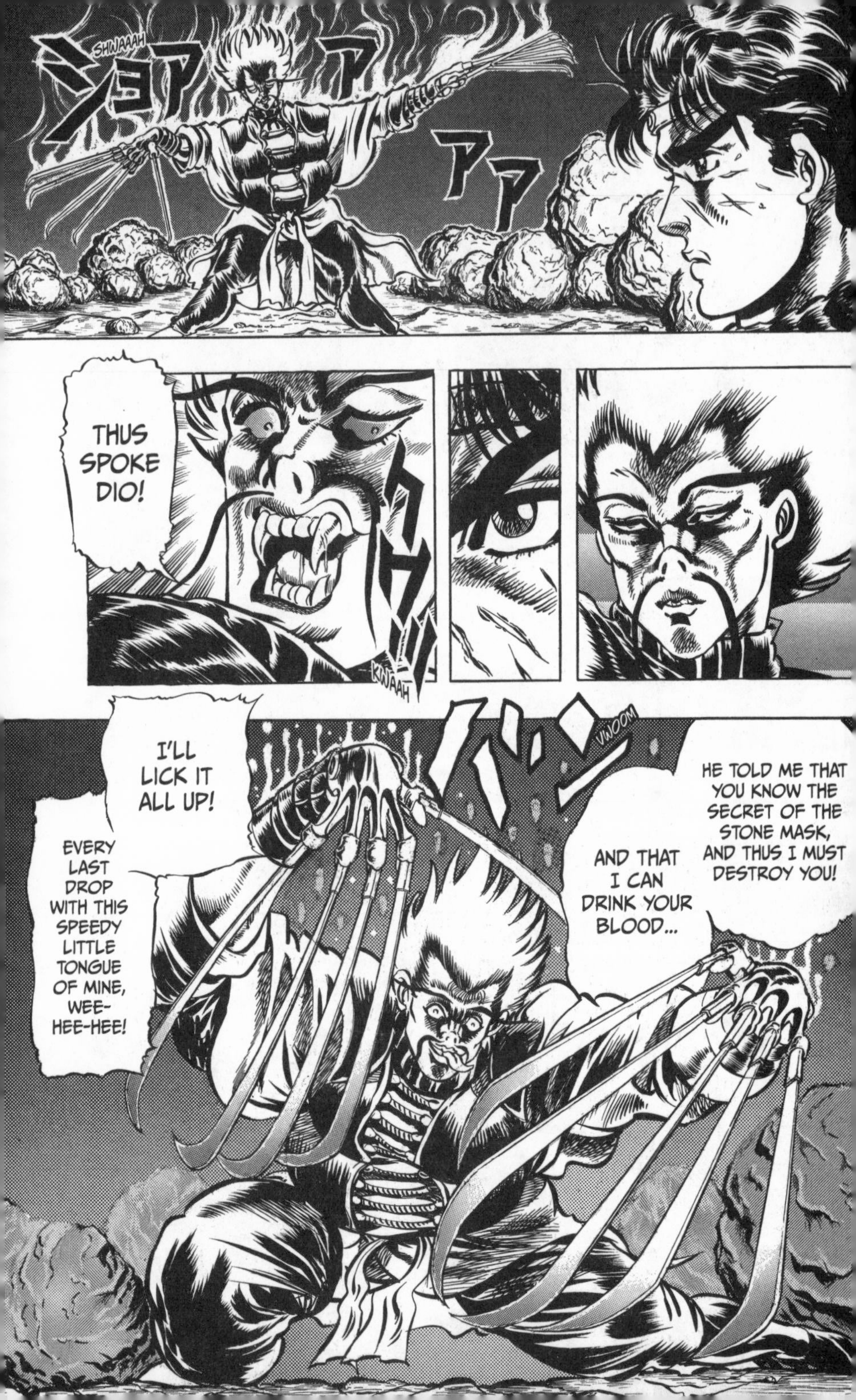
SHWAAAH
HE TOLD ME THAT YOU KNOW THE SECRET OF THE STONE MASK, AND THUS I MUST DESTROY YOU!
THUS SPOKE DIO!
KWAAH
VWOOM
AND THAT I CAN DRINK YOUR BLOOD...
I'LL LICK IT ALL UP!
EVERY LAST DROP WITH THIS SPEEDY LITTLE TONGUE OF MINE, WEE-HEE-HEE!

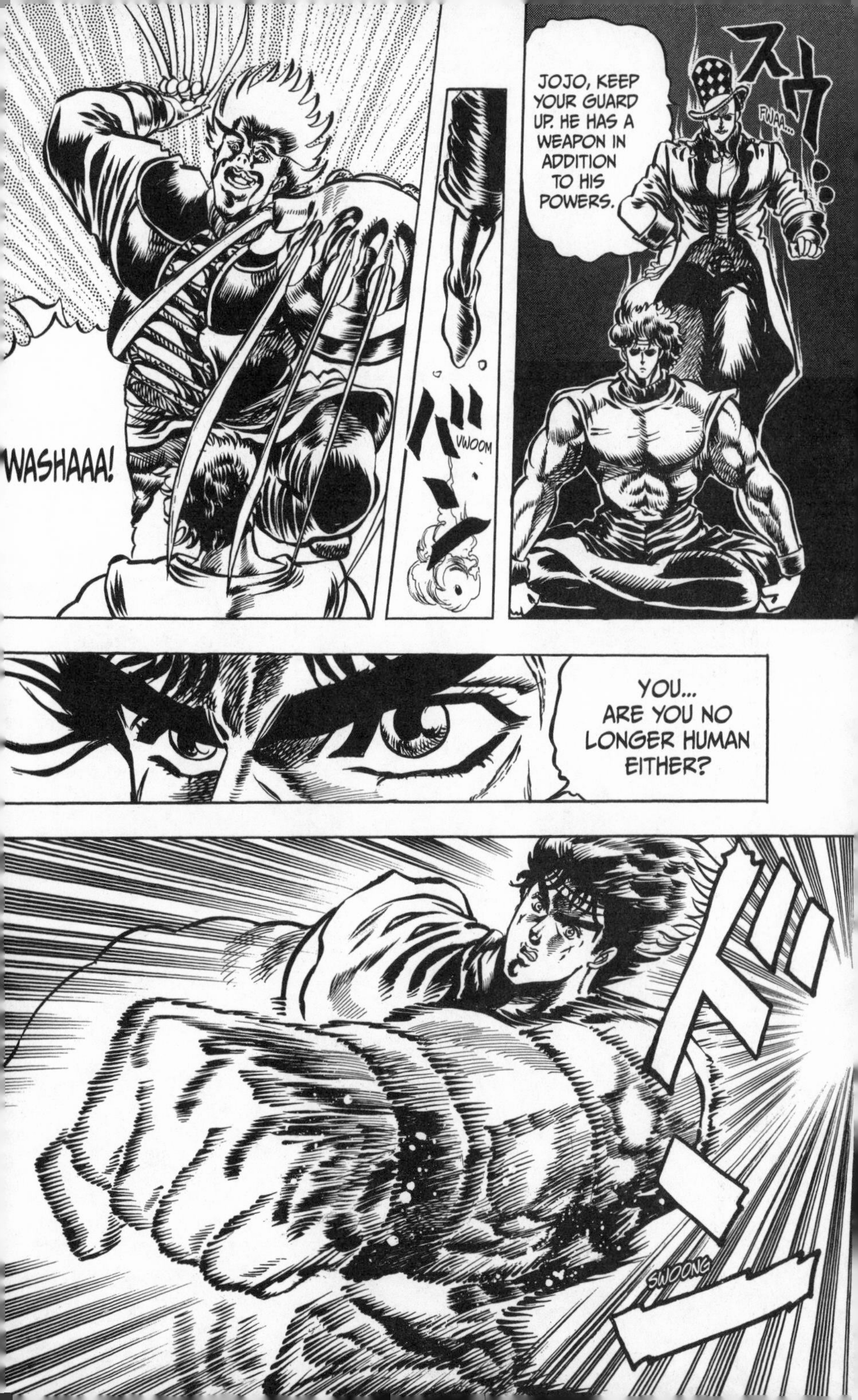
FWAA...
JOJO, KEEP YOUR GUARD UP. HE HAS A WEAPON IN ADDITION TO HIS POWERS.
VWOOM
WASHAAA!
YOU... ARE YOU NO LONGER HUMAN EITHER?
SWOONG

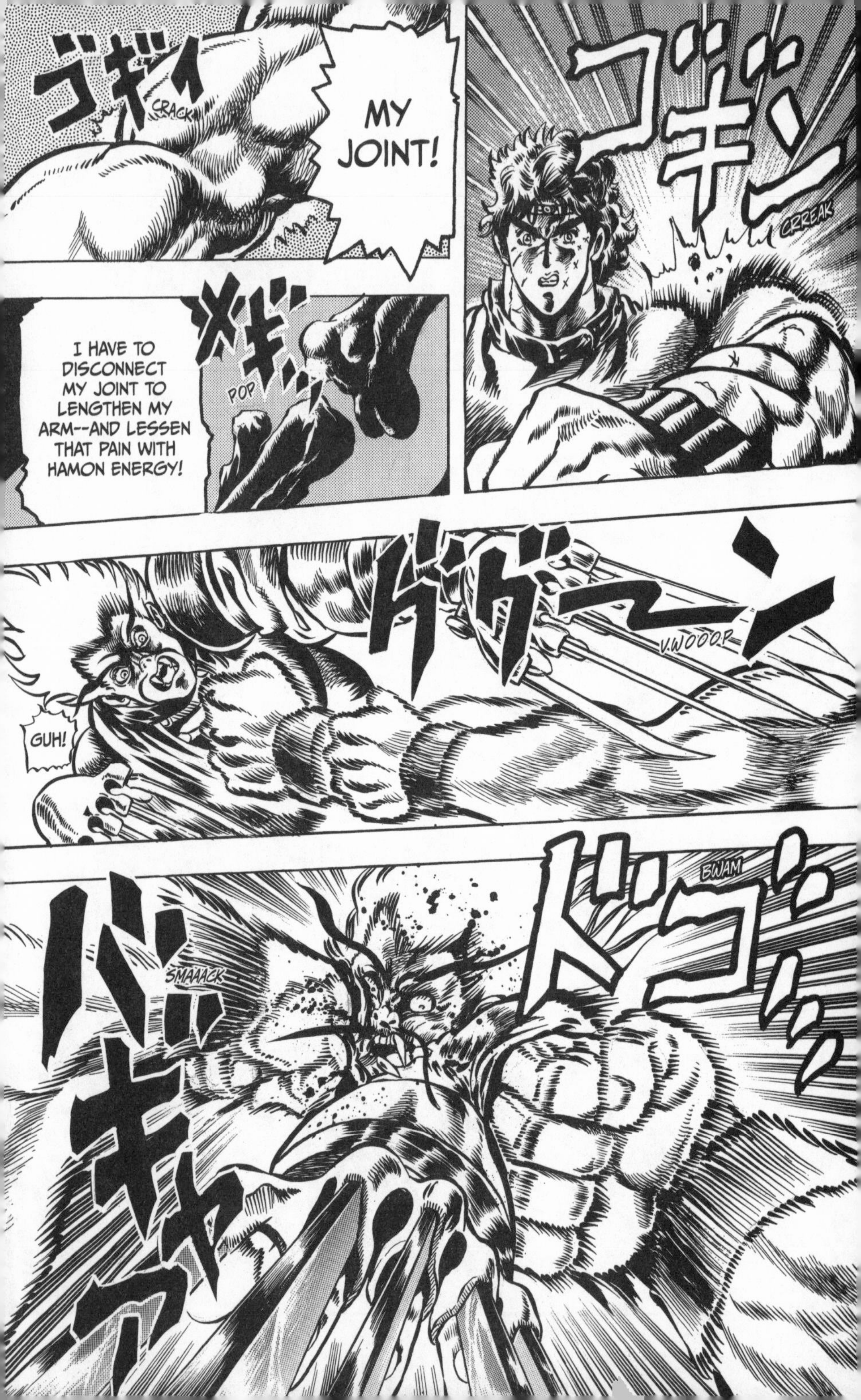
CRREAK
CRACK
MY JOINT!
POP
I HAVE TO DISCONNECT MY JOINT TO LENGTHEN MY ARM--AND LESSEN THAT PAIN WITH HAMON ENERGY!
V.WOOOP
GUH!
BWAM
SMAAACK

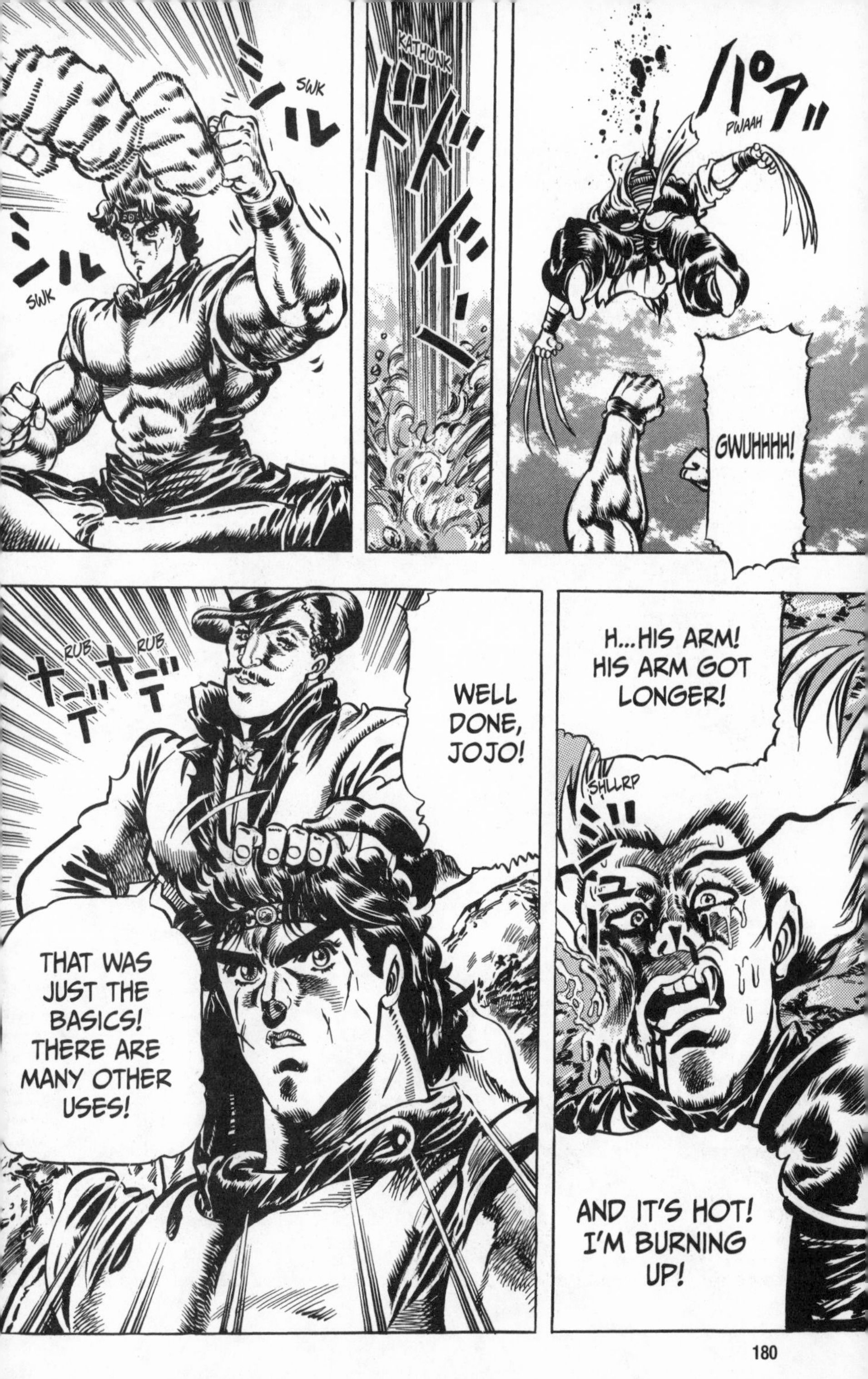
PWAAH
GWUHHHH!
KATHUNK
SWK
SWK
H...HIS ARM! HIS ARM GOT LONGER!
SHLLRP
AND IT'S HOT! I'M BURNING UP!
RUB RUB
WELL DONE, JOJO!
THAT WAS JUST THE BASICS! THERE ARE MANY OTHER USES!

CHAPTER 21: Jack the Ripper and Zeppeli the Strange PART 4

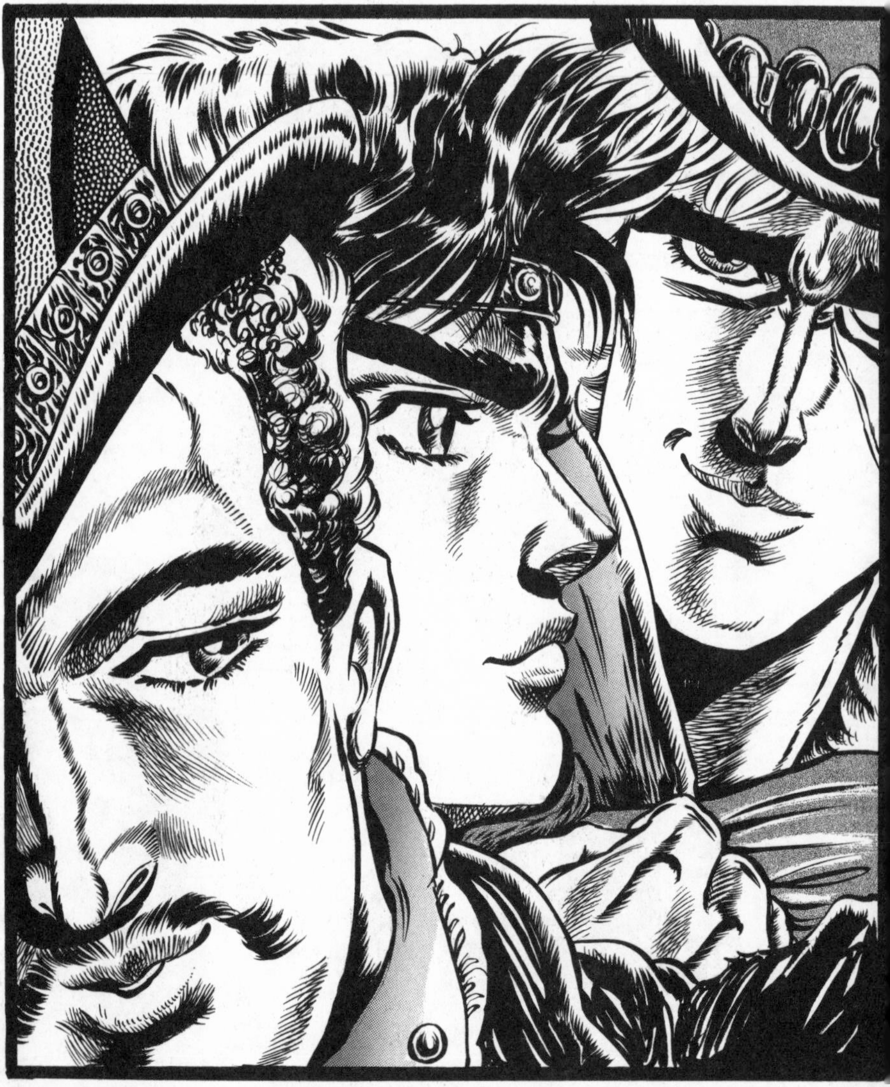

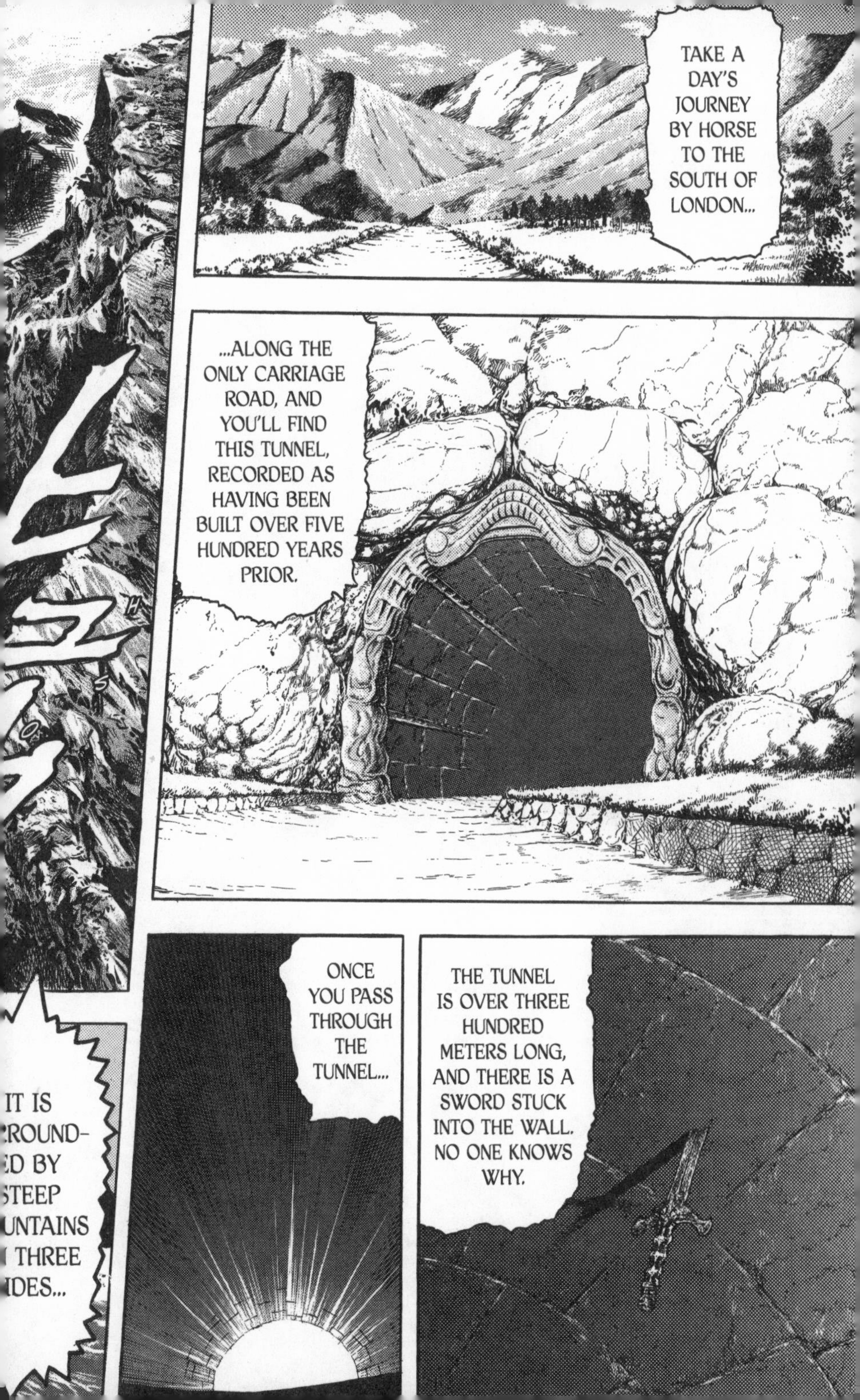
TAKE A DAY'S JOURNEY BY HORSE TO THE SOUTH OF LONDON...
...ALONG THE ONLY CARRIAGE ROAD, AND YOU'LL FIND THIS TUNNEL, RECORDED AS HAVING BEEN BUILT OVER FIVE HUNDRED YEARS PRIOR.
THE TUNNEL IS OVER THREE HUNDRED METERS LONG, AND THERE IS A SWORD STUCK INTO THE WALL. NO ONE KNOWS WHY.
ONCE YOU PASS THROUGH THE TUNNEL...
IT IS
ROUND-
D BY
STEEP
UNTAINS
THREE
IDES...

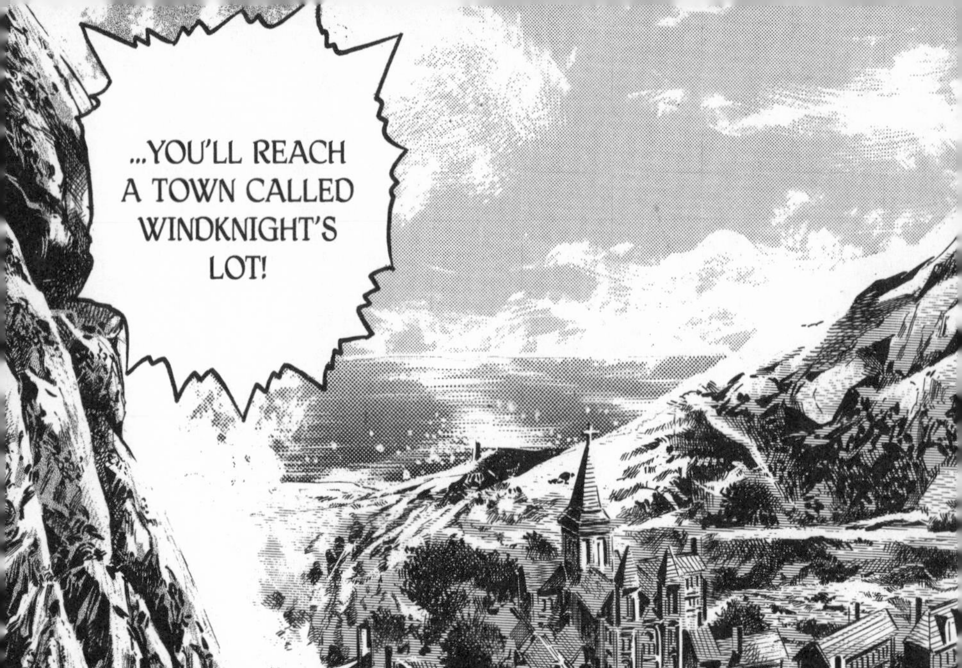
...YOU'LL REACH A TOWN CALLED WINDKNIGHT'S LOT!
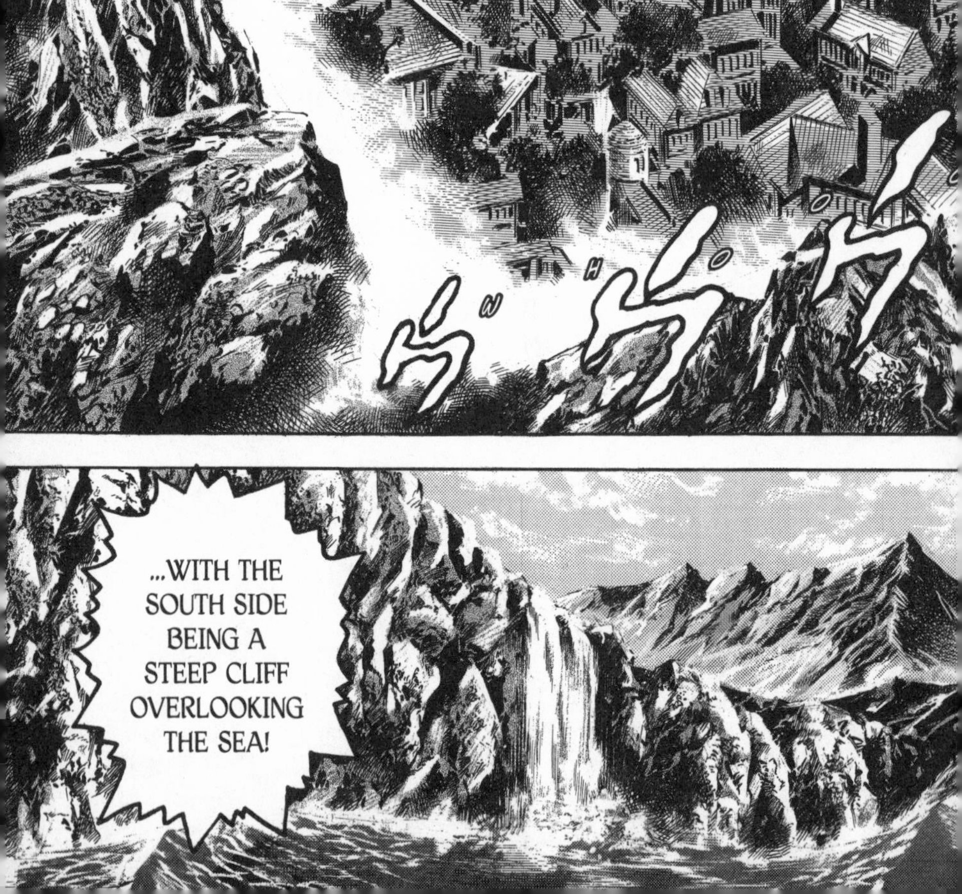
...WITH THE SOUTH SIDE BEING A STEEP CLIFF OVERLOOKING THE SEA!

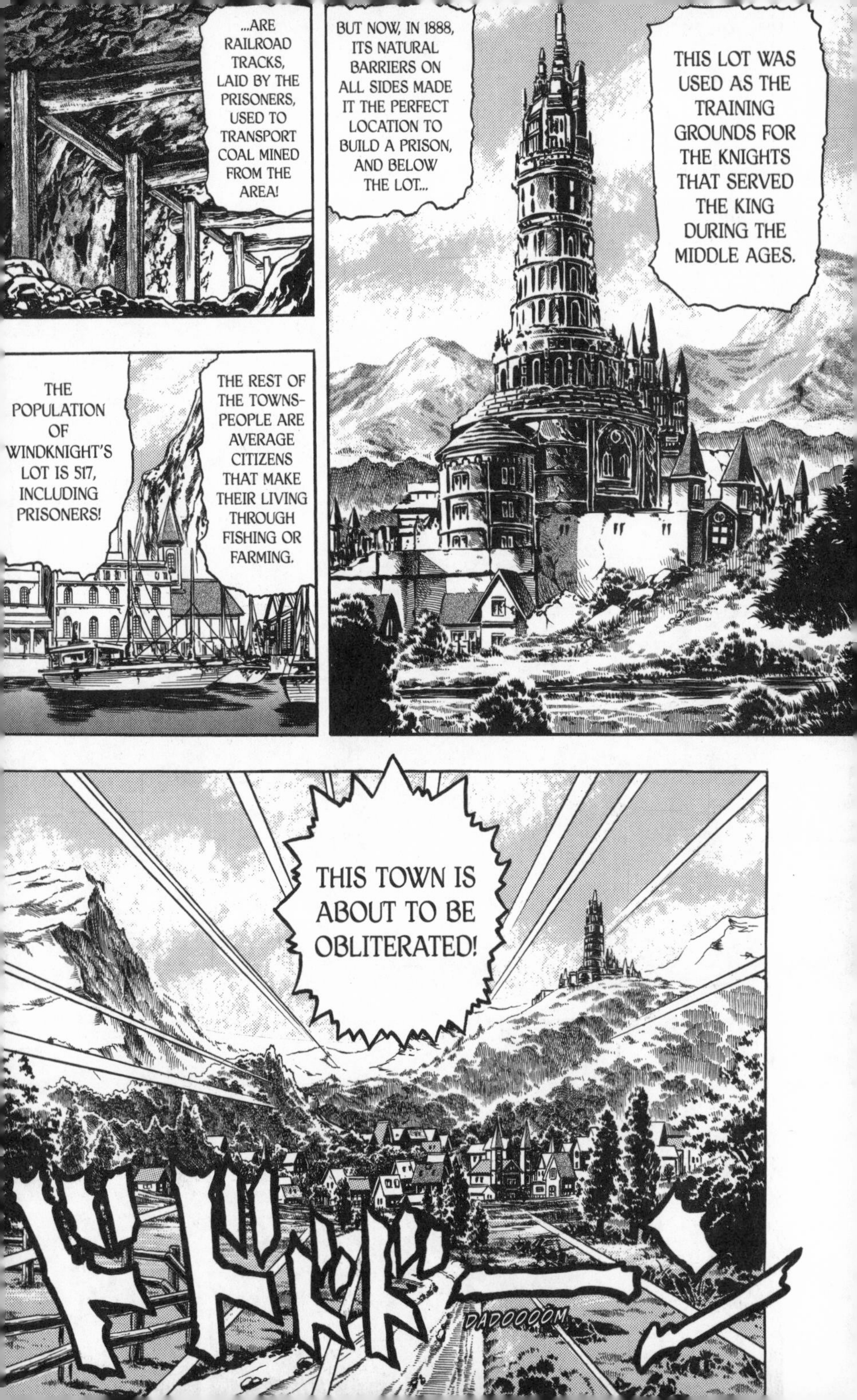
THIS LOT WAS USED AS THE TRAINING GROUNDS FOR THE KNIGHTS THAT SERVED THE KING DURING THE MIDDLE AGES.
BUT NOW, IN 1888, ITS NATURAL BARRIERS ON ALL SIDES MADE IT THE PERFECT LOCATION TO BUILD A PRISON, AND BELOW THE LOT...
...ARE RAILROAD TRACKS, LAID BY THE PRISONERS, USED TO TRANSPORT COAL MINED FROM THE AREA!
THE REST OF THE TOWNS-PEOPLE ARE AVERAGE CITIZENS THAT MAKE THEIR LIVING THROUGH FISHING OR FARMING.
THE POPULATION OF WINDKNIGHT'S LOT IS 517, INCLUDING PRISONERS!
THIS TOWN IS ABOUT TO BE OBLITERATED!
DADOOOOM

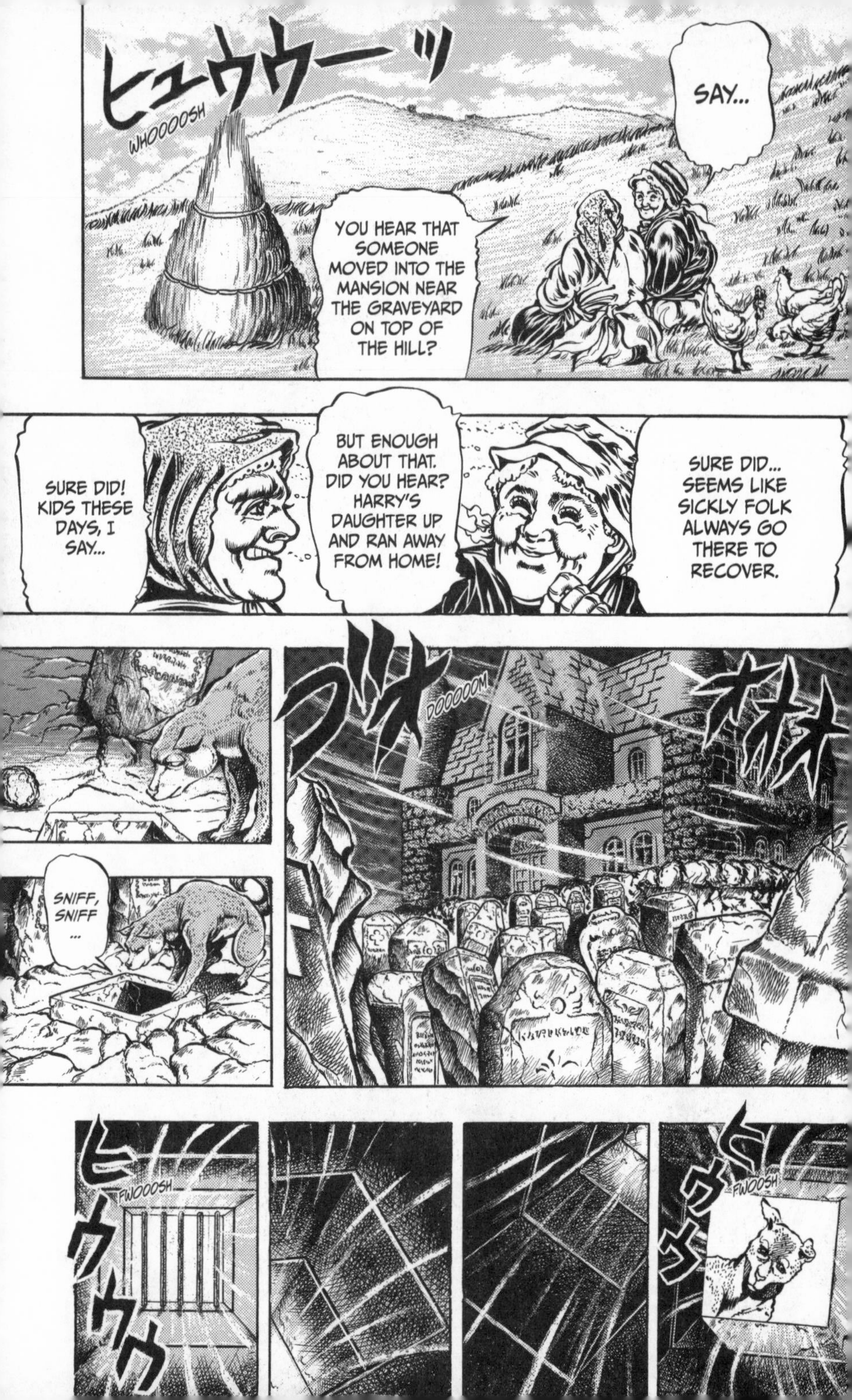
SAY...
YOU HEAR THAT SOMEONE MOVED INTO THE MANSION NEAR THE GRAVEYARD ON TOP OF THE HILL?
ヒュウウーーッ
WHOOOOSH
SURE DID... SEEMS LIKE SICKLY FOLK ALWAYS GO THERE TO RECOVER.
BUT ENOUGH ABOUT THAT. DID YOU HEAR? HARRY'S DAUGHTER UP AND RAN AWAY FROM HOME!
SURE DID! KIDS THESE DAYS, I SAY...
ゴオオオ
DOOOOOM
SNIFF, SNIFF ...
ヒュウ
FWOOSH
ヒュウウウ
FWOOSH

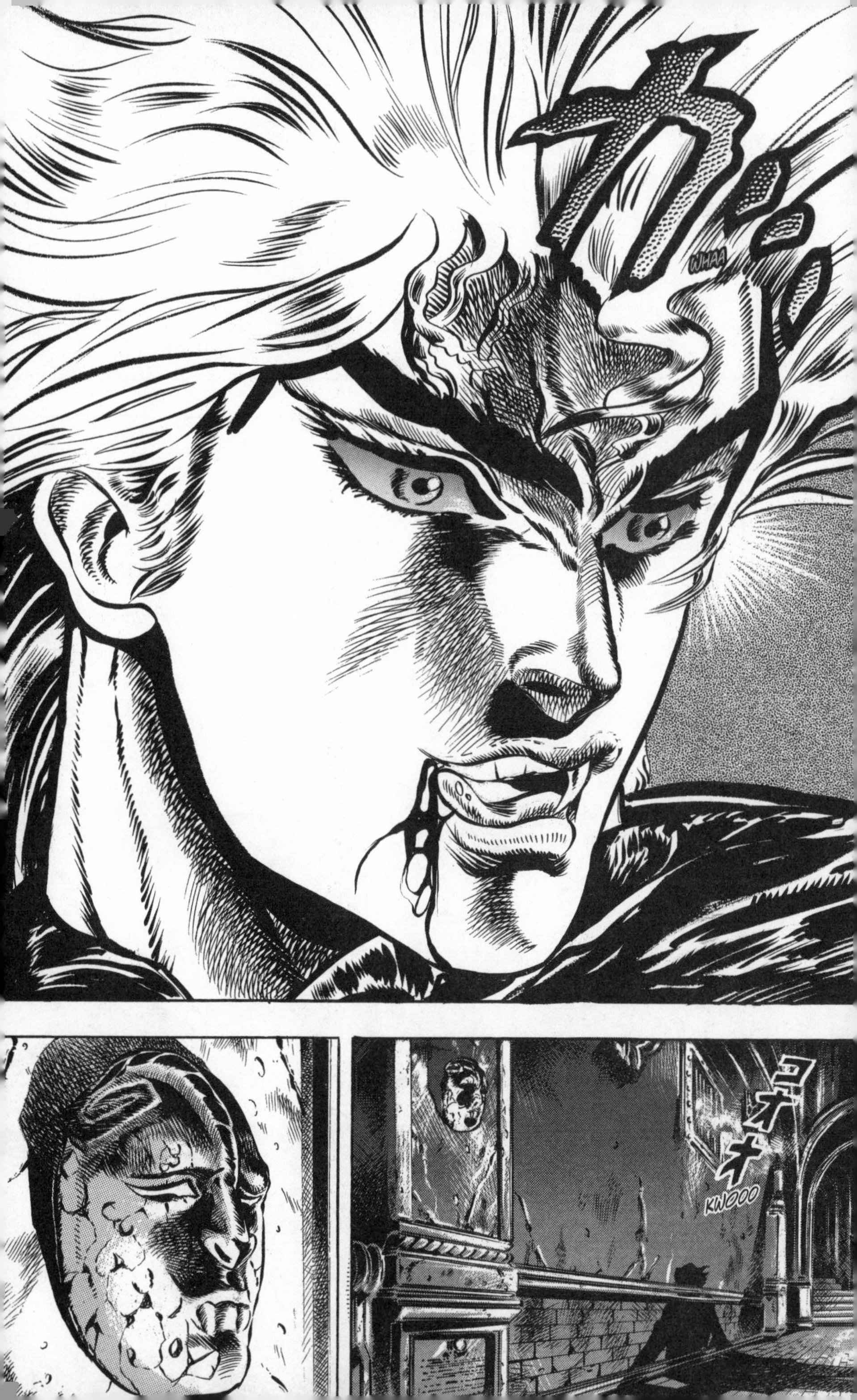
WHAA
KWOOO

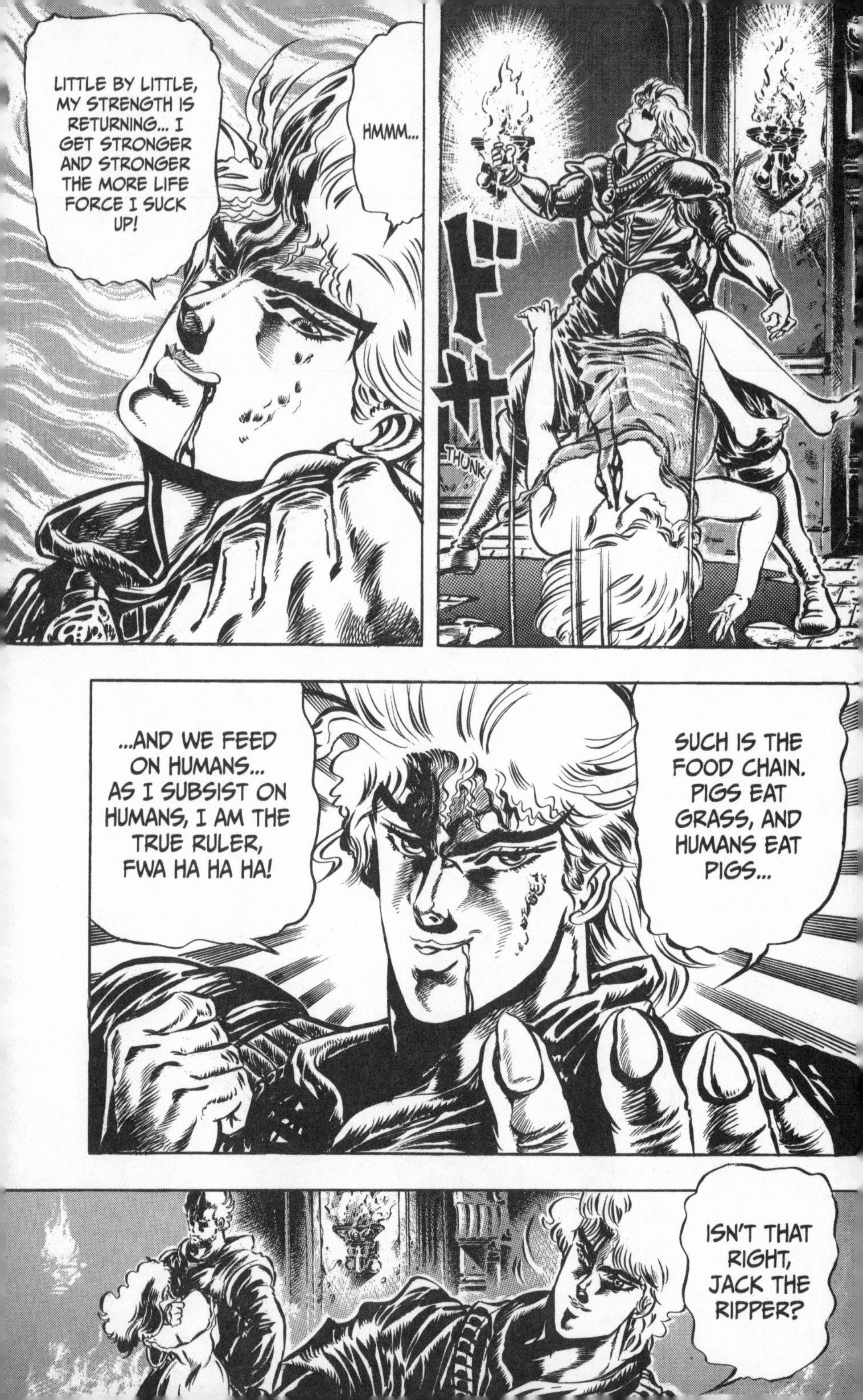
ドド
THUNK
HMMM...
LITTLE BY LITTLE, MY STRENGTH IS RETURNING... I GET STRONGER AND STRONGER THE MORE LIFE FORCE I SUCK UP!
SUCH IS THE FOOD CHAIN. PIGS EAT GRASS, AND HUMANS EAT PIGS...
...AND WE FEED ON HUMANS... AS I SUBSIST ON HUMANS, I AM THE TRUE RULER, FWA HA HA HA!
ISN'T THAT RIGHT, JACK THE RIPPER?

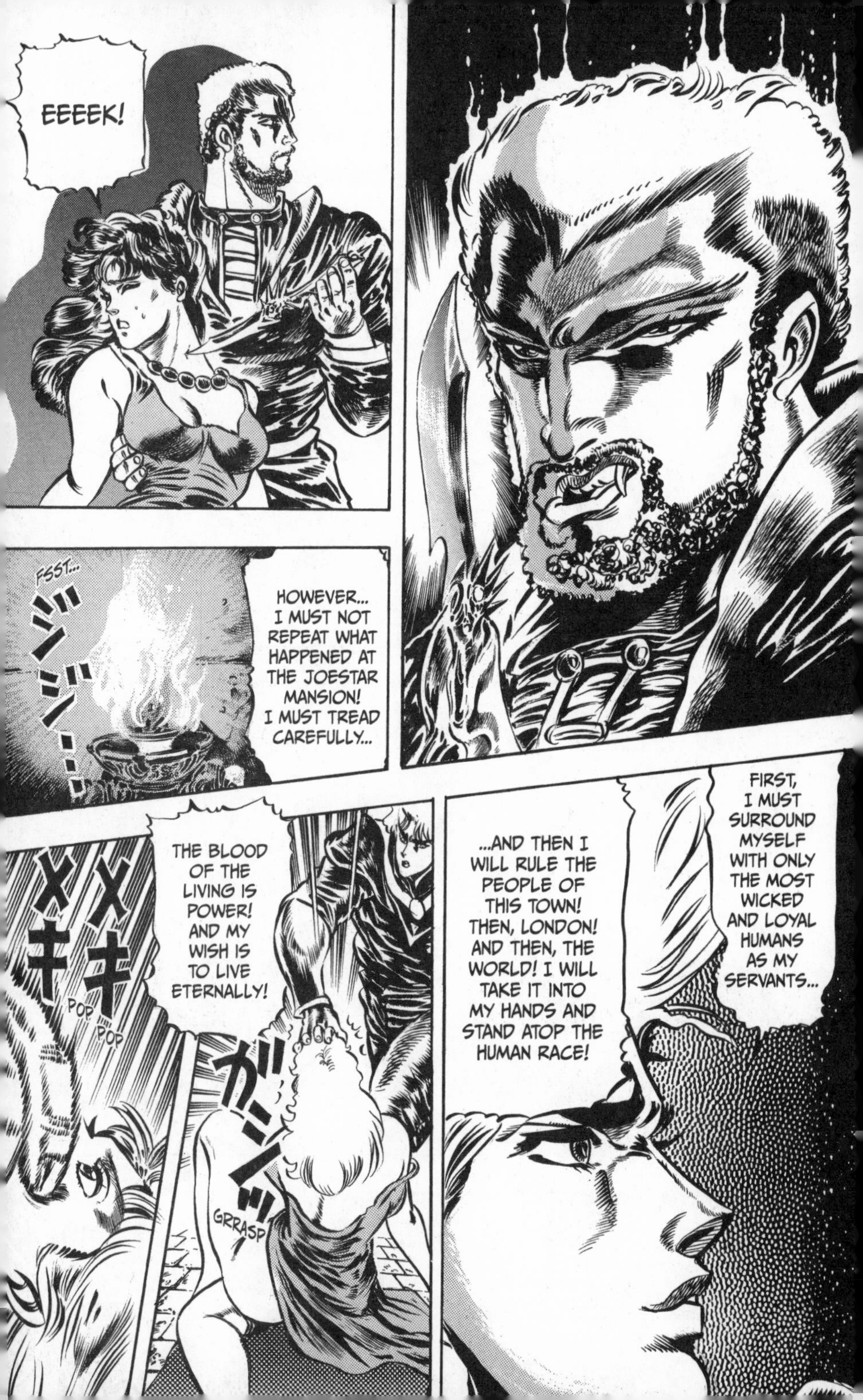
EEEEK!
FSST...
HOWEVER... I MUST NOT REPEAT WHAT HAPPENED AT THE JOESTAR MANSION! I MUST TREAD CAREFULLY...
FIRST, I MUST SURROUND MYSELF WITH ONLY THE MOST WICKED AND LOYAL HUMANS AS MY SERVANTS...
...AND THEN I WILL RULE THE PEOPLE OF THIS TOWN! THEN, LONDON! AND THEN, THE WORLD! I WILL TAKE IT INTO MY HANDS AND STAND ATOP THE HUMAN RACE!
THE BLOOD OF THE LIVING IS POWER! AND MY WISH IS TO LIVE ETERNALLY!
POP
POP
GRRASP

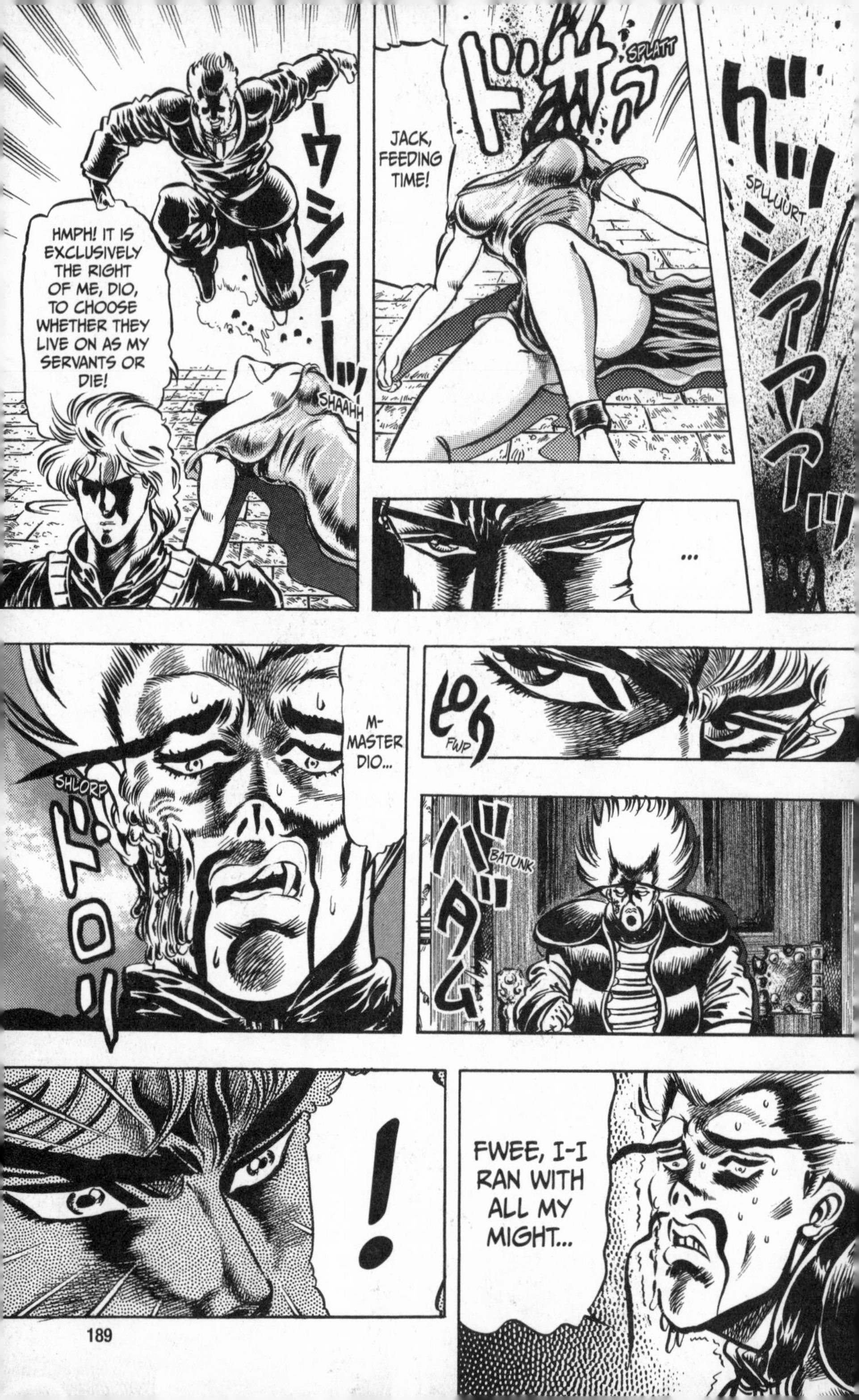
SPLLUURT
SPLATT
JACK, FEEDING TIME!
...
HMPH! IT IS EXCLUSIVELY THE RIGHT OF ME, DIO, TO CHOOSE WHETHER THEY LIVE ON AS MY SERVANTS OR DIE!
SHAAHH
FWP
BATUNK
M-MASTER DIO...
SHLORP
FWEE, I-I RAN WITH ALL MY MIGHT...
!

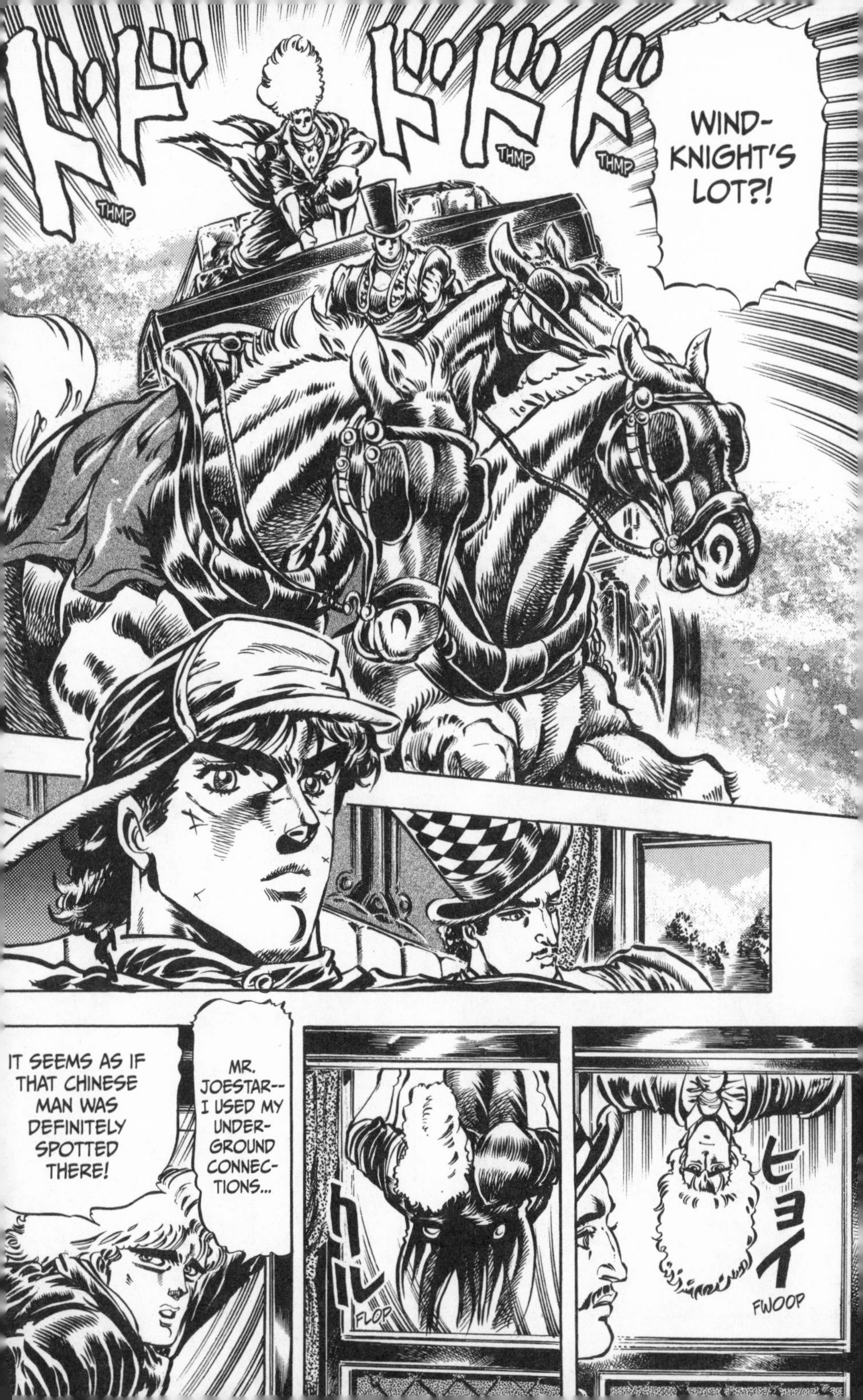
WIND-KNIGHT'S LOT?!
THMP
THMP
THMP
ヒョイ
FWOOP
FLOP
MR. JOESTAR-- I USED MY UNDERGROUND CONNECTIONS...
IT SEEMS AS IF THAT CHINESE MAN WAS DEFINITELY SPOTTED THERE!

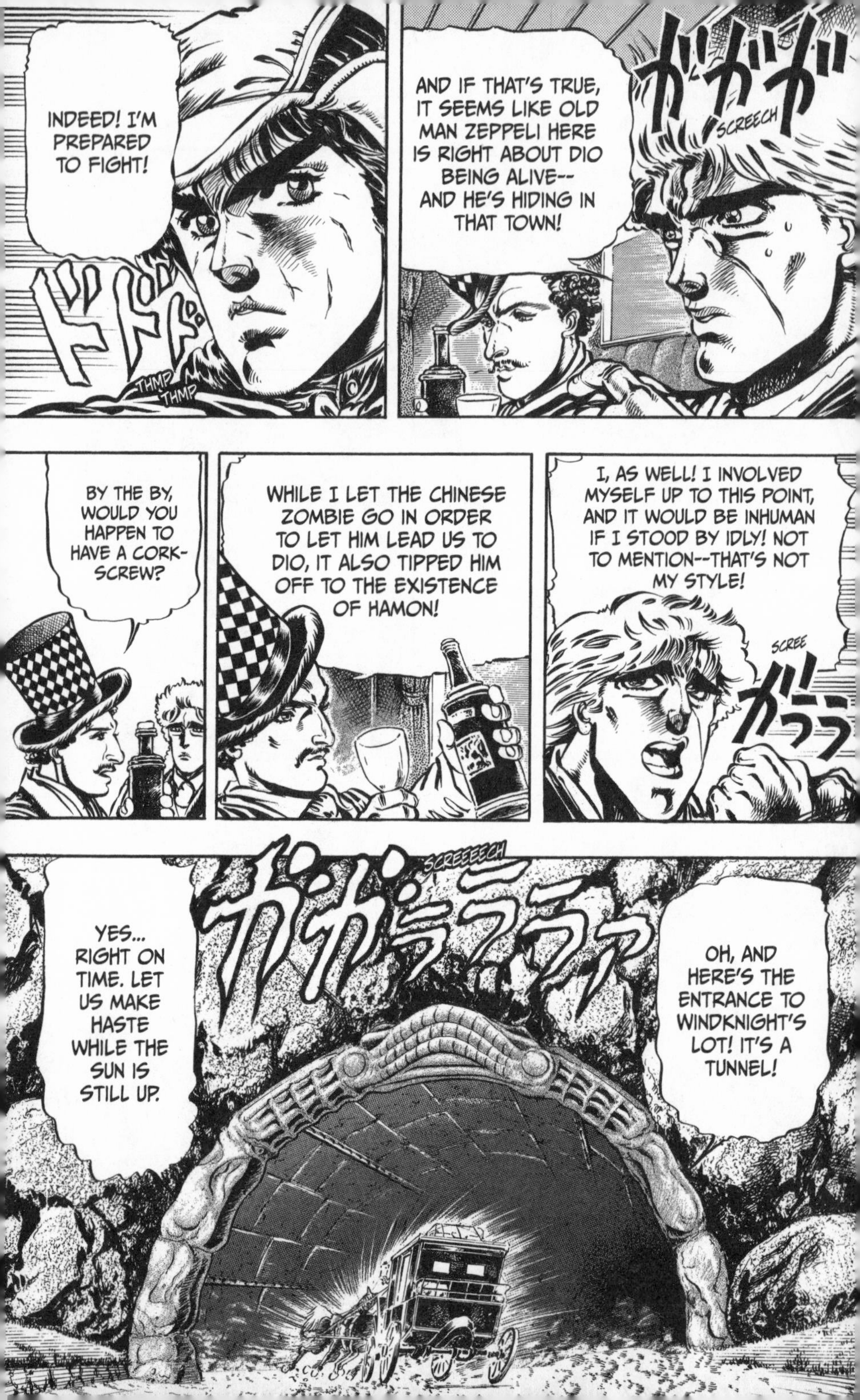
SCREECH
AND IF THAT'S TRUE, IT SEEMS LIKE OLD MAN ZEPPELI HERE IS RIGHT ABOUT DIO BEING ALIVE-- AND HE'S HIDING IN THAT TOWN!
INDEED! I'M PREPARED TO FIGHT!
THMP THMP
I, AS WELL! I INVOLVED MYSELF UP TO THIS POINT, AND IT WOULD BE INHUMAN IF I STOOD BY IDLY! NOT TO MENTION--THAT'S NOT MY STYLE!
SCREE
WHILE I LET THE CHINESE ZOMBIE GO IN ORDER TO LET HIM LEAD US TO DIO, IT ALSO TIPPED HIM OFF TO THE EXISTENCE OF HAMON!
BY THE BY, WOULD YOU HAPPEN TO HAVE A CORK-SCREW?
OH, AND HERE'S THE ENTRANCE TO WINDKNIGHT'S LOT! IT'S A TUNNEL!
SCREEEECH
YES... RIGHT ON TIME. LET US MAKE HASTE WHILE THE SUN IS STILL UP.

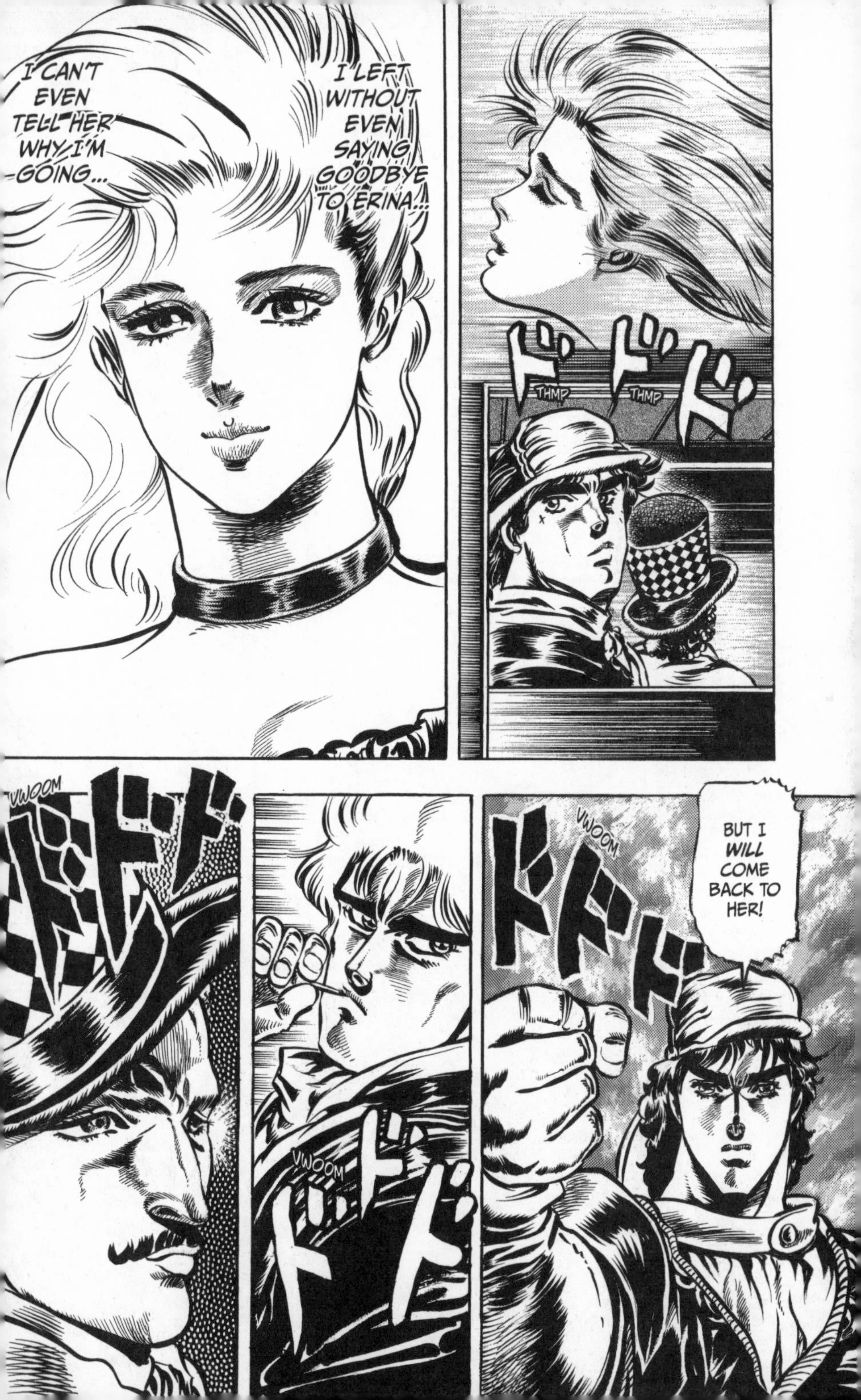
ドドドド
THMP
THMP
I LEFT WITHOUT EVEN SAYING GOODBYE TO ERINA...
I CAN'T EVEN TELL HER WHY I'M GOING...
ドドドド
VWOOM
BUT I WILL COME BACK TO HER!
ドドドド
VWOOM
ドドド
VWOOM

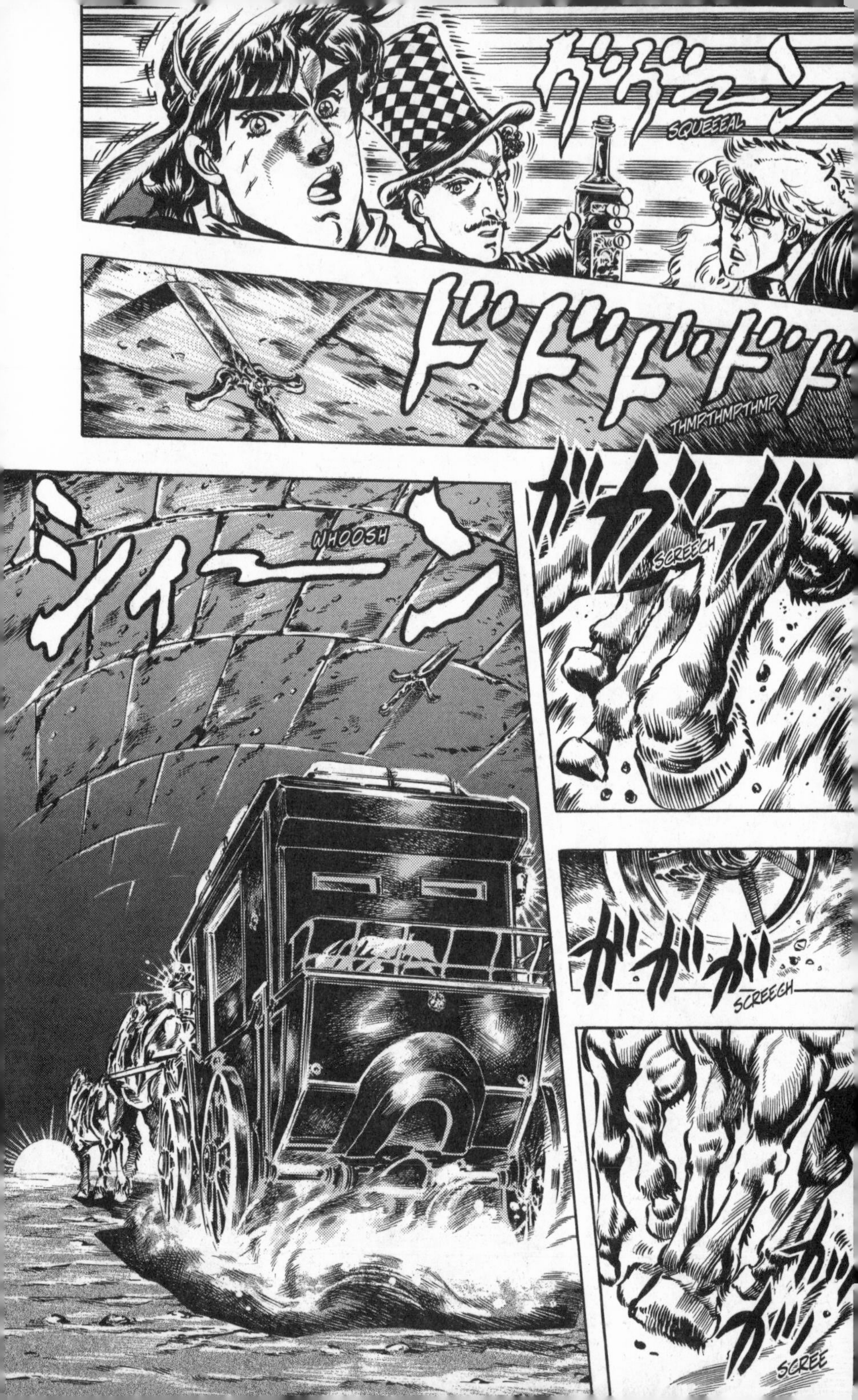
SQUEEEAL
THMPTHMPTHMP
SCREECH
SCREECH
SCREE
WHOOSH

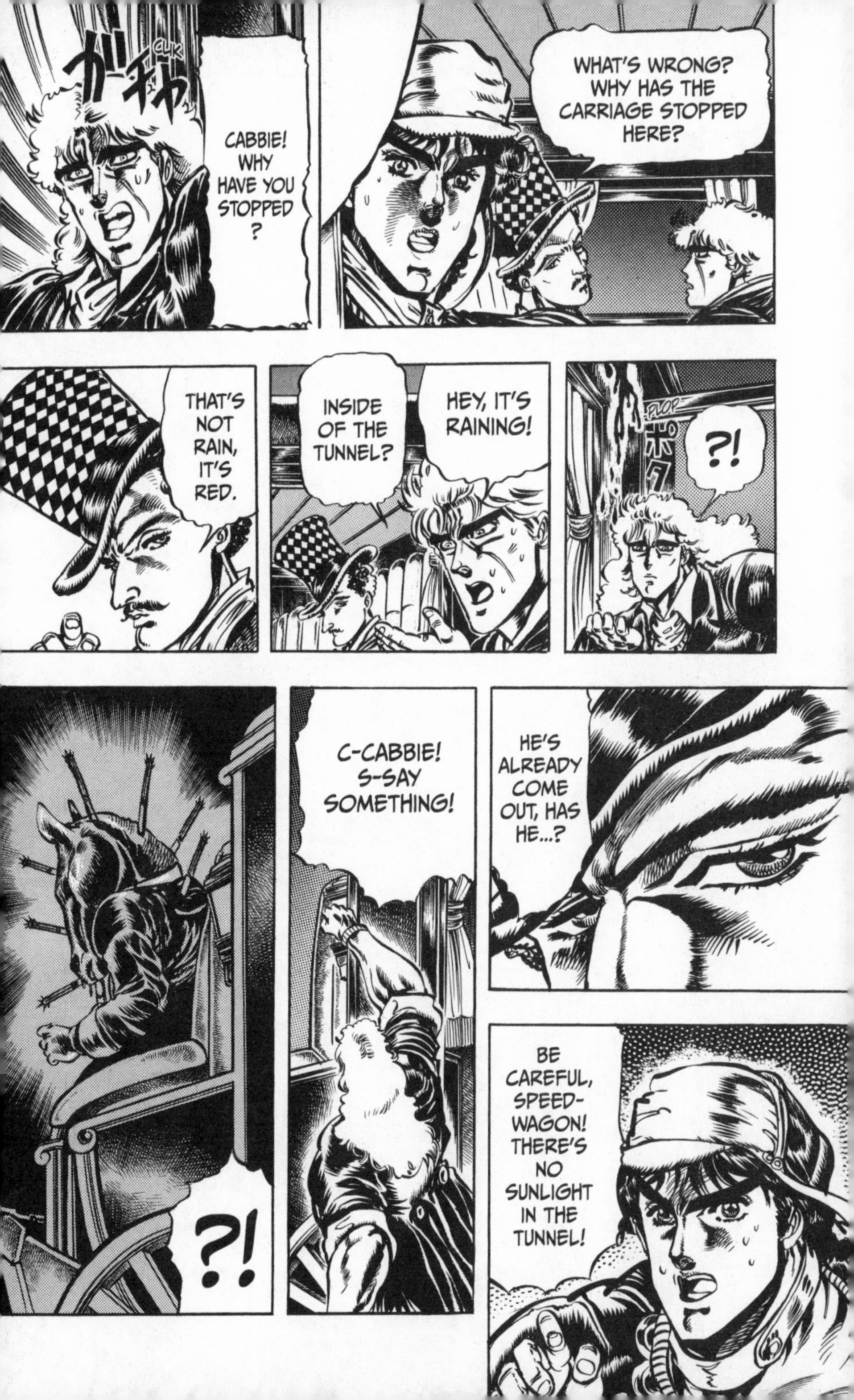
WHAT'S WRONG? WHY HAS THE CARRIAGE STOPPED HERE?
ガチャ
CLIK
CABBIE! WHY HAVE YOU STOPPED?
ポタ
PLOP
?!
HEY, IT'S RAINING!
INSIDE OF THE TUNNEL?
THAT'S NOT RAIN, IT'S RED.
HE'S ALREADY COME OUT, HAS HE...?
BE CAREFUL, SPEED-WAGON! THERE'S NO SUNLIGHT IN THE TUNNEL!
C-CABBIE! S-SAY SOMETHING!
?!

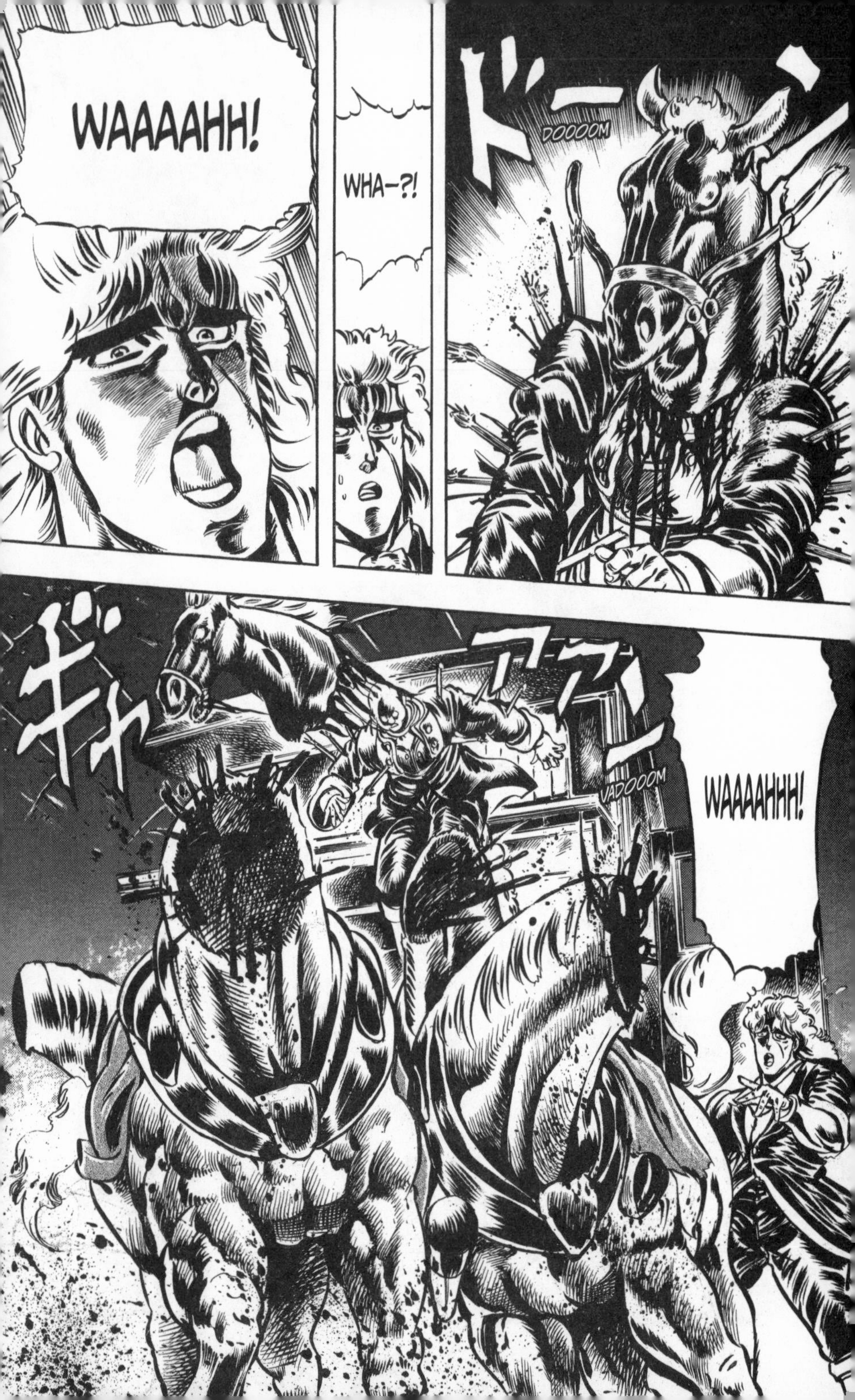

ドーン
DOOOOM
WHA-?!
WAAAAHH!
WAAAAHHH!
ギャアアー
VADOOOM

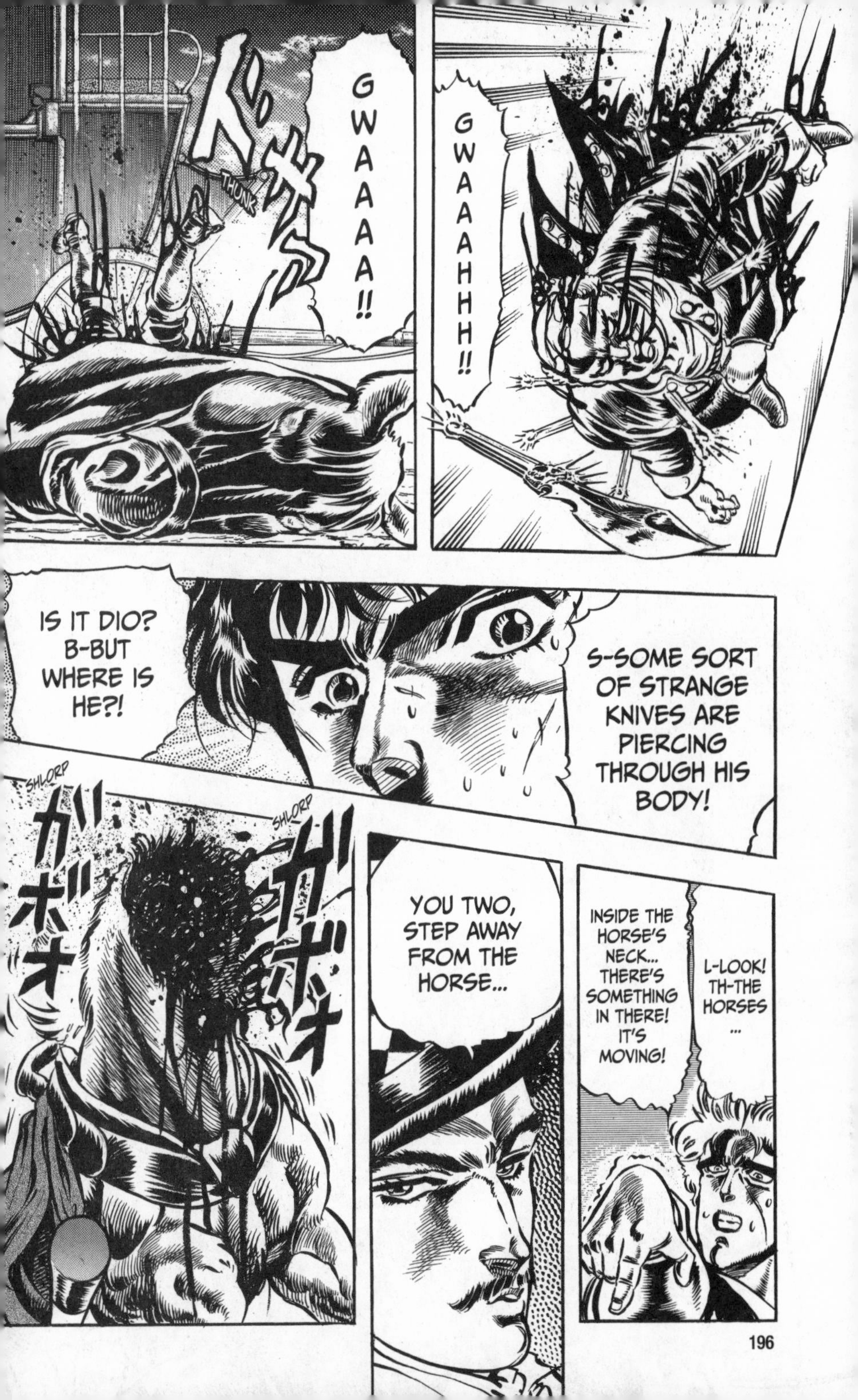
GWAAAAHHHH!!
GWAAAAA!!
THUNK
S-SOME SORT OF STRANGE KNIVES ARE PIERCING THROUGH HIS BODY!
IS IT DIO? B-BUT WHERE IS HE?!
L-LOOK! TH-THE HORSES ...
INSIDE THE HORSE'S NECK... THERE'S SOMETHING IN THERE! IT'S MOVING!
YOU TWO, STEP AWAY FROM THE HORSE...
SHLORP
SHLORP

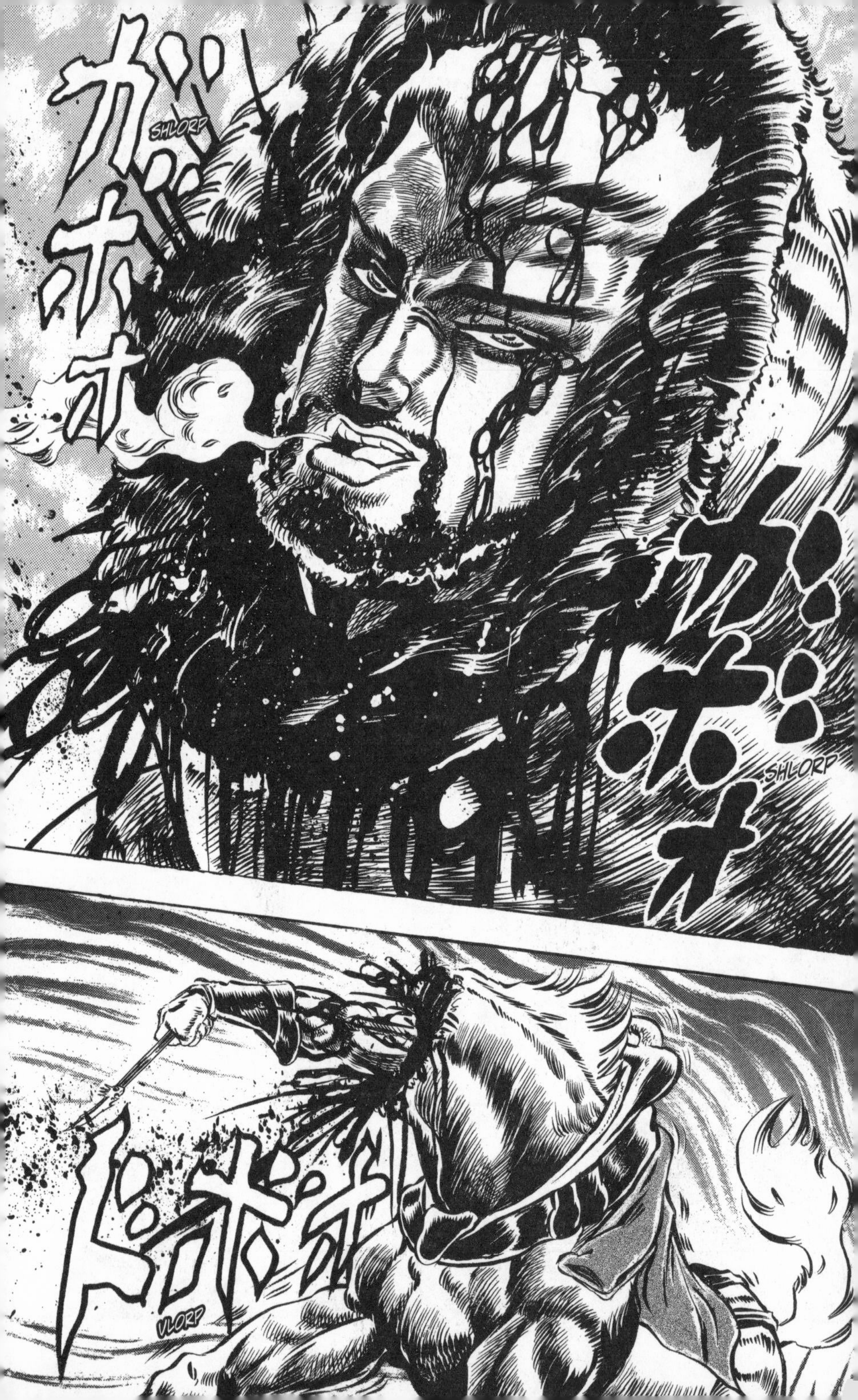
SHLORP
SHLORP
VLORP

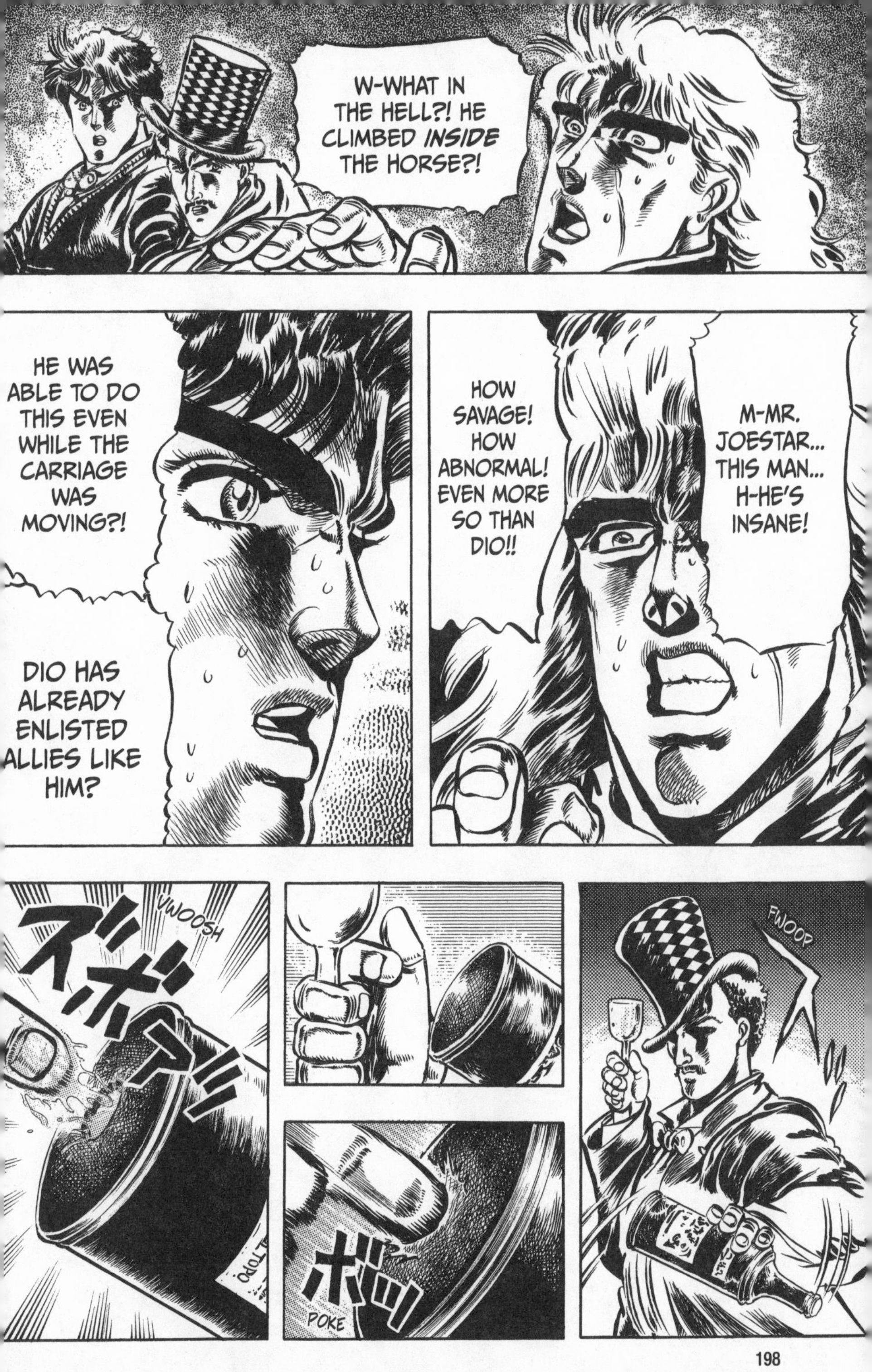
W-WHAT IN THE HELL?! HE CLIMBED *INSIDE* THE HORSE?!
M-MR. JOESTAR... THIS MAN... H-HE'S INSANE!
HOW SAVAGE! HOW ABNORMAL! EVEN MORE SO THAN DIO!!
HE WAS ABLE TO DO THIS EVEN WHILE THE CARRIAGE WAS MOVING?!
DIO HAS ALREADY ENLISTED ALLIES LIKE HIM?
FWOOP
POKE
VWOOSH

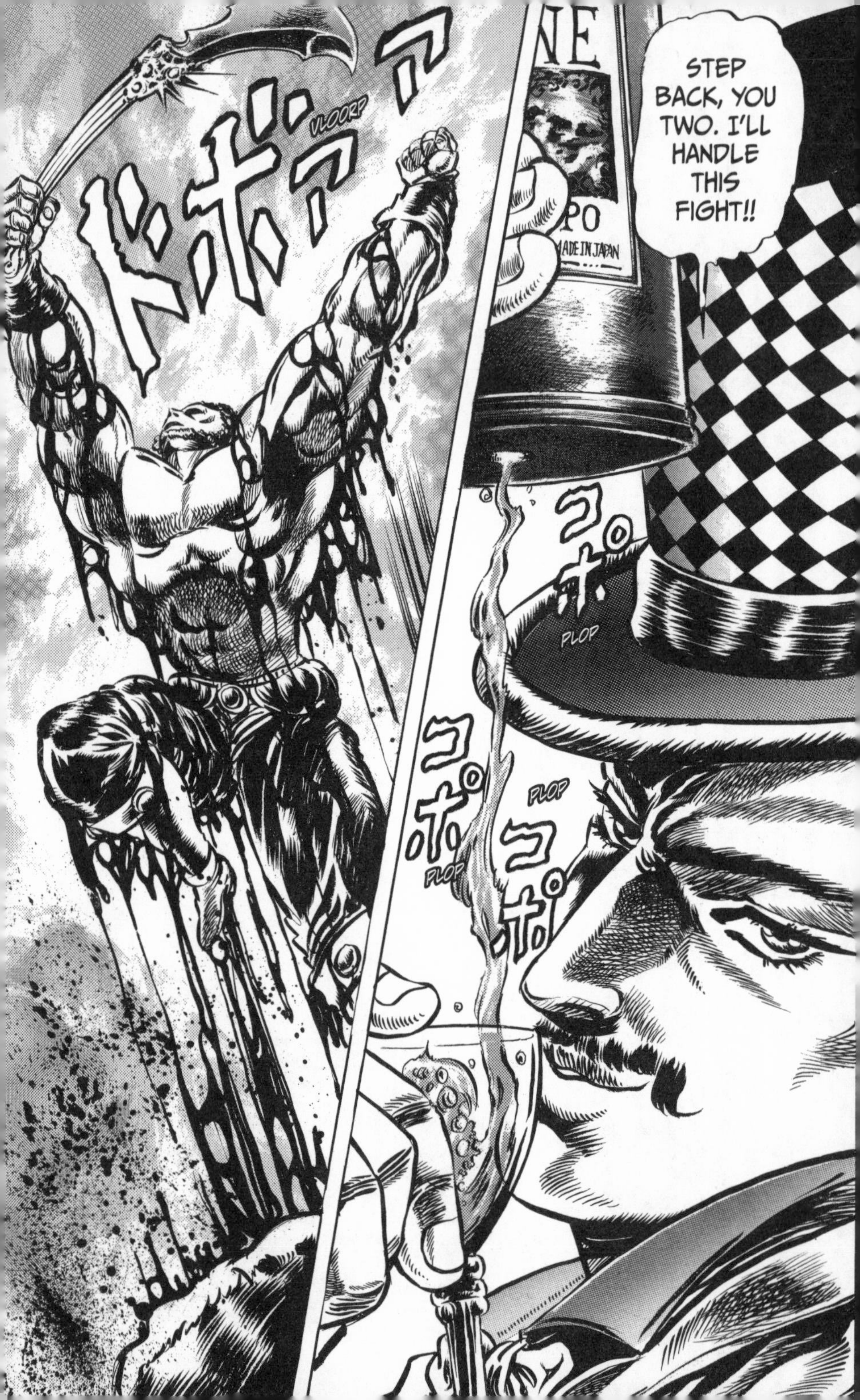
STEP BACK, YOU TWO. I'LL HANDLE THIS FIGHT!!
MADE IN JAPAN
コポ
PLOP
コポ
PLOP
コポ
PLOP
ドボァ
VLOORP

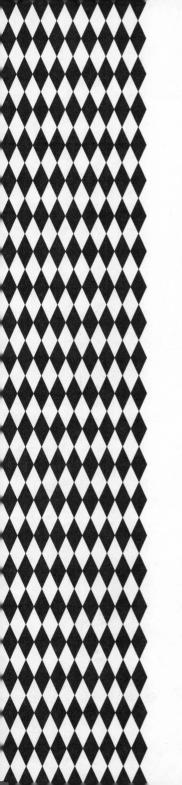

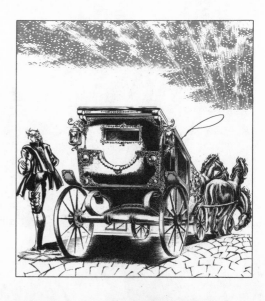

CHAPTER 22: Jack the Ripper and Zeppeli the Strange PART 5

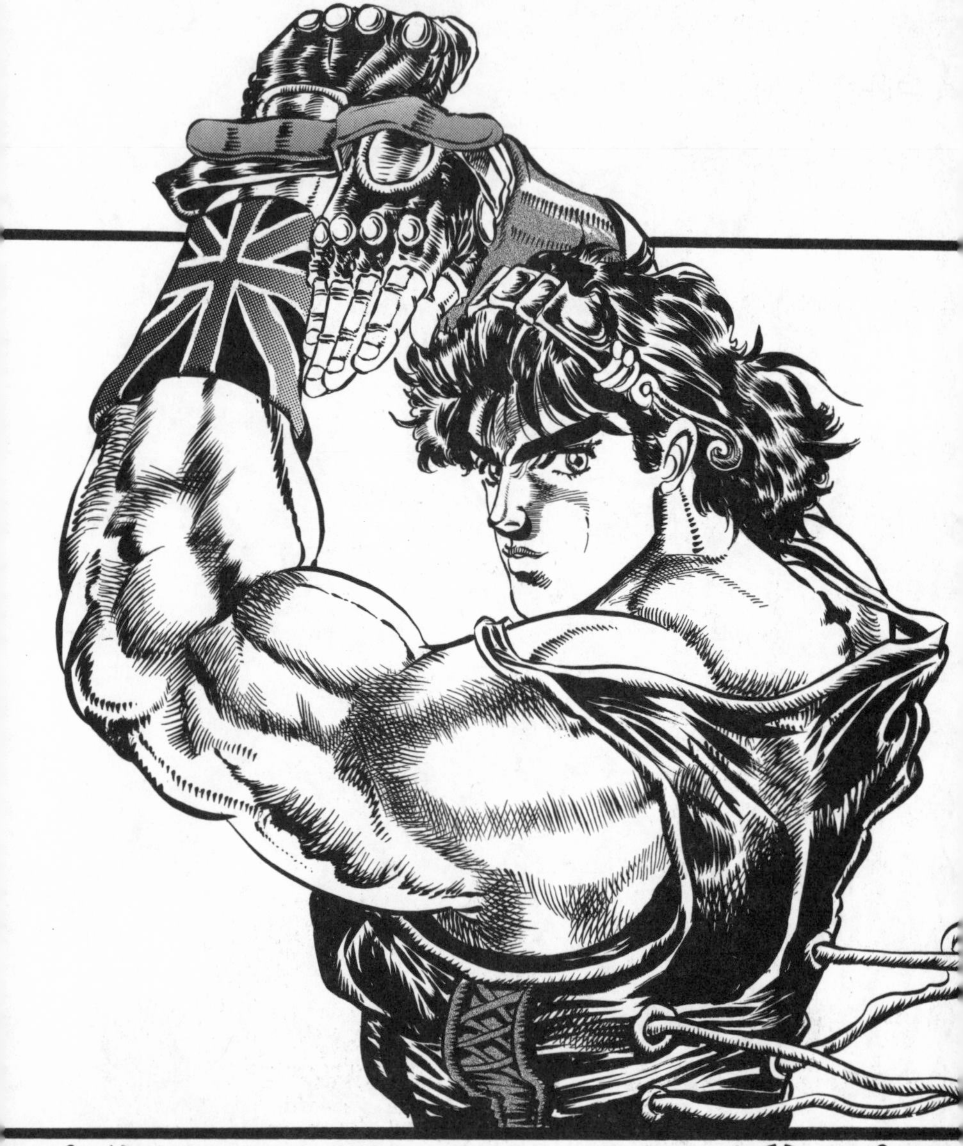

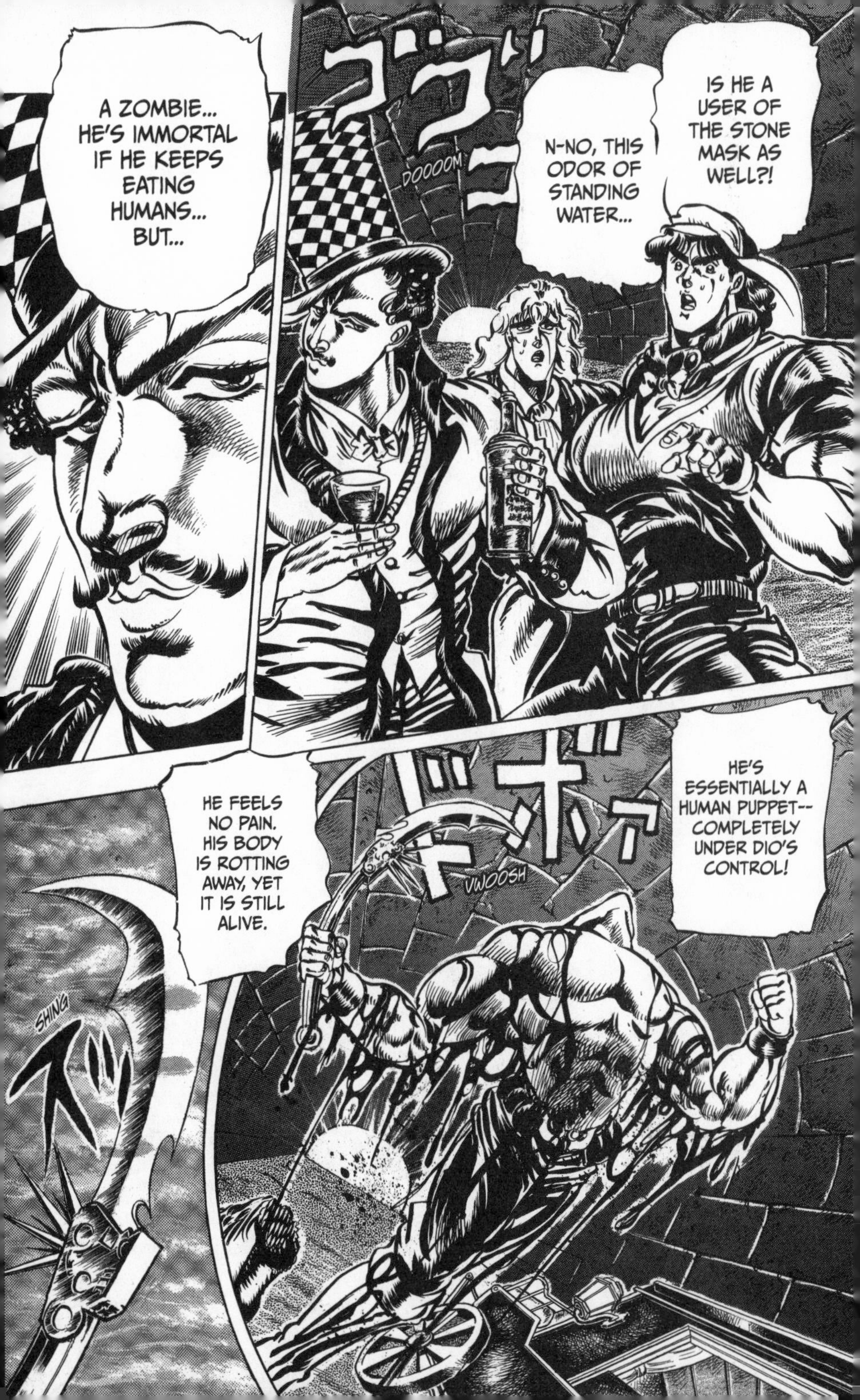
IS HE A USER OF THE STONE MASK AS WELL?!
N-NO, THIS ODOR OF STANDING WATER...
DOOOOM
A ZOMBIE... HE'S IMMORTAL IF HE KEEPS EATING HUMANS... BUT...
HE'S ESSENTIALLY A HUMAN PUPPET-- COMPLETELY UNDER DIO'S CONTROL!
VWOOSH
HE FEELS NO PAIN. HIS BODY IS ROTTING AWAY, YET IT IS STILL ALIVE.
SHING

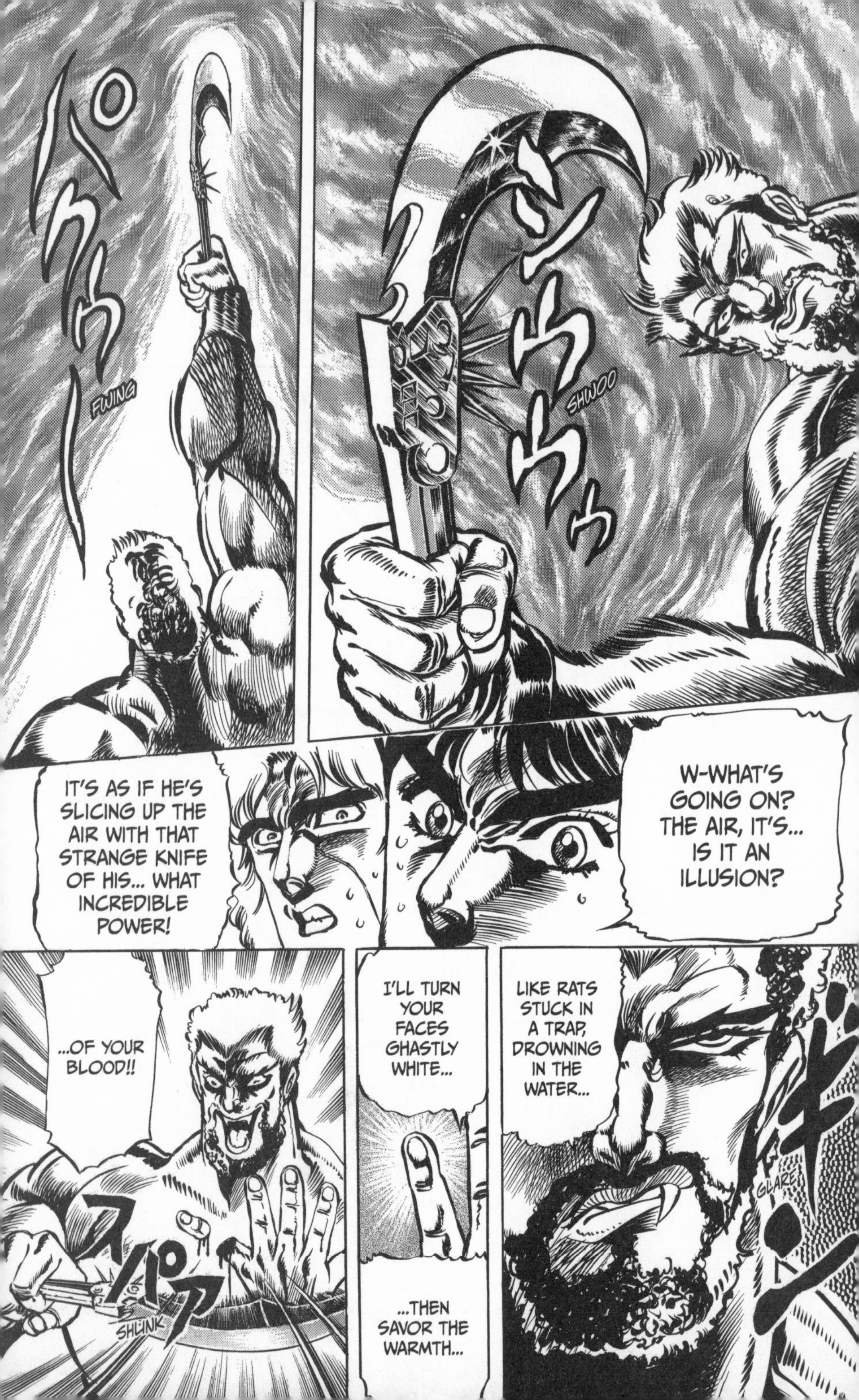
SHWOO
FWING
W-WHAT'S GOING ON? THE AIR, IT'S... IS IT AN ILLUSION?
IT'S AS IF HE'S SLICING UP THE AIR WITH THAT STRANGE KNIFE OF HIS... WHAT INCREDIBLE POWER!
GLARE
LIKE RATS STUCK IN A TRAP, DROWNING IN THE WATER...
I'LL TURN YOUR FACES GHASTLY WHITE...
...THEN SAVOR THE WARMTH...
...OF YOUR BLOOD!!
SHLINK

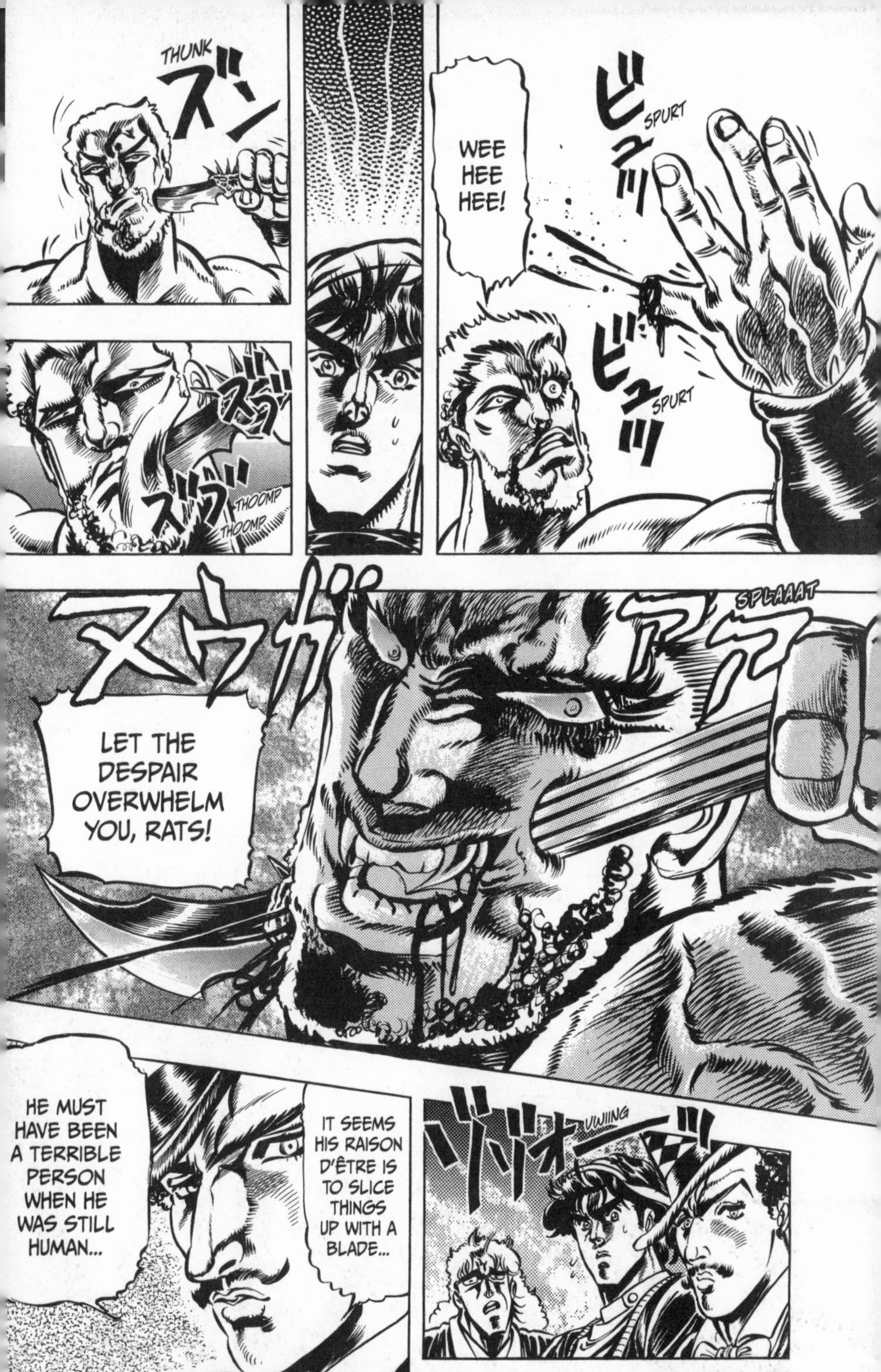
SPURT
WEE HEE HEE!
SPURT
THUNK
THOOMP THOOMP
SPLAAAT
LET THE DESPAIR OVERWHELM YOU, RATS!
VWIING
IT SEEMS HIS RAISON D'ÊTRE IS TO SLICE THINGS UP WITH A BLADE...
HE MUST HAVE BEEN A TERRIBLE PERSON WHEN HE WAS STILL HUMAN...

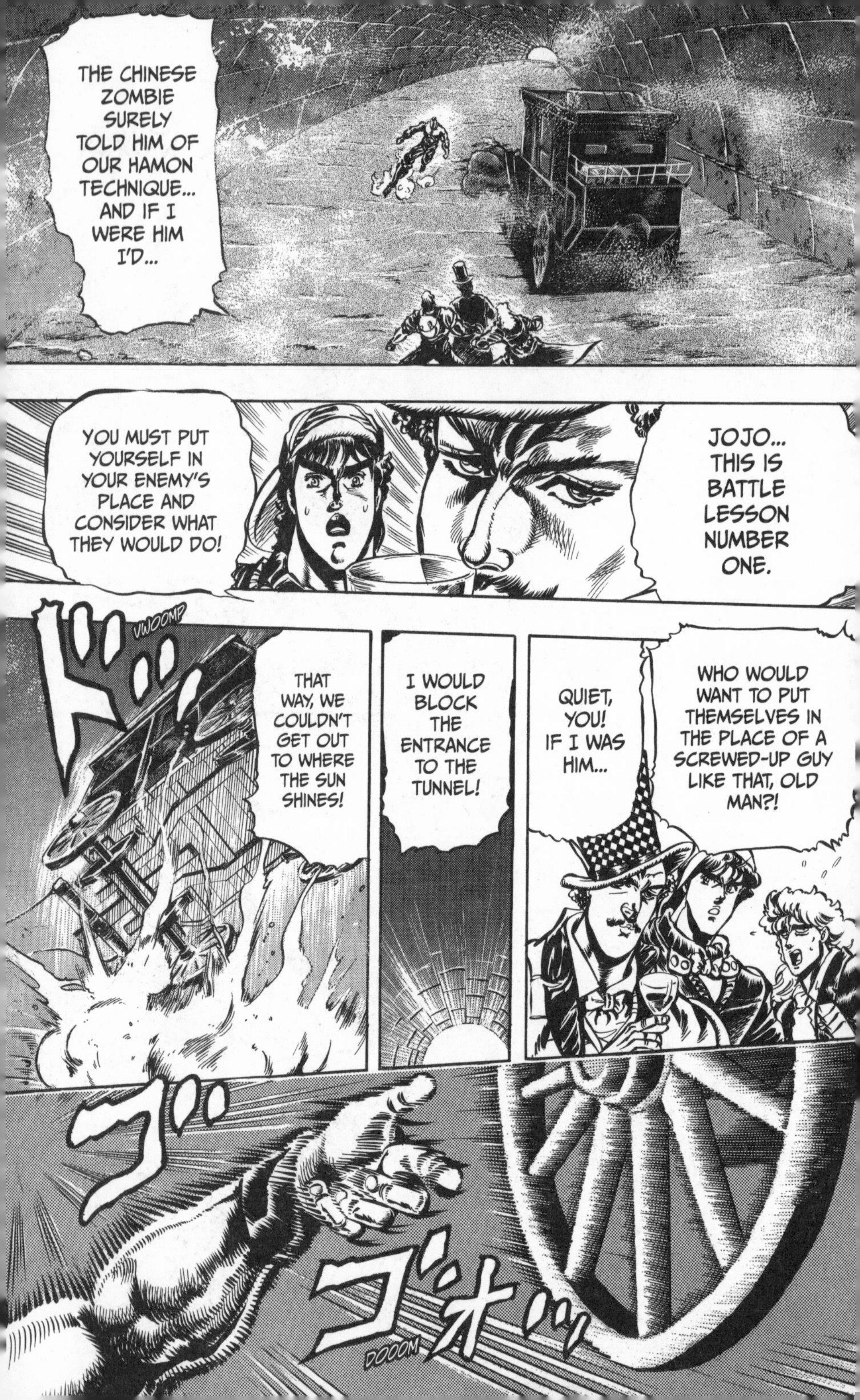
THE CHINESE ZOMBIE SURELY TOLD HIM OF OUR HAMON TECHNIQUE... AND IF I WERE HIM I'D...
JOJO... THIS IS BATTLE LESSON NUMBER ONE.
YOU MUST PUT YOURSELF IN YOUR ENEMY'S PLACE AND CONSIDER WHAT THEY WOULD DO!
WHO WOULD WANT TO PUT THEMSELVES IN THE PLACE OF A SCREWED-UP GUY LIKE THAT, OLD MAN?!
QUIET, YOU! IF I WAS HIM...
I WOULD BLOCK THE ENTRANCE TO THE TUNNEL!
THAT WAY, WE COULDN'T GET OUT TO WHERE THE SUN SHINES!
VWOOMP
DOOOM

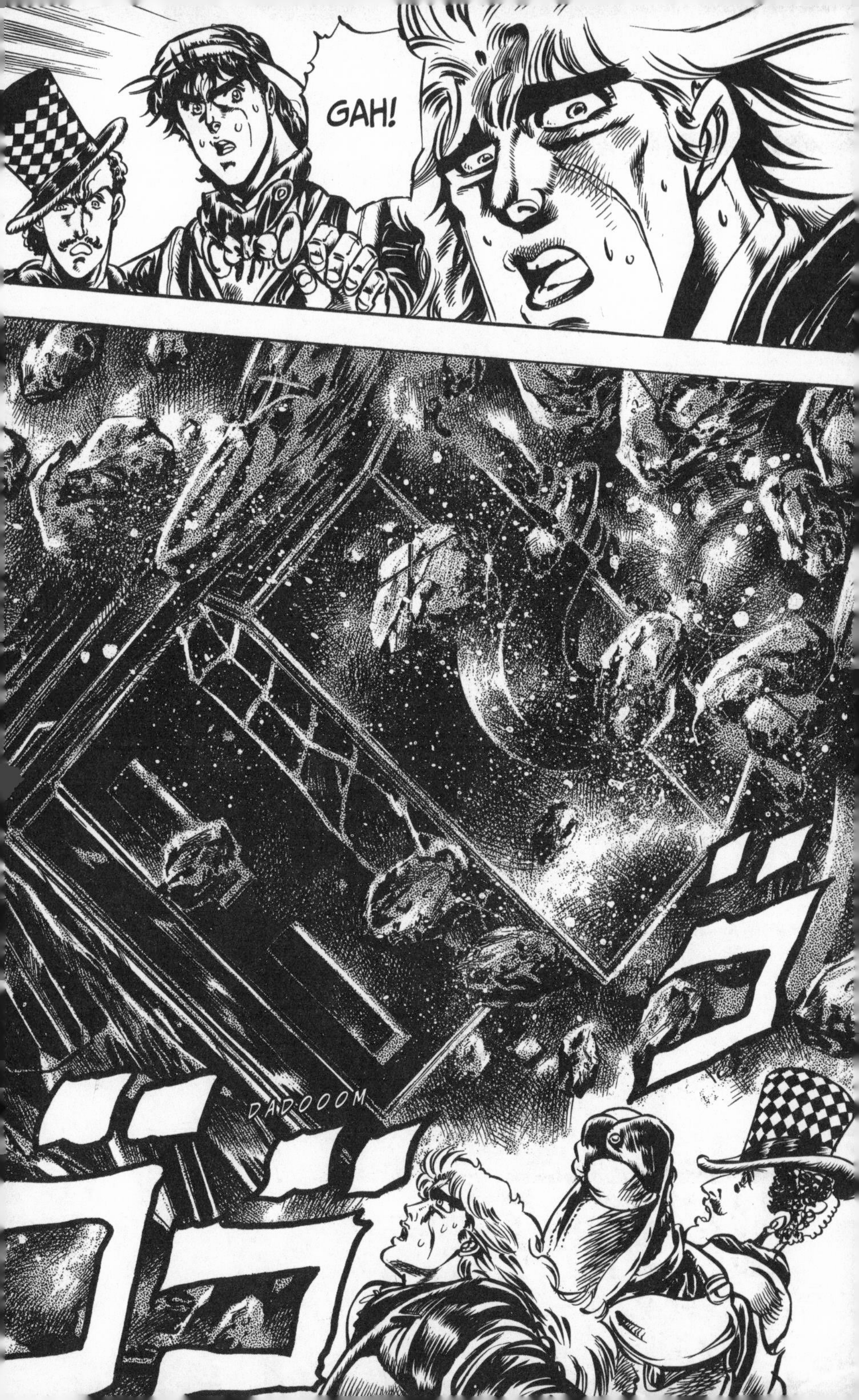
GAH!
DADOOOM

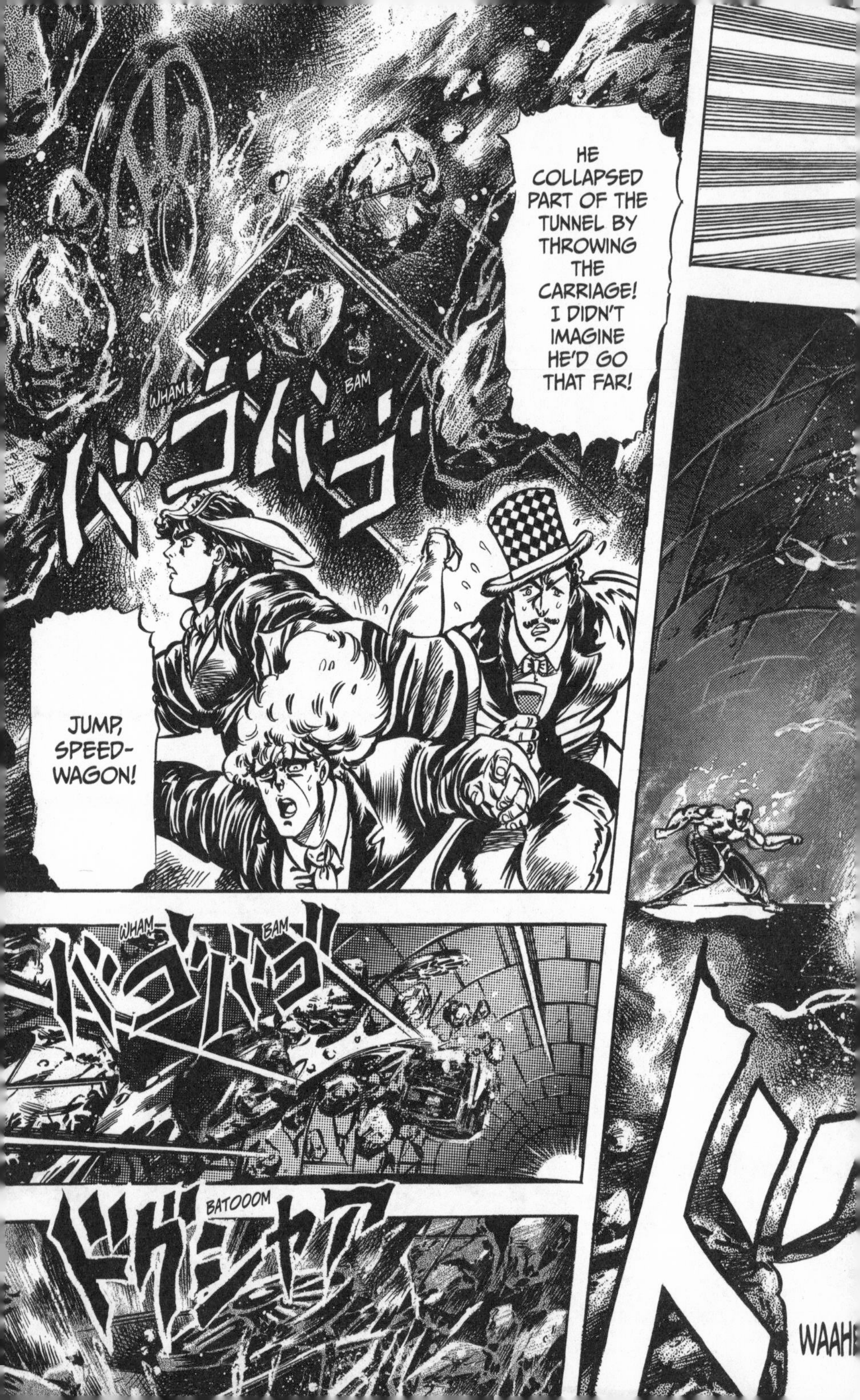
WAAH
HE COLLAPSED PART OF THE TUNNEL BY THROWING THE CARRIAGE! I DIDN'T IMAGINE HE'D GO THAT FAR!
BAM
WHAM
JUMP, SPEED-WAGON!
BAM
WHAM
BATOOOM

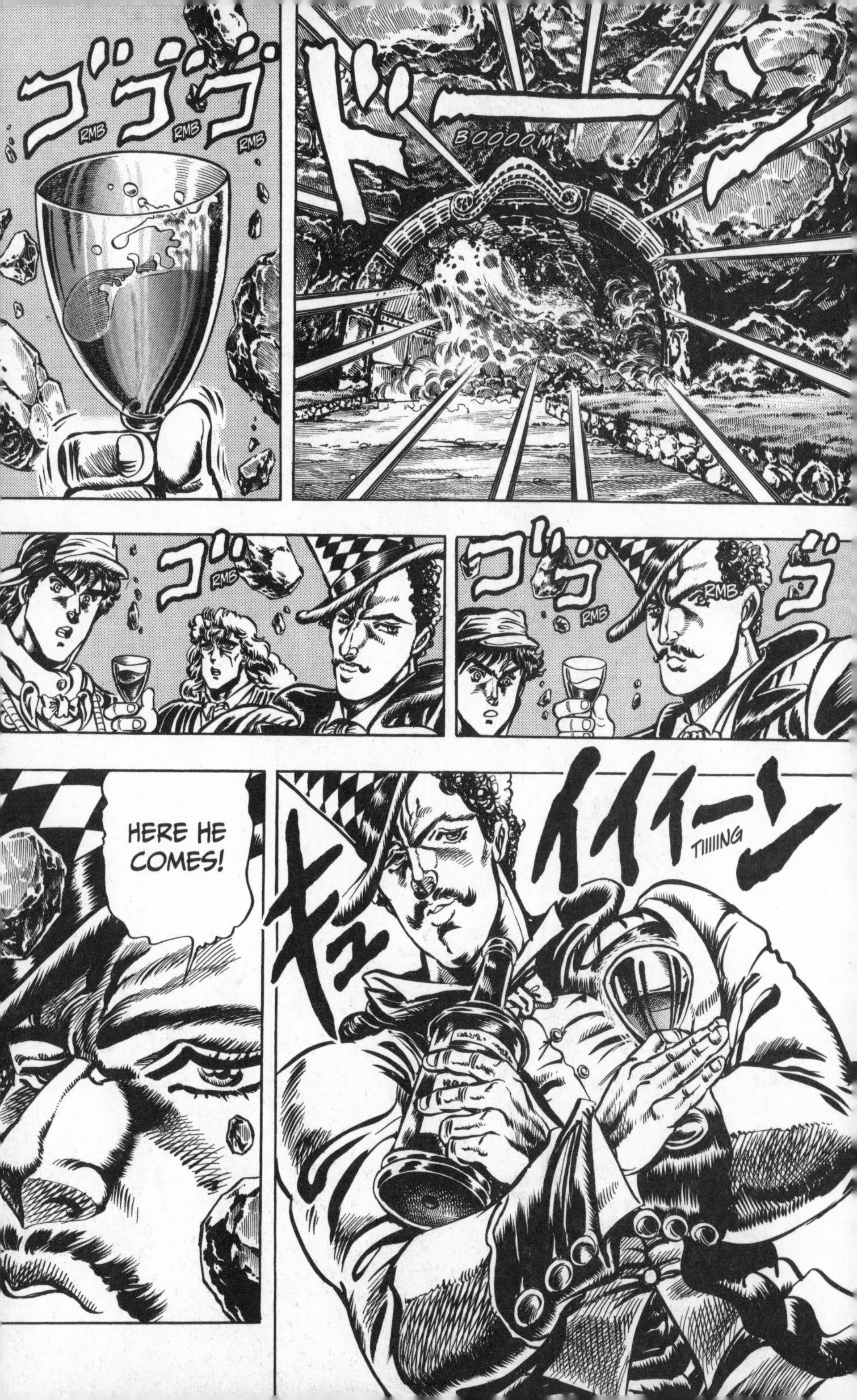
BOOOOM
RMB
RMB
RMB
RMB
RMB
RMB
TIIIING
HERE HE COMES!

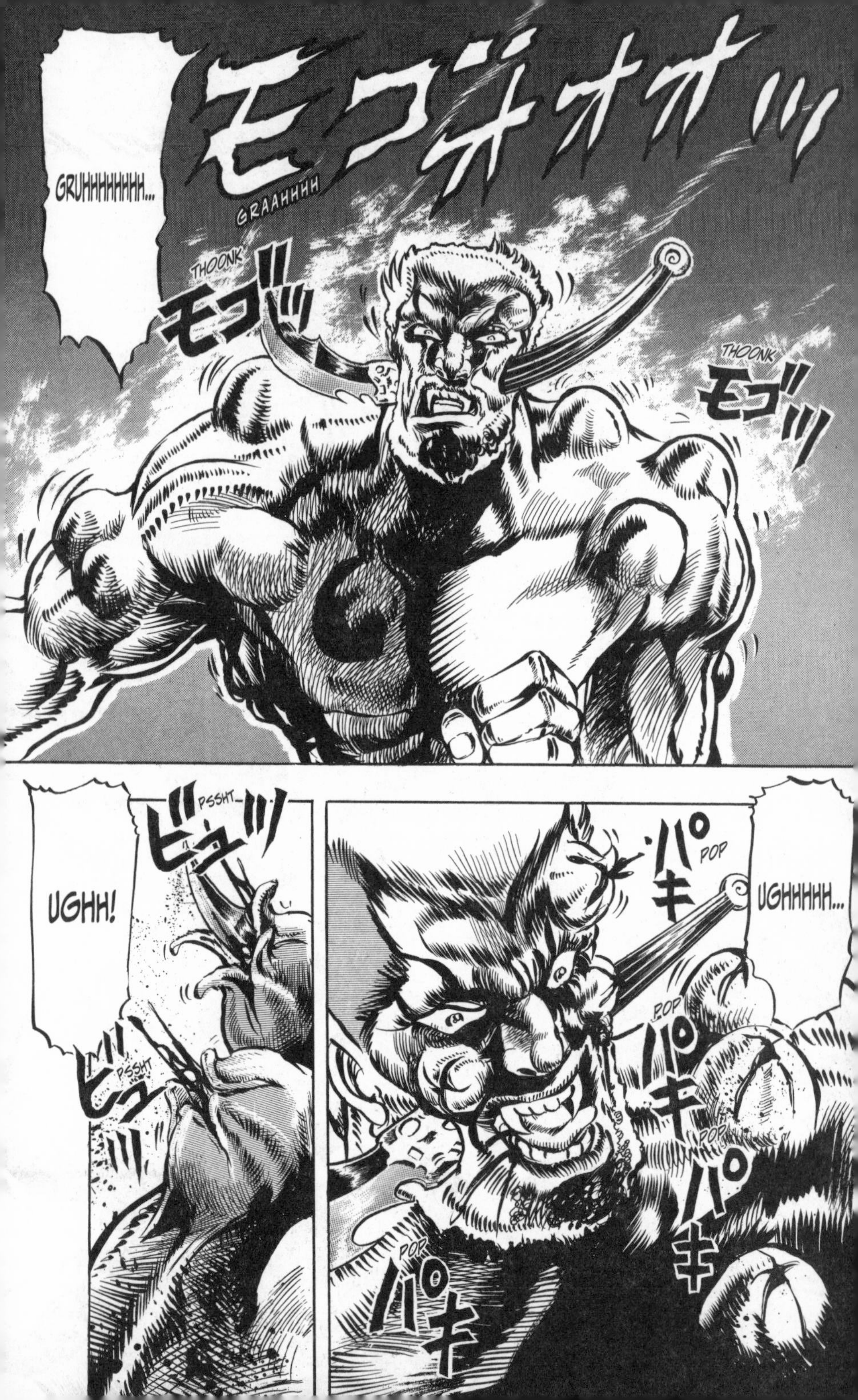
GRAAHHHH
GRUHHHHHHHH...
THOONK
THOONK
UGHHHHH...
POP
POP
POP
POP
PSSHT
UGHH!
PSSHT

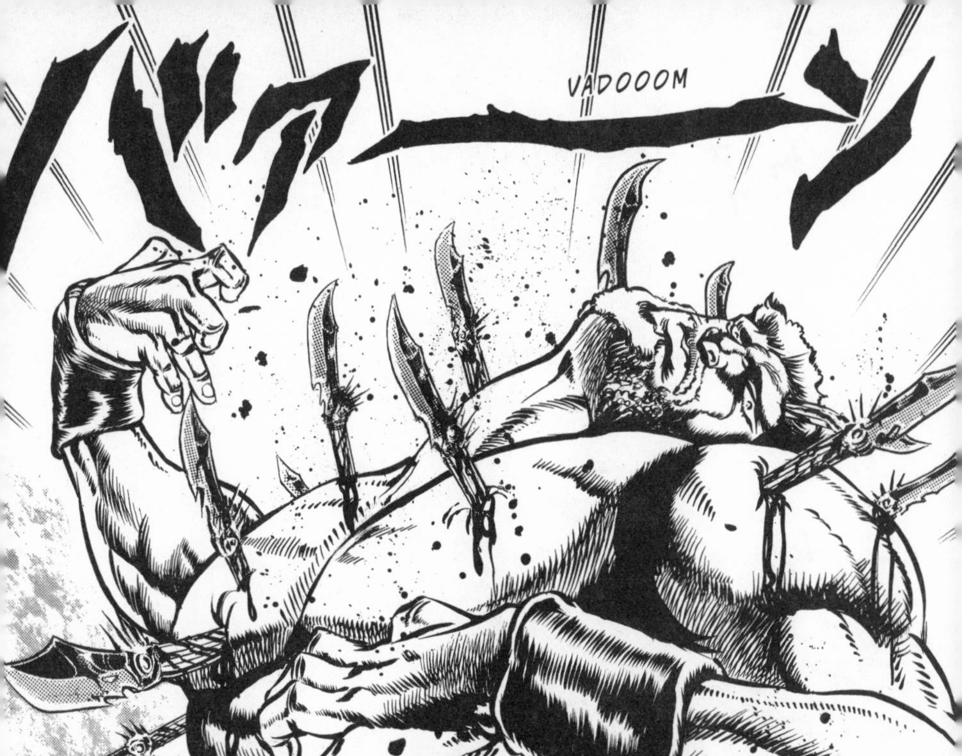
VADOOOM

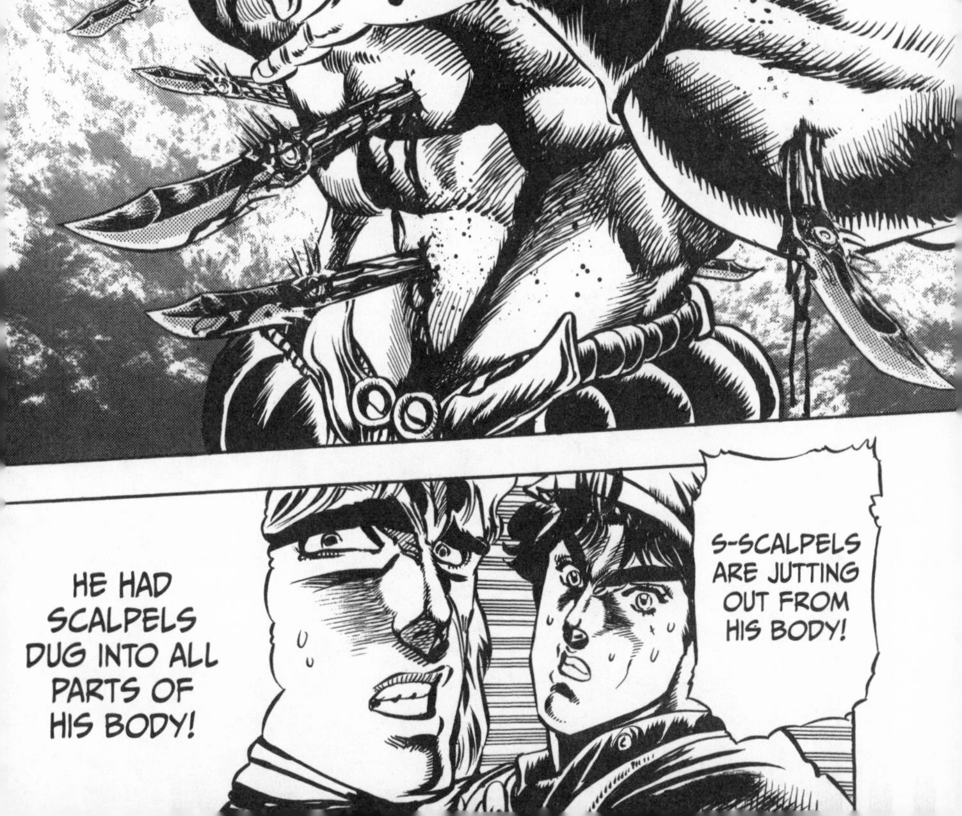
S-SCALPELS ARE JUTTING OUT FROM HIS BODY!
HE HAD SCALPELS DUG INTO ALL PARTS OF HIS BODY!

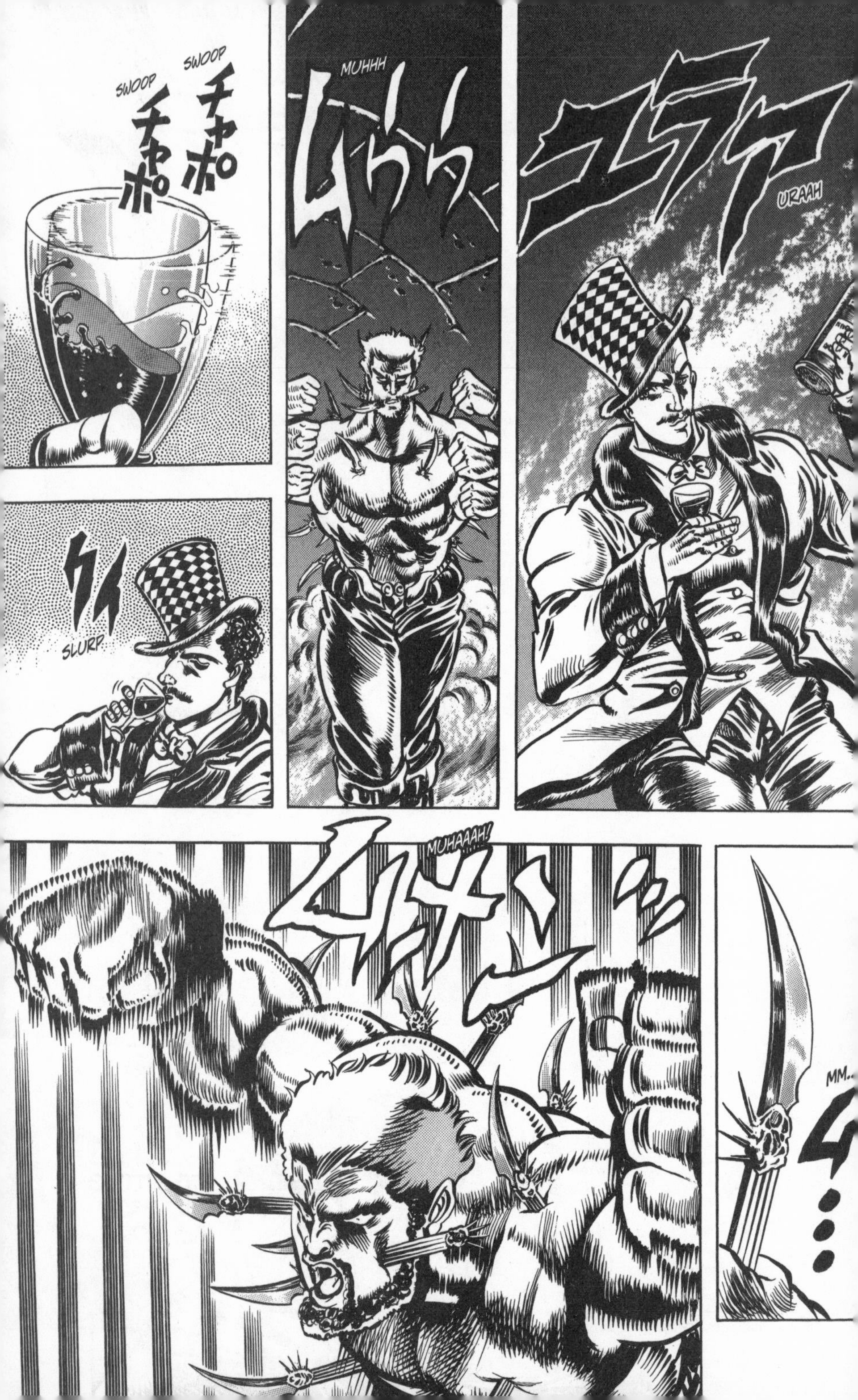

ウラァ
URAAH
ムゥゥ
MUHHH
チャポ
SWOOP
チャポ
SWOOP
グイ
SLURP
MM...
MUHAAAH!

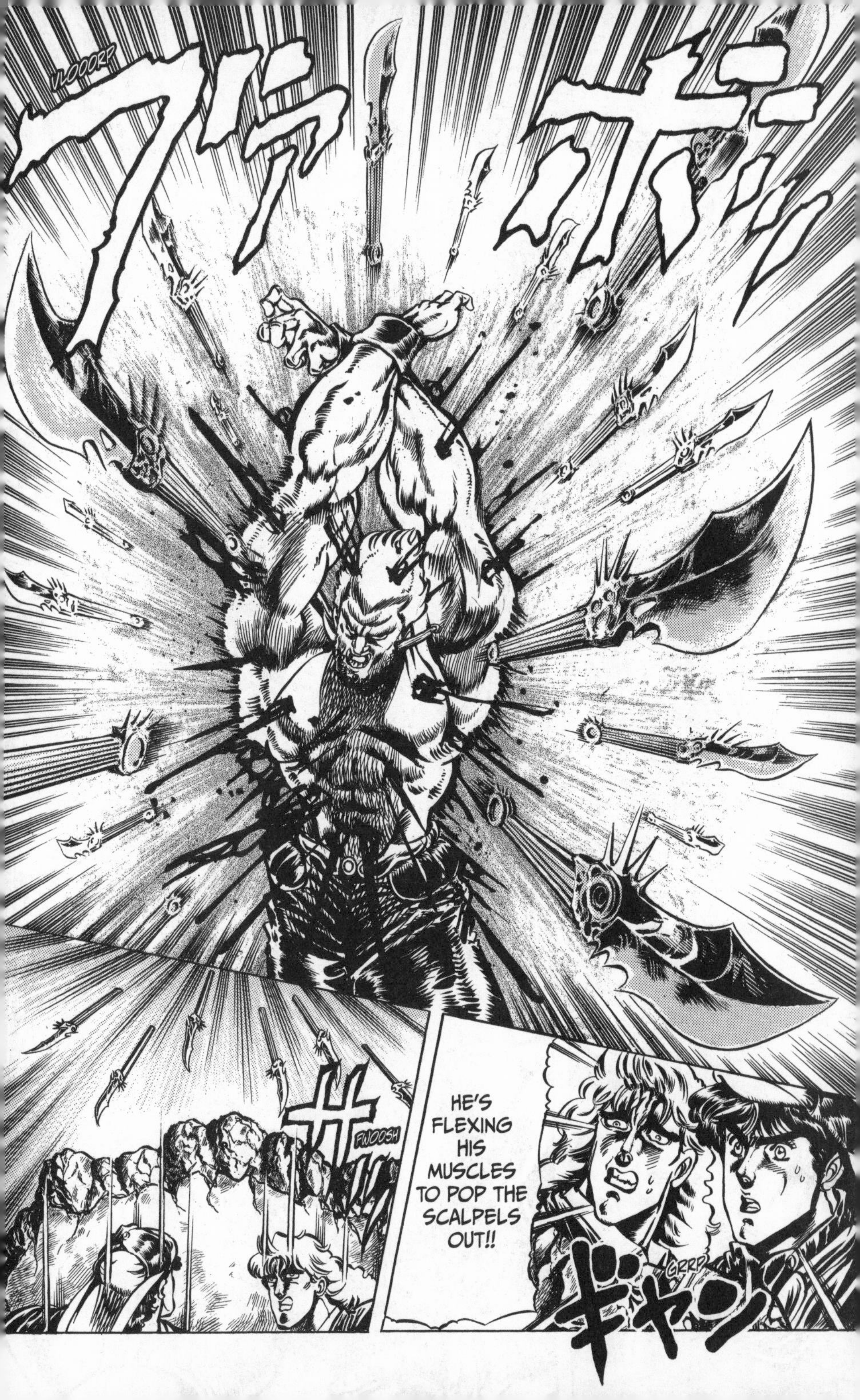
ULOOORP
HE'S FLEXING HIS MUSCLES TO POP THE SCALPELS OUT!!
GRRP
FWOOSH

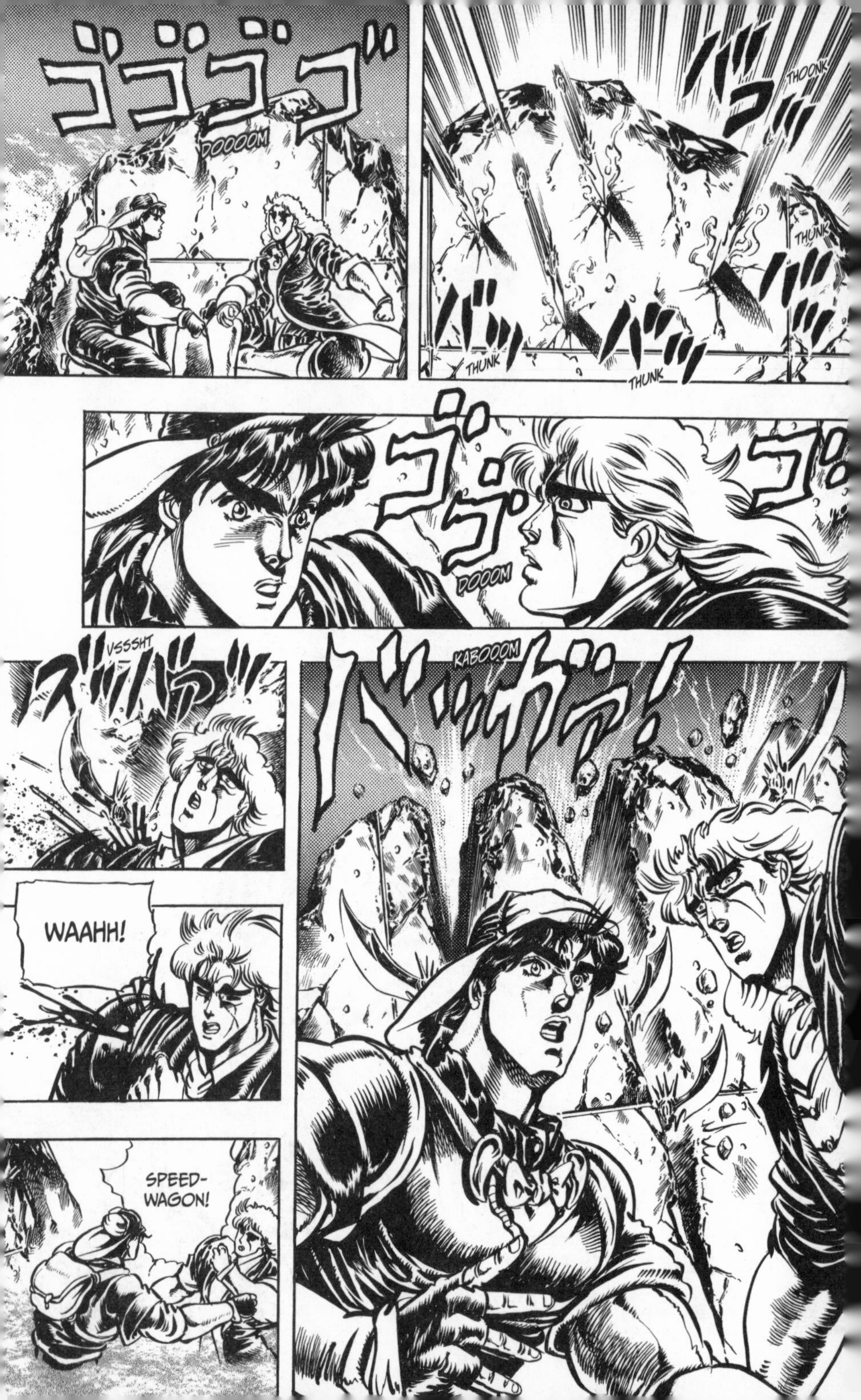
THOONK
THUNK
THUNK
THUNK
ゴゴゴゴ
DOOOOM
DOOOM
KABOOOM
バッガァ!
VSSSHT
WAAHH!
SPEED-WAGON!

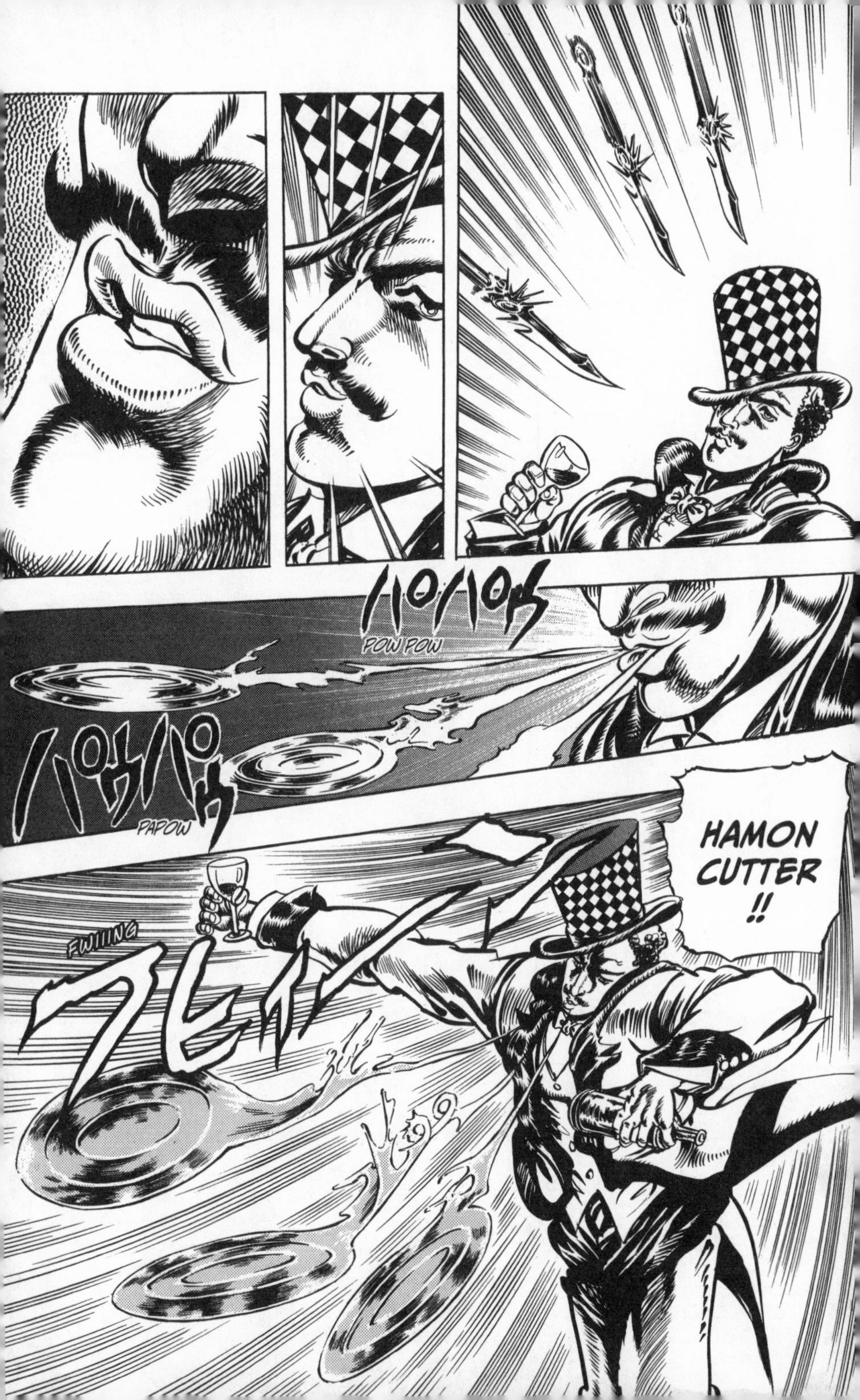
POW POW
PAPOW
HAMON CUTTER !!
FWIIING

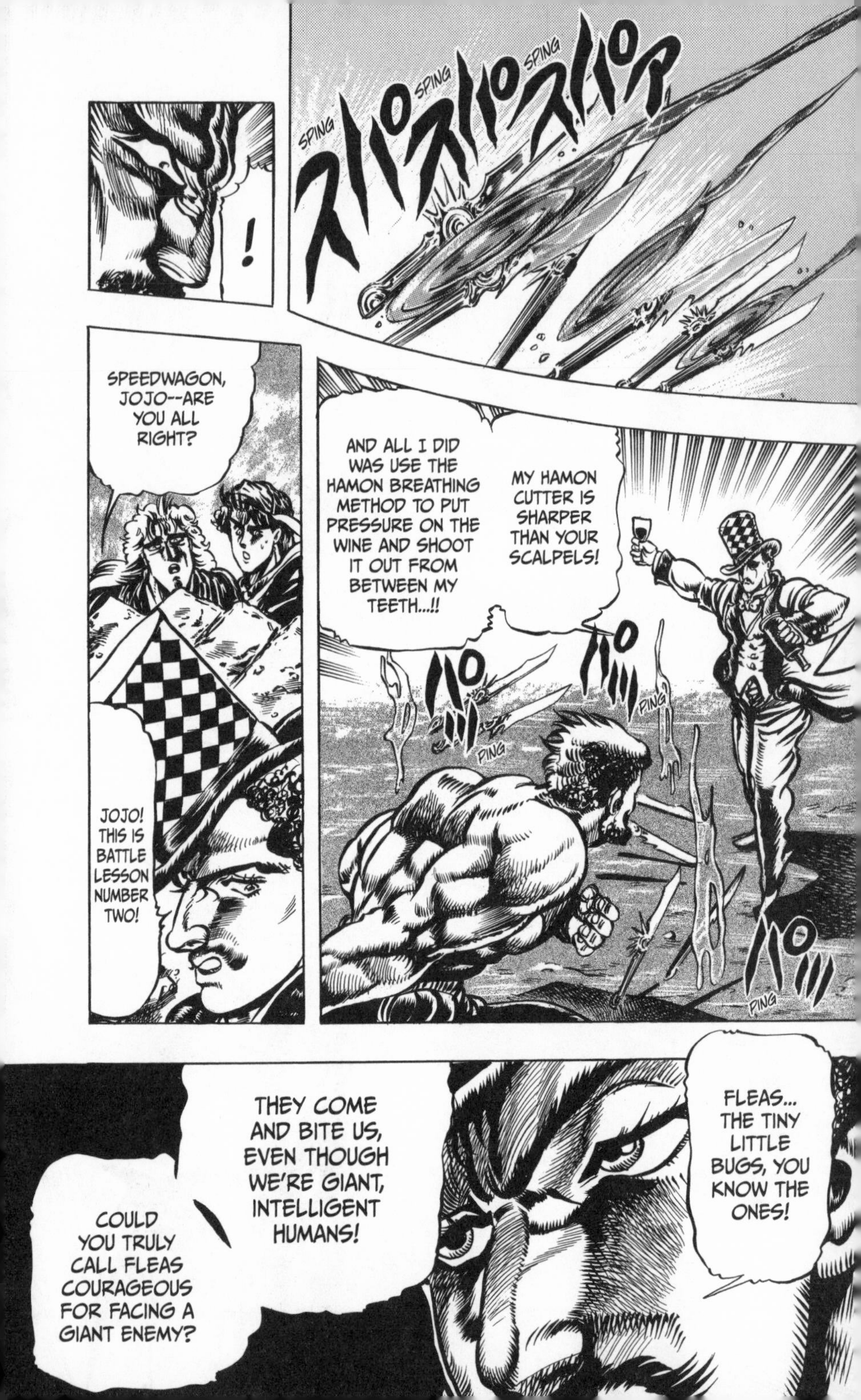

SPING SPING SPING
スパスパスパ
!
MY HAMON CUTTER IS SHARPER THAN YOUR SCALPELS!
AND ALL I DID WAS USE THE HAMON BREATHING METHOD TO PUT PRESSURE ON THE WINE AND SHOOT IT OUT FROM BETWEEN MY TEETH...!!
PING
PING
PING
SPEEDWAGON, JOJO--ARE YOU ALL RIGHT?
JOJO! THIS IS BATTLE LESSON NUMBER TWO!
FLEAS... THE TINY LITTLE BUGS, YOU KNOW THE ONES!
THEY COME AND BITE US, EVEN THOUGH WE'RE GIANT, INTELLIGENT HUMANS!
COULD YOU TRULY CALL FLEAS COURAGEOUS FOR FACING A GIANT ENEMY?

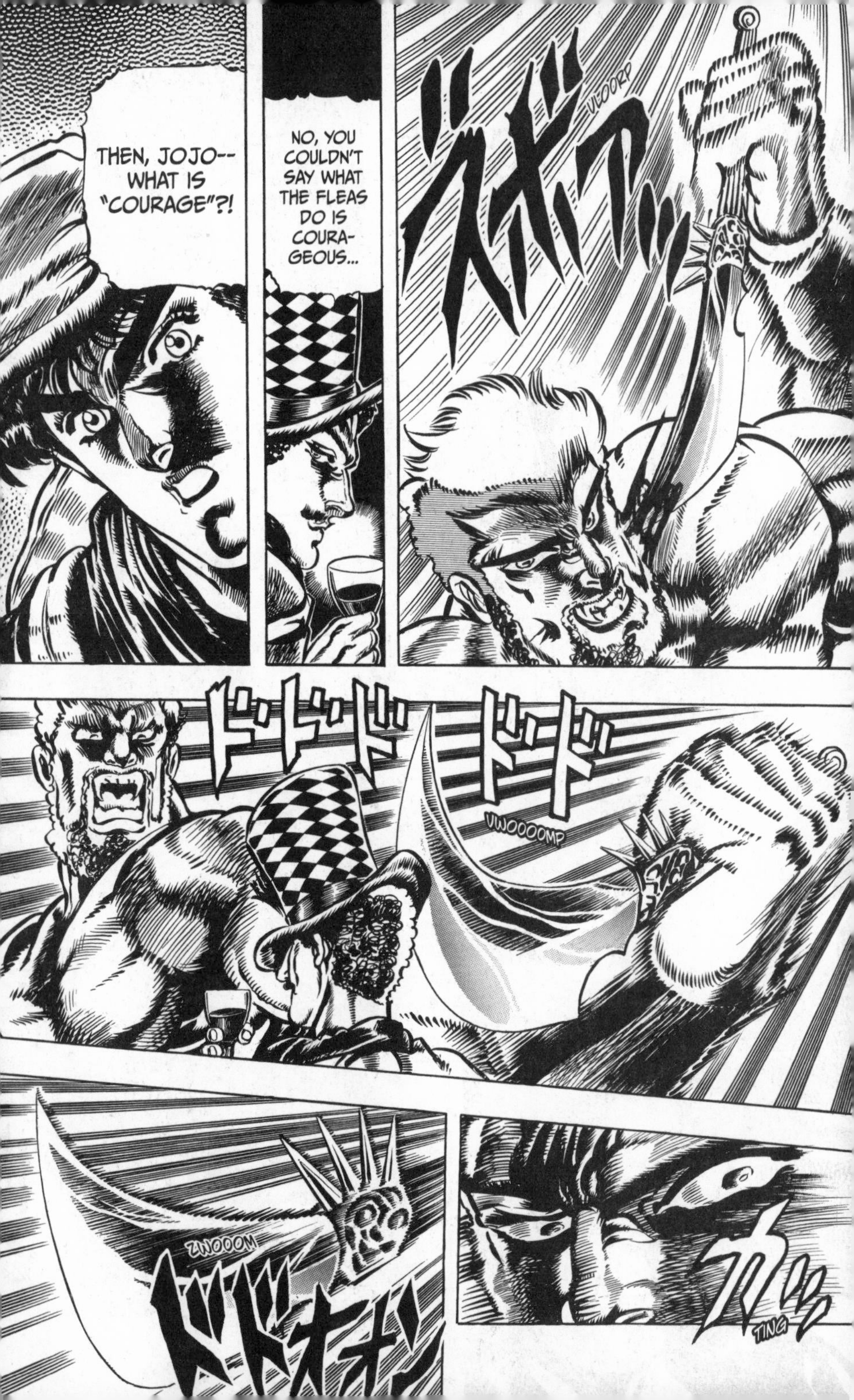
VUOORP
NO, YOU COULDN'T SAY WHAT THE FLEAS DO IS COURAGEOUS...
THEN, JOJO-- WHAT IS "COURAGE"?!
ドドドド ドドド
VWOOOOMP
TING!
ZWOOOM

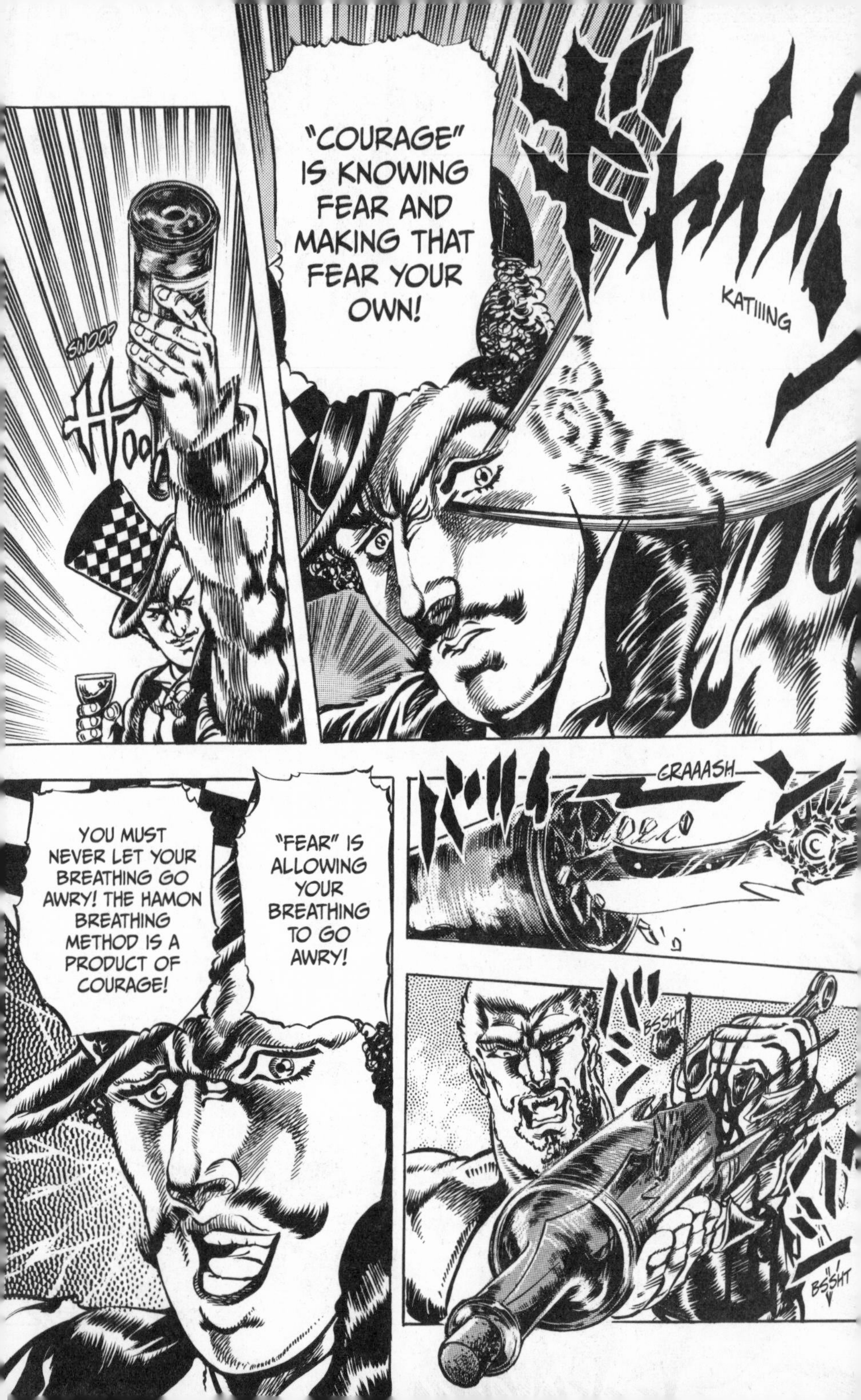

"COURAGE" IS KNOWING FEAR AND MAKING THAT FEAR YOUR OWN!
KATIIING
SWOOP
GRAAASH
BSSHT
BSSHT
"FEAR" IS ALLOWING YOUR BREATHING TO GO AWRY!
YOU MUST NEVER LET YOUR BREATHING GO AWRY! THE HAMON BREATHING METHOD IS A PRODUCT OF COURAGE!

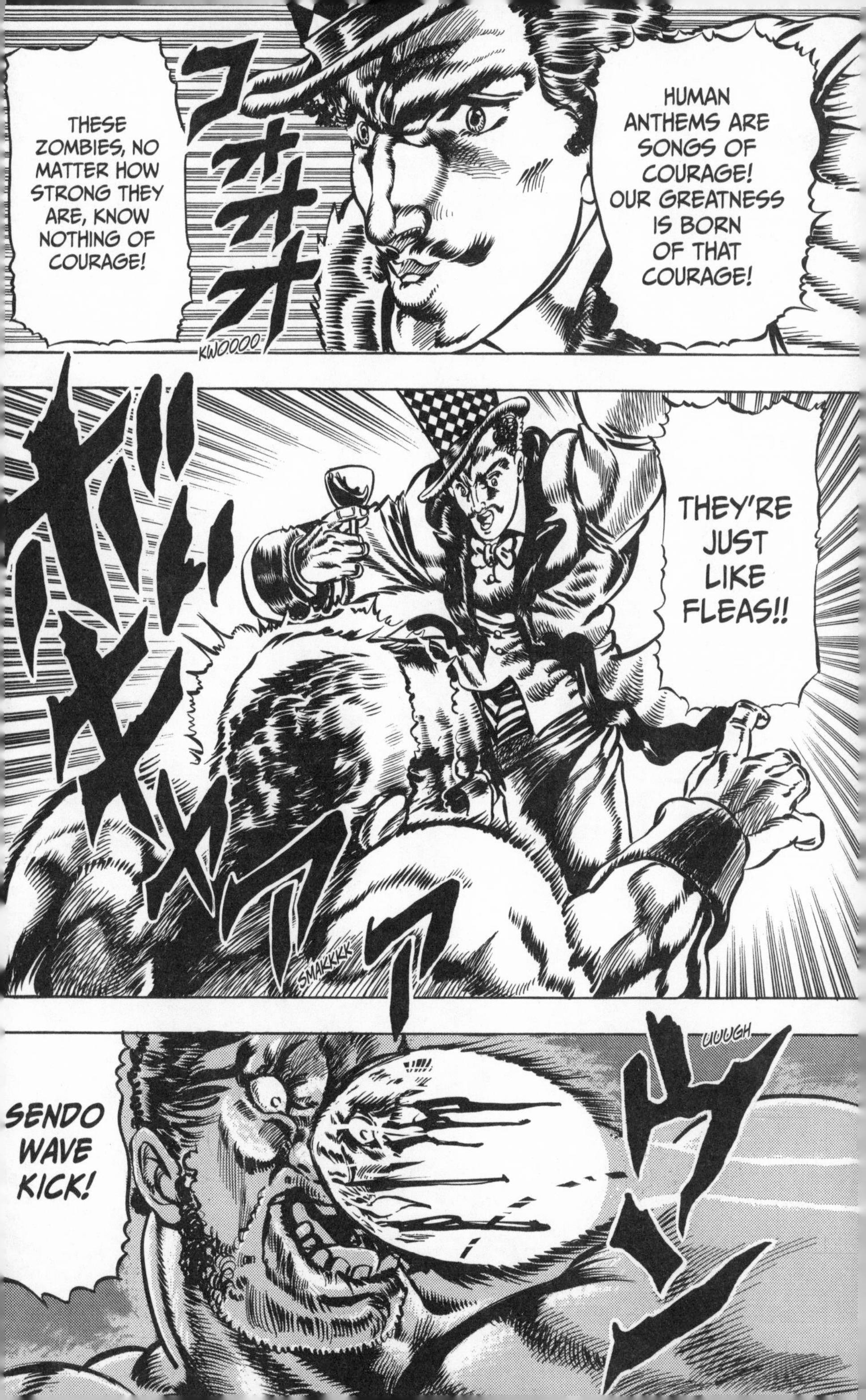
HUMAN ANTHEMS ARE SONGS OF COURAGE! OUR GREATNESS IS BORN OF THAT COURAGE!
THESE ZOMBIES, NO MATTER HOW STRONG THEY ARE, KNOW NOTHING OF COURAGE!
KWOOOO
THEY'RE JUST LIKE FLEAS!!
SMAKKKK
UUUGH
SENDO WAVE KICK!

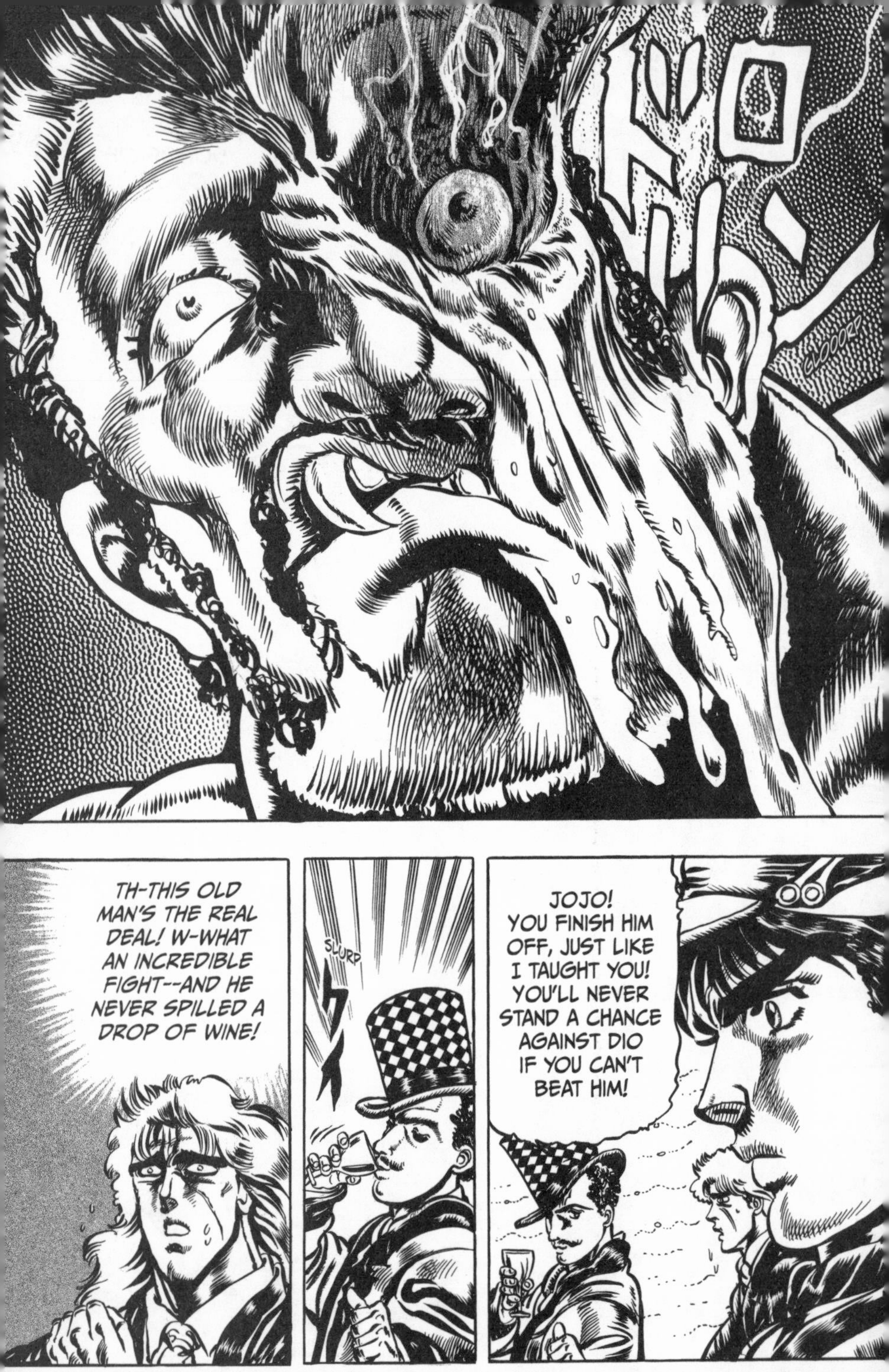
GLOOORP
JOJO! YOU FINISH HIM OFF, JUST LIKE I TAUGHT YOU! YOU'LL NEVER STAND A CHANCE AGAINST DIO IF YOU CAN'T BEAT HIM!
SLURP
TH-THIS OLD MAN'S THE REAL DEAL! W-WHAT AN INCREDIBLE FIGHT--AND HE NEVER SPILLED A DROP OF WINE!

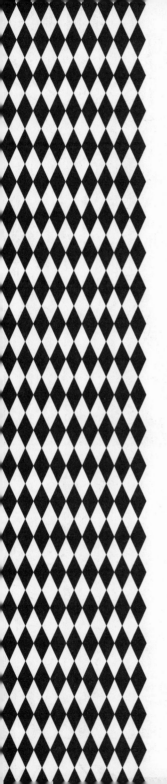

JoJo's
BIZARRE ADVENTURE

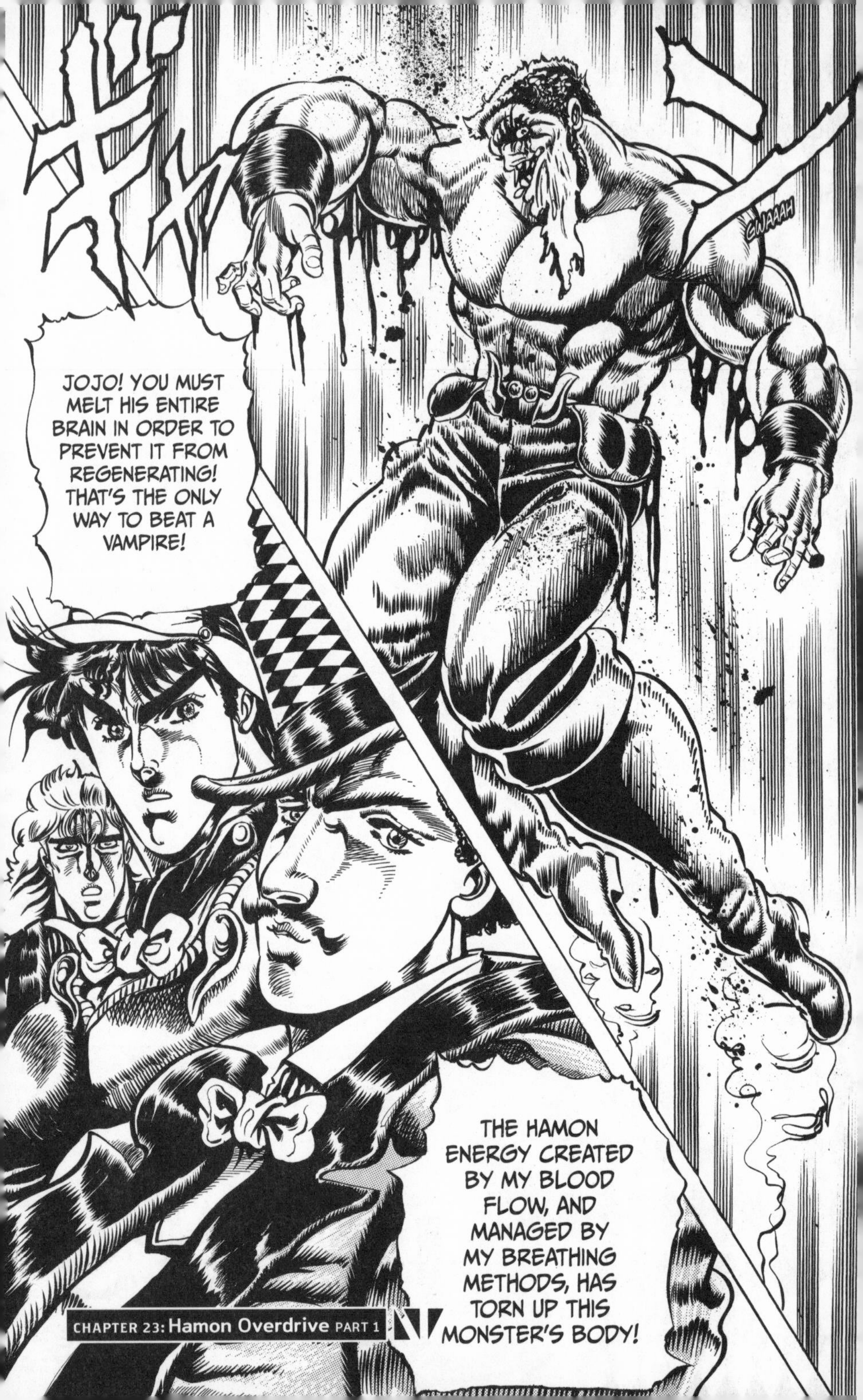
GWAAAH
JOJO! YOU MUST MELT HIS ENTIRE BRAIN IN ORDER TO PREVENT IT FROM REGENERATING! THAT'S THE ONLY WAY TO BEAT A VAMPIRE!
THE HAMON ENERGY CREATED BY MY BLOOD FLOW, AND MANAGED BY MY BREATHING METHODS, HAS TORN UP THIS MONSTER'S BODY!
CHAPTER 23: Hamon Overdrive PART 1

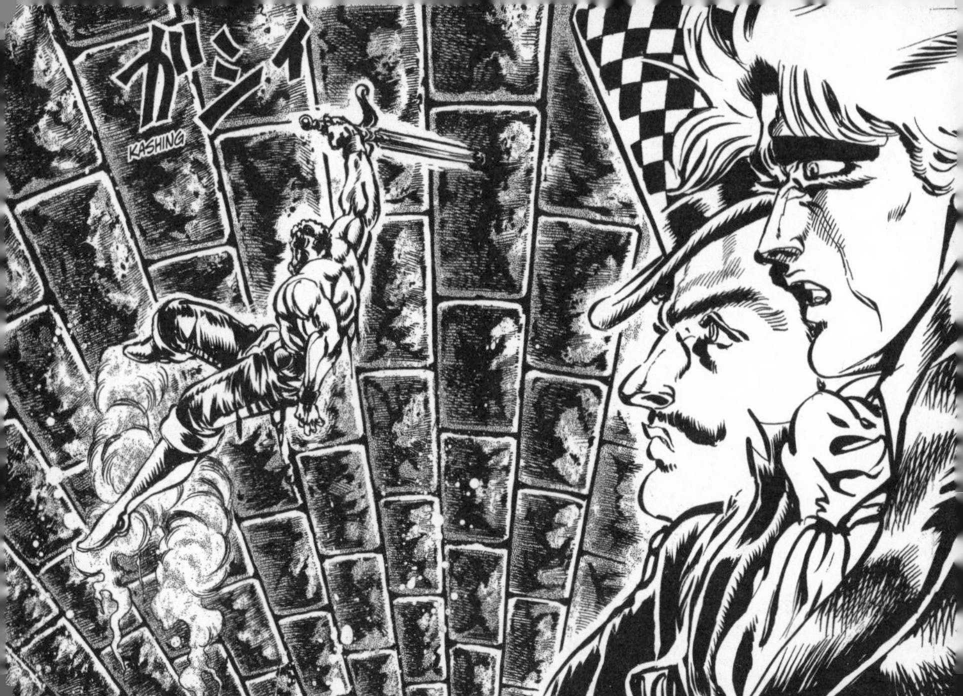
ガシィ
KASHING
CHAPTER 23: Hamon Overdrive PART 1

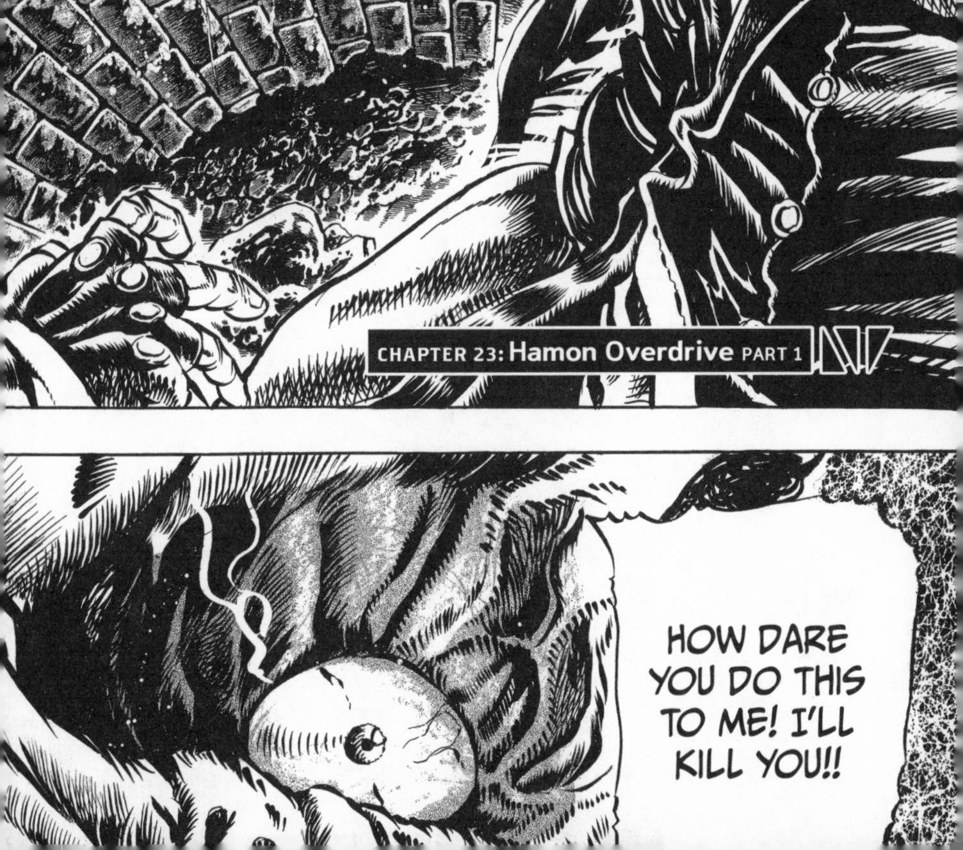
HOW DARE YOU DO THIS TO ME! I'LL KILL YOU!!

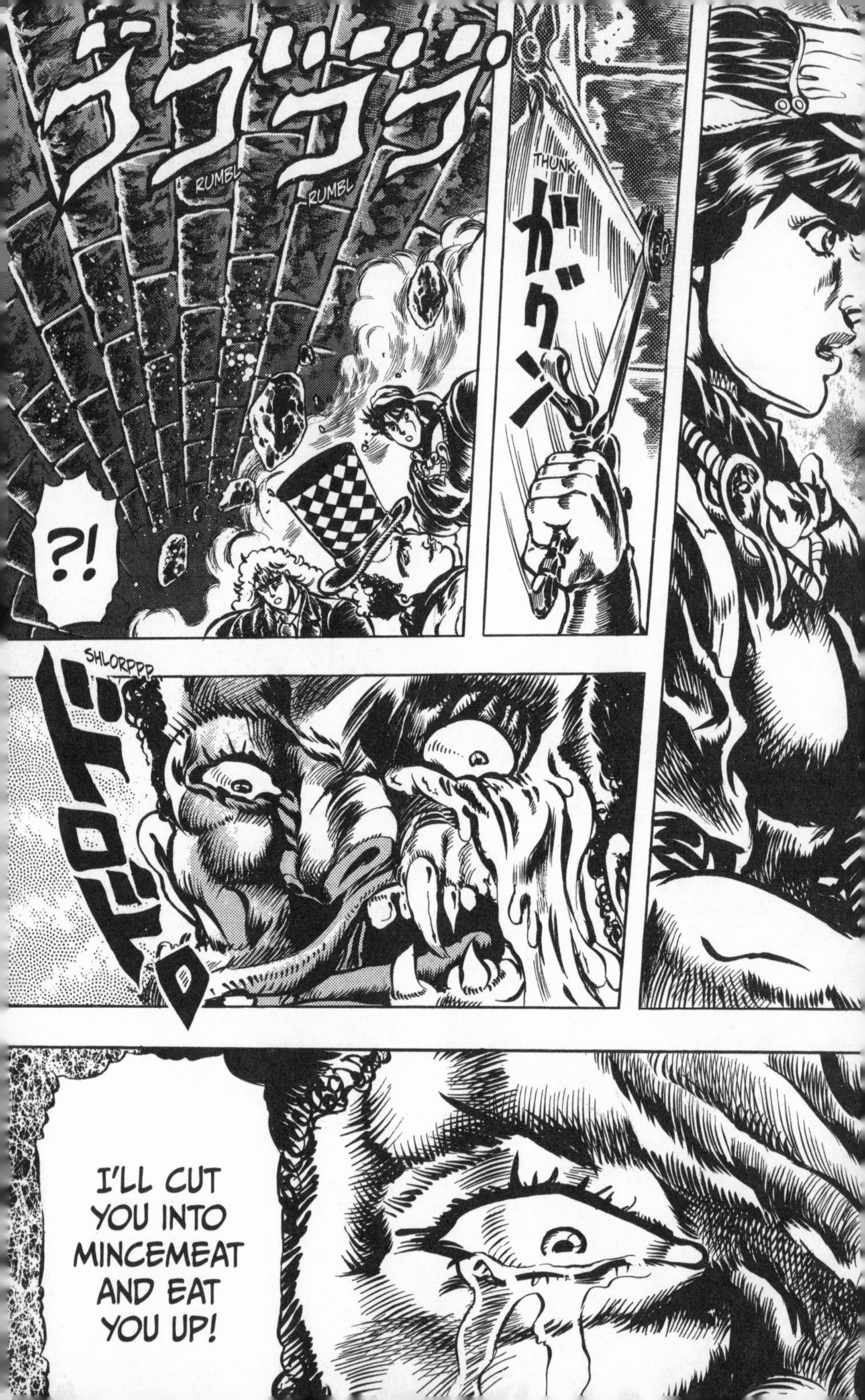
THUNK
ガグン
ゴゴゴゴ
RUMBL
RUMBL
?!
SHLORPPP
I'LL CUT YOU INTO MINCEMEAT AND EAT YOU UP!

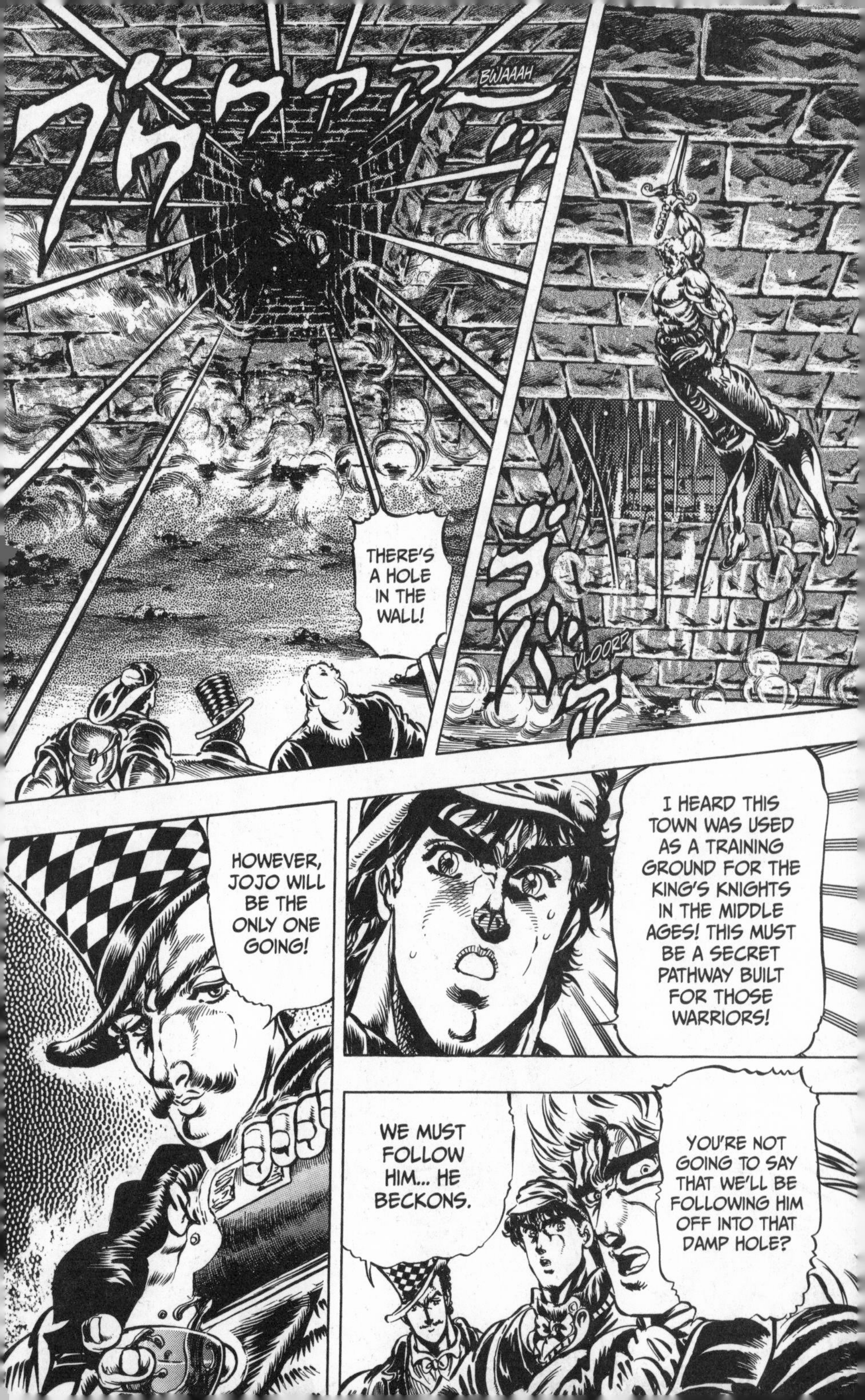
VLOORP
BWAAAH
THERE'S A HOLE IN THE WALL!
I HEARD THIS TOWN WAS USED AS A TRAINING GROUND FOR THE KING'S KNIGHTS IN THE MIDDLE AGES! THIS MUST BE A SECRET PATHWAY BUILT FOR THOSE WARRIORS!
YOU'RE NOT GOING TO SAY THAT WE'LL BE FOLLOWING HIM OFF INTO THAT DAMP HOLE?
WE MUST FOLLOW HIM... HE BECKONS.
HOWEVER, JOJO WILL BE THE ONLY ONE GOING!

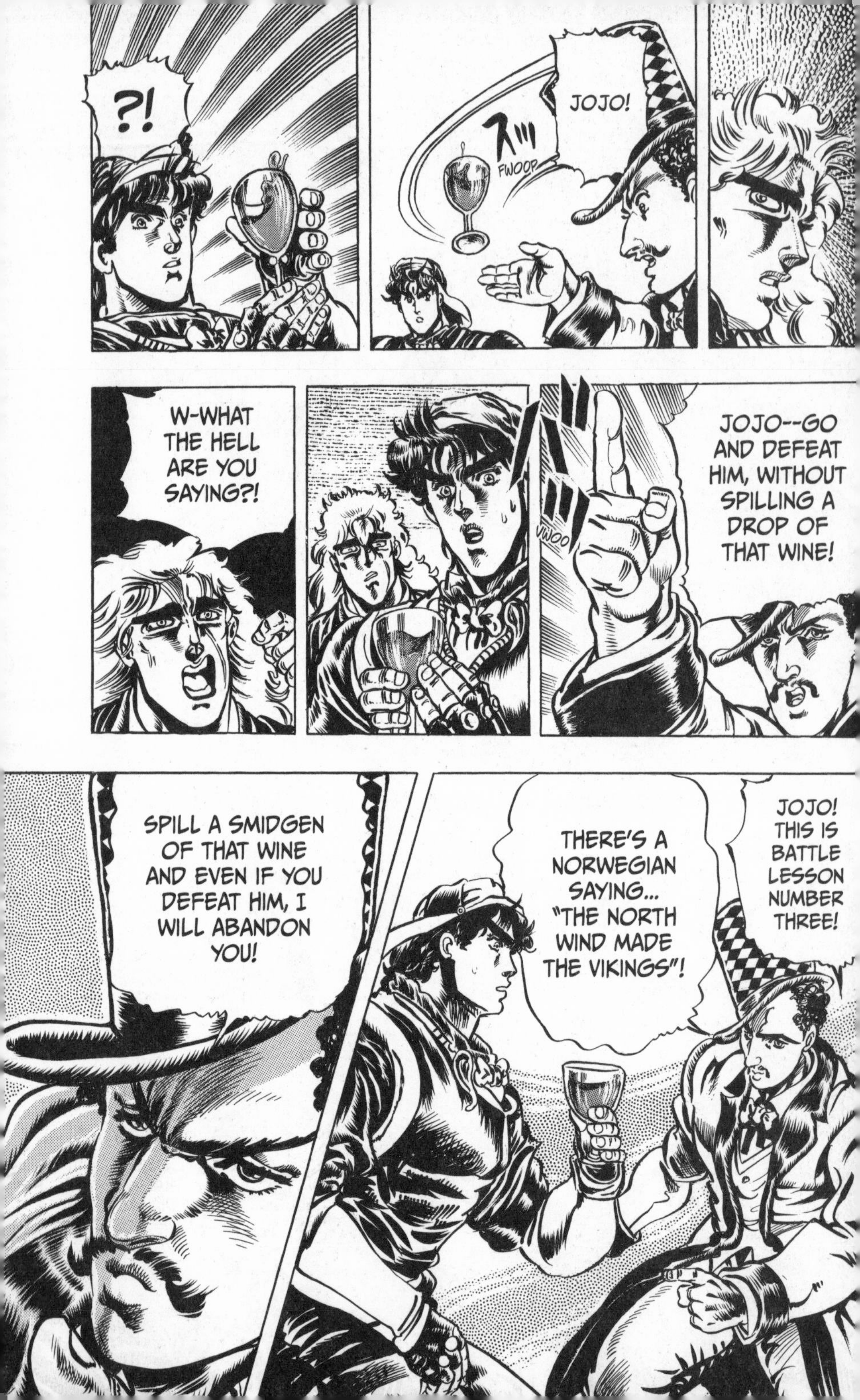
JOJO!
スッ
FWOOP
?!
JOJO--GO AND DEFEAT HIM, WITHOUT SPILLING A DROP OF THAT WINE!
VWOO
W-WHAT THE HELL ARE YOU SAYING?!
JOJO! THIS IS BATTLE LESSON NUMBER THREE!
THERE'S A NORWEGIAN SAYING... "THE NORTH WIND MADE THE VIKINGS"!
SPILL A SMIDGEN OF THAT WINE AND EVEN IF YOU DEFEAT HIM, I WILL ABANDON YOU!

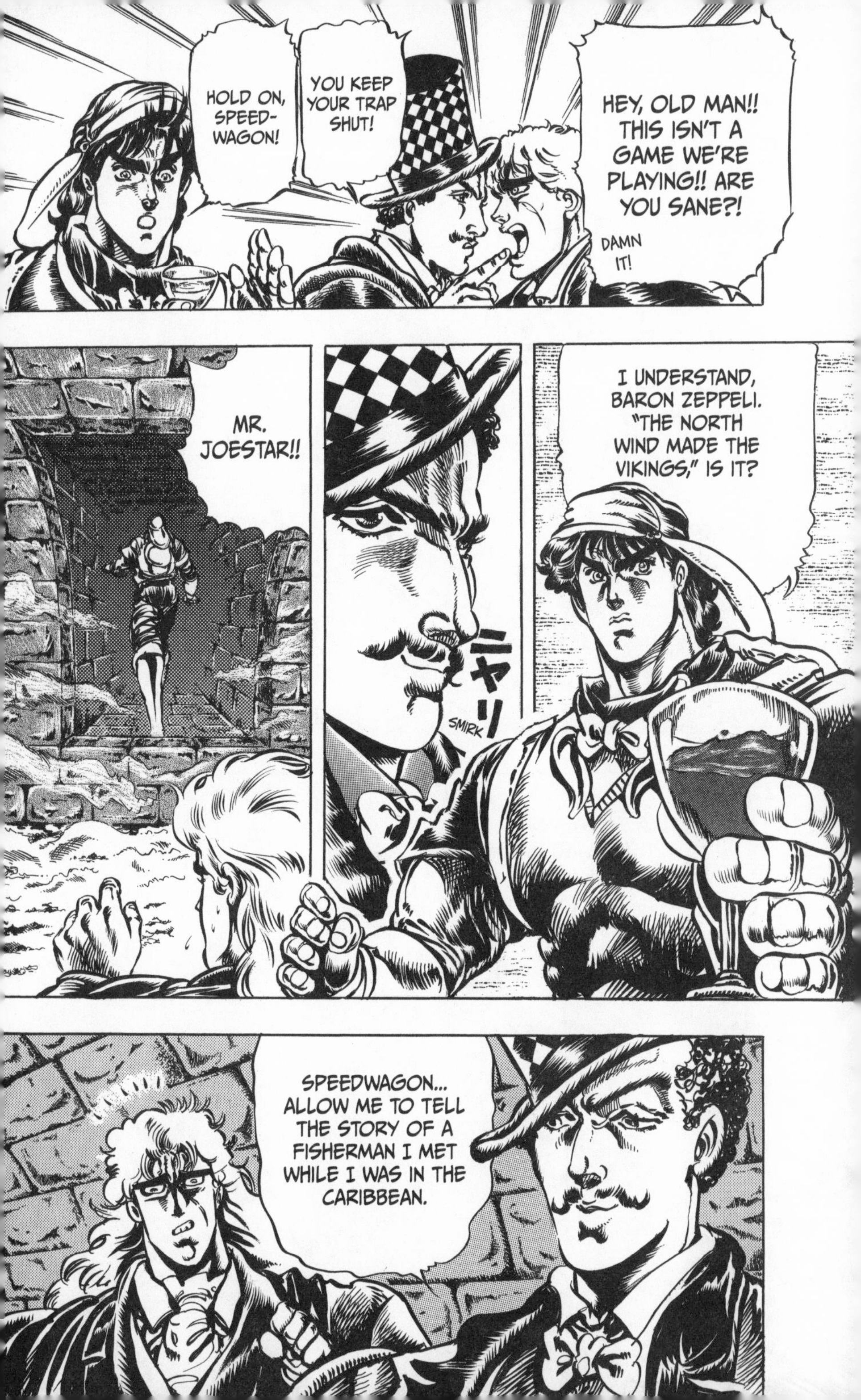
HEY, OLD MAN!! THIS ISN'T A GAME WE'RE PLAYING!! ARE YOU SANE?!
DAMN IT!
YOU KEEP YOUR TRAP SHUT!
HOLD ON, SPEED-WAGON!
I UNDERSTAND, BARON ZEPPELI. "THE NORTH WIND MADE THE VIKINGS," IS IT?
ニヤリ
SMIRK
MR. JOESTAR!!
SPEEDWAGON... ALLOW ME TO TELL THE STORY OF A FISHERMAN I MET WHILE I WAS IN THE CARIBBEAN.

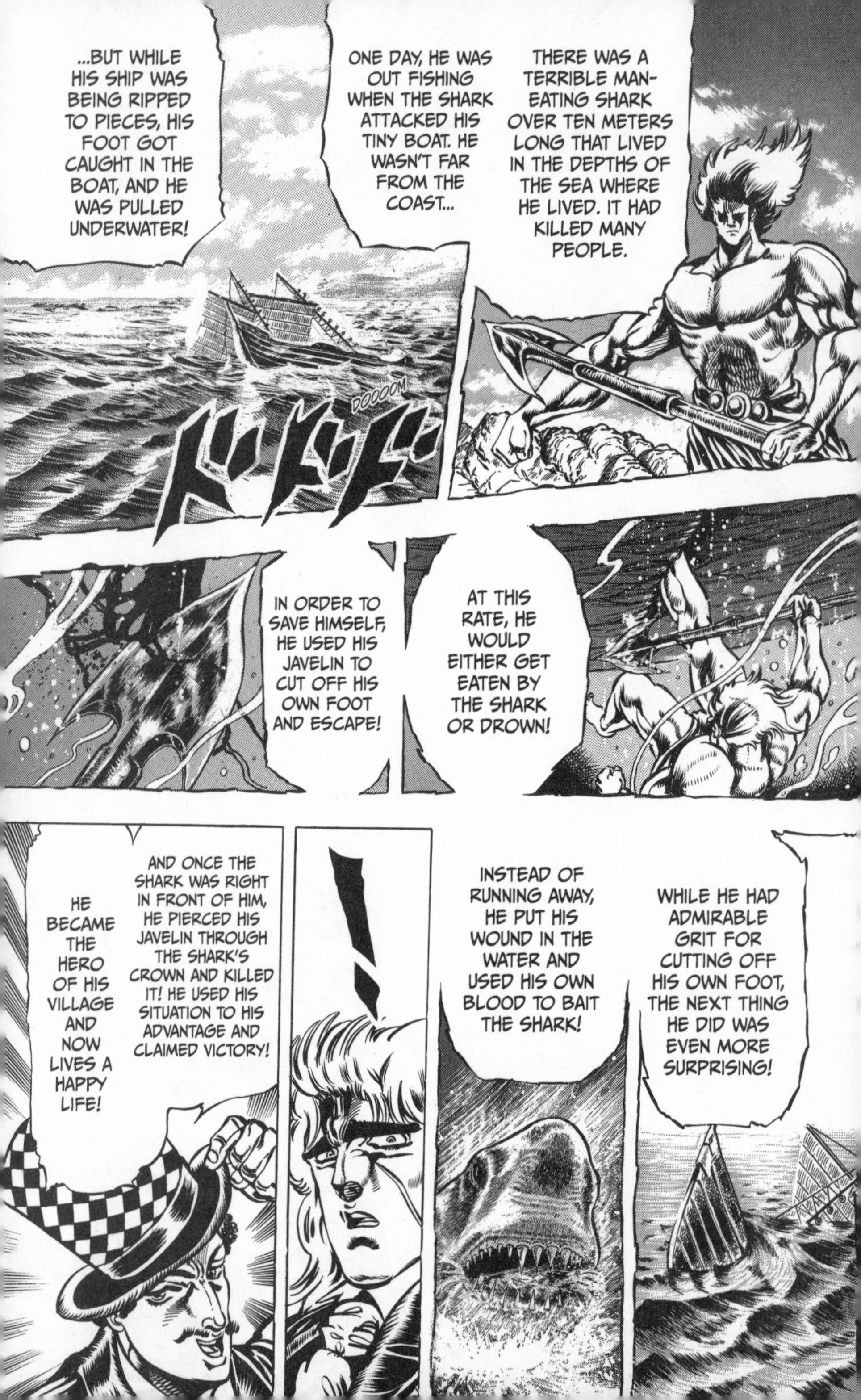
THERE WAS A TERRIBLE MAN-EATING SHARK OVER TEN METERS LONG THAT LIVED IN THE DEPTHS OF THE SEA WHERE HE LIVED. IT HAD KILLED MANY PEOPLE.
ONE DAY, HE WAS OUT FISHING WHEN THE SHARK ATTACKED HIS TINY BOAT. HE WASN'T FAR FROM THE COAST...
...BUT WHILE HIS SHIP WAS BEING RIPPED TO PIECES, HIS FOOT GOT CAUGHT IN THE BOAT, AND HE WAS PULLED UNDERWATER!
DOOOOM
AT THIS RATE, HE WOULD EITHER GET EATEN BY THE SHARK OR DROWN!
IN ORDER TO SAVE HIMSELF, HE USED HIS JAVELIN TO CUT OFF HIS OWN FOOT AND ESCAPE!
WHILE HE HAD ADMIRABLE GRIT FOR CUTTING OFF HIS OWN FOOT, THE NEXT THING HE DID WAS EVEN MORE SURPRISING!
INSTEAD OF RUNNING AWAY, HE PUT HIS WOUND IN THE WATER AND USED HIS OWN BLOOD TO BAIT THE SHARK!
!
AND ONCE THE SHARK WAS RIGHT IN FRONT OF HIM, HE PIERCED HIS JAVELIN THROUGH THE SHARK'S CROWN AND KILLED IT! HE USED HIS SITUATION TO HIS ADVANTAGE AND CLAIMED VICTORY!
HE BECAME THE HERO OF HIS VILLAGE AND NOW LIVES A HAPPY LIFE!

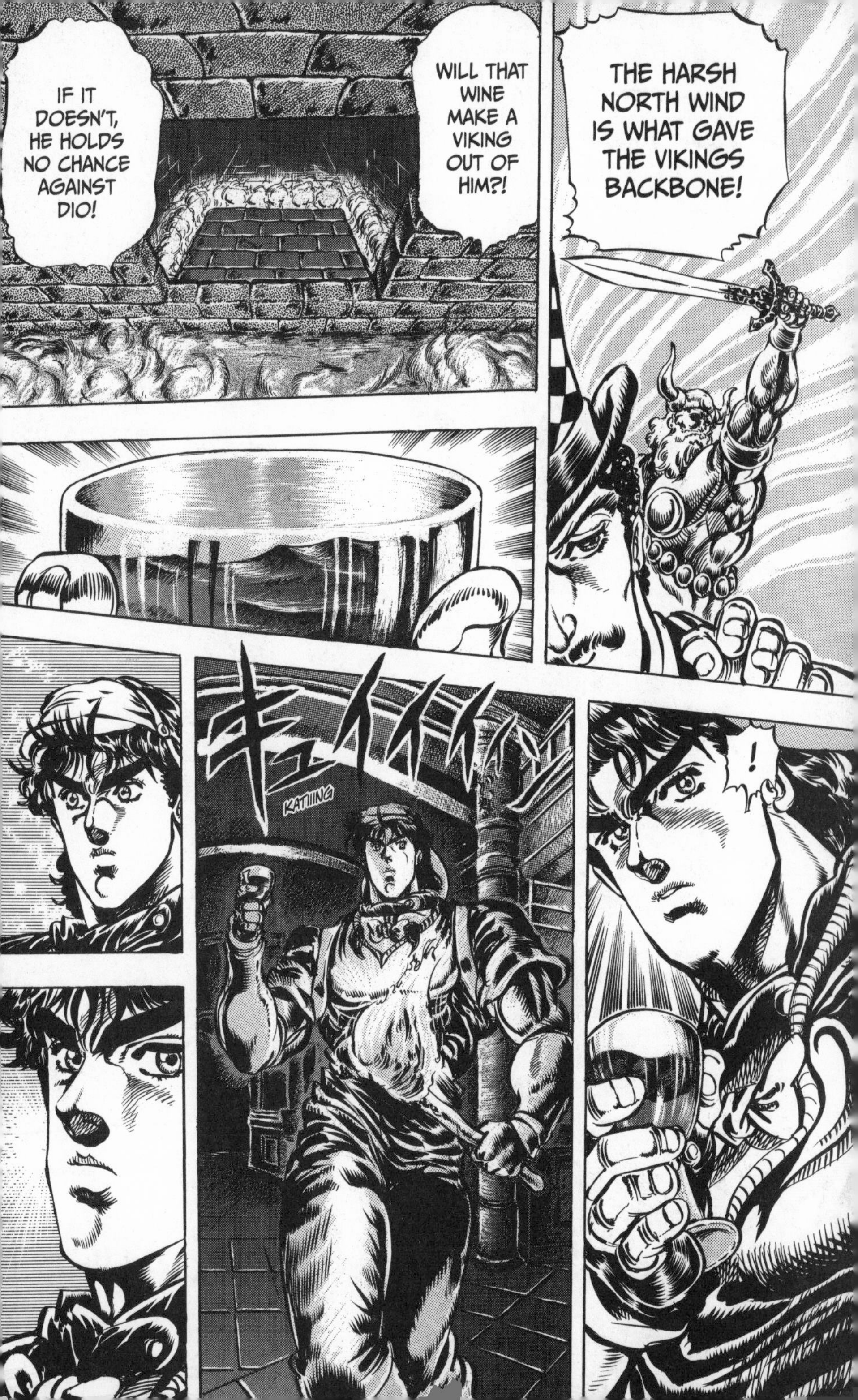
THE HARSH NORTH WIND IS WHAT GAVE THE VIKINGS BACKBONE!
WILL THAT WINE MAKE A VIKING OUT OF HIM?!
IF IT DOESN'T, HE HOLDS NO CHANCE AGAINST DIO!
!
KATIIING

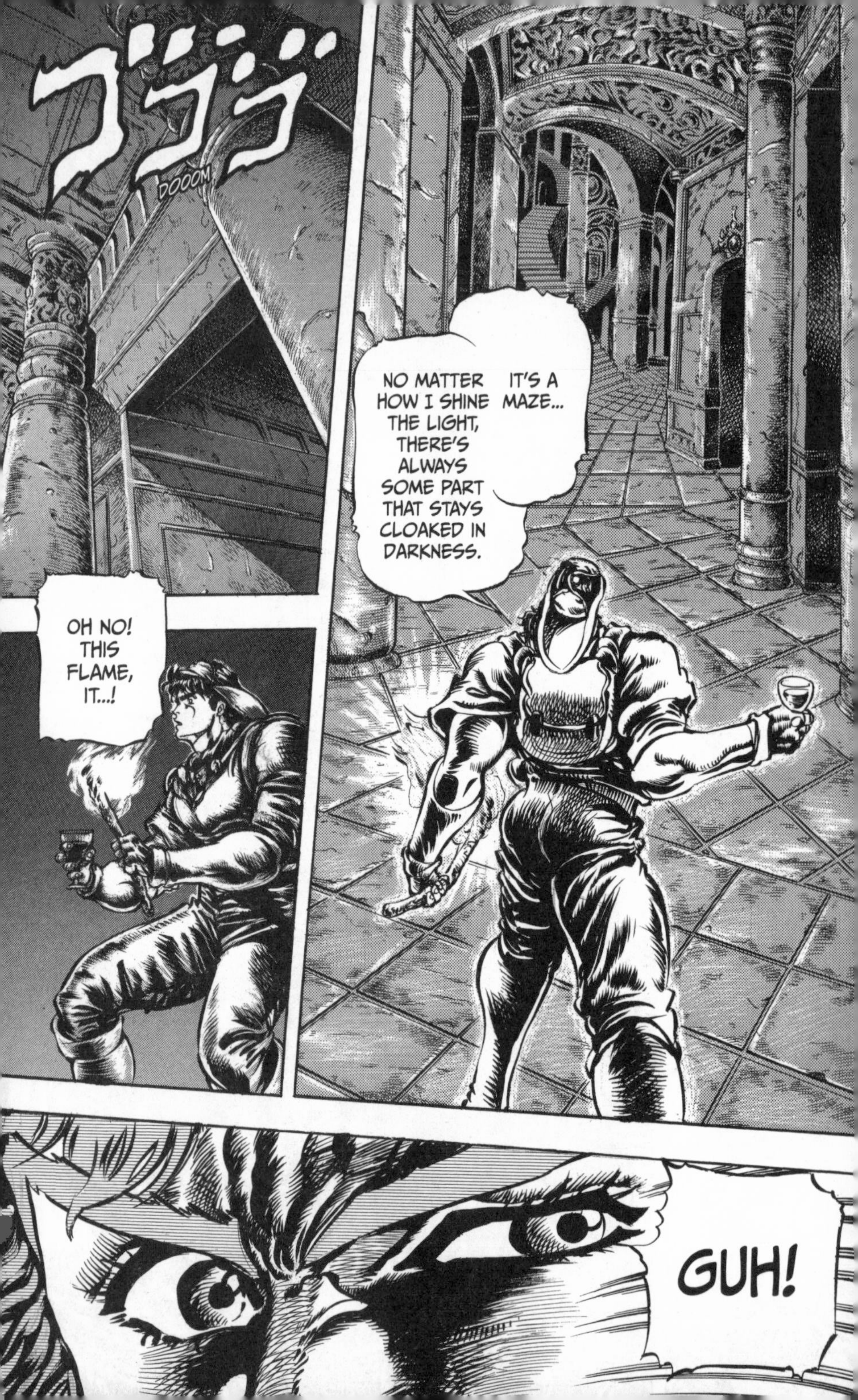
IT'S A MAZE...
NO MATTER HOW I SHINE THE LIGHT, THERE'S ALWAYS SOME PART THAT STAYS CLOAKED IN DARKNESS.
ゴゴゴ
DOOOM
OH NO! THIS FLAME, IT...!
GUH!

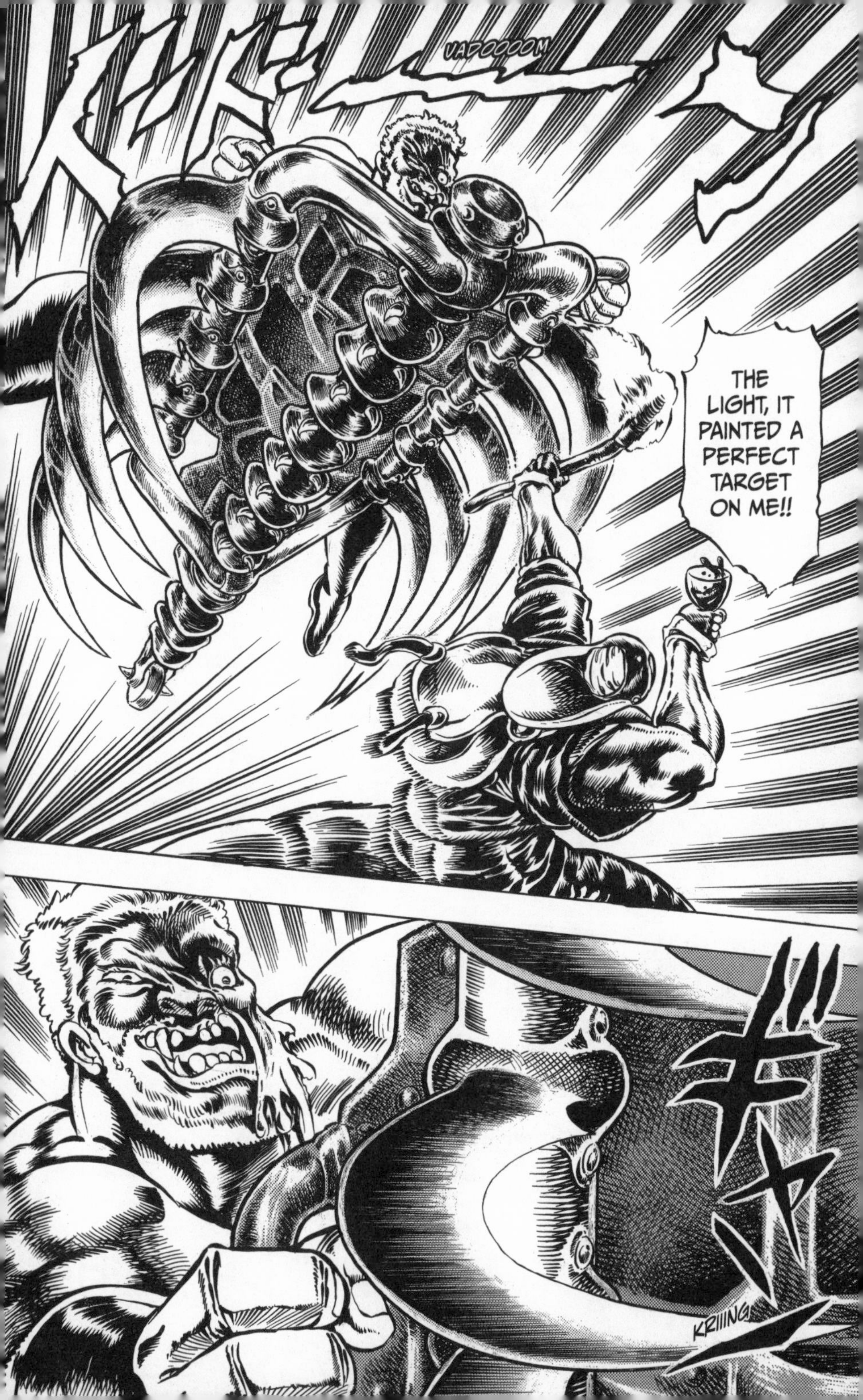
VADOOOOOM
THE LIGHT, IT PAINTED A PERFECT TARGET ON ME!!
KRIIING

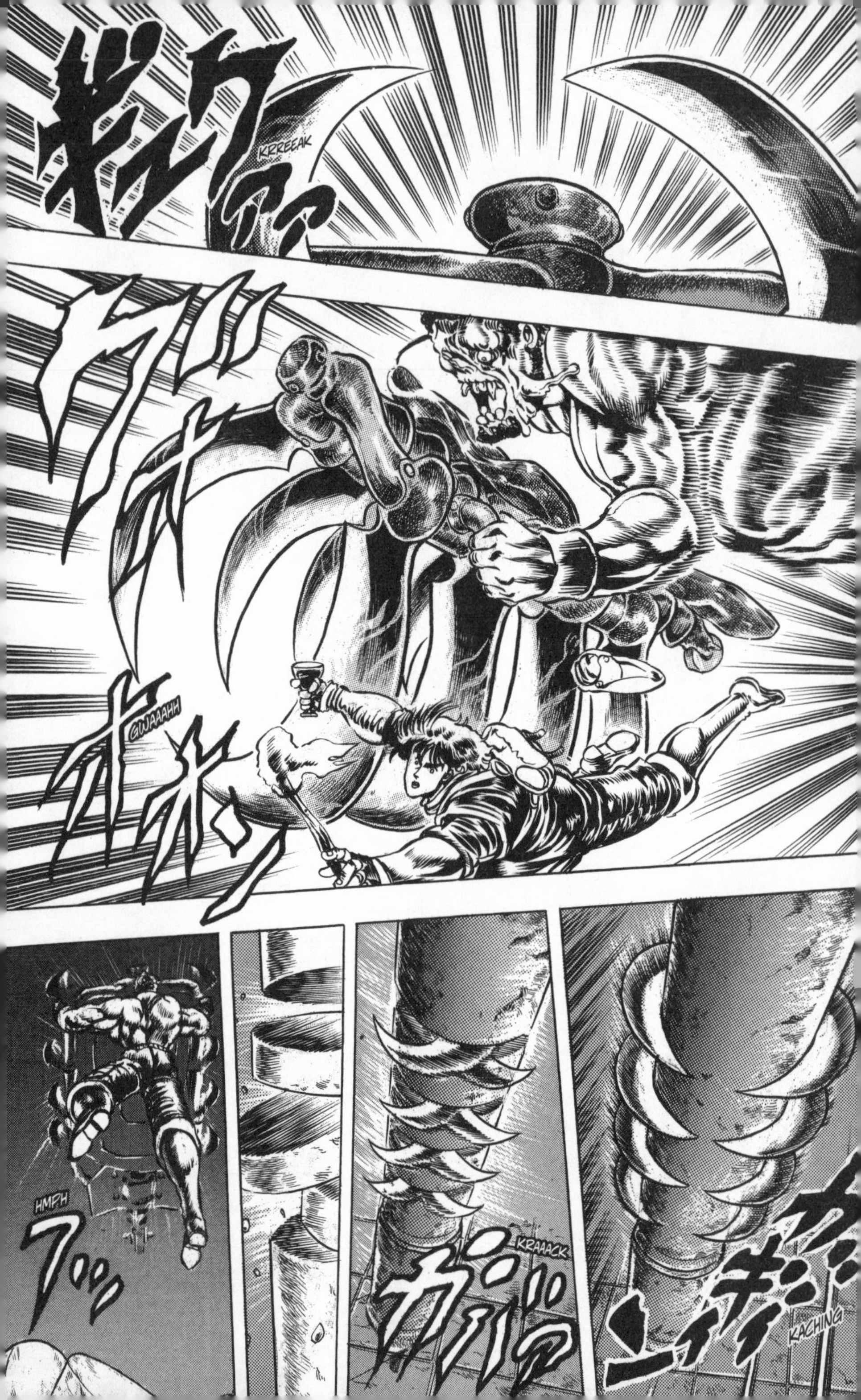
KRREEAK
GWAAAHH
KACHING
KRAAACK
HMPH

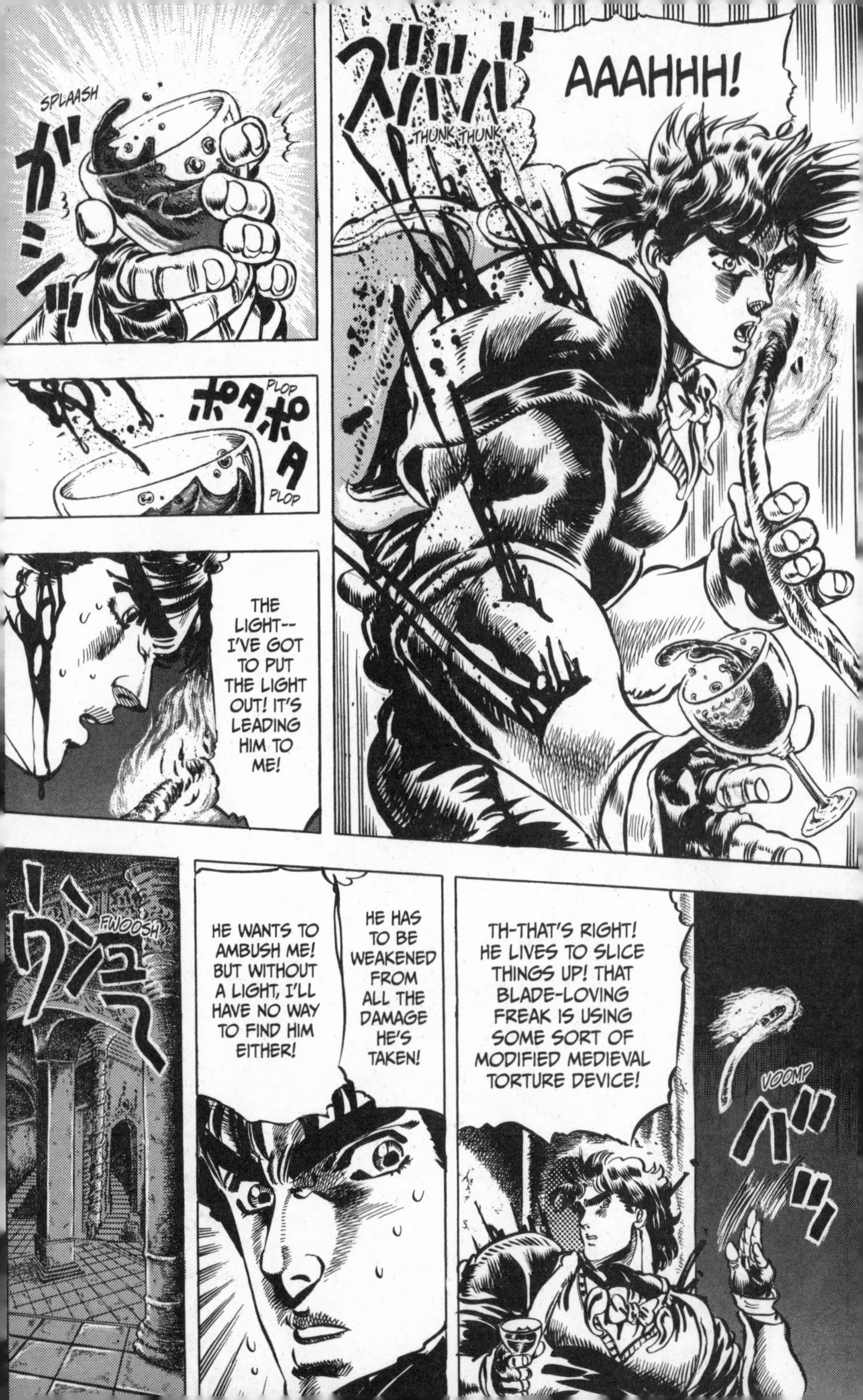
THUNK THUNK
AAAHHH!
SPLAASH
PLOP
PLOP
THE LIGHT-- I'VE GOT TO PUT THE LIGHT OUT! IT'S LEADING HIM TO ME!
TH-THAT'S RIGHT! HE LIVES TO SLICE THINGS UP! THAT BLADE-LOVING FREAK IS USING SOME SORT OF MODIFIED MEDIEVAL TORTURE DEVICE!
VOOMP
HE HAS TO BE WEAKENED FROM ALL THE DAMAGE HE'S TAKEN!
HE WANTS TO AMBUSH ME! BUT WITHOUT A LIGHT, I'LL HAVE NO WAY TO FIND HIM EITHER!
FWOOSH

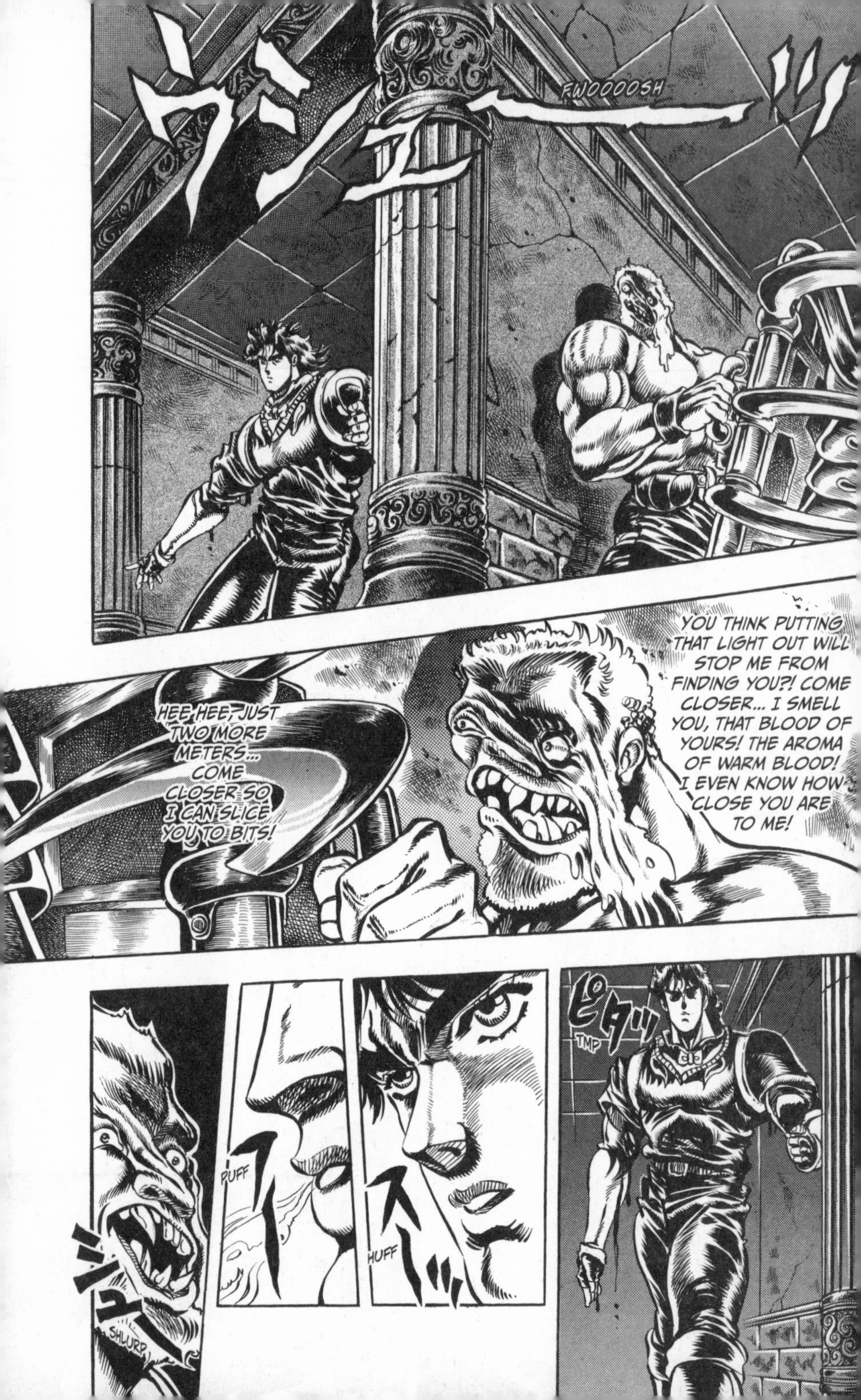
FWOOOOSH
YOU THINK PUTTING THAT LIGHT OUT WILL STOP ME FROM FINDING YOU?! COME CLOSER... I SMELL YOU, THAT BLOOD OF YOURS! THE AROMA OF WARM BLOOD! I EVEN KNOW HOW CLOSE YOU ARE TO ME!
HEE HEE, JUST TWO MORE METERS... COME CLOSER SO I CAN SLICE YOU TO BITS!
ピタッ
TMP
HUFF
PUFF
SHLURP

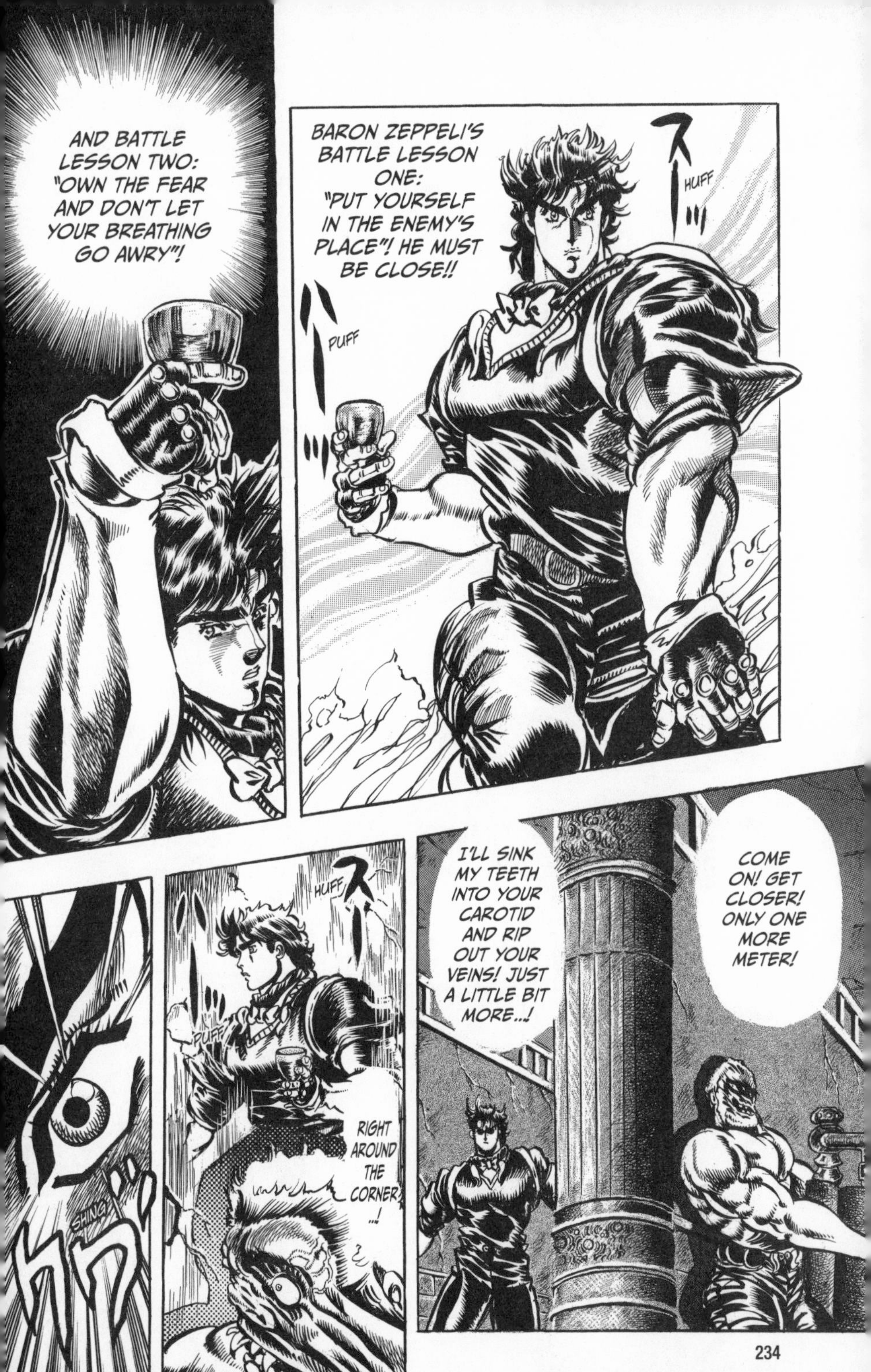
BARON ZEPPELI'S BATTLE LESSON ONE: "PUT YOURSELF IN THE ENEMY'S PLACE"! HE MUST BE CLOSE!!
HUFF
PUFF
AND BATTLE LESSON TWO: "OWN THE FEAR AND DON'T LET YOUR BREATHING GO AWRY"!
COME ON! GET CLOSER! ONLY ONE MORE METER!
I'LL SINK MY TEETH INTO YOUR CAROTID AND RIP OUT YOUR VEINS! JUST A LITTLE BIT MORE...!
HUFF
PUFF
RIGHT AROUND THE CORNER...!
SHING

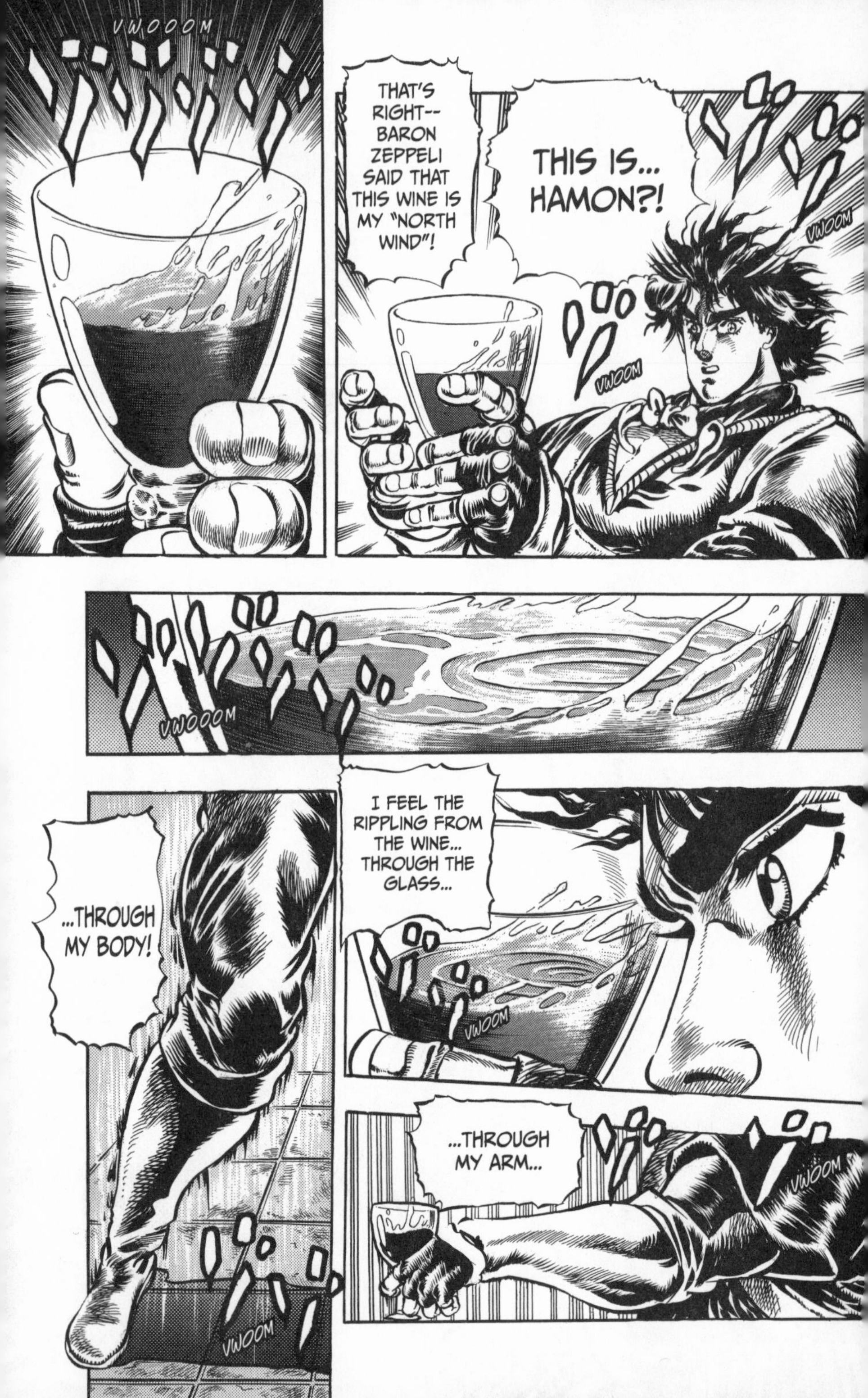
THIS IS... HAMON?!
THAT'S RIGHT-- BARON ZEPPELI SAID THAT THIS WINE IS MY "NORTH WIND"!
VWOOM
VWOOM
VWOOOM
VWOOOM
I FEEL THE RIPPLING FROM THE WINE... THROUGH THE GLASS...
VWOOM
...THROUGH MY ARM...
VWOOM
...THROUGH MY BODY!
VWOOM

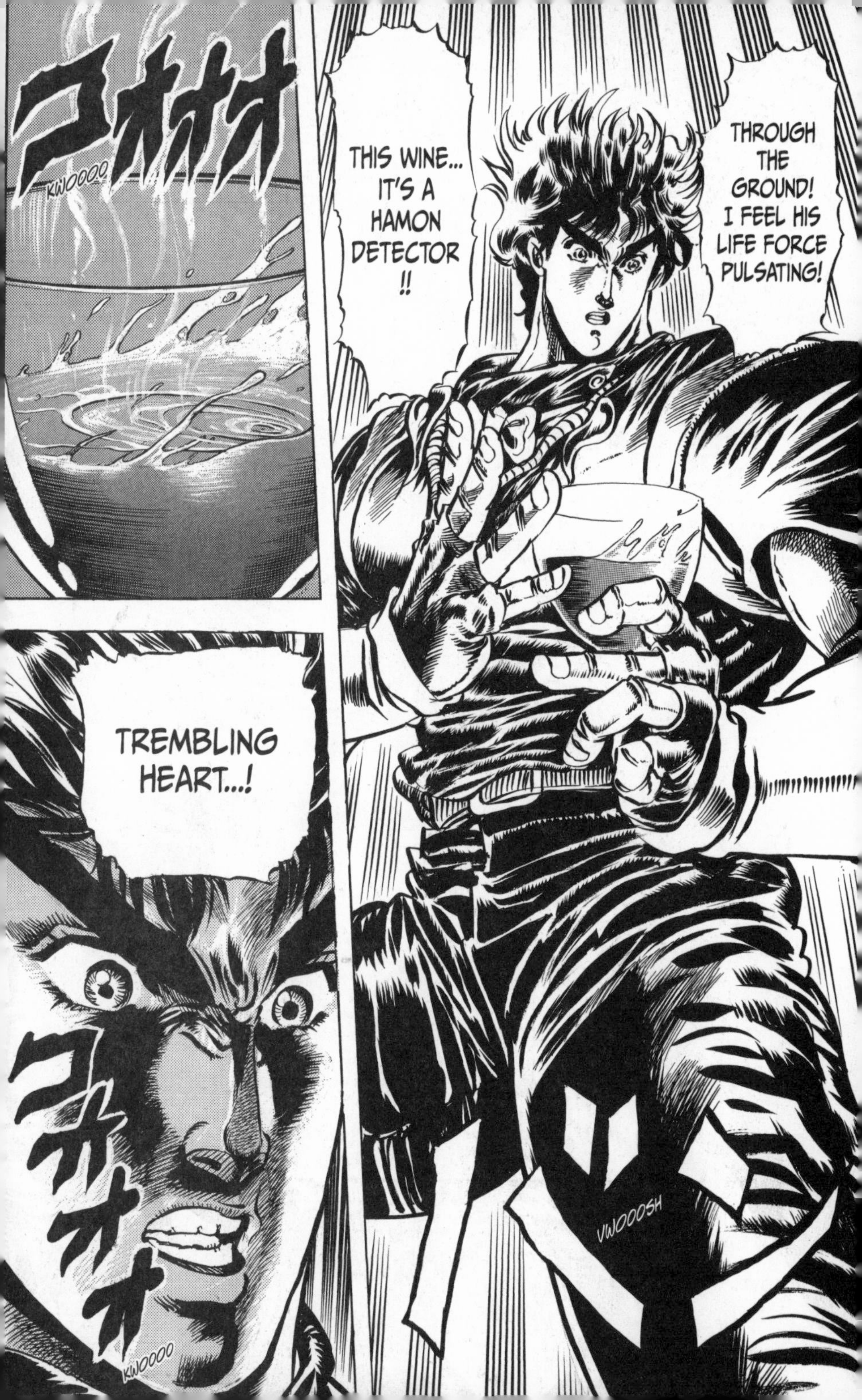
THROUGH THE GROUND! I FEEL HIS LIFE FORCE PULSATING!
THIS WINE... IT'S A HAMON DETECTOR !!
VWOOOSH
KWOOOO
TREMBLING HEART...!
KWOOOO

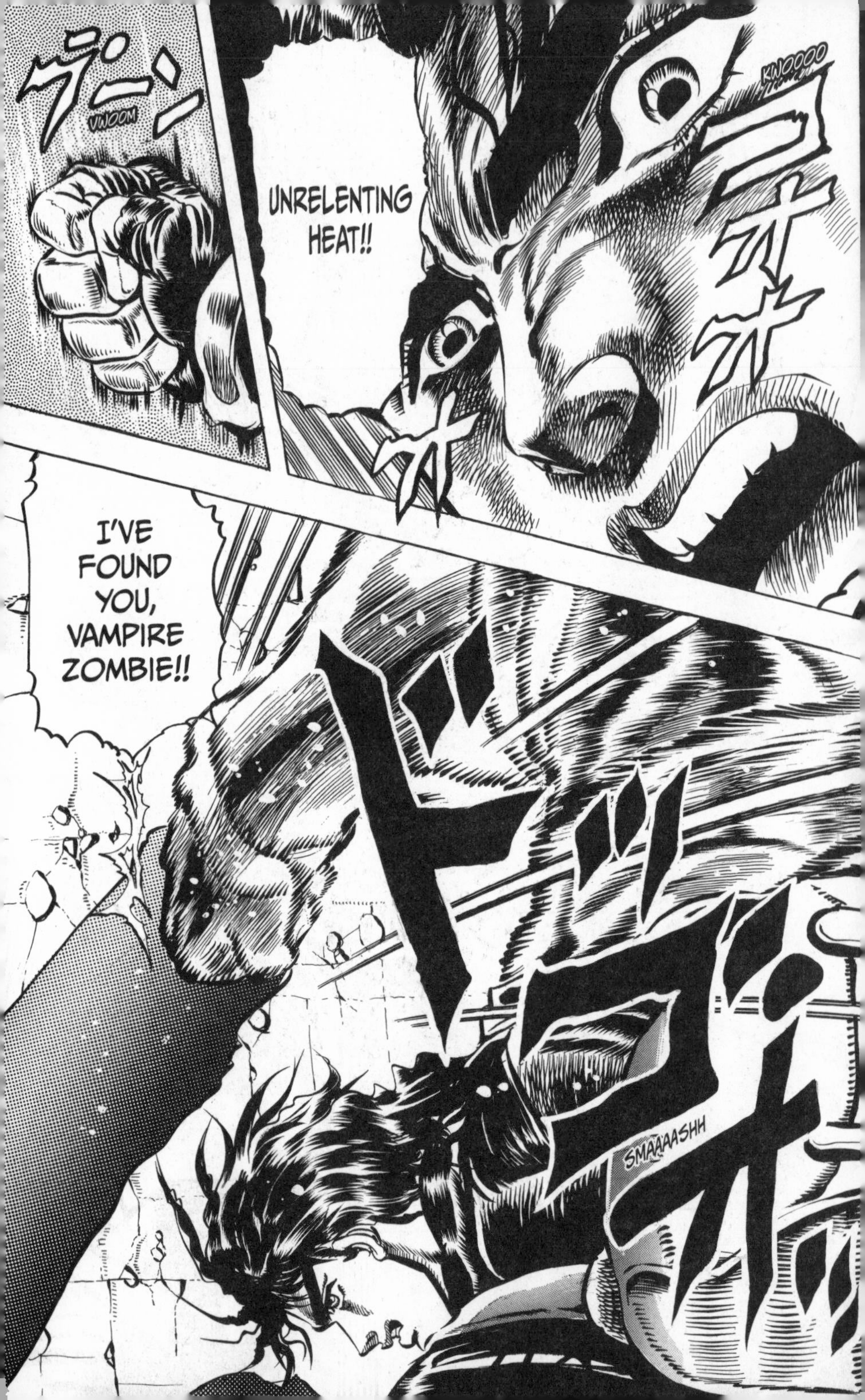
KWOOOO
UNRELENTING HEAT!!
VWOOM
I'VE FOUND YOU, VAMPIRE ZOMBIE!!
SMAAAASHH

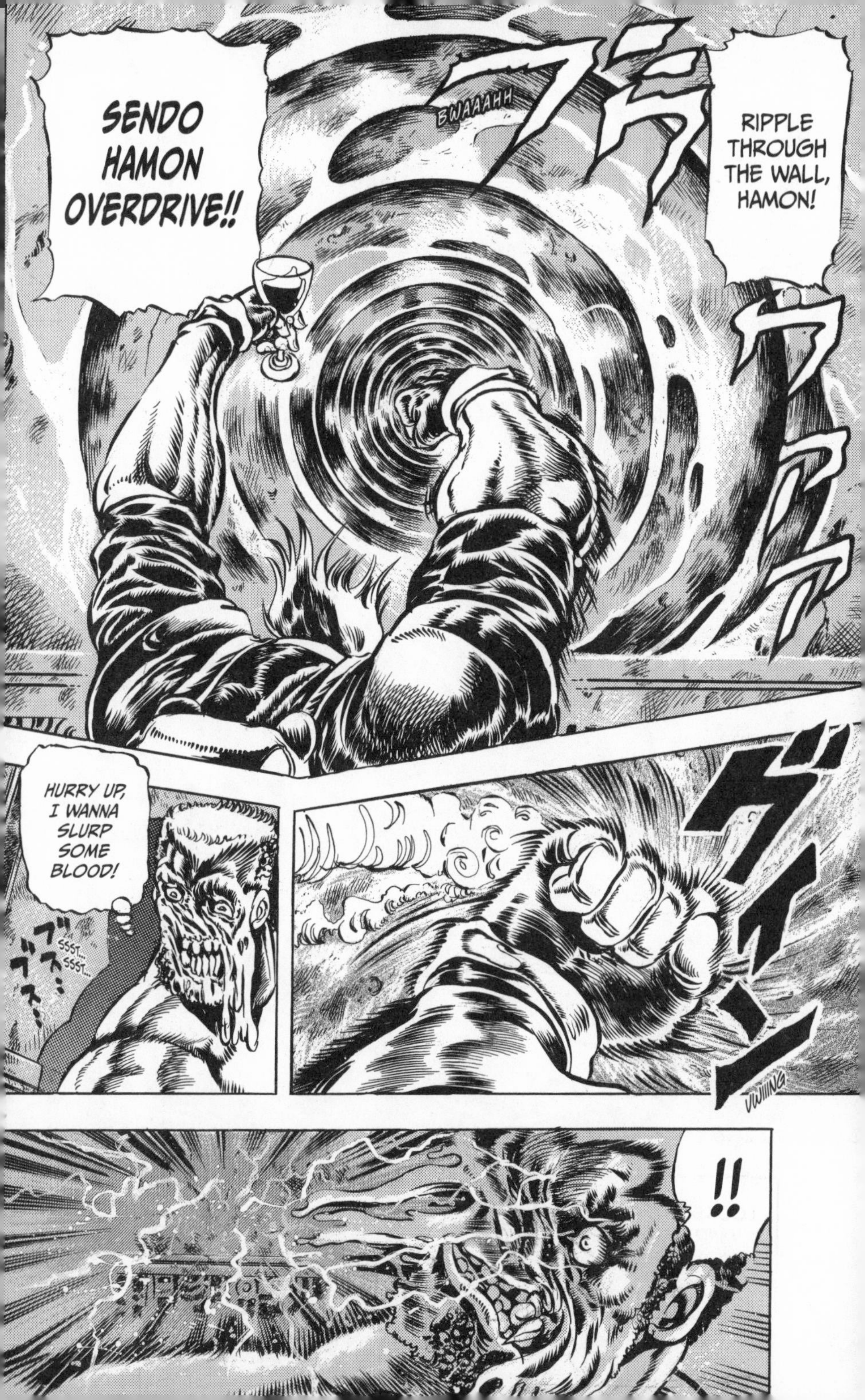
RIPPLE THROUGH THE WALL, HAMON!
BWAAAHH
SENDO HAMON OVERDRIVE!!
VWIIING
HURRY UP, I WANNA SLURP SOME BLOOD!
SSSST... SSSST...
!!

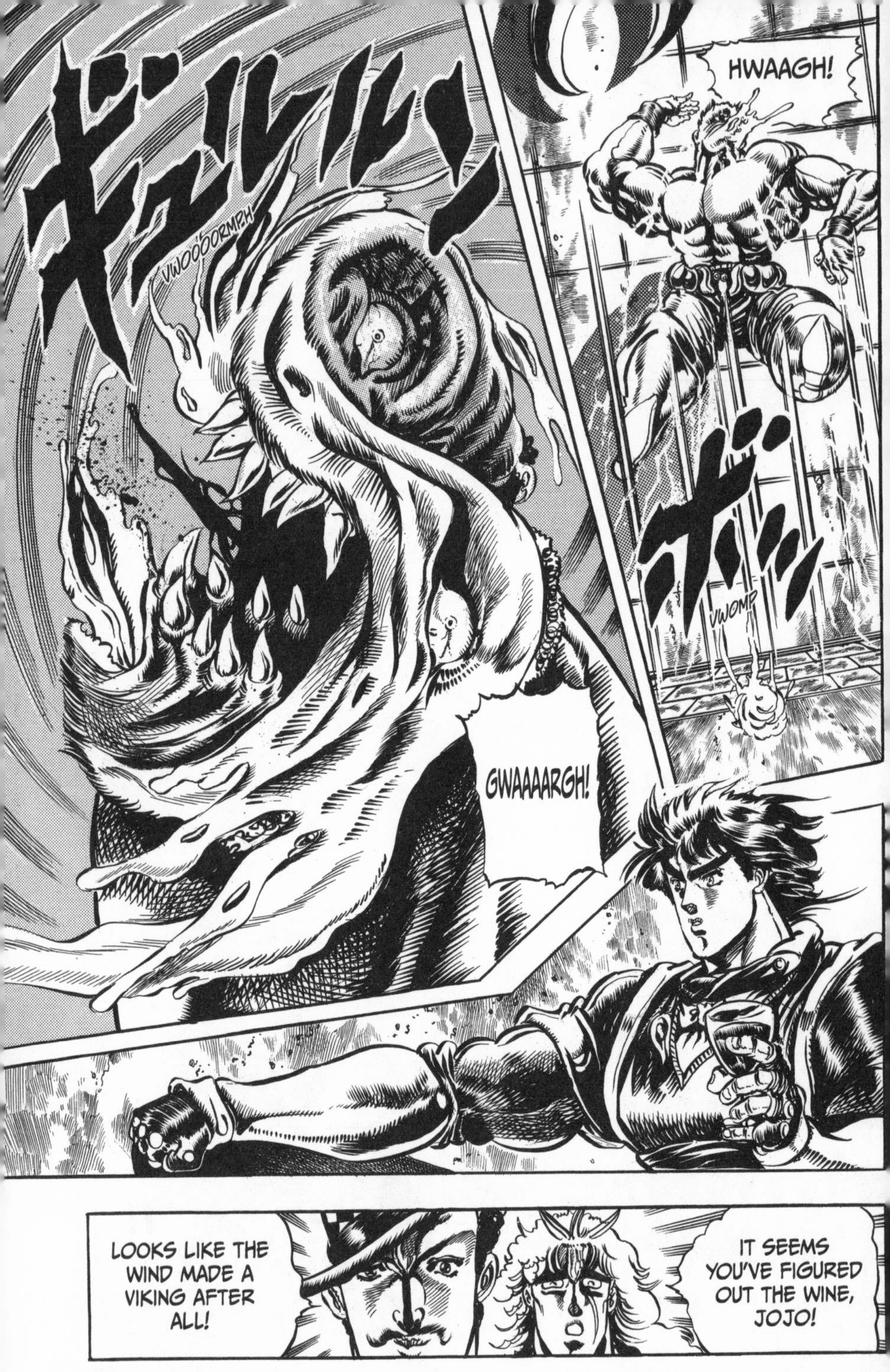
HWAAGH!
VWOMP
VWOOOORMPH
GWAAAARGH!
IT SEEMS YOU'VE FIGURED OUT THE WINE, JOJO!
LOOKS LIKE THE WIND MADE A VIKING AFTER ALL!

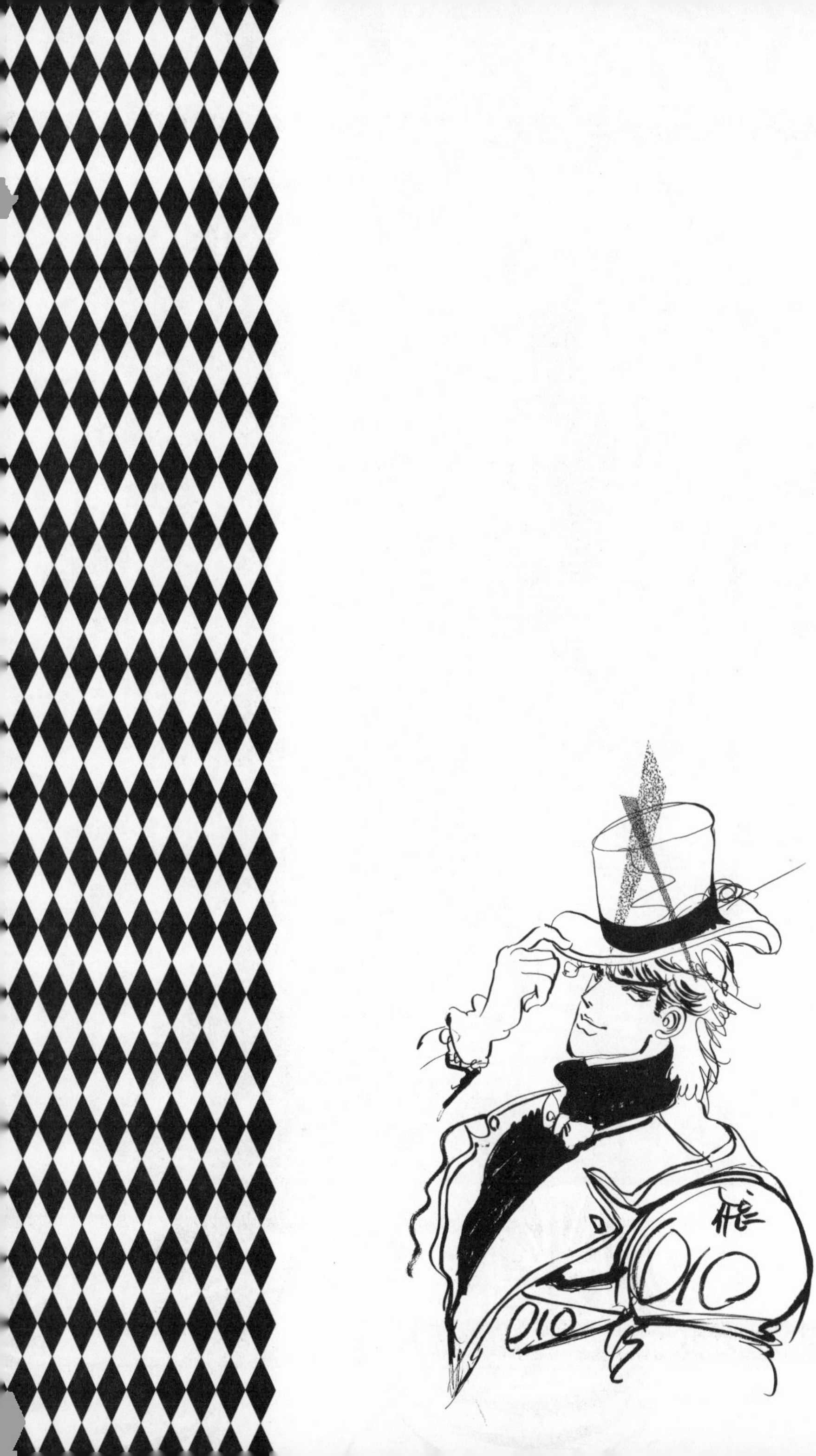
DIO
DIO

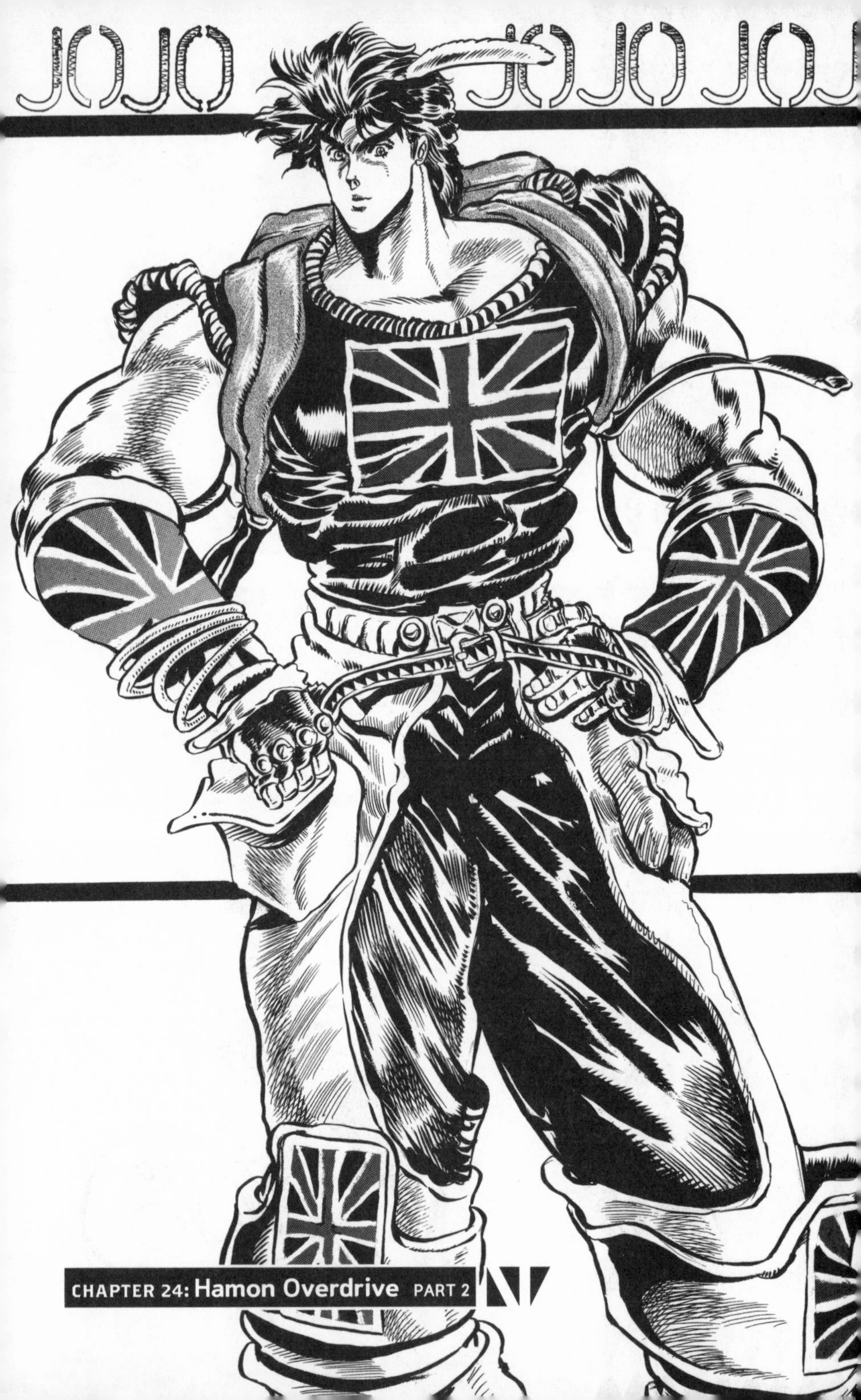
JOJO JOJO JOJO JOJ
CHAPTER 24: Hamon Overdrive PART 2

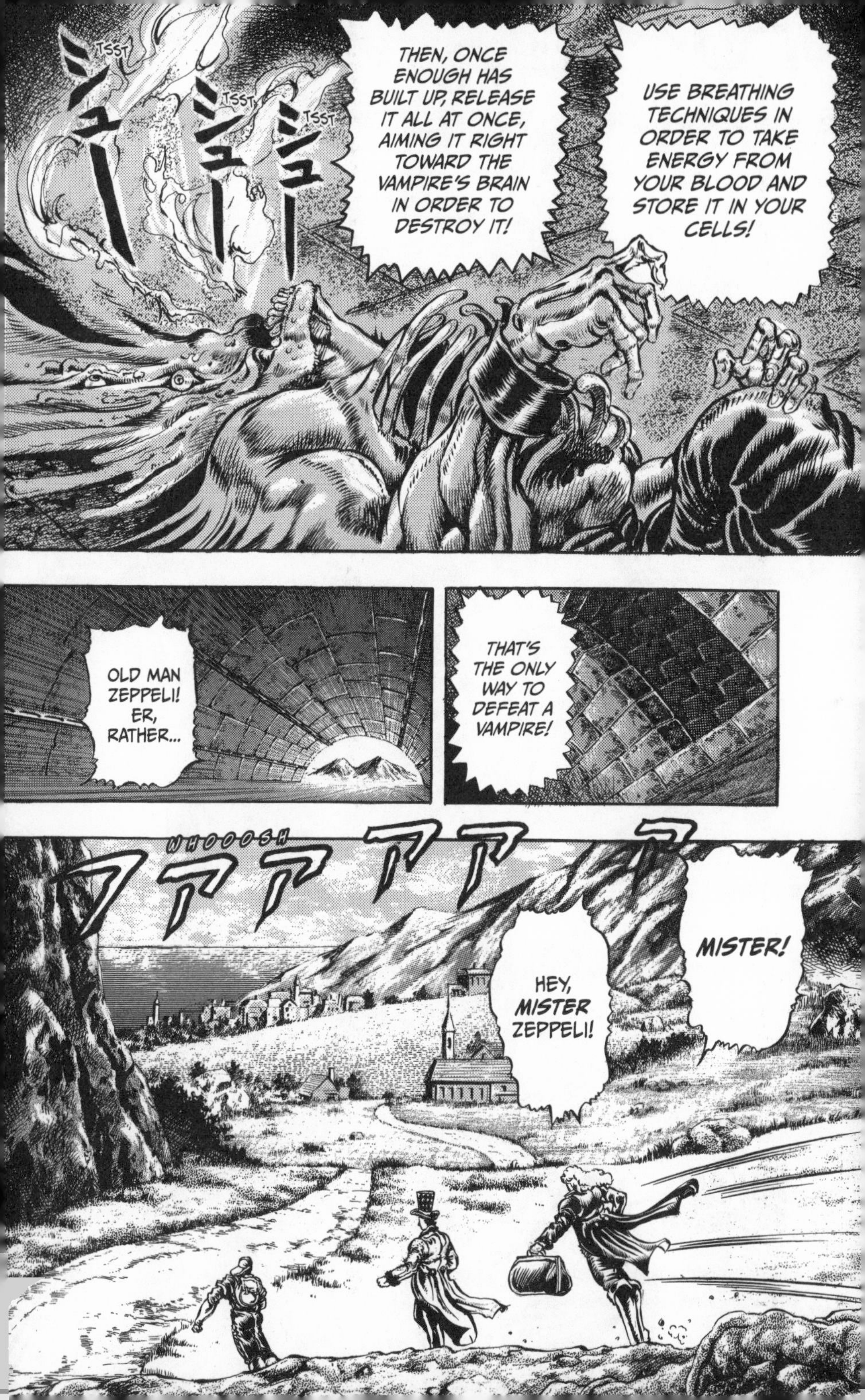
USE BREATHING TECHNIQUES IN ORDER TO TAKE ENERGY FROM YOUR BLOOD AND STORE IT IN YOUR CELLS!
THEN, ONCE ENOUGH HAS BUILT UP, RELEASE IT ALL AT ONCE, AIMING IT RIGHT TOWARD THE VAMPIRE'S BRAIN IN ORDER TO DESTROY IT!
TSST
TSST
TSST
THAT'S THE ONLY WAY TO DEFEAT A VAMPIRE!
OLD MAN ZEPPELI! ER, RATHER...
MISTER!
HEY, MISTER ZEPPELI!
WHOOOSH

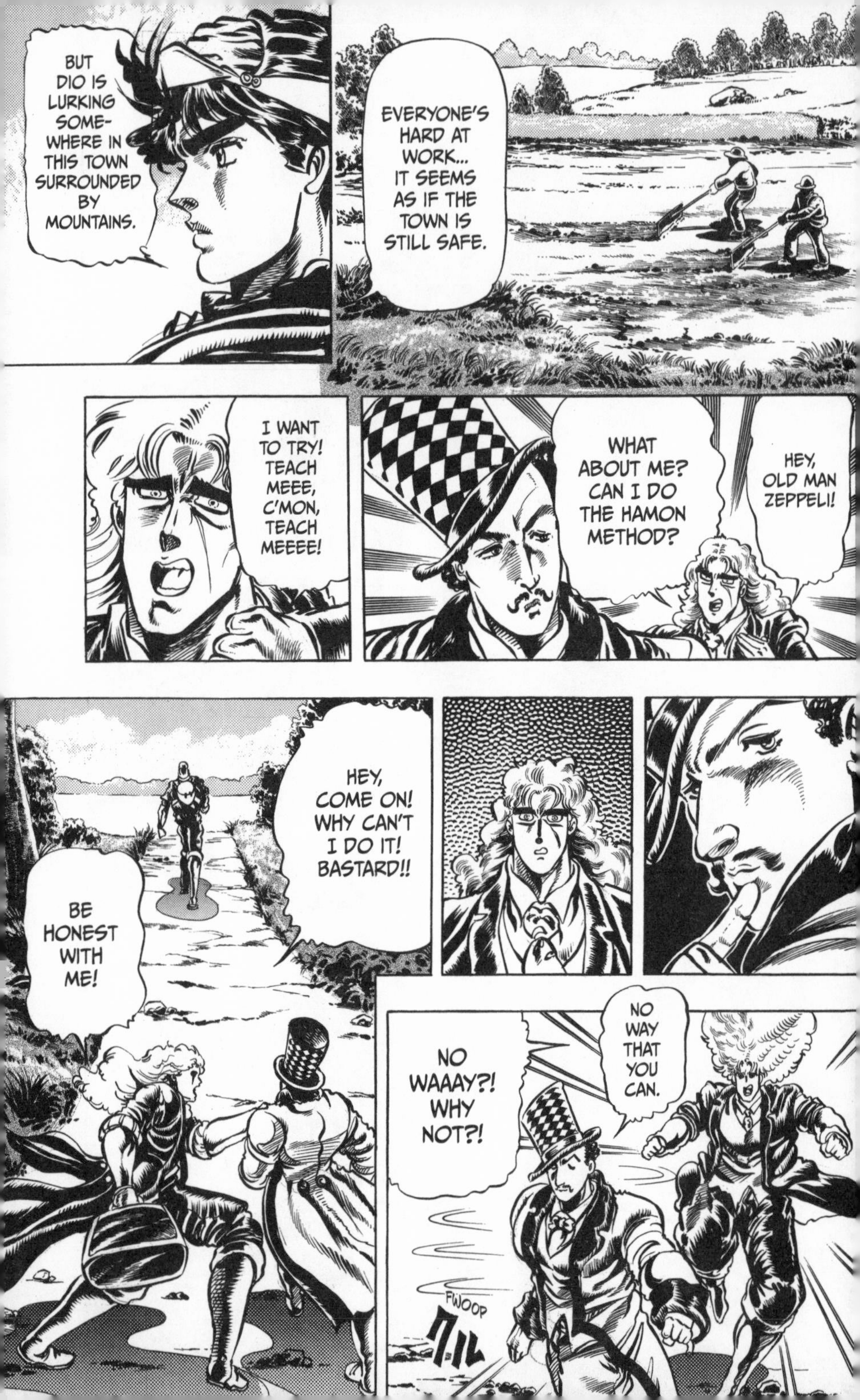
EVERYONE'S HARD AT WORK... IT SEEMS AS IF THE TOWN IS STILL SAFE.
BUT DIO IS LURKING SOME-WHERE IN THIS TOWN SURROUNDED BY MOUNTAINS.
HEY, OLD MAN ZEPPELI!
WHAT ABOUT ME? CAN I DO THE HAMON METHOD?
I WANT TO TRY! TEACH MEEE, C'MON, TEACH MEEEE!
NO WAY THAT YOU CAN.
NO WAAAY?! WHY NOT?!
FWOOP
HEY, COME ON! WHY CAN'T I DO IT! BASTARD!!
BE HONEST WITH ME!

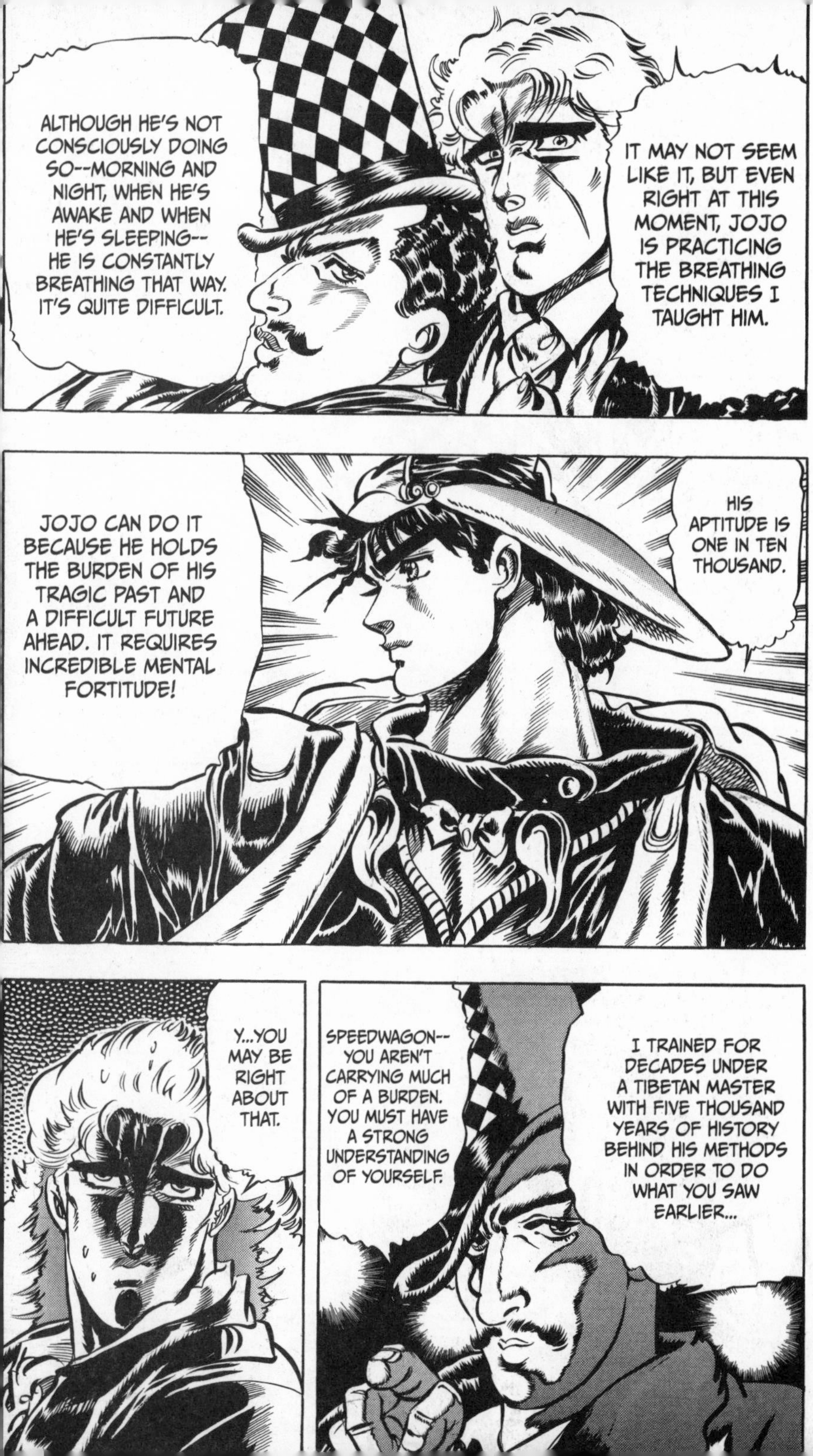
IT MAY NOT SEEM LIKE IT, BUT EVEN RIGHT AT THIS MOMENT, JOJO IS PRACTICING THE BREATHING TECHNIQUES I TAUGHT HIM.
ALTHOUGH HE'S NOT CONSCIOUSLY DOING SO--MORNING AND NIGHT, WHEN HE'S AWAKE AND WHEN HE'S SLEEPING--HE IS CONSTANTLY BREATHING THAT WAY. IT'S QUITE DIFFICULT.
HIS APTITUDE IS ONE IN TEN THOUSAND.
JOJO CAN DO IT BECAUSE HE HOLDS THE BURDEN OF HIS TRAGIC PAST AND A DIFFICULT FUTURE AHEAD. IT REQUIRES INCREDIBLE MENTAL FORTITUDE!
I TRAINED FOR DECADES UNDER A TIBETAN MASTER WITH FIVE THOUSAND YEARS OF HISTORY BEHIND HIS METHODS IN ORDER TO DO WHAT YOU SAW EARLIER...
SPEEDWAGON--YOU AREN'T CARRYING MUCH OF A BURDEN. YOU MUST HAVE A STRONG UNDERSTANDING OF YOURSELF.
Y...YOU MAY BE RIGHT ABOUT THAT.

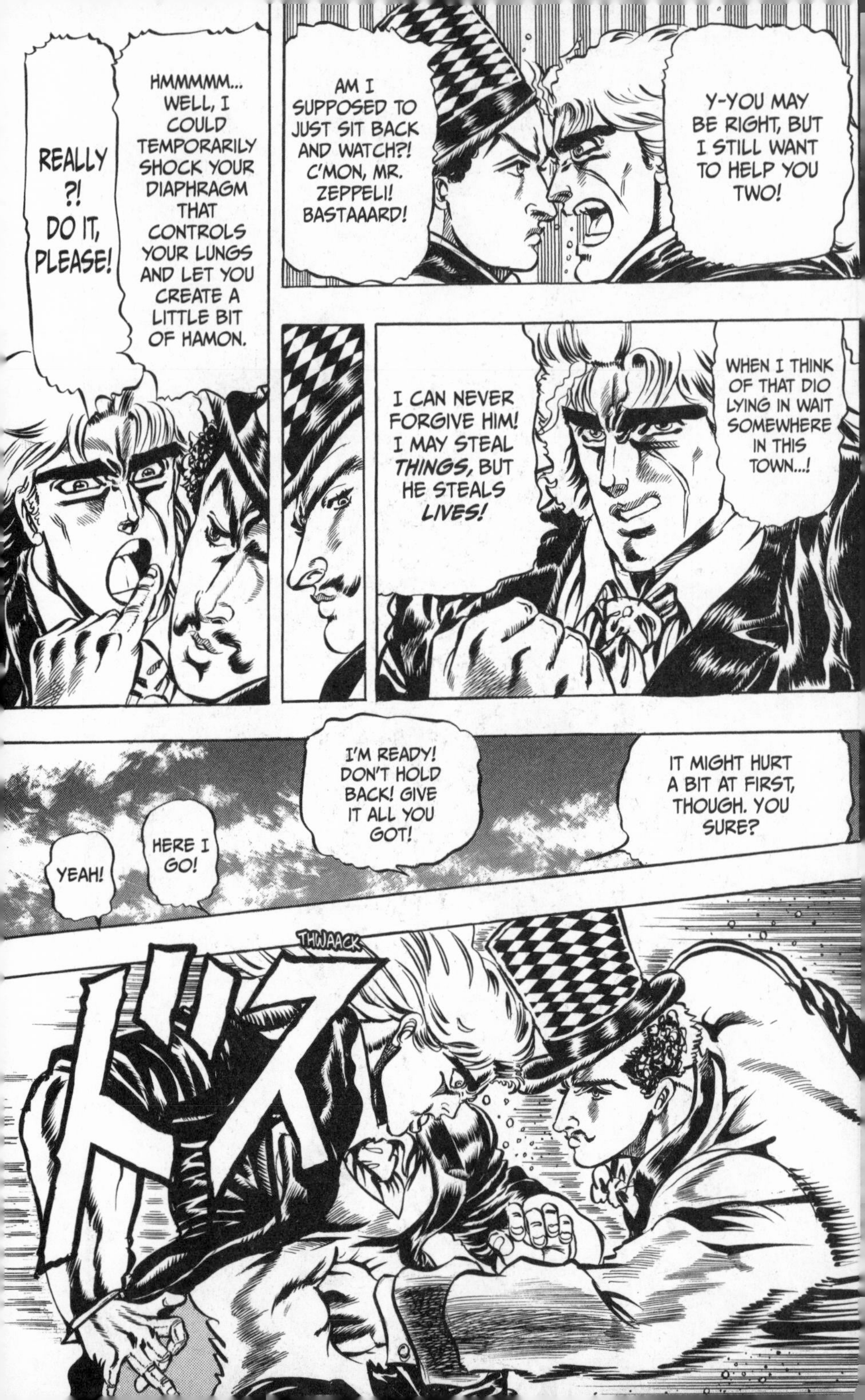
Y-YOU MAY BE RIGHT, BUT I STILL WANT TO HELP YOU TWO!
AM I SUPPOSED TO JUST SIT BACK AND WATCH?! C'MON, MR. ZEPPELI! BASTAAARD!
WHEN I THINK OF THAT DIO LYING IN WAIT SOMEWHERE IN THIS TOWN...!
I CAN NEVER FORGIVE HIM! I MAY STEAL *THINGS*, BUT HE STEALS *LIVES*!
HMMMMM... WELL, I COULD TEMPORARILY SHOCK YOUR DIAPHRAGM THAT CONTROLS YOUR LUNGS AND LET YOU CREATE A LITTLE BIT OF HAMON.
REALLY ?! DO IT, PLEASE!
IT MIGHT HURT A BIT AT FIRST, THOUGH. YOU SURE?
I'M READY! DON'T HOLD BACK! GIVE IT ALL YOU GOT!
HERE I GO!
YEAH!
THWAACK

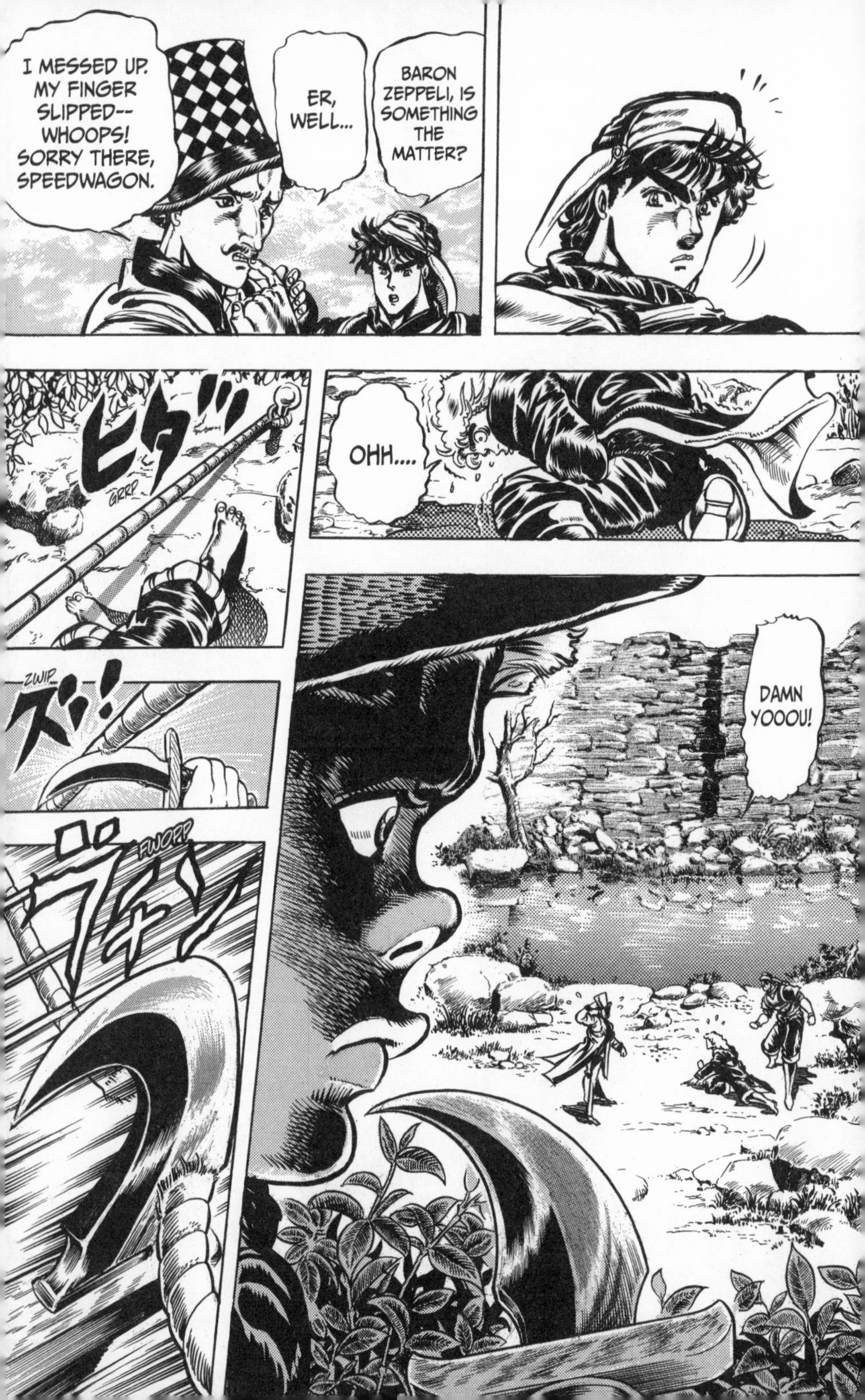
BARON ZEPPELI, IS SOMETHING THE MATTER?
ER, WELL...
I MESSED UP. MY FINGER SLIPPED-- WHOOPS! SORRY THERE, SPEEDWAGON.
OHH....
ビタッ
GRRP
DAMN YOOOU!
ズッ!
ZWIP
ヴォン
FWOPP

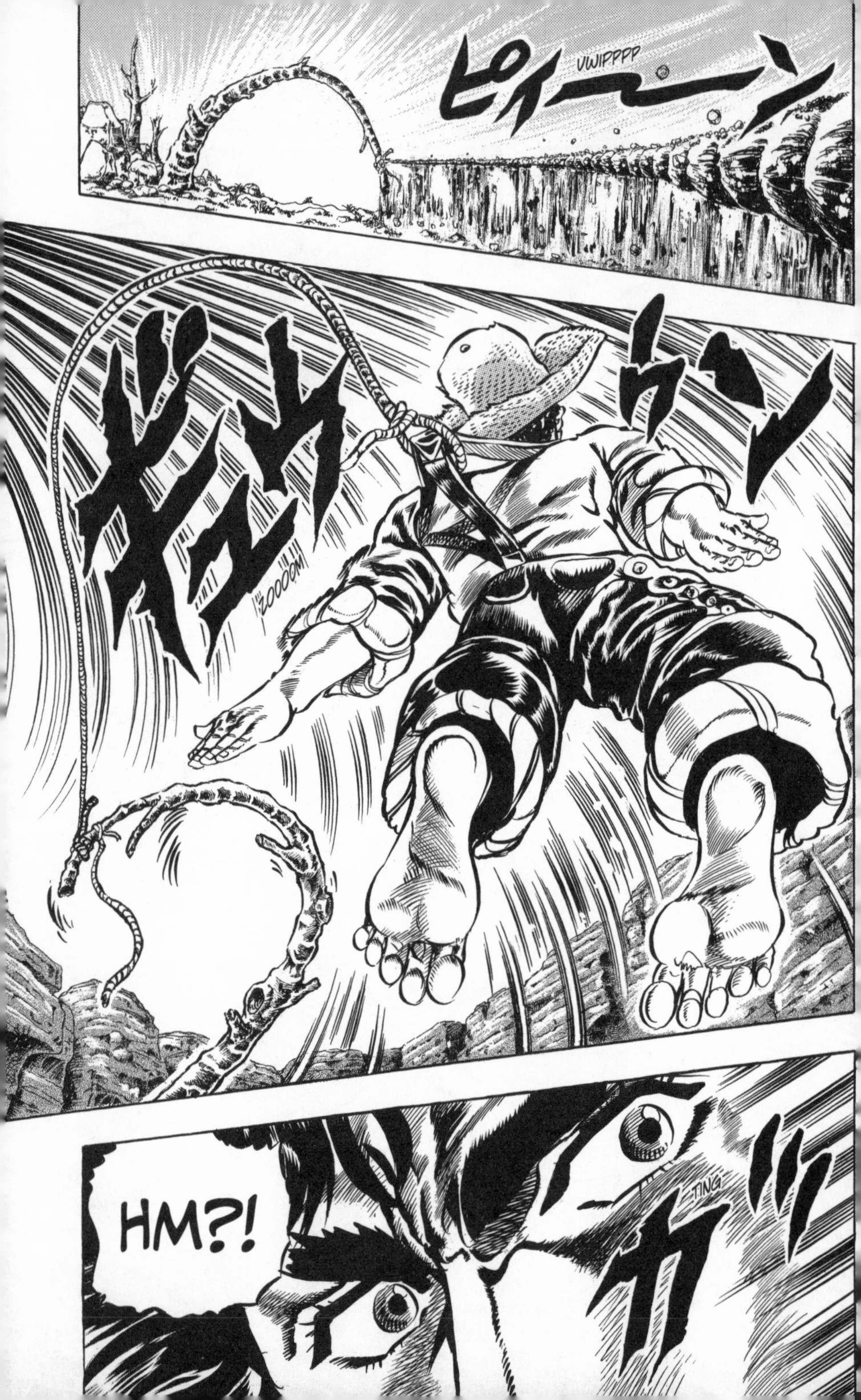
UWIPPPP
ZOOOOM
TING
HM?!

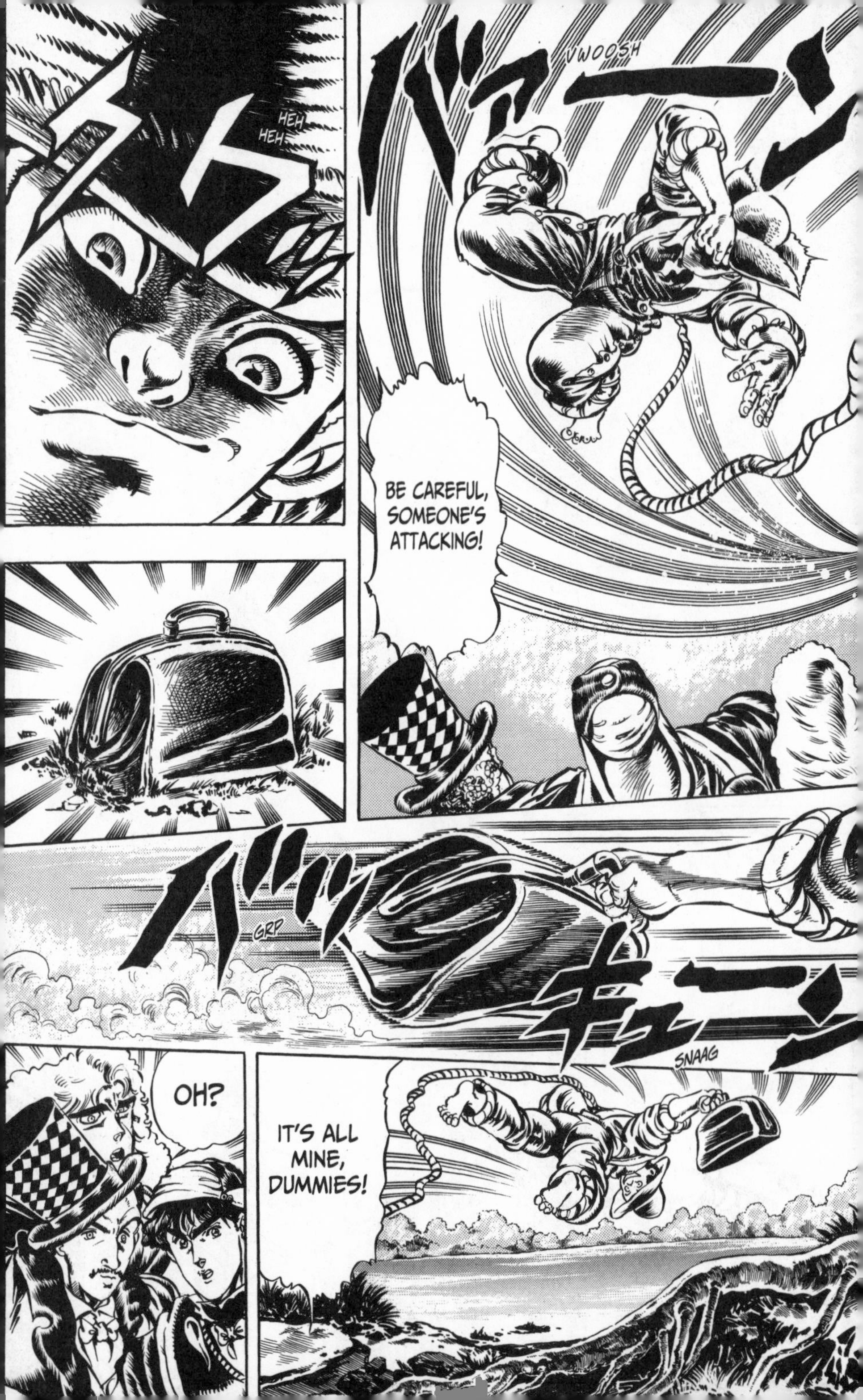
VWOOSH
BE CAREFUL, SOMEONE'S ATTACKING!
HEH HEH
GRP
SNAAG
IT'S ALL MINE, DUMMIES!
OH?

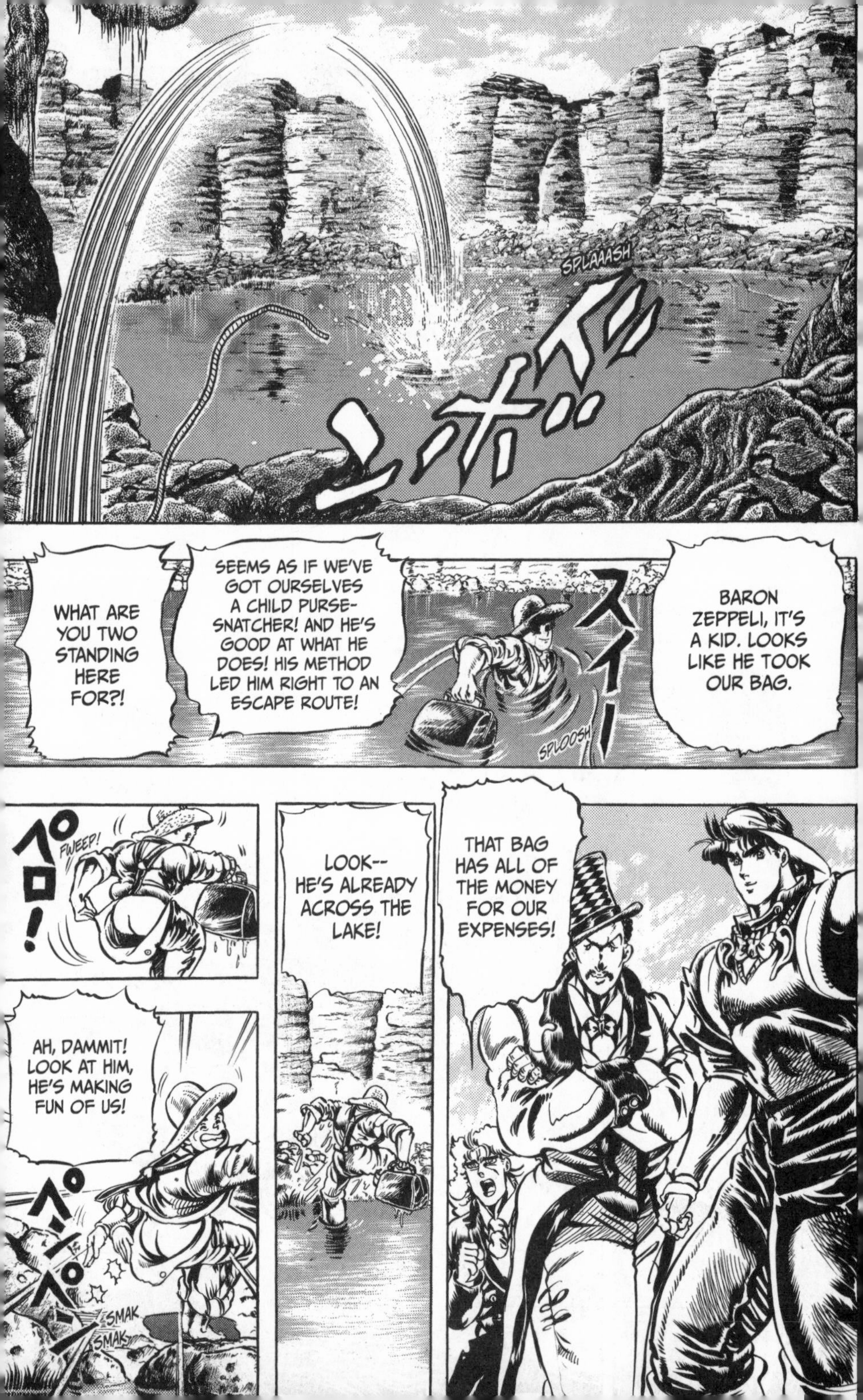
SPLAAASH
BARON ZEPPELI, IT'S A KID. LOOKS LIKE HE TOOK OUR BAG.
SPLOOSH
スイー
SEEMS AS IF WE'VE GOT OURSELVES A CHILD PURSE-SNATCHER! AND HE'S GOOD AT WHAT HE DOES! HIS METHOD LED HIM RIGHT TO AN ESCAPE ROUTE!
WHAT ARE YOU TWO STANDING HERE FOR?!
THAT BAG HAS ALL OF THE MONEY FOR OUR EXPENSES!
LOOK-- HE'S ALREADY ACROSS THE LAKE!
FWEEP!
ペロ!
AH, DAMMIT! LOOK AT HIM, HE'S MAKING FUN OF US!
SMAK
SMAK

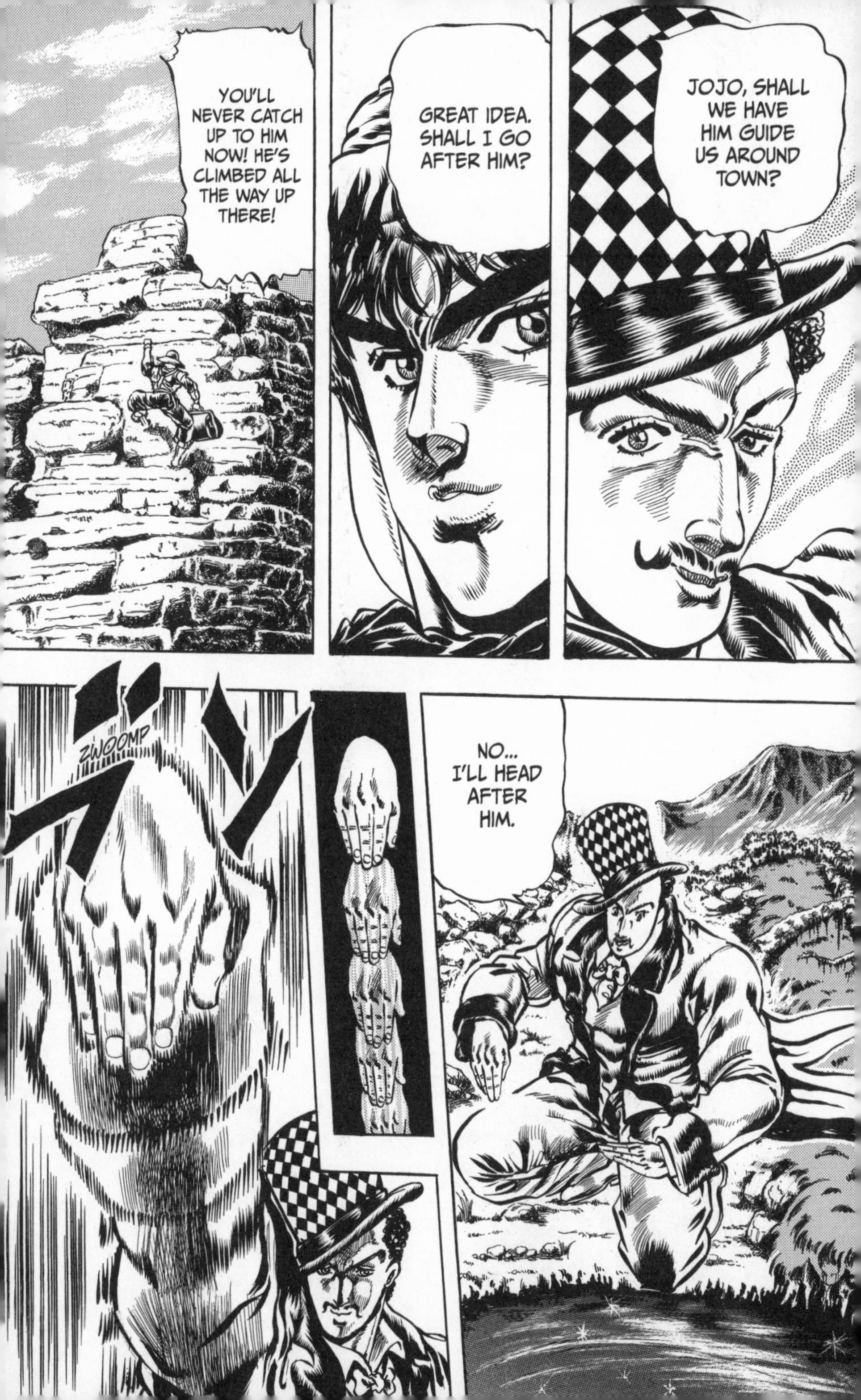
JOJO, SHALL WE HAVE HIM GUIDE US AROUND TOWN?
GREAT IDEA. SHALL I GO AFTER HIM?
YOU'LL NEVER CATCH UP TO HIM NOW! HE'S CLIMBED ALL THE WAY UP THERE!
NO... I'LL HEAD AFTER HIM.
ZWOOMP

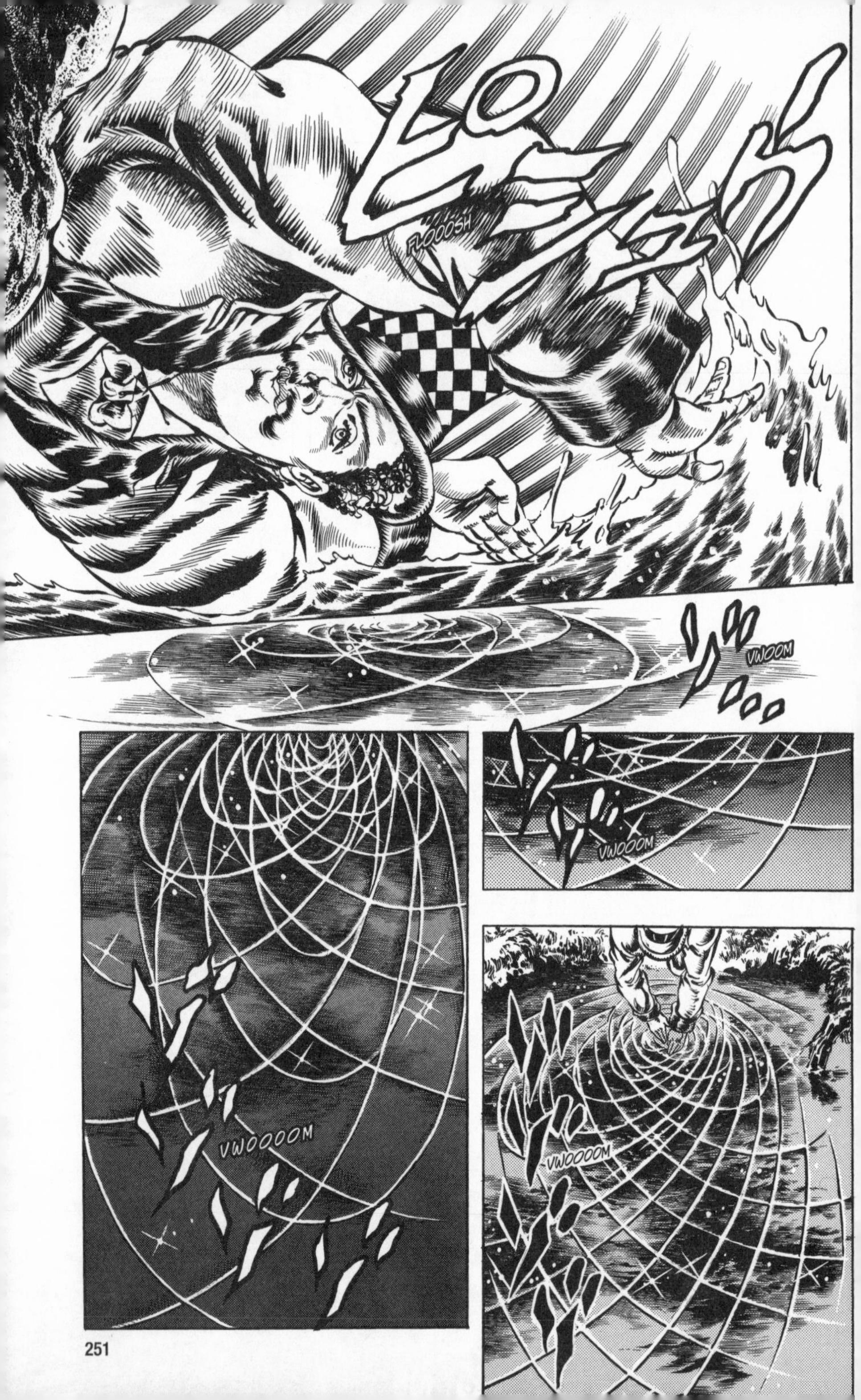
FLOOOSH
VWOOM
VWOOOM
VWOOOOM
VWOOOOM

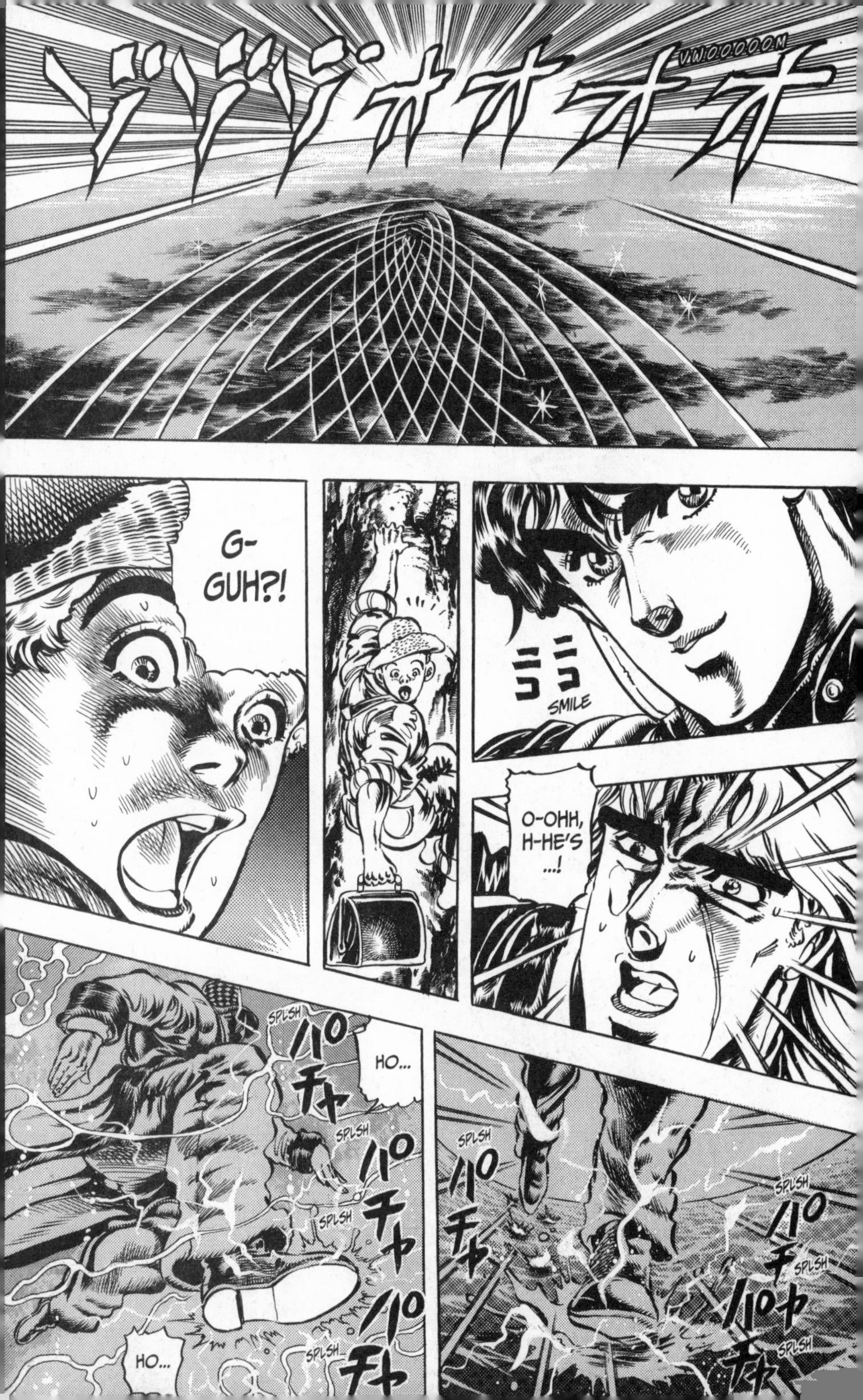
VWOOOOOM
SMILE
O-OHH, H-HE'S ...!
G-GUH?!
SPLSH
SPLSH
SPLSH
SPLSH
SPLSH
HO...
SPLSH
SPLSH
SPLSH
HO...

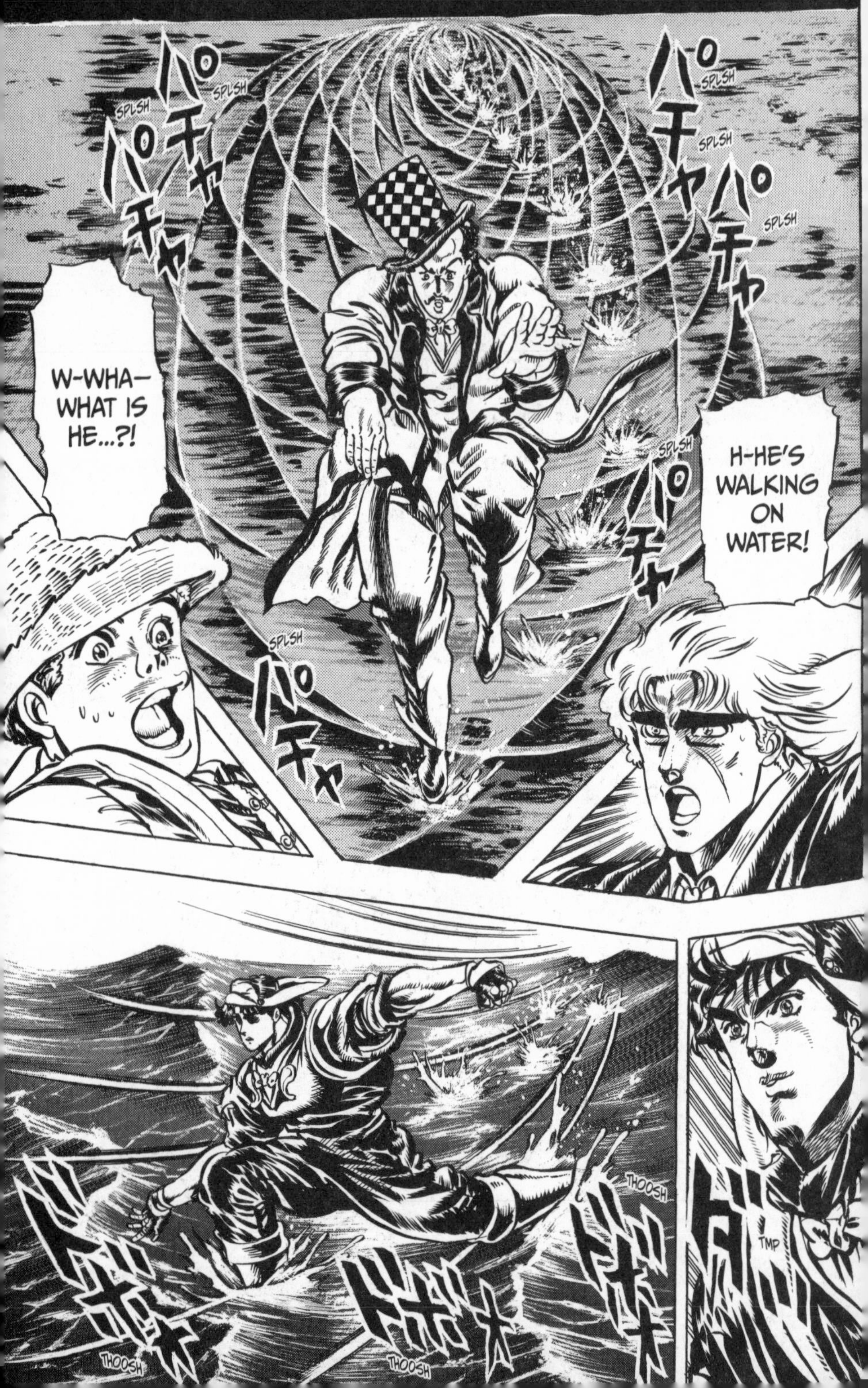
パチャパチャ
SPLSH
SPLSH
パチャパチャ
SPLSH
SPLSH
H-HE'S WALKING ON WATER!
W-WHA— WHAT IS HE...?!
SPLSH
パチャ
SPLSH
パチャ
TMP
THOOSH
THOOSH
THOOSH

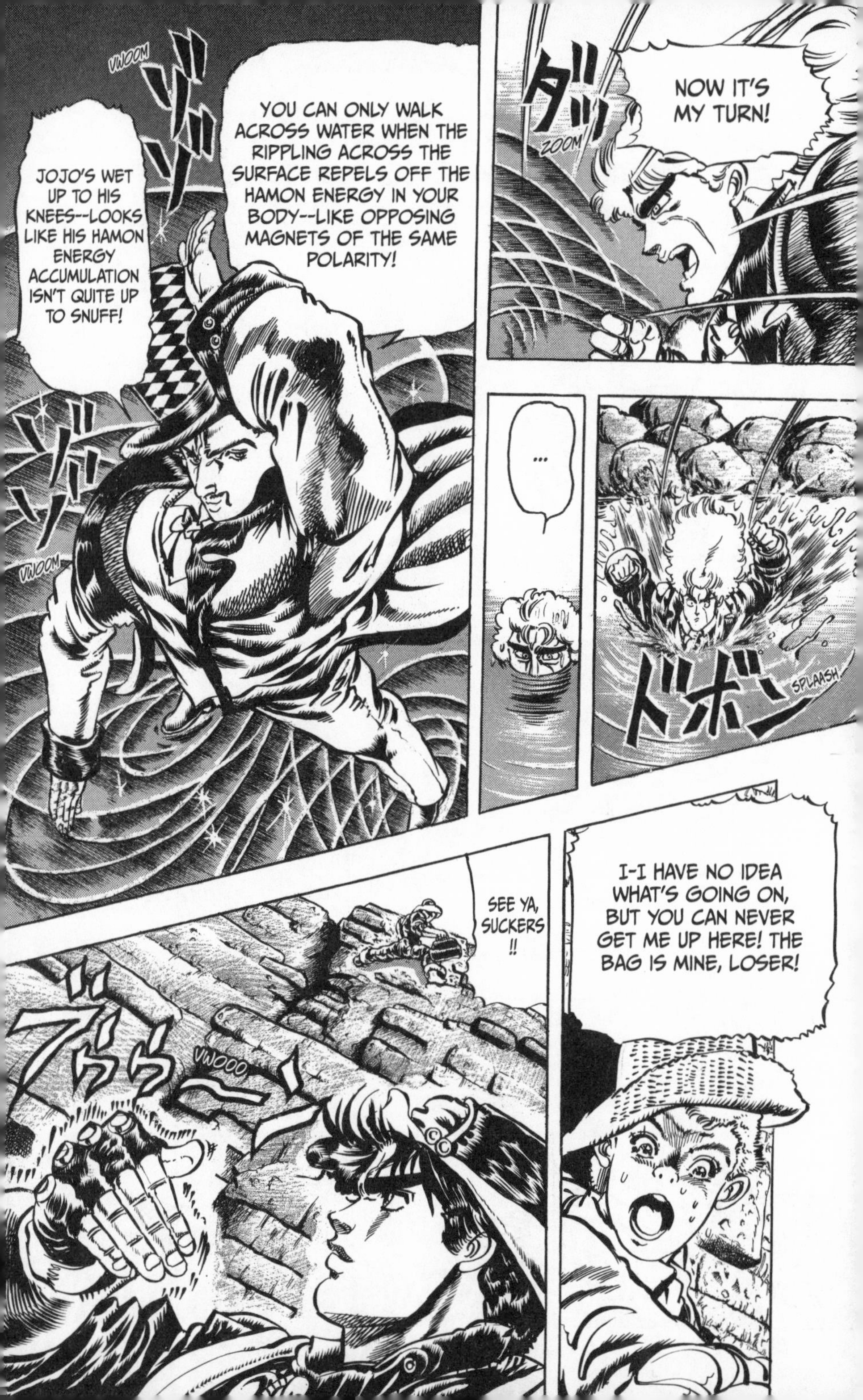
ダッ
ZOOM
NOW IT'S MY TURN!
ドボン
SPLAASH
...
YOU CAN ONLY WALK ACROSS WATER WHEN THE RIPPLING ACROSS THE SURFACE REPELS OFF THE HAMON ENERGY IN YOUR BODY--LIKE OPPOSING MAGNETS OF THE SAME POLARITY!
VWOOM
JOJO'S WET UP TO HIS KNEES--LOOKS LIKE HIS HAMON ENERGY ACCUMULATION ISN'T QUITE UP TO SNUFF!
VWOOM
I-I HAVE NO IDEA WHAT'S GOING ON, BUT YOU CAN NEVER GET ME UP HERE! THE BAG IS MINE, LOSER!
SEE YA, SUCKERS !!
VWOOO

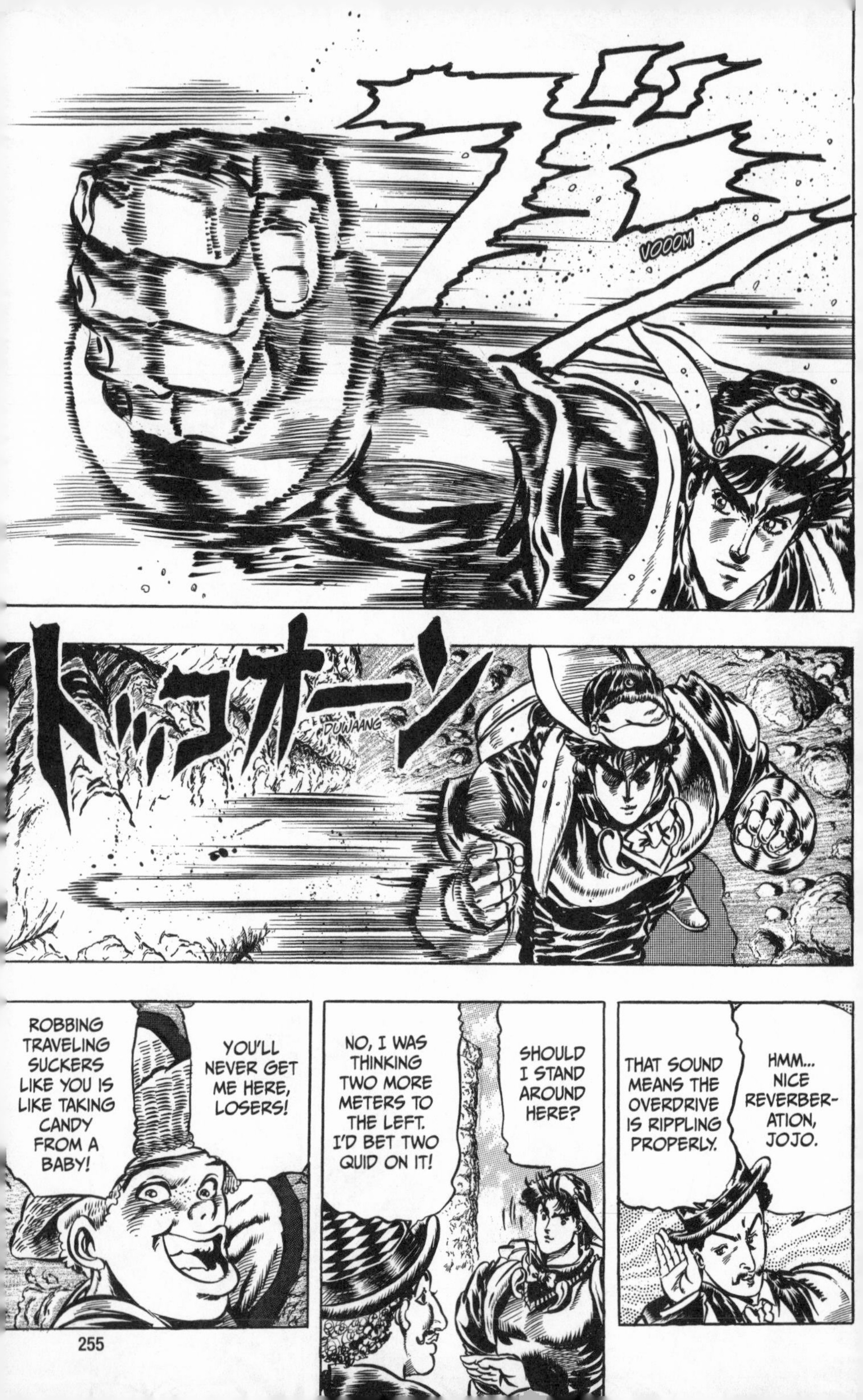
VOOOM
ドッゴオーン
DUWAANG
HMM... NICE REVERBERATION, JOJO.
THAT SOUND MEANS THE OVERDRIVE IS RIPPLING PROPERLY.
SHOULD I STAND AROUND HERE?
NO, I WAS THINKING TWO MORE METERS TO THE LEFT. I'D BET TWO QUID ON IT!
YOU'LL NEVER GET ME HERE, LOSERS!
ROBBING TRAVELING SUCKERS LIKE YOU IS LIKE TAKING CANDY FROM A BABY!

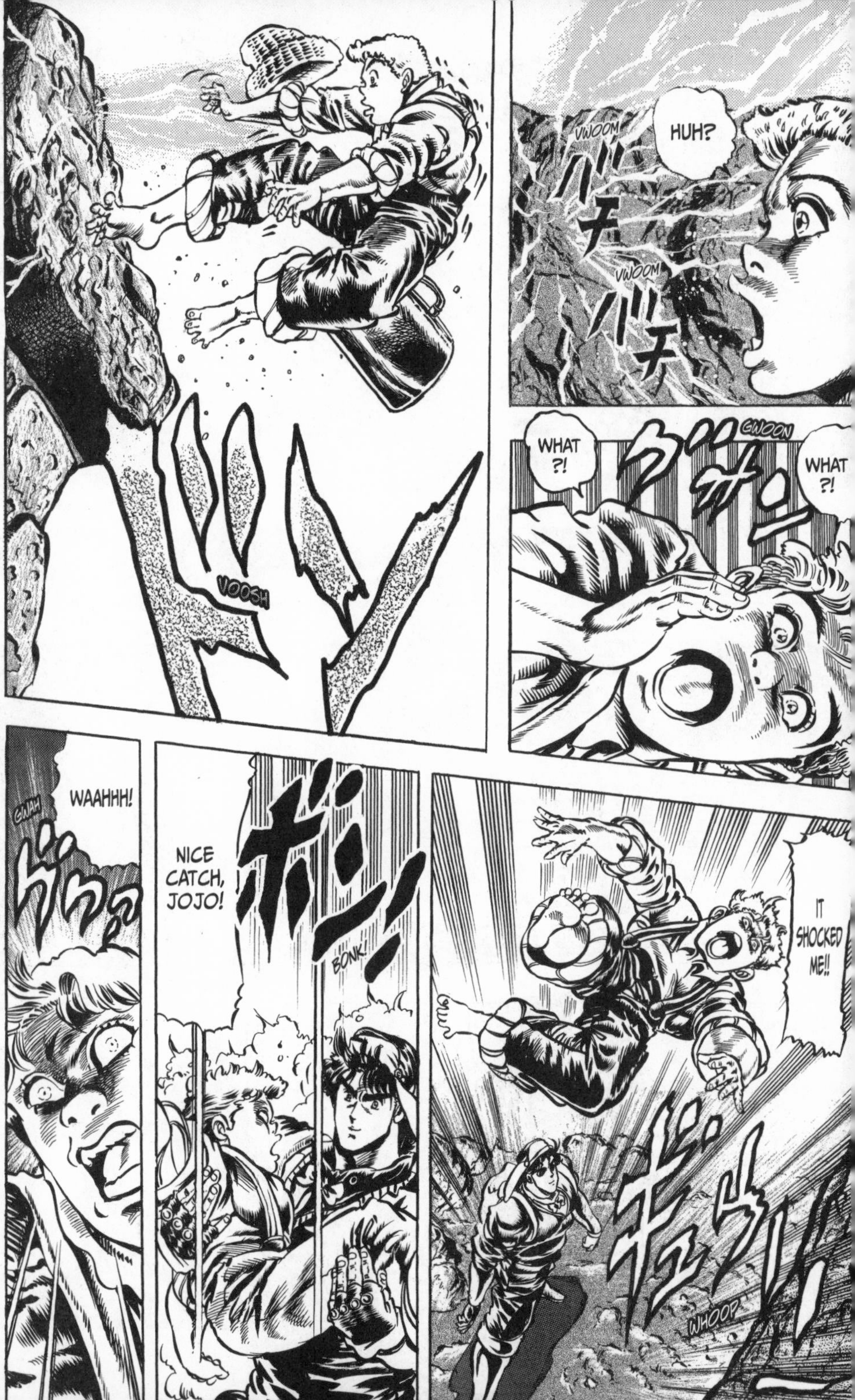

HUH?
VWOOM
VWOOM
WHAT ?!
GWOON
WHAT ?!
VOOSH
IT SHOCKED ME!!
WHOOP
NICE CATCH, JOJO!
BONK
WAAHHH!
GWAH

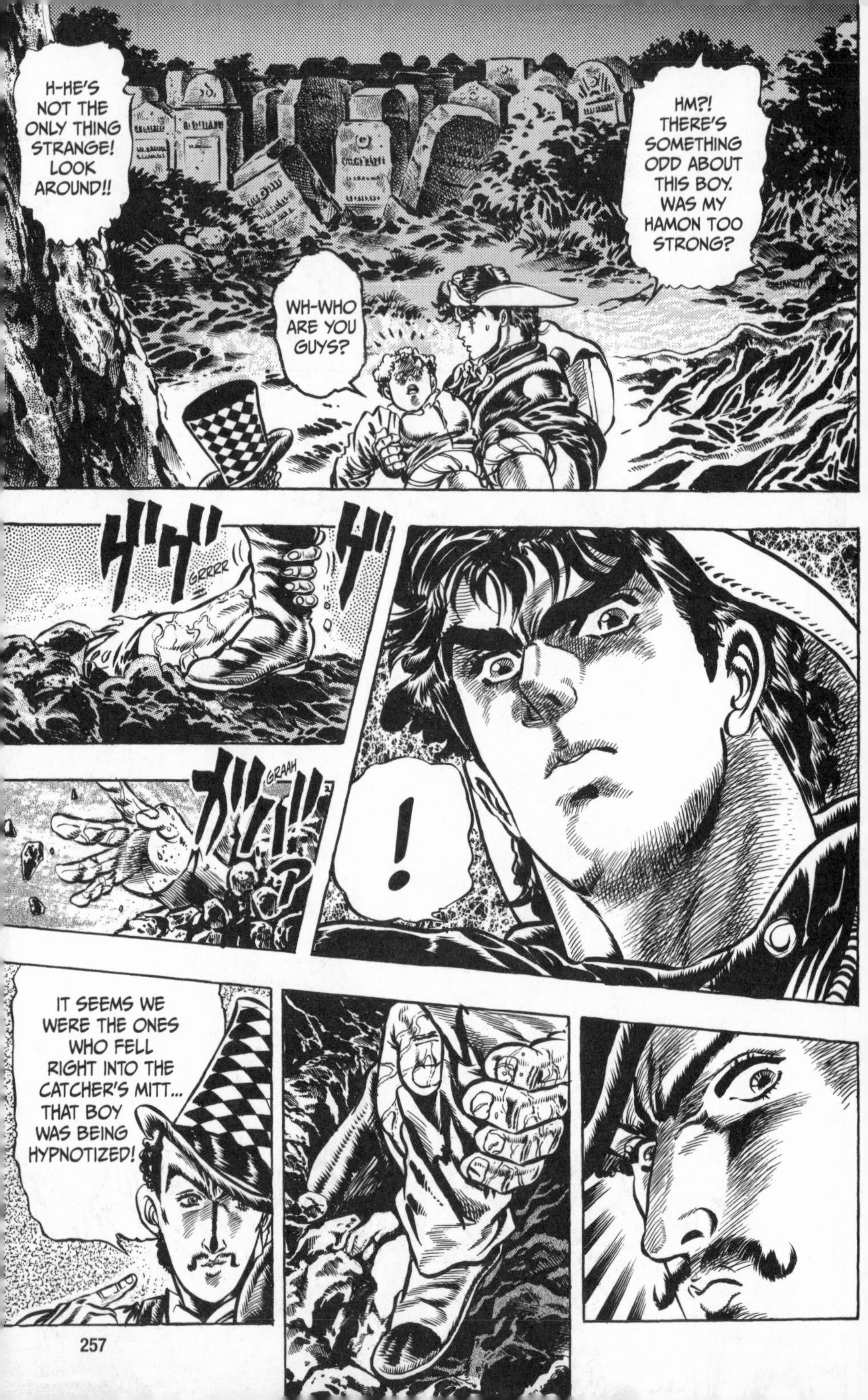
HM?! THERE'S SOMETHING ODD ABOUT THIS BOY. WAS MY HAMON TOO STRONG?
H-HE'S NOT THE ONLY THING STRANGE! LOOK AROUND!!
WH-WHO ARE YOU GUYS?
!
GRRRR
GRAAH
IT SEEMS WE WERE THE ONES WHO FELL RIGHT INTO THE CATCHER'S MITT... THAT BOY WAS BEING HYPNOTIZED!

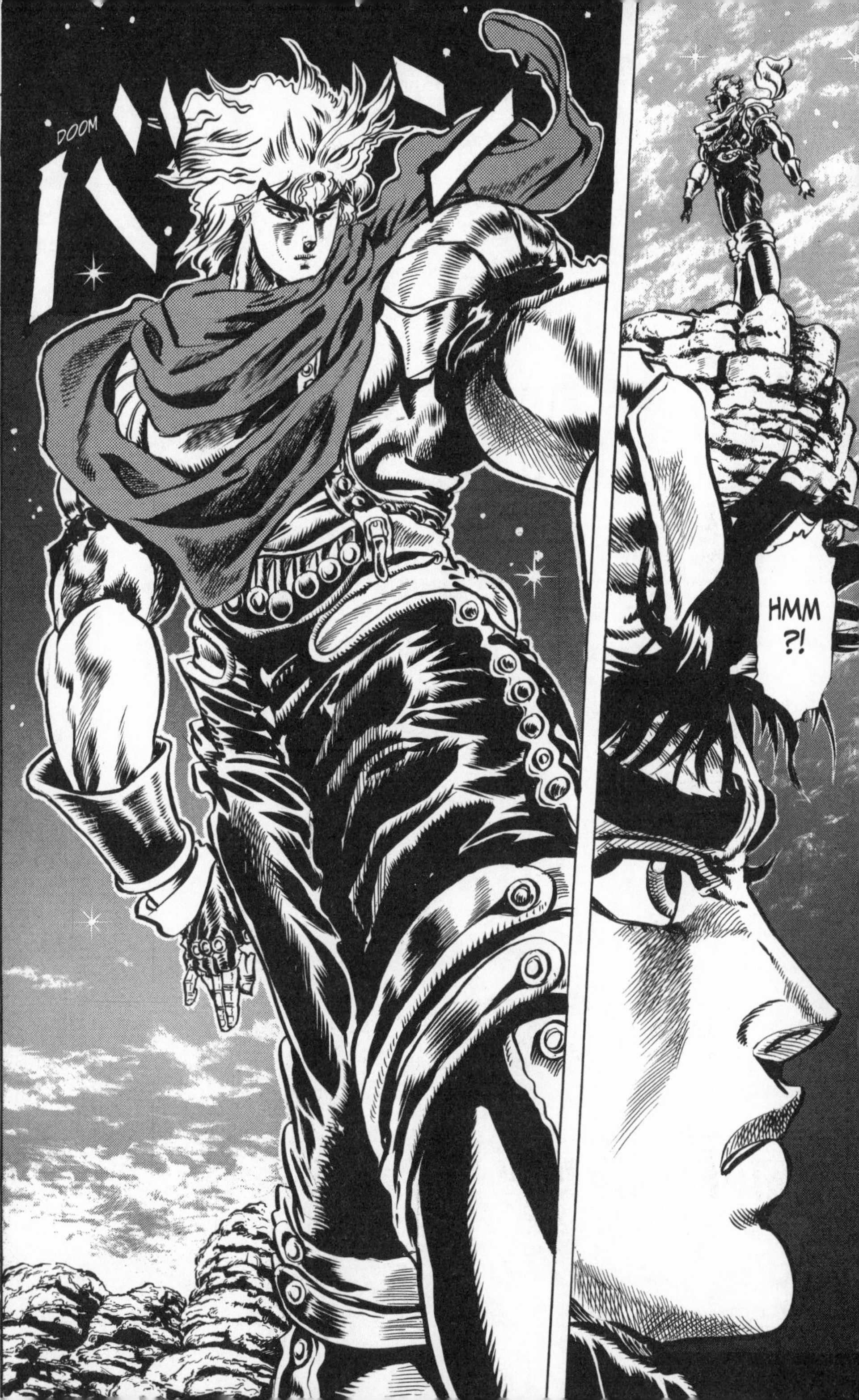
HMM ?!
DOOM

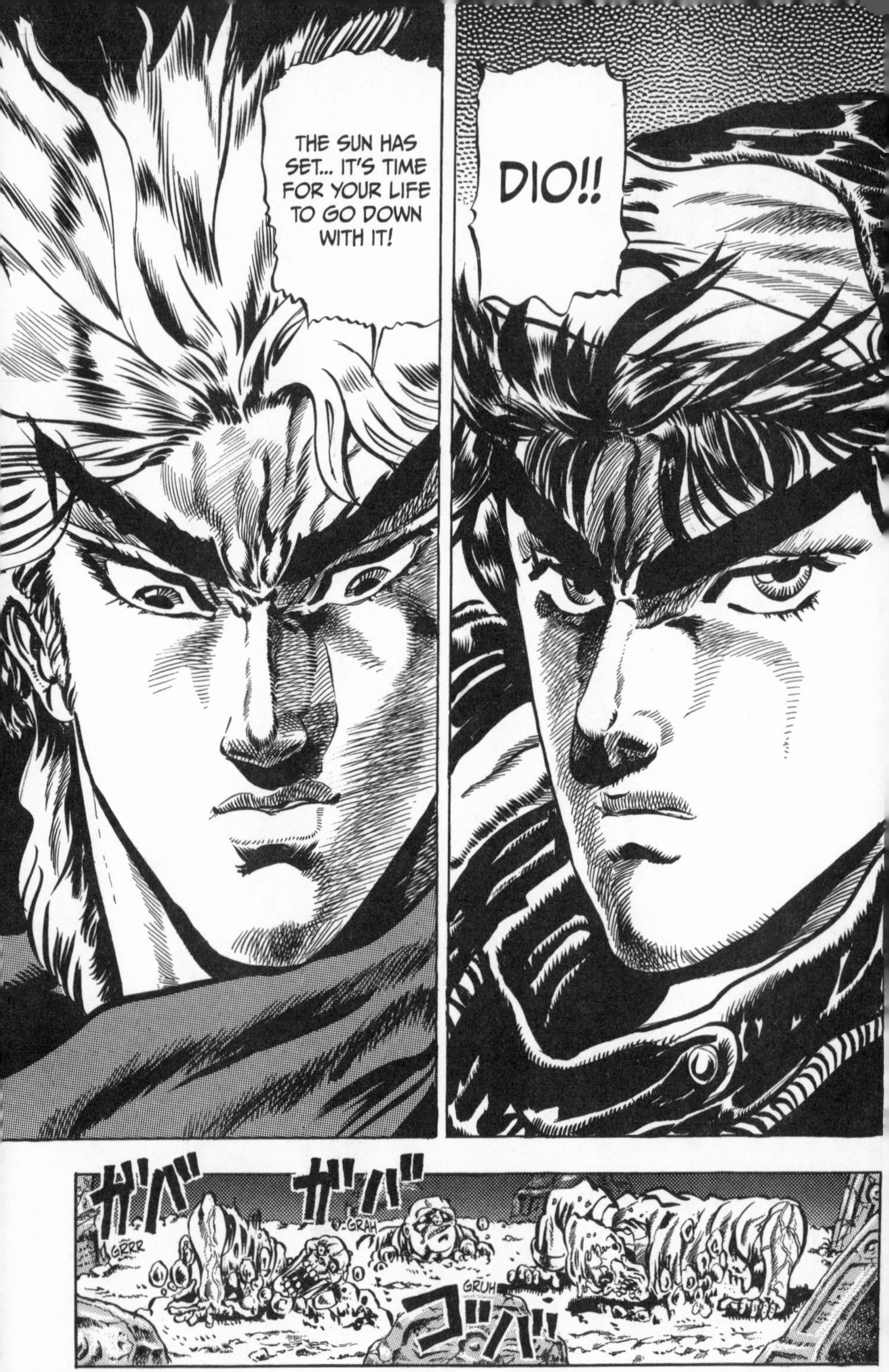
DIO!!
THE SUN HAS SET... IT'S TIME FOR YOUR LIFE TO GO DOWN WITH IT!
ガバ
GRAH
ガバ
GRRR
GRUH
ゴバ

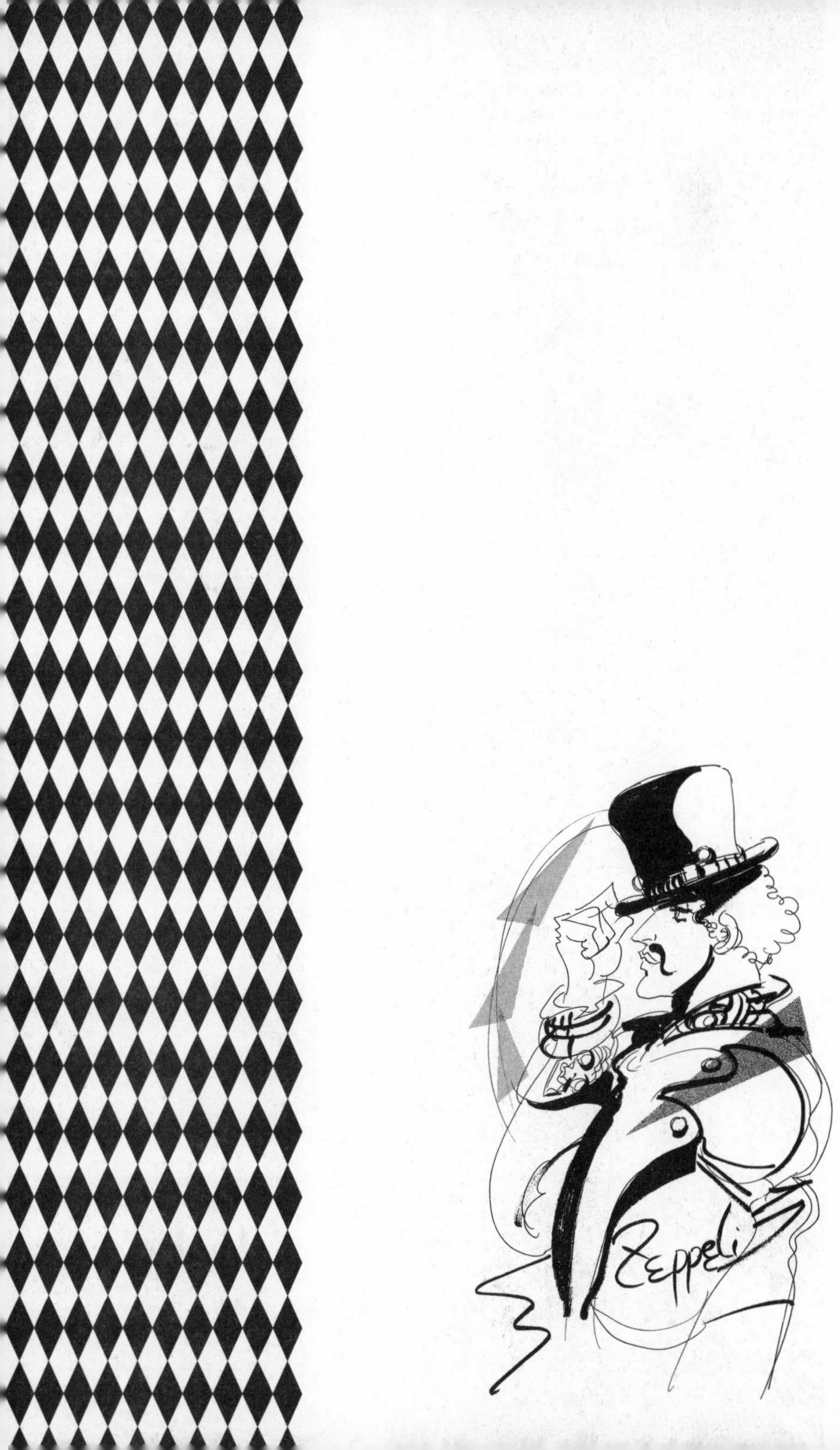
Zeppeli

CHAPTER 25: Hamon Overdrive PART 3

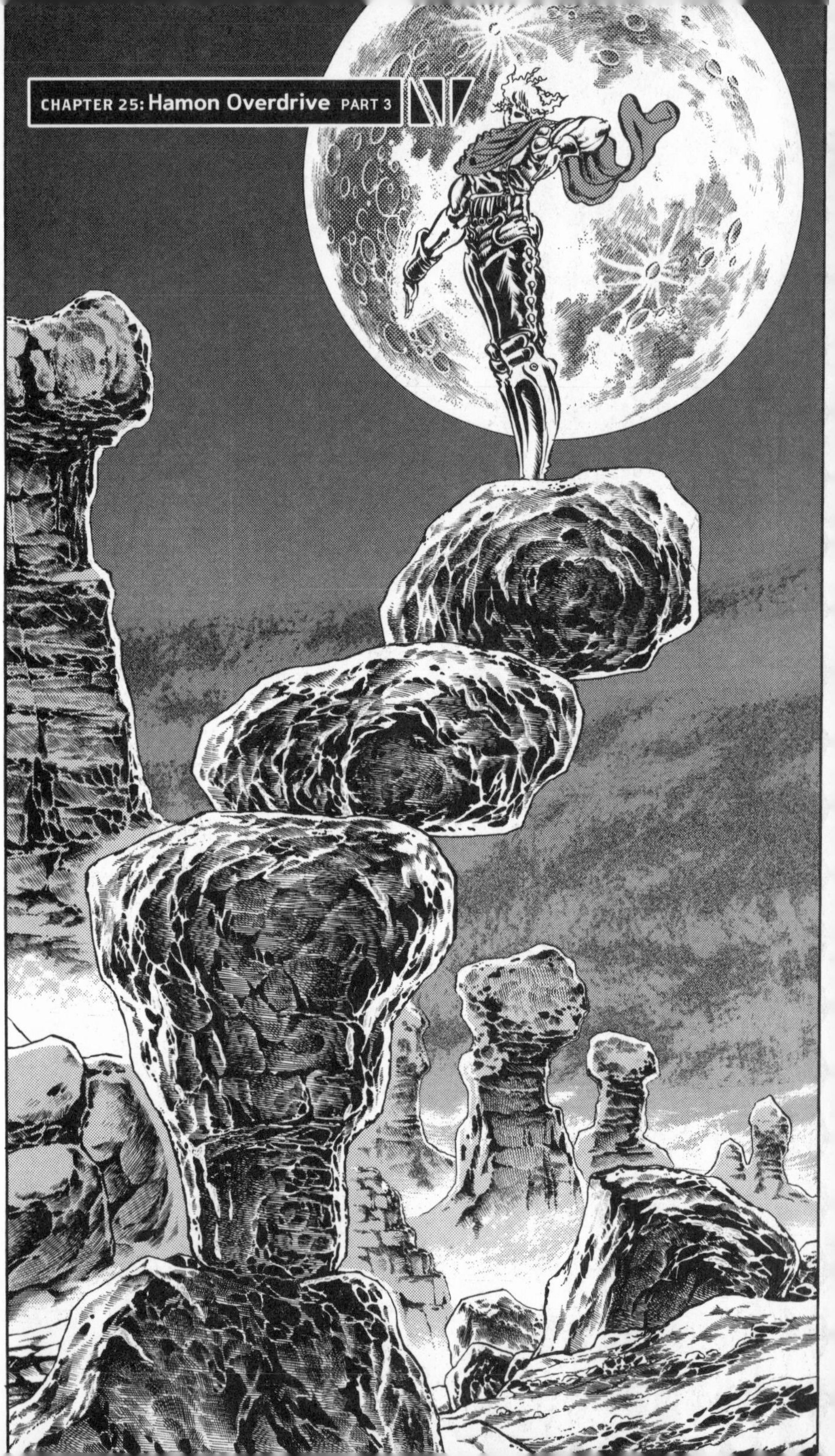

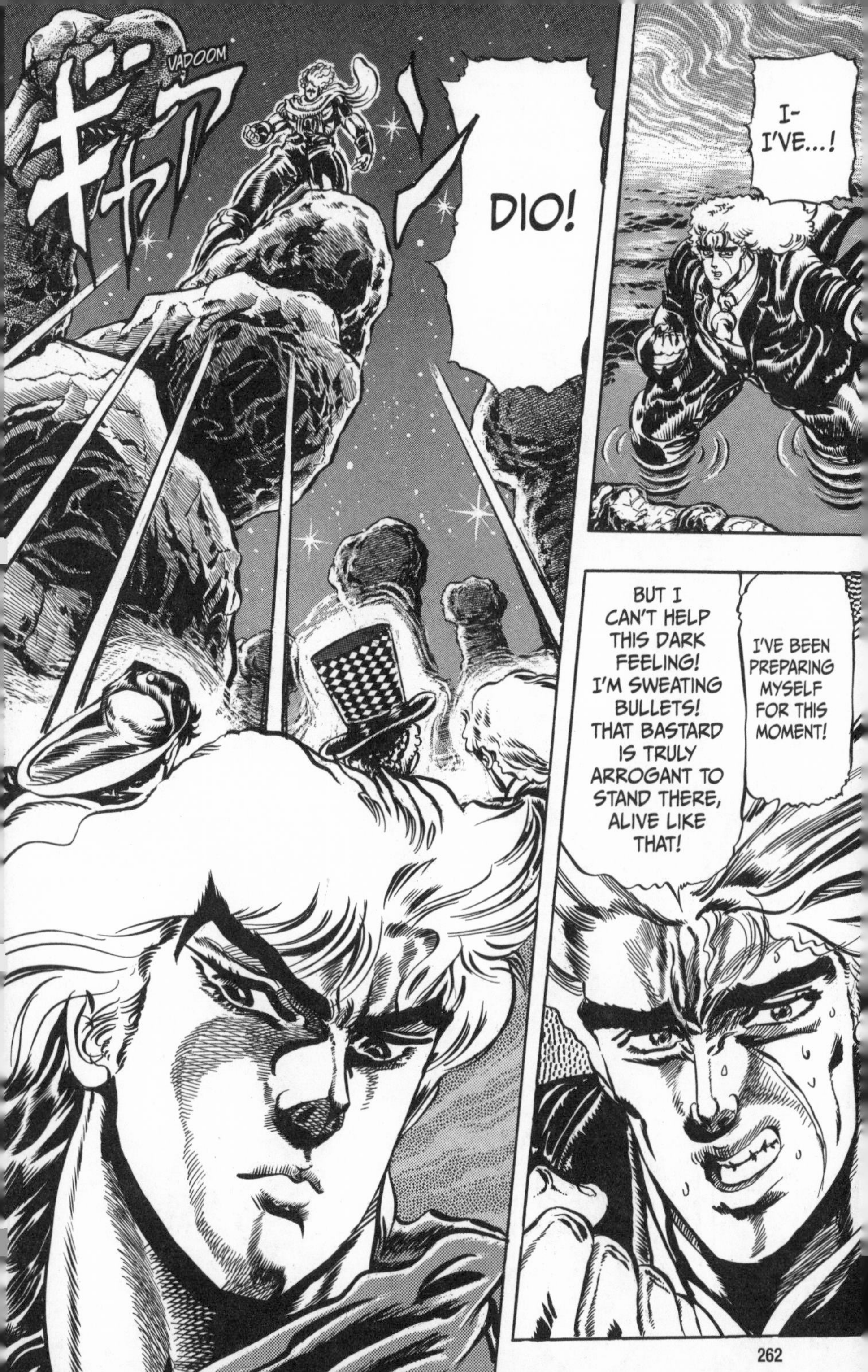
I- I'VE...!
I'VE BEEN PREPARING MYSELF FOR THIS MOMENT!
BUT I CAN'T HELP THIS DARK FEELING! I'M SWEATING BULLETS! THAT BASTARD IS TRULY ARROGANT TO STAND THERE, ALIVE LIKE THAT!
DIO!
VADOOM

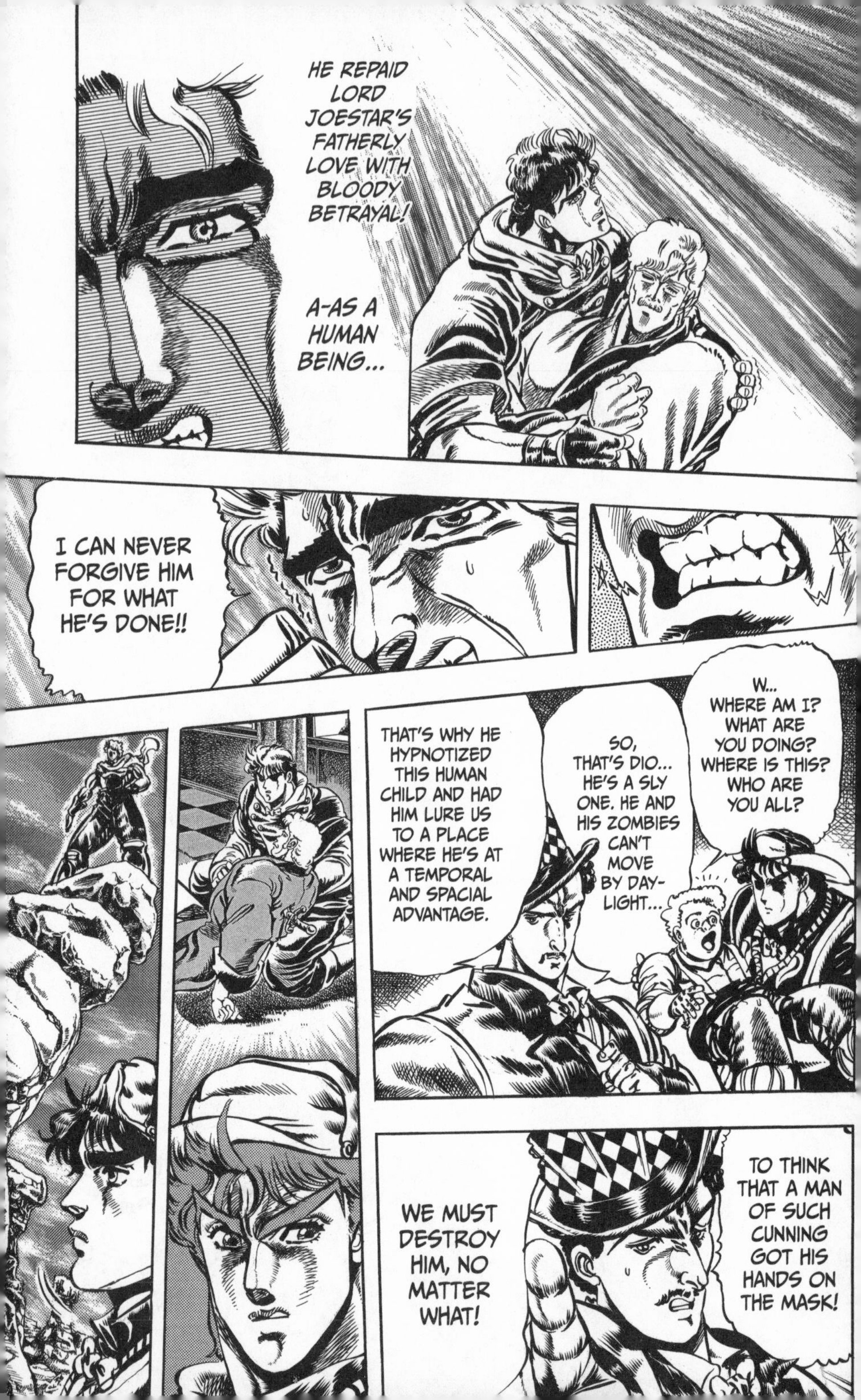
HE REPAID LORD JOESTAR'S FATHERLY LOVE WITH BLOODY BETRAYAL!
A-AS A HUMAN BEING...
I CAN NEVER FORGIVE HIM FOR WHAT HE'S DONE!!
W... WHERE AM I? WHAT ARE YOU DOING? WHERE IS THIS? WHO ARE YOU ALL?
SO, THAT'S DIO... HE'S A SLY ONE. HE AND HIS ZOMBIES CAN'T MOVE BY DAY-LIGHT...
THAT'S WHY HE HYPNOTIZED THIS HUMAN CHILD AND HAD HIM LURE US TO A PLACE WHERE HE'S AT A TEMPORAL AND SPACIAL ADVANTAGE.
TO THINK THAT A MAN OF SUCH CUNNING GOT HIS HANDS ON THE MASK!
WE MUST DESTROY HIM, NO MATTER WHAT!

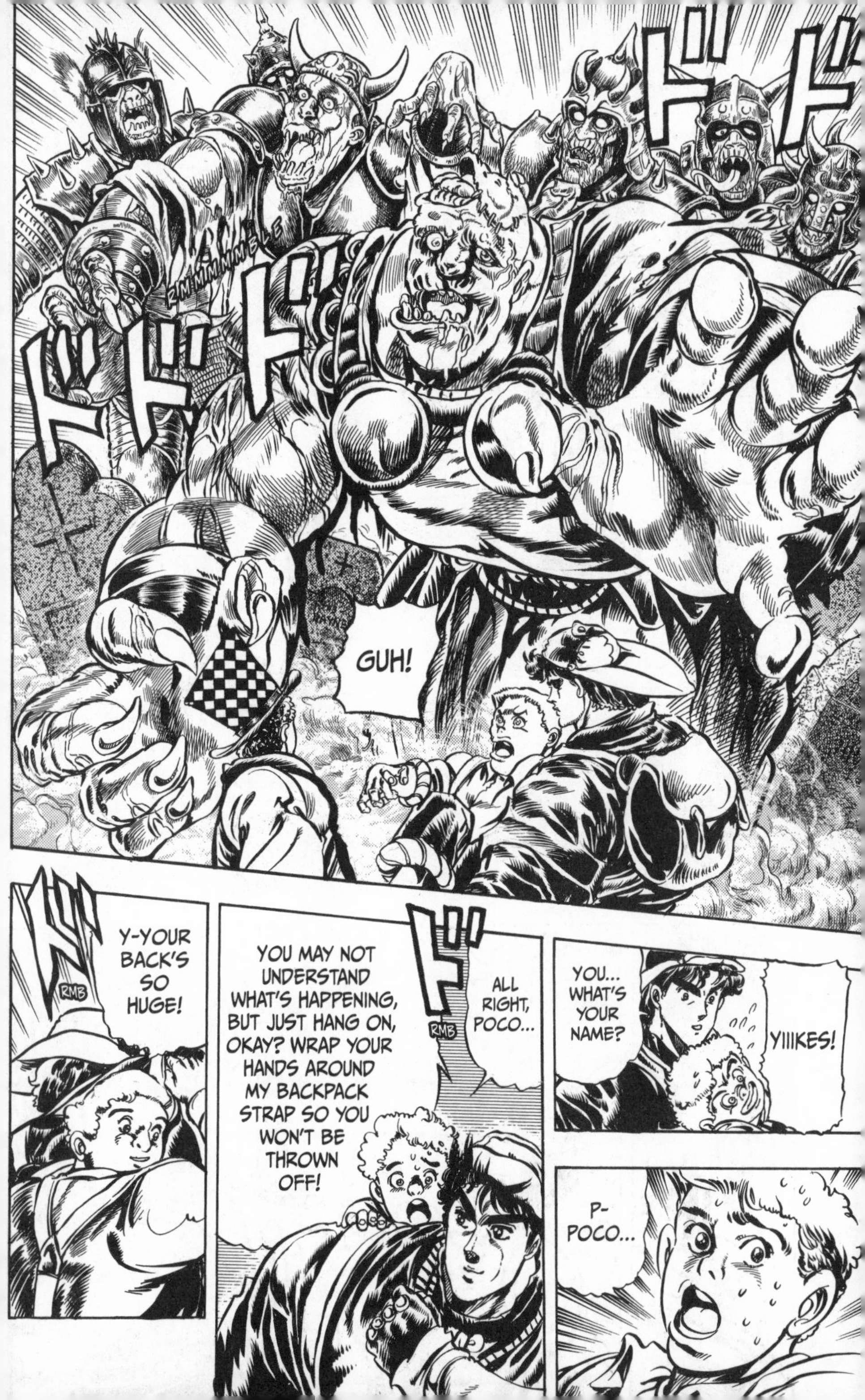
RMMMMMBLE
GUH!
YIIIKES!
YOU... WHAT'S YOUR NAME?
P-POCO...
RMB
ALL RIGHT, POCO...
YOU MAY NOT UNDERSTAND WHAT'S HAPPENING, BUT JUST HANG ON, OKAY? WRAP YOUR HANDS AROUND MY BACKPACK STRAP SO YOU WON'T BE THROWN OFF!
RMB
Y-YOUR BACK'S SO HUGE!

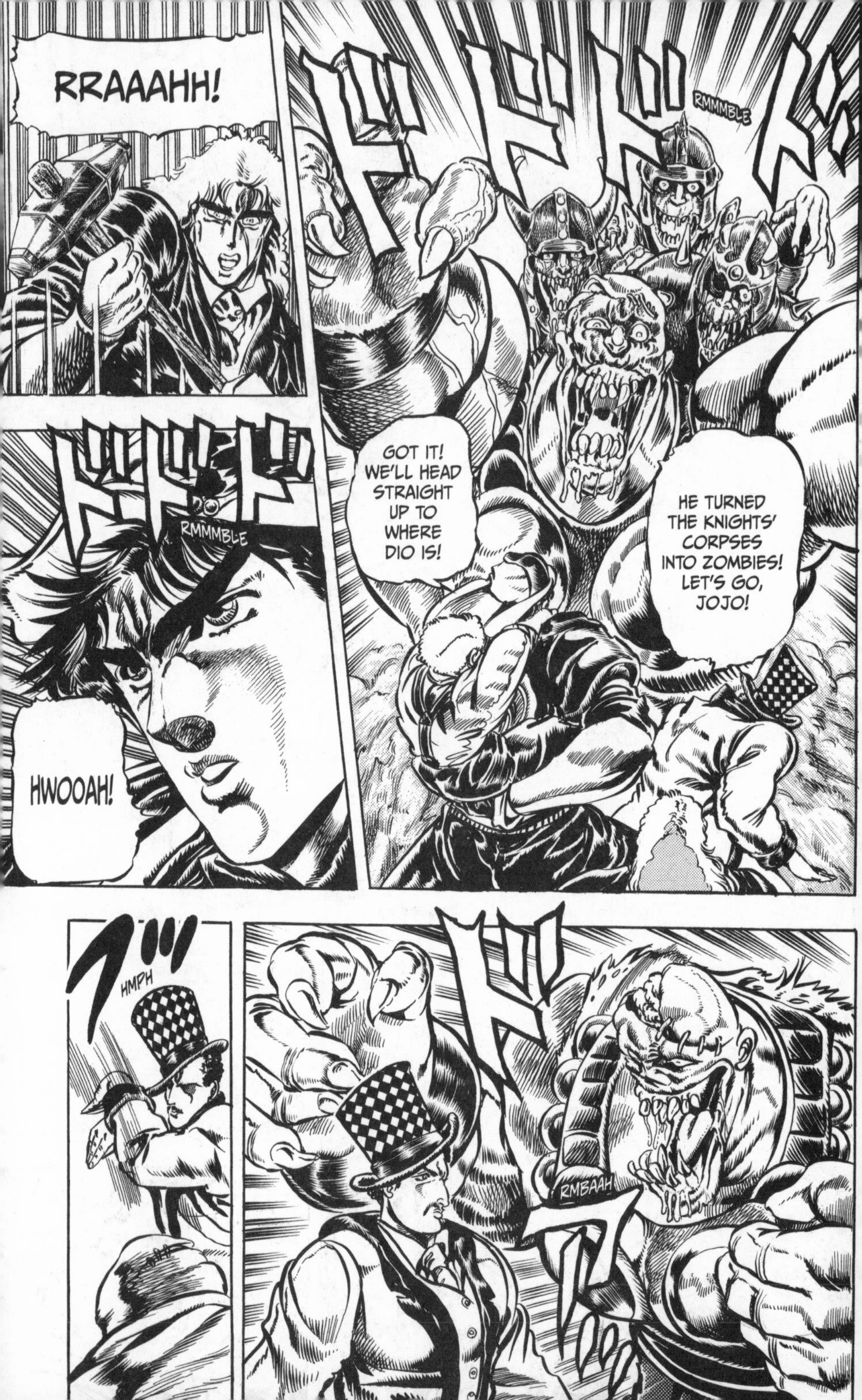
RMMMBLE
HE TURNED THE KNIGHTS' CORPSES INTO ZOMBIES! LET'S GO, JOJO!
GOT IT! WE'LL HEAD STRAIGHT UP TO WHERE DIO IS!
RRAAAHH!
RMMMBLE
HWOOAH!
RMBAAH
HMPH

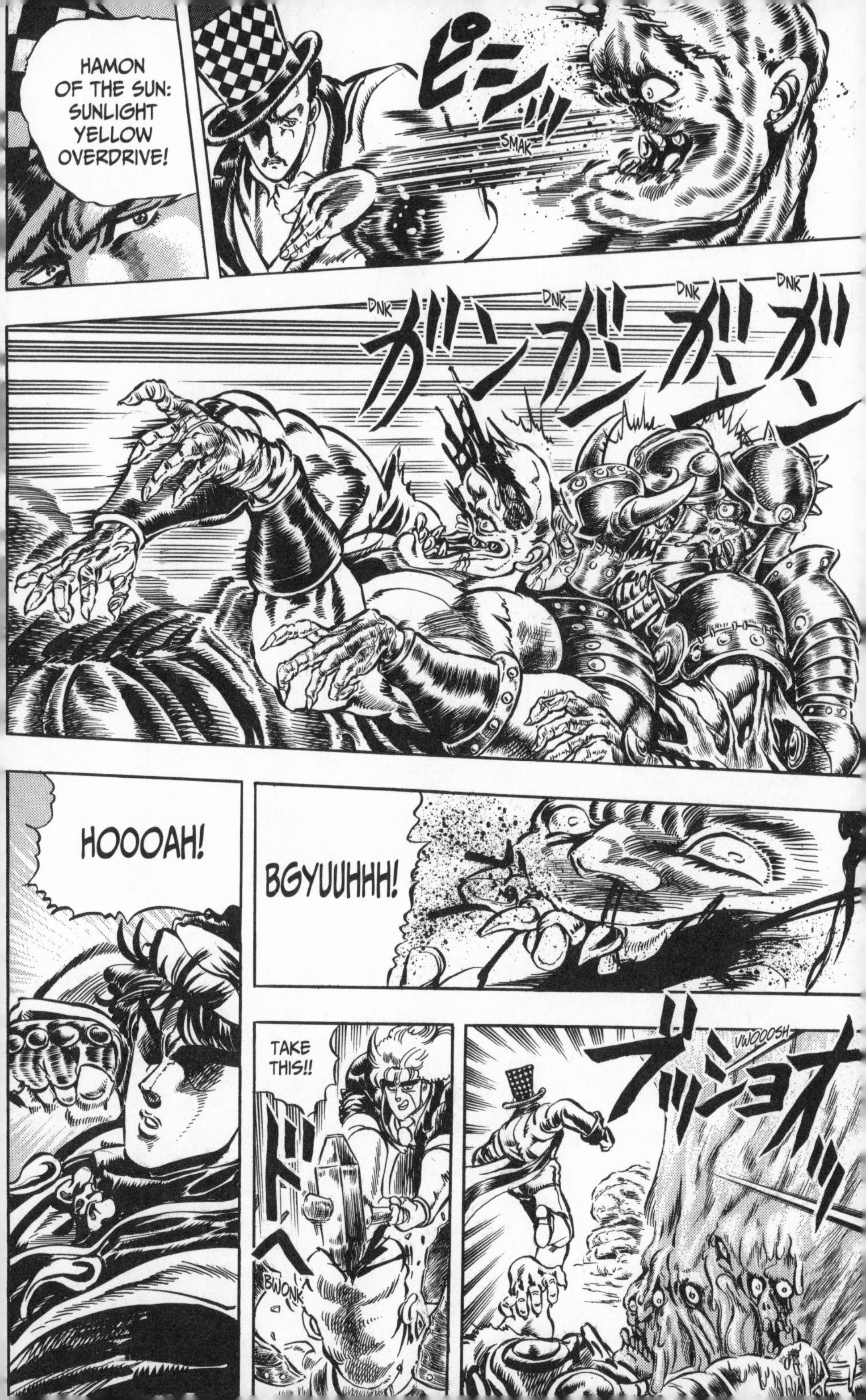
SMAK
HAMON OF THE SUN: SUNLIGHT YELLOW OVERDRIVE!
DNK
DNK
DNK
DNK
BGYUUHHH!
VWOOOSH
TAKE THIS!!
BWONK
HOOOAH!

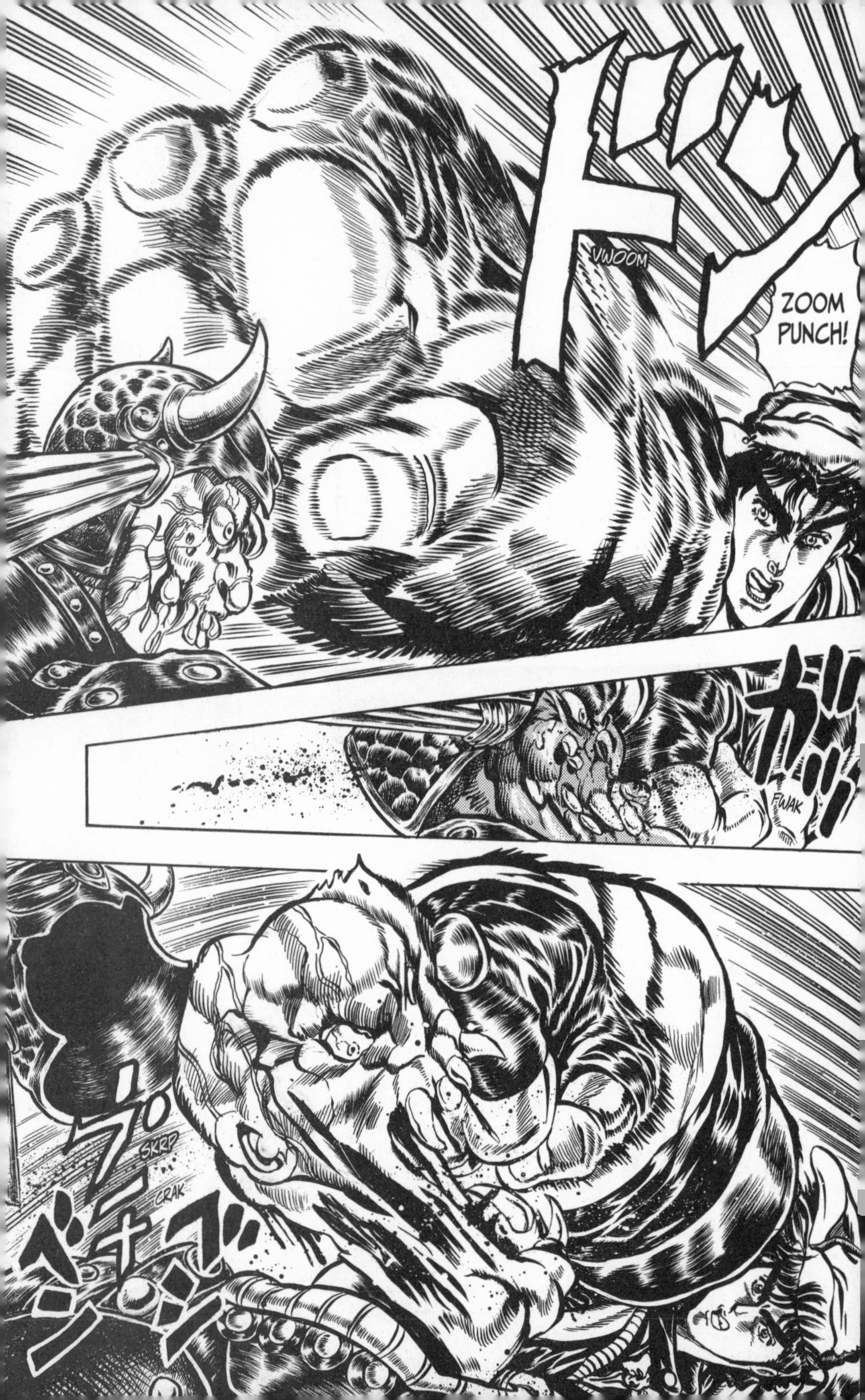
ZOOM PUNCH!
VWOOM
FWAK
SKRP
CRAK

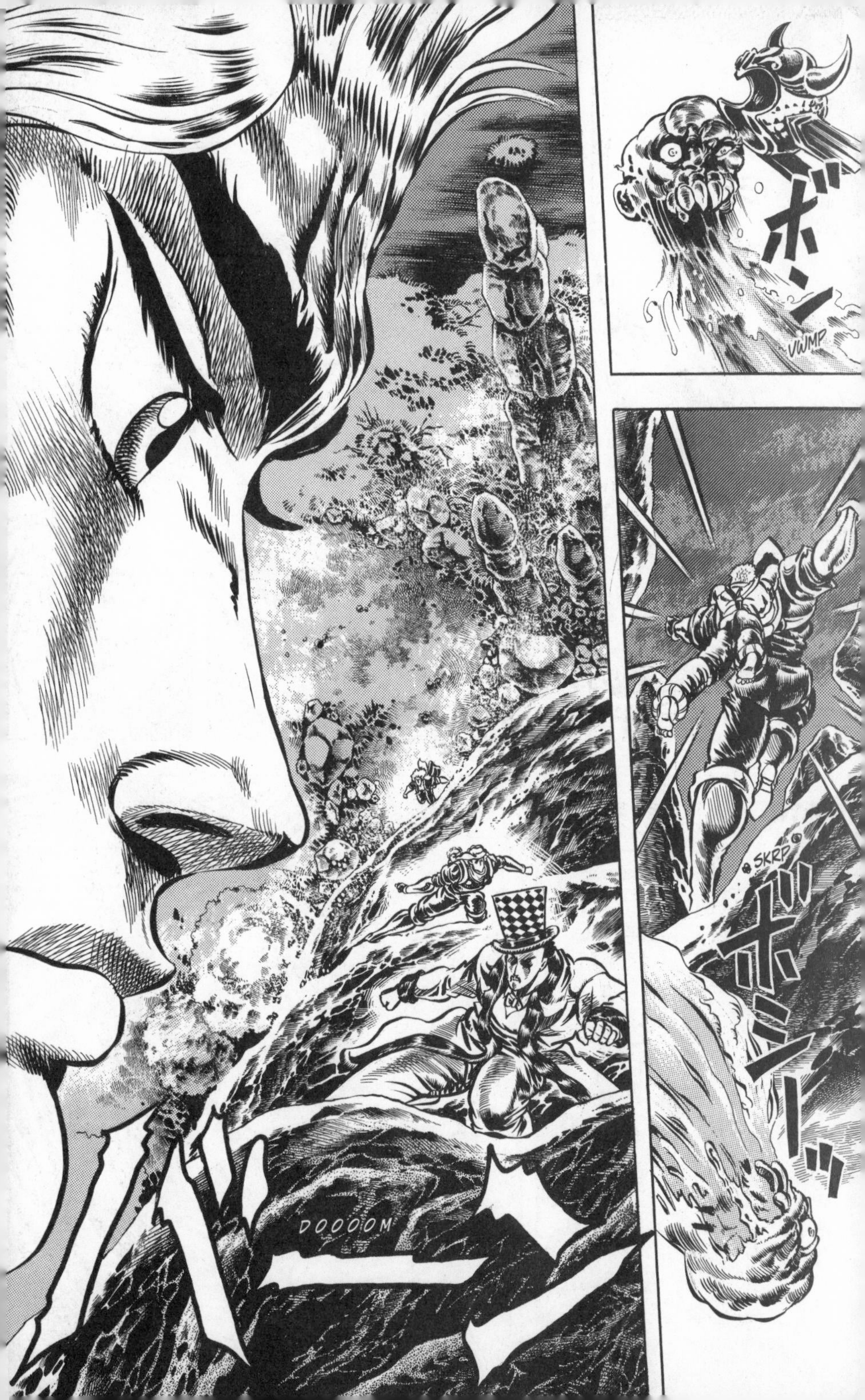
VWMP
SKRP
DOOOOM

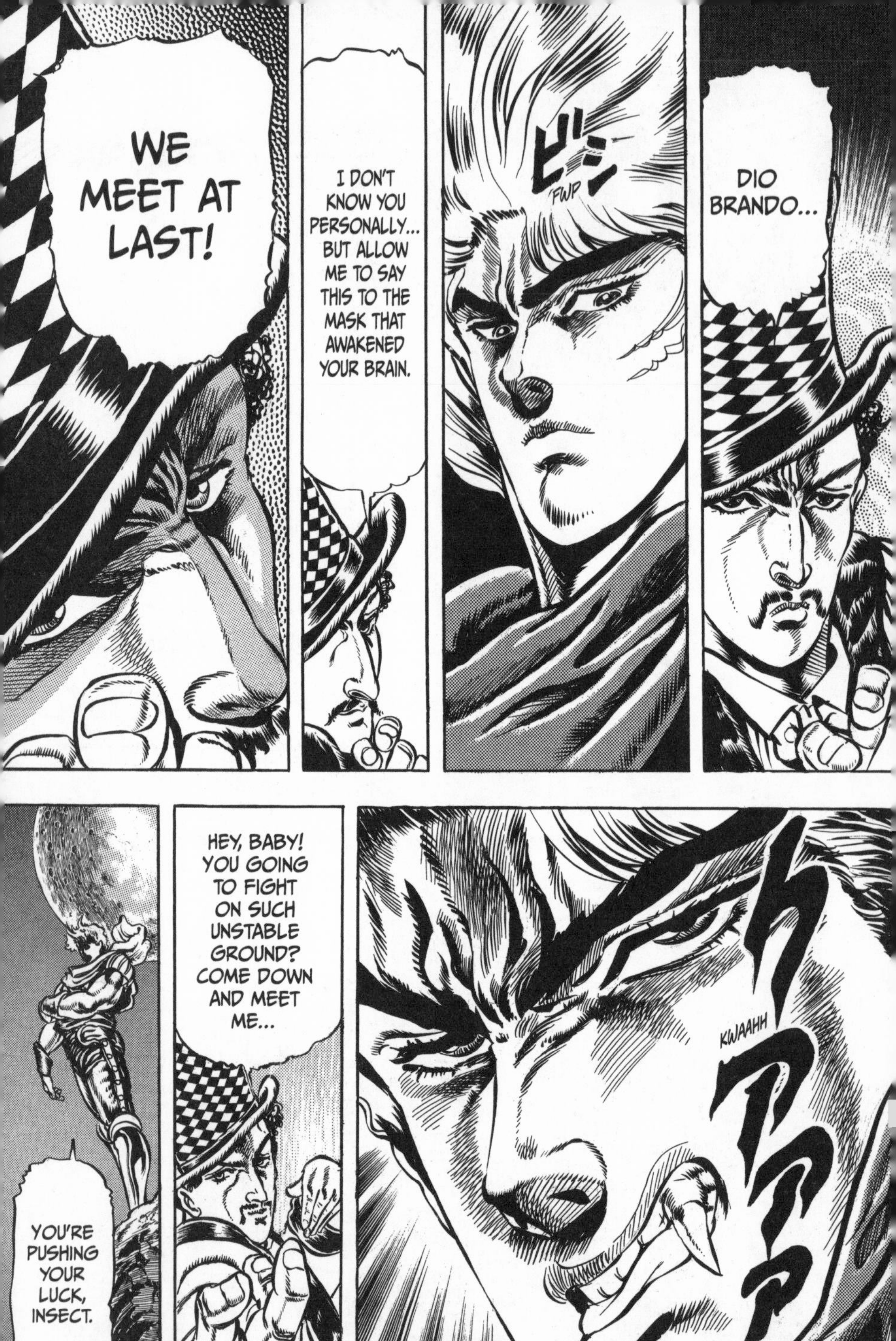
DIO BRANDO...
FWP
I DON'T KNOW YOU PERSONALLY... BUT ALLOW ME TO SAY THIS TO THE MASK THAT AWAKENED YOUR BRAIN.
WE MEET AT LAST!
KWAAHH
HEY, BABY! YOU GOING TO FIGHT ON SUCH UNSTABLE GROUND? COME DOWN AND MEET ME...
YOU'RE PUSHING YOUR LUCK, INSECT.

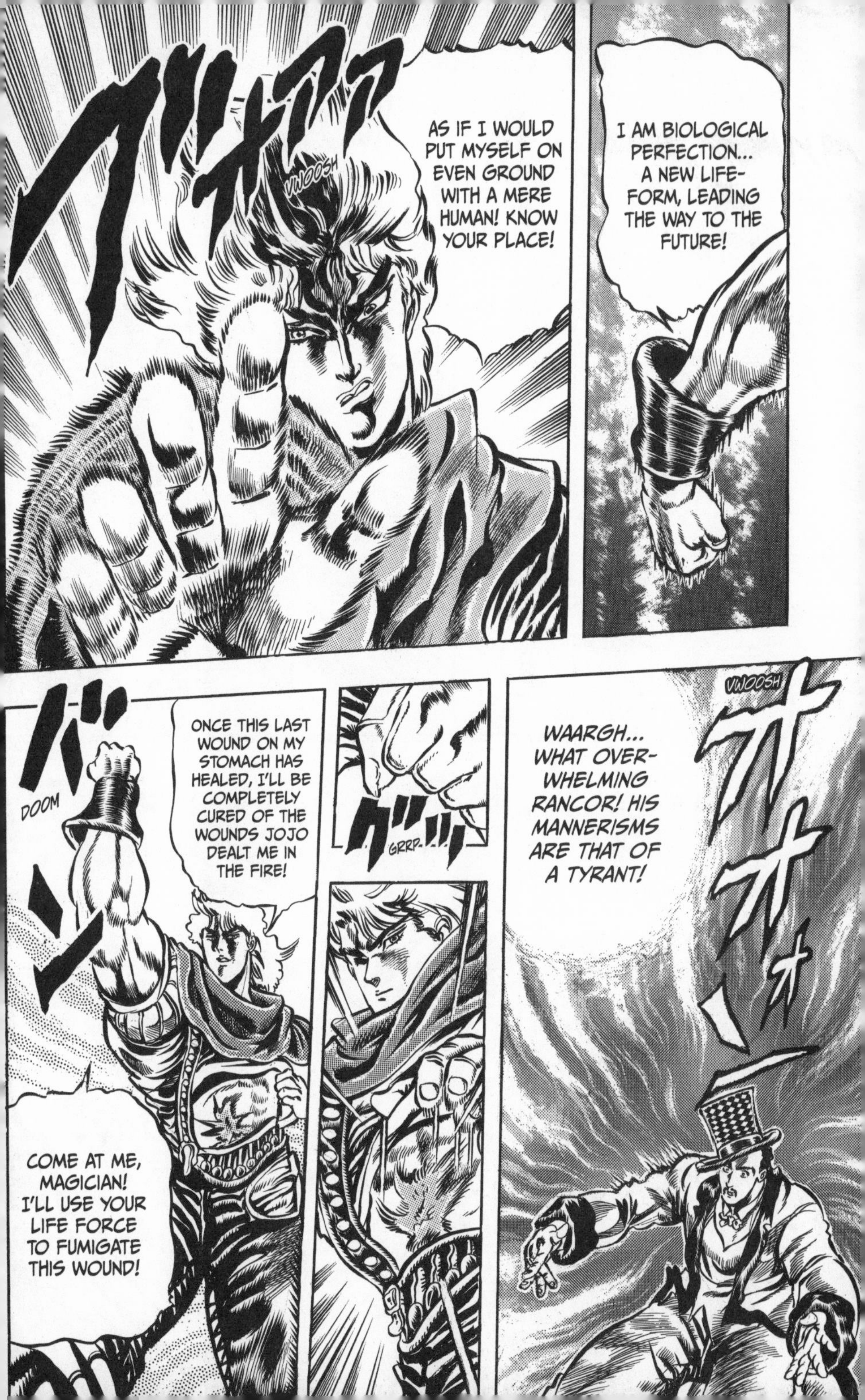
I AM BIOLOGICAL PERFECTION... A NEW LIFE-FORM, LEADING THE WAY TO THE FUTURE!
AS IF I WOULD PUT MYSELF ON EVEN GROUND WITH A MERE HUMAN! KNOW YOUR PLACE!
VWOOSH
VWOOSH
WAARGH... WHAT OVER-WHELMING RANCOR! HIS MANNERISMS ARE THAT OF A TYRANT!
GRRP
ONCE THIS LAST WOUND ON MY STOMACH HAS HEALED, I'LL BE COMPLETELY CURED OF THE WOUNDS JOJO DEALT ME IN THE FIRE!
DOOM
COME AT ME, MAGICIAN! I'LL USE YOUR LIFE FORCE TO FUMIGATE THIS WOUND!

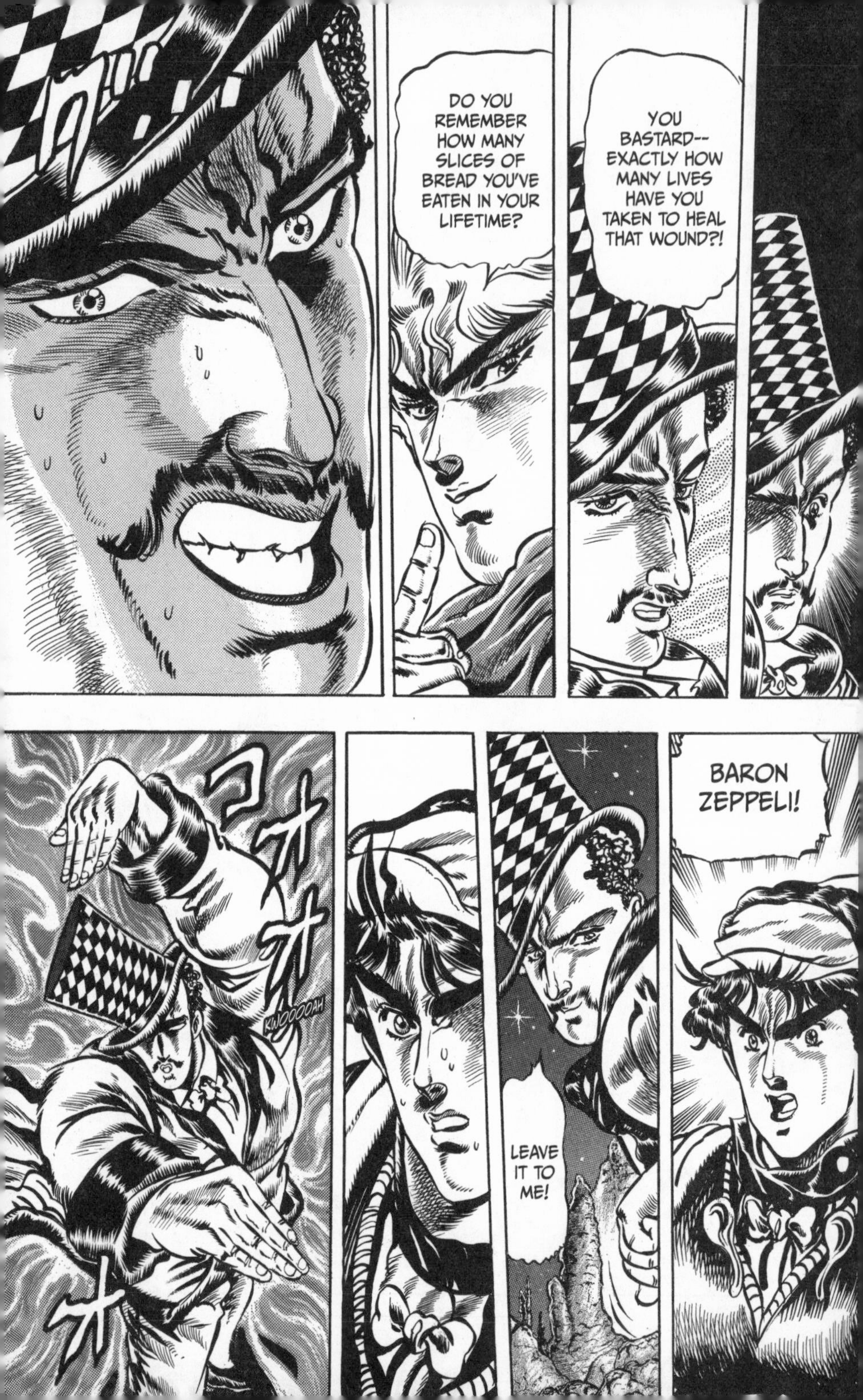
YOU BASTARD-- EXACTLY HOW MANY LIVES HAVE YOU TAKEN TO HEAL THAT WOUND?!
DO YOU REMEMBER HOW MANY SLICES OF BREAD YOU'VE EATEN IN YOUR LIFETIME?
BARON ZEPPELI!
LEAVE IT TO ME!
KWOOOOAH

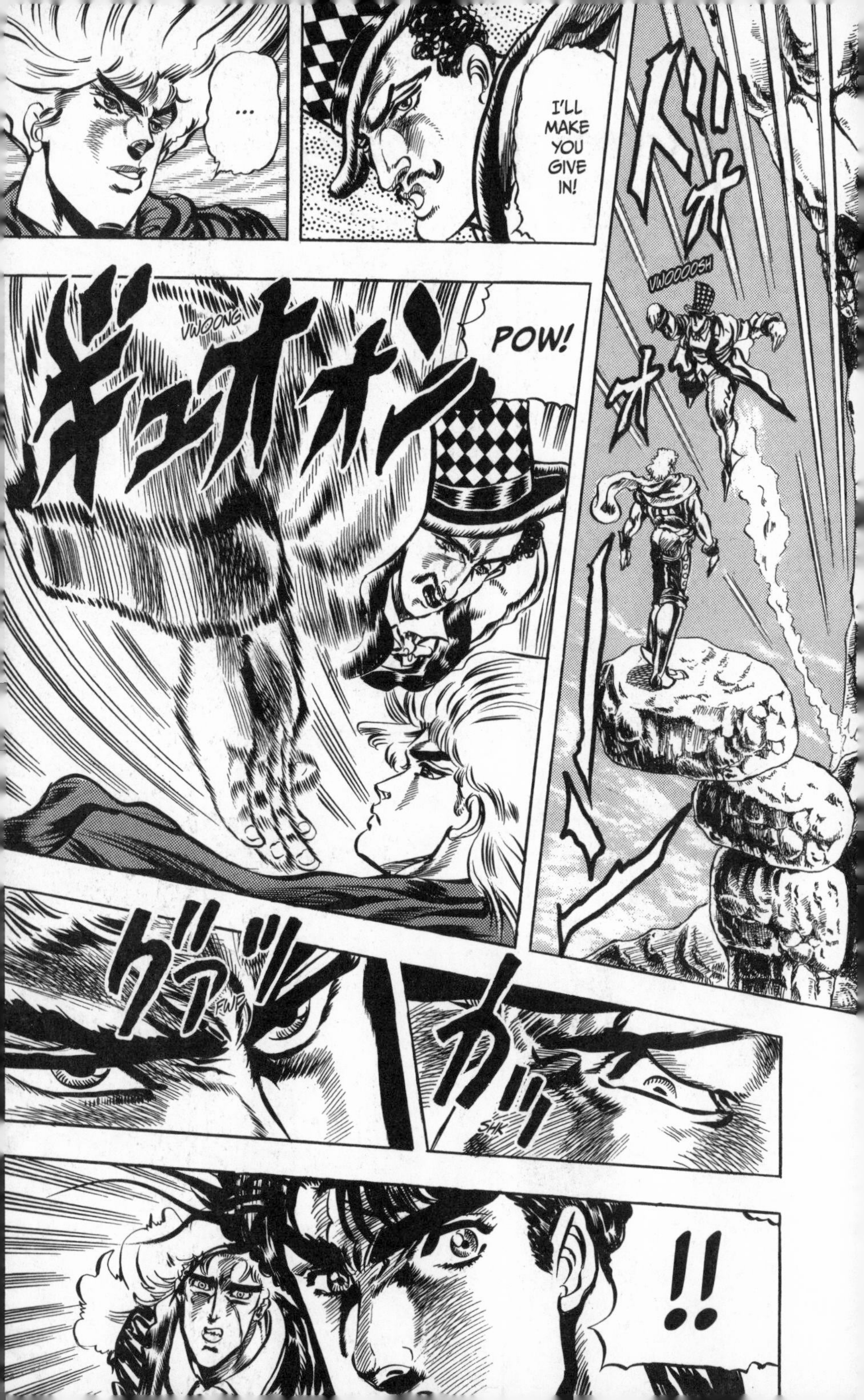
VWOOOOSH
I'LL MAKE YOU GIVE IN!
...
VWOONG
POW!
FWP
SHK
!!

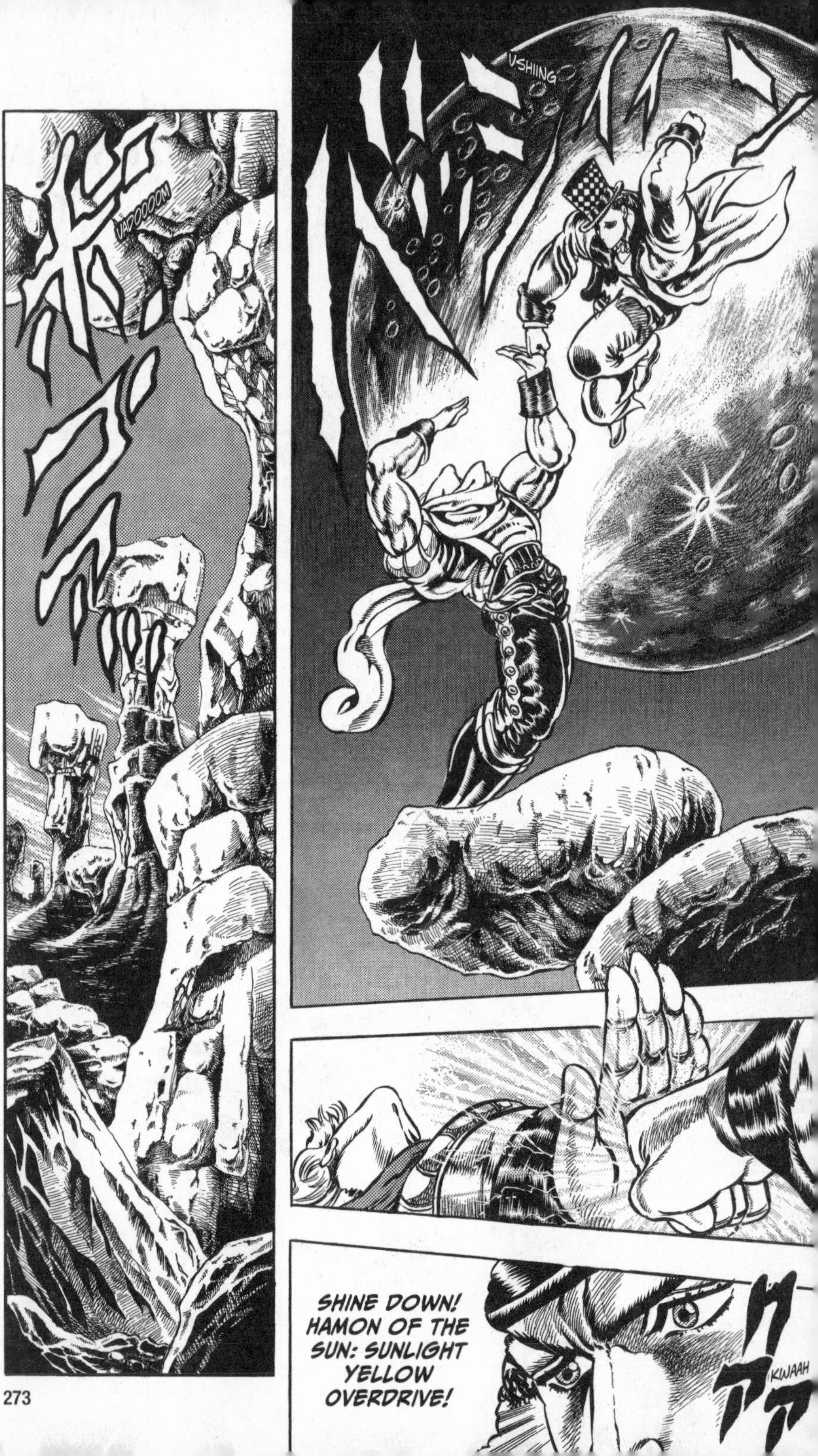

VSHIING
SHINE DOWN! HAMON OF THE SUN: SUNLIGHT YELLOW OVERDRIVE!
KWAAH
VAPOOOOM

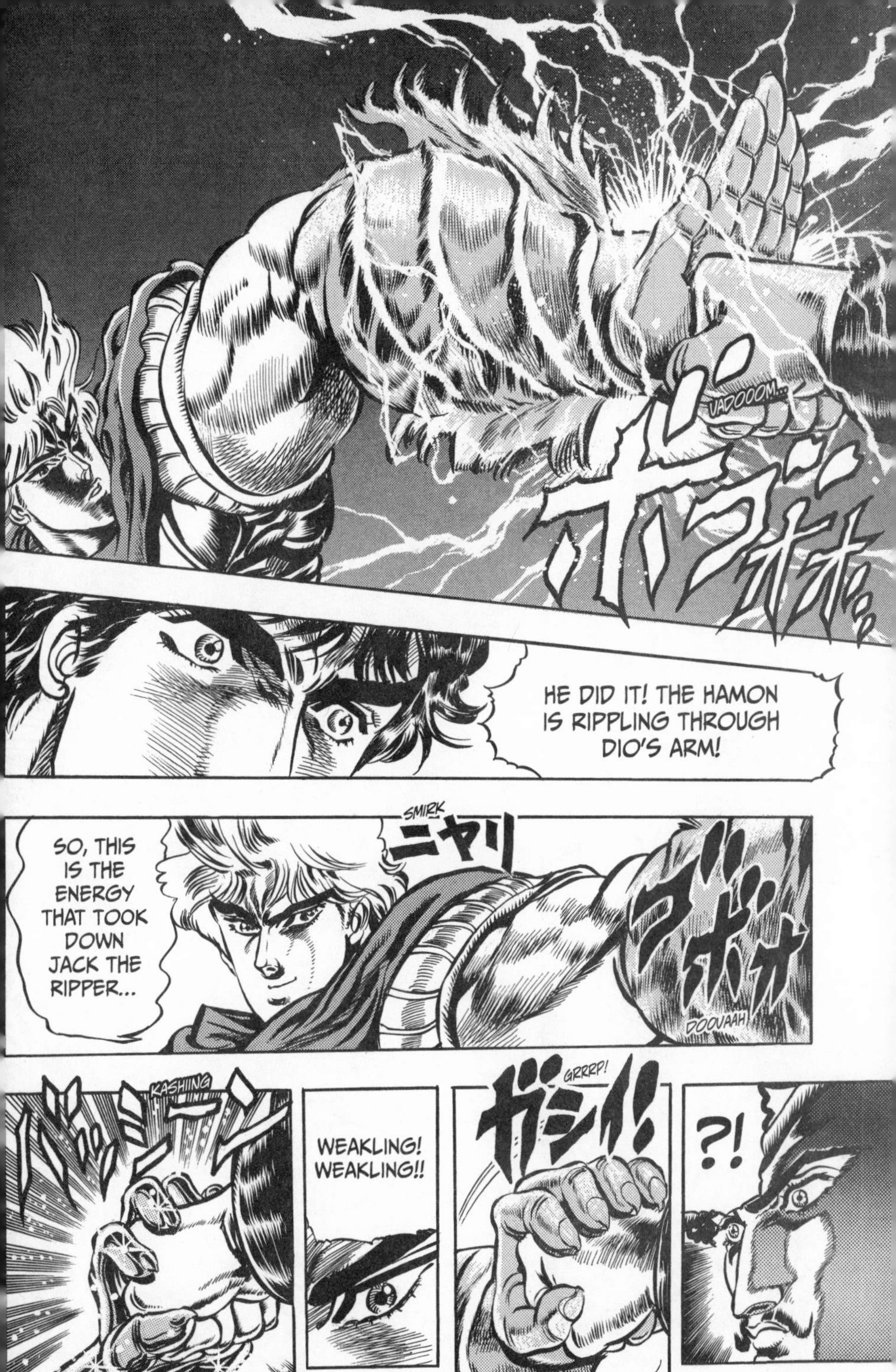
VADOOOM...
HE DID IT! THE HAMON IS RIPPLING THROUGH DIO'S ARM!
DOOUAAH
SMIRK
ニヤリ
SO, THIS IS THE ENERGY THAT TOOK DOWN JACK THE RIPPER...
?!
GRRRP!
ガシィ!
WEAKLING! WEAKLING!!
KASHIING

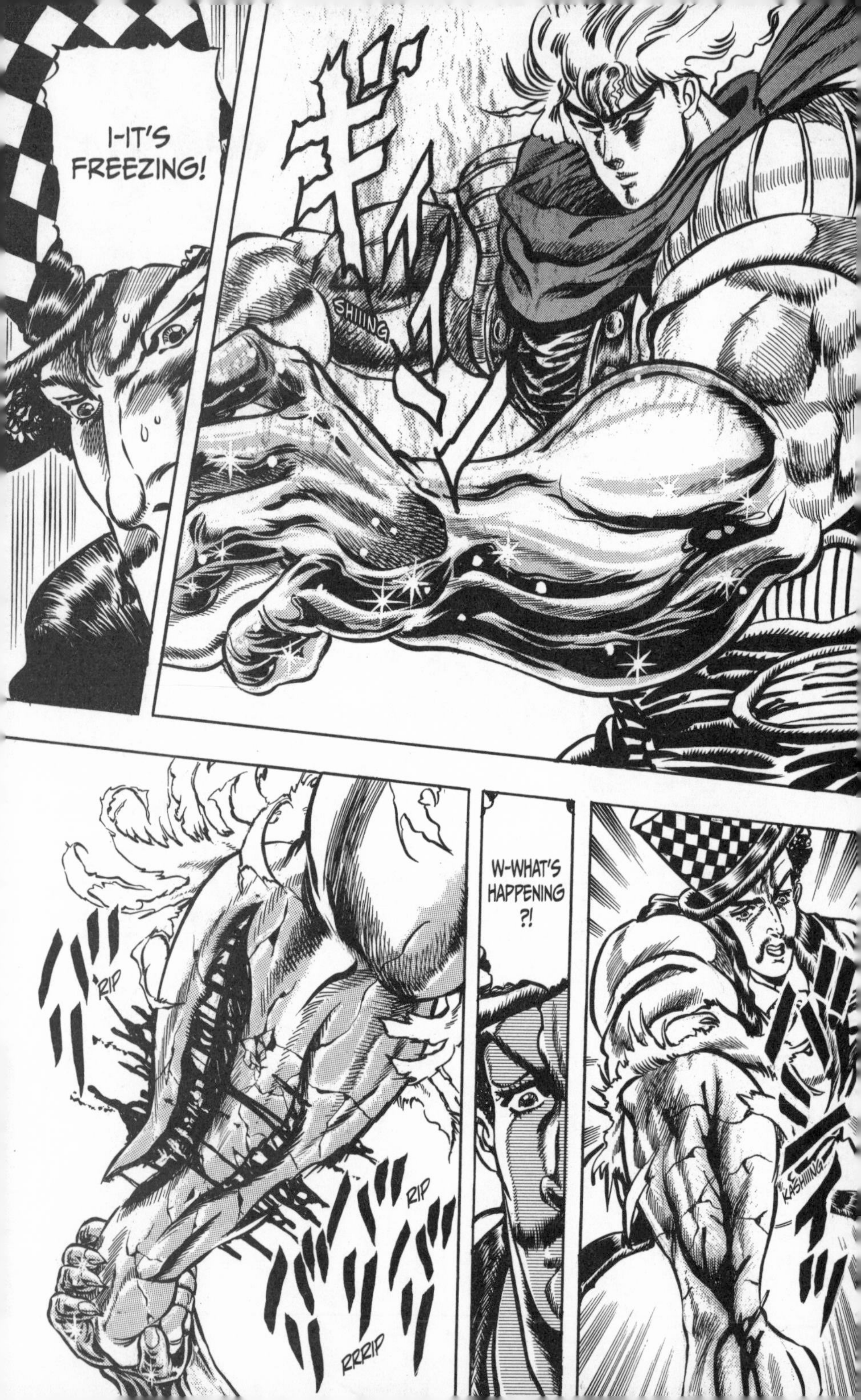
SHIIING
I-IT'S FREEZING!
KASHIING
W-WHAT'S HAPPENING ?!
RIP
RIP
RRRIP

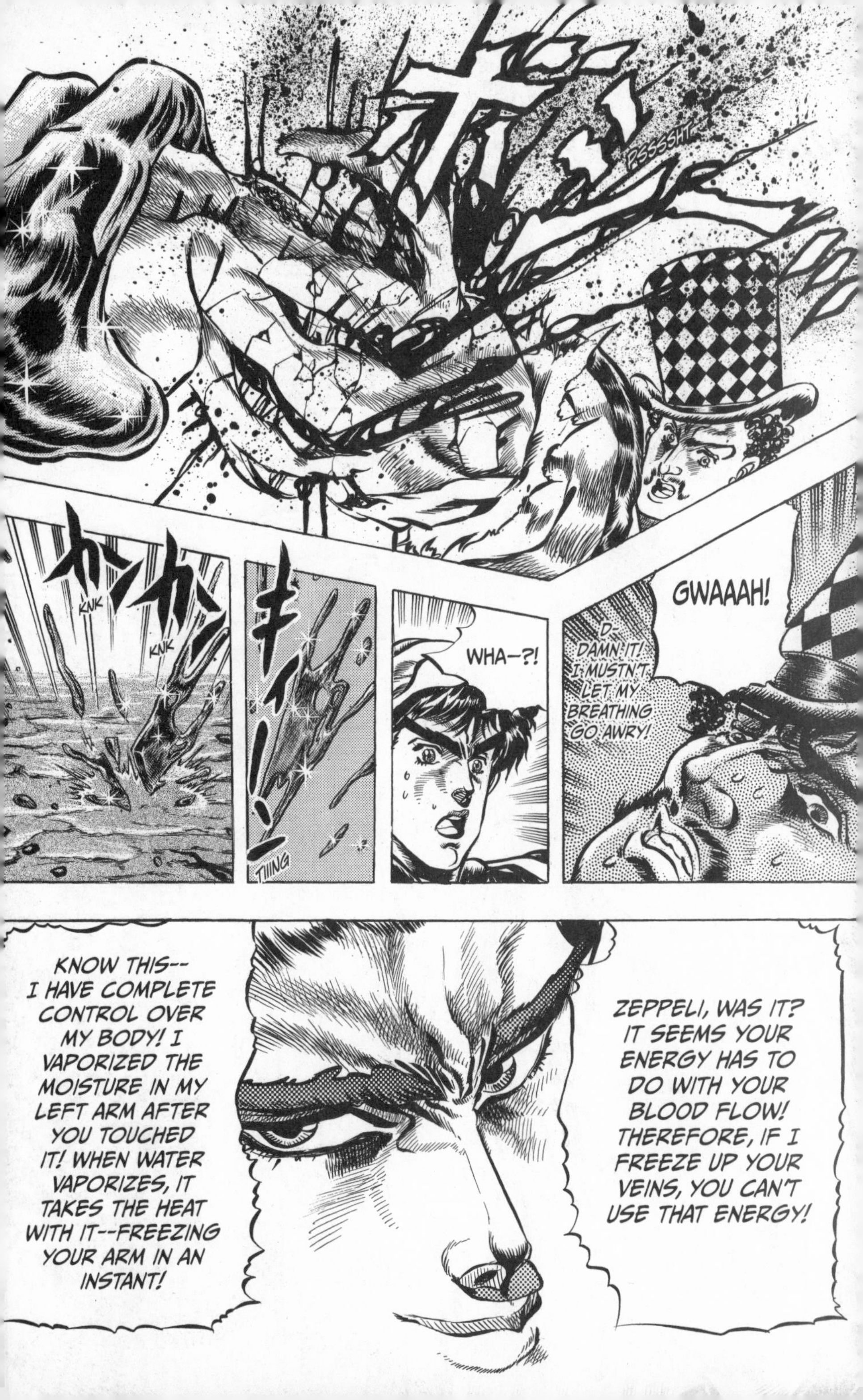
PSSSSHT
GWAAAH!
D-DAMN IT! I MUSTN'T LET MY BREATHING GO AWRY!
WHA-?!
TIIING
KNK
KNK
ZEPPELI, WAS IT? IT SEEMS YOUR ENERGY HAS TO DO WITH YOUR BLOOD FLOW! THEREFORE, IF I FREEZE UP YOUR VEINS, YOU CAN'T USE THAT ENERGY!
KNOW THIS-- I HAVE COMPLETE CONTROL OVER MY BODY! I VAPORIZED THE MOISTURE IN MY LEFT ARM AFTER YOU TOUCHED IT! WHEN WATER VAPORIZES, IT TAKES THE HEAT WITH IT--FREEZING YOUR ARM IN AN INSTANT!

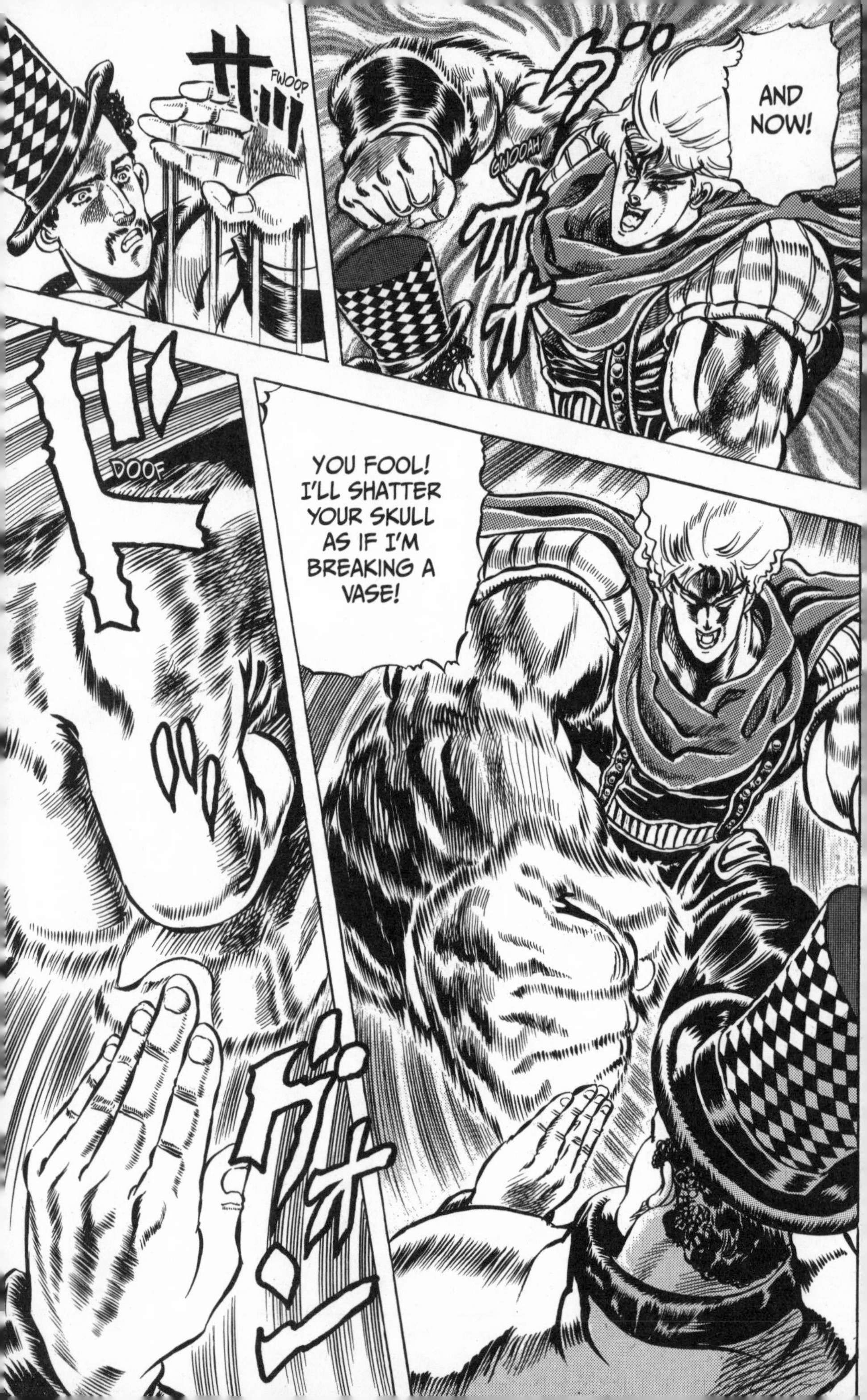
AND NOW!
GWOOAH
FWOOP
YOU FOOL! I'LL SHATTER YOUR SKULL AS IF I'M BREAKING A VASE!
DOOF

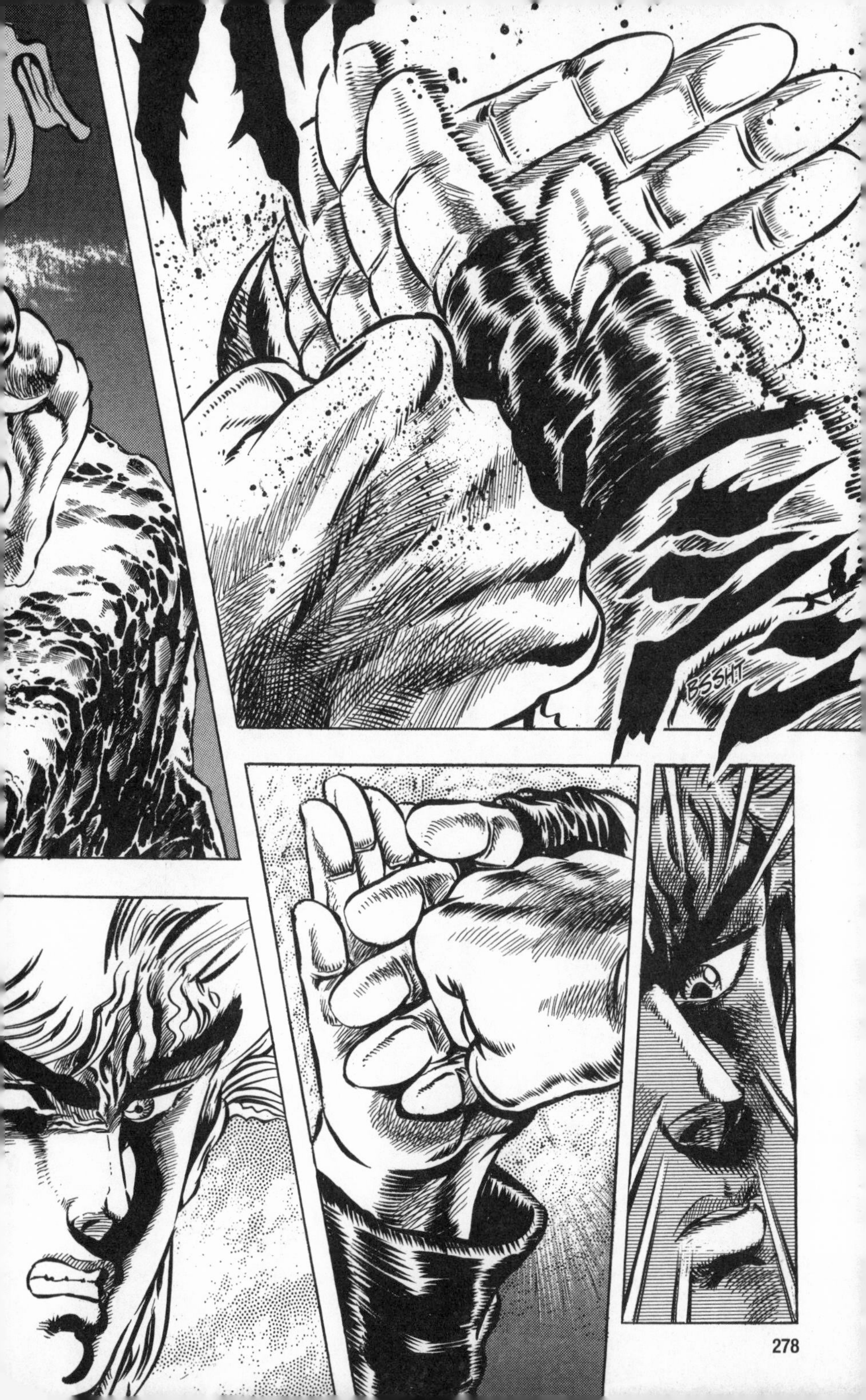
BSSHT

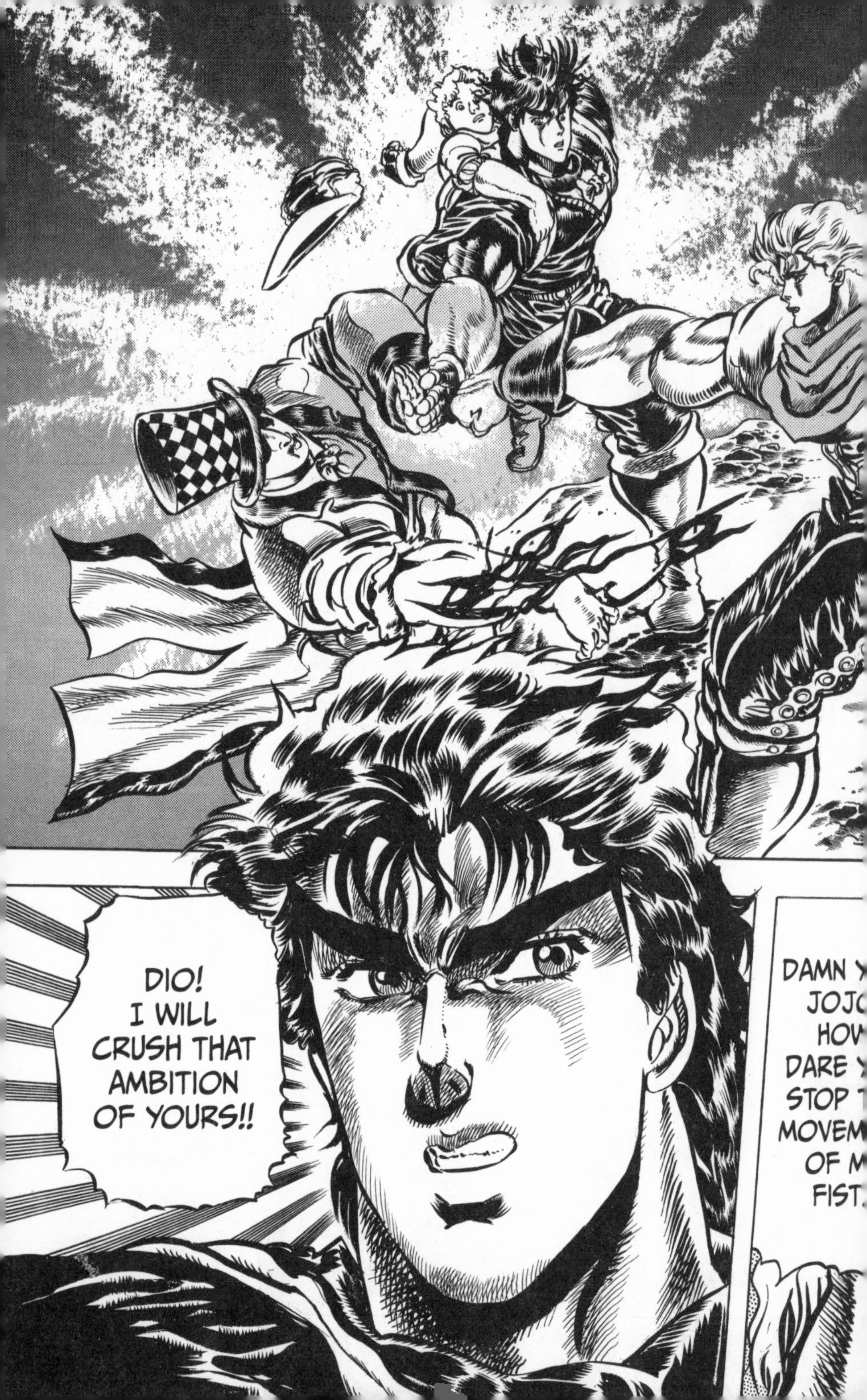
DAMN Y JOJC HOW DARE Y STOP T MOVEM OF M FIST.
DIO! I WILL CRUSH THAT AMBITION OF YOURS!!

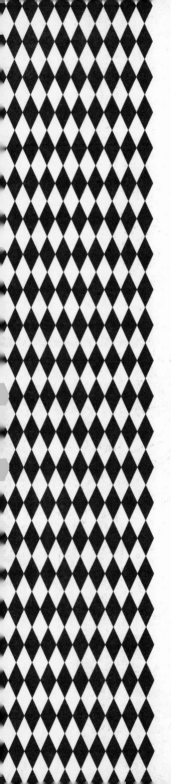

JoJo's
BIZARRE ADVENTURE

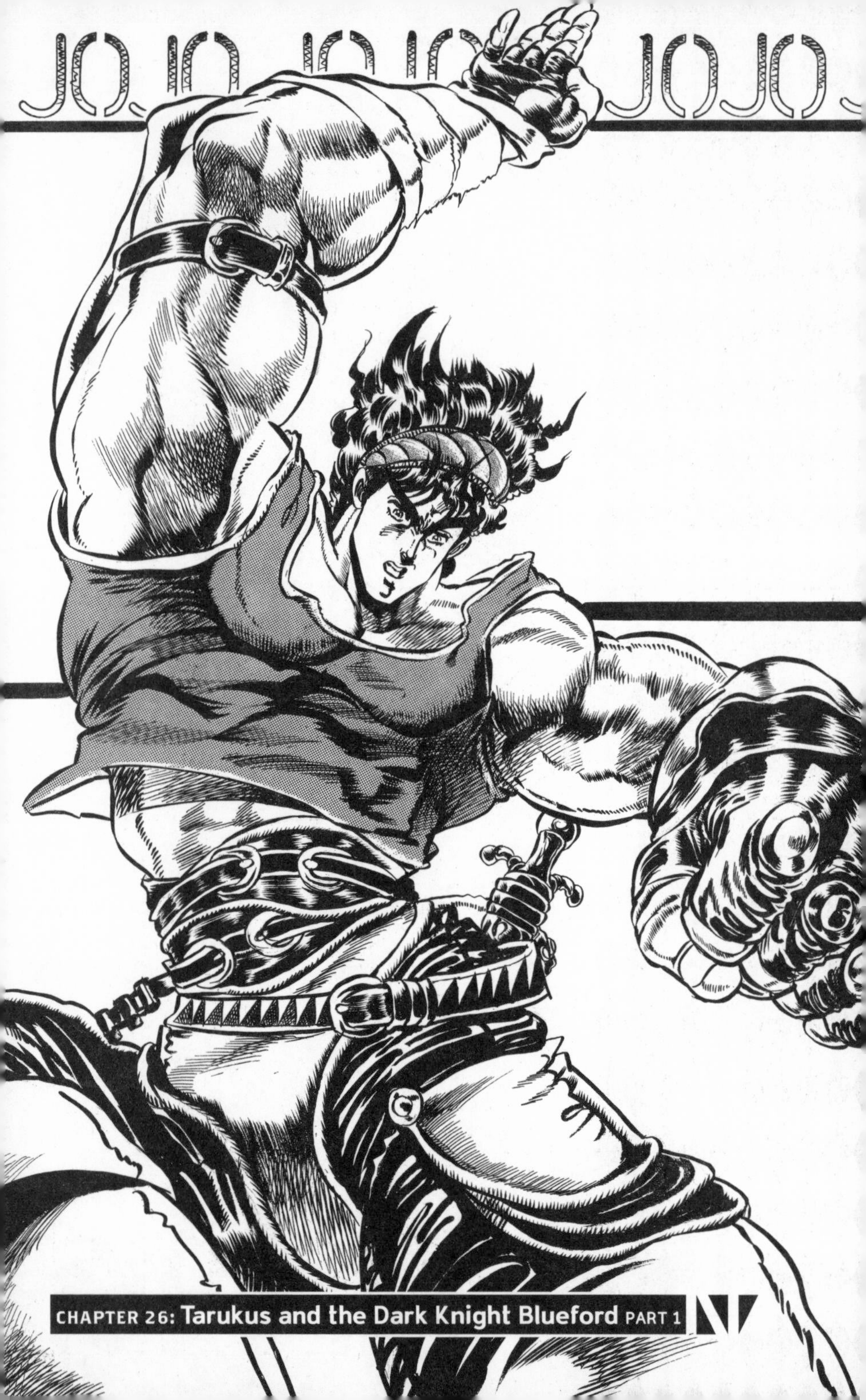
JOJO JOJO JOJO

CHAPTER 26: Tarukus and the Dark Knight Blueford PART 1

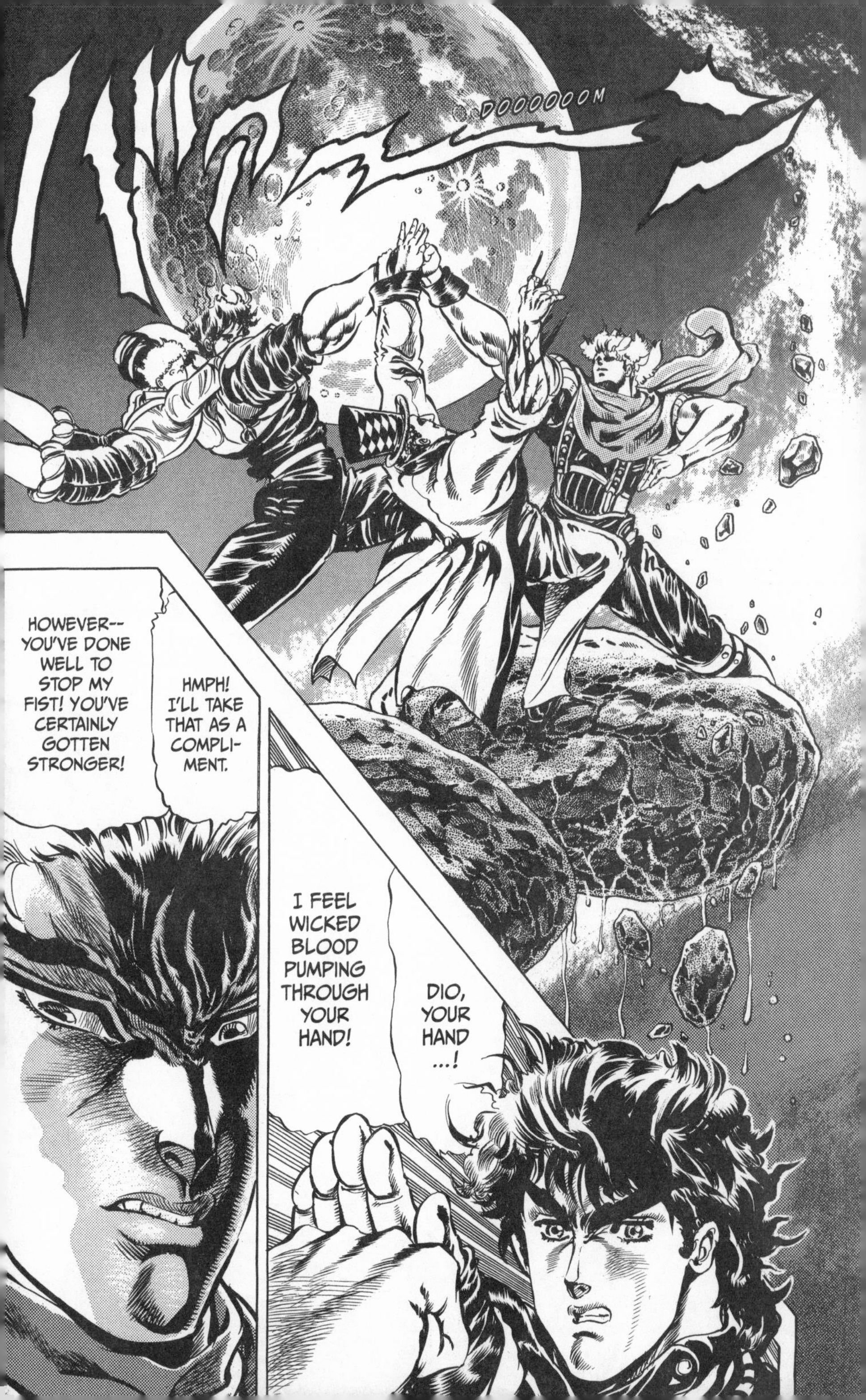
DOOOOOOOM
DIO, YOUR HAND ...!
I FEEL WICKED BLOOD PUMPING THROUGH YOUR HAND!
HMPH! I'LL TAKE THAT AS A COMPLI- MENT.
HOWEVER-- YOU'VE DONE WELL TO STOP MY FIST! YOU'VE CERTAINLY GOTTEN STRONGER!

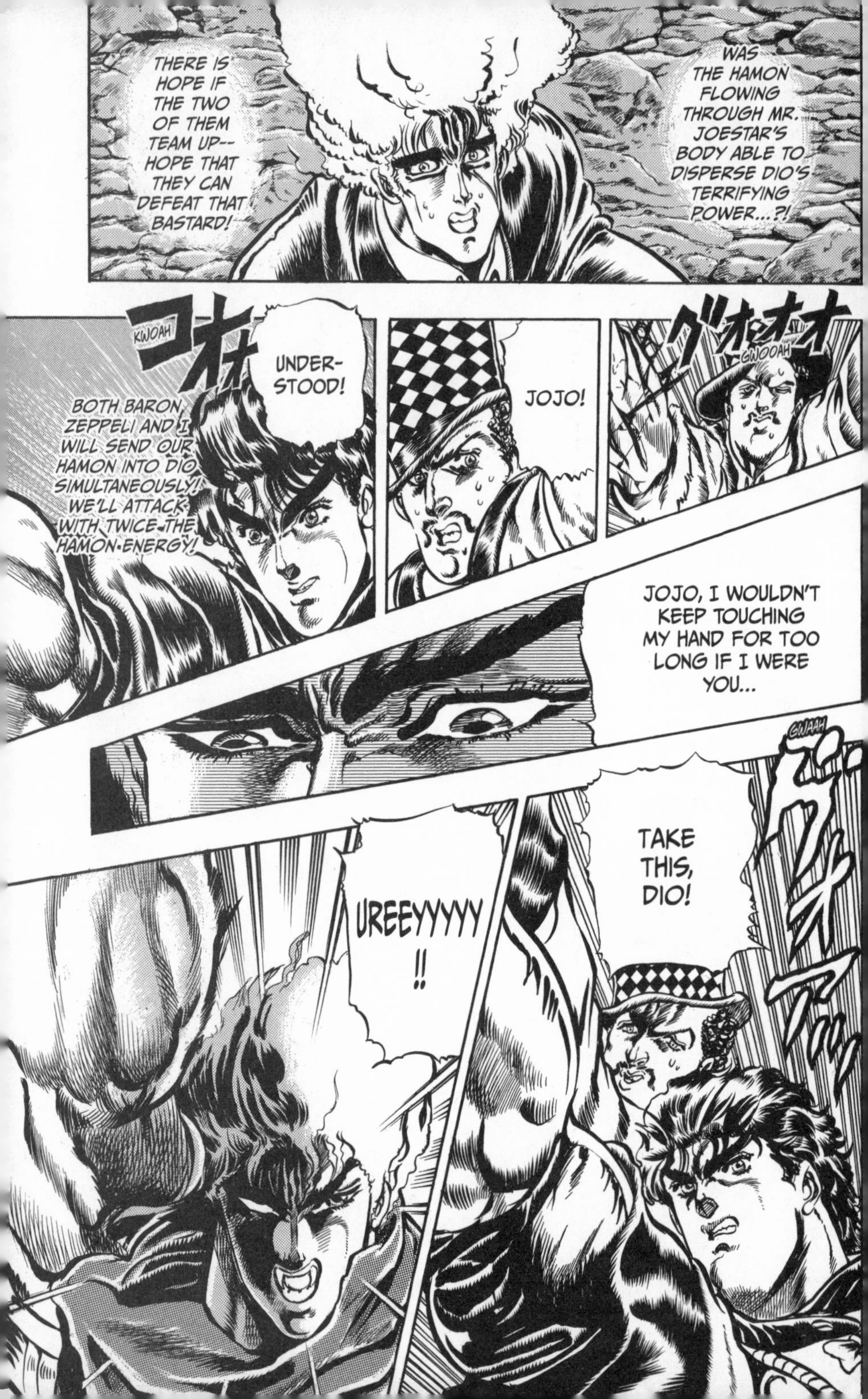
WAS THE HAMON FLOWING THROUGH MR. JOESTAR'S BODY ABLE TO DISPERSE DIO'S TERRIFYING POWER...?!
THERE IS HOPE IF THE TWO OF THEM TEAM UP-- HOPE THAT THEY CAN DEFEAT THAT BASTARD!
GWOOAH
JOJO!
UNDER-STOOD!
KWOAH
BOTH BARON ZEPPELI AND I WILL SEND OUR HAMON INTO DIO SIMULTANEOUSLY! WE'LL ATTACK WITH TWICE THE HAMON ENERGY!
JOJO, I WOULDN'T KEEP TOUCHING MY HAND FOR TOO LONG IF I WERE YOU...
GWAAH
TAKE THIS, DIO!
UREEYYYYY !!

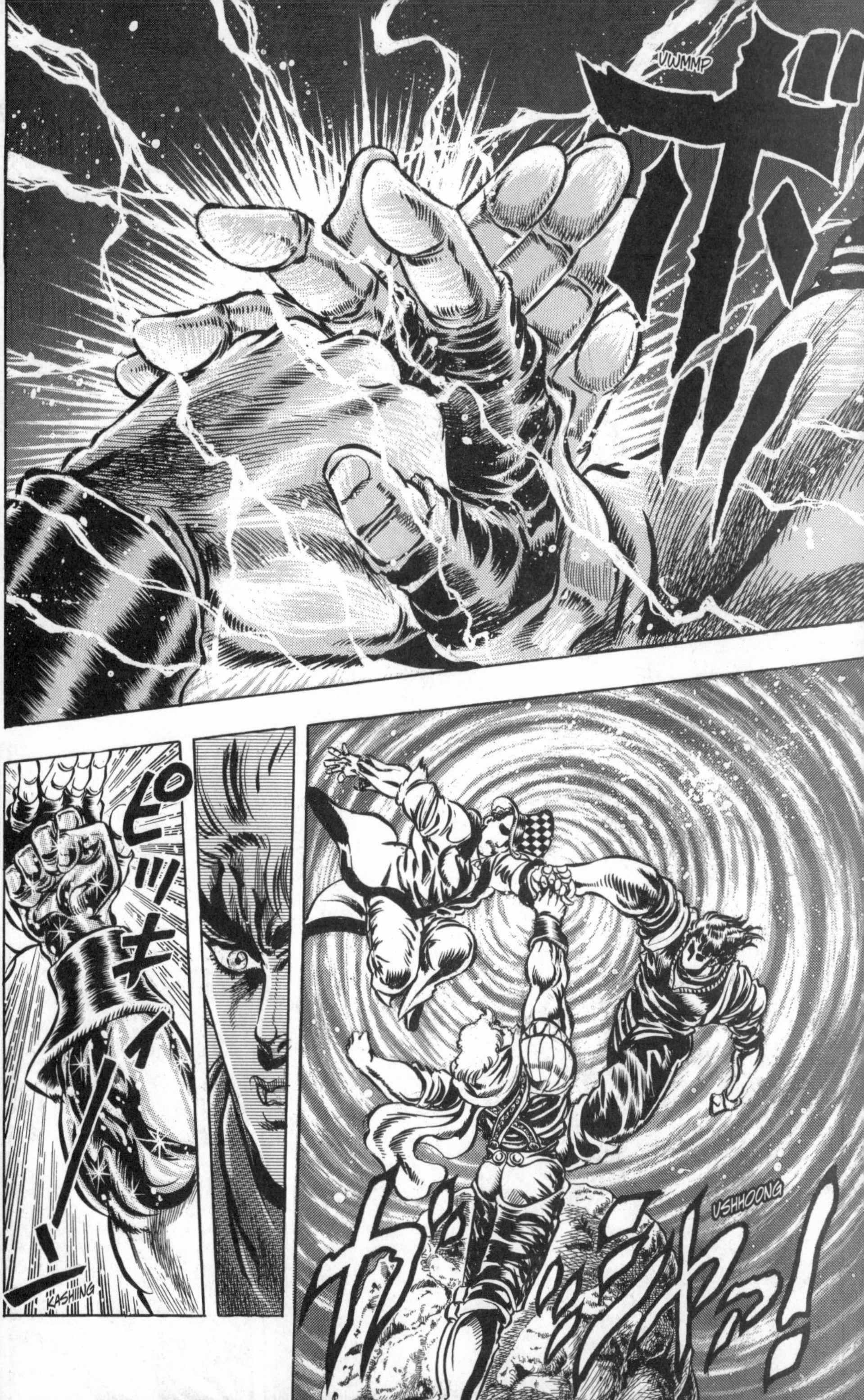
VWMMP
USHHOONG
KASHIING

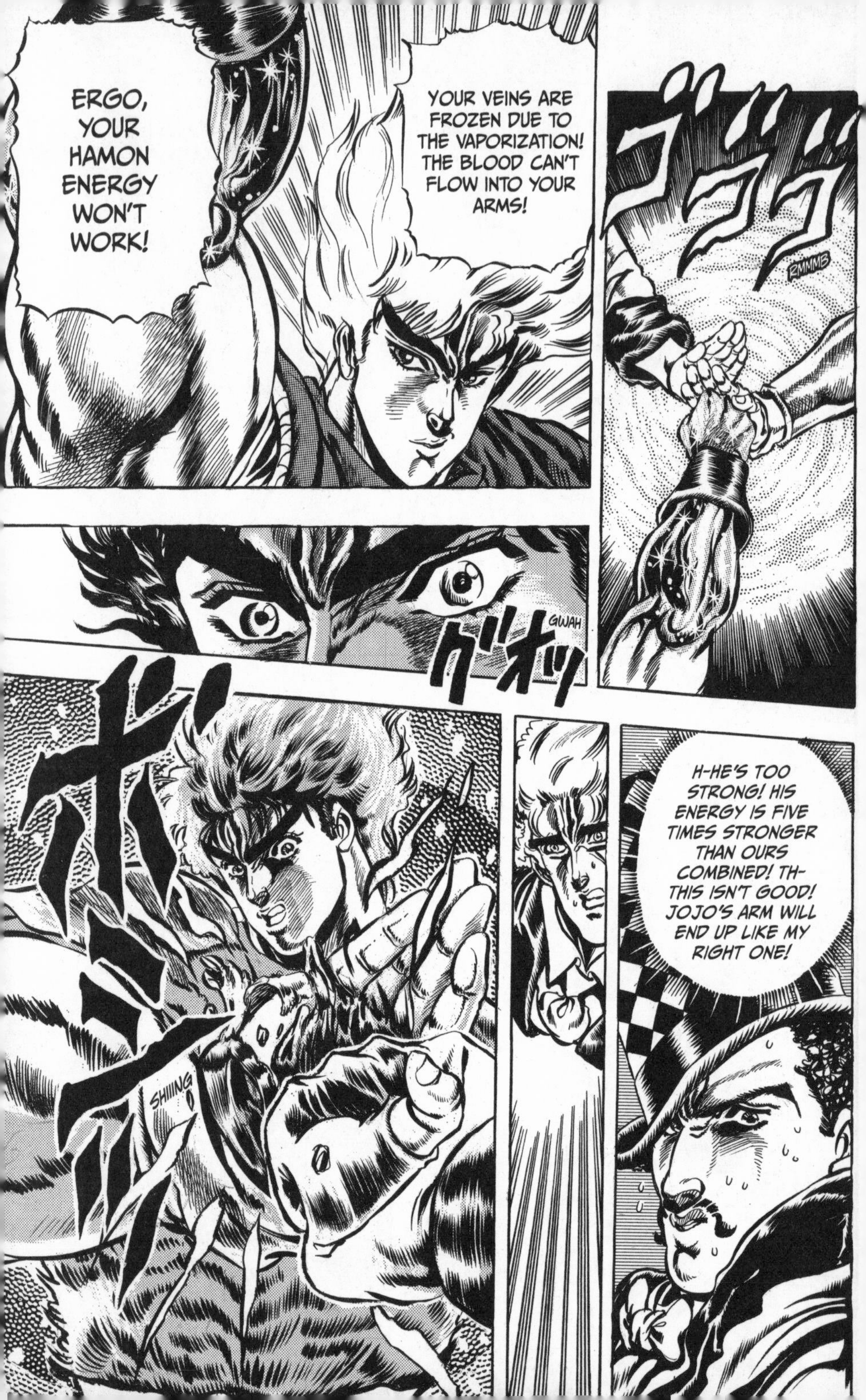
RMMMB
YOUR VEINS ARE FROZEN DUE TO THE VAPORIZATION! THE BLOOD CAN'T FLOW INTO YOUR ARMS!
ERGO, YOUR HAMON ENERGY WON'T WORK!
GWAH
H-HE'S TOO STRONG! HIS ENERGY IS FIVE TIMES STRONGER THAN OURS COMBINED! TH-THIS ISN'T GOOD! JOJO'S ARM WILL END UP LIKE MY RIGHT ONE!
SHIING

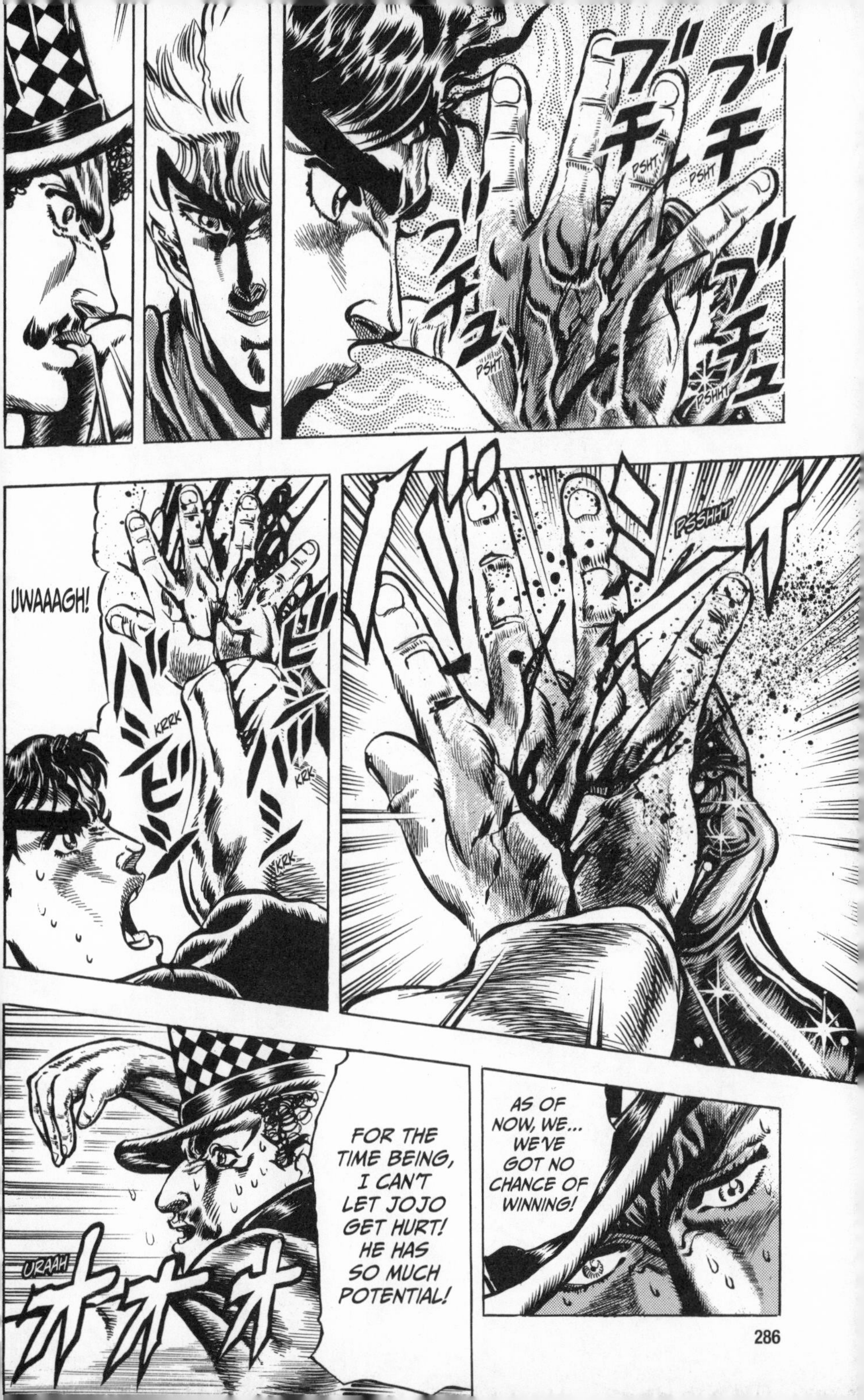
PSHT
PSHT
PSHT
PSHHT
PSSHHT
UWAAAGH!
KRRK
KRK
KRK
AS OF NOW, WE... WE'VE GOT NO CHANCE OF WINNING!
FOR THE TIME BEING, I CAN'T LET JOJO GET HURT! HE HAS SO MUCH POTENTIAL!
URAAH

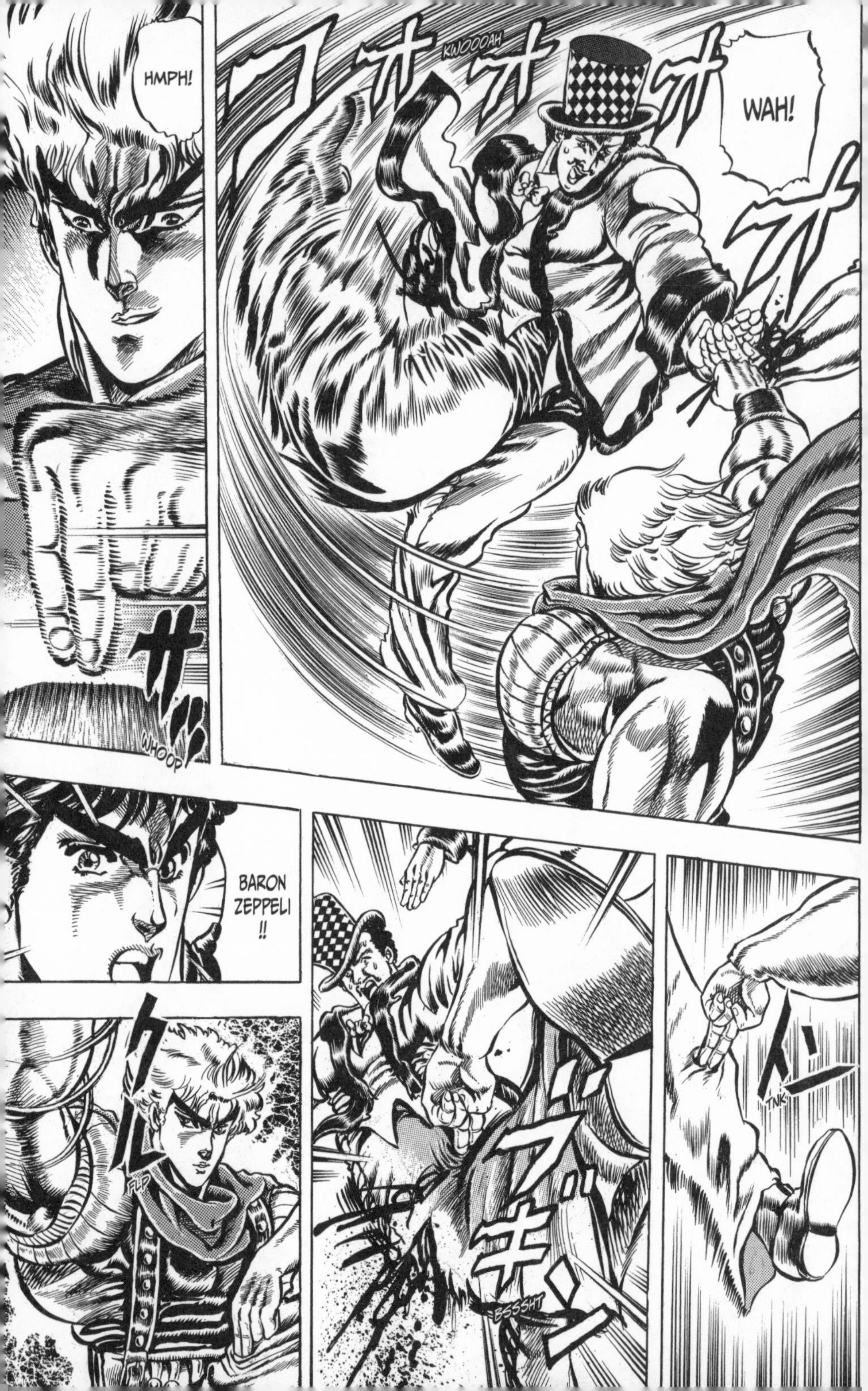
WAH!
KWOOOAH
HMPH!
WHOOP
TNK
BSSSHT
BARON ZEPPELI !!
FLP

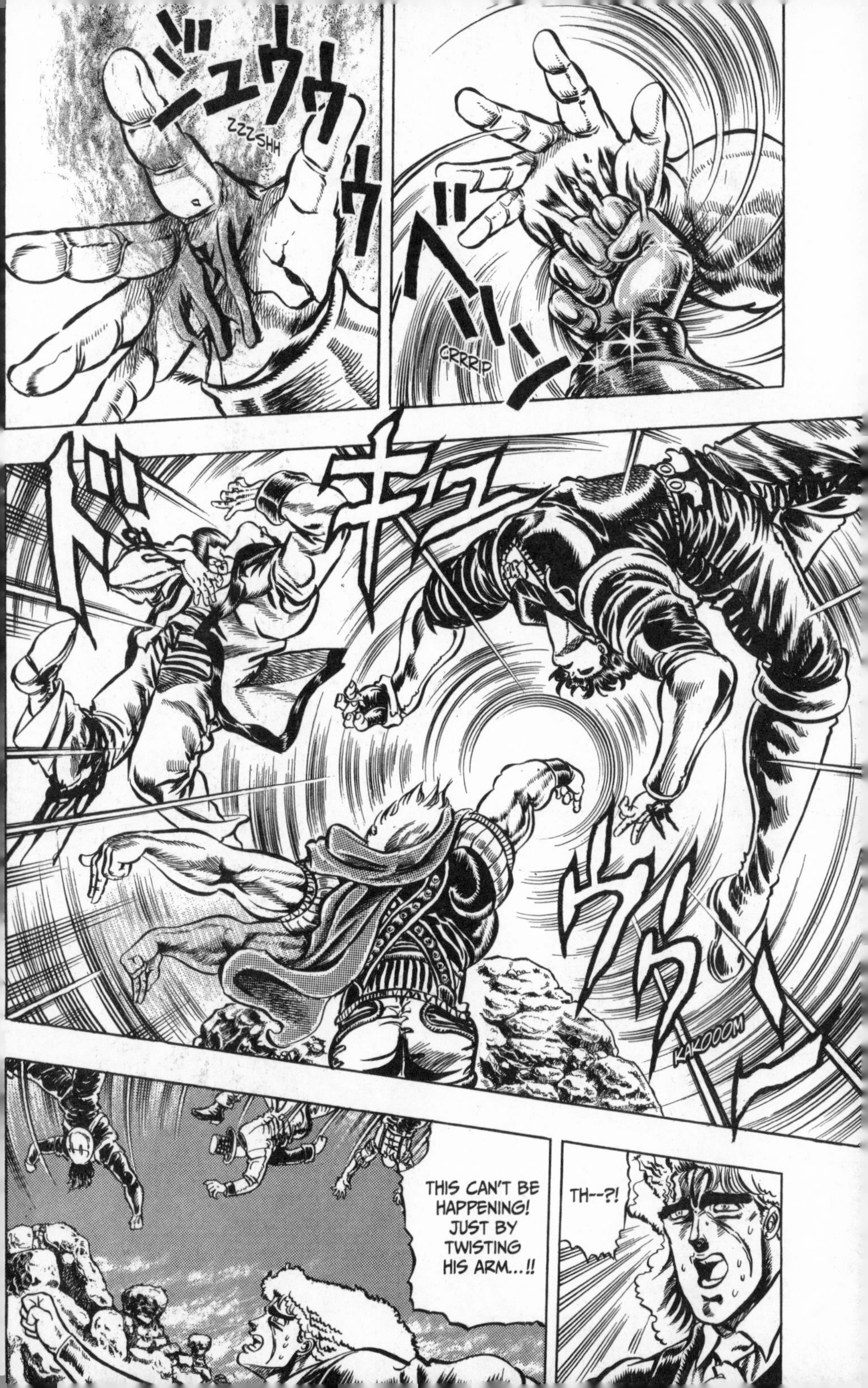
CRRRIP
ジュウウウ
ZZZSHH
KAKOOOM
TH--?!
THIS CAN'T BE HAPPENING! JUST BY TWISTING HIS ARM...!!

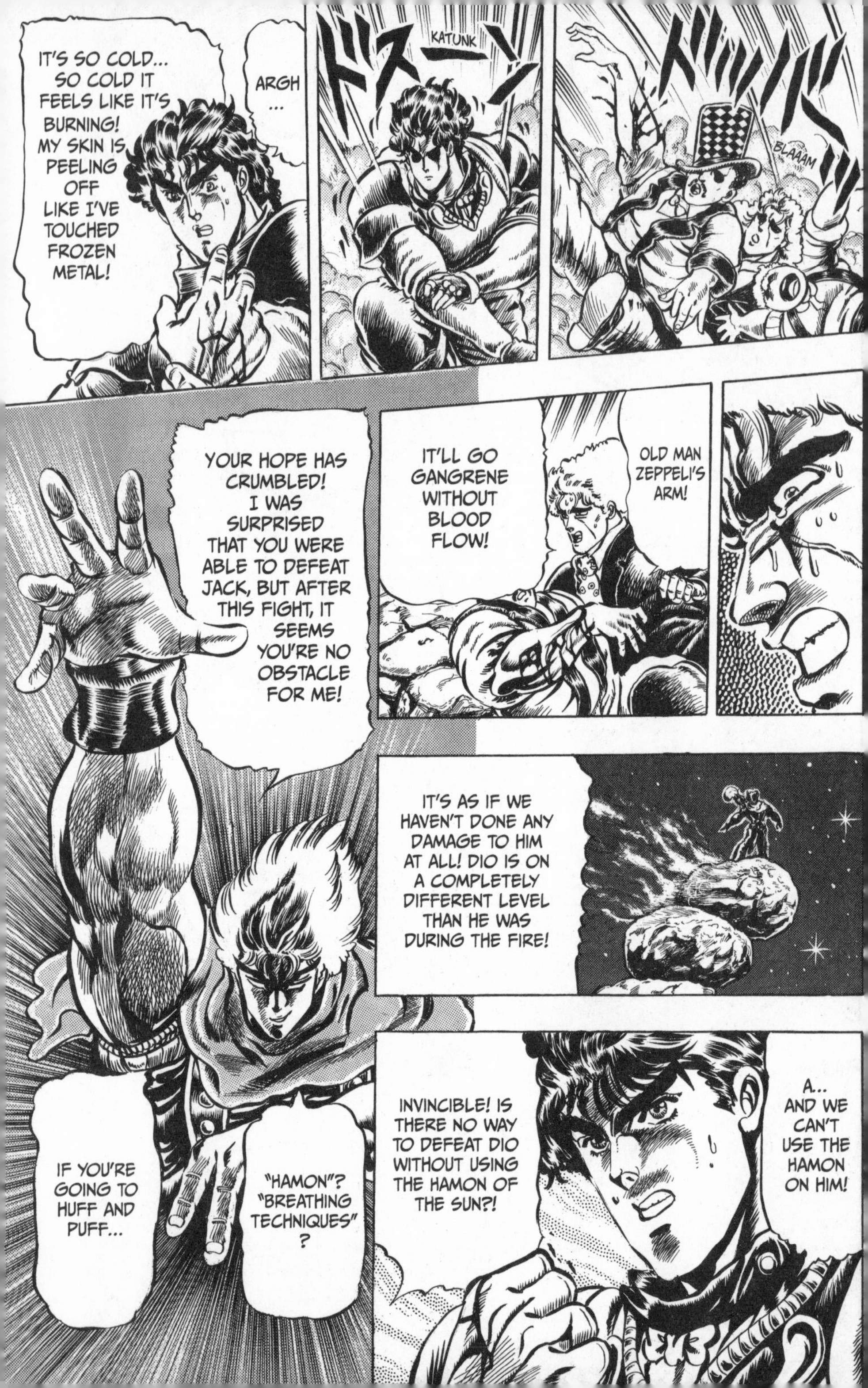
BLAAAM
KATUNK
ドスーン
ARGH ...
IT'S SO COLD... SO COLD IT FEELS LIKE IT'S BURNING! MY SKIN IS PEELING OFF LIKE I'VE TOUCHED FROZEN METAL!
OLD MAN ZEPPELI'S ARM!
IT'LL GO GANGRENE WITHOUT BLOOD FLOW!
IT'S AS IF WE HAVEN'T DONE ANY DAMAGE TO HIM AT ALL! DIO IS ON A COMPLETELY DIFFERENT LEVEL THAN HE WAS DURING THE FIRE!
A... AND WE CAN'T USE THE HAMON ON HIM!
INVINCIBLE! IS THERE NO WAY TO DEFEAT DIO WITHOUT USING THE HAMON OF THE SUN?!
YOUR HOPE HAS CRUMBLED! I WAS SURPRISED THAT YOU WERE ABLE TO DEFEAT JACK, BUT AFTER THIS FIGHT, IT SEEMS YOU'RE NO OBSTACLE FOR ME!
"HAMON"? "BREATHING TECHNIQUES"?
IF YOU'RE GOING TO HUFF AND PUFF...

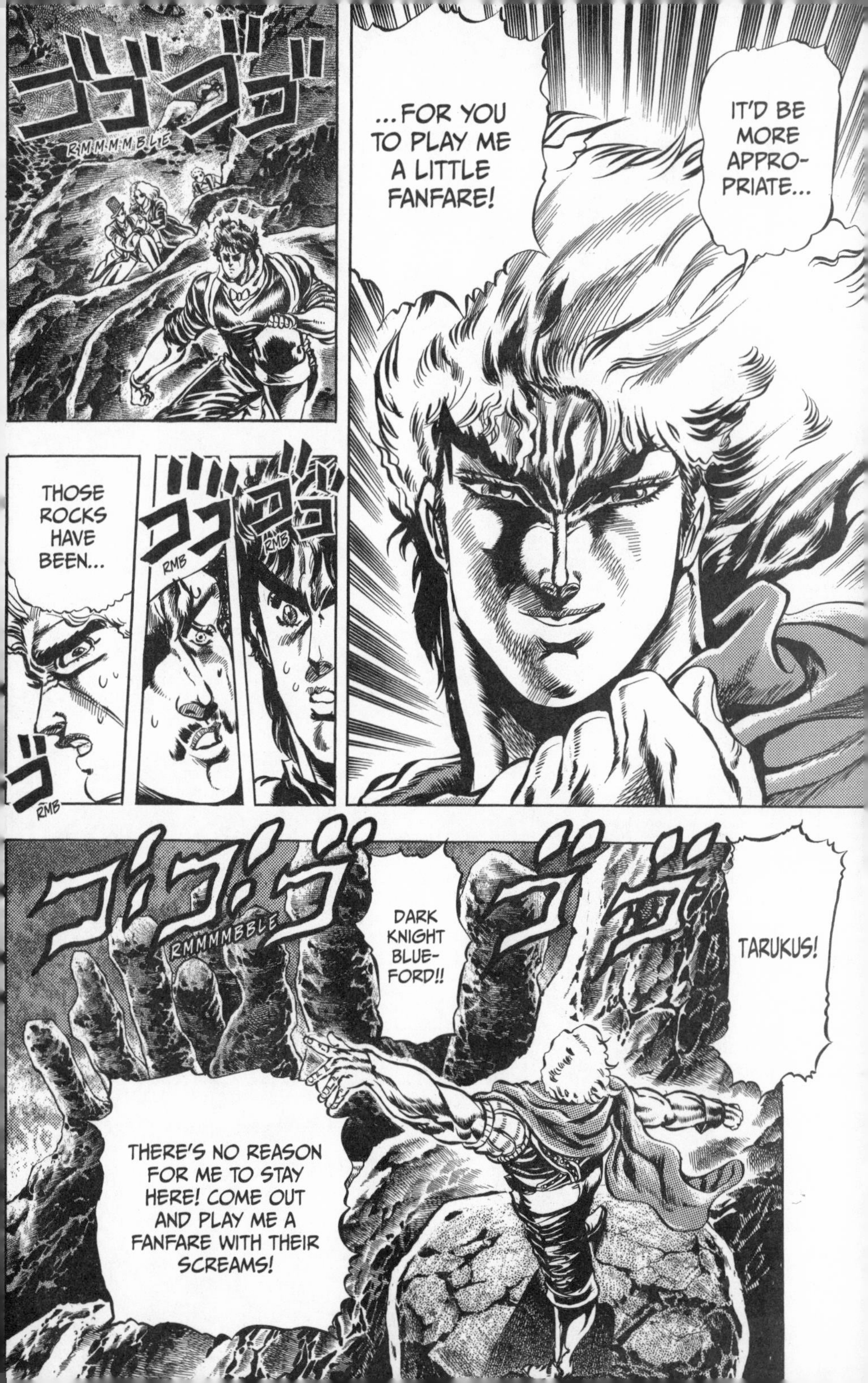
IT'D BE MORE APPROPRIATE...
...FOR YOU TO PLAY ME A LITTLE FANFARE!
RMMMMBLE
RMB
RMB
THOSE ROCKS HAVE BEEN...
RMB
TARUKUS!
DARK KNIGHT BLUEFORD!!
RMMMMBBLE
THERE'S NO REASON FOR ME TO STAY HERE! COME OUT AND PLAY ME A FANFARE WITH THEIR SCREAMS!

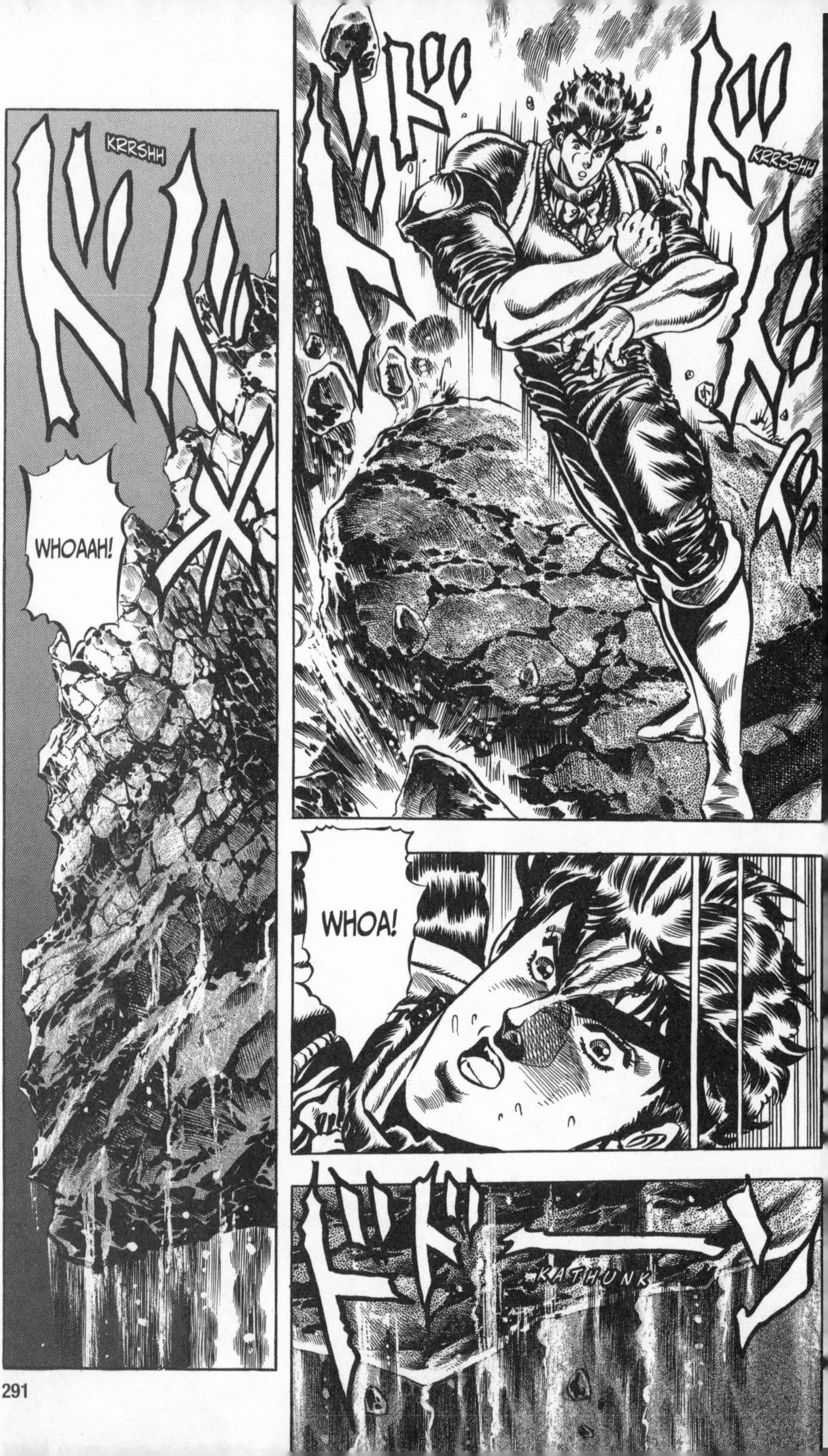
KRRSSHH
WHOA!
KATHUNK
KRRSHH
WHOAAH!

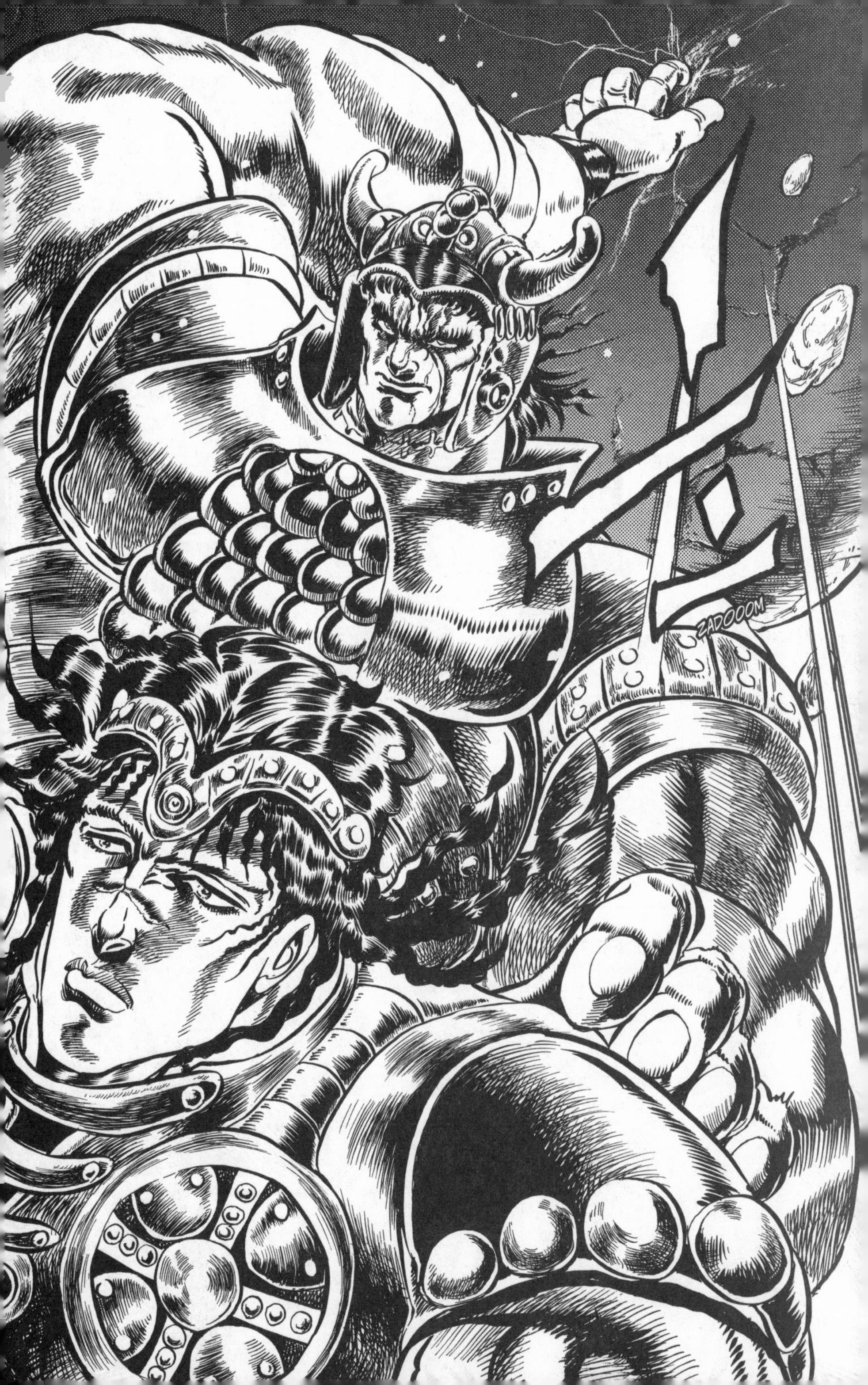
ZADOOOM

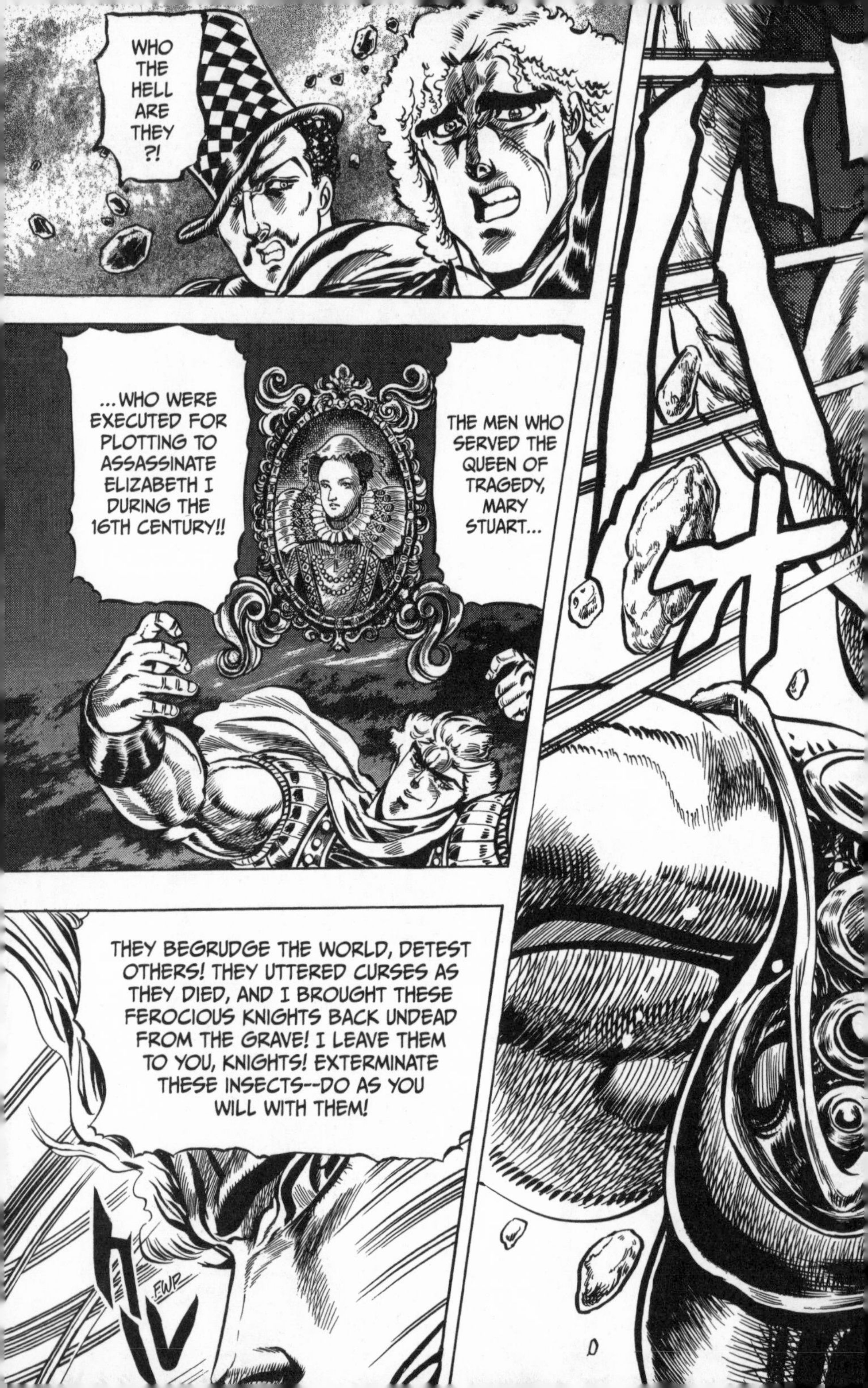
WHO THE HELL ARE THEY ?!
THE MEN WHO SERVED THE QUEEN OF TRAGEDY, MARY STUART...
...WHO WERE EXECUTED FOR PLOTTING TO ASSASSINATE ELIZABETH I DURING THE 16TH CENTURY!!
THEY BEGRUDGE THE WORLD, DETEST OTHERS! THEY UTTERED CURSES AS THEY DIED, AND I BROUGHT THESE FEROCIOUS KNIGHTS BACK UNDEAD FROM THE GRAVE! I LEAVE THEM TO YOU, KNIGHTS! EXTERMINATE THESE INSECTS--DO AS YOU WILL WITH THEM!
FWP

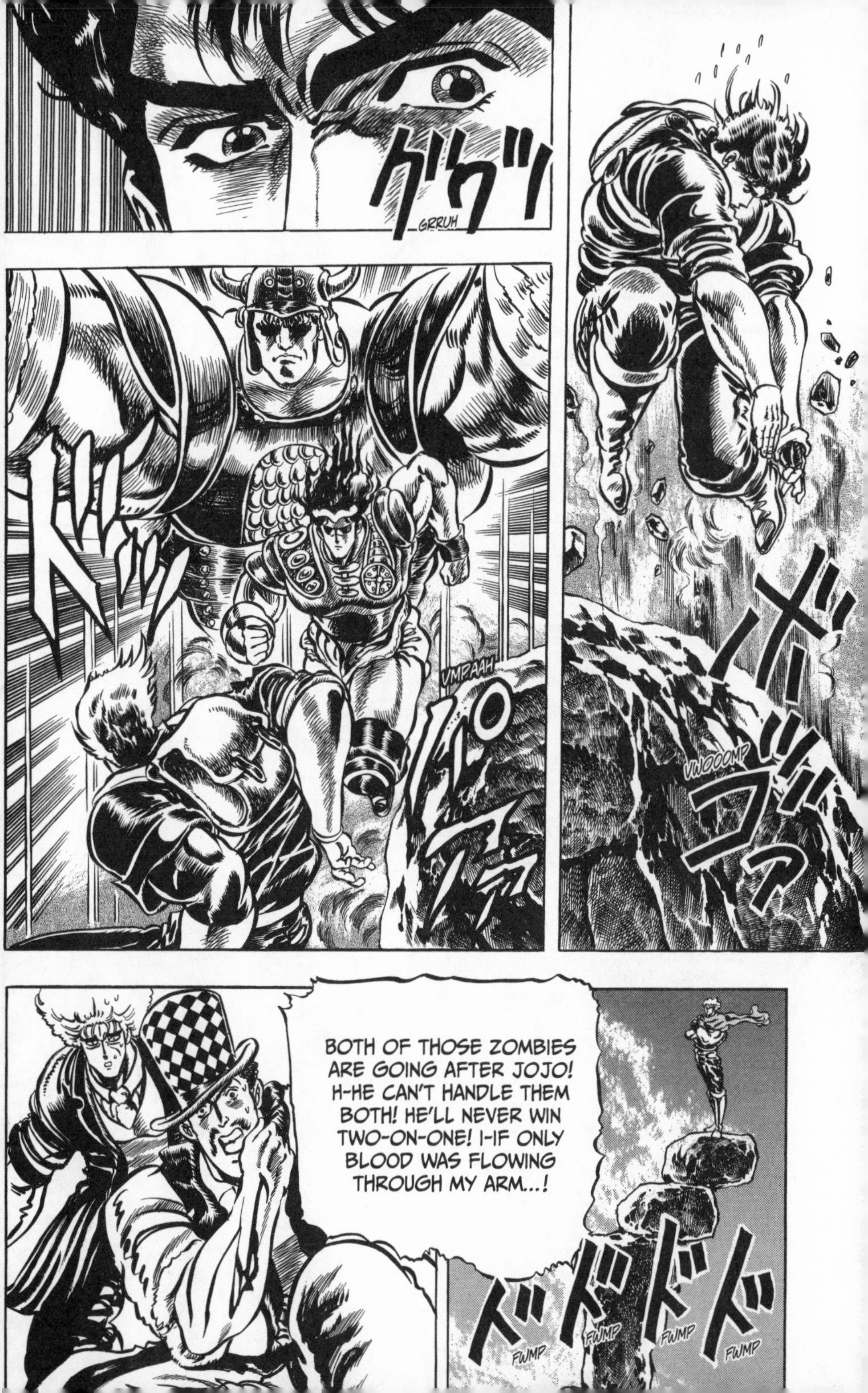
VWOOOMP
GRRUH
UMPAAH
BOTH OF THOSE ZOMBIES ARE GOING AFTER JOJO! H-HE CAN'T HANDLE THEM BOTH! HE'LL NEVER WIN TWO-ON-ONE! I-IF ONLY BLOOD WAS FLOWING THROUGH MY ARM...!
FWMP
FWMP
FWMP
FWMP

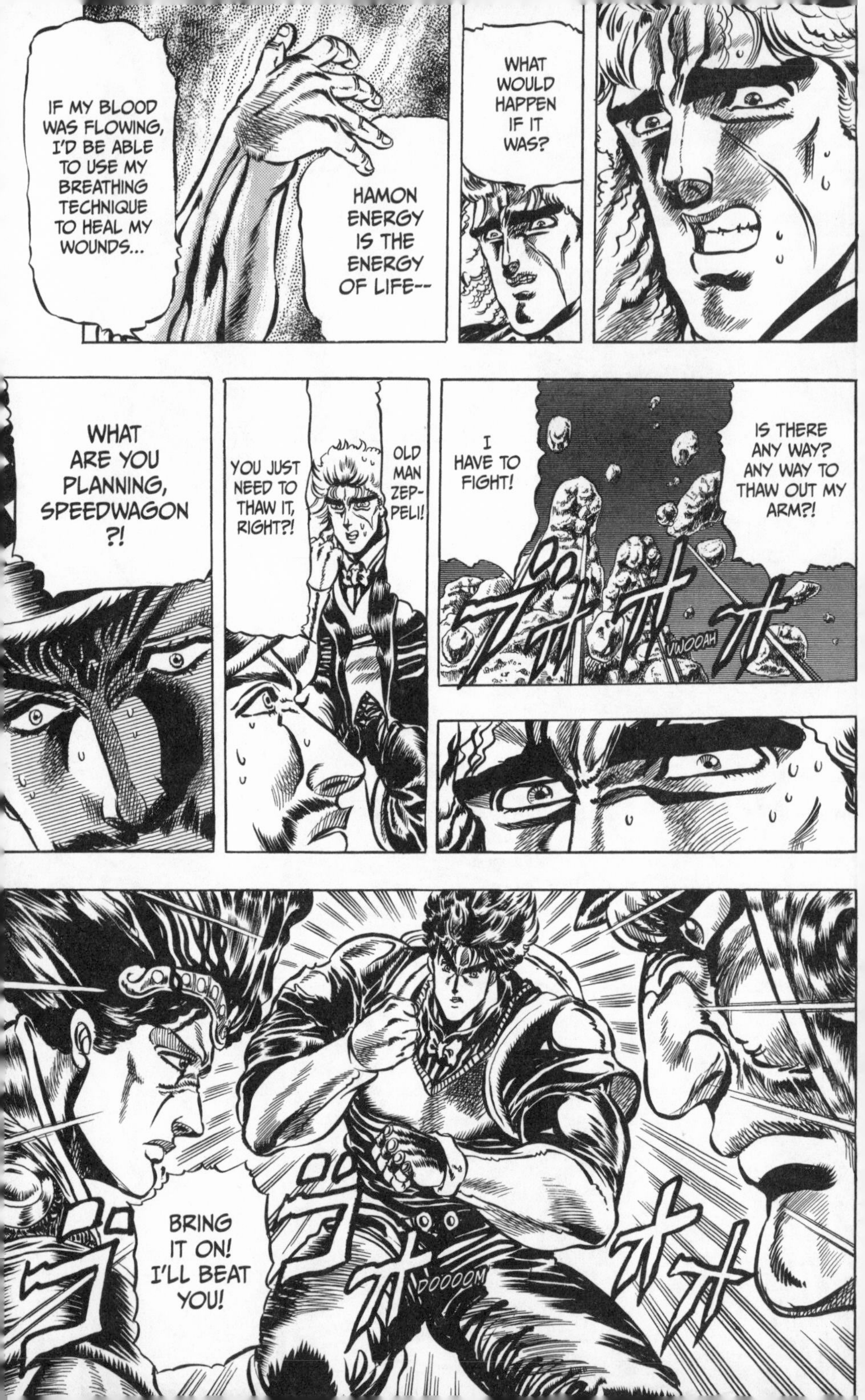
WHAT WOULD HAPPEN IF IT WAS?
HAMON ENERGY IS THE ENERGY OF LIFE--
IF MY BLOOD WAS FLOWING, I'D BE ABLE TO USE MY BREATHING TECHNIQUE TO HEAL MY WOUNDS...
IS THERE ANY WAY? ANY WAY TO THAW OUT MY ARM?!
I HAVE TO FIGHT!
VWOOAH
OLD MAN ZEP-PELI!
YOU JUST NEED TO THAW IT, RIGHT?!
WHAT ARE YOU PLANNING, SPEEDWAGON ?!
DOOOOM
BRING IT ON! I'LL BEAT YOU!

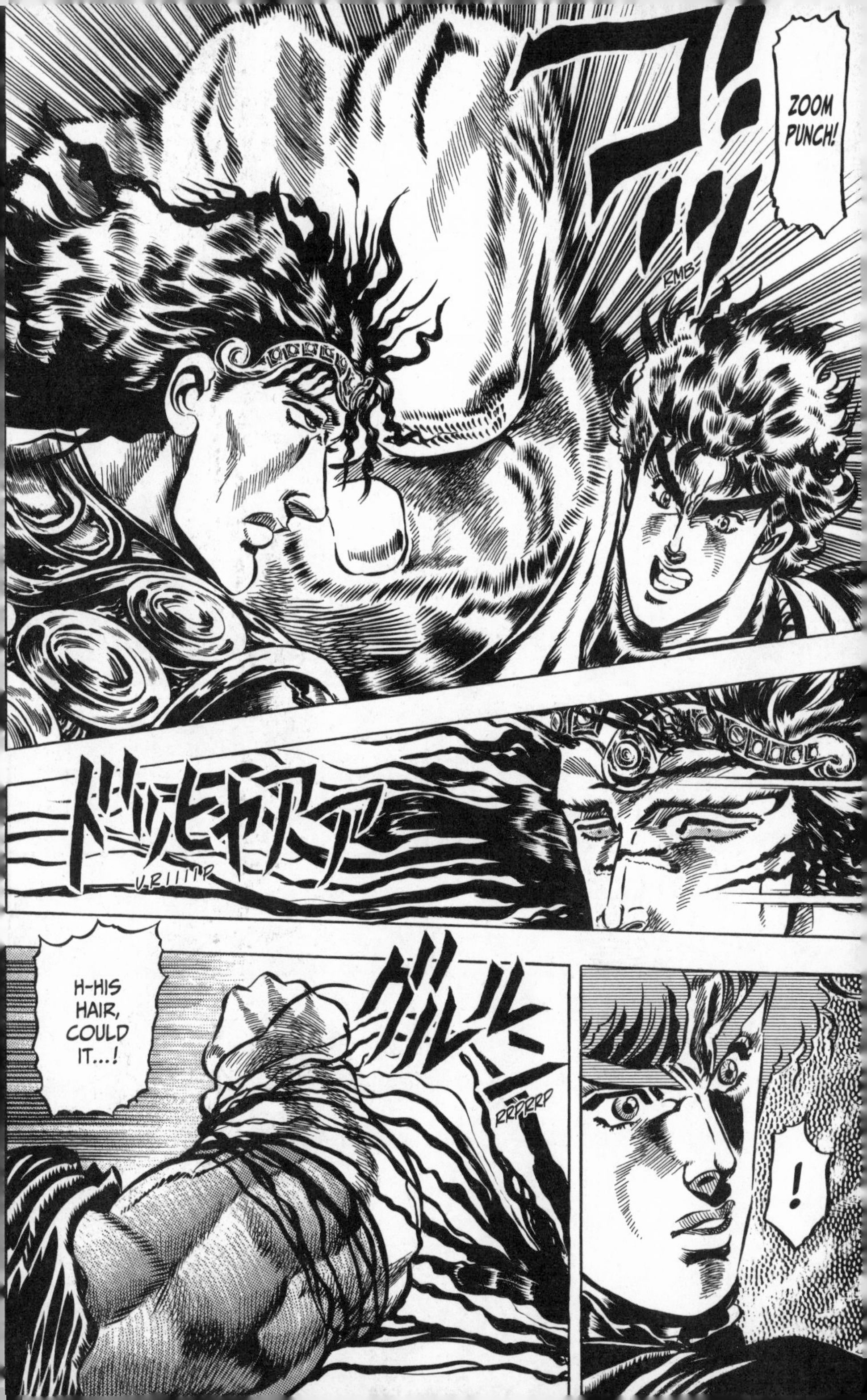
ZOOM PUNCH!
RMB
U.RIIIIP
!
H-HIS HAIR, COULD IT...!
RRPRRP

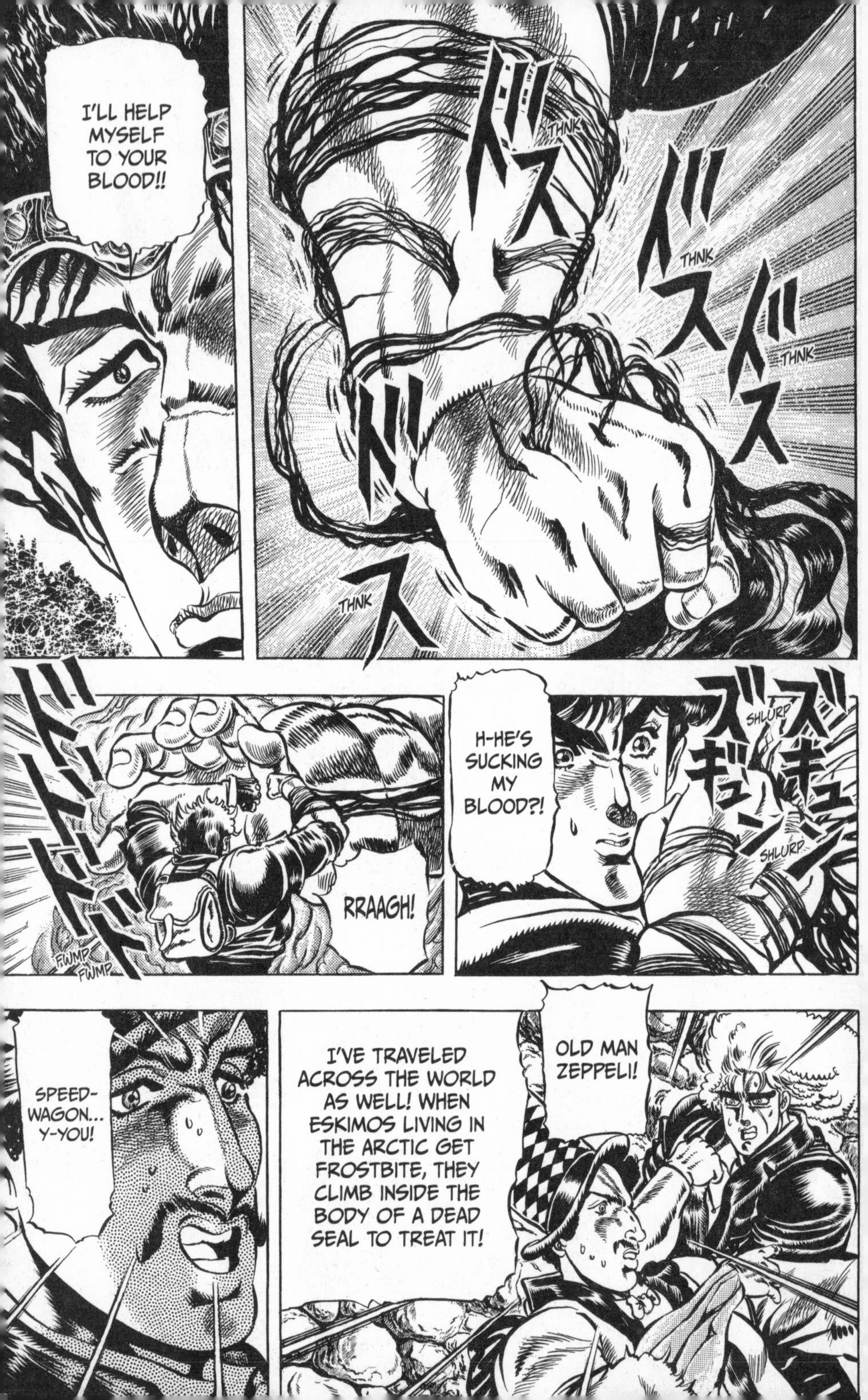

THNK
THNK
THNK
THNK
I'LL HELP MYSELF TO YOUR BLOOD!!
H-HE'S SUCKING MY BLOOD?!
SHLURP
SHLURP
RRAAGH!
FWMP FWMP
OLD MAN ZEPPELI!
I'VE TRAVELED ACROSS THE WORLD AS WELL! WHEN ESKIMOS LIVING IN THE ARCTIC GET FROSTBITE, THEY CLIMB INSIDE THE BODY OF A DEAD SEAL TO TREAT IT!
SPEED-WAGON... Y-YOU!

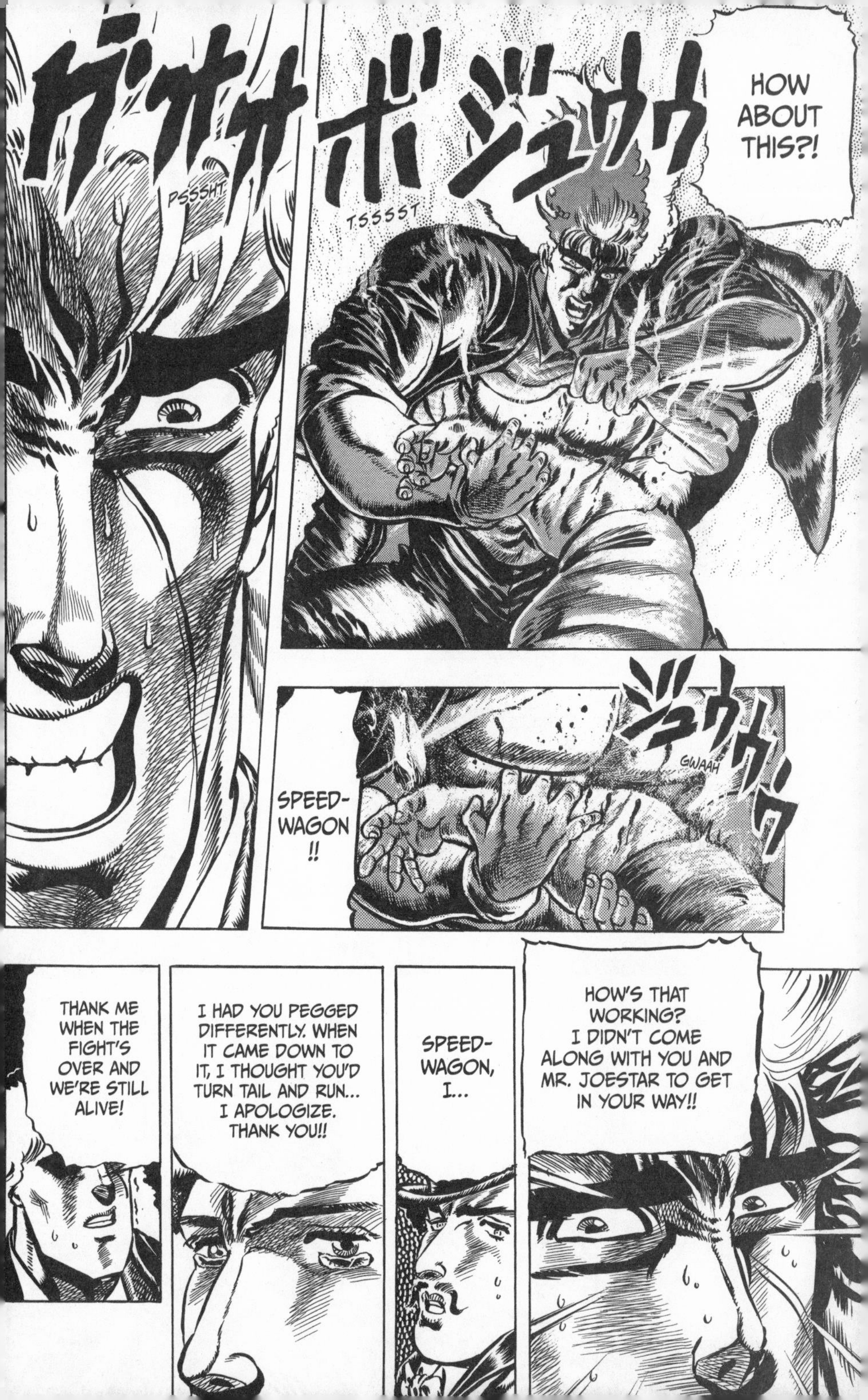
ボジュウウ
T.S.S.S.S.T
HOW ABOUT THIS?!
ジュウウウウ
GWAAH
SPEED-WAGON !!
PSSSHT
HOW'S THAT WORKING? I DIDN'T COME ALONG WITH YOU AND MR. JOESTAR TO GET IN YOUR WAY!!
SPEED-WAGON, I...
I HAD YOU PEGGED DIFFERENTLY. WHEN IT CAME DOWN TO IT, I THOUGHT YOU'D TURN TAIL AND RUN... I APOLOGIZE. THANK YOU!!
THANK ME WHEN THE FIGHT'S OVER AND WE'RE STILL ALIVE!

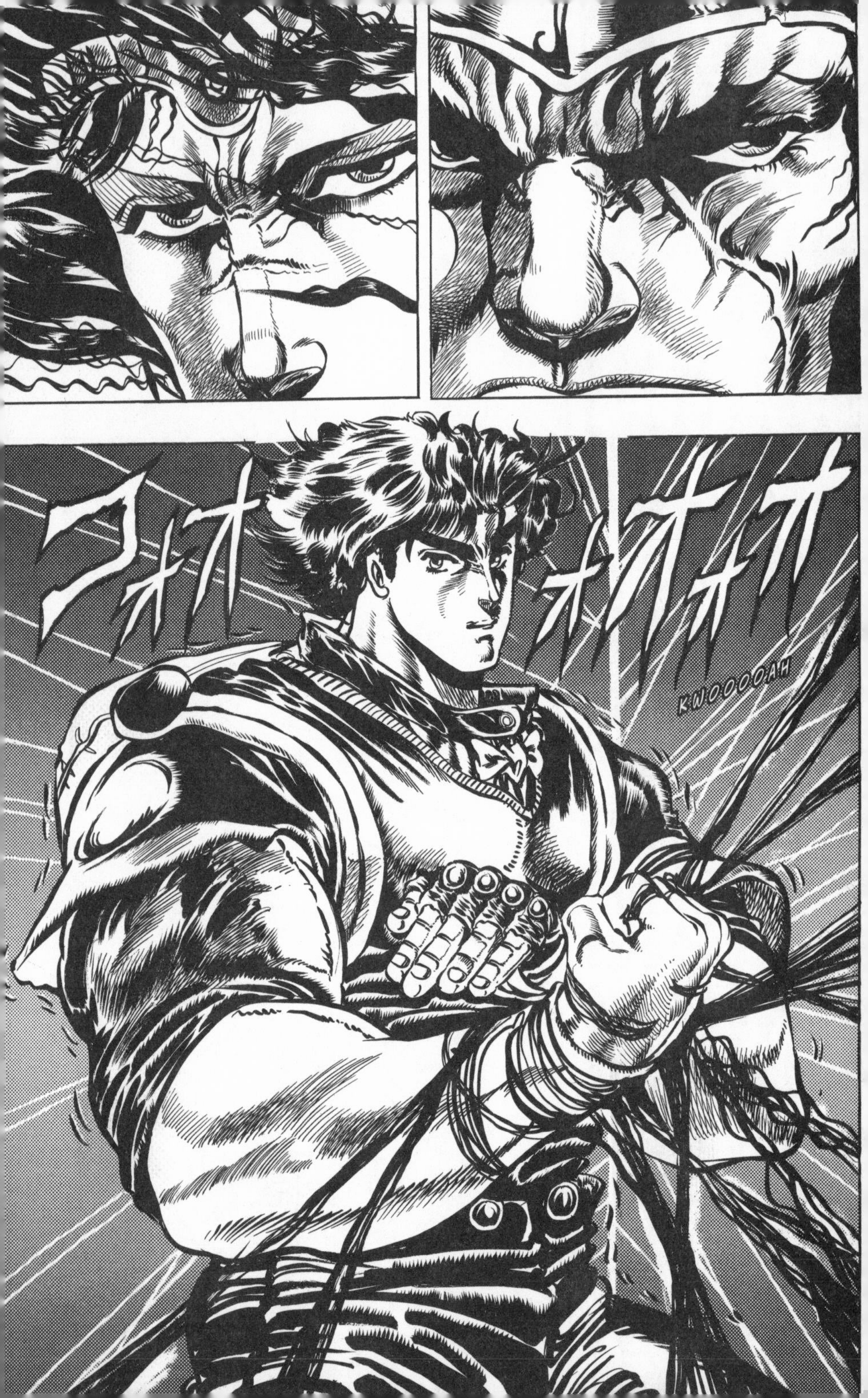
ウォオ
オォオォオ
KWOOOOOAH

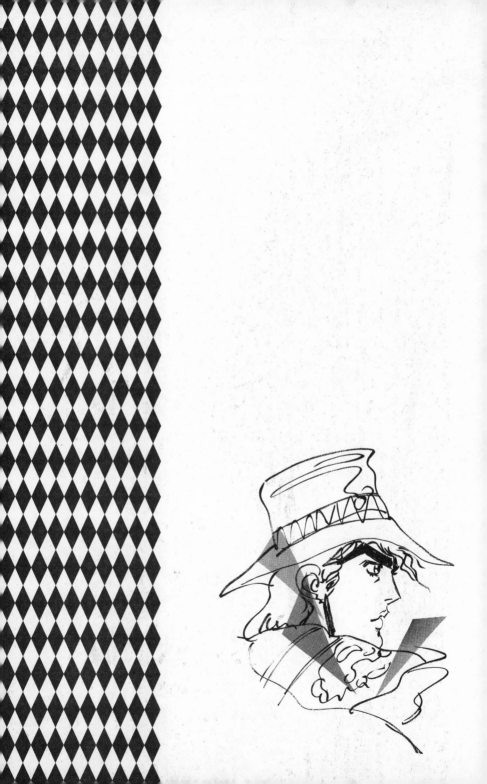

CHAPTER 27: Tarukus and the Dark Knight Blueford PART 2

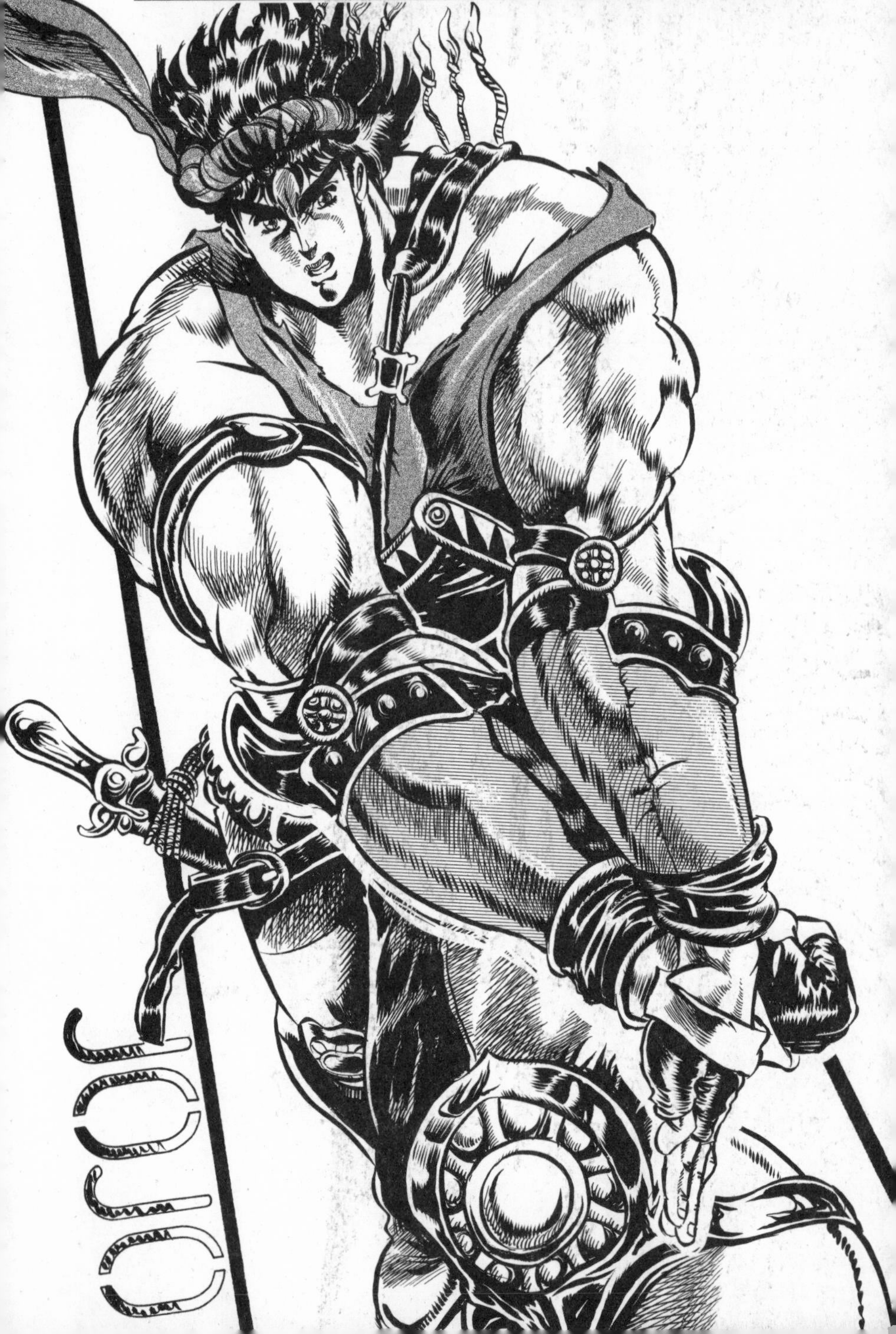

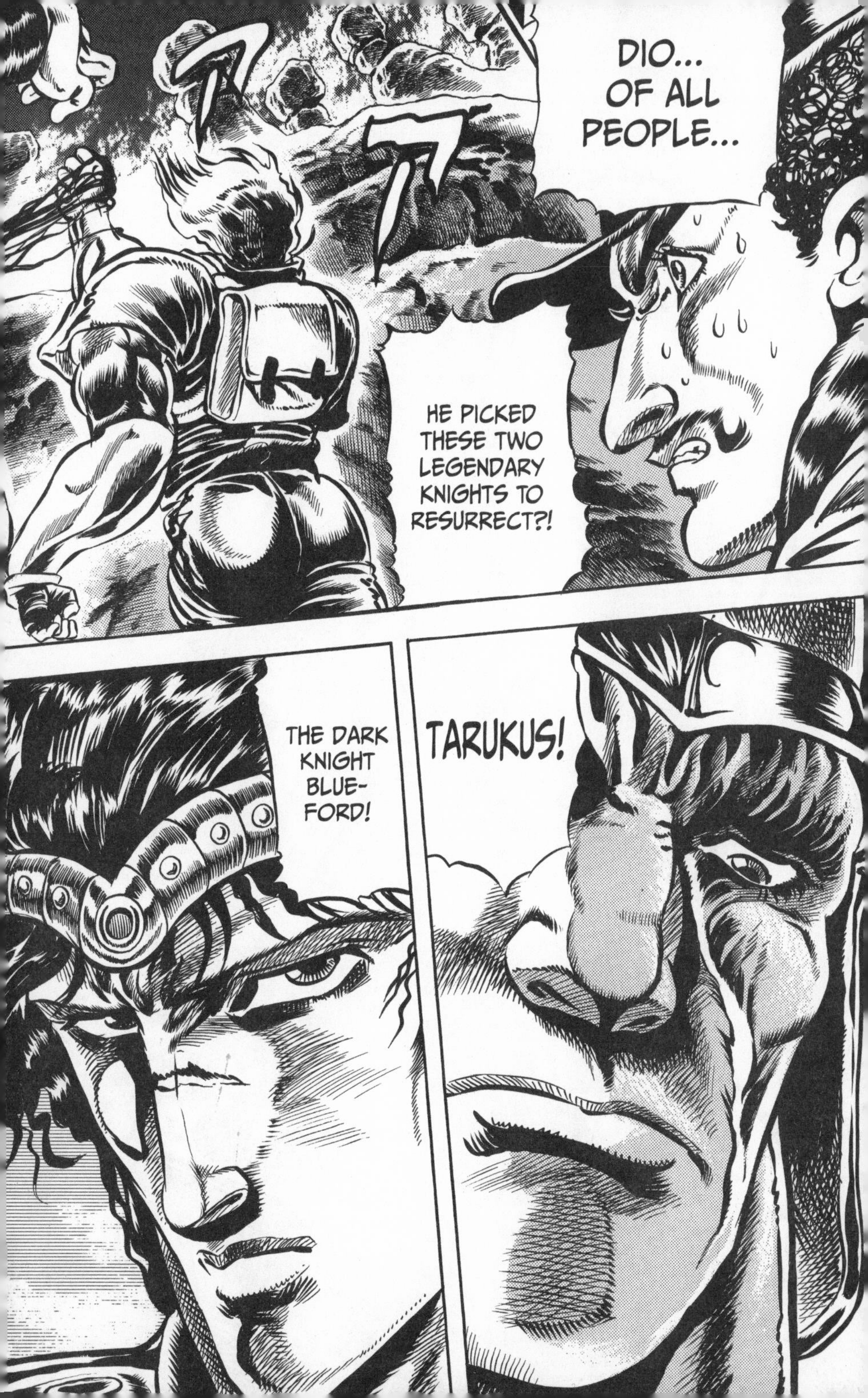
DIO... OF ALL PEOPLE...
HE PICKED THESE TWO LEGENDARY KNIGHTS TO RESURRECT?!
TARUKUS!
THE DARK KNIGHT BLUE-FORD!

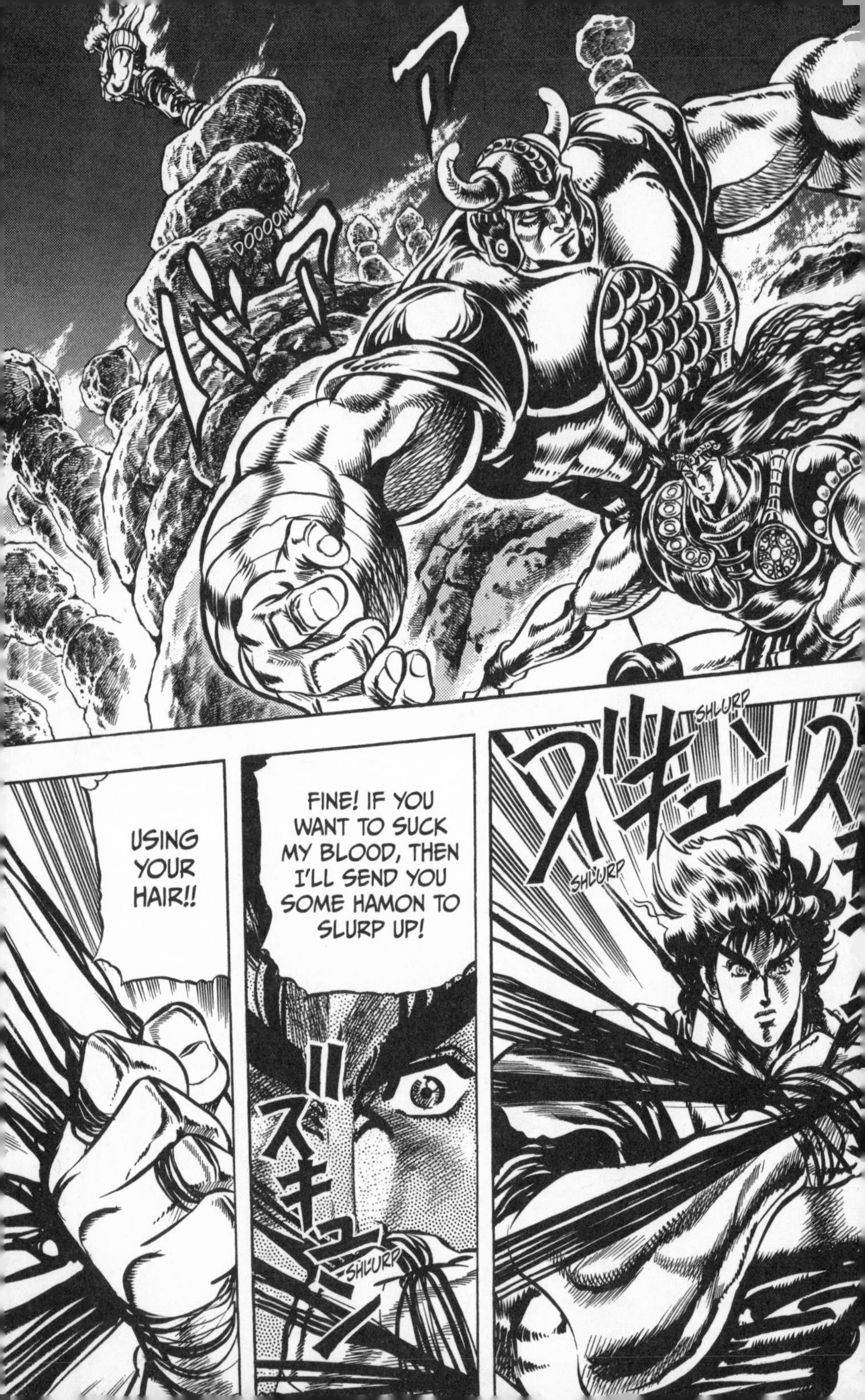
DOOOOM
SHLURP
SHLURP
FINE! IF YOU WANT TO SUCK MY BLOOD, THEN I'LL SEND YOU SOME HAMON TO SLURP UP!
SHLURP
USING YOUR HAIR!!

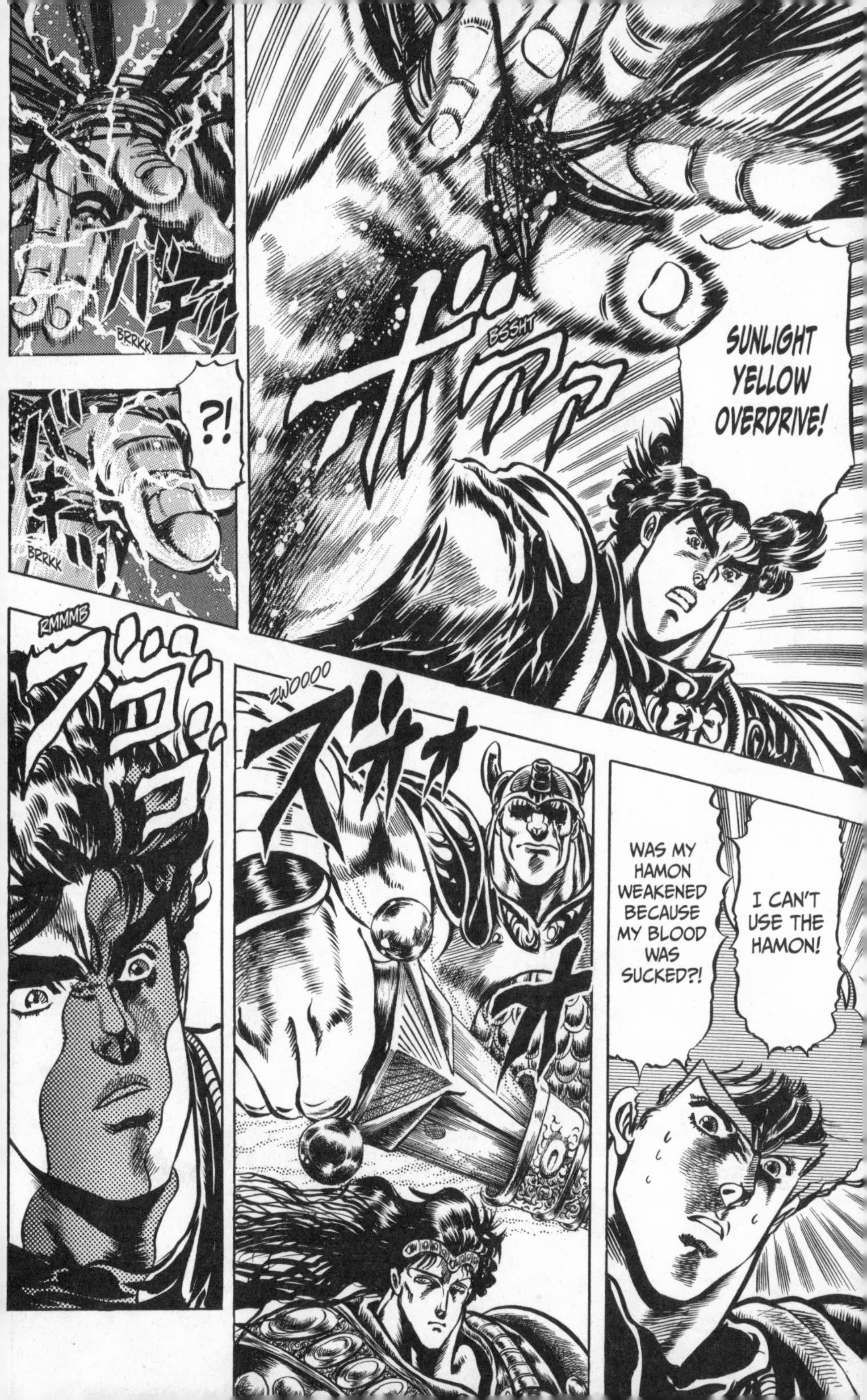
BSSHT
SUNLIGHT YELLOW OVERDRIVE!
BRRKK
?!
BRRKK
I CAN'T USE THE HAMON!
WAS MY HAMON WEAKENED BECAUSE MY BLOOD WAS SUCKED?!
ZWOOOO
RMMMB

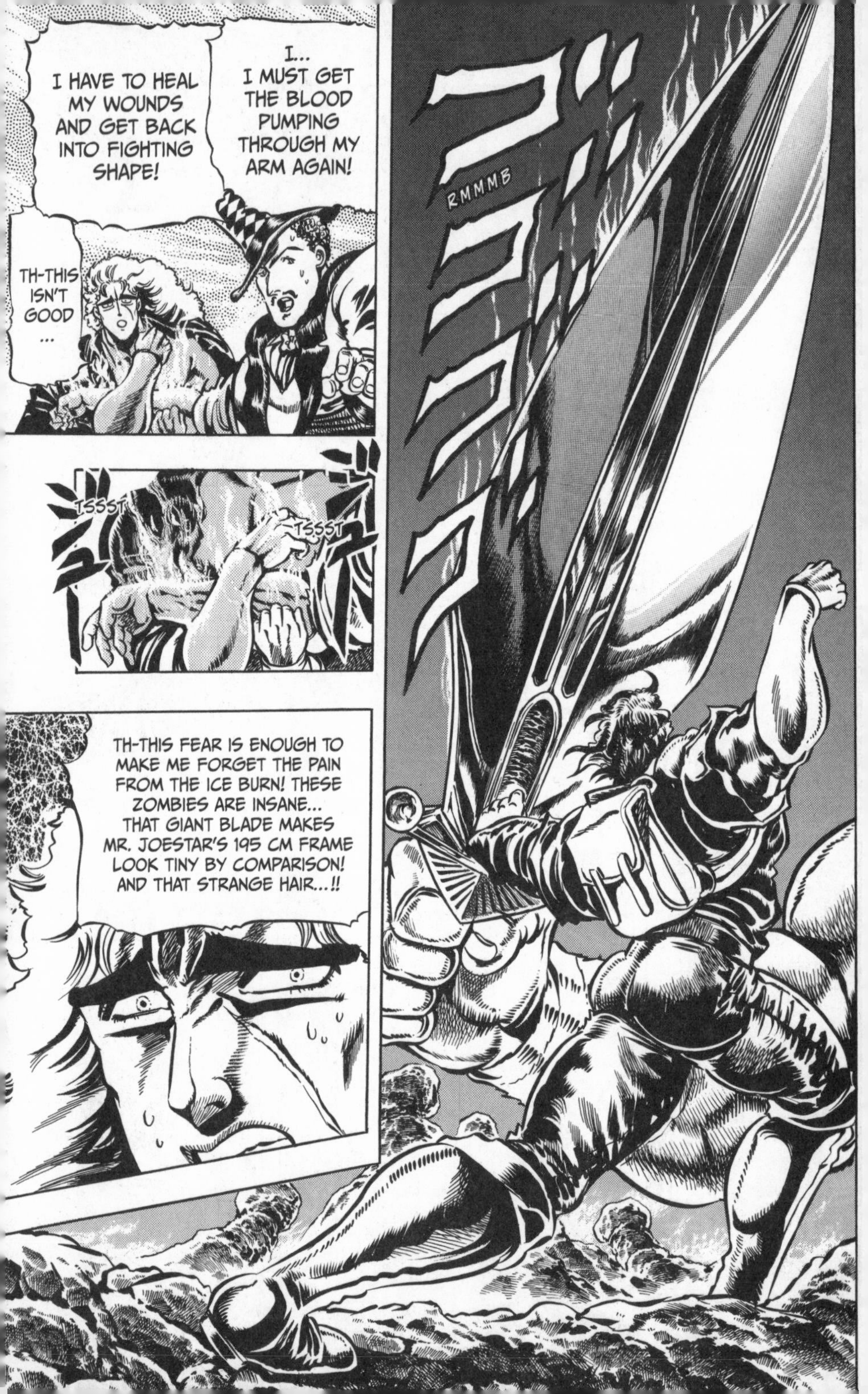
RMMMB
I... I MUST GET THE BLOOD PUMPING THROUGH MY ARM AGAIN!
I HAVE TO HEAL MY WOUNDS AND GET BACK INTO FIGHTING SHAPE!
TH-THIS ISN'T GOOD ...
TSSST
TSSST
TH-THIS FEAR IS ENOUGH TO MAKE ME FORGET THE PAIN FROM THE ICE BURN! THESE ZOMBIES ARE INSANE... THAT GIANT BLADE MAKES MR. JOESTAR'S 195 CM FRAME LOOK TINY BY COMPARISON! AND THAT STRANGE HAIR...!!

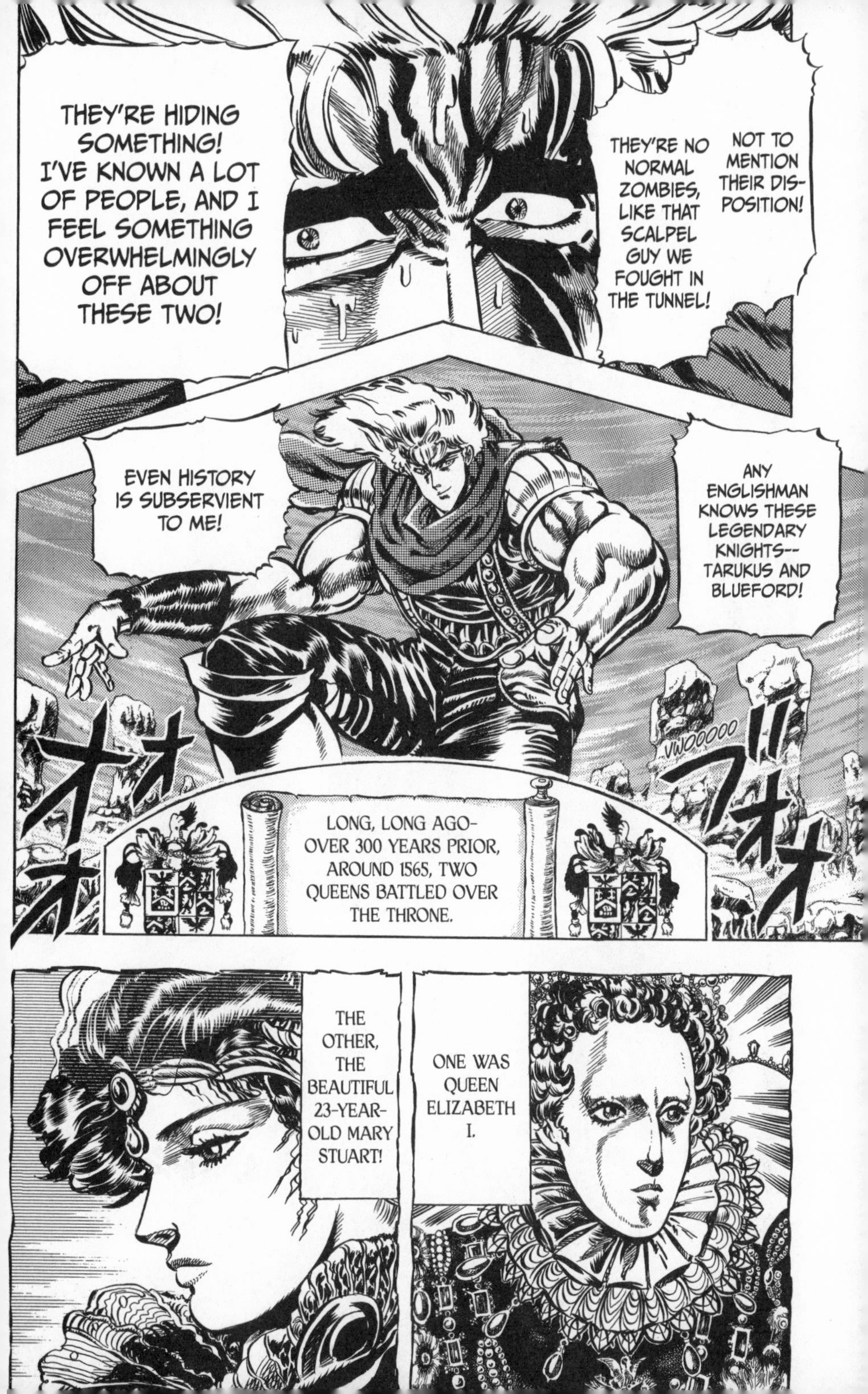
NOT TO MENTION THEIR DISPOSITION!
THEY'RE NO NORMAL ZOMBIES, LIKE THAT SCALPEL GUY WE FOUGHT IN THE TUNNEL!
THEY'RE HIDING SOMETHING! I'VE KNOWN A LOT OF PEOPLE, AND I FEEL SOMETHING OVERWHELMINGLY OFF ABOUT THESE TWO!
ANY ENGLISHMAN KNOWS THESE LEGENDARY KNIGHTS-- TARUKUS AND BLUEFORD!
EVEN HISTORY IS SUBSERVIENT TO ME!
ブオオオ
VWOOOOO
オオオ
LONG, LONG AGO- OVER 300 YEARS PRIOR, AROUND 1565, TWO QUEENS BATTLED OVER THE THRONE.
ONE WAS QUEEN ELIZABETH I.
THE OTHER, THE BEAUTIFUL 23-YEAR-OLD MARY STUART!

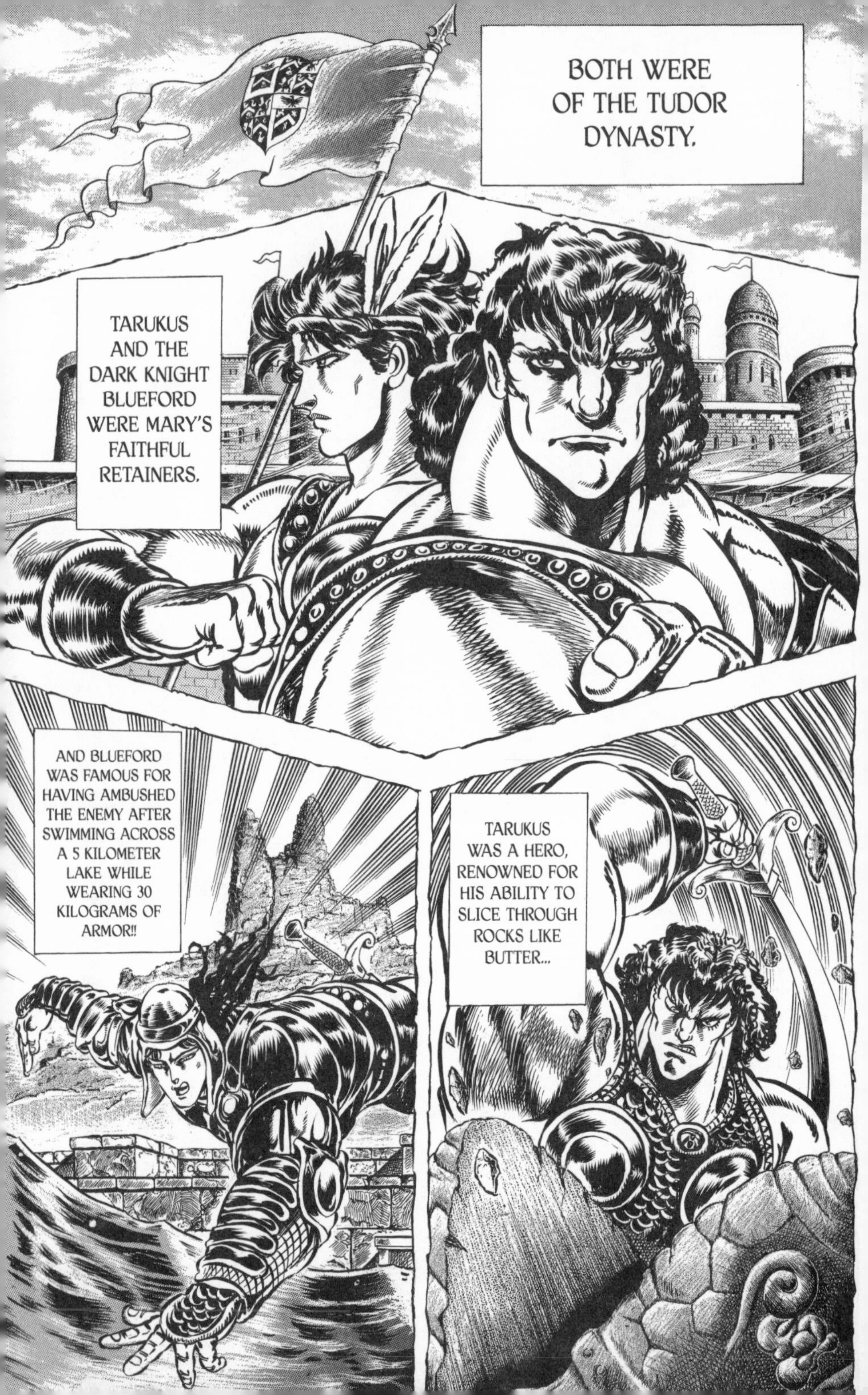

BOTH WERE OF THE TUDOR DYNASTY.
TARUKUS AND THE DARK KNIGHT BLUEFORD WERE MARY'S FAITHFUL RETAINERS.
TARUKUS WAS A HERO, RENOWNED FOR HIS ABILITY TO SLICE THROUGH ROCKS LIKE BUTTER...
AND BLUEFORD WAS FAMOUS FOR HAVING AMBUSHED THE ENEMY AFTER SWIMMING ACROSS A 5 KILOMETER LAKE WHILE WEARING 30 KILOGRAMS OF ARMOR!!

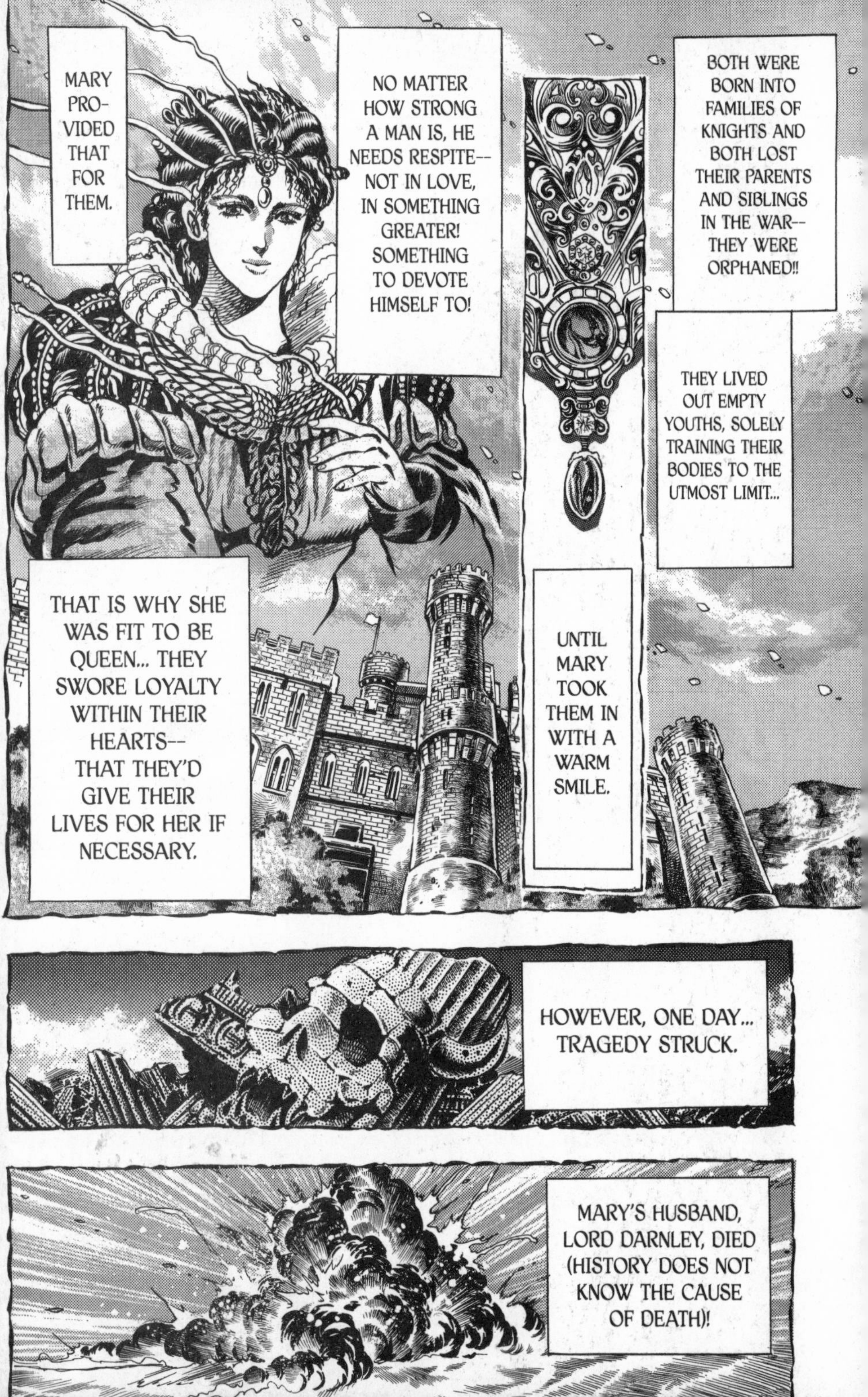
BOTH WERE BORN INTO FAMILIES OF KNIGHTS AND BOTH LOST THEIR PARENTS AND SIBLINGS IN THE WAR-- THEY WERE ORPHANED!!
THEY LIVED OUT EMPTY YOUTHS, SOLELY TRAINING THEIR BODIES TO THE UTMOST LIMIT...
UNTIL MARY TOOK THEM IN WITH A WARM SMILE.
NO MATTER HOW STRONG A MAN IS, HE NEEDS RESPITE-- NOT IN LOVE, IN SOMETHING GREATER! SOMETHING TO DEVOTE HIMSELF TO!
MARY PRO-VIDED THAT FOR THEM.
THAT IS WHY SHE WAS FIT TO BE QUEEN... THEY SWORE LOYALTY WITHIN THEIR HEARTS-- THAT THEY'D GIVE THEIR LIVES FOR HER IF NECESSARY.
HOWEVER, ONE DAY... TRAGEDY STRUCK.
MARY'S HUSBAND, LORD DARNLEY, DIED (HISTORY DOES NOT KNOW THE CAUSE OF DEATH)!

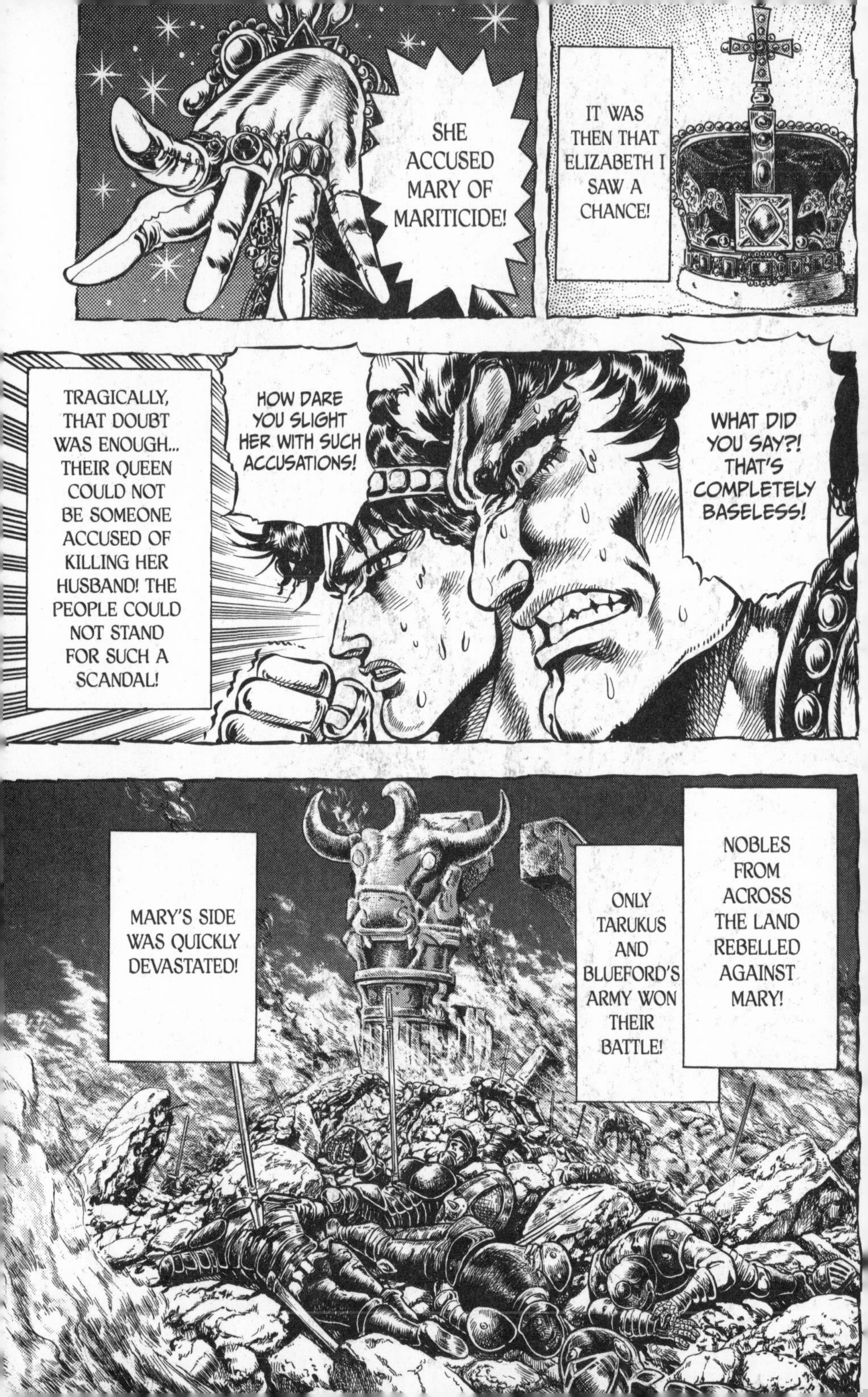
IT WAS THEN THAT ELIZABETH I SAW A CHANCE!
SHE ACCUSED MARY OF MARITICIDE!
WHAT DID YOU SAY?! THAT'S COMPLETELY BASELESS!
HOW DARE YOU SLIGHT HER WITH SUCH ACCUSATIONS!
TRAGICALLY, THAT DOUBT WAS ENOUGH... THEIR QUEEN COULD NOT BE SOMEONE ACCUSED OF KILLING HER HUSBAND! THE PEOPLE COULD NOT STAND FOR SUCH A SCANDAL!
NOBLES FROM ACROSS THE LAND REBELLED AGAINST MARY!
ONLY TARUKUS AND BLUEFORD'S ARMY WON THEIR BATTLE!
MARY'S SIDE WAS QUICKLY DEVASTATED!

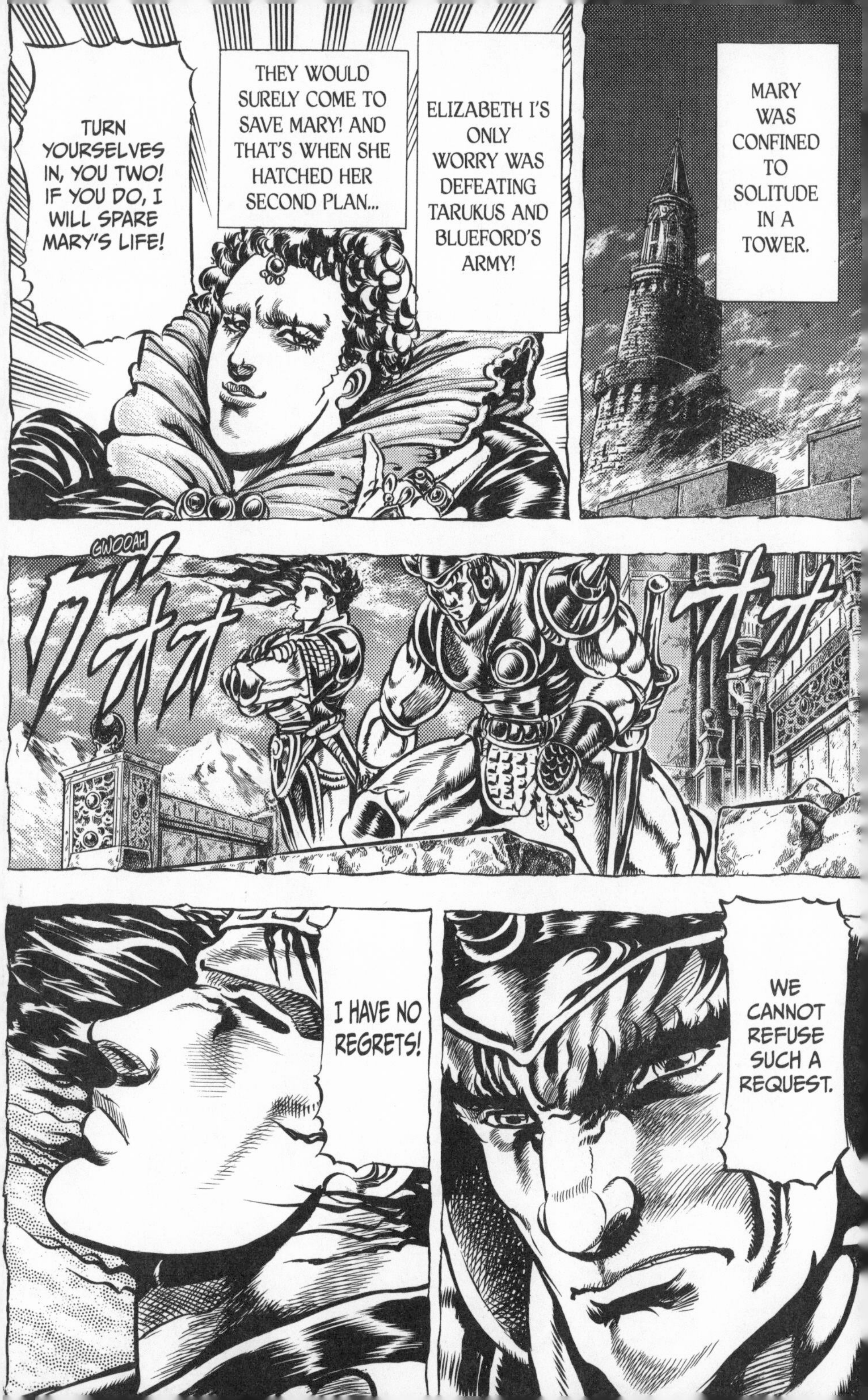

MARY WAS CONFINED TO SOLITUDE IN A TOWER.
ELIZABETH I'S ONLY WORRY WAS DEFEATING TARUKUS AND BLUEFORD'S ARMY!
THEY WOULD SURELY COME TO SAVE MARY! AND THAT'S WHEN SHE HATCHED HER SECOND PLAN...
TURN YOURSELVES IN, YOU TWO! IF YOU DO, I WILL SPARE MARY'S LIFE!
GWOOAH
WE CANNOT REFUSE SUCH A REQUEST.
I HAVE NO REGRETS!

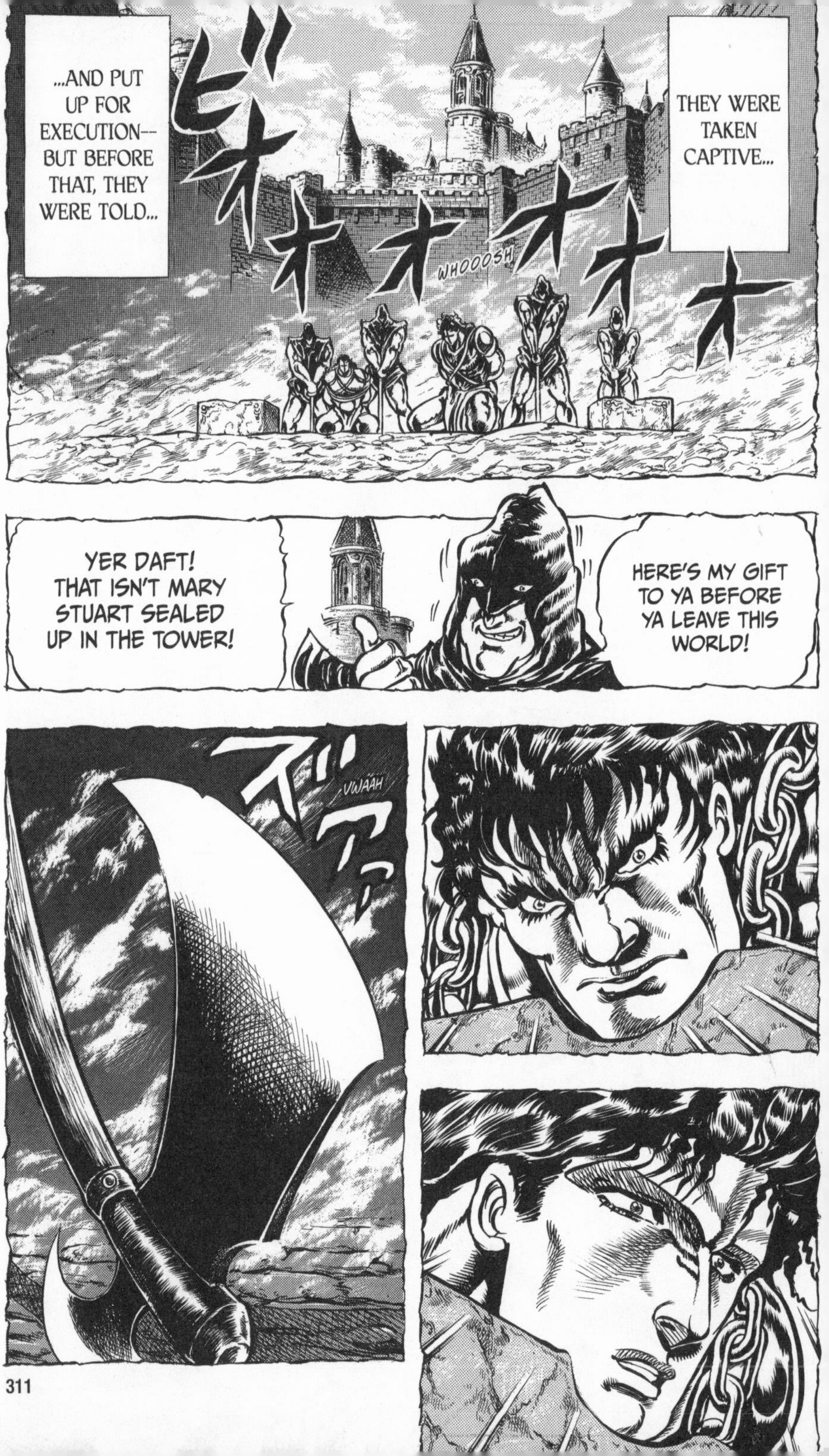
THEY WERE TAKEN CAPTIVE...
...AND PUT UP FOR EXECUTION-- BUT BEFORE THAT, THEY WERE TOLD...
WHOOOSH
HERE'S MY GIFT TO YA BEFORE YA LEAVE THIS WORLD!
YER DAFT! THAT ISN'T MARY STUART SEALED UP IN THE TOWER!
VWAAH

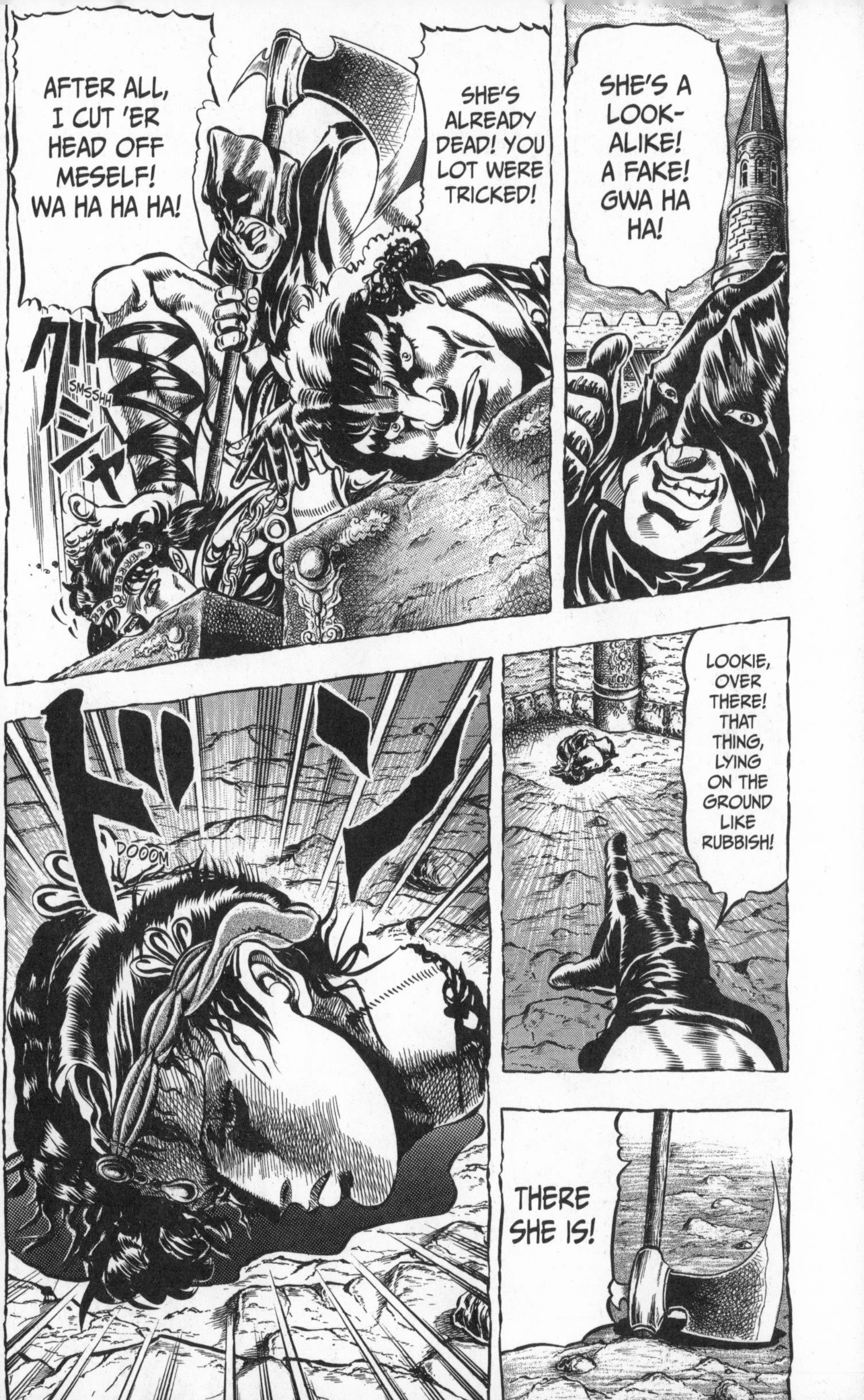
SHE'S A LOOK-ALIKE! A FAKE! GWA HA HA!
SHE'S ALREADY DEAD! YOU LOT WERE TRICKED!
AFTER ALL, I CUT 'ER HEAD OFF MESELF! WA HA HA HA!
SMSSHH
LOOKIE, OVER THERE! THAT THING, LYING ON THE GROUND LIKE RUBBISH!
THERE SHE IS!
DOOOM

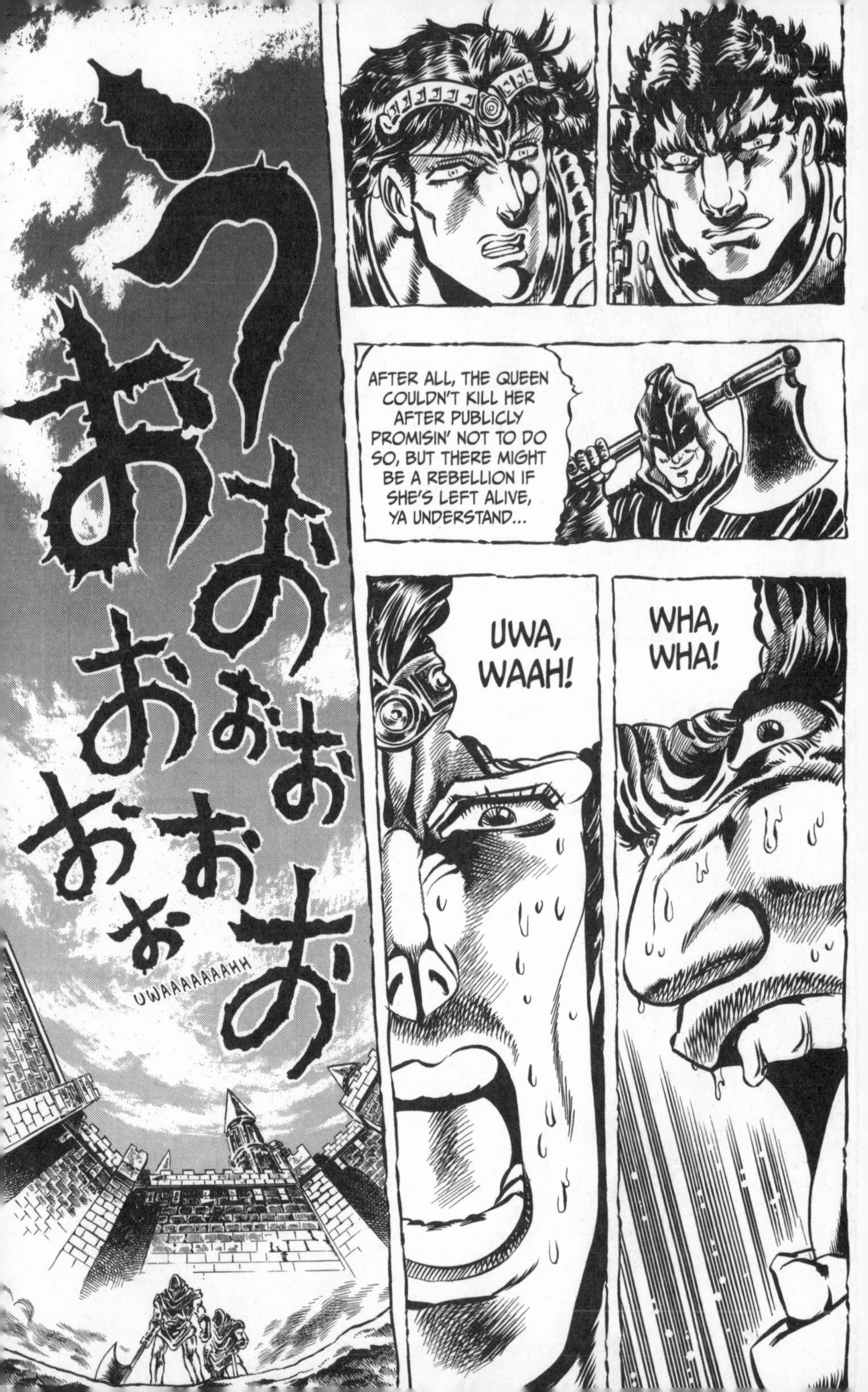
AFTER ALL, THE QUEEN COULDN'T KILL HER AFTER PUBLICLY PROMISIN' NOT TO DO SO, BUT THERE MIGHT BE A REBELLION IF SHE'S LEFT ALIVE, YA UNDERSTAND...
WHA, WHA!
UWA, WAAH!
UWAAAAAAAHH

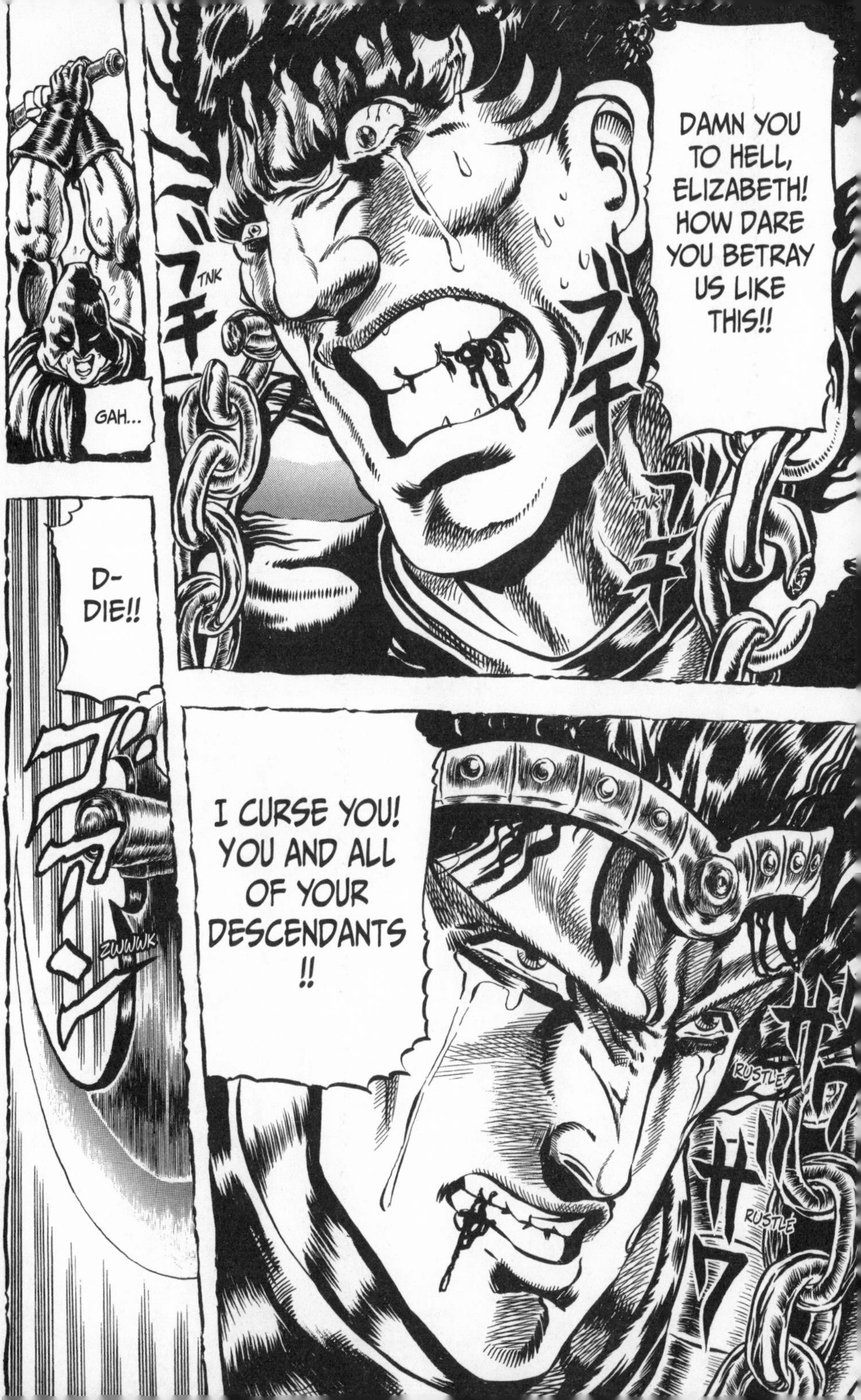
DAMN YOU TO HELL, ELIZABETH! HOW DARE YOU BETRAY US LIKE THIS!!
TNK
TNK
TNK
GAH...
I CURSE YOU! YOU AND ALL OF YOUR DESCENDANTS !!
RUSTLE
RUSTLE
D- DIE!!
ZWWWK

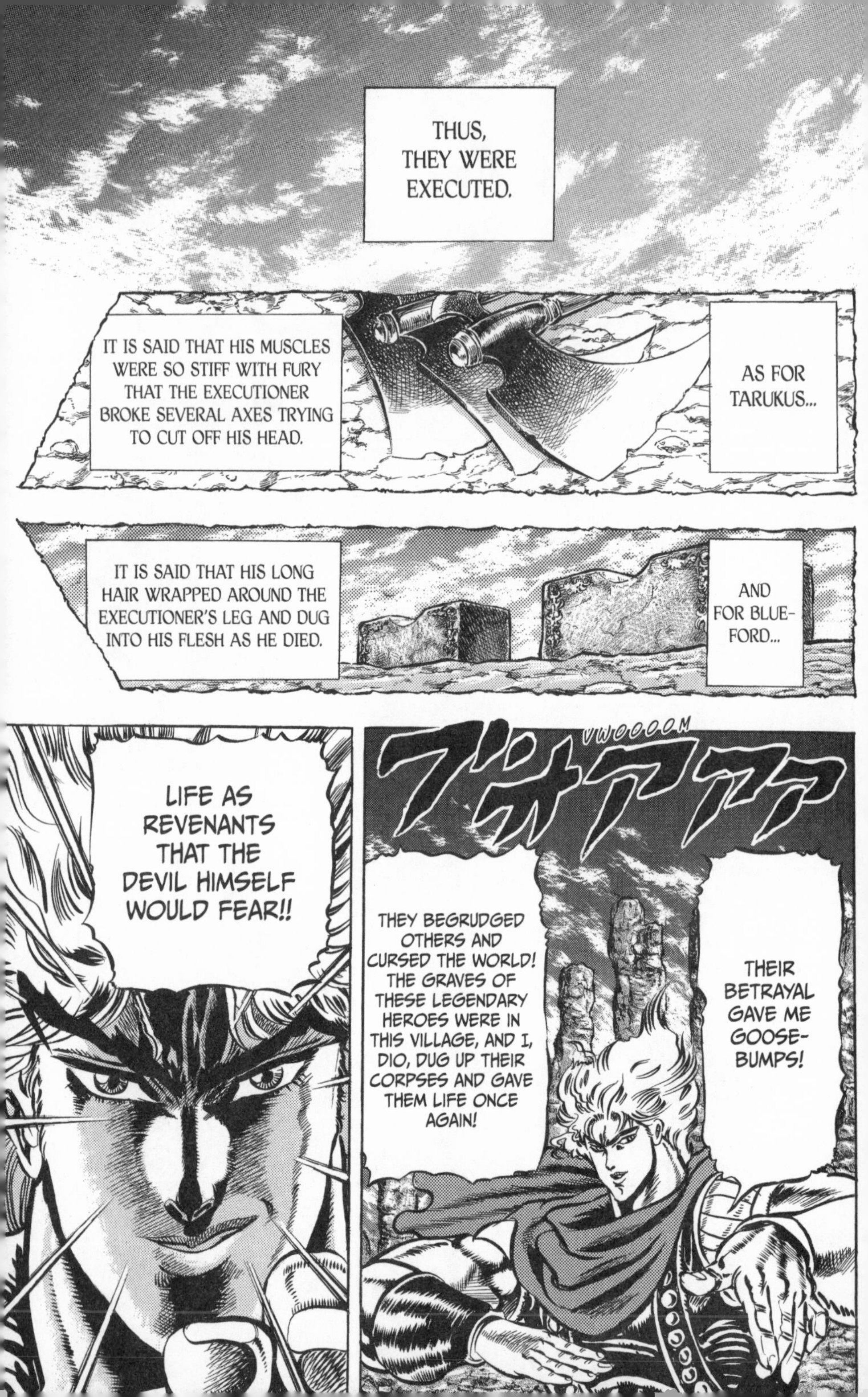
THUS, THEY WERE EXECUTED.
AS FOR TARUKUS...
IT IS SAID THAT HIS MUSCLES WERE SO STIFF WITH FURY THAT THE EXECUTIONER BROKE SEVERAL AXES TRYING TO CUT OFF HIS HEAD.
AND FOR BLUE-FORD...
IT IS SAID THAT HIS LONG HAIR WRAPPED AROUND THE EXECUTIONER'S LEG AND DUG INTO HIS FLESH AS HE DIED.
ブォアアア
VWOOOOM
THEIR BETRAYAL GAVE ME GOOSE-BUMPS!
THEY BEGRUDGED OTHERS AND CURSED THE WORLD! THE GRAVES OF THESE LEGENDARY HEROES WERE IN THIS VILLAGE, AND I, DIO, DUG UP THEIR CORPSES AND GAVE THEM LIFE ONCE AGAIN!
LIFE AS REVENANTS THAT THE DEVIL HIMSELF WOULD FEAR!!

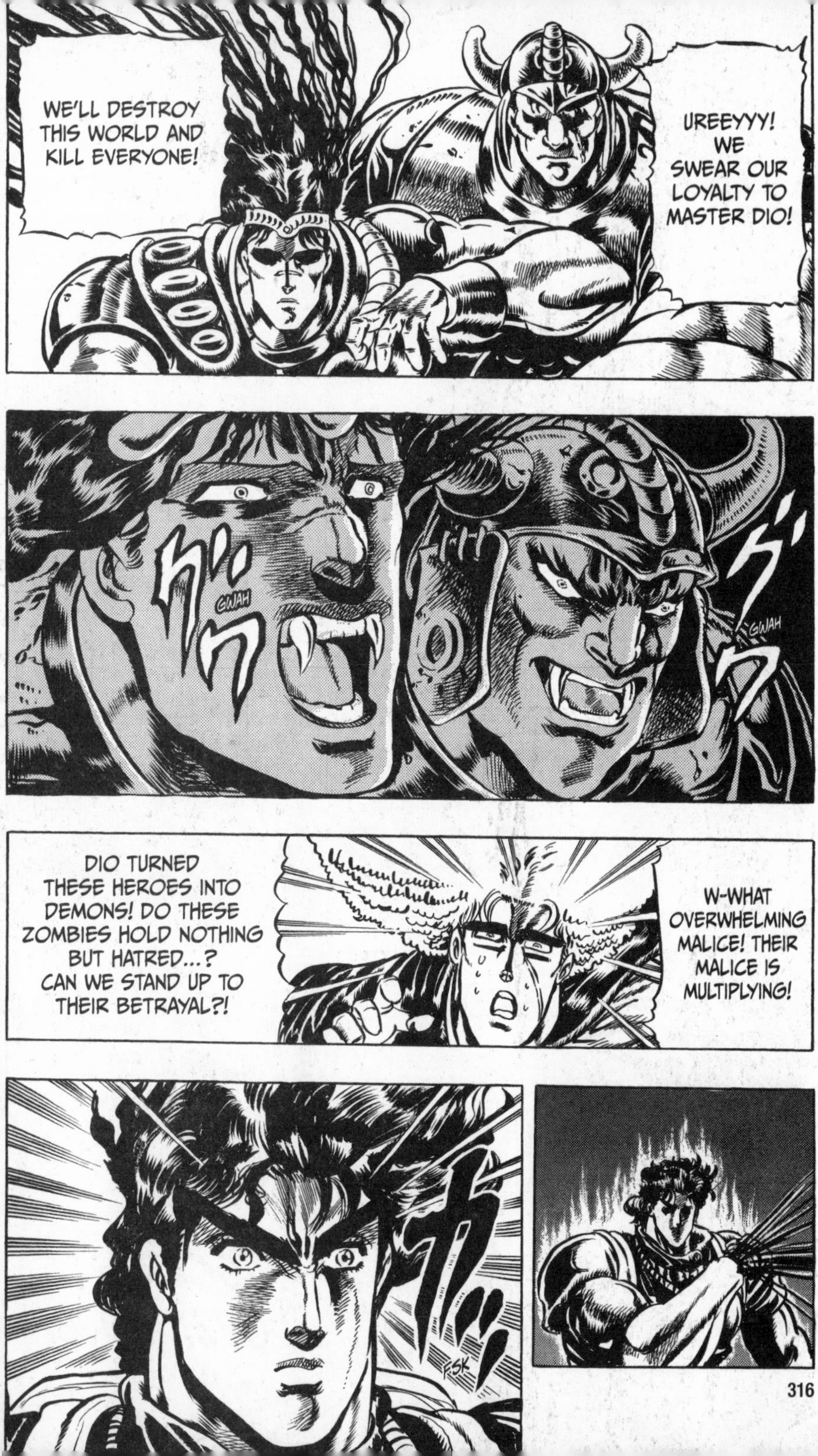
UREEYYY! WE SWEAR OUR LOYALTY TO MASTER DIO!
WE'LL DESTROY THIS WORLD AND KILL EVERYONE!
GWAH
GWAH
W-WHAT OVERWHELMING MALICE! THEIR MALICE IS MULTIPLYING!
DIO TURNED THESE HEROES INTO DEMONS! DO THESE ZOMBIES HOLD NOTHING BUT HATRED...? CAN WE STAND UP TO THEIR BETRAYAL?!
F-SK

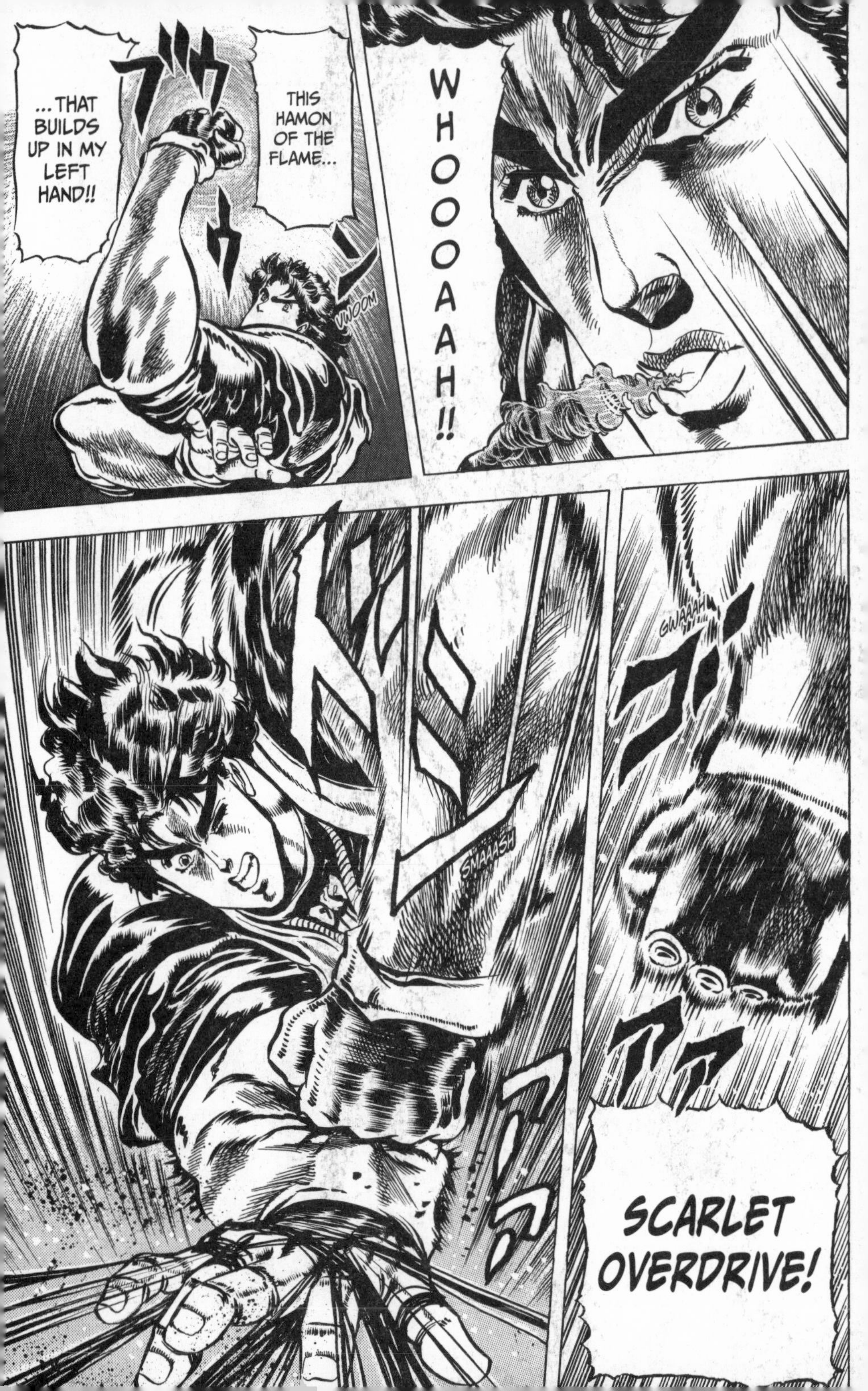
WHOOOAAH!!
THIS HAMON OF THE FLAME...
...THAT BUILDS UP IN MY LEFT HAND!!
VWOOM
GWAAAH
SCARLET OVERDRIVE!
SMAAASH

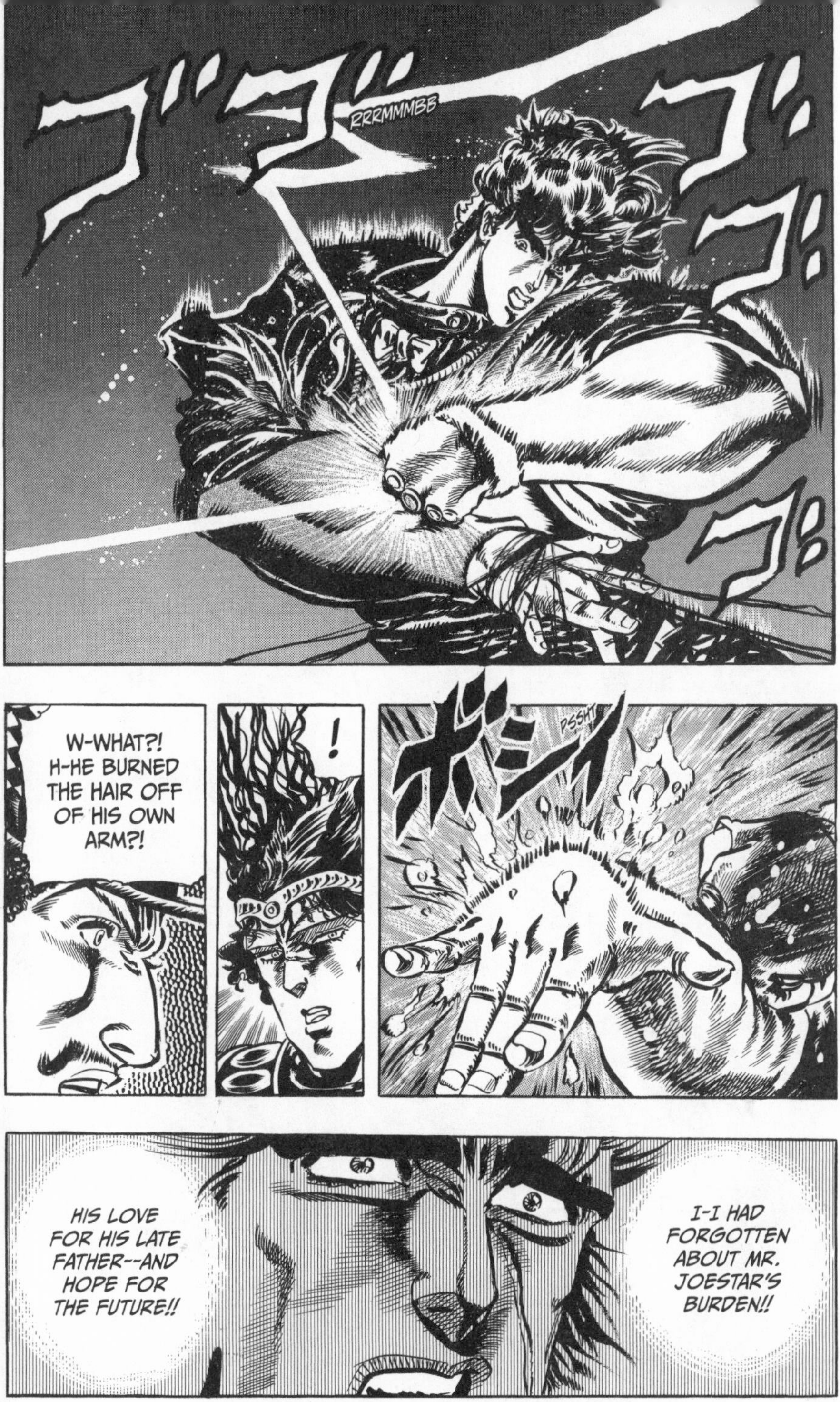
RRRMMMBB
PSSHT
!
W-WHAT?! H-HE BURNED THE HAIR OFF OF HIS OWN ARM?!
I-I HAD FORGOTTEN ABOUT MR. JOESTAR'S BURDEN!!
HIS LOVE FOR HIS LATE FATHER--AND HOPE FOR THE FUTURE!!

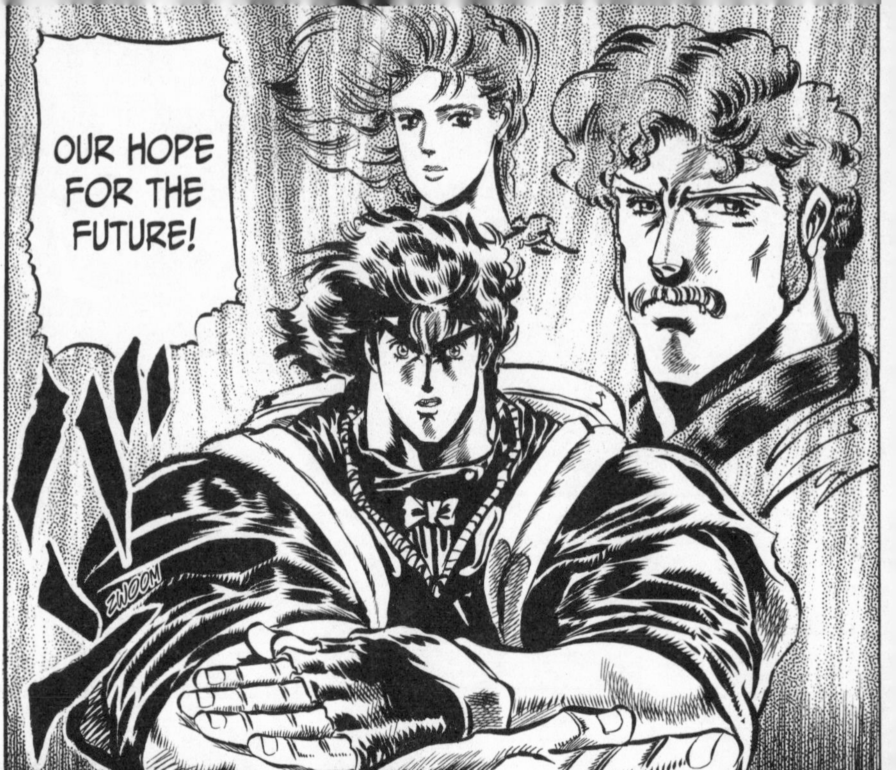
OUR HOPE FOR THE FUTURE!
ZWOOM

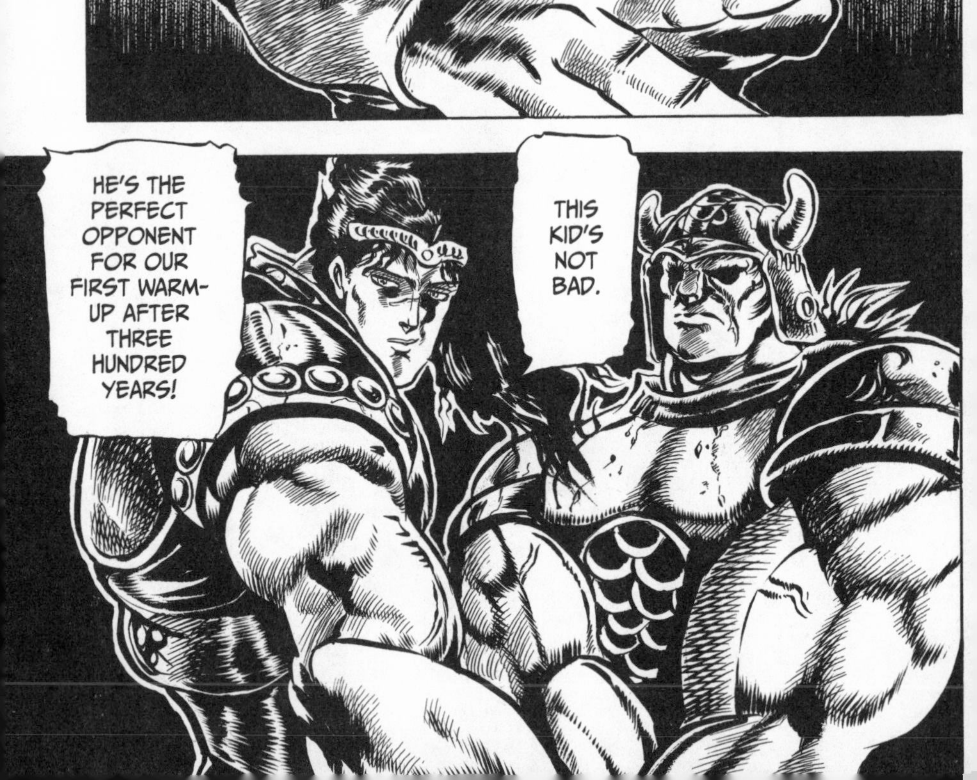
THIS KID'S NOT BAD.
HE'S THE PERFECT OPPONENT FOR OUR FIRST WARM-UP AFTER THREE HUNDRED YEARS!

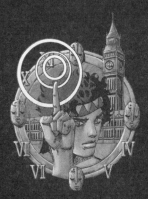

JOJO'S
BIZARRE ADVENTURE

02

END

To Be Continued

JoJo's BIZARRE ADVENTURE

02

Ze

荒木飛呂彦が語るキャラクター誕生秘話

Hirohiko Araki talks about character creation!

JoJo's BIZARRE ADVENTURE
PART 1
PHANTOM BLOOD

02

Zeppeli

"ZEPPELI'S MUSTACHE WAS A HUGE GAMBLE"

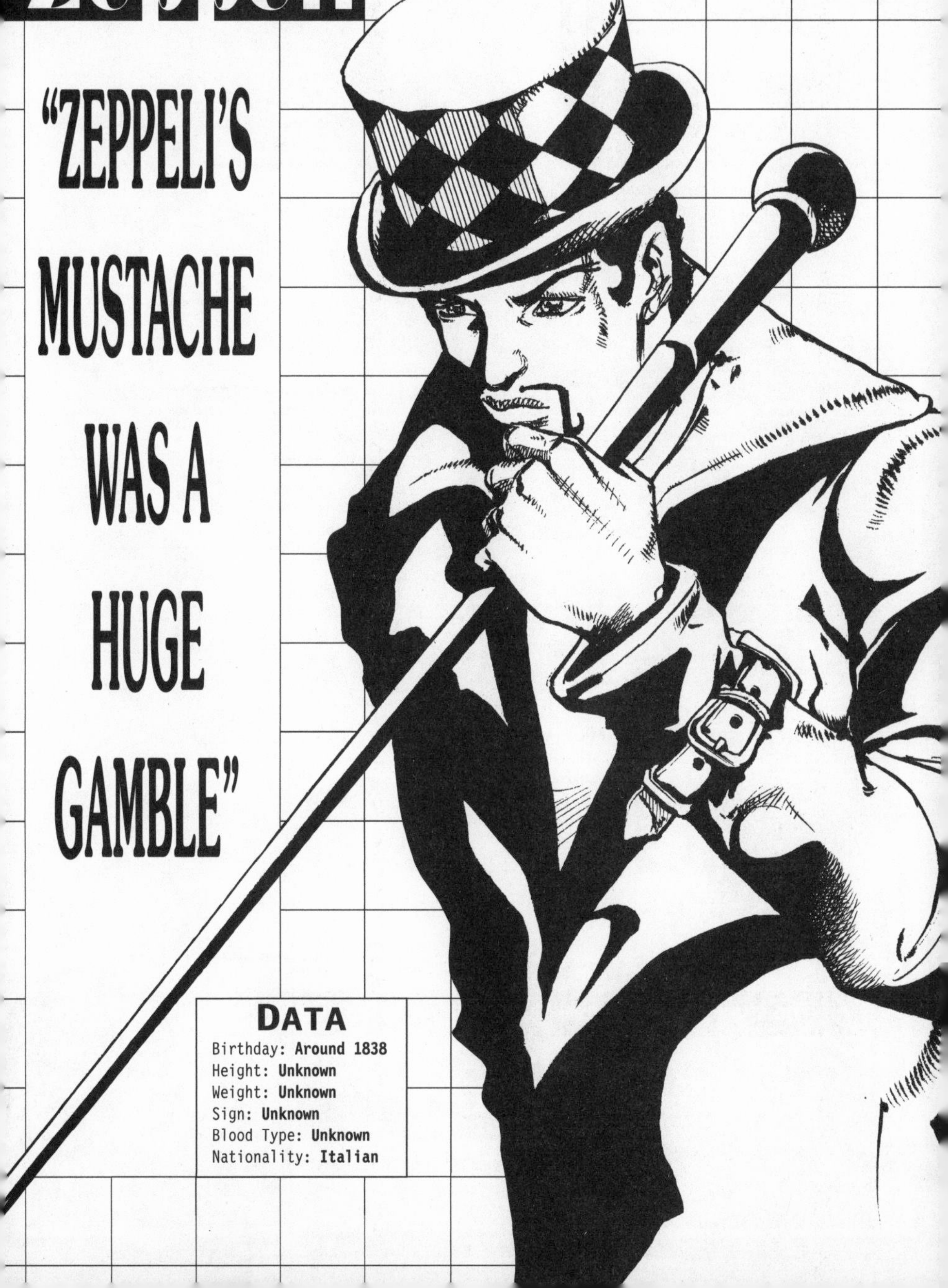

DATA

Birthday: **Around 1838**
Height: **Unknown**
Weight: **Unknown**
Sign: **Unknown**
Blood Type: **Unknown**
Nationality: **Italian**

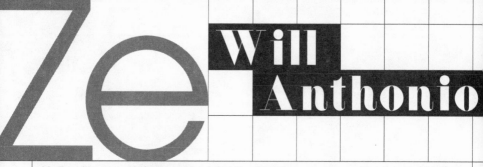

Ze Will Anthonio

Mr. Zeppeli* was named after the rock band "Led Zeppelin." They are top-tier musicians to me, so I felt I had to reference their name with this character, albeit it's really a shame I used it so early--kind of like playing the Joker right at the beginning of a card game. Therefore, I had to resolve myself to that when I debuted Mr. Zeppeli. It's also important how the name sounds; there are a lot of "J" names in the series like JoJo, Jonathan and Joestar that are similar, so I wanted to balance out the names with a "Z" like Zeppeli. I made sure to do the same thing with Speedwagon.

Mr. Zeppeli teaches the Hamon to Jonathan and leads him on his quest to destroy the stone mask. I like teachers who are silly and make you wonder whether or not they're missing a screw up there. Like in Jackie Chan movies, the master's always a drunkard--so how can he be so strong? Same thing in *The Karate Kid*. Their outside appearance may be a little off, but it's what's underneath that is deserving of respect. These characters have charm because of the gap between their exterior and interior, and because you can't judge them by their covers. Mr. Zeppeli may look weak at first glance, but he's actually strong, even though I dressed him like a magician and gave him the mustache of a snake oil salesman. His mustache was actually inspired by those worn by the painter Salvador Dali and *Osomatsu-kun's* Iyami.

However, the mustache requires a lot of courage to pull off in a shonen magazine. Mainly because it makes the character look older and untrustworthy, no matter the type of mustache. As for Mr. Zeppeli—while he serves as JoJo's master, it's not like he's an old man far older than JoJo. He's also the lead supporting character. I might have turned readers off with him, so it took courage. He's a type of character that I haven't really used in any of my other work, but one that I wanted to use for the reasons I mentioned above. Thinking about it now, it may have been a "gamble" or "adventure" on my part. Back then I probably figured, "Eh, it's JoJo, it'll work out." It is a *Bizarre Adventure*, after all.

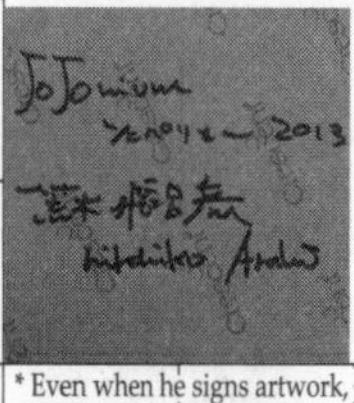

Lastly, to my credit, JoJo's Bizarre Adventure (*JoJo no Kimyou na Bouken*) came out **before** the Japanese TV drama series *Bizarre Stories in This World* (*Yonimo Kimyou na Monogatari*).
Let's get that straight.

* Even when he signs artwork, Zeppeli is the only character that Araki Sensei refers to as "Mr." (*San* in Japanese)

The story behind the new illustration for **JoJo 02!**

Q. Could the sphere on his cane be...?

A. It's a steel ball from *Steel Ball Run.*

Zeppeli is known for his silken top hat. It's a cool shape and if you curve the diamond design, it looks three-dimensional.

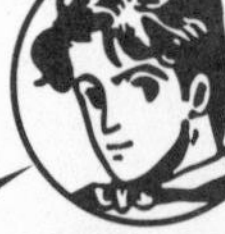

Hirohiko Araki

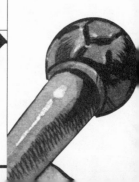

JOJO'S BIZARRE ADVENTURE

PART I PHANTOM BLOOD

BY

HIROHIKO ARAKI

Translation ☆ Evan Galloway
Touch-Up Art & Lettering ☆ Mark McMurray
Design ☆ Fawn Lau
Editor ☆ Urian Brown

JOJO'S BIZARRE ADVENTURE © 1986 by Hirohiko Araki
All rights reserved.
First published in Japan in 1986 by SHUEISHA Inc., Tokyo.
English translation rights arranged by SHUEISHA Inc.

Original Japanese cover design by
MITSURU KOBAYASHI (GENI A LÒIDE)

The stories, characters and incidents mentioned
in this publication are entirely fictional.

No portion of this book may be reproduced or
transmitted in any form or by any means without
written permission from the copyright holders.

Printed in the U.S.A.

Published by VIZ Media, LLC
P.O. Box 77010
San Francisco, CA 94107

IO
First printing, April 2015
Tenth printing, February 2022

PARENTAL ADVISORY
JOJO'S BIZARRE ADVENTURE PART ONE PHANTOM BLOOD
is rated T+ for Older Teen and is recommended for ages 16 and up.
This volume contains graphic violence and some mature themes.

www.viz.com

SHONEN JUMP
ADVANCED
www.shonenjump.com

JO

ドッギャーン!

JO

THIS IS THE LAST PAGE

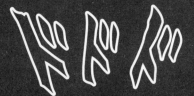

JoJo's Bizarre Adventure
has been printed in the original
Japanese format in order to
preserve the orientation of the
original artwork.

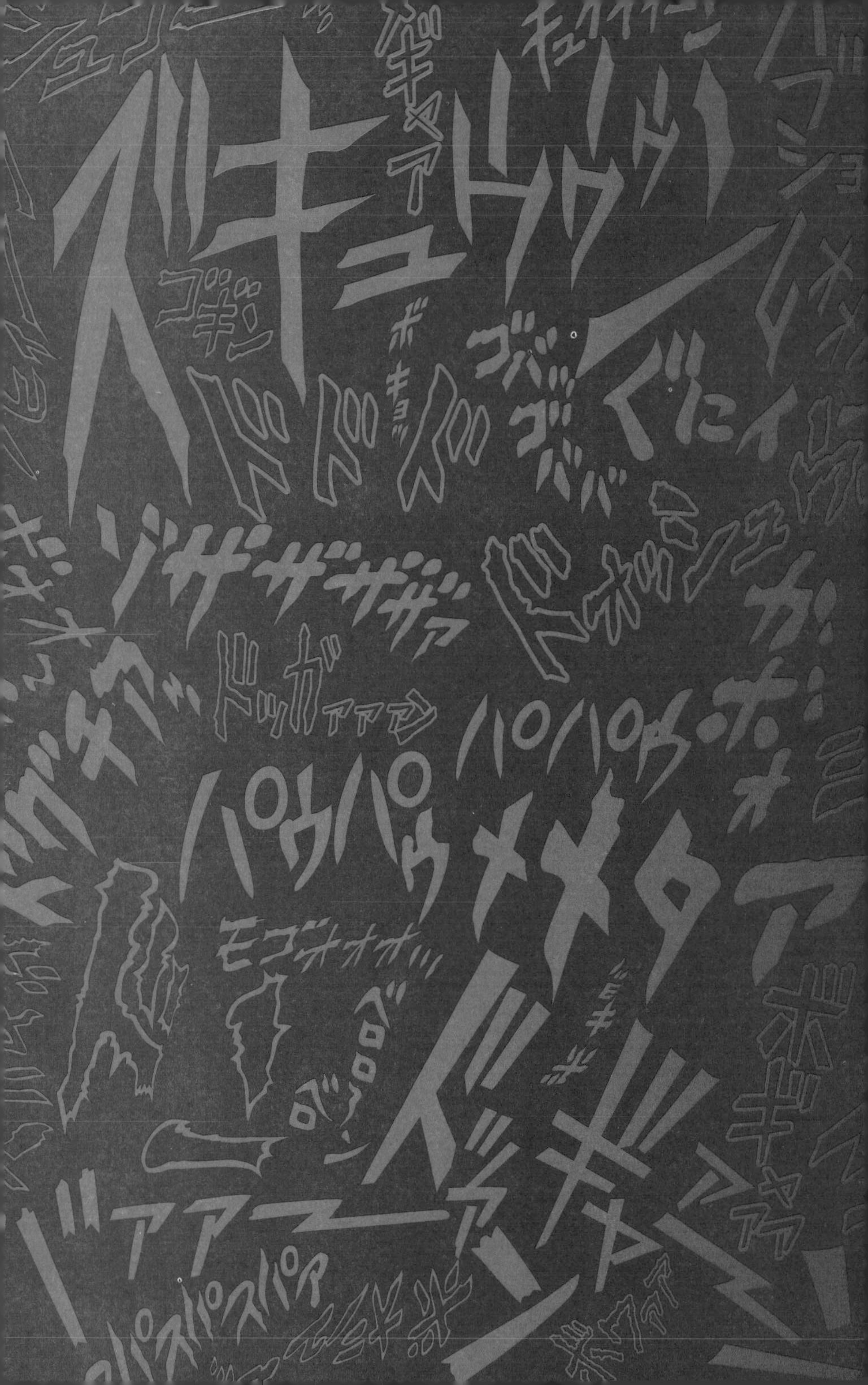
ゴバゴバババ
ザザザザァ
パウパウ
メメタァ
モゴオオオッ
パスパスパァ

W9-CLC-307